How to Use the Companion CD

The companion CD and the software included on it have been designed to run on Windows 95, NT, and 3.x systems using a Web browser and Internet connection. System requirements for the various types of software vary widely depending on what you download from the CD. Please review all software readme files before installing software directly to your machine.

Because this CD has been produced in HTML you may still view much of the contents using a browser. Note that some software on this CD may be 95 and NT specific.

Recommended System

- Pentium PC

- Windows 95, NT, or 3.x operating system

- 4x CD-ROM drive

- 16MB RAM

CD START INSTRUCTIONS

1. Place the CD-ROM in your CD-ROM drive.

2. Launch your Web browser.

3. From your Web browser, select Open File from the File menu. Select your CD-ROM drive (usually drive D), then select the file called welcome.htm.

Network
Buyer's Guide

Network
Buyer's Guide

Strategic Research Corporation

Ziff-Davis Press

**An imprint of Macmillan
Computer Publishing USA**

Emeryville, California

Writer	Dennis Casey
Publisher	Stacy Hiquet
Acquisitions Editor	Paula Hardin
Editor	Deborah Craig
Table Editor	Abby Johnston/Creative Solutions
Technical Reviewer	Wade Ellery
Production Editor	Ami Knox
Proofreader	Jeff Barrash
Cover Illustration and Design	Megan Gandt
Book Design	Laura Lamar/MAX, San Francisco
Illustrators	Sarah Ishida and Mina Reimer
Page Layout	M. D. Barrera
Indexer	Christine Spina

Ziff-Davis Press, ZD Press, the Ziff-Davis Press logo, PC Magazine, and the PC Magazine logo are trademarks or registered trademarks of, and are licensed to Macmillan Computer Publishing USA by Ziff-Davis Publishing Company, New York, New York.

Ziff-Davis Press imprint books are produced on a Macintosh computer system with the following applications: Frame-Maker®, Microsoft® Word, QuarkXPress®, Adobe Illustrator®, Adobe Photoshop®, Adobe Streamline™, MacLink® *Plus*, Aldus® FreeHand™, Collage Plus™.

Ziff-Davis Press, an imprint of
Macmillan Computer Publishing USA
5903 Christie Avenue
Emeryville, CA 94608

ISBN 1-56276-438-1

Manufactured in the United States of America
10 9 8 7 6 5 4 3 2 1

CONTENTS AT A GLANCE

TABLE OF CONTENTS

TABLE OF CONTENTS

TABLE OF CONTENTS

TABLE OF CONTENTS

TABLE OF CONTENTS

TABLE OF CONTENTS

TABLE OF CONTENTS

TABLE OF CONTENTS

TABLE OF CONTENTS

TABLE OF CONTENTS

ACKNOWLEDGMENTS

It took many committed people to put together this product guide and their work is greatly appreciated. First is a credit to the Network Buyer's Guide on the Internet, which served as the foundation for the research on this project. I greatly appreciate Ziff-Davis Press for tackling the daunting task of putting this material into print and onto CD-ROM, and for giving us the opportunity to write it. Their exceptional editing and layout teams certainly helped make this book a success. Thanks to Paula Hardin, Ami Knox, Deborah Craig, Abby Johnston of Creative Solutions, M. D. Barrera, and Christine Spina.

Product vendors and network administrators also deserve praise for providing timely information and feedback that helped keep us on the right track. A big thanks to the Strategic Research Corporation (SRC) research team—Pat Campion, Malcolm Cross, Bryan Farley, Michael Mahin, Joe Raffetto, and Lisa Schechter. They all made a big commitment to this project. Michael Peterson, President of SRC, contributed some of his expertise by writing Chapter 11.

Finally, thank you Jennifer, Jack, and Katrina for your love and support through the long hours on this book.

Author: Dennis C. Casey
Dennis has been a Research Analyst at Strategic Research Corporation for eight years. He has researched and written many studies and reports on computer storage and networking. He is the Director of the Network Buyer's Guide on the Internet, a Web site that facilitates gathering purchase information for network and system administrators.

NBG Sample on CD ROM :
Scott Cerny

INTRODUCTION

This book was written for people confronted with the task of buying computer networking equipment. The choices are many, and we're here to help! This material focuses on the buying process, the key purchase criteria to consider for networking components, and specifications on many products on the market. This book is a reference for people of all skills levels, whether you're new to networking or a savvy networking professional.

The book is packaged with a CD-ROM that provides a searchable version of the book. It also includes several software tools from Interpose Inc. and Imagenet Corporation to assist in network planning and purchases. In addition, the CD-ROM contains detailed company profiles taken from the Network Buyer's Guide (NBG) on the Internet (www.sresearch.com).

Please remember that this publication is a buyers guide, not a training manual on how to network. Our objective here is to help you find and assess products. For more information on networking, take a look at books such as *PC Magazine's Guide to Connectivity,* 3rd. Edition.

How This Book Is Organized

The first two chapters of this book provide a basic overview of networking and what networking has to offer. Chapter 3 establishes a methodology for making the best possible purchase decisions; it should help make you a critical buyer and save you time in the process.

Chapters 4 through 12, the bulk of this published work, consist of product information. These chapters begin by discussing each product class and describing its role in networking. They also identify the key features of the equipment so you know what to look for when making a purchase. Finally, the chapters include comprehensive tables of networking products and their specifications as provided by equipment vendors.

The book finishes up with several appendices. Appendix A is a contact list of all the companies whose products are mentioned in the book. Appendix B is a collection of forms that you can copy and use to help you make purchase decisions; it also includes detailed explanations of how to use the forms. Appendix C describes the contents of the CD-ROM and explains how to install it.

Using the Product Information Chapters

In Chapters 4 through 12, each network component is presented using three elements: an introduction, a key product features discussion, and product specification tables. After introducing the network product class, we discuss its key features. For each feature, there's a heading that includes the same six words—"Performance," "Reliability," "Manageability," "Scalability," "Flexibility," and "Value"—just to the right of the feature name. These words represent key product criteria. The criteria in bold are those addressed by that particular feature.

Here is a sample feature heading for file servers:

Processor Speed and RAM

Performance	Reliability	Manageability	Scalability	Flexibility	**Value**

The feature in this sample is a computer's processor speed and RAM. The heading suggests that this feature set primarily addresses the product's performance and overall value. The text underneath each heading explains the feature or features in greater detail.

After this description of important features and purchase criteria are the product specification tables. These tables provide a good sampling of available products and list some of the factors that differentiate them. You can reach these vendors by looking up their contact information in Appendix A or by trying the NBG on the Internet (www.sresearch.com) for a link to their Web site.

1 WHY NETWORK?

NETWORKING IS AN EVOLUTIONARY step in the use of desktop computers. Before the PC, mainframes or mini-computers commonly provided central processing with attached terminals. Most computing was done in large businesses and was focused on mission critical applications. With the advent of the PC, businesses and institutions of all sizes could afford to computerize. Large companies also adopted PCs and business information began disseminating to the desktop. The need for shared access to this information and the economic benefits of sharing resources were the driving forces to network.

WHY NETWORK?

Resource Sharing

Networking is about sharing resources, whether equipment such as a printer or information such as a spreadsheet file. Sharing resources can increase productivity, cut costs, and give you a competitive advantage.

Printers and Other Hardware Resources

The most common piece of shared equipment is the printer. If five people need to use a printer, it makes sense to buy just one and give everyone access to it. One strategy would be to patch the five printer cables to a box that users could switch manually—enabling one person at a time to print. But it makes more sense to use a print-sharing device to route print requests and queue the print jobs without manual intervention. This arrangement allows several people at once to use the printer—without swapping cables or flipping switches.

Building a network infrastructure that allows you to share many resources gives you room for growth and flexibility. Even if you just want to share a printer today, before long you'll probably want to share other equipment such as CD-ROM drives, tape drives, and so on.

Software Applications

Networks also enable you to share software. Software applications designed to run on server-based networks are often referred to as client/server applications. They can provide users with a consistent interface. In addition, they let the network administrator manage just one copy of the software on a server rather than many single workstation versions. Network software applications can also allow several people to use files and information simultaneously. For instance, a database application may permit many people to view the same record simultaneously, but allow only one person at a time to edit it. A networked word processor may let several people annotate a document, color-coding the edits to indicate who made them.

Information

Networks make it simple to share information, or data. Information is often a company's most valuable resource. Invoices, inventories, product specifications, and marketing data are just a few examples. Getting the most out of this information means sharing it with the appropriate people and departments. If your customer service department can instantly call up information for a customer on the phone, you may have a strategic advantage in the service you're able to provide. Networking is an important piece in making this possible for most businesses.

In addition to sharing information on internal networks, companies are using the biggest network of all, the Internet, to help serve customers

WHY NETWORK?

with accurate and updated information. Copying files to a disk or tape and then mailing them just isn't as efficient as sending information electronically. It's nearly impossible to share and manage your information without networking. In a server-based model, you can store information centrally on the server where it is much easier to manage and protect than if it's distributed across desktops.

The Benefits of Networking

The key reason for networking is improved productivity. This can sometimes be hard to measure. For people, it may mean saving 10 minutes on a daily task so they can now spend that time on other work. For equipment, it's operating at 80 percent rather than 40 percent capacity. For information, it's getting the right stuff to the right people faster and in the right form. A good business network improves the productivity of everyone, even clients, by letting them make the best use of their time and resources. The sections that follow describe some of the advantages you'll gain from networking.

Leveraged Resources

When a resource is networked, it's available to many people. This allows for *more* usage with *less* equipment. For example, if one printer is connected to a single computer, the printer may be idle for much of the time. On a network serving many people, the printer spends more time printing.

Improved Communications

The telephone revolutionized communications by allowing you to carry on a conversation with someone who wasn't right there with you. Networking makes possible electronic mail (e-mail), another revolutionary tool for communicating the written word in similar speed and range. With e-mail, you can easily send messages and files to others. These messages are delivered almost instantly, even if they're going around the world. You can also broadcast a single message to many people without much additional effort. And you can send and read e-mail messages at your convenience.

Instant Access to Information

Instant information has become part of modern culture. CNN provides fast access to the world's news. Most business customer service departments can provide instant access to order status, ship dates, inventory, and other information. For many organizations, fast access to information has gone from being a strategic advantage to being a minimum standard for survival. Networking plays a major role in facilitating the fast access to information demanded today.

WHY NETWORK?

Lower Costs
Networking helps lower costs in a number of ways, particularly by enabling you to share resources. For example, you can buy several modems and make them accessible to a dozen or more people rather than buying each person a modem. In the case of software, it can be less expensive to buy a network license than to buy individual copies for all your workstations. In almost all cases, sharing means saving.

Resource Management
Networks can make it easier to manage resources. Instead of managing a printer for every workstation, for example, you'll be managing a smaller number of shared printers. In addition, with networks, management and control can become more centralized. For example, through network software, I may be able to configure distributed printers remotely from the network administrator console. I might even get a notice via e-mail or pager if something goes wrong. I may be able to check a report that tells me about who is using what printer and how much so I can maximize print traffic and use.

A Competitive Edge
Customer service is critical to the success of many organizations. A good network can provide timely information to assist technical support calls, provide and maintain order information, and so on. This type of service is now standard in many industries, but your company can still distinguish itself from the rest by having the kind of information access you only get by networking. Tying into the Internet and creating a Web presence is another example of networks providing a competitive edge, not only for marketing but for providing online service such as software updates, technical support, and the like.

The Drawbacks of Networking
Most businesses that use more than one or two computers will benefit from some form of networking. But there are always some drawbacks, even if the benefits far outweigh them.

Installation
Networks are usually installed to streamline work flow. In some cases, the installation may be part of a reengineering process that can radically change business operations. Physically installing network hardware will inevitably disrupt business activity. Planning ahead can minimize the impact of the installation. Install as much equipment as you can during off hours. Also consider doing the installation in increments to affect fewer people at a time.

WHY NETWORK?

Maintenance

Like all equipment, networks need maintenance. Someone must back up data, assign and reassign users, install software, and troubleshoot equipment problems. Having maintenance done under a service contract is a good option for many. Even so, there are things that someone internally needs to take care of, such as changing backup tapes or changing user passwords. Fear of maintenance is a common argument against networking. But networking is not the arcane process it used to be. With today's simple and reliable network solutions, the benefits of networking far outweigh the costs. Because networks are now reasonably simple and reliable, you can consider doing maintenance in house, and you can still use an outside service for the "big stuff." Once again, planning is key. Determine the maintenance issues ahead of time so you can make informed decisions.

Dependency

When work flow and productivity are tied to the network, they are clearly affected when the network goes down. How will you get your data? How can you print? These concerns are legitimate, but there are strategies that can protect you from network downtime and improve restore times if downtime occurs. For example, many people are very concerned about losing the data that their company has become so dependent on. Backing up to tape daily, or, better yet, storing the same information on more than one hard disk minimizes risks of data loss and provides ways of quickly getting back on line. The increased productivity you gain from networking should make the inevitable disruptions acceptable.

Commitment

Networking requires certain commitments in terms of time, effort, and money. You need to choose a network topology, network software, and so on. If for some reason you have to change to a different system down the line, it could get expensive. A good way to ensure that your network won't become obsolete is to invest in widely used nonproprietary architectures. Then you can install the newer technologies when company growth demands it while retaining overall connectivity to older systems. This way you can gradually migrate to the new technology, instead of having to scrap your entire system in favor of a new one.

Do You Need To Network?

You may wonder what you'll gain from networking. You can get a pretty good picture by asking the right questions. Talk with a company of similar size that has networked and listen to what they say. Have a consultant or system integrator put together a conceptual plan based on your business

WHY NETWORK?

activity. If you have three or more computer users, you can probably benefit from networking. The fact that today's computer operating systems
now include basic networking capabilities makes it easy to begin.

The Wait-and-See Approach

The wait-and-see approach can work well for new technology and applications. It's not always great to be the first one using a new product. You
may end up spending a lot of time fixing something that wasn't quite
ready for market. Or the product may bomb after you've invested a great
deal of money in installation and training. But the wait-and-see approach
doesn't really make sense for basic networking, the core bugs and problems of which have been overcome. If you use the wait-and-see approach
to networking, you risk being left behind by the competition. Some form
of networking will provide the cost benefit you are looking for. Install too
little and your needs are not met. Install too much and you've sunk capi-
tal into a quickly depreciating asset. The key is finding the right fit and
using a strategy that accommodates an incremental growth plan.

The Costs of Not Networking

You can also decide whether it makes senses to network by asking the
question "What are the costs of not networking?" Things may "work"
now but what productivity gains and business opportunities can you
achieve with better information technology? Usually the question is not
whether to network, but what level of networking you could benefit from.
Some businesses require extensive networking. Others may only need to
share a printer. Determine what's best for you by considering the size of
your operation and what your business currently does. Stay informed on
computing in your industry.

CHAPTER

2 NETWORK BASICS

THIS CHAPTER COVERS BASIC networking concepts and terminology. You'll review the basic network components necessary for all networks that should meet the needs for most networks under 100 people. These include cables, file servers, network operating system software, and more. Larger sites may have special needs such as integrating mainframe systems, integrating remote sites into the network, and wireless connections. These are covered briefly as well.

NETWORK BASICS

BY NO MEANS DOES this chapter cover everything you need to know to set up and run a network! Before you can install even a basic network you need to do more reading, be able to follow detailed instructions, and go through some trial and error. In fact, it's always a good choice to have your network installed professionally, whether you hire someone from outside or have someone within your company who specializes in installing and maintaining networks. Even if you plan to take on networking responsibilities, it pays to have the network set up by a professional while you watch, learn, and participate in the process. If you do decide to use a professional for installation or service, be sure you get one with knowledgeable network engineers and at least some experience installing medium to large sites. And make sure to check references! Spend some time on the phone with satisfied customers. Better yet, take them to lunch so they'll relax and really spend some time with you.

Networking Overview

As illustrated in Figure 2.1, networking means connecting computers together to share information and resources. Doing this requires a connection (cable), hardware that enables these connections (network interface cards, hubs, and/or routers), and software to control and manage the sharing process.

The two basic forms of networking are peer-to-peer and server-based. In a *peer-to-peer network*, computers are attached to each other and can communicate and share resources among themselves. Peer-to-peer networking can be an inexpensive way to network; a starter kit for five systems costs as little as $600 (not including computers of course). But this type of network tends to be slow, especially with many users carrying out many shared operations. This is because your workstation may be performing functions for others on the network while you're using it. If your sharing needs are light and mostly consist of printing and e-mail, and you're attaching under ten computers, peer-to-peer is a viable option.

In a *server-based network*, the user' computers are attached to one or more computers (servers) dedicated to providing shared resources. Most networks today are server-based, requiring you to dedicate at least one computer to serve your users. Server-based networks are faster and often more reliable than peer-to-peer networks. Client workstations no longer have to serve others and the server system can be optimized to provide network services exclusively.

If you're deciding between server-based and peer-to-peer networking, here is some advice: If you can afford it, go with a server-based network. A typical, server-based PC LAN network for ten users costs around $15,000 installed (this includes everything but the workstations). Even though your up front costs are higher than with peer-to-peer, better performance and expandability make this a good value (see Table 2.1).

NETWORK BASICS

■ Figure 2.1   Networking technologies

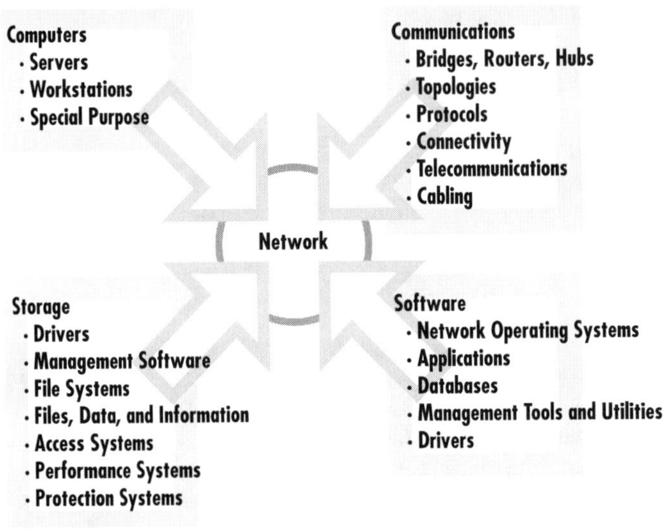

Computers
- Servers
- Workstations
- Special Purpose

Communications
- Bridges, Routers, Hubs
- Topologies
- Protocols
- Connectivity
- Telecommunications
- Cabling

Network

Storage
- Drivers
- Management Software
- File Systems
- Files, Data, and Information
- Access Systems
- Performance Systems
- Protection Systems

Software
- Network Operating Systems
- Applications
- Databases
- Management Tools and Utilities
- Drivers

■ Table 2.1   Server Versus Peer-to-Peer Networks

	Server-Based	Peer-to-Peer
Purchase and installation cost	Medium	Low
Scalability (number of users)	Low to high	Low to medium
Input/output load	High	Low
Performance	High	Low
Maintenance costs	Medium to high	Low
Client/Server applications	Yes	Yes, but slow
Resource availability	Medium to high	Low to medium
Resource sharing	High	Medium

Basic Network Components
Figure 2.2 shows the basic components for networking. You'll learn more about these components in the sections that follow.

Workstations
A *workstation* is a computer that an individual uses to do his or her work. When you connect these workstations so they can share information

NETWORK BASICS

■ Figure 2.2 Simple networks

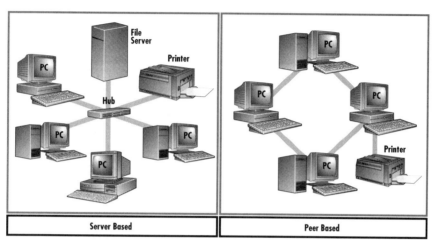

and/or resources, you have networked them. Today, workstations usually have their own processors and storage and can operate on their own if they're not connected to a network. They often run applications like word processing programs and spreadsheets locally, but use and store their files on the server. Diskless workstations are less common today. These machines are often called terminals, and rely completely on the network to function. Files stored on the server can be shared with other workstations on the network. In peer-to-peer networking, workstations can act as servers, providing other computers with their information and resources.

File Servers

File servers are a critical part of the network. These special, network computers are dedicated to processing and managing shared information, applications, and network resources. For this reason, servers tend to be high-performance computers with fast processors, lots of memory, and fast I/O. This high performance helps maintain fast access when many people are connected.

File servers can come from many computing platforms, including PC, UNIX, and even mainframe systems. PC and UNIX are the most common platforms for file servers and networking. Administrators take extra precautions to keep their servers running and their data secure because an outage would affect many people. The servers themselves often incorporate fault-tolerant features such as redundant interfaces, buses, power supplies, and disk storage.

NETWORK BASICS

Network Interface Cards

The network interface card (NIC) is a circuit board that plugs into an existing slot on the workstation. This card enables the computer to transmit and receive information across the network. The type of NIC you use depends on the *hardware protocol* of your network (Ethernet and Token Ring are examples of hardware protocols—the methods by which electrical transmissions are made throughout the network). NICs vary in performance, and support different types of cabling and connectors.

Cabling

Cabling is the wiring used to make the connections between machines. The most common cabling used today is *twisted-pair*, which is like standard telephone wiring. However, there is a sizable installed base of *coaxial cable* in use as well. This cable looks just like TV cable but it's specially rated for network use. Cable types can vary in the bandwidth they can handle. *Bandwidth* refers to the range of frequencies a circuit will pass. As with plumbing, the larger the pipe, the more water can pass through it. Cabling is a large part of network costs and an important consideration in the network planning process. Even though the actual cost of the cable is not too high (although its significant), the labor involved in laying it into walls and ceilings, hooking up wall jacks, and testing it add quite a bit to the cost. Figure 2.3 illustrates the common cable and connection types.

Twisted-Pair Cable   Unshielded twisted-pair (UTP) cable is the most common cabling used for today's network installations for two reasons: First, buildings are usually wired with UTP for telephone systems so it's convenient to use it for networking. (But you should make sure to test existing cable to see if it is properly rated for network applications.) Second, UTP is inexpensive relative to coaxial and fiber-optic cabling, and is still sufficient for today's typical network. The downside to UTP is that it is susceptible to electrical noise or interference. It also might not support the high-speed rates fiber-optic is capable of, although it is adequate for 10 Mbps and high-speed 100 Mbps networkings.

Coaxial Cable   Coaxial cable (sometimes called "coax") consists of a central copper wire surrounded by insulation and shielding layers. It provides somewhat better shielding from electrical noise than UTP and can support higher data transmission rates (although typical network speeds are within the capabilities of both). For this reason, coaxial may still be chosen over UTP in environments of high electrical interference. Its speed advantage is insignificant because the difference is small and it's the other network equipment that usually prohibits high network speeds.

NETWORK BASICS

■ Figure 2.3 Cable and connection types

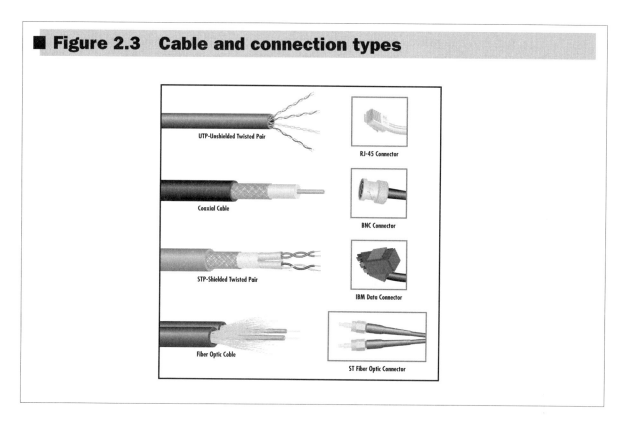

Fiber-Optic Cable   Fiber-optic technology differs significantly from the technology used for UTP and coax cable. These cables transmit signals using light beams instead of copper wire. The key advantages of fiber-optic cable are very high transmission speeds and immunity to electrical interference. In addition, fiber-optic cable can support long distances, is highly resistant to corrosion, and is more secure than wire-based cable. The downsides are its higher cost, the high cost of components that can use it, and added complexity in configuring connections. Fiber-optic is used in only specialized networking applications.

Hub

The *hub* (sometimes referred to as an MAU for IBM equipment) is a device that workstation cables are plugged into (when workstations are connected in a "star" configuration). This hub then connects to a server. Hubs often employ LEDs to show active connections, electronic traffic, and other information. It is common to "stack" hubs as more connections are needed. Some networks are actually configured without hubs, and workstations are instead chained together through a main cable running

NETWORK BASICS

throughout the office. This configuration is less common because a downed station or connection can affect others in the chain; in contrast, the hub isolates these problems to each particular workstation.

Network Operating System (NOS)

Computers need operating system software to function. Desktop PCs commonly use Windows or System 7 for Macintosh. Although Windows has some built-in networking capabilities, people typically use software specially designed to manage the flow of information over the network. This is called the network operating system (NOS). It resides on both servers and workstations, enabling the sharing of information and re-sources. The most common network operating software for the PC is Nov-ell's NetWare. The UNIX environment is different in that it has complete built-in networking capabilities. Because workstations run the same code as servers, there's no need for additional NOS software.

Network Applications

Network applications are those designed for client/server computing. These are applications such as e-mail, groupware, and databases that focus on sharing information. You can buy general application software—like word processing or spreadsheet programs—for single users or for use by many people on a network. Network versions of applications have spe-cial features that make it easier to share information.

Storage Devices

Although information storage is a critical part of the network, it is rarely thought of as a network component; often it is a component of the file server. Storage may not seem related to connectivity, but without it there is little reason to network. Files and data form the network's most impor-tant asset. Information on the network is contained in disk drives built into the file server or storage server. Tape drives also form part of virtu-ally every network because tape is relatively inexpensive and well-suited for backing up the information on the disk drives. Optical technology is also common in networks, particularly CD-ROMs, which provide refer-ence information, software distribution, and other functions.

Network Printers

Like storage, network printers are often thought of as peripherals rather than network components. However, printing is an important network function and print services are often a key reason that a business chooses to network. You can connect a stand-alone printer to a network with con-nectivity equipment. You can also use network printers, which have built-in network connectivity equipment and are usually "industrial grade" to handle the increased load of being used by many people.

NETWORK BASICS

Advanced Network Components

Large networks, networks that need to integrate with many computer types, and businesses with special network needs need more advanced networking equipment. Some of these advanced components can still be plug-and-play, but their function is more specialized than basic connectivity needs. Figure 2.4 illustrates a more complex network with additional equipment.

Application Servers

As networks grow, they need additional servers to accommodate the increased number of workstations. The ratio of servers to workstations depends on computing needs. At a certain point it makes more sense to have different servers perform specific functions. For instance, a network may be more efficient with a print server, a communications server, and a storage server than with three file servers handling all three functions.

■ Figure 2.4   A complex network

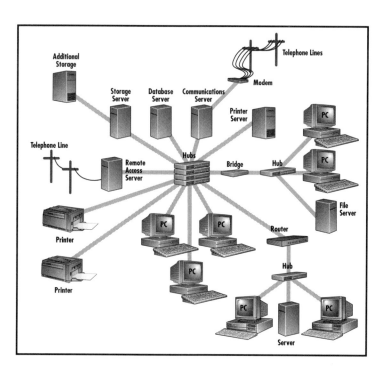

NETWORK BASICS

Servers with a sole purpose or application are called *application servers*. Here are some examples of application servers:

- A **print server** is a server dedicated to managing printers and printer requests.

- A **fax server** is a server dedicated to managing fax modems and fax requests.

- A **terminal server** is a server dedicated to communicating with mainframes and minicomputers.

- A **storage server** is a server dedicated to providing a file storage repository (and possibly backup operations).

- A **database server** is a server dedicated to handling a large database with many I/O requests.

- A **remote access server** is a server dedicated to managing remote network connections via modems.

- An **Internet server** is a server dedicated to providing Internet access and/or presenting information on the Internet.

Connecting to Other Networks

Connecting small network segments of the same type can be relatively easy—you can probably use a simple router to connect them. But often network segments need to be connected to different computing platforms—maybe a mainframe or minicomputer. Many tools enable these types of connections. Gateways, terminal servers, and other types of equipment that fall into this category are discussed in more detail in Chapter 5.

Wide area networking (WAN) is networking over great distances, usually distances of over a mile. For example, I may have a LAN at corporate headquarters and several at other sales offices. If I hook these LANs together via phone lines or other means, I have created a WAN. The use of WANs has become quite common in Fortune 1000 companies and even many small organizations can afford to create a WAN. Managing a WAN implies managing more than one LAN. However, LAN management may still be done locally with a network administrator, leaving management of the WAN, the connections between different sites, to another person or department. WAN management is usually done at headquarters, or where there is a central repository of shared information. Wide area networking is sometimes referred to as inter-networking.

NETWORK BASICS

Wireless LANs

Wireless technology exchanges information without using cables. The technologies used to achieve wireless connections are radio frequencies, infrared waves, or microwave technologies. Each vary in distance and performance capabilities. Wireless technology is primarily used for networking over great distances with microwave technology. Infrared and radio wave technologies are suitable for short-distance wireless links. See Chapter 5 for a more detailed description of these technologies and their applications.

Management Tools

Managing a network involves using software tools that provide you with information and the means to make changes. Network operating software has a number of built-in tools for managing everything from the server system to networked peripherals. However, additional software applications that specialize in system or network management can provide more robust features and capabilities that medium to large installations may require. Management tools are covered in more detail in Chapter 7.

Platforms Defined

Open systems computing consists of basically two platforms: PCs (IBM- and Mac-like personal computers) and UNIX workstations (more powerful computers from Sun Microsystems, Hewlett-Packard, and others that are used in engineering, financial, and other computing intensive markets). PCs are more prevalent and offer entry level to relatively powerful computing. UNIX machines are typically more powerful than even high-end PCs, although multiprocessing PCs and operating systems such as Windows NT are closing this gap. Minicomputers and mainframes are at the high end of the computing power spectrum. These include VAX systems from Digital Equipment Corporation, mainframe systems from IBM, and others. Networking is primarily focused at PC and UNIX environments as business move to a more distributed computing model. However, midrange and mainframe systems still have certain advantages and they are often integrated, at least for the near term, with the desktops.

Physical Topology

Physical topology refers to how workstations and computers are wired together. As illustrated in Figure 2.5, there are basically two types of physical topologies used in networking today: star and bus.

Star is the most common network configuration; it gets its name from the star shape of many cables coming to a common point. In this topology, cables from each workstation extend to a central connection called a hub, which is connected to the file server. An advantage of this wiring method is that if one workstation connection fails, the others are not

NETWORK BASICS

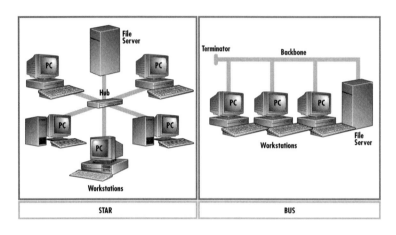

■ **Figure 2.5   Network topologies**

affected. In bus topology, each workstation cable (Tap) is attached to a single cable (backbone) that runs throughout the facility. This layout usually requires less cable than the star layout, but has its drawbacks: When a piece of equipment fails on the network, it can be difficult to isolate if your network has a bus configuration. In addition, failures can affect other workstations that wouldn't normally be affected in a star topology.

Hardware Protocol

Protocol on a network is the manner in which information exchanges occur. *Hardware protocol* is the physical format used to transmit electronic signals (information) over the network. There are three major hardware protocols currently in use: Ethernet, Token-Ring, and ARCnet. Others are now emerging and will become tomorrow's standard.

Ethernet

Ethernet is the most common protocol used today. With this method, network messages are constantly sent between the workstations and servers. Colliding messages are resent at random intervals. Each workstation reads the message addresses and accepts the ones addressed to it. Although this method appears more disorganized than others, it is actually quite fast, efficient, and relatively inexpensive. There are several Ethernet standards, the popular 10Base, which operates at 10 Mbps, and the high-speed 100Base, which operates at 100 Mbps. The extensions (10Base2,

NETWORK BASICS

10Base5, 10BaseT, and so on) refer to the cable type and corresponding standard. For example, 10BaseT refers to the IEEE specification for running Ethernet over unshielded twisted-pair cabling.

Token-Ring

In the Token-Ring protocol, network messages are carried around the network by an information packet called a token. A workstation can send data only when it gets the token. Regardless of the physical topology (star or bus), information passes from computer to computer rather than directly to a server, creating a "ring." Each time the token reaches a workstation, that station reads the address, processing it if it's for that workstation or passing it along if it's for another.

ARCnet

Like Ethernet, ARCnet provides a direct communication path between any two nodes (a node is simply a workstation on the network). Yet it uses a token similar to Token-Ring's for broadcasting.

High-Speed Standards

Most network communications occur at 10 Mbps. This speed is adequate for most applications, such as a single workstation communications to and from a server or another workstation. Equipment that performs at this speed is also much cheaper than the high-speed alternatives. But higher speeds, like the 100 Mbps formats, are becoming increasingly affordable and can help relieve bottlenecks created by a concentration of slower signals. Of course, 100 Mbps rates will one day be the standard on all networks. Figure 2.6 maps out a network speed comparison.

100BaseT

The 100BaseT standard functions just like 10BaseT, but more advanced technology allows it to perform at ten times the speed. 100BaseT is not yet widely used because 10BaseT meets the price and performance needs of most LANs. At the moment, 100BaseT is used to alleviate certain network bottlenecks, such as high traffic to and from centralized server environments, certain LAN-to-LAN or WAN applications, or specialized applications that require very high speeds (such as the high-speed backup of large amounts of data in a relatively short amount of time).

Fiber-Distributed Data Interface (FDDI)

Fiber-Distributed Data Interface (FDDI) also performs like 100BaseT, providing 100Mbps network speeds. It uses a star cable configuration, Token-Ring-like communications, and fiber-optic cable. FDDI offers high speed and reliability, but it is costly. Its implementation is generally limited

NETWORK BASICS

■ **Figure 2.6   Network speed comparison**

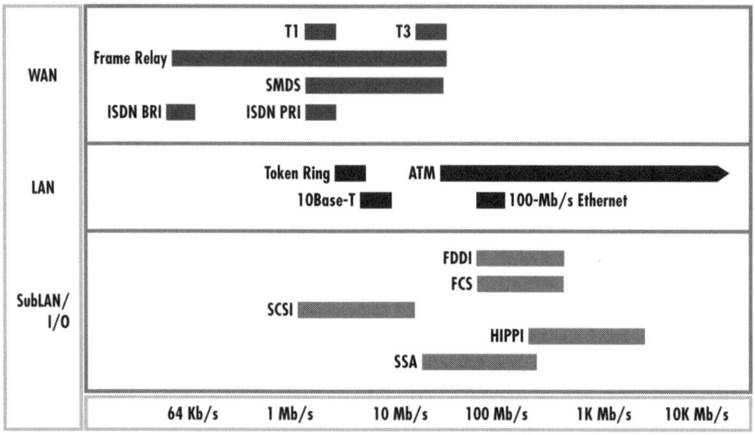

WAN	T1 T3 · Frame Relay · SMDS · ISDN BRI ISDN PRI
LAN	Token Ring ATM · 10Base-T 100-Mb/s Ethernet
SubLAN/ I/O	FDDI · FCS · SCSI · HIPPI · SSA

64 Kb/s	1 Mb/s	10 Mb/s	100 Mb/s	1K Mb/s	10K Mb/s

---

to special applications and high-speed internetworking between LANs or WANs. FDDI will continue to become less expensive as competing technologies vie for market share in the 100 Mbps market.

Asynchronous Transfer Mode (ATM)

Asynchronous Transfer Mode (ATM) touts extremely fast speeds, the flexibility to communicate at different speeds, and a single protocol for LAN or WAN communications. It is quite expensive and is used only for special networking needs.

3

THE BUYING PROCESS

WHEN PERSONAL COMPUTERS FIRST came on the market in the early 1980s, the choices of what to buy and where to buy it were fairly limited. Today, you can buy personal computers of all kinds from many sources. PCs appear on most business desktops, and have become household items even for "nontechies." If you're new to computers, buying a PC can still be somewhat daunting. But if you have computer experience, the decision is fairly straightforward.

THE BUYING PROCESS

TODAY MOST OFFICES USE networks of interconnected computers to share information and resources. Buying equipment for your network requires much more planning than purchasing a PC, because the equipment needs to work with the existing system, and any problems will affect, not just you but dozens or more people on the network. This doesn't mean that you have to produce a 10-page report every time you want to buy a cable. It does, however, mean that you need to consider purchases as part of a larger network plan that includes a sound buying method.

Before buying networking equipment you should have a network plan. The network plan prepares you for everything, from buying equipment to installing it to maintaining it. You use the plan and a sound buying methodology to make purchase decisions. Network plans and buying methodologies are both discussed in more detail in this chapter.

Establishing a Network Plan

Whether you're putting together your first network or buying something new for an established one, it's essential to have a network plan. Creating such a plan forces you to address the business needs of your organization and to consider which information technology will meet those needs. Even if someone outside the organization will install and maintain your network, someone within the organization should be involved in the network planning process. After the network is installed, you should maintain your plan to log changes, keeping an updated reference on your network. Table 3.1 lists the key elements of a network plan.

Assessing Current and Future Needs

Is the network meeting your current needs? Do you know how these needs might change in the next year or two? It is essential to assess existing equipment to determine what must change and what, instead, would merely be nice to change. You will probably discover gaps in the current systems that need to be addressed in the network plan.

Once you assess your current needs, think about how your network will grow. It is often more cost effective to buy now for some of your future needs, assuming the equipment you buy won't become obsolete. For instance, total storage on a typical network grows at 50 percent per year. Although you can add additional disk storage fairly easily, you don't want to have to open up walls and ceilings again later, which you would have to do when adding cable. It makes more sense to add extra cable and jacks the first time around. Past growth can give you some indication of future growth, but you should also take into account what the business intends to do.

THE BUYING PROCESS

Considering the Business Solution

It's easy to get busy and overlook the big picture. This often happens to IS managers, who spend so much time managing daily technical needs and crises that they have little time for network planning. No matter how overworked you are, you need to make sure that your network equipment meets your business objectives. This isn't always easy because both business goals and network needs may change.

The person in charge of network planning should meet regularly with department heads to understand their business objectives. These business objectives should drive the development and planning of information technology, enabling IS managers to anticipate needs instead of constantly having to put out fires. Used properly, information technology can make your business more competitive by enabling you to offer better customer service and helping you to lower operating costs.

It's fairly standard to have to cost-justify computer and networking purchases. Market research is revealing important information about things such as network management costs and network downtime costs. This information lets you assess equipment purchases on the basis of payback and other traditional measurements. There are now software products that automate and simplify this otherwise tedious process. One such product, C/S Solutions Advisor, created by Interpose Inc., is provided on

■ Table 3.1   Key Elements of Your Network Plan

Component	Description
Physical layout of the office	A document showing the office layout and indicating cable drops, workstation and printer locations, and so on.
A network needs assessment	A summary of network needs based on an outline of business objectives. It should include some basic plans for growth. It should also include the overall performance needs of the network so you know the level of capability needed in the products you buy.
Equipment list	An inventory of existing equipment and an assessment of the number and type of different network components you need. You can use this equipment list to assess the products on the market. Once you decide which products to buy, this list becomes an inventory of your network equipment. You should update the list when you upgrade the network.
Installation plan	A summary of the installation plan, including the stages and timing of installation. A good installation plan will minimize work disruptions and allow you to test network segments throughout the installation.
Maintenance requirements	Understanding the maintenance requirements will help you determine your staffing needs and prepare for potential downtimes or disasters. Your maintenance requirements may affect the sources you buy equipment from. If you outsource maintenance and assistance, you'll probably want to buy equipment from sources that provide these services.

THE BUYING PROCESS

the CD-ROM packaged with this book. You can find other such tools on The Network Buyer's Guide on the Internet (http://www.sresearch.com).

Using Network Planning Tools

If you have a small network, your network plan need not be complex. You may just need pen, paper, an office layout, and a sound planning process. However, if you are designing or maintaining a medium- to large-sized network, it can be extremely helpful to use specialized planning tools. Chapter 7 covers some of these network planning tools. In addition, some network management applications include tools for network planning. Planning tools can help you map out cabling, servers, workstation groups, compatibility, and so on.

The enclosed CD-ROM includes sample planning software from Imagenet. Their product is well-suited for ground up network planning. In addition to layout planning, it includes performance simulation and cost estimates based on the equipment you select.

Getting Help

It is important to never go it alone. Even experienced network administrators get opinions or assistance from peers, vendors, and others. You should establish sources of support early on. You want to know whom to call if something goes wrong *before* it goes wrong.   Try to get a mix of sources, including vendors, peers, and system integrators, who will spend time with you when you need it.

From Network Plan To Purchasing

With your network plan in place, you're ready to evaluate and purchase products. Of course you need to decide what equipment you need—as established in the network plan. Next you have to evaluate the products on the market and decide what to buy. You also need to decide how much you can afford and what your time frame is. And, you need a sound buying methodology.

Buying Methodology

Having a buying methodology simply means having a thorough system for deciding what to buy. In fact, you already follow such a method when making everyday purchases. For example, your grocery shopping strategy may include finding the item you want, inspecting ingredients, checking fat grams, determining calories, and considering price. This process is shaped by your knowledge of the products, the item's importance, and its cost. The five components of a sound buying methodology are

- Identifying a need

THE BUYING PROCESS

- Collecting information

- Establishing purchase criteria

- Selecting products

- Choosing a source

Identifying a Need

Identifying a need—whether it's solving a problem, increasing performance, and so on—is something that you initially address in the network plan for a new network. For existing networks, new needs are discovered and then become part of the evolving network plan. For example, if you decide you need access to the Internet you'll need a modem. At this point you may think you are deciding on things such as baud rate, whether to buy an internal or external modem, and so on. But what if you also want to fax directly through your computer, send database files via modem to your office headquarters, and hook up your modem to your laptop? Suddenly, one need has turned into ten. If you're lucky, a single product can satisfy several needs. But be sure your most important needs are met first so budget constraints don't interfere.

A good way to do this is to prioritize your needs, as shown here:

1	Internet access	Critical
2	Fax with my computer	Important
3	Database file transfers	Important
4	Portable	Nicety
5	Interface with a laptop	Nicety

Once you identify your priorities, you may decide to meet just your critical need of Internet access. Or, it may turn out that there's enough money in the till to get a modem that also has fax capabilities.

Fit the Particular Solution In with Your Network Objectives   Because you're operating in a network environment, you always have to consider how purchases fit in with the network. For example, if you decide that the modem will be a shared resource, you must consider the modem's impact on the network as well as the communications objectives of others. Will the modem require additional software? Will one modem be enough? What will be the network downtime for setup and maintenance?

Finally, most purchases come with hidden costs. With a modem, the hidden costs may be installation time, learning new communications software, maintenance, and network downtime. If the modem will be a network resource, there may be additional hidden costs. If it will cost $1,500

THE BUYING PROCESS

to network a $150 modem, you may decide against it if just a few people will be using it.

Collecting Information

Once you've established your needs, you can begin collecting information about products and prices. Products and brands that you are already familiar with, and happy with, are often a good place to start.

As you collect information, you may want to reassess your needs. In the modem example, you realized that the modem, sharing software, fax software, and installation would cost $3,500. If only three people will use the modem, you may be better off buying each person a modem, or you may decide to buy just one modem and have one person will handle modem communications. Your budget is always an important consideration, but don't automatically feel bound by it. If you can present a good argument for increased productivity and fast payback, the budget might turn out to be somewhat flexible.

Using Multiple Sources   You should collect information from both vendors and independent sources. Vendor-supplied information includes product literature, advertisements, and white papers. You can also gather information by consulting with sales reps, product managers, technical support personnel, resellers, trade associations, and consultants. Information from independent sources includes trade press articles, independent product comparisons, buyer's guides, and product reviews. You may also want to seek out users groups, Internet and other electronic chat lines, and current users of the product.

Vendor-provided information will undoubtedly be biased but tends to be detailed. It usually clearly states the benefits of the product—and highlights the competition's weaknesses—but downplays any drawbacks. Vendors typically have extensive technical background material on their products, but the competitive data they supply is sometimes misleading. In addition, vendors may provide expert help in implementing their products, but, as you may know from experience, product support personnel are not always knowledgeable. Your job is to sift through the hype, ask the right questions to obtain more information if necessary, and extract the useful information.

Independently provided information may be less biased but might not be as complete and may not show products at their optimal configuration. Current users of the product can verify vendor claims and expose product drawbacks. Most vendors will happily supply lists of satisfied (but not unsatisfied) customers. In addition, you can use the Internet to tap into user forums and users groups relevant to the product in question. Trade periodicals often provide product comparisons that provide close to real environment testing.

THE BUYING PROCESS

Also look for case studies in the various trade publications. Don't forget to take opinions with a grain of salt and to keep in mind any peculiarities of your own situation.

Finding Out What's Not in the Literature   Although marketing literature should accurately list product features and applications, you will want to know things that are probably not in the literature. For example, the literature often doesn't cover installation. Check with a salesperson or technical support person about how easy installation really is. The literature also rarely describes ongoing maintenance that the ongoing management costs. It's a good idea to write down the product's potential effect on your network. This becomes a helpful reference as you go through the literature and other sources of information. If the literature does not answer your questions, refer to another source.

Establishing Purchase Criteria

Once needs are assessed and product information gathered, the product selection criteria and required feature set have to be identified. These requirements must be balanced against budget constraints and the capabilities of the available products. The general rule of "buy the best your budget allows" holds true. Follow this sequence to work through the decision making process:

1. Match available features to your needs.

2. Prioritize *required* features above *nice to have* features.

3. Compare products using specifications and other sources.

4. Compare price, availability, service, and support.

5. Narrow the field.

6. Evaluate the top candidates if possible.

7. Make your choice.

Matching Features to Your Needs and Priorities   It can be relatively easy to match product features to your needs if you've done the prep work. Of course, you eliminate products that don't have the features you need. You are left with ones that meet your needs and ones that exceed them. The natural inclination is to keep stepping up to the next level of performance and features. For example, "If I'm going to go with the 166 MHz instead of the 133 MHz machine, I should upgrade the RAM and video card as well." It doesn't take long to move up the list quickly! Price usually keeps things in perspective.

THE BUYING PROCESS

Compare Product Specifications   Product specification sheets or data sheets are a key source for product feature information. Most should have the key criteria for that product class. By creating a table with product features on the left column and corresponding products along the right, you can build your own features table for comparing the products you're considering. This table also makes it easy to identify products that are missing key features you need.

If you are missing information from your comparison table, go back to your information sources for more input. You may have some questions regarding features not listed in the specifications, or have more detailed questions now that you know about the products in general. At this point, it's also a good idea to review your objectives to check that your initial goal is still intact.

By this time in the process, you've identified needs, gathered information, and assessed products. You might already have a good idea of which product you want. If not, narrow the choices.

Narrowing the Field   If you haven't done so already, eliminate products that don't absolutely meet your needs, budget, or fail on other criteria. Compare your needs with the product features table. If this is not adequate, then expand your criteria to include other factors such as availability, service, support, brand name, or reseller and peer recommendations. Figure out what additional information will give you the confidence to make a decision about what to buy.

Brand names may imply quality or reliability and buying brand names is often a safe choice. If specific brands provide you with peace of mind, it may be worth it to pay a higher price for them. For network equipment, however, there are rarely "generic" brands. Vendor brands tend to focus on different areas of the market, such as "low-end" or "high-end." Just because a company has top brand reputation in one area does not mean they are the best choice in another. You should consider them on the merits of their products as well as their reputation for standing behind them.

Product Evaluation   If you *really* want to test your choice, make arrangements to evaluate the product at your site. You'd be surprised how many vendors are willing to do this. You can try evaluating a few products at the same time and keep only the one that works best for you. It takes some effort to participate in an evaluation, and there's a possible risk to network stability unless you establish a test environment. Have a clear plan for measuring product performance. Be sure you're ready to buy if you're satisfied after the evaluation so your efforts are worth it.

THE BUYING PROCESS

Deciding Where to Buy

When collecting product information, you will undoubtedly find out about prices and about where you can buy products. Most people settle on a few sources and use them regularly. If your most important concern is price, you will probably use large suppliers that have competitive prices. If you like lots of help, you'll tend to buy from sources that emphasize service, even though they may not have the cheapest prices. It makes sense to have both types of sources, so you can choose the source that provides the appropriate service and prices.

Retail   If you're buying retail, you have a variety of options from which to choose:

- Computer retail stores generally focus on single systems and not so much on networking. These types of stores tend to have decent pricing with focus on service such as sales assistance and service departments. Examples include local independent stores and chains such as ComputerLand and Egghead Software.

- Consumer electronics stores such as Circuit City and Good Guys often carry computer equipment these days. However, do not expect to find much in the way of networking equipment.

- Computer/electronics superstores such as Fryes Electronics build their business on volume. They focus on single computer systems rather than networks, but they typically have some networking equipment, including complete networking starter kits. Prices are usually excellent and you can purchase installation support.

- Systems integrators/value added resellers (VARs) are a popular choice for networking equipment because they often specialize in network services. They tend to install and use certain brands of equipment because once they are familiar with a certain product, the installation and service becomes much easier. Specialization and service will vary. They are a good source for purchasing equipment because of their broad knowledge of products, what's new, and their experience with products and installation.

- Like system integrators or VARs, independent consultants can provide service. But they do not have the business infrastructure of other groups. Finding someone committed to it as a business is important, otherwise you may end up with someone who will not be there for you in the long run. They may purchase equipment for you through the same retail or wholesale channels as an end user. Dealing with returns and getting help can be difficult if your consultant is just a one-person

THE BUYING PROCESS

operation. Pricing can vary, but it is usually competitive. The best way to find a good consultant is to get references from retailers or other sources.

- Mail order services have become a popular way to buy equipment. Pricing is always quite good and most mail order businesses have good return policies. Technical help varies, but you can usually turn to the manufacturer for more detailed help. Online mail order through the Internet is emerging as yet another source for products.

- Manufacturers are increasingly selling directly to the public (PC manufacturers are a good example), but networking equipment is still sold mostly through channels because service needs are still high. Pricing from manufacturers varies, but is usually competitive.

Wholesale   If you're buying wholesale you have a whole different set of choices:

- General distributors such as Merisel, Ingram/Micro, and Tech Data carry a wide range of computer and computer-related equipment. Pricing is good because of high sales volume. Technical assistance will vary and assistance programs are often available.

- Specialty distributors tend to be smaller than general distributors and have a more focused product line for more specific needs. They are more likely to carry leading edge and small volume product lines than general distributors. Their knowledge and support is usually quite good and pricing is competitive.

- More and more people are opting to deal directly with manufacturers for purchases and support, whether they are buying wholesale or retail. As your network grows, so will the list of different vendor equipment that you need. Service will sometimes be excellent and sometimes frustrating. Dealing with many vendors is more difficult than dealing with a single source, such as a system integrator. You should have a good understanding of how to maintain and troubleshoot your network. Buying direct from the manufacturer means being a little more on your own when it comes to integrating that purchase with your current network.

Assessing Your Current Buying Sources   From time to time, it makes sense to assess the sources you buy from. If any source is really giving you trouble, another can probably take its place. Loyalty will generally get you better service and pricing in the long run, but don't be afraid to try new sources.

Even if you're happy with your current sources, it's a good idea to get information from sources you don't typically use. This validates your

THE BUYING PROCESS

choice in sources and keeps you up to date on new ones. Not all sources can meet all of your needs all of the time, so it's important to know of alternative sources.

A good strategy is to have more than one source for purchasing network equipment. This way, you can use the source that best fits the needs for that particular purchase. For instance, when buying an item such as cable that has no service needs, you can choose a favorite low price source—maybe you can buy mail order. For a new server setup, you may choose a system integrator who will test and install the machine because the services included with the purchase may be important. If you need something within 24 hours, product availability may determine which source you choose. Once again, the key is to have a number of sources with different characteristics so you can choose a source according to your varying needs.

4

SERVER SYSTEMS

SERVERS ARE A CRITICAL part of the network, and your buying decision here is an important one. A server can be from any computing platform, but PCs and UNIX systems make up most the market. Which server platform and type you should use depends on your computing power and connectivity needs.

SERVER SYSTEMS

THIS BUYER'S GUIDE CLASSIFIES server systems into three main categories:

- **File servers** are single processor systems that perform multiple serving functions.

- **Super servers** are multiprocessor systems that perform multiple serving functions.

- **Application servers** are servers that provide a single server function and can be single or multiprocessing systems.

File Servers

File servers follow the traditional server paradigm where one computer manages all serving functions such as printing, e-mail, modem access, backup, and so forth. They still represent a large part of the server market, although this is changing. As demand on the server increases and performance suffers, networks require additional servers. This section just discusses single processor computers and they are listed under PC, UNIX, and midrange platforms (multiprocessing file servers appear under the super server section). In the PC platform, Pentium processor machines with 32MB of RAM and at least 2GB of disk space are basic configurations. A computer like this can typically serve 25 workstations efficiently. Prices for files servers range from approximately $4,000 to $15,000.

Super Servers

There is a growing market for multiprocessing or parallel computing systems, which this guide refers to as "super servers." These systems have more than one processor; their processors work in parallel, increasing system performance significantly. This class of computers can be used as file or application servers. There are several multiprocessing methods. Symmetrical Multiprocessor (SMP) computers have multiple processors that share the system memory and I/O. "Massively parallel computers" have multiple system memory and I/O components in addition to multiple processors. A "cluster" of servers—a group of servers that act as one—are like massively parallel computers in that they work together as one system. SMP servers are by far the most common because they are relatively inexpensive and easy to use (you don't need special software to take advantage of the multiprocessing features). Super servers can also be distinguished by fault-tolerant features such as redundant power supplies, controllers, and so on. These machines are particularly well-suited for handling mission critical applications or serving a large number of workstations. Prices for these servers are $10,000 and up, depending on configuration and computing platform.

SERVER SYSTEMS

Application Servers

Network administrators have found that it is more efficient to divide tasks among servers than to add more general-purpose servers that do "everything." Each of these specialized servers, or "application servers," performs a specific function, such as printing or modem communications.

The typical application server is a computer, sold as an ordinary file server, that the network administrator custom configures and dedicates to a specific application. A small but growing portion of application servers are computers designed and preconfigured as servers for specialized functions. Some application servers—such as low-cost, plug-in print servers—are simple devices with basic electronics that can cost less than $500. On the high end are multiprocessing database servers that can cost over $100,000. Application servers are the fastest growing server market. Before you decide what to buy you should gauge the anticipated demand for the application and subsequent load on the network.

Communications Servers

Communications servers are primarily used for remote access and modem use. Remote access refers to providing network access to mobile users or remote sites. Many communications servers primarily provide modem use for people on the network at a given site. This typically includes desktop faxing and modem access to public or private networks like the Internet or CompuServe. Many communications servers are made from standard server class computers and configured for communications by the purchaser. They vary widely in cost and application.

Database Servers

Database servers make up a large part of specialized server applications, but systems are rarely packaged as such. Database servers are usually created by configuring a powerful server class computer for optimized database access and management. Some of this optimization might include multiple I/O buses for speed and redundant components for fault tolerance and accessibility.

Internet/Web Servers

Web servers—also called Internet servers—are a fast emerging class of products. The many resources on the Internet and the market exposure it offers fuel much of the interest in it. In addition, companies are finding valuable ways to use Web technology on their internal network for information sharing. Internal Webs are called intranets. UNIX computers, in particular from Sun Microsystems, have been the traditional server systems for Internet and intranet applications. But there are a number of different brands and computer platforms serving this market today. In

SERVER SYSTEMS

addition, you can now get low-cost Internet server "boxes" that have everything you need for plug-and-play operation. Although not as robust as their full-fledged counterparts, these inexpensive products provide you basic Internet/intranet server capabilities without requiring that you configure a server with all the necessary software and connectivity hardware.

Print Servers

Print server systems, the most common application server, are a varied group. The low end begins with simple plug-and-play hardware tools that accommodate small workgroups for a few hundred dollars. These systems have little computing power but perform well at their designated function. They are usually used when there is no network and network accessible files are not important. The typical network will have print services built into the network, provided by the file server. When printing needs are heavy or the network environment is large, you can dedicate a server to handling just print requests and management.

Storage/Backup Servers

A storage server is a repository for data files and performs storage related tasks such as backup and archiving. Unlike an ordinary file server, it handles storage exclusively. These systems are server-class computers with lots of disk space and good storage management software. Often they manage large external storage devices such as disk farms, tape libraries, or optical jukeboxes. They also tend to be created by a systems or network administrator rather than purchased as a prepackaged storage server solution.

Key Criteria for Server Systems

Processor Speed and RAM

Performance	Reliability	Manageability	**Scalability**	Flexibility	**Value**

The computer's processor and memory (RAM) are the two most important factors contributing to its speed. The two common processor types today are Intel-based (Pentium, 486, 386) and Motorola-based (as found in UNIX systems). The Power PC chip bridges the two. Even when processors and the amount of RAM are identical, there are small differences in performance between brands because of the system's other components.

Choosing what level of performance you need in a server can be difficult because there are so many outside factors involved (number of users, network traffic, and so on). A common buying strategy for these important network components is to "buy the most you can afford." This means

SERVER SYSTEMS

that you should first consider processor speed. You should also buy
enough RAM to operate comfortably and more if you can. But you can
add RAM later more easily than processing power. A basic Novell file
server for 10 workstations could have 16MB of RAM, preferably 32MB.
The same servers running many applications and/or managing large
amounts of disk space may require 64MB or more. Seeing network performance and monitoring caching levels will tell you if they have the right
amount of RAM.

Computer Components					
Performance	**Reliability**	Manageability	Scalability	Flexibility	Value

A network server must have quality components; they are the foundation of system integrity. It is hard enough to integrate components reliably without having to contend with component failure. Components
should also be "well-matched." Their quality and performance levels
should be equal, so that a low performing component does not reduce the
value of other components. But it is not always easy to get good quality
and well-integrated components. For this reason, many people prefer to
buy major brands or to rely on system integrators who have a reputation
for building quality machines. Asking for references and talking with people who are using products you are considering is an excellent way to
learn about component reliability and performance.

Servers are often marketed as "certified" for various operating systems. This means that they have been tested, and run successfully, under
the specified operating system or network operating system. Certification
is not a guarantee that the machine has superior components than an un-
certified machine. It is, however, another level of assurance that the machine will function well in the environment for which it has been certified.

Machine Upgradability					
Performance	Reliability	Manageability	**Scalability**	**Flexibility**	**Value**

Some computers are designed to be easy to upgrade. They may include an upgradable chipset, extra slots for RAM, room for additional
components, and so on. An upgradable machine will have a longer life, incremental upgrade costs, and more. RAM is the most common computer
upgrade and you don't need any special upgrade features to add RAM to
your machine. It's a good idea to buy a machine that has extra RAM slots
so you can add RAM without having to replace existing RAM modules.
Keep in mind that computers and their components age more from the

SERVER SYSTEMS

availability of newer and faster technology than they do from use. The machine you bought two years ago probably performs pretty much as well as it did the day you bought it, but now it's slow compared to what you can buy today. Also remember that new software has a tendency to put greater demands on memory and processing power.

All components age together. For instance, I can add RAM to a two-year-old machine to extend its life, but the other components—such as the processor, the video cards, and so forth—are still two years old. Sometimes it is more cost effective to buy a new machine and use the older one for a less computer-intensive task. It is always wise to have an upgrade or replacement plan in place before you buy.

I/O Architecture					
Performance	Reliability	Manageability	**Scalability**	Flexibility	Value

The server's main function is managing input and output (I/O) requests, whether it's to internal memory, the disk drive, or to other machines. The three common internal bus architectures (from oldest to newest) are 16-bit ISA, 32-bit EISA, and 32-bit PCI. Newer is usually better and 32-bit PCI is pretty much today's standard. A PC must also communicate with peripherals such as storage. EISA bus hard drives are common on the desktop, but SCSI is the general standard on server systems because of its superior performance. The third key I/O piece of the server is the network interface. Fortunately, the server's network card can be just like those on your workstations. There is no advantage to having a souped up network card on the server, but the card should be reliable, like all the cards on your network!

Storage					
Performance	Reliability	Manageability	**Scalability**	Flexibility	Value

Storage, more specifically hard-disk storage, is a critical part of your server. Hard-disk storage has become incredibly reliable and inexpensive. Even so, it seems to barely keep ahead of the demand for increased capacity from new software applications and the large data files they create. For this reason, you should buy at least twice your current capacity to accommodate for some growth. But that may only last you a year since typical server storage requirements increase at approximately 35 percent annually. The low cost of disk drives has also helped fuel the market for fault-tolerant disk storage as part of the typical file server. Disk "duplexing," or "mirroring," is the practice of writing information to two separate

SERVER SYSTEMS

hard drives so, if one should fail, the other will continue operation without downtime. This is the first level of using redundant disk drives to achieve fault tolerance, referred to as RAID (Redundant Array of Inexpensive Disks). There are more advanced levels of RAID, as described in Chapter 10. Storage options are an important consideration when choosing a server.

Communications Servers ∎

Manufacturer	3Com	3Com
Model	Office Connect Remote (510, 520, 530)	AccessBuilder 2000
General Description and Benefits	For single Web or workgroup access, from remote LAN to any size of central site	Features 4 or 8 high-speed asynchronous ports. The AccessBuilder 2000 belongs to 3Com's SuperStack and can be easily configured as a stand-alone device or a leaf node on a larger network.
CPU Type	Motorola	I 960 Processor
Ports	ISDN BRI Voice (fax or modem) Leased line	4 or 8 port options
Protocols	Routes IP/IPX; bridges all others	SUP, ARA 1.0/2.0/2.1, PAP, CHAP
Network Connectivity	LAN—10BASE-T (RJ-45), 10BASE2 (BNC)	Ethernet
Bundled Software	Configuration tool, and all software included in price.	Remote Access Client 6.2, NetWare Bindery/Windows NT/NDS Security Support
Comments	Optimised for use over ISDN. Approved for connection in USA, Japan, and Europe.	
Warranty	1 year	1 year
Price	$1,095 (510), $1,295 (520), $1,495 (530)	$2,795–$3,895

Manufacturer	3Com	3Com
Model	AccessBuilder 4000	AccessBuilder 5000
General Description and Benefits	For large branch locations of corporate remote networking applications. The chassis can handle a mix of up to 16 asynchronous and ISDN connections simultaneously in either Ethernet or Token Ring environments. The product supports a range of NOS-based and third-party external security servers.	Brings together multisegment LAN switching and 256 WAN ports. The 17-slot chassis supports Ethernet and Token Ring networks. It accommodates hot-swappable WAN media modules to mix and match asynchronous, ISDN, PRI, and T1/E1 connections in a fault-tolerant enclosure.
CPU Type	I 960 Processor	I 960 Processor
Ports	4, 8, or 16 port options	From 48 to 256 ports available
Protocols	PPP, MCPPP, SUP, ARA 1.0/2.0/2.2, IP, IPX, BCP, PPTP, PAP, CHAP	PPP, MCPPP, SLIP, ARA 1.0/2.0/2.1, IP, IPX, BCP, PPTP, PAP, CHAP
Network Connectivity	Ethernet or Token Ring	Ethernet or Token Ring, DOS/Windows 3.1/Windows 95 client support
Bundled Software	Remote Access Client 6.2, NetWare Bindery/Windows NT/NDS Security Support.	Remote Access Client 6.2, NetWare Bindery/Windows NT/NDS Security Support
Comments		
Warranty	1 year	1 year parts and labor
Price	$6,795–$7,795	$24,995–$29,995

Manufacturer	APT Communications, Inc.	Aurora Technologies, Inc.
Model	DS3	Solaris x86 Communication/ WAN Server
General Description and Benefits	3 port dial-in and dial-out, stand-alone, server for Macintosh. Connects to Ethernet. Supports Apple Remote Access 1.0 and 2.0, network, zone, and device level filters for each user group	Attach up to 8 high-speed sync or async WAN links to an Intel/Solaris x86 machine for WAN communications-ideal for Telco. Connect to terminals, printers, modems, DSU/CSU, ISDN terminal adapters, routers
CPU Type	Motorola 68302	N/A
Ports	3 RS-232 serial asynchronous	4 or 8 port ISA/EISA. Sync and/or async. Up to 128kbps per line
Protocols	ARA 1.0 and 2.0	PPP, X.25, SNA, HDLC, SDLC

N/A—Not applicable   INA—Information not available

Table Continues →

■ Communications Servers

Manufacturer	APT Communications, Inc.	Aurora Technologies, Inc.
Network Connectivity	Ethernet 10BASE-T, 10BASE2, AUI	DB-25, RS-232 standard. RS-422/485 optional
Bundled Software	Software for server, dial-out client for Macintosh, management software	Single-command install device driver.
Comments	Auto detection ARA 1.0 or 2.0, enhanced security includes call back, password aging, manual pass words; zone, network	High-speed sync or async selectable/port. Large, dual-ported DMA buffers. Flow control processing. Full modem support all lines.
Warranty	2 year	1 year
Price	$1,500	$1,000

Manufacturer	Aurora Technologies, Inc.	Axis Communications
Model	Solaris x86 Terminal Server	Axis 850 (Ethernet)/950 (Token Ring) CD ROM servers
General Description and Benefits	Attach up to 8 high-speed async serial peripherals (printers, terminals, modems) to an Intel/x86 machine for communication-intensive applications like modem banks, Internet	32-bit RISC
CPU Type	N/A	Up to 32MB
Ports	4 or 8 port ISA/ EISA. Async. Up to 115.2Kbps per line	1MB
Protocols		7
Network Connectivity	DB-25, RS-232 standard. RJ-45 optional	SCSI
Bundled Software	Single-command install device driver	Ethernet, Token Ring
Comments	Dedicated RISC communications controllers. Large double buffers. Flow control processing. Full modem support.	
Warranty	1 year	5 year
Price	$500	$799–$999

Manufacturer	The Bristol Group
Model	IsoFax Fax Tower
General Description and Benefits	A network-ready fax solution includes NT operating system and IsoFax server software, and fax modems. Supports Windows, Windows 95, Windows NT, Sun, Hewlett-Packard, IBM, and Mac clients.
CPU Type	Pentium processor, 32MB of RAM, 1.2GB hard drive
Ports	Up to 16 internal fax modems, up to 128 fax modems in a single tower
Protocols	TCP/IP
Network Connectivity	TCP/IP 10BASE- T, TCP/IP 100BASE-T, 10 MBit, thick or thin Ethernet
Bundled Software	Includes NT operating system, IsoFax server software, and client software
Comments	FaxTower includes administrative tools, modem management, complete, complete logging information, queue management, fax distribution, intelligent transmission features, e-mail-to-fax gateway, and APIs.
Warranty	1 year on-site
Price	$6,995 with an internal fax modem

N/A—Not applicable   INA—Information not available

Communications Servers ■

Manufacturer	Brooktrout Technology, Inc.	Brooktrout Technology, Inc.
Model	TR114 Series, TruFax Series	TruFax200, TR114
General Description and Benefits	Tr114 Series universal port boards offer full fax and voice processing on a single, multichannel board for high-performance LAN fax servers. TruFax Series feature 2 channels of fax per board and workshop servers.	TruFax200 features 2-channel fax board. TR114 offers 2- to 8-channel fax and voice processing, speech record, and playback. Both V.17, 14.4bps
CPU Type	Each channel on a TR114 board has a dedicated 32-bit microprocessor with embedded DSP core and real-time operating system.	None
Ports	TR114 Series boards are available in 2 and 4 channel analog configurations with loop starter or DID and 2, 4, 8 channel digital configurations with MVIP or PEB, TruFax is a 2-channel fax analog card.	TruFax200: 2 loop start interface. TR114: 2-4 loop start or DID, 2-8 PEB or MVIP
Protocols	TR114 Series supports V.17, V.21, V.27, V.29 TruFax Series supports V.17, V.33, V.29, V.27, V.21	TruFax200 supports T.30, MH TR114 supports T.30, MH, MR, MMR, ECM
Network Connectivity	N/A, application dependent	Loop start, DID, T1, E1, and ISDN
Bundled Software	The Brooktrout API supports Unix, UnixWare, Solaris, SCOUNIX, SCOxenix, QNX, OS/2, Windows, Windows NT, and DOS.	Supports all major LAN fax applications software
Comments		
Warranty	1 year	1 year
Price	TR114 Series starts at $1,995. TruFax starts at $799	TruFax200: $799 TR114: $1,995

Manufacturer	Calculus, Inc.	CallWare Technologies, Inc.
Model	EZ-Fax for networks	Series 5 - Model 3000
General Description and Benefits	Hardware\software combo providing true network fax-server functions (not simple modem sharing) optimized for outbound applications.	Advanced-level plug and play, voice and call processing system, with CallWare 5.2 pre-installed and pre configured. CallWare provides voice messaging, automated attendant, audiotext, fax, pager notification, and enhanced AMIS networking.
CPU Type	ISA-bus machine, MS-DOS v.5x or v6.x, 1024k RAM	CPU 100 Pentium MHz 32MB RAM 2GB hard drive
Ports	Includes coprocessor fax card using Intel I8051 microprocessor	4 ports, upgradeable to 48
Protocols	Protocol independent	TCP/IP SPX/IPX
Network Connectivity	Certified on Novell NetWare, Artisoft LANtastic, Banyan Vines. Runs on WFW, Windows NT, Windows 95, MS LanMan, OS\2 LAN server, PowerLAN, Invisible Network, others	NetWare 4.x
Bundled software	Includes DOS fax-server software, and DOS and Windows client software	CallWare 5.2 software offers full-featured voice messaging, Internet, fax, and GroupWise integration is optional.
Comments	Optimized for outbound applications such as purchasing, sales, insurance, escrow, and mass faxing. Especially useful for faxing from legacy DOS apps under either DOS or Windows.	CallWare series 5 Model 1000 is available in 500, 1000, and 5000, and 10,000 user configurations.
Warranty	1 year	90 days from installation
Price	Base $699	Prices begin at approximately $32,945

N/A—Not applicable   INA—Information not available

Table Continues →

■ Communications Servers

Manufacturer	**CallWare Technologies, Inc.**	**CallWare Technologies, Inc.**
Model	Series 5—Model 2000	Series 5—Model 1000
General Description and Benefits	Mid-level plug and play, voice and call processing system, with CallWare 5.2 pre-installed and pre-configured. CallWare provides voice messaging, automated attendant, audiotext, fax, pager notification, and enhanced AMIS networking.	Entry-level plug and play, voice and call processing system, with CallWare 5.2 pre-installed and pre-configured. CallWare provides voice messaging, automated attendant, audiotext, fax, pager notification, and enhanced AMIS networking.
CPU Type	CPU 100 Pentium MHz 32MB RAM 1.2GB hard drive	CPU 80486 DX/2-66MHz 16MB RAM 1.08GB hard drive
Ports	4 ports, upgradeable to 48	4 ports, upgradeable to 12
Protocols	TCP/IP SPX/IPX	TCP/IP SPX/IPX
Network Connectivity	NetWare 4.x	NetWare 4.x
Bundled software	CallWare 5.2; GroupWise integration is optional.	CallWare 5.2; GroupWise integration is optional.
Comments	Available in 50, 100, and 500 user configurations	Available in 10, 25, 50, and 100 user configurations
Warranty	90 days from installation	90 days from installation
Price	$9,945+	$4,945+

Manufacturer	**CASTELLE**	**CASTELLE**
Model	FaxPress Family 1000, 1500, 2000, and 3000	OfficeConnect Fax Server
General Description and Benefits	FaxPress is a compact, self-contained fax server that connects directly to a LAN and is accompanied by software that is installed from any personal computer or workstation on the LAN.	A self-contained, network fax server designed to provide comprehensive fax services and fax management features to LANs up to 50 users.
CPU Type	FaxPress systems utilize M68xxx CPUs with 9600bps or 14.4Kbps modems	Motorola MC68302 CPU with a Rockwell 14.4 fax modem
Ports	1-4 RJ-45 lines	1 10BASE-T RJ-45 port, 1 BNC port for 10BASE-2
Protocols	802.3 and 802.3SNAP8137 Ethernet IIsource/non-source routing in Token Ring environments plus others	802.3 and 802.2SNAP8137 Ethernet IIsource/non-source routing in Token Ring environments plus others
Network Connectivity	NetWare 2.x, 3.x, 4.x as well as Windows NT	NetWare 2.x, 3.x and 4.x as well as Windows NT
Bundled Software	Proprietary client/server software included with every unit	Proprietary client/server software included with every unit
Comments		"Clippable" OfficeConnect product line includes fax and print servers and 3Com's remote routers and hubs.
Warranty	1 year	1 year
Price	$1,995–$5,495	$1,695

Manufacturer	**Chase Research**	**Cayman Systems**
Model	10LAN+10LAN Rack+	Marina 130
General Description and Benefits	Connects serial devices (e.g., terminals, printers, modems, PCs, SLIP/PPP lines, or any RS232 device) remotely or locally to LAN.	Provides remote branch offices and mobile users with connections to their LAN and network services including e-mail, remote printing, file sharing, internal WWW, and the Internet.
CPU Type	25MHz Intel 38625 processor	16MHz Motorola MC68302 processor
Ports	8 or 16 DB25 (stand-alone) or RJ-45 (rackmount) connectors with surge protection and 115.2Kbps port speed	3 WAN ports and 1 Ethernet hi-media LAN port, supports a variety of configuration needs using RS-232 asynchronous interfaces for easy installation.

N/A—Not applicable   INA—Information not available

Communications Servers ■

Manufacturer	Chase Research	Cayman Systems
Protocols	TCP/IP (rlogin, Telnet), SLIP, CSLIP, PPP, PAP, RCP, LPD, SNMP, DNS, PING	TCP/IP over PPP, AppleTalk
Network Connectivity	AUI, BNC and 10BASE-T network interfaces built-in with "auto-sensing" or Ethernet LAN connectivity	Marina 130 supports the industry standard TCP/IP. This provides access to popular network services such as Telnet, FTP, Internet, e-mail WAIS, Gopher, and WWW.
Bundled Software	Printer, modems, and bi-directional devices configured as local ports on Unix host	It incorporates MarinaView management software which uses a GUI for easy network administration and remote management.
Comments	Provides enhancements to "authentication security," "port activity logging," "dial on demand." Has Flash ROM support for simplified upgrades. Free firmware upgrades and technical support.	Features fast and seamless connectivity including both dial-in remote access and dial-out routing on demand. Addresses needs of non-technical PC users for easy remote connection of Microsoft Windows 3.1, Windows 95, Macintosh, and Unix systems with PPP-based client software.
Warranty	Lifetime	2 year
Price	$2,145, $1,595	$995

Manufacturer	Chase Research	ChatCom, Inc
Model	10LAN Terminal Server	ChatterBox Corporate Series 2000: Models 2010,2020,2040. Office Series 200: Models 204,210.
General Description and Benefits	Allows PCs, SLIP/PPP lines, or any RS232 device to be directly connected to LANs.	ChatterBox Corporate and Office Series products offer five models, ranging from a 4-slot enclosure housing with 8 Pentium processors up to a 56-slot enclosure with 112 Pentium processors.
CPU Type	16MHz Intel 80c186 processor	Range available from 66MHz '486 to 200MHz Pentium Pro
Ports	4, 8, 16 DB25 connections with surge protection and 57.6Kbps port speeds on all ports	Depends on configuration—can be up to hundreds.
Protocols	Supports TCP/IP (rlogin, Telnet), SLIP, RCP, LPD, DNS, PING	Can support any LAN/WAN protocol via installed software: IP Stack, IPX Stack, SNA/SDLC, Frame Relay, ATM, etc.
Network Connectivity	BNC and AUI network interfaces for Ethernet LAN connectivity	Can support any LAN/WAN via installed PCI/ ISA bus cards: Ethernet 10/100, Token Ring, T1 (sync), ISDN, high-speed async, etc.
Bundled Software	Printer, modems, and bi-directional devices configured as local ports on Unix host	Can support any PC-compatible server application: Notes, Exchange, Netscape, Internet Information Server, pcAnywhere, and others.
Comments	SNMP network managed with MIB1 and MIB2. Provides full bi-directional modem support on all ports. Has simple to use menu-driven interface, allows for quick installation. Free upgrades and support.	Systems are fully scalable, since the same-server subsystems are used in all models. Server modules are upgradable to faster processors.
Warranty	Lifetime	1 year hardware and software
Price	$1,195–$1,750	$5,000–$100,000+

Manufacturer	Citrix Systems Inc.	Computone Corp.
Model	WinFrame/Enterprise	IntelliServer, Slimline, and PowerRack
General Description and Benefits	Based on Windows NT server, WinFrame Enterprise extends the reach of business applications beyond the LAN to remote users of the existing enterprise network, corporate Intranet or Internet.	IntelliServer is an expandable line of asynchronous communications servers. It combines the functionality of a terminal server with the extended capabilities of an Ethernet remote access communications server.
CPU Type	Intel Pentium-286 PC with 640K of RAM	High-performance RISC workstation with 32-bit MIPS-R3000 compatible CPU

N/A—Not applicable   INA—Information not available

Table Continues →

■ Communications Servers

Manufacturer	Citrix Systems Inc.	Computone Corp.
Ports	15 users per single processor. Provides support for symmetrical multiprocessing systems.	IntelliServer Slimline provides 64 physical ports, 96 login sessions, and up to 32 PPP/SLIP connections. IntelliServer PowerRack is expandable with three additional sixteen-port serial card for a total of 64 physical ports, 96 login sessions, and up to 64 PPP/SLIP connections.
Protocols	SPX, IPX, TCP/IP, NetBEUI, NetBIOS, Citrix ICA	Protocol support includes rlogin, Telnet, Telnetd, reverse Telnet, SNMP, RADIUS, RIP, and full PPP, SLIP and CSLIP support.
Network Connectivity	Asynchronous dial-up, WANs (T1, T3, 56K, X.25), broadband connections (ISDN, Frame Relay, ATM), LANs, Internet, Intranet	IntelliServer provides transparent remote access to Ethernet LANs, easy access to Internet services, and routes TCP/IP traffic using the industry standard PPP protocol
Bundled Software	Supports DOS, Windows 3.1, Windows 95, Windows NT, Windows for Workgroups, Client/Server, legacy application	Resident multi-session manager: IntelliView. IntelliServer requires no special operating system device drivers to simplify upgrades and TCP/IP host cross-platform connectivity.
Comments	Win/Frame Enterprise is based on a network-centric computing model, which includes Citrix's ICA-based, thin-client software that works in conjunction with WinFrame/Enterprise multiuse application server software.	Surge/spike protection on all transmit and receive signals (optional on SlimLine, included with PowerRack). PowerRack can communicate at baud rates of 921.6Kbps full-duplex, SlimLine up to 200Kbps.
Warranty	60 day	1 year
Price	$595 for 15 concurrent users	INA

Manufacturer	Copia International	Corollary, Inc.
Model	Faxfacts	60-0203-01, 60-0202-01
General Description and Benefits	Faxfacts Server provides a client/server environment that consolidates maintenance and control at one or more "host" or fax-server CPUs and links access to an unlimited number of "client" workstations.	CNS-1600 LAN-attached multiport. CNS-1610 terminal server.
CPU Type	Can drive from 2 to 24 lines per CPU, 486 66MHz or better with 4MB RAM	Internal 16MHz 960 Processor
Ports	No com1 and com2 limitations	(1b) Serial, RS-423 W/RJ-45 connectors. (2) Parallel, Centronics compatible.
Protocols	Fax	1600: PX, SPX. 1610: TCP/IP-Telnet, rlogin, PPP, SLIP, CSLIP.
Network Connectivity	Supports LANs, Novell, LANtastic, Token Ring, Banyan Vines, etc. Links TCP/IP workstations to any network or installs directory on Windows NT server.	10BASE-T and AUI Ethernet interfaces
Bundled Software	Licensed by phone line and workstation	TCP/IP with PPP, SLIP and CSLIP.
Comments	The base system includes broadcast faxing, on-the-fly faxing, status reports, and cover sheet attachments.	Connection station, terminal servers, all terminals, printers, modems, and serial devices to access any host system on the TCP/IP, Ethernet Network
Warranty	90 day	3 year
Price	2 lines, 4 users $1,985	$590–$1,600, $2,290–$1,610

Manufacturer	Cubix Corporation	Cubix Corporation
Model	WorldDesk Commuter	ERS/FT II
General Description and Benefits	A secure remote access server appliance for Microsoft and Novell networks featuring built-in security and fault tolerance	Fault-tolerant platform for network speciality servers and services
CPU Type	486DX/2	Up to 8 Pentium 150MHz uni-processor computers

N/A—Not applicable   INA—Information not available

Communications Servers ■

Manufacturer	Cubix Corporation	Cubix Corporation
Ports	Serial: 6 or 12 ports. Max trans rate: 460.8Kbps. Uart: 16c552 Concurrent rate: 115KbpsBuffering: 16 byte	2 to 128 ports per chassis
Protocols	IPX, TCP/IP, NetBEUI	IPX/SPX, TCP/IP, NetBEUI
Network Connectivity	10BASE-T interface	Built-in 10BASE-T, add-in 100BASE-T, FDDI or ATM cards as required
Bundled Software	WorldDesk remote access client/unlimited user license supports DOS 5.0 or greater, Windows 3.x, Windows 95 and Windows for Workgroups.	Available with NetWareConnect, MPR, or ReachOut
Comments	Free graphical user management package, WorldDesk Manager. WorldDesk Commuter can be purchased with integrated V.34 modems, and it supports Int 14, NASI, and Windows #.x Comm redirector.	Open architecture design allows third- party hardware and software used with the Cuvix product Integration.
Warranty	Return to manufacturer	1 year
Price	$1,995–$2,795	$3,995

Manufacturer	Equinox	Equisys USA
Model	ELS Products	ZETAFAX
General Description and Benefits	Ethernet terminal server products.	A fax server that originates from a true client/server architecture allowing high-performance sending and receiving of faxes from any workstation
CPU Type	Custom ICP	485 DC, 6MB RAM
Ports	8 to 48 ports per unit. Speeds to 38.4Kbps	Supports Brooktrout, Chiliport, DIG, and other multi-port boards.
Protocols	TCP/IP, LAT, IPX, SLIP, PPP	Client/server architecture; essentially protocol independent.
Network Connectivity	Ethernet to serial async	Windows, WFWG, Windows NT, OS/2, Windows 95, and other NetBIOS networks
Bundled Software	Works in UNIX, Novell, Windows NT, and DEC environments.	INA
Comments		
Warranty	3 year	Full 30-day money-back warranty
Price	$1,795–$5,400	5-user system starts at $525

Manufacturer	Evergreen Systems, Inc.	FaxBack, Inc
Model	CAPserver	FaxBack, FaxCenter
General Description and Benefits	CAPserver is a multifunction communication server that provides dial-in, remote node, remote control, modem pooling, fax, e-mail gateway, WAN router and Web server functions.	Including Windows client interface, DID routing, e-mail integration, NetWare or NT compatible, inbound/outbound notification and more
CPU Type	Base unit uses a 486 DX4-100MHz. Up to 19 additional application processors can be added (486 or Pentium).	Pentium 90 server or higher, 16MB RAM
Ports	Supports up to 128 ports per server	2 port minimum to 256 in rackmount
Protocols	IPX, TCP/IP, AppleTalk	File based. No low level protocols required.
Network Connectivity	NetWare, Windows NT, AppleTalk	Novell NetWare or Windows NT compatible. FaxCenter operates as client application on LAN.
Bundled Software	Includes Remote Control, Remote Node and Management software. SNMP also available.	Sold as turnkey solutions only. Server and client software shipped on server.

N/A—Not applicable   INA—Information not available

Table Continues →

■ Communications Servers

Manufacturer	Evergreen Systems, Inc.	FaxBack, Inc
Comments	Multi-CPU, multi-function communications platform also supports e-mail hubs, WAN routers, and Web servers. Hot-swappable/fault-tolerant power supply option.	FaxCenter provides inbound/outbound fax processing as well as high-volume fax broadcasting and fax on demand.
Warranty	2 year	90 day, extended plans available
Price	Starts at $4,395	$4,995 including server and 10-user software

Manufacturer	Gamma-Link	Kelaur Netcom Corporation
Model	CPD/220, CP-4/LSI Series 2, Cpi/200	DATAFAX
General Description and Benefits	Communication fax boards	Provides for in- and outbound network fax, fax on demand, outbound modem pooling, inbound datacom, inbound application server, in- and outbound virtual networking, bridging, routing, terminal server, and video server.
CPU Type	Communicates with the CPU via programmed I/O instead of using serial port interrupts. 20MHz on-board microprocessor.	Multiple Z86, RISC, Pentium, up to 200MHz
Ports	The Gamma-Link product line scales from 1 to 12 lines on digital, T-1 and direct inbound dialing (DID) interfaces	2-96 fax and/or 4-64 data, simultaneously.
Protocols	T.30 software protocol enables systems to transmit faxes more rapidly and enhances compatibility to more fax devices.	Windows NT, Novell, NetBuei, TCP/IP, NASI, LAN Manager, Pathworks, Banyan Vines, Unix.
Network Connectivity	2 direct inbound dial ports and 2 analog ports in a single slot with 512K of RAM enabling 32 ports, a loop-start interface (LSI), four-port fax board for LAN capabilities, multi-port fax board can support up to 30 separate fax channels	Ethernet (up to 100Mbps), Token Ring
Bundled Software	Various	Complete software provided for all system configurations.
Comments	Gamma-Links fax server partner (FSP) program combines Gamma-Link's hardware technology with those of the fax server software vendors.	Fully integrated hardware/software turnkey network communications gateway systems. Field upgradeable.
Warranty	3 year	2–5 year
Price	$2,995/$2,995/$1,395	$5,000–$12,000

Manufacturer	Lantronix	Lantronix
Model	LRS2	LRS 16
General Description and Benefits	Two-port branch office remote access server for LAN-to-LAN, remote node, remote control, and Internet access applications	16-port central site remote access server for LAN-to-LAN, remote node, remote control, and Internet access applications
CPU Type	Motorola 68302	ID 3081
Ports	2 115Kbps serial ports	16 115.2Kbps serial ports (RJ-45)
Protocols	Routes TCP/IP and IPX, supports PPP, SLIP/CSLIP	Routes TCP/IP and IPX, supports PPP, SLIP/CSLIP
Network Connectivity	10BASE-T, 10BASE2, AUI ports	10BASE-T, 10BASE2, AUI ports
Bundled Software	EZCon configuration software included	EZCon configuration software included
Comments	Includes multilink PPP, and link time out management features. Tiered security: Radius, Secur ID, dial-back.	All 16 ports can operate at full speed simultaneously. Link Management features include link timeout multilink PPP supported. Security: Radius, SecurID, dial back.
Warranty	5 year	5 year
Price	$995	$2,495

N/A—Not applicable   INA—Information not available

Communications Servers ■

Manufacturer	**LeeMah DataCom Security Corporation**	**Linksys**
Model	BandWagon Remote Access Server	LANgate
General Description and Benefits	BandWagon enables remote PC users to access corporate enterprise networks and resources.	Dial-in and dial-out access point for Novell networks. Built-in thin coax/10BASE-T.
CPU Type	Pentium 90 (main processor), 386 auxiliary (async)	N/A
Ports	86 simultaneous connections, up to 32 modem ports at 115.2Kbps, up to 54 ISDN connections	1 modem port, up to 115.2Kbps
Protocols	IP, IPX, NetBBUI, NetBIOS, SLIP, PPP, MLPPP, RIP, SAP, DES, TACAS, RADIUS, PAP, CHAP, SNMP, INT 14	IPX
Network Connectivity	LAN interface: one 10MBps Ethernet3 media connection. WAN support: modem 8-32 ports ISDN, 0-2 Quad BRI cards, 0-1 single/dual PRI card, and 0-2 T1/E1	Novell only
Bundled Software	Non-preemptive kernel supports broad range of client and management software: Windows, Windows 95, Windows NT	DOS, Windows-based standard CDI stack. All software included.
Comments	Dial-in, dial-out, and LAN-to-LAN access for up to 86 simultaneous users, with integrated user authentication security	None
Warranty	2 year	1 year
Price	Base system $5,800	$399

Manufacturer	**Livingston Enterprises**	**Livingston Enterprises**
Model	Livingston Portmaster2/ 2R/ 25	Livingston Enterprises2E/ 2ER
General Description and Benefits	Ethernet communications servers	Modular Ethernet communications servers
CPU Type	Intel 386 DX40	Intel 386 DX40
Ports	Portmaster2 fixed configuration 10 ports.Portmaster2R has 10 asynchronous ports, 1 synchronous routing port (up to T1/E1), and 1 Ethernet port. Portmaster25 has 25 ports 115.2Kbps.	Modular,up to 30 asynchronous ports; modular platform with up to 10, 20, 30 asynchronous ports, 1 synchronous routing port (up to T1/E1) and 1 Ethernet port 115.2Kbps
Protocols	TCP/IP, Novell, IPX	TCP/IP, Novell, IPX
Network Connectivity	Ethernet, 10BASE-T, 10BASE2, AUI	Ethernet, 10BASE-T, 10BASE2, AUI
Bundled Software	Pmconsole management utility available for: MS Windows, HP/UX, DEC Alpha, SunOS, AIX, Ultrix	Pmconsole management utility available for: MS Windows, HP/UX, DEC Alpha, SunOS, AIX, Ultrix
Comments	Portmaster25's high- density port connectors provide connectivity to modem racks. Included at no extra charge: Radius accounting server ChoiceNet, ComOS, Pmconsole	Included at no extra charge: Radius accounting server ChoiceNet, ComOS, Pmconsole
Warranty	Free lifetime support and software upgrades	Free lifetime support and software upgrades
Price	$2,495/$3,295/$3,495	$2,695/$3,495

Manufacturer	**Microcom, Inc.**	**Microdyne**
Model	LANexpress4000 release 4.0	ACS4400
General Description and Benefits	Scaleable and interoperable with any network or PC and provides a simultaneous remote node and remote control solution.	Microdyne's asynchronous communication server ACS4400 is a complete dial-in, dial-out remote access solution for NetWare users
CPU Type	486 66MHz	Intel 486-25/8MB RAM
Ports	2–12 ports	4 RS-232 ports

N/A—Not applicable   INA—Information not available Table Continues →

■ Communications Servers

Manufacturer	Microcom, Inc.	Microdyne
Protocols	AppleTalk remote access protocol, PPP, SLIP	IPX-802.2 and 802.3 frame types
Network Connectivity	AppleTalk, LAN Server, NetWare, LAN Manager, Windows NT advanced server, DecNet, Banyan Vines, XNS, OS/400, 802.2/ILC	Remote node and remote control dial-in connectivity. Dial-out via NASI and Int.14
Bundled Software	LANexpress client software (includes remote node, remote control, terminal emulation in single call) and Express Watch management software	NetWare Connect, NetWare
Comments	Client and server management, parallel port interface, auto-detect on incoming calls for x.75 vs.v.120 vs.async or synch	List of security and configuration features includes surge/spike protection on all transmit and receive signals (optional on SlimLine, included with PowerRack). IntelliServer allows network users to work anywhere and gain access to corporate network for remote client access, multi-user host access, and remote office access. PowerRack can communicate at baud rates of 921.6Kbps full-duplex, SlimLine up to 200Kbps.
Warranty	1 year hardware, 90 day software	5 year
Price	$3,995–$10,995	16 port SlimLine: $2,695 (2MB) or $2,995 (4MB) 16 port PowerRack $3,995(4MB)

Manufacturer	Modular Industrial Solutions, Inc.	Motorola ISG
Model	N-1000, Network resource platform	925 AccessWay™ System with 925 LANRover/8E
General Description and Benefits	Multi-purpose server is passive-backplane based utilizing multi-I/O CPU cards allowing integration, modularity, serviceability and upgradability. Runs PCI, ISA, and EISA bus platforms.	A sophisticated remote access and wide area networking system, linking corporate sites with data, voice, and video communications across high-speed lines.
CPU Type	486 and Pentium to 200MHz with on-board I/O, VGA, and SCSI	68040
Ports	Supports any PC server compatible. I/O ports (latest 586SBC includes Ultra Wide SCSI).	Expandable in increments of 8 or less; no overall limit per network. 10BASE-T; UI.
Protocols	Open	IPX, TCP/IP, AppleTalk, PPP, Multilink PPP, NetBELOI, NetBIOS, ARAIO,2.0, 802.2/ 802.3 UC, SLIP
Network Connectivity	Supports any PC compliant network I/O requirement	T1, BRI, analog tip or ring, EI, PRI, 10BASE-T
Bundled Software	OS/2, NetWare, LAN Manager, Windows for Workgroups, Windows NT, UNIX, MS DOS, Lanux	Shiva: NetManager, Remote Dial-In, Dial-Out, LanConnect Novell: NetWare Client, TCP/IP Client; any PPP client
Comments	Enables multiple servers or server and dedicates external processes to share a single cabinet, power supply and user interface (with optional keyboard, monitor, and mouse).	Supports data, voice, video, analog, T1, E1, PRI, Fraction T1, ISDN, Drop & Insert. The 925 AccessWay starts as a modem pool but expands with user's needs. Custom systems available.
Warranty	2 year	2 year hardware, 90 day software
Price	$1,250–$15,500	24 port begins at $27,995

Manufacturer	Multi-Tech Systems, Inc.	Multi-Tech Systems, Inc.
Model	RNGCOM	RNI08
General Description and Benefits	Dedicated 4-port communication server with an Ethernet NIC (model EN301CT16C,) for a TCP/IP or IPX LAN. Automatically detects remote-node or remote-control session. supports dial-in PPP LAN access.	Dedicated 8-port communication server with an ISI608 and Ethernet NIC for a TCP/IP or IPX LAN. Automatically detects remote-node or remote-control session. supports dial-in PPP LAN access. Expands to 32 ports in eight-port increments via the RNGEXP server expansion kit.
CPU Type	386 DX 33 through Pentium 166	386 DX 33 through Pentium 166
Ports	4 standard PC Com port	8 high speed port modems, DSU's, ISON, MUKs can be used.

N/A—Not applicable   INA—Information not available

Communications Servers ■

Manufacturer	Multi-Tech Systems, Inc.	Multi-Tech Systems, Inc.
Protocols	IPX or IP	IPX or IP
Network Connectivity	Ethernet 10BASE2 or 10BASE-T	Ethernet 10BASE2 or 10BASE-T
Bundled Software	Complete with remote node and remote control plus PPP client.	Complete with remote node and remote control plus PPP client.
Comments	Requires a user suplied PC with one to four 16550 COM ports	Requires a user suplied PC with one to four 16550 COM ports
Warranty	2 year	2 year
Price	$290	$600

Manufacturer	Multi-Tech Systems, Inc.	Multi-Tech Systems, Inc.
Model	MMLNOV2111	RNI08M
General Description and Benefits	Self contained single-port data/fax communications server, remote-node server, async, LAN bridge, fax server or remote-control host for IPX networks. Async router operation via third software. Internal V.34(28.8Kbps) data/fax modem, and Ethernet combo (10BASE-T/Thinnet) NIC.	Dedicated 8-port communication server with a multi-ModemISI (models ISI2834/4 and ISI2834/4a) and Ethernet NIC for a TCP/IP or IPX LAN. Requires a user suplied PC. Automatically detects remote-node or remote-control session. Supports dial-in PPP LAN access. Expands to 32 ports in eight-port increments via the RNGEXP server expansion kit.
CPU Type	486 DX4/100	386 DX 33 through Pentium 166
Ports	2 ports, internal with 28.8 built in modem, external RJ232 connection	8 ports complete with 8 modems on an internal high speed card
Protocols	IPX or IP	IPX or IP
Network Connectivity	Ethernet 10BASE2 or 10BASE-T	Ethernet 10BASE2 or 10BASE-T
Bundled Software	Complete with remote node and remote control plus PPP client	Complete with remote node and remote control plus applicant
Comments	Connectors for video, keyboard, and amouse or external modem. Modem-sharing software handles up to two modems. Included DOS 6.22, modem-sharing, Int6B/INT14 redirector, site-licensed datacomm, and bridging software.	
Warranty	2 year	2 year
Price	$1,500	$1,950

Manufacturer	Multi-Tech Systems, Inc.	Multi-Tech Systems, Inc.
Model	MA4CWR 4002	MAYCWR4010
General Description and Benefits	Four-slot mini-tower case equipped with MT75E single board computer. Minimum 32MB RAM, 1GB hard drive. Operates on NT, NetBioiu, or IPX LAN.	Four-slot mini-tower case equipped with MT75E single board computer. Minimum 32MB RAM, 1GB hard drive. Operates on NT, NetBioiu, or IPX LAN.
CPU Type	Pentium 133	Pentium 133
Ports	5 user 5 high speed ports compete with modems (33.6)	5 user 5 high speed ports compete with modems (33.6)
Protocols	ICA 3 over IP or IPX	ICA 3 over IP or IPX
Network Connectivity	Ethernet 10BASE2 or 10BASE-T	Ethernet 10BASE2 or 10BASE-T
Bundled Software	CITRIX WINFRAME and Windows NT server includes zetafax and spartacom	CITRIX WINFRAME and Windows NT server includes zetafax and spartacom
Comments		
Warranty	2 year	2 year
Price	$8,900	$8,900

N/A—Not applicable   INA—Information not available

T a b l e   C o n t i n u e s →

■ Communications Servers

Manufacturer	Multi-Tech Systems, Inc.	Multi-Tech Systems, Inc.
Model	MAYCWR4010/5010	MAYCWR4005/5005
General Description and Benefits	Four-slot mini-tower case equipped with MT75E single board computer. Minimum 32MB RAM, 1GB hard drive. Operates on NT, NetBiois, or IPX LAN.	Four-slot mini-tower case equipped with MT75E single board computer. Minimum 32MB RAM, 1GB hard drive. Operates on NT, NetBiois, or IPX LAN.
CPU Type	Pentium 133 (4010), Pentium 166 (5010)	Pentium 133 (4010), Pentium 166 (5010)
Ports	10 users; 10 ports	5 users; 8 ports
Protocols	ICA 3 over IP or IPX	ICA 3 over IP or IPX
Network Connectivity	Ethernet 10BASE2 or 10BASE-T	Ethernet 10BASE2 or 10BASE-T
Bundled Software	CITRIX WINFRAME and Windows NT server includes zetafax and spartacom	CITRIX WINFRAME and Windows NT server includes zetafax and spartacom
Comments		
Warranty	2 year	2 year
Price	$9,500 (4010) $9,999 (5010)	$7,700 (4005) $8,170 (5005)

Manufacturer	Multi-Tech Systems, Inc.	Multi-Tech Systems, Inc.
Model	MAYCWR5002	MAYCWR5009
General Description and Benefits	Four-slot mini-tower case equipped with MT75E single board computer. Minimum 32MB RAM, 1GB hard drive. Operates on NT, NetBiois, or IPX LAN.	Four-slot mini-tower case equipped with MT75E single board computer. Minimum 32MB RAM, 1GB hard drive. Operates on NT, NetBiois, or IPX LAN.
CPU Type	Pentium 166	Pentium 5009
Ports	5 users; 5 high speed ports-complete with modems (33.6)	10 users; 16 ports
Protocols	ICA 3 over IP or IPX	Ethernet, 10BASE2 or 10BASE-T
Network Connectivity	Ethernet 10BASE2 or 10BASE-T	ICA3 over IP or IPX
Bundled Software	CITRIX WINFRAME and Windows NT server includes zetafax and spartacom	CITRIX WINFRAME and Windows NT server includes zetafax and spartacom
Comments		
Warranty	2 year	2 year
Price	$8,870	$10,100

Manufacturer	Multi-Tech Systems, Inc.	Multi-Tech Systems, Inc.
Model	MAYNWC 3008	MAYNWC 3012
General Description and Benefits	Four-slot mini-tower case equipped with MT75E single board computer. Minimum 32MB RAM, 1GB hard drive. Operates on IPX LAN.	Four-slot mini-tower case equipped with MT75E single board computer. Minimum 32MB RAM, 1GB hard drive. Operates on IPX LAN.
CPU Type	AMD 586/133	AMD 586/133
Ports	8 high speed serial ports	4 high speed ports complete with modems (33.6)
Protocols	Ethernet 10BASE2 or 10BASE-T	Ethernet 10BASE2 or 10BASE-T
Network Connectivity	ICA3 over IP or IPX	IP or IPX
Bundled Software	Novell NetWare connect 8 user version	Novell NetWare connect

N/A—Not applicable   INA—Information not available

Communications Servers ■

Manufacturer	Multi-Tech Systems, Inc.	Multi-Tech Systems, Inc.
Comments		
Warranty	2 year	2 year
Price	$5,190	$5,720

Manufacturer	Network Products Corporation	Network Products Corporation
Model	ACS2+INS	ACS2/SA
General Description and Benefits	Dial-out modem server, dial-in remote-node server for NetWare	Compact, dial-out communication server for PCs
CPU Type	Z80	80188, Z80
Ports	Up to 16 RS-232, 115, 200 baud	2 RS-232, DB-9, 115,200 baud
Protocols	NCSI, IPX	NCSI, IPX, NetBEUI
Network Connectivity	Dial-out, dial-in remote node, dial-in remote control	Dial-out, dial-in remote control
Bundled Software	Complete server, unlimited client, comprehensive utilities	Complete server, unlimited client, comprehensive utilities
Comments	Use for remote access, terminal emulation, Internet, fax, paging, remote control, specialty information access	Use for terminal emulation, Internet, fax, paging, remote control, specialty information access
Warranty	1 year	1 year
Price	Base $2,690	$995

Manufacturer	Networks Product Corporation	Networks Product Corporation
Model	XCS2	NMP2 and ACS2/4
General Description and Benefits	X.25 communication server for PCs	Software dial-out modem servers for PCs
CPU Type	N/A	N/A
Ports	2 64k physical links, 32 virtual circuits	NMP2: 1 port. ACS2/4: up to 4 ports. Both use standard COMn ports
Protocols	NCSI, IPX, NetBIOS, X.25, X.3, X.28, X.29	NCSI, IPX, NetBIOS, Banyan IPC
Network Connectivity	LAN to X.25	Dial-out, dial-in remote control
Bundled Software	Complete server, unlimited client, comprehensive utilities	Complete server, unlimited client, comprehensive utilities
Comments	Use for host connectivity, terminal emulation, specialty information access, etc.	Use for terminal emulation, Internet, fax, paging, remote control, specialty information access
Warranty	1 year hardware and software, lifetime support	NMP2: 6 month software ACS2/4: 1 year software, lifetime support
Price	$3,790	$49/$349

Manufacturer	Networks Product Corporation	Paralon Technologies Inc.
Model	ACS2	PathKey Remote Access Server—PK-RAS Model 2m
General Description and Benefits	Software and modem server for PCs	Multi-protocol, 8 port PCMCIA-based remote access server integrating PathKey® Technology for authentication, access control and real-time data encryption security with comprehensive RAS services and V.34 PC-card modems

N/A—Not applicable   INA—Information not available

Table Continues →

■ Communications Servers

Manufacturer	Networks Product Corporation	Paralon Technologies Inc.
CPU Type	Z80	Motorola 68360, Data encryption Standard (DES) processors
Ports	Up to 32 RS-232, 115,200 baud	Eight (8) type II or four (4) Type III PCMCIA
Protocols	NCSI, IPX, NetBIOS, Banyan IPC	IPX, NACS\NASI, ARA, AND TCP/IP (PPP, SLIP, and CSLIP)
Network Connectivity	Dial-out, dial-in remote control	Auto or user-selectable Ethernet 10BASE-T, AUI, or Coax
Bundled Software	Complete sever, unlimited client, comprehensive utilities	Novell-compatible software for DOS/Windows/WIN95 clients; Windows-based PathKey RAS manager system configurator software
Comments	Use for terminal emulation, Internet, fax, paging, remote control, specialty information access	Supports 5,000 PathKey Domain Series Clients; FIPS 140-1 compliant; Platform, OS, application, and protocol independent; unlimited port densities via Server Replication features; NIST-approved.
Warranty	1 year hardware and software, lifetime support	1 year
Price	Base $2,190	$5,795 with 2 V.34 modems

Manufacturer	Penril Datability Networks	Penril Datability Networks
Model	Access Beyond 1000/RA	RAM Rack
General Description and Benefits	Stand-alone remote access servers with 4, 8, or 16 async ports	The RAM (Remote Access Modem) Rack server offers 8 to 32 integrated V.34 modems in a small 5"-high rackmount chassis.Designed for high-density dial-in/dial-out LAN access.
CPU Type	Motorola 68360	Multiple Intel 386 (1 per port)
Ports	Ethernet Port: AUI and 10BASE-T, 4, 8, or 16 RS-232 async	Ethernet Port: AUI, BNC and 10BASE-T, 8 to 32 integrated V.34 modems
Protocols	IP, Novell IPX, AppleTalk, PPP, SLIP, Telnet, NACS/NASI	IP, Novell IPX, AppleTalk, PPP, SLIP, Telnet, NACS/NASI
Network Connectivity	Novell and IP Ethernet networks	Novell and IP Ethernet
Bundled Software	LinkIPX remote IPX client included, unlimited license	LinkIPX remote IPX client included, unlimited license
Comments	Comprehensive security and accounting support. Includes Windows-based, SNMP configuration tool.	Comprehensive security and accounting support. Includes Windows-based, SNMP configuration tool.
Warranty	1 year	1 year
Price	$1,600–$2,300	$6,500–$23,500

Manufacturer	Penril Datability Networks	PLEXCOM, Inc.
Model	Access Beyond 2400 Modular Access Chassis	2008SX
General Description and Benefits	The Access Beyond 2400 provides complete remote LAN access with support for integrated async, V.34 modems, and ISDN support.	TCP-IP and DEC LAT Terminal Server with 8 RS-232 ports. 2 ports have full modem control. All ports have partial modem control. Network interface is 10Mb Ethernet.
CPU Type	Motorola 68360	I960 RISC
Ports	4 backbone interfaces for LAN and WAN connectivity. 2 port module slots for ISDN, V.34 and async connectivity.	8 RS-232 ports with DC to 38.4 Kbps. Utilizes RJ-45 connectors.
Protocols	IP, Novell IPX, AppleTalk, PPP, SLIP, Telnet, NACS/NASI	TCP-IP, DEC LAT, PPP, SLIP, CSLIP
Network Connectivity	Ethernet, PPP, ISDN, V.34 modems, async, Frame Relay, X.25	TCP-IP or DEC LAT over 10 Mbps Ethernet. AUI, 10BASE-T, 10BASE-FL/FOIRL and 10BASE2. Thinnet interfaces are available.

N/A—Not applicable   INA—Information not available

Communications Servers ◼

Manufacturer	**Penril Datability Networks**	**PLEXCOM, Inc.**
Bundled Software	LinkIPX remote IPX client included, unlimited license. Windows configuration and management tool included.	Telnet, BootP, TFTP Network host or self-load units
Comments	Modular chassis provides complete remote LAN access solution in a single box.	Stand-alone or modular-chassis-based terminal server with modem control for remote access, dial-in applications. Supports PPP, SLIP, CSLIP, TCP-IP, and DEC LAT.
Warranty	1 year	1 year
Price	$2,800–$12,500 depending on configuration and level of integration	$2,595

Manufacturer	**Polywell Computers, Inc.**	**Polywell Computers, Inc.**
Model	Poly500FX	PolyAlpha300RS
General Description and Benefits	Fax server for up to 8 ports and 1,000 users	Remote access server for Internet access and communication
CPU Type	Pentium 133MHz	DEC Alpha 21164- 300MHz, 128MB RAM, 20GB HD Raid5
Ports	1- to 8-port 14,400 fax	Ethernet, T1
Protocols	IPX, NetBEUI, TCP/IP	TCP/IP, NetBEUI, IPX/SPX
Network Connectivity	Ethernet 10/100MB	Ethernet
Bundled Software	NetWare, NT, OS/2	DEC Unix, NT, Netscape
Comments		CPU intensive access server
Warranty	3 year	3 year
Price	$3,000–$6,000	$15,000

Manufacturer	**RNS**	**Rad Data Communications**
Model	NetHopper NH-RAS Remote Access Server	LAN Ranger Series
General Description and Benefits	Connects remote users or LANs over dial-up analog phone lines for file sharing and file transfer.	Internet and remote access servers for Token Ring and Ethernet LANs; modular interfaces for synchronous and asynchronous, leased or dial ups, ISDN, Frame Relay, 4-wire sync. modems, PCMCIA slots; up to 8 WAN links.
CPU Type	Intel 486sx	Motorola 68302 with a RISC communications processor
Ports	NH-RAS 510N has 1 RJ-11 connecton. NH-RAS 550 has 5 RJ-11 ports.	Modular WAN ports; up to 8 ports per device; rates to 115.2Kbps async, 512Kbps sync.
Protocols	IP/IPX	Transparent bridging; ODI and NDIS clients; IP/IPX routing over SLIP, CSLIP, and PPP.
Network Connectivity	Auto senses AUO or 10BASE-T Ethernet connection.	Token Ring: STP and UTP. Ethernet: AUI or BNC or UTP
Bundled Software	Includes stamped Remote Office Gold, remote node software	ODI and NDIS Client software for PCs running DOS, Windows, OS/2
Comments	Includes PPP, CHAP, Compression, IP Firewall, IPX Spoofing. Supports SNMP MIB-11, SecurID, RADIUS	Modular interfaces; supports Internet and remote access from same device over LAN and WAN service; plug-and-play installation; multilevel security; management agent: NMP or Telnet.
Warranty	2 year hardware, 90 day software	1 year
Price	$1,795–$3,795	Starts at $890 (1 Ethernet, 1 serial link)

N/A—Not applicable   INA—Information not available

Table Continues →

Communications Servers

Manufacturer	SFA DataComm, Inc.	**Manufacturer**	SFA DataComm. Inc.
Model	XenoLink Access Server	FaxConnX
General Description and Benefits	XAS is a remote LAN access server that allows remote users to access corporate LAN through dial-up modem, X.25, Frame Relay. ISP can use XAS to provide remote access to Internet.	A communicaiton platform for routing facsimile traffic over private and public networks. It provides A/D conversion, alternate routing, stored and forward, and broadcast functions.
CPU Type	MC68360	V.35 NEC processor, 1MB RAM, 512K ROM, 32K SRAM, 210MB / 1.2GB HD
Ports	8-32	4 RJ-11, supports G3 Fax up to 9.6Kbps
Protocols	TCP/IP, IPX/SPX, RIP, TSR, TSR, X.25, FR	G3 Fax up to 9.6Kbps
Network Connectivity	X.25, FR or asynch	DB25/RS-232, synch or asynch, 1.2 - 64 Kbps
Bundled Software	Proprietary	Proprietary for both FaxConnX and the NMS
Comments	XAS allows telecommuters and traveling users to dial in to connect to the corporate LAN to retrieve and deposit e-mail, files and Internet resource access.	Can be connected to PBX or to fax machines.Combines the features of a data router with the networking capabilities of WAN and telephone switches.
Warranty	1 year	1 year
Price	$1,995–$4,500	$4,000

Manufacturer	Shiva Corp.	SVEC Computer Corp.
Model	LanRover/Plus	FD7000 Remote Access Server
General Description and BenefitsGeneral Description	A multi-protocol remote access server supporting hundreds of remote access users. It provides analog and digital dial-in, dial-out and LAN-to-LAN connectivity. Benefits include ease-of-use and deployment, performance, security, and stability.	Connections provided through a 4-in-1 modem and MS Windows NT RAS function
CPU Type CPU Info	Motorola 68 020	Pentium 100
PortsPort Info	2, 4, 8 and stackable for up to 128	Plus 4-port async card
Protocols	IP, IPX, TCP/IP, NetBEUI, AppleTalk, 802.2/LLC	Supports PPP, NetBEUI, IPX/SPX, TCP/IP
Network Connectivity	Virtual connections provide user with transparent access to information due to digital call set up times. Also Shiva Tariff Management is designed to allow companies to control telecommunications costs.	MS Windows-based network
Bundled Software	Shiva PPP Client software	RAS-MS Windows NT
Comments		
Warranty	1 year server, 90 days software	5 year
Price	$1,999+	$4,900

Manufacturer	Sonic System Inc.	Spartacom USA
Model	QuickStream/3	SAPS-Spartacom Synchronous Port Sharing
General Description and Benefits	3 high-speed modem ports for dial-in connection; 115.2	SAPS provides modem pooling/sharing capabilities for Windows, Windows NT, Windows 95, and all NetB105 networks. One common-moded pool supports Microsoft RAS and dial out across the entire network.
CPU Type	68 EN 360 Motorola	PC with Intel 386 compatible processor or higher, 4MB RAM, 3.5 disk drive
Ports	3 RS-232 serial, 1 RJ-45 Ethernet, 1 BNC Ethernet	Compatible with most synchronous multi-port cards operating under Windows and Windows NT
Protocols	AppleTalk, TCP/IP; PPP, SLIP, CSLIP; multilink PPP; proprietary; ARA	Requires NetB105. Also supports TCP/IP.

N/A—Not applicable   INA—Information not available

Communications Servers ▪

Manufacturer	Sonic System Inc.	Spartacom USA
Network Connectivity	10BASE-T, RJ-45; 10BASE2; BNC	Windows, WFUG, Windows NT, and Windows 95. Supports all NetB105 networks.
Bundled Software	Mac management program; Mac dial-in client; optional upgrade port-share pro stalker	Compatible with communications software supporting Microsoft's Windows Comm Drivers
Comments	Supports both AppleTalk and TCP/IP which allows access to all AppleTalk resources (file servers, databases, printers), as well as Ethernet-based TCP/IP services (Internet Mail, WWW, FTP, etc.)	
Warranty	Lifetime warranty	Full 30-day, money-back warranty
Price	$999	$594+

Manufacturer	Stallion Technologies	Stallion Technologies
Model	ECS	EasyServer ETS
General Description and Benefits	ECS family are stand-alone terminal servers which provide local and remote connectivity.	Provides connection of serial devices (terminals, printers, modems, and personal computers) to an Ethernet network
CPU Type	N/A	N/A
Ports	8 or 16 ports full modem control and RS-423 signalling	RJ-11
Protocols	TCP/IP, DEC LAT, and AppleTalk	N/A
Network Connectivity	802.3 Ethernet, DB15 female AUI Connector	Thinnet 10BASE2 BNC or 10BASE-T UTP
Bundled Software	N/A	N/A
Comments		N/A
Warranty	5 year	5 year
Price	$1,745–$2,795	$890–$1,090

Manufacturer	Stallion Techologies	Texas Micro
Model	Easyreach	SP 6013
General Description and Benefits	Provides local and remote work group connectivity for Intel-based Unix systems	Rackmounted, passive backplane, dual processor (SMP), server platform; features 5 EISA and PCI I/O slots, 3 n+1 redundant hot swap power supplies, 4 redundant hot swap SCA SCSI-2 drives, redundant hot swap fans
CPU Type	N/A	1-2 Intel Pentium Pro processors, SMP 166to 200Mhz
Ports	DB25	1-parallel, 2-series, PS/2 keyboard and mouse, 5-EISA and 6 PCI slots (all primary)
Protocols	N/A	User defined
Network Connectivity	N/A	Any utilizing PCI or EISA interface cards
Bundled Software	SCO OpenserverR5, SCO Unix, SCO Xenix, SCO UnixWare, Unix SVR4.0, SVR4.2, Interactive Unix	NetWare, Windows NT, OS/2, Solaris, QNX
Comments	N/A	
Warranty	5 year	1 year
Price	$2,295	$11,000–$15,000

N/A—Not applicable   INA—Information not available

Table Continues →

■ Communications Servers

Manufacturer	Texas Micro	U.S. Robotics
Model	SP5018P	Total Control NETserver8 and NETserver16
General Description and Benefits	Rackmounted, passive backplane, server platform; features 11 ISA and 6 PCI I/O slots, Intel Pentium processors from 100 to 200MHz, dual redundant hot swap power supplies, 6 hot swap SCA SCSI-2 hard drives, redundant hot swap fans	8/ 16 port Ethernet LAN access solution with integrated V.34 modem technology, Netstarter auto configuration wizard for automatic installation
CPU Type	Intel Pentium 100 to 200MHz with up to 512k L2 cache, PCI/ISA	486 CPU
Ports	11-ISA, 6-PCI slots serial, parallel, PS/2 keyboard and mouse, PCI F/W SCSI-2, PCI video	8 or 16 port V.everything with V.34 modem providing connection speed up to 33.6Kbps
Protocols	User defined	IPS, IPX, PPP, or SLIP/CSLIP, VJ header compression, Telnet (client and host), radius, DNS, NIS, SNMP
Network Connectivity	Any utilizing ISA or PCI interface cards	10MB Ethernet using 10BASE2 or 10BASE-T
Bundled Software	NetWare, Windows NT, OS/2, Solaris, QNX	Remote Office Gold client software from Stampede
Comments	Rackmount, server platform ISA/EISA/PCI and custom-split backplanes available	Netserver combines remote LAN dial access, LAN-to-LAN routing and terminal server functions with management, security, and accounting capabilities.
Warranty	1 year	2 year
Price	$4,500–$7,000	8/$4,495 16/$8,495

Manufacturer	U.S. Robotics	U.S. Robotics
Model	Total Control Enterprise Network Hub	Sportster ISDN 128K with integrated NT-1 and U interface
General Description and Benefits	Enterprise access server allows remote access to IP and IPX networks utilizing T1PRI or analog connectivity	Provides connectivity to an ISDN BRI and allows simultaneous voice and data communications. Equipped with an RJ-11 jack, the Sportster can be used with a telephone, a fax machine over the digital network
CPU Type	Multiprocessor architecture, multi bus architecture	PC 386 CPU-based or higher
Ports	230 BRI connections, 60 analog connections in a single chassis	U interface, analog device port
Protocols	IP, IPX, Frame Relay, X.25	Multilink, PPP, compression, Stal, Microsoft, ascend, PPP, synchronous PPP
Network Connectivity	10BASE-T Ethernet, Token Ring, X.25, Frame Relay	BRI ISDN, PPP, Multilink PPP
Bundled Software	Free client software—Stampede Remote Node Remote control Total control manager. Net. Mgmt. Software for NMS, SunNet Mgr., HP OpenView	Sportster 128k manager, Windows 95 drivers
Comments		Dynamic voice override feature assigns bandwidth to a voicecall only when the call is being made or received. As soon as call is completed the 120k automatically returns the bandwidth to the data application.
Warranty	2 year	5 year
Price	$18,000–$65,000	$549

Manufacturer	U.S. Robotics	U.S. Robotics
Model	AllegraBRI for Windows NT with NT-1	AllgraBRI for NetWare with NT-1
General Description and Benefits	Integrates within Windows NT server running RAS and ISDN RAS. Integrates within a Windows NT Workstation for single-user remote access, telecommuting, or Internet access. Integrates analog and NT-1 ports. Simultaneous voice and data.	Integrates within a Novell NetWare server. Supports up to 2 ISDN-based remote users simultaneously, analog device port and integrated NT-1. Simultaneous voice and data.
CPU Type	486 CPU	486 CPU

N/A—Not applicable   INA—Information not available

Communications Servers ■

Manufacturer	U.S. Robotics	U.S. Robotics
Ports	1 RJ-11 for phone, fax machine, modem, answering machine 1 U interface ISDN RJ-45	1 RJ-11 for phone, fax machine, modem, answering machine 1 U interface ISDN RJ-45
Protocols	PPP, MultiLink, compression	PPP, MultiLink
Network Connectivity	Supports up to 2 ISDN-based remote users simultaneously	Can be used as an ISDN remote access server or an ISDN router or both with appropriate software
Bundled Software	NT drivers for RAS	Novell NetWare Connect software Novell MultiProtocol Router software
Comments	Target market is a small- or medium-sized business that has Windows NT and has requirements for connecting multiple LAN-based sites together or providing LAN access to remote employee.	Target market is a small- or medium-sized business that has Windows NT and has requirements for connecting multiple LAN-based sites together or providing LAN access to remote employee.
Warranty	5 year	5 year
Price	$549	$549

Manufacturer	Whitaker Xyplex	Whittaker Xyplex
Model	1600 Maxserver	720 Remote Access Server for Network 9000 Hub
General Description and Benefits	Family of remote access and terminal servers. Connections up to 115.2Kbps are supported	Multiprocessor server for remote and terminal server functions to connect devices to Ethernet LANs. Modems not included.
CPU Type	68020/20MHz	68020/20MHz
Ports	40 WAN ports 1 LAN port	Up to 280
Protocols	PPP, SLIP, CSLIP, ARA, TCP/IP, IPX, AppleTalk, Decnet, SPX	PPP, SLIP, CSLIP, ARA, TCP/IP, IPX, AppleTalk, Decnet, SPX
Network Connectivity	N/A	N/A
Bundled Software	Stampede Remote Office	Remote Node/Remote Control software included (Stampede Remote Office)
Comments	Dial back, password authentication, derverus, secureID, dial-in, dial-out supported	Dial-in, dial-out supported
Warranty	3 year	3 year
Price	$1,995–$4,995	$1,095–$1,995

Manufacturer	Xylogics, A Bay Networks Company	Xylogics, A Bay Networks Company
Model	Remote Annex 2000	Remote Annex 4000
General Description and Benefits	Remote Annex provides user with transparent dial-in access to Ethernet LANs. Users can access e-mail, databases, and file servers residing on Novell NetWare, TCP/IP and AppleTalk LANs as if they were directly connected to the network.	Remote Annex provides users with transparent dial-in access to Ethernet LANs. Users can access e-mail, databases, and file servers residing on Novell NetWare, TCP/IP, and AppleTalk LANs as if they were directly connected to the network.
CPU Type	80486SLC (4 ports); 80486SXLC2 (8 or 16 ports)	80486SXLC2 motherboard; 80486SLC (serial boards)
Ports	Either 4, 8, 16 RS-232 ports; speeds up to 115.2Kbps	From 18 to 72 RS-232 ports; spedes up to 115.2Kbps.
Protocols	TCP/IP, IPX, ARA, LAT, TN3270	TCP/IP, IPX, ARA, LAT, TN3270
Network Connectivity	Ethernet	Ethernet
Bundled Software	Rel 11.1, bundled clients- FASTLINK-II Remote Node; Proxy Remote Control- unlimited right to distribute.	Rel 11.1, bundled clients- FASTLINK-II Remote Node; Proxy Remote Control- unlimited right to distribute.

N/A—Not applicable   INA—Information not available

Table Continues →

Communications Servers

Manufacturer	Xylogics, A Bay Networks Company	Xylogics, A Bay Networks Company
Comments	Extended support programs	Extended support programs
Warranty	Limited lifetime	Limited lifetime
Price	$1,995–$6,285	$4,795–$12,885

Manufacturer	Xylogics, A Bay Networks Company	Xylogics, A Bay Networks Company
Model	Annex 3; MicroAnnexXL, MicroAnnex ELS	Remote Annex 6100
General Description and Benefits	The Annex family provides local and remote multiuser system access, connecting asynchronous devices such as terminals, printers, and modems to multipro-tocol Ethernet LANs	Remote Annex provides users with transparent dial-in access to Ethernet LANs. Users can access e-mail, databases, and file servers residing on Novell Net-Ware, TCP/IP, and AppleTalk LANs as if they were directly connected to the network.
CPU Type	80387 SX	80486SXLC2 motherboard; 80486SLC (serial boards)
Ports	8 to 63 RS232 serial ports; speeds to 57.6Kbps	INA
Protocols	TCP/IP, LAT, TN3270	TCP/IP, IPX, ARA, LAT, TN3270
Network Connectivity	Ethernet	Ethernet
Bundled Software	Rel. 10.0	Rel 11.1, bundled clients- FASTLINK-II Remote Node; Proxy Remote Control- unlimited right to distribute.
Comments	Extended support programs	Extended support programs
Warranty	Limited lifetime	Limited lifetime
Price	$1,595–$7,685	$4,795–$12,885

N/A—Not applicable   INA—Information not available

End ■

File Servers ■

Manufacturer	ALR	ALR
Model	Evolution 5ST 100,120,133,150,166	Evolution 6 150
CPU Type	Intel Pentium 100,120,133, 150,166MHz	Intel Pentium Pro 150MHz
Cache	256K	256K (integrated)
Memory	8MB std 128MB max	16MB std 128MB max
Disk Controller	Fast Wide SCSI-2 Adaptec AHA2940W	Fast Wide SCSI-2 Adaptec AHA2940W
Expansion Slots	4 ISA,3 PCI 1 shared	2 ISA, 3 PCI 1 shared
Disk Drives	2–9GB	2–9GB
Disk/CD ROM	1.44MB/4X CDROM	1.44MB/4X CDROM
NIC	Cogent EM110 RJ-45, 10BASE-T AUI	Cogent EM110 RJ-45, 10BASE-T AUI
Power Supply	250w	200w
Enclosure	Mini-Tower	Mini-Tower
Comments		
Warranty	5 year	5 year
Price	$1,400–$4,000	$3,500–$4,500

Manufacturer	Bull	Bull
Model	Estrella Server Series	Escala Server
CPU Type	PPC 604 100,133MHz	PPC 604 112MHz
Cache	256,512K	1MB
Memory	16MB std 256MB max	32MB std 512MB max
Disk Controller	SCSI-2	SCSI-2
Expansion Slots	2 EISA, 2 PCI 1 shared	6 MCA
Disk Drives	(1) 4.3GB	(1) 4.2GB
Disk/CD ROM	1.44MB/600MB	1.44MB/600MB
NIC	10BASE-T 10BASE5 Ethernet	10BASE-T Ethernet
Power Supply	230VA	380VA
Enclosure	Mini-Tower, desktop	Mini-Tower
Comments		
Warranty	1 year	1 year
Price	$5,000–$7,000	$17,000–$20,000

Manufacturer	Compaq	Compaq
Model	ProLiant 1500, 5/75, 5/100	ProLiant 1500, 5/133, 5/166
CPU Type	Intel Pentium 75,100MHz	Intel Pentium 133,166MHz
Cache	256K	512K

N/A—Not applicable   INA—Information not available

Table Continues →

■ File Servers

Manufacturer	Compaq	Compaq
Memory	16MB std 208MB max	256MB std
Disk Controller	32bit Smart, Smart-2 Fast SCSI-2	Fast Wide SCSI, Smart-2
Expansion Slots	5 EISA, 2 PCI 1 shared	5 EISA, 2 PCI 1 shared
Disk Drives	(2) 2.1GB	(2) 4.3GB
Disk/CD ROM	1.44MB/4x	1.44MB/4x
NIC	RJ-45 NetFlex2 ENET-TR	RJ-45, BNC NetFlex3/P
Power Supply	325w	325w
Enclosure	Tower, rack	Tower, rack
Comments	Other File servers ProLiant 4500; ProLiant 4000/R; ProLiant 2000/R; ProLiant 1000, and ProSignia VS	Other File servers ProLiant 4500; ProLiant 4000/R; ProLiant 2000/R; ProLiant 1000, and ProSignia VS
Warranty	3 year	3 year
Price	$4,976	$6,226–$7,249

Manufacturer	Compaq	Compaq
Model	ProSignia 300 5/75, 5/90, 5/120	ProSignia 500 5/120, 5/150
CPU Type	Intel Pentium 75, 90, 120MHz	Intel Pentium 120,150 MHz
Cache	256K	256K
Memory	16MB std 208MB max	16MB std 208MB max
Disk Controller	32bit Fast SCSI 2/P	32bit Fast SCSI-2/P
Expansion Slots	3 EISA, 1 PCI 1 shared	3 EISA, 1 PCI 1 shared
Disk Drives	(2) 2.1GB	(2) 2.1GB
Disk/CD ROM	1.44MB/4x	1.44MB/4x
NIC	RJ-45, BNC NetFlex-L ENET	RJ-45, BNC NetFlex-L ENET
Power Supply	280w	280w
Enclosure	Mini-Tower	Tower,Desktop
Comments	Other File servers ProLiant 4500; ProLiant 4000/R; ProLiant 2000/R; ProLiant 1000, and ProSignia VS	Other File servers ProLiant 4500; ProLiant 4000/R; ProLiant 2000/R; ProLiant 1000, and ProSignia VS
Warranty	3 year	3 year
Price	$2,333–$2,556	$3,556

Manufacturer	CSS Lakes	Cubix
Model	MaxPro 1500,800,1000	ERS/FT 2 4x3
CPU Type	Intel Pentium 100, 166MHz	Pentium 90,120,150 MHz
Cache	512K	256K
Memory	16MB std 256MB,384MB max	384MB max
Disk Controller	Fast SCSI-2 Adaptec 3940w	Fast SCSI-2, IDE32bit internal PCI
Expansion Slots	4 EISA, 4 ISA, 2 PCI, 1 shared	2 PCI, 1 shared ISA/PCI

N/A—Not applicable   INA—Information not available

File Servers ■

Manufacturer	CSS Lakes	Cubix
Disk Drives	(2) 2.1GB	(1) 4GB std (8) 2GB max
Disk/CD ROM	1.44MB/6x	1.44MB/4x Opt.
NIC	CSS EtherPro 10/100 RJ- 45	10BASE-T Ethernet
Power Supply	Dual 300w hot swap	350w
Enclosure	Tower	Rack
Comments		
Warranty	3 year	1 year
Price	$6,000–$8,000	$8,190

Manufacturer	Cubix	Data General
Model	ERS/FT 2 2x5	AV2000
CPU Type	Pentium 90,120,150 MHz	Intel Pentium 133, 166MHz
Cache	256K	256K
Memory	384 max	16MB std 256MB max
Disk Controller	Fast SCSI-2, IDE 32bit internal PCI	Fast SCSI-2
Expansion Slots	0-4 ISA field segmentable, 5 PCI	6 EISA, 3 PCI 1 shared
Disk Drives	(1) 4GB	(1) 4GB
Disk/CD ROM	1.44MB/4x Opt.	1.44MB/4x
NIC	10BASE-T Ethernet	Ethernet
Power Supply	350w	230w
Enclosure	Rack	Tower
Comments		
Warranty	1 year	3 year
Price	$8,290	$4,865

Manufacturer	Dell	Dell
Model	PowerEdge XE-2	PowerEdge XL
CPU Type	100,133,166MHz	133MHz
Cache	512K	512K
Memory	16MB std 512MB ECC	32MB std 768MB ECC
Disk Controller	32bit Fast SCSI-2	32bit Fast Wide SCSI-2
Expansion Slots	7 EISA, 1 PCI 1 shared	4 EISA, 2 PCI 1 shared
Disk Drives	1–9GB	1–9GB
Disk/CD ROM	1.44MB/6x	1.44MB/6x
NIC	Etherlink 10MB PCI, Lanstemer, PCI, SMC Etherez ISA	Etherlink 10MB PCI,Etherlink 10/100MB, Lansteamer PCI, EtherExpress Pro 100MB
Power Supply	530w	525w

N/A—Not applicable   INA—Information not available

Table Continues →

■ File Servers

Manufacturer	Dell	Dell
Enclosure	Deskside	Tower
Comments		
Warranty	3 year	3 year
List Price	$3,949–$4,749	$9,949–$11,949

Manufacturer	Dell	Dell
Model	PowerEdge SP-2	PowerEdge EL
CPU Type	100,133,166MHz	75,90,100, 120,133MHz
Cache	256K std 512K max	256K
Memory	16MB std 512MB ECC	16MB std 256MB max
Disk Controller	32bit Fast SCSI-2	32bit Fast SCSI-2
Expansion Slots	5 EISA, 1 PCI 1 shared	4 ISA, 2 PCI 2 shared
Disk Drives	1–9GB	1–4GB
Disk/CD ROM	1.44MB/6x	1.44MB/6x
NIC	Etherlink 10MB PCI,Etherlink 10/100MB, Lansteamer PCI, EtherExpress Pro 100MB	Etherlink EISA,Etherlink 10MB PCI,Etherlink 10/100MB, Lansteamer PCI, EtherExpress Pro 100MB
Power Supply	300w	244w
Enclosure	Tower	Mini-Tower
Comments		
Warranty	3 year	3 year
Price	$3,189–$4,159	$2,987–$2,649

Manufacturer	Digital Equipment Corporation	Digital Equipment Corporation
Model	AlphaServer 1000	AlphaServer 400 4/166, 4/233
CPU Type	Alpha 266MHz	Alpha 166,233MHz
Cache	16K, 2MB ECC	8K
Memory	1GB ECC max	384MB max
Disk Controller	Fast SCSI-2, Fast Wide SCSI	SCSI-2
Expansion Slots	7 EISA, 2 PCI, 1 shared	3 ISA, 2 PCI 1 shared
Disk Drives	2–8GB	2–8GB
Disk/CD ROM	Both	1.44MB
NIC	Ethernet, FDDI, Token Ring, SNA, X.25, TCP/IP, DEC-net/OSI, WAN	Ethernet, FDDI, Token Ring, WAN X.25, SNA, TCP/IP, DECnet.OSI
Power Supply	450w	345w
Enclosure	Tower, Rack	Mini-Tower
Comments	Internet Alpha Server software available	Internet Alpha Server software available
Warranty	3 year	3 year
Price	$9,999–$17,980	$8,500–$8,980

N/A—Not applicable   INA—Information not available

File Servers ∎

Manufacturer	Falcon	Hewlett Packard
Model	Fastfile Pro	Netserver 5100 LH
CPU Type	100MHz	Intel Pentium 100MHz
Cache	16MB	512K
Memory	32MB std 224MB max	32MB std 192MG max
Disk Controller	32bit PCI Fast Wide SCSI	Fast 5 SCSI-2
Expansion Slots	6 EISA, 4 PCI	4 PCI, 4 EISA, 1 shared
Disk Drives	1,2,4 or 9GB	1GB, 2GB, or 4GB
Disk/CD ROM	1.44MB/4x	4x
NIC	Fiber Channel, FDDI, ATM, HiPPI, Ethernet 100/10BASE-T	PCI, EISA
Power Supply	1200w	350w
Enclosure	Tower, Rack	Tower
Comments		
Warranty	1 year	3 year
Price	$18,995	$7,199

Manufacturer	Hewlett Packard	IBM
Model	NetServer 5/133 LH	8641MZO; MZV/ 8641-MZS; MZE; MZL
CPU Type	Intel Pentium 133MHz	Intel Pentium 100MHz
Cache	256K	512K
Memory	32MB std 192MB max	32MB ECC
Disk Controller	Fast Wide SCSI-2	Fast Wide SCSI-2
Expansion Slots	4 EISA, 4PCI 1 shared	6 Micro Channel, 2 PCI
Disk Drives	(4) 2GB	(1-6) 2.25GB, open bay
Disk/CD ROM	4x	4x
NIC	PCI, EISA	Ethernet, Token Ring
Power Supply	350w	434w
Enclosure	Tower	Tower
Comments		IBM also manufactures the PC Server 320 series
Warranty	3 year	3 year
Price	$16,989	$7,400–$12,500

Manufacturer	IBM	IBM
Model	8641-EZO; EZV 8641-EZ1; EZS; EZE	8639-OZO 8639-OZT/ODT
CPU Type	Intel Pentium 100MHz	Intel Pentium 100, 133, 166MHz
Cache	512K	256K
Memory	32MB ECC	16MB std 192MB max

N/A—Not applicable　INA—Information not available

Table Continues →

■ File Servers

Manufacturer	IBM	IBM
Disk Controller	Fast Wide SCSI, PCI RAID Adapter 2	Fast Wide SCSI-2
Expansion Slots	4 EISA, 1 PCI 1 shared	3 ISA, 2 PCI
Disk Drives	(1-4) 2.25GB, open bay	Open bay/1.08GB
Disk/CD ROM	4x	4x
NIC	Ethernet, Token Ring	Ethernet
Power Supply	434w	200w
Enclosure	Tower	Mini-Tower
Comments		
Warranty	3 year	3 year
Price	$7,400–$13,600	$36,000

Manufacturer	Maximum Strategy	Maximum Strategy
Model	proFile XL	proFile L
CPU Type	Motorola 68060	Motorola 68060
Cache	120MB max	24MB max
Memory	64MB std	32MB std
Disk Controller	Fast Wide SCSI-2	Fast Wide SCSI-2
Expansion Slots	N/A	N/A
Disk Drives	(24 to 96) 9GB	(8 or 16) 9GB
Disk/CD ROM	4.3GB	4.3GB
NIC	FTP and NFS over TCP or UDP/IP ATM,Fibre Channel,HiPPI	FTP and NFS over TCP or UDP/IP ATM,Fibre Channel,HiPPI
Power Supply	4.85 KVA max	1.2 KVA max
Enclosure	Tower	Tower
Warranty	3 year	3 year
Price	$1–$3/MB starting at $100,000	$1–$3/MB starting at $100,000

Manufacturer	NCR	NCR
Model	S10DT	S10MT
CPU Type	75,100,13, 166MHz	75,100,13, 166MHz
Cache	256K	256K
Memory	192MB	192MB
Disk Controller	Fast Wide SCSI-2	Fast Wide SCSI-2
Expansion Slots	4 EISA, 2PCI, 1 shared	4 EISA, 2PCI, 1 shared
Disk Drives	(2)4GB	(2)4GB
Disk/CD ROM	600MB/ 4x	600MB/ 4x
NIC	Single ended or differential, PCI SCSI adapters	Single ended or differential, PCI SCSI adapters
Power Supply	200w	200w

N/A—Not applicable   INA—Information not available

File Servers ∎

Manufacturer	NCR	NCR
Enclosure	Desktop	Mini-Tower
Comments		
Warranty	3 year	3 year
Price	$4,340	$4,340

Manufacturer	NCR	NEC
Model	S10XL	ProServa V Series
CPU Type	100,133, 166 MHz	Pentium 100 MHz
Cache	256K	245K
Memory	256MB	16,32MB std 256MB max
Disk Controller	Hot pluggable SCSI-2	Fast Wide SCSI-2
Expansion Slots	4 EISA, 2 PCI, 1 shared	5 EISA, 2 PCI, 1 shared
Disk Drives	(2)4GB	2-4GB multiple drive options
Disk/CD ROM	1.44MB/4x	1.44MB/4x
NIC	Single ended or differential, PCI SCSI adapters	Ethernet
Power Supply	250w	300w
Enclosure	Mini-Tower	Mid-Tower
Comments		
Warranty	3 year	3 year
Price	$10,780	$2,500–$51,000

Manufacturer	NEC	NEC
Model	ProServe PH Series	ProServa SH Series
CPU Type	Pentium 133MHz	Pentium Pro 166,200MHz
Cache	1MB perCPU	256,512K
Memory	16,32MB std 768MB max	64MB std 1GB max
Disk Controller	Fast Wide SCSI-2 128bit	Fast Wide SCSI-2
Expansion Slots	4 EISA, 2 PCI, 2 shared	6 EISA, 1 PCI
Disk Drives	(1–4) 2GB	INA
Disk/CD ROM	1.44MB/4x	1.44MB/4x
NIC	Ethernet	Ethernet
Power Supply	525w	(2)325w
Enclosure	Full Tower	Full Tower
Comments		
Warranty	3 year	3 year
Price	$8,400–$18,000	INA

N/A—Not applicable   INA—Information not available

Table Continues →

■ File Servers

Manufacturer	Network Appliance	Network Appliance
Model	NetApp F220	NetAppF330
CPU Type	Intel 75	Intel 90
Cache	256K	512K
Memory	32HB	64MB
Disk Controller	INA	INA
Expansion Slots	10/100BASE-T FDDI, CBBI	10/100BASE-T FDDI, CBBI
Disk Drives	(4) 4GB	(4) 4GB
Diskette/CD ROM	1.44MB/4x Opt.	1.44MB/4x Opt.
NIC	RJ-45	RJ-45
Power Supply	INA	INA
Enclosure	Rack	Rack
Comments	INA	INA
Warranty	INA	INA
Price	$17,950	$34,950

Manufacturer	Polywell Computers	Network Appliance
Model	PolyAlpha 400s	NetApp540
CPU Type	DEC Alpha 21164A 400MHz	Intel 275
Cache	2MB	2 HB, 2MB
Memory	64-128MB std 512MB max	64MB
Disk Controller	SCSI-3	
Expansion Slots	3 ISA, 4 PCI	10/100BASE-T FDDI, CBBI
Disk Drives	4–20GB	(4) 4GB
Disk/CD ROM	INA	1.44MB/4x
NIC	1–4 Channel 100Mb Ethernet	RJ-45
Power Supply	800w	INA
Enclosure	INA	Rack
Comments	INA	INA
Warranty	2 year	INA
Price	$9,500–$1,800	$52,950

Manufacturer	Polywell Computers	Polywell Computers
Model	Poly 500F1	Poly 560F1
CPU Type	Intel Pentium 180MHz	Intel Pentium 166MHz
Cache	256K	512K
Memory	16MB std 128MB max	32MB std 512MB max
Disk Controller	EIDE	EIDE

N/A—Not applicable   INA—Information not available

File Servers ■

Manufacturer	Polywell Computers	Polywell Computers
Expansion Slots	5 ISA, 4 PCI 1 shared	5 ISA, 4 PCI 1 shared
Disk Drives	(1) 2.1GB	(2) 2.1GB
Disk/CD ROM	1.44/4x	1.44/6x
NIC	Ethernet RJ-45 BNC	Ethernet RJ-45 BNC
Power Supply	250w	300w
Enclosure	Tower, rack	Tower, rack
Comments		
Warranty	3 year	3 year
Price	$1,995	$2,850

Manufacturer	Sun Microsystems	Sun Microsystems
Model	SPARC Server 20	SPARC Server 5
CPU Type	Super SPARC 2 75,150MHz	Micro SPARC 2 110MHz
Cache	1MB std 512K max	24K
Memory	32MB std 512MB max	32MB std 256MB max
Disk Controller	Fast SCSI-2	Fast SCSI-2
Expansion Slots	4 SBUS	3 SBUS
Disk Drives	(2) 2.1GB	(2) 2.1GB
Disk/CD ROM	1.44MB/ 2x	1.44MB/ 2x
NIC	Ethernet	Ethernet
Power Supply	150w	150w
Enclosure	Desktop	Desktop
Comments	Also available, NFS 150 Server offering highly reliable features such as an integrated uninterruptible power supply, RAID5, and an easy to use HTML administration interface	Also available, NFS 150 Server offering highly reliable features such as an integrated uninterruptible power supply, RAID5, and an easy to use HTML administration interface
Warranty	1 year	1 year
Price	$14,995	$7,495

Manufacturer	Sun Microsystems	Sun Microsystems
Model	Ultra Enterprise 1/150	Ultra Enterprise 1/170/ Netra NFS 150
CPU Type	Ultra SPARC 167MHZ	Ultra SPARC 167MHz
Cache	512K	512K
Memory	32MB std 1GB max	64MD std 512MB max
Disk Controller	Fast Wide SCSI-2	Fast Wide CSI
Expansion Slots	3 SBUS	3 SBUS
Disk Drives	(2) 2.1GB/ 25.2GB Hot Plug	(4) 2.1GB

N/A—Not applicable   INA—Information not available

Table Continues →

ZIFF-DAVIS PRESS

■ File Servers

Manufacturer	Sun Microsystems	Sun Microsystems
Disk/CD ROM	644MB/ 4x	2.1GB/ 4x
NIC	Fast Ethernet 10MB/sec/ Fast Wide Ethernet 100MB/sec	10BASE-T Ethernet, 10/100BASE-T Fast Ethernet, 9 10BASE-T, 2 100BASE-T, 2 FDDI,2 Token Ring
Power Supply	180w/350w	100-240 VAC
Enclosure	Desktop/tower, rack	Tower, rack
Comments		
Warranty	1 year	1 year
Price	$15,495–$16,245	$24,395

Manufacturer	Unisys	Zenith Data Systems
Model	Clear Path SMP 5200/ SMP 5200	WL
CPU Type	Intel Pentium 100,133MHz	Intel 120,150,200MHz
Cache	16K std 256K max	256,512K
Memory	16MB std 256MB max	16MB std, 256MB max
Disk Controller	PCI Fast Wide SCSI	32-bit Ultra Wide SCSI-3, 16-bit Fast SCSI-2
Expansion Slots	5 EISA 2 PCI 1 shared	5 EISA, 2 PCI 1 shared
Disk Drives	1–12GB	1,2,4GB
Disk/CD ROM	1.44MB/4x	1.44MB/4x
NIC	Ethernet 100Mbps	Optional
Power Supply	300w	300w
Enclosure	Tower/Desktop	Tower
Comments		
Warranty	1 year	3 year
Price	$2,709	INA

N/A—Not applicable   INA—Information not available

End ■

Print Servers ■

Manufacturer	Axis Communications	Axis Communications
Model	Axis 150/152	Axis 540/640
CPU Type	32bit RISC	32bit RISC
Memory	128K	256K
NIC	Ethernet 10Mbps	Ethernet 10Mbps or Token Ring 4/16 Mbps
Protocols	IPX/SPX	IPX/SPX, TCP/IP, NetBIOS/NetBEUI, EtherTalk, HTTP
Printer Interfaces	2 high-speed parallel 1EEE 1228	1 high-speed parallel 1EEE 1284
OS/NOS	NetWare including NDS, all Windows platforms, LAN Server and LAN Manager	NetWare including NDS, Unix, all Windows platforms, LAN Server and LAN Manager. In addition, the + models support Apple EtherTalk as well.
Setup and Mgt. Utility	Windows, NetWare, OS/2	Unix, Windows, NetWare, OS/2
Hardware/Software	Hardware with embedded software	Hardware with embedded software
Price	$399	$349/$499

Manufacturer	Axis Communications	Axis Communications
Model	Axis 560/660	Axis 570/670
CPU Type	32bit RISC	32bit RISC
Memory	256K	512K
NIC	Ethernet 10Mbps or Token Ring 4/16Mbps	Ethernet 10 Mbps or Token Ring 4/16Mbps
Protocols	IPX/SPX, TCP/IP, NetBIOS/NetBEUI, EtherTalk	SNA, IPX/SPX, TCP/IP, NetBIOS/NetBEUI, EtherTalk
Printer Interfaces	2 high-speed parallel 1EEE 1228, 1 high-speed serial	2 high-speed parallel 1EEE 1228, 1 high- speed serial
OS/NOS	NetWare including NDS, Unix all Windows platforms, LAN Server and LAN Manager, Apple EtherTalk	IBM Mainframe and AS/400 (Native SNA), NetWare including NDS, Unix, all Windows platforms, LAN Server and LAN Manager, Apple EtherTalk
Setup and Mgt. Utility	Unix, Windows, NetWare, OS/2	Unix, Windows, NetWare, OS/2
Hardware/Software	Hardware with embedded software	Hardware with embedded software
Price	$599/$699	$899/$999

Manufacturer	Castelle	Castelle
Model	Office Connect	LANpress 2+1/ LANpress 3+1
CPU Type	16MHz Motorola 68302	16MHz Intel 80186
Memory	512K Flash ROM, 1MB RAM	256K Flash ROM, 1MB RAM
NIC	Ethernet 10BASE-T/BNC Autoselect	Ethernet 10BASE-T/BNC,AUI, Token Ring, 16/4Mbps
Protocols	Ethernet, IPX/SPX, TXP/IP, Telnet, RARP, TFTP	EtherTalk, IPX/SPX, TCP/IP, Telenet, RARP, TFTP
Printer Interfaces	2 bi-directional IEEE parallel	2 centronics parallel, 1 RS-232 serial
OS/NOS	Windows NT, NetWare,Unix TCP/IP, Telnet, ZARP,TFTP, Novell	Windows NT, NetWare,Unix, EtherTalk
Setup and Mgt. Utility	DOS, Windows	DOS, Windows
Hardware/Software	Both	Both
Comments	One of the Office Connect "clippable" family	
Warranty	2 year	2 year, extended available
Price	$499	$499–$719

N/A—Not applicable   INA—Information not available

Table Continues →

■ Print Servers

Manufacturer	Castelle	Castelle
Model	LANpress JR	LANpress IP
CPU Type	12MHz Intel 80186	12MHz Intel 80186
Memory	256K Flash ROM, 1MB RAM	256K Flash ROM, 1MB RAM
NIC	Ethernet 10BASE-T/BNC Autoselect	Ethernet 10BASE-T/BNC Autoselect
Protocols	EtherTalk, IPX/SPX, TCP/IP, Telnet, RARP, TFTP	EtherTalk, IPX/SPX, TCP/IP, Telnet, RARP, TFTP
Printer Interfaces	1 centronics direct connect	1 centronics parallel port
OS/NOS	Windows NT, NetWare (with NDS compatibility) Unix, EtherTalk	Windows NT, NetWare (with NDS compatibility) Unix, EtherTalk
Setup and Mgt. Utility	DOS, Windows	DOS, Windows
Hardware/Software	Both	Both
Comments	Multi-protocol external print server with flash memory	Multi-protocol external print server with flash memory
Warranty	2 year, extended available	2 year, extended available
Price	$379	$389

Manufacturer	Chase Research	D Link
Model	10PRINTZ	DE-960
CPU Type	16MHz Motorola MC 68340	16MHZ AMD 80c188
Memory	INA	16K buffer
NIC	10BASE-T, BNC	Ethernet 10Mbps UTP,BNC
Protocols	IPX/SPX, NetBEUI, TCP/IP, Apple EtherTalk	TCP/IP, IPX/SPX
Printer Interfaces	2 RS-232, 2 bi-parallel (1EEE 1284)	2 LPT and com ports
OS/NOS	TCP/IP, IPX, EtherTalk, Windows NT, Unix	Novell, Windows NT, TCP/IP
Setup and Mgt. Utility	Windows, SNMP	DOS, Windows NT, Unix, Telnet
Hardware/Software	Both	Both
Comments		
Warranty	Lifetime	1 year
Price	$665	$395

Manufacturer	Digi International, Inc.	Digital Products Inc.
Model	Fast Port Family (9 models)	JexPrint 1000
CPU Type	16MHz Intel 80186	16MHz Motorola 68340
Memory	256K RAM, 2K (non-volatile)	512K
NIC	Ethernet 10Mbps Token Ring 416MB	Ethernet 10BASE-T/2, Token Ring
Protocols	IPX/SPX, EtherTalk, TCP/IP, NetBEUI, TokenTalk	IPX/SPX, TCP/IP
Printer Interfaces	1 parallel, 1 serial; 2 parallel	IEEE 1284 bi-di parallel andserial
OS/NOS	OS/2, LAN Manager, Windows NT, Windows for Workgroups	NetWare, Unix, TCP-IP, Windows NT, Banyan Vines, Apple
Setup and Mgt. Utility	ACT for NetWare, DOS, Unix included	DOS, Windows, Telnet, MacIntosh

N/A—Not applicable   INA—Information not available

Print Servers ■

Manufacturer	**Digi International, Inc.**	**Digital Products Inc.**
Hardware/Software	External housing 802.3, 802.2	Both
Comments		Toll-free customer service, overnight replacement
Warranty	5 year	3 year
Price	$395–$945	$349–$795

Manufacturer	**Digital Products Inc.**	**Digital Products Inc.**
Model	NetPrint	NetPrint 10
CPU Type	16MHz Motorola 68340	16MHz Motorola 68340
Memory	512K	512K
NIC	Ethernet 10BASE-T/2, Token Ring	Ethernet 10BASE-T/2, Token Ring
Protocols	IPX/SPX, TCP/IP, Telnet, FTP	IPX/SPX
Printer Interfaces	IEEE 1284 bi-directional parallel and serial	IEEE 1284 bi-directional parallel and serial
OS/NOS	Solaris, Ultrix, HP-UX, AIX, SCO, DOS, Alpha OSF, NetWare, Unix, Windows NT, Banyan Vines	NetWare
Setup and Mgt. Utility	DOS, Windows	DOS, Windows
Hardware/Software	Both	Both
Comments		
Warranty	Toll-free customer service, overnight replacement. 3 year (std), 6 year (with return).	Toll-free customer service, overnight replacement. 3 year.
Price	$345–$795	$245

Manufacturer	**Digital Products Inc.**	**Digital Products Inc.**
Model	NetPrint 1000	NetCommuter 1
CPU Type	16MHz Motorola 68340	16MHz Motorola 68340
Memory	512K	1MB
NIC	Ethernet 10BASE-T/2, Token Ring	Ethernet
Protocols	IPX/SPX, TCP/IP, Telnet, MOP	IPX/SPX, IXP/PPP, Windows 95 PPP
Printer Interfaces	IEEE 1284 bi-directional parallel and serial	IEEE 1284 bi-directional parallel and serial
OS/NOS	NetWare, Unix, Windows NT, Banyan Vines, Apple, LAT, Solaris, Ultrix, HP-UX, AIX, SCO, DOS, Alpha OSF	NetWare, Unix, Windows NT, Apple
Setup and Mgt. Utility	DOS, Windows, MacIntosh,	DOS, Windows, MacIntosh
Hardware/Software	Both	Both
Comments	External print server. Toll-free customer service, overnight replacement.	Multi-functional remote access print server. Toll-free customer service, overnight replacement.
Warranty	3 year (std), 6 year (with return)	3 year
Price	$495-$1,095	$795

Manufacturer	**Emulex**	**Emulex**
Model	NETQue Token Ring	NETQue Pro2
CPU Type	4/16MHz AMD 80186	20MHz AMD 80186
Memory	11/2MB RAM, 1MB Flash (non-volatile)	1MB RAM, 1MB Flash (non-volatile)

N/A—Not applicable   INA—Information not available

Table Continues →

■ Print Servers

Manufacturer	Emulex	Emulex
NIC	Token Ring 4/16 Mbps, UTP and STP	Ethernet 10Mbps (10BASE-T UTP and 10BASE2BNC)
Protocols	IPX/SPX, TCP/IP, AppleTalk, NetBEUI/NetBIOS, UDP, ICMP, ARP, RARP, BootP, TFTP, DHCP, "1pr/1pd"	IPX/SPX, TCP/IP, AppleTalk, NetBEUI/NetBIOS, UDP, ICMP, ARP, RARP, BootP, TFTP, DHCP, "1pr/1pd"
Printer Interfaces	IEEE 1284 high speed parallel, high-speed serial (115.2kpbs)	2 IEEE 1284 high speed parallel, high-speed serial, 1 high speed Serial (115.2kpbs)
OS/NOS	NetWare 2.x, 3.x, 4.x (NDS/NEST), Unix, "1pd", Windows NT, Windows for Workgroups, AppleTalk, LAN Manager, LAN Server, OS/2 Warp Connect Server	NetWare 2.x, 3.x, .x (NDS/NEST), Unix, "1pd", Windows NT, Windows for Workgroups, AppleTalk, LAN Manager, LAN Server, OS/2 Warp Connect Server, digital-licensed LAT
Setup & Mgt. Utility	Emulex NET wizard printer server administrator, Pconsole, NWAdmin, TES Kermit, Emulex proprietary "enstall" (Unix installation script, ARP, RARP, BootP, DHCP, Telnet)	Emulex NET wizard printer server administrator, Pconsole, NWAdmin, TES Kermit, Emulex proprietary "enstall" (Unix installation script, ARP, RARP, BootP, DHCP, Telnet, Flash Upgrade Utility)
Hardware/Software	Both	Both
Warranty	2 year	2 year
Price	$695	$599

Manufacturer	Emulex	Emulex
Model	NETJet	NETQue
CPU Type	10MHz AMD 80186	10MHz AMD 80186,
Memory	1MB RAM, 1MB Flash (non-volatile)	1MB RAM, 1MB Flash (non-volatile)
NIC	Ethernet 10Mbps (10BASE-T UTP and 10Base2BNC)	Ethernet 10Mbps (10BASE-T UTP and 10BASE2 BNC)
Protocols	IPX/SPX, TCP/IP, AppleTalk, NetBEUI/NetBIOS, UDP, ICMP, ARP, RARP, BootP, TFTP, DHCP, "1pr/1pd"	IPX/SPX, TCP/IP, Appletalk, Digitalilicensed LAT, NetBEUI/NetBIOS, UDP, ICMP, ARP, RARP, BootP, TFTP, DHCP, "1pr/1pd"
Printer Interfaces	Hewlett-Packard MIO, high-speed serial (115.2Kps)	IEEE 1284 high-speed parallel, high-speed serial (115.2Kps)
OS/NOS	NetWare 2.x, 3.x, 4.x (NDS/NEST), Unix, "1pd", Windows NT, Windows for Workgroups, AppleTalk, LAN Manager, LAN Server, OS/2 Warp Connect Server, Digital-licensed LAT	NetWare (NDS/NEST), Unix, "1pd", Windows NT, Windows for Workgroups, AppleTalk, LAN Manager, LAN Server, OS/2 Warp Connect Server, Digital-licensed LAT
Setup and Mgt. Utility	Emulex NET wizard printer server administrator, Pconsole, NWAdmin, TES Kermit, Emulex propriety "enstall" (Unix installation script, ARP, RARP, BootP, DHCP, Telnet, Flash Upgrade Utility	Emulex NET wizard printer server administrator, Pconsole, NWAdmin, TES Kermit, Emulex propriety "enstall" (Unix installation script, ARP, RARP, BootP, DHCP, Telnet, Flash Upgrade utility
Hardware/Software	Both	Both
Warranty	2 year	2 year
Price	$499	$549

Manufacturer	Emulex	Extended Systems
Model	NETQue Mate	Pocket Print Server
CPU Type	10MHz AMD 80186	Intel 80188 10Mhz
Memory	1MB RAM, 1MB Flash (non-volatile)	128K
NIC	Ethernet 10Mbps (10BASE-T UTP)	Ethernet 10Mbps
Protocols	IPX/SPX, TCP/IP, AppleTalk, NetBEUI/NetBIOS, UDP, ICMP, ARP, RARP, BootP, TFTP, DHCP, "1pr/1pd"	IPX/SPX, TCP/IP, Vines IP
Printer Interfaces	IEEE 1284 high speed parallel, high-speed serial (115.2Kbps)	1 IEEE 1284 high-speed parallel

N/A—Not applicable   INA—Information not available

Print Servers ■

Manufacturer	Emulex	Extended Systems
OS/NOS	NetWare 2.x, 3.x, 4.x (NDS/NEST), Unix, "1pd", Windows NT, Windows for Workgroups, AppleTalk, LAN Manager, LAN Server, OS/2 Warp Connect Server	TCP/IP, NT, NetWare 3.x+4.x, Banyan Vines
Setup and Mgt. Utility	Emulex NET wizard printer server administrator, Pconsole, NWAdmin, TES Kermit, Emulex proprietary "enstall" (Unix installation script, ARP, RARP, BootP, DHCP, Telnet, Flash upgrade utility)	Windows, DOS
Hardware/Software	Both	Both
Comments		Direct attach, no cable
Warranty	2 year	5 year
Price	$399	$299–$595

Manufacturer	Extended Systems	Extended Systems
Model	ExtendNet DX. ExtendNet	ExtendNet MPX. ExtendNet SX
CPU Type	Intel 80188 20MHz	Intel 80186 16MHz/Intel 80188 20Mhz
Memory	512K	512K
NIC	Ethernet 10Mbps, Token Ring 4/16MB	Ethernet 10Mbps, Token Ring 4/16MB
Protocols	IPX/SPX, TCP/IP, Banyan Vines IP, DLC, PAP, EtherTalk	IPX/SPX, TCP/IP, Banyan Vines IP, DLC, PAP, EtherTalk
Printer Interfaces	2 IEEE 1284. 1 internal MP Mid, 1 IEEE 1284	2 IEEE 1284, 2-parallel, serial. 1 IEEE 1284
OS/NOS	NetWare, Banyan Vines, LAN Server, LAN Manager	NetWare, Banyan Vines, LAN Server, LAN Manager
Setup and Mgt. Utility	Windows, DOS	Windows, DOS
Hardware/Software	Both	Both
Comments		
Warranty	5 year	5 year
Price	$499–$1,195/ $369–$895	$795–$1,195 /$395–$695

Manufacturer	Hewlett-Packard Company	Hewlett-Packard Company
Model	HP JetDirect M10 card for Ethernet, Token Ring, or Ethernet/LocalTalk	Hp JetDirect EX Plus (Multiprotocol support for Ethernet)
CPU Type	N/A	INA
Memory	N/A	1MB Flash EPROM
NIC	Ethernet 10Mbps, Token Ring 4/16MB	Ethernet 10Mbps
Protocols	IPX/SPX, TCP/IP, DLC/LLC, NetBios, Appletalk	IPX/SPX, TCP/IP, DLC/LLC, NetBios, Appletalk
Printer Interfaces	IEEE 1284, HP BiTronics parallel	HP High-speed IEEE 1284 compatible BiTronics parallel (3 of them)
OS/NOS	NetWare 3.x & 4.x, Windows NT, 95 & for workgroups, IBM LAN server & AIX, UNIX, LAN manager, IBM AIX/ LAN server, UNIX, MacIntosh, others	NetWare 3.x & 4.x, Windows NT, 95 & for workgroups, IBM LAN server & AIX, UNIX, LAN manager, Solaris, sunOS, HP-UX, MacIntosh for UNIX
Setup & Mgt. Utility	DOS, Windows, Terminal session	DOS, Windows, Terminal session, Mac OS
Hardware/Software	Hardware	Both (HP JetAdmin included)

N/A—Not applicable   INA—Information not available

Table Continues →

■ Print Servers

Manufacturer	Hewlett-Packard Company	Hewlett-Packard Company
Comments		200 K/s throughput
Warranty	3 years	3 years
Price	Ethernet—$369 Token Ring—$619 Ethernet/LocalTalk—$429	Ethernet—$349 Token Ring—$729 100-VG—$649

Manufacturer	Hewlett-Packard Company	Icon Resources, Inc.
Model	EX-Plus 3 for Ethernet, Token Ring, or 100 VG AnyLAN	ICO 411,ICO 450,ICO 493
CPU Type	NA	16MHz Motorola 68306
Memory	128K RAM, 512K RAM	512K, 8MB Flash
NIC	Ethernet 10Mbps, Token Ring 4/16MB, 100VG Any-LAN	Ethernet 10Mbps, Token Ring 416MB
Protocols	IPX/SPX, TCP/IP, DLC/LLC, NetBios, Appletalk	IPX/SPX, LAT, Banyan Vines, TCP/IP, Peur Token, EtherTalk
Printer Interfaces	HP High-speed IEEE 1284 compatible BiTronics parallel (3 of them)	IEEE 1284, 10BASE-T, 10BASE2, AUI, high-speed parallel
OS/NOS	NetWare 3.x & 4.x, Windows NT, 95 & for workgroups, IBM LAN server & AIX, UNIX, LAN manager, Solaris, sunOS, HP-UX, Macintosh for UNIX	Windows NT, Windows 95, Decums
Setup & Mgt. Utility	DOS, Windows, Terminal session, Appletalk	DOS, Windows 95, Telnet, NCP, serial port, BootP, ARP, RARP
Hardware/Software	Both (HP JetAdmin included)	Both
Comments		
Warranty	3 year	5 year
Price	Ethernet—$529 Token Ring—$729 100-Vg—$649	$249

Manufacturer	Infinite Technologies	Intel
Model	I-Queue!	Netport express PRO
CPU Type	N/A	Intel 386
Memory	2.5K	1MB Flash, 1MB RAM
NIC	10BASE-T Ethernet	Ethernet 10Mbps, Token Ring 4/16MB
Protocols	IPX/SPX	IPX/SPX, TCP/IP, NetBEUI, Unix
Printer Interfaces	2 serial, 3 parallel	2 parallel, 1 serial
OS/NOS	NetWare 3.x and 4.x	Windows NT, NetWare, Windows 3.1, Windows for Workgroups, Windows 95, LAN Manager, LAN Server, Unix, AppleTalk
Setup and Mgt. Utility	DOS, Windows	DOS, Windows
Hardware/Software	Software	Both
Comments		
Warranty	Unlimited	3 year
Price	$249	$499 external, $349 internal

N/A—Not applicable   INA—Information not available

Print Servers ∎

Manufacturer	Lantronix	Lantronix
Model	LPS1	MPSI/EPSI
CPU Type	10MHz Motorola 68000	10MHz Motorola 68000/ National 32000
Memory	512K, 2K non-volatile	512K, 2K non-volatile
NIC	Ethernet 10Mbps	Ethernet 10Mbps
Protocols	IPX, TCP/IP	IPX,TCP/IP, AppleTalk, NetBIOS, NetBEUI, LAT
Printer Interfaces	1 parallel port RJ-45 connector	1 parallel port RJ-45, Ethernet/1 parallel port, 1 serial port, RJ-45 and AUI
OS/NOS	NetWare,Unix, Windows 95	NetWare,Unix, DEC,Macantosh, LanManager, Windows 95/NT
Setup and Mgt. Utility	DOS, NetWare, Windows 95,Unix	DOS, NetWare, Macintosh,Unix, Windows 95
Hardware/Software	Both	Both
Comments		
Warranty	5 year	5 year
Price	$299	$399–$495

Manufacturer	Linksys	Microdyne Corp.
Model	Pocket Print Server/Ethernet Print Server	NPE 400
CPU Type	N/A	10MHz Intel 80C188 Micro Controller
Memory	32K	1MB Flash Memory
NIC	Ethernet 10Mbps, 10BASE-T/BNC	IEEE 802.3, 10BASE2, 10BASE-T (auto sensing)
Protocols	IPX/SPX, SMB/ IPX/SPX	IPX/SPX
Printer Interfaces	1 parallel port 2 high-speed parallel, 1 serial	IEEE 1284, high-speed parallel port
OS/NOS	NovellNet	NetWare , any centronics 36-pin parallel port
Setup and Mgt. Utility	DOS, Windows	NetWare
Hardware/Software	Both	Both
Comments		
Warranty	1 year	5 year
Price	$247/$469	$399

Manufacturer	Microplex Systems Ltd.	Microplex Systems Ltd.
Model	M204 PCMCIA/ M208 Workgroup	M205/M206
CPU Type	16MHz Motorola 68340	10MHz Motorola 68EC000
Memory	256K, 512K 1MB Flash	512K, 512K Flash
NIC	10Mbps Ethernet, 16/4MB Token Ring	10Mbps Ethernet
Protocols	TCP/IP, IPX/SPX, EtherTalk, NetBIOS over TCP/IP	TCP/IP, IPX/SPX, EtherTalk, NetBIOS over TCP/IP
Printer Interfaces	IEEE 1284 high-speed parallel, 2 serial	IEEE 1284 high-speed parallel
OS/NOS	Unix, Novell, Windows NT, Windows 95, AppleTalk, OS/2	Unix, Novell, Windows NT, Windows 95, AppleTalk, OS/2

N/A—Not applicable   INA—Information not available

Table Continues →

■ Print Servers

Manufacturer	Microplex Systems Ltd.	Microplex Systems Ltd.
Setup and Mgt. Utility	Windows, Unix Shell Script	Windows, Unix Shell Script
Hardware/Software	Both	Both
Comments	PCMCIA cards, supports Token Ring and Ethernet simultaneously	
Warranty	6 year	6 year
Price	$720	$375

Manufacturer	Microplex Systems	NetFrame
Model	M202/ M212	8510/8520
CPU Type	16MHz Motorola 68340	100MHz Intel Pentium
Memory	256K RAM 512K Flash	64MB–1GB
NIC	10Mpbs Ethernet	Ethernet, Token Ring, SCSI-IiSCSI-II single-coded buses + SCSI. devices + Fast/Wide differentiated SCSI buses. FDDI Backbone
Protocols	TCP/IP, IPX/SPX, EtherTalk, Appletalk, NetBIOS over TCP/IP	TCP/IP, IPX/SPX, NetBIOS, AppleTalk NetBEUI, SNMP
Printer Interfaces	2 IEEE 1284 high-speed parallel,2 serial	Through print server support
OS/NOS	Unix, NetWare, Windows(NT, W95), Mac OS, OS/2	NetWare, Windows NT
Setup and Mgt. Utility	Windows and Unix Shell Script	Maestro Mgmt Suite
Hardware/Software	Both	Both
Comments		Can also serve as a file server and an application server. Supports SNMP.
Warranty	6 year	1 year
Price	$595 (M202/M212)	$14,950

Manufacturer	NetFrame	Pacific Data
Model	8570/8590	Direct Net X10/ Direct NetMIO
CPU Type	150MHz Intel Pentium	10MHz Motorola 68000
Memory	64MB–1GB	512K, 256K Flash
NIC	Ethernet, Token Ring, SCSI-IiSCSI-II single-coded buses + SCSI. devices + Fast/Wide differentiated SCSI buses. FDDI backbone	Ethernet 10Mbps
Protocols	TCP/IP, IPX/SPX, NetBIOS, AppleTalk, NetBEUI, SNMP	IPX/SPX, TCP/IP, EtherTalk
Printer Interfaces	Through print server support	HP X10/ HP M10
OS/NOS	NetWare,1SMP, Windows NT	N/A
Setup and Mgt. Utility	Maestro Mgmt Suite	Windows, DOS
Hardware/Software	Both	Both
Comments	Can also serve as a file server and an application server	Also includes direct Web-based print mgmt. software
Warranty	1 year	3 year
Price	$29,950	$369

N/A—Not applicable   INA—Information not available

Print Servers ■

Manufacturer	Pacific Data	Pacific Data
Model	Direct Net EX2	DirectNET, PEPS3 Family
CPU Type	16MHz Motorola 68306	16MHz Motorola 68306
Memory	512K 512K Flash	256K, 512K Flash
NIC	Ethernet 10Mbps	Ethernet 10Mbps
Protocols	IPX/SPX, TCP/IP, EtherTalk	IPX/SPX, TCP/IP, AppleTalk
Printer Interfaces	2 IEEE 1284 high-speed parallel	IEEE 1284 high-speed parallel
OS/NOS	NA	NetWare 2.x, 3.x (Binday and NDS); Sun 03, 4P-UX, Windows NT with DHCP, Unix-TCP/IP, IBMAIX, Scoo-mix; AppleTalk.
Setup and Mgt. Utility	Windows	Windows
Hardware/Software	Both	Both
Comments		
Warranty	3 year	3 year
Price	$449	$199–$299

Manufacturer	Pacific Data	Patton Electronics
Model	PEPS1, PEPS2	2127
CPU Type	20MHz 8188 NECV25	INA
Memory	512K, 512K Flash	INA
NIC	Ethernet 10Mbps	Ethernet 10Mbps (10BASE-FL, Fiber)
Protocols	IPK/SPX, TCP/IP, NetBEUI	IPX/SPX, PING, Telnet, FTP
Printer Interfaces	IEEE 1284 high-speed parallel	Standard centronics parallel
OS/NOS	NetWare 2.x, 3.x, 4.x. Sun OS, HP-UX, Unix TCP/IP, IBM AIX, SCOUnix, LAN Manager, LAN Server.	Concurrent Novell and TCP/IP
Setup and Mgt. Utility	DOS	UConnect
Hardware/Software	Both	Plug-in device
Comments		Single-port server Flash. Eprom upgrade.
Warranty	Lifetime	1 year
Price	$399–$499	$625

Manufacturer	Patton Electronics	Polywell Computers
Model	2125/2126	Poly 500PSR
CPU Type	INA	100MHz Intel Pentium
Memory	INA	16MB
NIC	Ethernet 10Mbps 10BASE-T, RJ-45, BNC	Ethernet 10/100MB, Token Ring 4/16MB
Protocols	IPX/SPX, PING, Telnet	DCC, IPX/SPX, NetBEUI
Printer Interfaces	Standard centronics parallel	IEEE 1286, EEP and EPC high-speed parallel
OS/NOS	Concurrent Novell TCP-IP	Windows NT, NetWare, OS/2
Setup and Mgt. Utility	UConnect	DOS, Windows 95, OS/2

N/A—Not applicable   INA—Information not available

Table Continues →

■ Print Servers

Manufacturer	Patton Electronics	Polywell Computers
Hardware/Software	Both	Both
Comments	Plug-in device. Single port server,Flash-EPROM Upgrade.	Supports up to 4 parallel and 4 serial printers
Warranty	1 year	3 year
Price	$425	$150

Manufacturer	Protec Microsystems	Protec Microsystems
Model	PSC	PSM-2E/PSM-Hub
CPU Type	2180 MPU 216C35 (4DMA)	PSM-2E: 2180 MPU PSM-Hub: 2180 MPU 216C35 (4DMA)
Memory	256K	256K
NIC	Ethernet 10Mbps, Token Ring, ARCnet. Ethernet 10Mbps, 10BASE-T, 10BASE2	Ethernet 10Mbps, 10BASE-T, 10BASE2 Ethernet, 10Mbps, AUI, 16 RJ-45, BNC,
Protocols	TCP/IP, LPD/LPR, IPX/SPX	TCP/IP, LPD/LPR, IPX/SPX
Printer Interfaces	4 high-speed parallel, 1 serial	1 parallel,1serial RS-232 (PMS-2E). 4 high-speed parallel, 1 serial (PSM-Hub)
OS/NOS	TCP/IP, Windows NT/95, NetWare, TCP/IP, Windows NT/95, Windows for Workgroups	PSM-2E, NetWare, TCP/IP, Windows NT/95, Windows for Workgroups
Setup and Mgt. Utility	DOS, Windows, Novell	DOS, Windows, Windows 95
Hardware/Software	Both	Both
Comments	Printers can be located up to 1,000 ft. away.	Printers can be located up to 1,000 ft. away.
Warranty	INA	INA
Price	5 year $649/$775	5 year $435/$995

Manufacturer	Rose Electronics	Siemens/Nixdorf Printing Systems
Model	Microserve	9000 Server
CPU Type	10MHz NEC V25+	133MHz Pentium
Memory	INA	32MB
NIC	Ethernet 10Mbps, Token Ring 4/16MB	Ethernet, Token Ring
Protocols	IPX/SPX, TCP/IP	TCP/IP
Printer Interfaces	ARCnet serial/parallel NetWare TCP/IP	Proprietary
OS/NOS	Novell NetWare, Windows NT, Unix	SCO, Unix
Setup and Mgt. Utility	DOS, Windows	DOS, Windows
Hardware/Software	Hardware	Both
Comments		
Warranty	1 year	TBA
Price	$395–695	INA

N/A—Not applicable   INA—Information not available

Print Servers ■

Manufacturer	SVEC	SVEC
Model	FD2100-N	FD2110-N
CPU Type	81088	80188
Memory	256K	256K
NIC	Ethernet 10Mbps, AUI/BNC, RJ-45	Ethernet 10Mbps, AUI/BNC, RJ-45
Protocols	IPX/SPX, NDIS, TCP/IP, AppleTalk	IPX/SPX, NDIS, TCP/IP, AppleTalk
Printer Interfaces	2 high-speed centronics, 1 serial	1 high-speed centronics
OS/NOS	NetWare, Unix, Windows NT	NetWare, Unix, Windows NT
Setup and Mgt. Utility	DOS	DOS
Hardware/Software	Both	Both
Comments		
Warranty	5 year	5 year
Price	$279	$179

Manufacturer	TRENDware	Vivid Image
Model	TE-300	Dahlia/ Imagebox EX
CPU Type	12MHz Intel 80c:88	100MHZ DEC Alpha RISC/25MHz WEITEK
Memory	32K, 128K Flash	16MB std 64MB max
NIC	Ethernet 10Mbps	Ethernet 10BASE-T, 10BASE2 parallel
Protocols	IPX/SPX	EtherTalk, IPX/SPX
Printer Interfaces	2 parallel	2 parallel
OS/NOS	NetWare	NetWare, Windows NT, LAN Server, WFW, Windows 95, Mac, Unix
Setup and Mgt. Utility	DOS, Windows	Macintosh, Windows 3.11, Windows 95, Windows NT
Hardware/Software	Both	Both
Comments		
Warranty	5 year	1 year
Price	$319	$5,995/$3,995

Manufacturer	Whittaker Xyplex	Xcd
Model	1450 Print Server	Xconnect II Lite
CPU Type	Motorola 6800	16MHz Motorola 68306
Memory	1 or 3MB DRAM	256K, 512K Flash
NIC	External dDevice	Ethernet
Protocol	TCP/IP, CAT, IPX/SPX, Telnet	TCP/IP, IPX/SPX
Printer Interfaces	2 female DB-25 connectors centronics/IBM PC compatible	1 parallel, 1 serial
OS/NOS	NetWare 23.x	Variable

N/A—Not applicable   INA—Information not available

Table Continues →

■ Print Servers

Manufacturer	**Whittaker Xyplex**	**Xcd**
Setup and Mgt. Utility	Xyplex, control port, SNMP manager	DOS, Windows
Hardware/Software	Both	Both
Comments	Easy set-up. Software is downloadable from a host or from memory card.	
Warranty	3 year	1 year
Price	$1,695	$325

Manufacturer	**Xcd**	**Xcd**
Model	Xconnect II	XJet
CPU Type	16MHz Motorola 68306	16MHz Motorola 68306
Memory	156K, 512K Flash	256K, 512K Flash
NIC	Ethernet	Ethernet
Protocol	TCP/IP, IPX/SPX, AppleTalk, DEC, LAT, Banyan Vines	TCP/IP, PPX/SPX, AppleTalk, DEC, LAT, Banyan Vines
Printer Interfaces	1284 parallel, RS-232 serial	Lexmark IOP
OS/NOS	Variable	Variable
Setup and Mgt. Utility	DOS, Windows	DOS, Windows
Hardware/Software	Both	Both
Comments		
Warranty	1 year	1 year
Price	$495	$495

Manufacturer	**Xcd**
Model	XMark
CPU Type	16MHz Motorola 68306
Memory	256K, 256K Flash
NIC	Ethernet
Protocol	TCP/IP, IPX/SPX, AppleTalk, DEC, LAT, Banyan Vines
Printer Interfaces	1284 parallel, RS-232 serial
OS/NOS	INA
Setup and Mgt. Utility	DOS, Windows
Hardware/Software	Both
Comments	
Warranty	1 year
Price	$325

N/A—Not applicable   INA—Information not available

E n d ■

Super Servers ▪

Manufacturer	ALR	ALR	ALR
Model	Evolution Dual 6	Revolution Quad6	Revolution Q-SMP/
CPU Type	Intel Pentium Pro 150,200MHz	Intel Pentium Pro 166,200MHz	Intel Pentium 100,133,166MHz
Number of Processors	1–2	1–4	1–4
Cache	256K (INT)	256K, 512K (INT)	256K,1MB, 2MB
Memory	16MB std 512MB max	64MB std 2GB max	16MB std 2GB max
Bus Type	ISA, PCI	2 EISA/PCI	2 EISA/PCI
Expansion Slots	3 PCI, 3 EISA, 1 shared	7 PCI, 7 EISA, 1 shared	3 PCI, 5 EISA, 1 shared
Internal Disk Storage	Variable	Variable	Variable
Redundant Components (Fault Tolerance)	ECC Memory, RAID Option	Power ECC, RAID Option	Power, ECC RAID Option
NIC	Ethernet, 100Mbps	Ethernet 100Mbps	Ethernet 100Mbps
Server Management Software Included?	Yes	Yes	No
OS/NOS	Netware, Windows NT, Unix	Netware, Windows NT, Unix	Netware, Windows NT, Unix
Power Supply	315w	575w	575w
Comments		Integrated hardware. Server management with youch screen control panel. Rack mountable.	Rack mountable
Warranty	5 year	5 year	5 year
Price	$3,200–$5,000	$15,000–$50,000	$6,000–$20,000

Manufacturer	ALR	Auspex	CCNS
Model	Revolution MP	H57000 Series	Series 3
CPU Type	Intel Pentium 100,133,166MHz	Sparc 100MHz	Intel Pentium 75,90,100,120,133, 150,166MHZ
Number of Processors	1–2	4–16	1–2
Cache	512K	256K	256K
Memory	8MB std 512MB max	72MB std 1704MB max	32MB std 256MB max
Bus Type	EISA/PCI	VME-64 = Patented Enhanced Mode	EISA/PCI
Expansion Slots	3 PCI, 3 EISA, 1 shared	VME-12	8 total EISA/PCI
Internal Disk Storage	Variable	4.3GB std 900GB max	2GB Wide SCSI
Redundant Components (Fault Tolerance)	RAID Option	DataGuard: Reboot Unix without interrupting NFS client data access. ServerGuard:Patented transparent server hot standby replication	RAID Mass Storage Sub Systems

N/A—Not applicable   INA—Information not available

Table Continues →

■ Super Servers

Manufacturer	ALR	Auspex	CCNS
NIC	Ethernet 100Mbps	Ethernet, 100BASE-T, FDDI, CDDI, ATM	10/100 Ethernet, PCI
OS/NOS	Netware, Windows NT, Unix	Unix, NFS, ONC	Your choice
Server Management Software Included?	No	Yes	Yes
Power Supply	300w	1800w	350w
Comments			
Warranty	5 year	90 day	1 year
Price	$2,800–$3,800	Base $39,900	INA

Manufacturer	CCNS	Data General	Data General
Model	Series2	AV4700 Enterprise	AV4800 Enterprise
CPU Type	Intel Pentium Pro 150,166,180, 200MHZ	Intel Pentium 133,166MHz	Intel Pentium 133,166MHz
Number of Processors	1–2	1–2	1–4
Cache	256K	512MB	512MB
Memory	32MB std 512MB max	32MB std 1GB max	64MB std 2.5GB max
Bus Type	ISA, PCI	6 PCI	CBUS 2
Expansion slots	8 total ISA, PCI	6 PCI	6 PCI
Internal Disk Storage	4GB Wide SCSI	INA	INA
Redundant Components (Fault Tolerance)	RAID, Mass Storage Sub Systems	Cooling, fault tolerance disk array, fast file recovery	Cooling, fault tolerance disk array, fast file recovery
NIC	10/100 Ethernet, PCI	Ethernet, 10/100BASE-T, SCSI, FDDI, Token Ring	Ethernet, 10/100BASE-T, SCSI, FDDI, Token Ring
Server Management Software Included?	Yes	Yes	Yes
OS/NOS	Your choice	Unix, Windows NT	Unix, Windows NT
Power Supply	408w	960w	960w
Comments			
Warranty	1 year	1 year	1 year
Price	Variable	$19,900	$32,900S

Manufacturer	Data General	Data General	Digital Equipment Corporation
Model	AV3000	AV5800	AlphaServer 2100A 4/275,5/250,5/300
CPU Type	Intel Pentium 100,133,166MHz	Intel Pentium 166MHz	275-300MHz
Number of Processors	1–4	2–8	1–4
OS / NOS	Unix,Windows NT, Netware	Unix, Windows NT	Digital Unix, OpenVMS, Windows NT
Cache	16K	16K	4MB per processor

N/A—Not applicable   INA—Information not available

Super Servers ■

Manufacturer	Data General	Data General	Digital Equipment Corporation
Memory	32MB std 768MB max	256MB std 2.56GB max	2GB max
Bus Type	PCI, EISA	CBUS 2	PCI, EISA
Expansion slots	4 PCI, 4 EISA	6 PCI	8 PCI, 3 EISA
Internal Disk Storage	INA	INA	16 hot swap disks for 69GB, 3 removeable media
Redundant Components (Fault Tolerance)	Power, RAID	Power, cooling, on board controllers	Auto reboot, thermal management, redundant power system, remote system management, RAID, disk hot swap
NIC	Ethernet 10/100Mbps	Ethernet, 10/100BASE-T, SCSI, FDDI, Token Ring	Ethernet, FDDI, Token Ring, synchronous comms., ATM
Server Management Software Included?	No	No	Yes
Power Supply	525 w	960w	(2) 600w
Comments			Other super-servers from DEC: AlphaServer 2000 4/275, 5/250, 5/300
Warranty	3 year	1 year	3 year
Price	$9,850–$27,000	$69,900	$27,930–$59,000

Manufacturer	Digital Equipment Corporation	Digital Equipment Corporation	Digital Equipment Corporation
Model	AlphaServer 8200 5/300	AlphaServer 8400 5/300	AlphaServer 4100, 5/300
CPU Type	300 or 350MHz	300 or 350MHz	Pentium 300-400MHz
Number of Processors	1–6	1–12	1–4
Cache	4MB per processor	4MB per processor	1-4MB per processor
Memory	6GB max	14GB max	4GBmax
Bus Type	PCI, EISA	PCI, EISA, XMI, Futurebus	PCI
Expansion Slots	9 PCI, 8 EISA	132 PCI, 8 EISA	5 PCI, 3 shared EISA/PCI
Internal Disk Storage	16GB 39TB max	192GB 39TB max	21 hot-swap disks for 90GB
Redundant Components (Fault Tolerance)	Auto reboot, thermal management, redundant power system, remote system management, RAID, disk hot swap	Auto reboot, thermal management, redundant power system, remote system management, RAID, disk hot swap	System auto reboot, thermal management, redundant power system, remote system management, RAID, disk hot swap
NIC	Ethernet, FDDI, Token Ring, HiPPI, Fiberchannel, sync.	CI, Ethernet, FDDI, Token Ring, HiPPI, Fiberchannel, sync.	Ethernet, Fast Ethernet, FDDI, Token Ring, sync. comms, ATM
Server Management Software Included?	Yes	Yes	Yes
OS / NOS	Digital Unix, OpenVMX	Digital Unix, OpenVMX	Digital Unix, OpenVMS, Windows NT
Power Supply	240w	150w	450w
Comments			
Warranty	1 year	1 year	3 year
Price	$100,000	$201,000	$44,300–$55,000

N/A—Not applicable   INA—Information not available

Table Continues →

■ Super Servers

Manufacturer	Concurrent Computer Corporation	Concurrent Computer Corporation	Concurrent Computer Corporation
Model	Night Hawk 4800	Night Hawk 4400/4400s	Night Hawk 5800/5800s
CPU Type	Motorola 88,100MHz	Motorola 88,100MHz	Motorola 88,100MHz
Number of Processors	1–8	1–4	1–8
Cache	32,128KB	32,128KB	2256KB, 1MB
Memory	16MB std 1.5GB max	16MB std 192MB max	16MB std 512MB max
Bus Type	1 or 2 VME	VME	1 or 2 VME
Expansion Slots	5–40 VME	5–21VME	5–40 VME
Internal Disk Storage	1GB–32GB	1GB–32GB	1GB–32GB
Redundant Components (Fault Tolerance)	Disks, power supplies	Disks, power supplies	Disks, power supplies
NIC	Ethernet, FDDI	Ethernet, FDDI	Ethernet, FDDI
Server Management Software Included?	Optional	Optional	Optional
OS/NOS	CX/UX	CX/UX	CX/UX
Power Supply	400w–1500w	400w–1500w	400w–1500w
Comments	High-performance, real-time, Unix-based systems	High-performance, real-time, Unix-based systems	High-performance, real-time, Unix-based systems
Warranty	1 year	1 year	1 year
Price	INA	INA	INA

Manufacturer	Harris Computer Systems Corporation	Hewlett-Packard	Hewlett-Packard
Model	Night Hawk 6800	Netserver 5/133 LS2 and LS$	Netserver 5/100 LS2 and LS$
CPU Type	Power PC 604 100MHz	Intel Pentium 133MHz dual SMNP card	Intel Pentium 133MHz dual SMNP card
Number of Processors	1–8	2–4	2–4
Cache	16K	1 MB write-back for each processor	1 MB write-back for each processor
Memory	32MB std 1GB max	64MB std 68MB max	64MB std 768MB max
Bus Type	1 or 2 VME	2 PCI, 4 EISA, 2 shared	2 PCI, 4 EISA, 2 shared
Expansion Slots	5–40 VME	External PCI fast/wide SCSI-2. 2 9-pin RS-232	External PCI fast/ wide SCSI-2. 2 9-pin RS-232
Internal Disk Storag	1GB–32GB	2 PCI fast/wide SCSI-2	2 PCI fast/wide SCSI-2
Redundant Components (Fault Tolerance)	Disks, power supplies,	Disk array option	Disk array option
NIC	Ethernet FDDI	All	All

N/A—Not applicable   INA—Information not available

Super Servers ■

Manufacturer	Harris Computer Systems Corporation	Hewlett-Packard	Hewlett-Packard
Server Management Software Included?	Optional	Netserver assistant	Netserver assistant
OS/NOS	Power UX	Banyan Vines, Windows NT, Netware, Netware UnixWare, and others	Banyan Vines, Windows NT, Netware, Netware UnixWare, and others
Power Supply	400w-1500w	470w	470w
Comments	High-performance, real-time, Unix-based systems		
Warranty	1 year	3 year	3 year
Price	INA	$14,198	$12,299

Manufacturer	IBM	IBM	IBM
Model	PC Server 720 8642-0EN/8642-0E1/ 8642-2E1	PC Server 720 8642-ODN/ 8642-ODO	PC Server 704 8650-4BW/ 8650-7AX
CPU Type	Intel Pentium 133MHz	Intel Pentium 133MHz	Intel Pentium Pro 66,166MHz
Number of Processors	1–6	1–6	2
Cache	512K	512K	512K per processor
Memory	128MB std 1GB max	64MB std 1GB max	64MB std 1GB max
Bus Type	PCI, Micro Channel	PCI, Micro Channel	PCI, EISA
Expansion Slots	7 PCI Micro Channel	7 PCI Micro Channel	6 PCI, 4 EISA
Internal Disk Storage	49.5GB	49.5GB	4.28GB/8.56GB
Redundant Components (Fault Tolerance)	Power, cooling	Power, cooling	Power, cooling
NIC	Ethernet, Token Ring	Ethernet, Token Ring	100/10Mbps Ethernet
Server Management Software Included?	Yes	Yes	Yes
OS/NOS	Netware, OS/2, Unix, Windows NT, SCO, Solaris	Netware,OS/2, , Unix, Windows NT, SCO, Solaris	OS/2, Windows NT
Power Supply	470w	470w	(2) 420w
Comments			Other super servers manufactured by IBM: PC Server 720 8642-2DS, 8642-0Z0, 8642-1Z0, 8642-2ZS, 8642-4ZS
Warranty	3 year	3 year	3 year
Price	$11,269–$28,789	$11,269–$28,789	$18,995–$31,445

N/A—Not applicable   INA—Information not available

Table Continues →

■ Super Servers

Manufacturer	Polywell Computers	Sequent Computer Systems, Inc.	Sun Microsystems
Model	Poly P6-200PS	Symmetry® 5000 Series	Ultra Enterprise 2
CPU Type	Intel Pentium Pro (2) 200Mhz (SMP)	Intel Pentium/166MHz	UltraSPARC 167,200MHz
Number of Processors	2	2–30	1 or 2
Cache	512K–1MB	4MB–60MB	512K, 1MB
Memory	64–128MB std. 1GB max	64 MB std 3.5GB max	64MB std 2GB max
Bus Type	PCI, EISA	1 Sequent's Highly Scalable Bus (HSB) (2-34) SCSI, (1-4) VME	SBUS, UPA
Expansion Slots	4 PCI, 4 ISA, 2 shared	HSB (20), SCSI (2-32), VME (5-29)	4 SBUS, 1 UPA
Internal Disk Storage	(4) 20GB 350GB max	1.7TBmax	(2) 2.1GB
Redundant Components (Fault Tolerance)	Power, disk drives, disk array, CPU	Power, processors, memory, mirrored disk, RAID disk	
NIC	1–4 100MB Ethernet	Ethernet, FDDI, Token Ring	Fast Ethernet 10MB/sec
Server Management Software Included?	Yes	Yes	Yes
OS/NOS	Windows NT, Netware, Unix, OS/2	DYNIX/ptx, Windows NT (WinServer5000)	Netra NFS Smart Serve
Power Supply	600w	2.17 kw	180w
Comments	Advanced SMP server		
Warranty	3 year	90	1 year
Price	$8,900–$16,000	$100,000 (SE40)–$millions	$20,995

Manufacturer	Sun Microsystems	Tac Systems	Texas Microsystems
Model	Ultra Enterprise 3000	HSTS	SP 5500
CPU Type	UltraSPARC	Intel 586/900 166MHz	Intel Pentium 586 (SMP) 100,200MHz
Number of Processors	1–6	1–2	1–4
Cache	32K,512K	512K	256K–2MB
Memory	64MB std 6GB max	32MB std 512MB max	0–768MB ECC
Bus Type	(1–6) SBUS	EISA, PCI	EISA, PCI (2)
Expansion Slots	2–9 SBUS 0–3 UPA	5 EISA 4 PCI	4 EISA 2 PCI 2 EISA/PCI
Internal Disk Storage	2.1GB	Up to 4GB SCSI	Up to 24GB, fast/wide SCSI-2, optional RAID controller
Redundant Components (Fault Tolerance)	Redundant, hot swap power, cooling, hot swap disk, mirrored disk	Mirrored, possible RAID level 5	Power supplies, fans, drive arrays (all hot swapable)

N/A—Not applicable   INA—Information not available

Super Servers

Manufacturer	Sun Microsystems	Tac Systems	Texas Microsystems
NIC	Ethernet 100Mbps	Your choice	Optional
Server Management Software Included?	Yes	Yes	INA
OS / NOS	Solaris	Netware, Windows NT, Unix	Netware, Windows NT, Unix, OS/2
Power Supply	750w	1250w	Redundant 400w hot swap
Comments		Includes 32-bay hotswap tower, CD, hard drive, tape drive, magneto-optical drives.	Rackmount open platform based on Intel extended express architecture
Warranty	1 year	1 year	1 year
Price	$39,100–$700,000	$13,320–$15,230	$8,000–$15,000

Manufacturer	Tricord	Unisys
Model	Power Frame Enterprise Server	Clear Path SMP 5400
CPU Type	133/166 SMP	Intel Pentium 100,133MHz
Number of Processors	1–12	1–4
Memory	64MB std 4GB max	16MB std 768MB max
Cache	2MB	16K
Bus Type	Powerbus with 7 slots, sypeak subsystem for PCI/EISA slots, 8 for either/or	PCI (dual)
Expansion Slots	4 expansion cabinets x 14 slots each	2 PCI 4 EISA 2 shared
Internal Disk Storage	+Gig, S.CS1-2 +200 Gig	1–24GB fast/wide SCSI-2
Redundant Components (Fault Tolerance)		
NIC	Ethernet 10/100, Token Ring, ATM, FDDI, CDDI, Power, disk controller, cooling, CPUs, NICs	Ethernet 100Mbps, Token Ring, ISDN, FDDI, ATM, Disk controller, software and hardware, RAID, U clusters
Server Management Software Included?	Yes	No
OS/NOS	Netware NT SMP for both	SVR4MP, Unix, Windows NT
Power Supply	1000w (std) 1200w (max)	750w
Comments		Wide range of hardware, communication and software options
Warranty	1,2, or 3 years Service 7 days a week, 24 hours a day	1 year
Price	$100,000	$5,995

N/A—Not applicable   INA—Information not available

Table Continues →

■ Super Servers

Manufacturer	Unisys	Zenith Data Systems
Model	Clear Path 6100	MX
CPU Type	Intel Pentium 150MHz/ Intel Pentium Pro 200MHz	Intel Pentium 133/166(SMP)
Number of Processors	2–10	1–4
Cache	128MB std 4GB max	1MB per processor
Memory	2–4MB	16–768MB ECC
Bus Type	SCM PCI dual	PCI/EISA
Expansion slots	7 PCI 5 EISA	2 PCI 4 EISA 2 shared
Internal Disk Storage	1–24GB fast/wide SCSI-2	Up to 6 4GB fast/wide SCSI hot plug
Redundant Components (Fault Tolerance)		ECC Memory, RAID option, hot plug disks
NIC	Ethernet 100Mbps, Token Ring, ISDN	Optional PCI cards
OS/NOS	RAID controller, U clusters	Netware, Windows NT, Solaris, Unix, OS/2, Banyan
Server Management Software Included?	No	Yes
Power Supply	SVR4MP, Unix, Windows NT, 1000w- 1400w	525w
Comments	Wide range of hardware, communication and software options	Won 3 AIM Hot Iron awards Feb '96
Warranty	1 year	3 year
Price	$65,709	$6,500–$25,000

N/A—Not applicable   INA—Information not available

End ■

Storage Servers ∎

Manufacturer	ECCS	ECCS	LSC,Inc
Model	Model 1300	Model 1600	Integrated Data Server IDS-S1000E/IDS-S20
CPU Type	Intel Pentium 133MHz	Intel Pentium 166MHz	SuperSPARC 60MHz 2–8 processors
Cache	256K	256K	1MB SuperCache
Memory	64K std 128K max	64K std 128K max	S1000E: 64MB std 2GB max S20: 64MB std 256MB max
Bus Type	4 PCI, 3 ISA	4 PCI, 3 ISA	1–4 Sbus, 1 SBus
Expansion Slots	2 PCI 3 ISA	2 PCI 3 ISA	12 SBus/ 4 SBus
Disk Controller(s)	Fast SCSI-2 16bit	Fast SCSI-2 16bit	Fast/wide SCSI-2 RAID
Disk Drives	(5) 2.1GB or (5) 4.2GB	(5) 2.1GB or (5) 4.2GB	(2) 2.1GB (4.2 GB to 1.5 TB)
Disk/CD ROM	1.44MB/6x	1.44MB /6x	1.44MB/6X CD-ROM
NIC	Ethernet 10/100 BASE-T, FDDI, CDDI, Token Ring	Ethernet 10/100 BASE-T, FDDI, CDDI, Token Ring	Ethernet, Fast Ethernet, ATM, FDDI, HiPPI, Fiber Channel
Storage Management Software	Synchronection 3.2	Synchronection 3.3	LSC SAM-FS Storage and Archive Manager
Power Supply	350w	350w	2,000w
Enclosure	Rackmount, desktop	Rackmount , desktop	Tower
Comments:			
Warranty	1 year	1 year	90 day
List Price	$34,000	$40,911	$113,155/$50,100

Manufacturer	LSC,Inc	Maximum Strategy	Maximum Strategy
Model	Integrated Data Server IDS-S5	Gen 5 XL/ S Serial XL	Gen 5 L/ S Series L
CPU Type	SuperSPARC 110MHz	Motorola 68060	Motorola 68060
Cache	24KB	120MB	1-24MB
Memory	64MB std 512MB max	N/A	N/A
Bus Type	1 SBus	2 x 200Mbps, internal data bus	2 x 200Mbps, internal data bus
Expansion Slots	3 SBus	N/A	N/A
Disk Controller(s)	Fast/wide SCSI-2, RAID	Fast/wide SCSI	Fast/wide SCSI
Disk Drives	(2) 2.1GB (4.2GB/750GB)	(24 to 96) 9GB	(8 or 16) 9GB
Disk/CD ROM	1.44MB/CD-ROM	1.44MB/CD-ROM	1.44MB/CD-ROM
NIC	Ethernet, Fast Ethernet, ATM, FDDI, HiPPI, Fiber Channel	HiPPI and Fiber Channel/SCSI Fast/Wide and Ultra Wide	HiPPI and Fiber Channel/SCSI Fast/Wide, Ultra Wide
Storage Management Software	LSC SAM-FS storage and archive manager	Proprietary	Proprietary
Power Supply	2,000w	40,850w	1200w

N/A—Not applicable   INA—Information not available

Table Continues →

■ Storage Servers

Manufacturer	LSC,Inc	Maximum Strategy	Maximum Strategy
Enclosure	Tower	Tower	Tower
Comments:			
Warranty	90 day	3 month	3 month
List Price	$32,100	Price per MB ($1–2.5/MB)	Price per MB ($1–2.5/MB)

Manufacturer	MTI	Polywell	Polywell
Model	Stingray SWSV-CI 3, SWSV-FD 3	Poly 560	Poly 2000FS
CPU Type	Intel I 960	Intel Pentium Dual 266 MHz	Intel Pentium Dual 200 MHz
Cache	1.5GB	512K	512K
Memory		64MB std 512MB max	128MB std 512MB max
Bus Type	12 SCSI	EISA/PCI	ISA/PCI
Expansion Slots		4 PCI 5 EISA	4 PCI 5 ISA
Disk Controller(s)	Fast SCSI-2	Fast SCSI-2 32-bit disk array	Fast SCSI-3 32-bit disk array
Disk Drives	2.1GB 4.3GB	(5) 2.1GB	(7) 4.3GB
Disk/CD ROM		1.44/6x	1.44/6x
NIC	CI, FDDI	Ethernet, Token Ring	Ethernet, Token Ring
Storage Management Software	N/A	Mylex Dac 950	Mylex Dac 950
Power Supply	238w	2 x 300W	2 x 400W
Enclosure	Rack, Tower	Tower or Rack	Tower or Rack
Comments:			
Warranty	1 year	3 year	3 year
List Price	$17,700	$9,500	$13,500

Manufacturer	Polywell	Procom Tech	Procom Tech
Model	Poly 500FS	CD Tower 21	CD Tower 14
CPU Type	Intel Pentium 133MHz	Intel Pentium 166,133MHz	Intel Pentium 133MHz
Cache	512K	256K	256K
Memory	32MB std 128MB max	32MB std 128MB max	16MB std 128MB max
Bus Type	ISA/PCI	EISA, ISA, PCI	
Expansion Slots	4 PCI 5 ISA	4 PCI, 3 ISA	2 PCI, 2 ISA
Disk Controller(s)	Fast SCSI-2 32-bit adapter	IDE 32-bit fast	IDE
Disk Drives	(2) 2.1GB	1.6GB	1.6GB
NIC	Ethernet, Token Ring	Token Ring, FDDI-1, FDDI-2, CDDI, Fast Ethernet, ATM	Token Ring, FDDI-1, FDDI-2, CDDI, Fast Ethernet, ATM
Disk/CD ROM	1.44/4x	1.44MB/ 4x, ,8x, 10x	1.44MB/ 4x, ,8x, 10x

N/A—Not applicable   INA—Information not available

Storage Servers ■

Manufacturer	Polywell	Procom Tech	Procom Tech
Storage Management Software	Mylex Dac 950	Your choice	Your choice
Power Supply	300w	650w redundant	400w redundant
Enclosure	Tower or Rack	Tower	Mini-Tower
Comments:		Available with CD force- embedded management software and hot-swap drive	Available with CD force- embedded management software and hot-swap drive
Warranty	3 year	1 year on site	1 year on site
List Price	$3,750	$14,995	$8,795

Manufacturer	ProcomTech	Protec Microsystems
Model	CD Tower-Rax-56	Network Backup Server
CPU Type	Intel Pentium 166, 133MHz	AMD 386 10MHz
Cache	256K	128K
Memory	64MB std 128MB max	2 MB
Bus Type	EISA, ISA, PCI	ISA
Expansion Slots	4 PCI, 3 ISA	N/A
Disk Controller(s)	IDE 32-bit fast	Fast SCSI-2
Disk Drives	(1)6GB	(2)6GB Optical
Disk/CD ROM	1.44MB/ 4x, 8x, 10x	Optical 2.6 GB
NIC	Token Ring, FDDI-1, FDDI-2, CDDI, Fast Ethernet, ATM	Ethernet, 10/100BASE-T, 10BASE2, Token Ring, BNC
Storage Management Software	Your choice	Protec Backup & Restore
Power Supply	2000w redundant	100w
Comments:	Available with CD force-embedded management soft- ware and hot-swap drive.	Optical network b Backup system has optional media tower
Warranty	1 year on site	1 year
List Price	$44,995	$4,985

Manufacturer	Symbios Logic	Symbios Logic	Symetrical Technologies Inc.
Model	SH1000	SH4000	SPANStor-HDD
CPU Type	Intel	Intel	Motorola 30Mhz
Cache	256K	256K	32MB max
Memory	32MB	64MB-128MB	8MB std 32MB max
Bus Type	PCI	PCI	Internal
Expansion Slots	PCI (4)	PCI (4)	N/A
Disk Controller(s)	(1–4)		Fast SCSI - 2
Disk Drives	4.2GB (6-40)	4.2GB (20-60)	(1,2,4,9) GB up to 7 drives

N/A—Not applicable   INA—Information not available

Table Continues →

■ Storage Servers

Manufacturer	Symbios Logic	Symbios Logic	Symetrical Technologies Inc.
Disk/CD ROM	1.44MB	1.44MB	N/A
NIC	10/100 Ethernet SA FDDI DA FDDI SA CDDI	10/100 Ethernet SA FDDI DA FDDI SA CDDI	10BASE-T, 10BASE2
Storage Management Software	jetworks™	jetworks™	Proprietary FFS
Power Supply	300 Watt	300 Watt	120v or 220v
Enclosure	56" rack mount	56"/72" rack mount	Product is direct network attach and and supports transparent file sharing across NFS, Netware, and NT
Comments:			
Warranty	1 year no charge	1 year no charge	3 year
List Price	$49,375	$102,650	$2,995–$15,495

Manufacturer	Transitional Technology	Zenith Data Systems
Model	NX Server	MX-133 XSM-9270-06/ MX-166 XSM 9770-08
CPU Type	Alpha AXP 21066A,166MHz	Intel Pentium 133MHz SMP/166MHz
Cache	8MB	1MB
Memory	32MB 192MB	64MB EDC std, 768MB ECC max
Bus Type	(2) 32bit PCI (5) Fast/wide SCSI (1) 64bit AlphaS	PCI/EISA
Expansion Slots	N/A	2 PCI 4 EISA 2 shared
Disk Controller(s)	Fast SCSI-2, SCSI-3	Fast/wide SCSI-2, dual channel RAID (optional)
Disk Drives	(5) 9GB	(up to 6) 1,2,4GB hot plug
Diskette/CD ROM	N/A	1.44MB/ 4x
NIC	10/100BASE-T Standard FDDI	Optional
Storage Management Software	Propiety	Optional
Power Supply	350w	525w
Enclosure	Tower or rackmount	Tower
Comments:		
Warranty	2 year	3 year
List Price	$35,000	$10,950/$11,950

N/A—Not applicable   INA—Information not available

End ■

Web Servers ■

Manufacturer	Apple Computer	Digital Equipment Corporation
Model	Workgroup Server 9150/120	Alphaserver 1000 4/40
CPU Type	Power PC 601	Intel Pentium 266MHz
Cache	1024K	16K
Memory	32MB	16-64MB
Bus Type	NuBus	PCI/EISA
Expansion Slots	4	10
Disk Controller	SCSI-2	SCSI
Disk Drives	1GB, 2GB, 4GB drives	1GB, 2GB, 4GB drives
NIC	Ethernet, EtherTalk	Ethernet, FDDI/ATM
Web Software	WebStar 1.2.4	Process Software Purveyor 1.1, FreeWare
Bundled Software	WebStar 1.2.4, Mac TCP, Applesearch, PageMill, BBE-dit, Adobe Acrobat, Apple Internet Mail Server, Netscape Navigator	FreeWare Products, Mosaic, Finger, NNTP News Server
OS/NOS	Mac OS	Windows NT Server 3.5.1
Comments		
Warranty	1 year	3 year
Price	INA	$19,995–$20,690

Manufacturer	Intergraph	NEC Technologies, Inc.
Model	TD-40	Privatenet Secure FW 2.0
CPU Type	Intel Pentium 133 MHz	P133
Cache	512K	256MB
Memory	32MB–256MB	16MB–32MB
Bus Type	PCI/ISA	PCI, ISA
Expansion Slots	10	5
Disk Controller	SCSI-2	SCSI-2
Disk Drives	1GB, 2GB, 4GB	1GB
NIC	Ethernet	10BASE-T; 10BASE2; AUI
Web Software	Netscape Communications Server 1.22, MS Word Internet Assistant.	N/A
Bundled Software	Netscape Communications Server 1.22, MS Word Internet Assistant.	PrivateNet FW S/W
OS/NOS	Windows NT	BSD/OS 2.1
Comments		
Warranty	3 year	1 year
Price	$9440–$10,640	$5,000–$15,000

Manufacturer	Silicon Graphics	Sun Microsystems
Model	Webforce Indy	Netra i 4
CPU Type	32MB–256MB	MicroSPARC II 110MHz
Cache	GIO32-bis	24K on chip
Memory	2	32MB std 160MB max

N/A—Not applicable   INA—Information not available

Table Continues →

■ Web Servers

Manufacturer	Silicon Graphics	Sun Microsystems
Bus Type	Ethernet	1 Sbus 32-bit
Expansion Slots	535MB, 1.05GB internal	2 RS-232C/RS-423 serial, 1 parallel
Disk Controller	Netscape	10Mbps Ethernet (10BASE-T or AUI) standard; Sun-FastEthernet, ISDN, HSI, FDDI, ATM, Token Ring optional; T1/E1 plug-in available from third party
Disk Drives	Iris Networker	SCSI-2
NIC	SCSI	4.2GB, 60GB
Web Software	INA	Netscape Navigator Gold 3.0 WYSIWYG authoring software Java Developer's kit, sample Java applets.
Bundled Software	INA	Netscape Enterprise Server, LiveWire Web site content management software. IPX Gateway software for NetWaree clients; TCP/IP. FireWall-First! Fire wall security software; TCP wrappers.
OS/NOS	Netscape Communications Server 1.22, WebMagic Pro, WebSpace author	Servers: Sun Solaris 2.5 Unix, optimized for Web serving. Clients: PC, Novell NetWaree, Macintosh, Unix.
Comments		Netra HTML-based graphical administration; recovery tooll; backup tool. Mail POP2/POP3 server, IMAP4 SERVER, SMTP Sendmail v8. Remote access services: Telnet, FTP, anonymous FTP server. Internet connectivity: asynchronous PPP, primary/secondary/ caching DNS server
Warranty	1 year	1 year standard, optional services
Price	$10,995	$7,495

Manufacturer	Sun Microsystems	Sun Microsystems
Model	Netra i140	Netra i 150
CPU Type	UltraSPARC II , 143MHz	UltraSPARC II 167Mhz
Cache	32K on chip; 512K external	16K on chip; 512K external
Memory	64MB std 1GB ECC max	64MB std 1GB ECC max
Bus Type	3 Sbus 64-bit	3 Sbus 64-bit
Expansion Slots	64-bit 2RS-232C/RS-423 Serial; 1 parallel	64-bit 2RS-232C/RS-423 Serial; 1 parallel
NIC	10Mbps Ethernet (10BASE-T or AUI) standard; Sun-FastEthernet, ISDN, HSI, FDDI, ATM, Token Ring optional; t1/e1 plug in available from third party	20Mbps fast/wide SCSI-2
Disk Controller	10Mbps fast SCSI-2	25GB, 349GB
Disk Drives	4.2GB, 324GB	10Mbps & 100Mbps Ethernet (BASE-T or MII) standard; ISDN, HSI, FDDI, ATM, Token Ring optional
Web Software	Netscape Navigator Gold 3.0 WYSIWYG authoring software. Java Developer's kit, sample Java applets.	Netscape Navigator Gold 3.0 WYSIWYG authoring software. Java Developer's kit, sample Java applets.
Bundled Software	Netscape Enterprise Server, LiveWire Web site content management software. IPX Gateway software for NetWare clients; TCP/IP. FireWall-First! Firewall security software; TCP wrappers.	Netscape Enterprise Server, LiveWire Web site content management software. IPX Gateway software for NetWare clients; TCP/IP. FireWall-First! Fire wall security software; TCP wrappers.
OS/NOS	Servers: Sun Solaris 2.5 Unix, optimized for Web serving. Clients: PC, Novell NetWaree, Macintosh, Unix.	Servers: Sun Solaris 2.5 Unix, optimized for Web serving. Clients: PC, Novell NetWaree, Macintosh, Unix.

N/A—Not applicable   INA—Information not available

Web Servers ■

Manufacturer	Sun Microsystems	Sun Microsystems
Comments	Netra HTML-based Graphical Administration; Recovery Tool; Backup tool. Mail POP2/POP3 server, IMAP4 SERVER, SMTP Sendmail v8. Remote access services: Telnet, FTP, anonymous FTP server. Internet Connectivity: Asynchronous PPP, Primary/Secondary/Caching DNS Server.	Netra HTML-based Graphical Administration; Recovery Tool; Backup tool. Mail POP2/POP3 server, IMAP4 SERVER, SMTP Sendmail v8. Remote access services: Telnet, FTP, anonymous FTP server. Internet Connectivity: Asynchronous PPP, Primary/Secondary/Caching DNS Server.
Warranty	1 year standard, optional services	1 year standard, optional services
Price	$13,995	$21,145

Manufacturer	Sun Microsystems	Sun Microsystems
Model	Netra i 5	Netra i 1/170E
CPU Type	MicroSPARC II 110MHz	UltraSPARC 167MHz
Cache	24K on chip	32K on chip; 512K external
Memory	32MB std 256MB max	64MB std 1GB ECC (max)
Bus Type	3 Sbus 32-bit	2 Sbus 64bit
Expansion Slots	2RS-232C/RS-423 Serial; 1 parallel	2RS-232C/RS-423 serial; 1 parallel
Disk Controller	SCSI-2	20Mbps Fast/wide SCSI-2
Disk Drives	4.2GB, 122GB	25GB, 349GB
NIC	10Mbps Ethernet (10BASE-T or AUI) standard; SunFastEthernet, ISDN, HSI, FDDI, ATM, Token Ring optional; t1/e1 plug in available from third party	10Mbps and 100Mbps Ethernet (BASE-T or MII) standard; ISDN, HSI, FDDI, ATM, Token Ring optional
Web Software	Netscape Navigator Gold 3.0 WYSIWYG authoring software. Java Developer's kit, sample Java applets.	Netscape Navigator Gold 3.0 WYSIWYG authoring software. Java Developer's kit, sample Java applets.
Bundled Software	Netscape Enterprise Server, LiveWire Web site content management software. IPX Gateway software for NetWare clients; TCP/IP. FireWall-First! Fire wall security software; TCP wrappers.	Netscape Enterprise Server, LiveWire Web site content management software. IPX Gateway software for NetWare clients; TCP/IP. FireWall-First! Fire wall security software; TCP wrappers.
OS/NOS	Servers: Sun Solaris 2.5 Unix, optimized for Web serving. Clients: PC, Novell NetWaree, Macintosh, Unix.	Servers: Sun Solaris 2.5 Unix, optimized for Web serving. Clients: PC, Novell NetWare, Macintosh, Unix.
Comments	Netra HTML-based Graphical Administration; Recovery Tool; Backup tool. Mail POP2/POP3 server, IMAP4 SERVER, SMTP Sendmail v8. Remote access services: Telnet, FTP, anonymous FTP server. Internet Connectivity: Asynchronous PPP, Primary/Secondary/Caching DNS Server.	Netra HTML-based Graphical Administration; Recovery Tool; Backup tool. Mail POP2/POP3 server, IMAP4 SERVER, SMTP Sendmail v8. Remote access services: Telnet, FTP, anonymous FTP server. Internet Connectivity: Asynchronous PPP, Primary/Secondary/Caching DNS Server.
Warranty	1 year standard, optional services	1 year standard, optional services
Price	$10,795	$24,395

Manufacturer	Tatung Science & technology	Texas Microsystems
Model	Microcompstation 5/11	NetSpresso 9730-140 and 9730-170
CPU Type	Sparc Technology Group MicroSparc II 110MHz	64-bit UltraSPARC microprocessor—140MHz and 167MHz
Cache	20K	16K min 512K max
Memory	16–256MB	up to 512MB
Bus Type	S-Bus	SCSI-2
Expansion Slots	3	Up to 24 32bit slots
Disk Controller	SCSI	2

N/A—Not applicable   INA—Information not available

Table Continues →

■ Web Servers

Manufacturer	**Tatung Science & technology**	**Texas Microsystems**
Disk Drives	1GB, 2BG, 4GB	INA
NIC	Ethernet	Ethernet
Web Software	Internet Gateway for Solaris 1	Netscape
Bundled Software	Internet Gateway for Solaris 1; Open Network Computing	INA
OS/NOS	Open Network Computing	Solaris/UNIX
Comments		Scalability, minimum configuration
Warranty	1 year	1 year
Price	$7,705–$8,635	Base systems start at $18,000

Manufacturer	**Zenith Data Systems**
Model	Z-Server MX IIS
CPU Type	Pentium 100MHz
Cache	256K
Memory	32 std 768 max
Bus Type	PCI, EISA
Expansion Slots	8
Disk Drives	(2) 1GB
Disk Controller	Fast/wide SCSI-2
NIC	32bit PCI Ethernet
Web Software	INA
Bundled Software	Microsoft Internet Information Server
OS/NOS	Windows NT
Comments	
Warranty	3 year
Price	

N/A—Not applicable   INA—Information not available

End ■

C H A P T E R

5 NETWORK CONNECTIVITY

THIS CHAPTER PRESENTS A vast array of products that make up a network's physical connections. You'll learn about everything from cabling to WAN multiplexors here. To make the network's physical connections you need a well-conceived network plan. For instance, the many connections must be able to handle the necessary communications protocols, of which your network may use more than one. Before you commit to a physical network structure you should attempt to anticipate how the network will evolve. Typically, you'll need to add networking segments and updated technology over time. You can minimize disruptions to the network infrastructure by planning ahead carefully and thinking about your future needs.

NETWORK CONNECTIVITY

Cables and Connectors

Cabling is often the most expensive part of installing a network. It is not uncommon for cabling to make up half of the total networking costs. Twisted-pair wiring is popular because of its relatively low cost and good performance. A key criteria for cable is its "category rating." Nearly all network cable sold today is rated "Category 5," which supports up to 100 Mbps performance. Buying Category 5 gives you some room to upgrade your network speed without having to replace wiring. Because cable varies little from vendor to vendor, you can make your choice based on price and service (warranty). Connectors, the "plugs" at each cable end, also have little to differentiate them besides price. Both cable and connector markets are dominated by brand name vendors.

Key Criteria

Cable Types					
Performance	Reliability	Manageability	Scalability	**Flexibility**	**Value**

First you need to decide which of the three basic types of cable you need—coaxial, twisted-pair, or fiber-optic. Coaxial and twisted-pair cabling yield similar network speeds. Coaxial may be better suited for environments with adverse conditions because it has better shielding and is more resistant to electrical interference. Twisted-pair is suitable for normal operating conditions, is relatively inexpensive, and is easy to work with. For these reasons, twisted-pair is the most common cable is use. Fiber-optic cabling is much faster and more expensive than the other two cable types. It is mostly used for specific applications such as handling especially high traffic areas of the network (such as centralized service connections) and/or for internetwork connectivity.

Cable Certification					
Performance	**Reliability**	Manageability	Scalability	Flexibility	Value

To assure cable reliability and performance for network applications, vendors conform to standards testing. The rating system identifies cable "categories" from which to choose. As mentioned, Category 5 is today's standard in cable performance for networking applications. Category 5 cable is certified to handle up to 100 Mbps. Because installing costs much more than buying a higher rated cable, it's wise to use at least Category 5 for new network installations. Even though most networking is currently

NETWORK CONNECTIVITY

done at 10 Mbps, 100 Mbps networking is available and will quickly become more common as the costs for equipment come down.

Price					
Performance	Reliability	Manageability	Scalability	Flexibility	**Value**

Most vendors carry the same cable types with the same ratings. Price can be a distinguishing feature, but its impact isn't usually significant unless you are installing over 10,000 feet. Cable guarantees are pretty standard and can range from 10 years to life. Extended guarantees are sometimes included free if you commit to buying a certain amount of cable over a specified period of time.

Supplier					
Performance	Reliability	Manageability	Scalability	Flexibility	**Value**

If you are buying and installing your network through a system integrator, they probably use a specific cable vendor. System integrators often make a volume commitment to the cable vendor to get better prices. Presumably your system integrator will also weed out any unreliable cables and cable vendors to avoid having to come back to fix any faulty cables. If you are buying cable yourself, seek out a brand name that you've heard is reliable and that will be backed by its vendor.

Converters and Transceivers

Converters and transceivers are devices that convert cable connections. Transceivers convert an AUI connector to other connector types, such as BNC or UTP. Converters change non-AUI connectors to other types of connectors. Both conversion devices tend to be quite reliable and relatively inexpensive, simply exchanging one medium for another. Converters can get more expensive than a typical transceiver if the media conversion is complex.

Overall, converters and transceivers are reliable and problem free. When shopping, you first need to determine whether the product will make the media conversion you need; after that, price and availability are often the most important determining factors.

NETWORK CONNECTIVITY

Network Interface Cards

The network interface card (NIC) provides the physical network connection at the computer workstation. There are a large number of vendors to choose from when selecting Ethernet NICs. It's common to stick with a single vendor. This usually results in better overall network reliability, simplified configuration, and easier troubleshooting due to familiarity with a common product. Software-based jumpers rather than actual jumpers on the card are usually preferred. LED indication of power and transmission is standard on most NICs. The most common network cards are 10BaseT Ethernet, providing 10 Mbps of network bandwidth.

Key Criteria

Network Topology					
Performance	Reliability	Manageability	Scalability	**Flexibility**	Value

Network cards can be grouped by which network topology (Ethernet, Token Ring, and so on) they run on. Once you decide on the topology of your network (or network segment), you can focus on the appropriate group of NICs. Because networks are predominantly Ethernet, the choice, availability, and pricing for this class of NICs are excellent.

Bit Architecture					
Performance	Reliability	Manageability	**Scalability**	Flexibility	Value

Within topologies, NICs are typically classified by bit architecture. 16-bit Ethernet cards are the most common today. Not long ago 8-bit cards were standard. The more expensive 32-bit cards can provide performance improvements, but the other network hardware must support the higher speeds to take advantage of it, so 16-bit cards are the norm for 10 Mbps Ethernet networking. It only makes sense to go to 32-bit cards if you're moving to 100 Mbps networking soon.

Connections					
Performance	Reliability	Manageability	Scalability	**Flexibility**	Value

Network cable connection to the card is dictated by the type of cabling you're using. Some cards offer multiple cable jacks of different types. Such cards are easy to integrate into existing environments and you can continue to use them even if you upgrade your cabling to another type.

NETWORK CONNECTIVITY

Once again, 10BaseT is a common standard today. (The "T" stands for twisted-pair, which uses an RJ-45 jack and UTP connection.) If you are buying for a network using all twisted-pair wiring for workstations, it's safe to commit to a single RJ-45 jack in your NIC.

Price

Performance	Reliability	Manageability	Scalability	Flexibility	**Value**

NICs, particularly the common 16-bit Ethernet class, are a commodity-like product. Because of competition they are a good value. People are influenced by price to different degrees when they buy NICs. Some people consistently choose the cheapest brands, saying performance is still consistent. Others stay loyal to name brands for what they feel is better reliability. It's a common practice to choose one brand and stick to it. The reasoning is that even though you may or may not have the "best" card, you know it well enough to simplify configuration, troubleshooting, and so on. In addition, many network administrators say that relibility in communications is better with "like" cards.

Hubs, Concentrators, and Switches

As the central point of network wiring (or at least workgroup wiring), hubs and concentrators need to be reliable and flexible to meet the needs of network growth. Network administrators often determine reliability by brand and product reputation in the market, a pattern in many network equipment decisions.

There are three basic categories of hubs:

- Simple hubs that act as a single segment and connection point

- Stackable hubs that allow multiple hubs to work together logically as one

- Managed hubs that incorporate management and monitoring features, usually through SNMP

Switches, or switching hubs, can increase network performance by providing individual workstations with full network bandwidth. They are either installed much like a hub, connecting workstations, or hooked to the network backbone to optimize uplink performance. The physical features of a switching hub are very similar to those of standard hubs (number of ports, stacking, and so on). Switches carry on more complex functions to achieve higher throughput and performance, and therefore tend to be more expensive than hubs. A switch's intelligence is usually embedded in the device using ASICs, their internal memory.

NETWORK CONNECTIVITY

Key Criteria

Topology					
Performance	Reliability	Manageability	Scalability	**Flexibility**	Value

When choosing a hub, you first need to consider topology (Ethernet, Token Ring, and so on). Ethernet is of course the most popular topology in use today. Some switches can provide uplink connections faster bandwidth technologies such as Fast Ethernet, ATM, or others.

Type of ports					
Performance	Reliability	Manageability	**Scalability**	**Flexibility**	Value

Once again, choosing twisted-pair as the network wiring dictates or at least narrows the choice of connector type. Hubs are usually a specific connection type while concentrators are modular units, allowing flexible and customizable mixes of port types (although the industry doesn't always stick to these terms as that distinction). Switches are often installed on existing LANs to increase performance on 10 Mbps Ethernet. Having multiple port types can simplify connection to existing wiring. For example, if your switch has an uplink port you can easily make connections to the network backbone.

Network Bandwidth and Throughput					
Performance	Reliability	Manageability	Scalability	Flexibility	Value

Hubs, concentrators, and switches are designed for specific bandwidths or network speeds. You need to match the hub's bandwidth to that of the other equipment on your network. Some offer multiple bandwidth capabilities. Switching hubs use technology to effectively increase throughput using the existing bandwidth. They may also provide a channel into higher network bandwidths. Data buffering and packet management can also affect throughput.

NETWORK CONNECTIVITY

Stackability/Modularity					
Performance	Reliability	Manageability	**Scalability**	**Flexibility**	Value

Many hubs are stackable, meaning that they can be "chained" together to create more connections. When stacking hubs, it's a good idea to stick with the same brands and models to simplify setup and interchangeability as well as avoid possible equipment conflicts. Modularity applies particularly to concentrators, which are defined as modular hubs (enabling flexible configurations of cable types and other capabilities). For concentrators, modularity means the number of modules the housing can support, the choice of modules, and the ease of use, including swapping out modules. For hubs, modularity means they can be stacked and indicates how many can be stacked.

Repeaters

Repeaters accept signals and retransmit them, extending the distance of the network connection. These devices are rather straightforward technologically speaking, and therefore tend to be reliable, plug-and-play solutions without a lot of features to compare. There are also repeating features in some multifunction devices that offer capabilities such as switching or routing in addition to repeating signals.

Key Criteria

Speed					
Performance	Reliability	Manageability	Scalability	**Flexibility**	Value

A repeater needs to retransmit its signals at the same rate as the network bandwidth. For instance, 10BaseT networks transmit at 10 Mbps so you need to buy a repeater designed for that transmission rate.

Distance					
Performance	Reliability	Manageability	Scalability	Flexibility	**Value**

The repeated signal can travel only a limited distance (without another "boost"). This distance varies depending on the medium you are boosting on (10BaseT, 10Base2, and so forth) and the repeater itself. Typical distance extensions a repeater provides on Ethernet are 200 to 500 meters. Because a repeater's sole purpose is to boost a signal, the length of the boost basically determines the repeater's value.

NETWORK CONNECTIVITY

Connections					
Performance	Reliability	Manageability	Scalability	**Flexibility**	Value

The repeater must of course be compatible with the network topology and the connectors you're using. Some products offer just one connector type, but most offer several choices built into one unit.

Price					
Performance	Reliability	Manageability	Scalability	Flexibility	**Value**

Price is of course a key consideration when you're making any purchase. With repeaters, price becomes more important because most repeaters are commodity-like products. Typical Ethernet repeaters range from $200 to $500. High-speed devices with many options, including fiber-optic, can cost a few thousand dollars. You can place more importance on other features such as distances, connections, and so on, rather than price for high-end devices.

Network Bridges

Bridges enable LANs to link to other LANs or networks running the same operating system. They extend the network and/or segment network traffic according to administrator set policies. Bridges are designed to connect two segments. Although one bridge can connect two local segments, bridging a WAN requires two bridges, one at each location. The complexity of these devices varies, from plug-and-play basic LAN extensions to bridging heterogeneous environments and integration into network monitoring and management. Switching technology has developed quickly and can provide bridging functions. For this reason, many buyers now use switching for both performance enhancements and LAN segmentation.

Key Criteria

Topology					
Performance	Reliability	Manageability	Scalability	**Flexibility**	Value

Connecting same topology LANs is simpler (and cheaper) than bridging different topologies. Most complexities are buried in the equipment and fairly transparent, however. The choice is dictated by the topologies to be bridged. Ease of setup and management can be important when your bridging needs are complex.

NETWORK CONNECTIVITY

Communication Protocol					
Performance	Reliability	Manageability	Scalability	**Flexibility**	Value

Bridges use the same communications protocol on each end of the link. These are usually standard WAN or LAN protocols, although some products have a proprietary WAN connection. The more protocol support a bridge offers, the more flexible its communication capabilities. This can be important if the network environment is dynamic.

Configuration Management					
Performance	Reliability	Manageability	Scalability	**Flexibility**	Value

Basic bridges don't really incorporate configuration management features and are designed for specific and simple links. The configuration management issue is more related to its modularity. More complex bridges channel signals according to administrator-defined policy. The ease of this management process can be important. Autoidentification of equipment can be quite valuable for larger sites. Even small sites can benefit when stations that are moved can be identified automatically and the signal routing tables are updated automatically.

Processing Power					
Performance	Reliability	Manageability	Scalability	Flexibility	Value

Some bridges are designed to be integrated into a computer while others incorporate their own processor, power supply, and so on. If your routing tables get complex, processing power can be important to maintaining network performance and not creating a bottleneck. The key to making the right choice is to assess the level of data flow through the bridge and the complexity of the routing tables. With this information, you can use processing power and the throughput rating provided by the vendor to assess your needs.

Speed/Throughput					
Performance	Reliability	Manageability	Scalability	Flexibility	Value

Bridges are designed for various network bandwidths. The actual speed of signal throughput depends on many factors, including signal routing complexity, hardware processing power, the volume of data, compression, and

NETWORK CONNECTIVITY

so on. Vendors present idealized throughput speeds by making assumptions about many of these factors. To get a more realistic assessment, talk with vendors about how the throughput number was derived and how your particular setup may compare.

Network Management					
Performance	Reliability	**Manageability**	Scalability	Flexibility	**Value**

You can obtain a great deal of information about network traffic and performance from the activity of a network bridge. This is not a feature found in basic LAN extension bridges since they are generally designed for plug-and-play, transparent operation. More complex bridges can report on the nature of their traffic for use in network planning and analysis. It can be quite useful to be able to integrate this information with other network management tools, which usually require reporting in a popular format such as SNMP.

Routers

Like bridges, routers link network segments together. But routers are a bit more complex than bridges because they can route many segments, not just two. In addition, routers can handle communications with more intelligence and flexibility than bridges. To do so, they must do more handling of data packets—for example, reading and repackaging them to get them to their destination and choose the best path for them to travel. For this reason, routers tend to handle data more slowly than bridges or switches. It's common for one product to perform bridging and routing functions. If you need both, these integrated products can be a good choice.

Key Criteria

Communication Protocol					
Performance	Reliability	Manageability	Scalability	**Flexibility**	Value

Like any network communications device, the communications protocol you use is important. It has to have the protocols you need. Most routers provide IPX/SPX or TCP/IP protocol communications. These two are sufficient for most applications, but some bridges offer many more. Multiprotocol routing can get complex, especially if you try to use multiple devices from different vendors. Routing to minicomputers or across a WAN may require special protocols.

NETWORK CONNECTIVITY

Routing Protocol

Performance   Reliability   **Manageability**   Scalability   **Flexibility**   Value

The routing protocol is the language routers use to communicate with each other. The two standard routing protocols used today are the routing information protocol (RIP) and Open Shortest Path First (OSPF). RIP is the older of the two, providing basic router identification. OSPF, which is becoming the new standard, can also identify other network features besides just router IDs, providing more services for network management applications. Some companies have implemented proprietary routing protocols, but these are rare and those products usually support one of the two industry standards in addition to their own.

Number of Ports

Performance   Reliability   Manageability   **Scalability**   **Flexibility**   Value

If you have basic router needs, the number of ports may not be critical. A single LAN and a single WAN port is a minimum configuration. Some routers specialize in either LAN or WAN communications and offer more ports to accommodate those needs. Yet another class of routers (or combination products such as bridge-routers and router-hubs) may offer connectivity modules. This enables you to custom configure and make changes as necessary. Some people use multiple routers instead of a single large device. This way, if one router fails, the others can carry on.

Network Management

Performance   Reliability   **Manageability**   Scalability   Flexibility   Value

Like bridges, routers can acquire a great deal of information about your network traffic and performance. Many routers can report on activity in a form that network management applications can use, such as SNMP. This can make them an important measurement tool in the network monitoring and management process. More and more communications products such as routers and switches include VLAN (Virtual LAN) capability. This allows you to segment the network "logically" regardless of its physical segmentation, giving you more flexibility to manage and configure your network in a way that works best for you. Routers can also provide network security measures through packet filtering, allowing only certain packets to pass by either an inclusion or exclusion list of packet types.

NETWORK CONNECTIVITY

WAN Media Support					
Performance	Reliability	Manageability	Scalability	**Flexibility**	Value

There are different protocol and media connection issues for routing over a WAN. If a WAN connection is based on fractional T1 lines, the router needs to support it. Some routers are designed specifically for WAN applications and will incorporate support for a variety of WAN connections.

Midrange Computing, Mainframe, and WAN Connections

Providing connectivity beyond the LAN often means making links to other sites or other computing platforms such as mainframe or midrange computers that are on other operating systems and network operating systems. The physical connection is usually achieved through a direct attached computer (gateway) that is also attached to the network. The rest of the workstations on the LAN then achieve access via terminal emulation software and communicate through the gateway machine.

There are many connectivity options for WAN links, from leased telephone and ISDN connections to radio and microwave wireless connections. Often you need specialized equipment to achieve these connections. For instance, if you're making connections through a high-speed T1 line, you need a multiplexor to subdivide the high-speed signal into separate voice and data communications channels.

Buying equipment and implementing these types of connections, particularly WAN links, involves much careful consideration and planning. This is a complex area of networking. This book includes product tables on gateways, terminal emulation, multiplexors, and WAN links.

Wireless LAN Systems

Wireless network connections can be for either LAN or WAN systems. When using wireless connections you need to decide which technology to choose. Distance, terrain, and network performance are key considerations. Today, wireless LANs are usually used for specialized workgroup situations that make cable connections difficult. They are also usually part of a larger, hard-wired, network. Because some wireless mediums have limited bandwidth and need error detection/correction schemes, they are usually slower than hard-wired LANs.

The environment plays a bigger role in wireless connections than in hard-wiring. Factors such as weather and electrical interference have more of an impact on wireless connections. Keep this in mind when considering which technology to choose.

NETWORK CONNECTIVITY

Radio Frequency Systems

You can use radio frequency connections for workgroup connectivity or LAN-to-LAN connectivity for relatively short distances. Radio wave connections can travel through solid objects, making this a viable option when physical interference is a problem. The frequencies used are in the 900MHz range. Radio communications are quite susceptible to electrical interference from mobile phones, radar, and other devices. Environmental control is an important issue.

The performance of radio frequency systems ranges from 0.6 to 2 Mbps. If you enhance signal forms you can boost these speeds to 4 to 6 Mbps. Many systems can provide single or multiple channels within the frequency bandwidth. The more channels you have, the more simultaneous transfers can take place but at a lower bandwidth (and performance). Some systems are designed for longer distances, up to several miles. At 2 Mbps, they can offer higher speeds than telephone-based connections at a lower cost.

It's pretty simple to interface wireless connections to a hard-wired LAN. You can use standard computer interfaces (a bus card, serial interface, and so on) or connections to standard hubs, routers, bridges, and so forth. Some people worry more about data security when passing information over airwaves. If this is a concern for you, look into security methods such as data encryption and frequency hopping.

Infrared Systems

Infrared wireless systems use infrared signals (wave forms just outside the visible light spectrum) to pass information. Unlike radio waves, infrared signals need to have a clear line of sight between sending and receiving devices. Because these signals are part of the optical spectrum, they are immune to electrical interference. They also have a higher network bandwidth than radio waves, less susceptibility to security breaches (due to a focused versus omnidirectional signal path), and very low power requirements. The current network speeds of infrared systems range from 0.6 to 16 Mbps. The theoretical limits are much higher but are not practical for current network applications.

Microwave Systems

Microwave systems are yet another option in wireless LAN connections. The distance between transceivers is 80 to 100 feet and you can extend these distances by increasing the number of "hops" to transceivers. Long-distance microwave towers can serve longer distances (about 35 miles). Like infrared systems, microwave links need to be relatively in line of site, although the signal travels in a wider beam and is easier to tune for connection. In addition, they are less susceptible to physical interference

NETWORK CONNECTIVITY

and can pass though semi-dense objects (cloth, some walls, and so on). They are, however, susceptible to interference from other microwave signals.

You must obtain a license to use a microwave frequency and the available frequencies are limited. Microwave systems can also be more expensive than the others.

■ Cables

Manufacturer	**AMP**	**AMP**
Cable Types	Twisted Pair, Fiber Optic	Twisted Pair, Fiber Optic
Coaxial	N/A	N/A
Twisted Pair	Category 5 4-pair 24 AWG unshielded riser cables. These cables are suitable for applications that may extend 100MHz and exceed the EIA/TIA-568A extended frequency requirements. UL and CSA listed. Suitable for 1EEE 802.5, Next at least 2 dB better than industry standard.	Category 5 4-Pair 26 AWG stranded shielded cables. This category 5 cable is designed to provide extended transmission distances over a broadened frequency range to 100MHz. Exceeds Crosstalk requirements of EIA/TIA-568A. Engineered for installation as general building wiring per NEC. UL and CSA listed.
Fiber Optic	50/125 micron singlemode riser. 3.5 atten. Max. 850 nm. 400 Bandwidth min. 1300. nm. 3.Dim. Nom. 598 Tensile load installation. 4.5 Bend radius min. install. 200 Crush resistance. Part number 503-016-2	100/140 micron single-mode riser. 5. atten. Max. 850 nm. 100 Bandwidth min. 1300. nm. 3. Dim. Nom. 598 Tensile load installation. 4.5 bend radius min. install. 200 Crush resistance. Part number 503-016-3.
Comments		
Warranty	5 year+	5 year+
Price	Twisted Pair—$85.76 a thousand feet Optical Fiber—$134.00 per hundred feet	Twisted Pair—$205.72 a thousand feet Optical Fiber–$390.00 per thousand feet

Manufacturer	**Belden Wire and Cable Company**	**Belden Wire and Cable Company**
Cable Types	Coaxial, Twisted Pair, Fiber Optic	Coaxial, Twisted Pair, Fiber Optic
Coaxial	Ethernet (TM) and IEEE 802.3 10BASE5/ ISO 8802.3 Coaxial cable. Product code 9880.	50 OHM Coaxial cable for IEEE 802.3/ISO 8802.3 10BASE2 (Thin Ethernet), RG 58/U Type. Product code 9907
Twisted Pair	Category 5 UTP, 4 Pair, #24 AWG solid bare copper, Polypropylene insulation, PVC jacket, ripcord, jacket sequentially marked at 2 foot intervals. Product code 1583A DATATWIST (R) Five.	4 PR UTP (Unshielded twisted pair) cable, 24AWG solid bare copper Polyolefin insulated, singles adjoined, rip-cord, PVC jacket. Jacket is sequentially marked at 2 foot intervals. Product code SM 1700A DATATWIST 350.
Fiber Optic	Lanlite fiber optic cable contains 2 PVC buffered 62.5/125 micron fibers. The fibers are stranded with aramid yarn, which provides cable tensile strength and impact resistance. The cable is jacketed with flame retardant PVC and is UL listed for riser applications. Product code 550263. Category 5.	4 fiber breakout style cable for plenum non-conduit installations. 4 color coded single fiber cable elements are stranded around fiberglass epoxy central strength member. A polyester separator tape is wrapped around the cable care and is covered with a Fluorocpolymer. Product code 225864. Category 5.
Comments	Multi-mode	Multi-mode
Warranty	10 year+	10 year+
Price (Sampling)	Coaxial—$5.88 per 500 feet Twisted Pair—$202.00 per 1000 feet Fiber Optic—$470.00 per 1000 feet	Coaxial—$4.00 per 500 feet Twisted Pair—$146.60 per 1000 feet Fiber Optic—$1,694.00 per 500 feet

Manufacturer	**Champlan Cable**	**Optical Cable, Corp.**
Cable Types	Shielded, Unshielded, Twisted Pair	Fiber Optic
Coaxial	N/A	N/A
Twisted Pair	UTP, F/UTP, S/STP, Plenum, Riser, 2-25 pair, CAT 3, 4, 5	N/A
Fiber Optic	N/A	Tight-buffered fiber optic cables suitable for both indoor and outdoor environments Both single and multi-mode.
Comments	High end product: CAT 5 Dataclear EF; 350MHz tested	
Warranty	15 year	INA

N/A—Not applicable   INA—Information not available

Cables ■

Manufacturer	Champlan Cable	Optical Cable, Corp.
Price	$30–$1500; call for pricing.	DX-Series Distribution Fiber Optic cable 6-fiber 62.5/125 Micron, 1K length riser-rated $.93 per feet; Plenum-rated $1.00 per feet BX Series Breakout Fiber Optic Cable 12-fiber 62.5/125 Micron, 1K length riser-rated $2.60 per feet; Plenum-rated $2.75 per feet GX Series subgrouping Fiber Optic Cable 12-fiber 62.5/125 Micron, 1K length riser-rated $5.53 per feet; Plenum-rated $6.10 per feet

Manufacturer	Lucent Technology	Lucent Technology
Cable Types	Coaxial, Twisted Pair, Fiber Optic	Coaxial, Twisted Pair, Fiber Optic
Coaxial	The 734A and 734B feature an impedance of 75ohms, small diameter, flame retardant PVC jacket, mechanical flexibility, 728-type transmission characteristics, Ul listed type CMR (734A) CSA, CXC Fta (734B).	Type 1247 18-pair Computer interconnect Cable is engineered to interconnect mainframe computers and high-speed peripherals operating at three megabits per second. Flexible, shielded dual foam with the latest copper technology and use of short twist lengths. 26 AWG solid tinned conductors. The inner jacket is wrapped in a polyester aluminum foil shield covered by a PVC outer jacket. A 24 AWG stranded tinned copper drain wire is located under the foil shield.
Twisted Pair	The 1061C+ Cable is composed of 24 AWG, bare; solid copper conductors insulate with high density polyolefin. The insulated conductors are twisted into pairs and jacketed with specially formulated material. UL listed type GM for general purpose use. Category 5.	The 2061+ four pair cable consists of 24 AWG, bare solid copper conductors insulated with Teflon FEP and Thermoplastic polymer. The insulated conductors are twisted into pairs and jacketed with low smoke PVC. UL verified Category 5, UL, and c(UL) listed type CMP for use in air return handling spaces.
Fiber Optic	ACCUMAX Cable 62.5/125 micron multimode fiber or depressed clad single mode fiber. Cable fiber counts are 1,2,4,6,8 and 12. Each micron fiber has the D-LUX 100 coating, bringing the diameter to 250 microns, and is proof tested at 100 kpsi. The coated fiber is buffered to 900 micron with PVC. The PVC buffer is color coated for identification. The buffered fibers are surrounded by aramid yarn for strength and over jacketed with PVC for protection.	ACCUMAX PLENUM Cable 62.5/125 micron multimode fiber or depressed clad single mode fiber. Cable fiber counts are 1,2,4,6,8 and 12. Each micron fiber has the D-LUX 100 coating, bringing the diameter to 250 microns, and is proof tested at 100 kpsi. The coated fiber is buffered to 900 micron with PVC. The PVC buffer is color coated for identification. The buffered fibers are surrounded by aramid yarn for strength and over jacketed with Plenum material for protection.
Comments	734A/B meet national electrical code requirements; spaced savings with reduced cable buildup in overhead racks and in rear of equipment framework. 20 AWG solid copper. 1061C+ has enhanced electrical performance exceeding Pair to Pair and power sum NEXT measurements, SRL and cable balance. The improved Power Sum cables are measured in accordance with ASTM D4566.	1061C+ has enhanced electrical performance exceeding Pair to Pair and power sum NEXT measurements, SRL, and cable balance. The improved Power Sum cables are measured in accordance with ASTM D4566.
Warranty	Up to 15 years	Up to 15 years
Price	Twisted Pair (1061C+)—$156.28 per 1000 feet Fiber Optic (Accumax)—$676.82 per 1000 feet	Twisted Pair (2061+)—$355.54 per 1000 feet Fiber Optic (plenum)—$823.96 per 1000 feet

Manufacturer	NORDX/CDT	NORDX/CDT
Cable Types	Twisted Pair, Fiber Optic	Twisted Pair, Fiber Optic
Coaxial	N/A	N/A
Twisted Pair	BDNFlex Plus: Category 5 CMP rated, 4 unshielded plenum rated cables, 24 AWG dual insulated design using FR Polymer as underlayer with FEP skin on all four pairs, and an overall flexible PVC jacket	BDN Plus: Category 5 CMR rated, 4 unshielded twisted pairs CMR-rated cables, 24 AWG PE insulated design, and an overall PVC jacket.

N/A—Not applicable   INA—Information not available   **Table Continues** →

■ Cables

Manufacturer	NORDX/CDT	NORDX/CDT
Fiber Optic	Fiber Distribution Series: for medium to high fiber count, intra-building installations. Offers a high degree of flexibility for backbone and horizontal applications. Available as 900 micron buffered fiber; 62.5/125 micron multi-mode fiber, single-mode fiber, or composite configurations.	Fiber Breakout Series: For medium to high fiber count, intra-building, harsh environment installations. Offers a high degree of flexibility for backbone and horizontal applications. Single or multi-mode. Available as 900 micron buffered fiber with a PVC jacket.
Comments	Offers Cat 5 plenum in 4 colors. The jacket is printed at intervals with a unique descending length marking starting at 1000 feet and ending at zero for box's and small spool, and at 2500 feet to 0 for large spool. Various connectors available. Available as riser rated or as plenum rated. Building telecommunications wiring standards.	Offers Cat 5 plenum in 4 colors. The jacket is printed at intervals with a unique descending length marking starting at 1000 feet and ending at zero for boxes and small spool, and at 2500 feet to 0 for large spool. Various connectors available. Available as riser rated or as plenum rated. Building telecommunications wiring standards.
Warranty	15 year	15 year
Price	Twisted Pair—$317.11 per 1000 feet	Twisted Pair—$108.33 per 1000 feet

Manufacturer	NORDX/CDT	NORDX/CDT
Cable Types	Twisted Pair(Mistake)Fiber Optic	Twisted Pair(Mistake)Fiber Optic
Coaxial	N/A	N/A
Twisted Pair	BDNFlex Plus: Category 5 CM rated, 4 unshielded plenum CM rated cables, 24 AWG PE insulated design and an overall flexible PVC jacket	BDN Plus 25 pair cable: Category 5 CMR rated, made up of 24 AWG copper thermoplastic insulated conductors that are assembled into one group of 25 pairs with an overall PVC jacket. Meet and exceed TIA/EIA-568-A NEXT PowerSum requirements.
Fiber Optic	Fiber interconnected cable: Single or multi-mode fiber. Designed for low fiber count premises environments. Small and very flexible and ideal for confined spaces. Suited for open applications.	Campus Series: Loose tube cables. Suited for outdoor applications such as direct burial, lashed aerial, or underground conduit. Available in three constructions. All-dielectric, indoor/outdoor riser rated or steel armored. Available as 62.5/125 micron multi-mode fiber or in composite configurations.
Comments	Offers Cat 5 plenum in Blue. The jacket is printed at intervals with a unique descending length marking starting at 1000 feet and ending at zero for box's and small spool. Various connectors available. Offers (EIA/TIA 568A) Comm. Building telecommunications wiring standards	Offers Cat 5 CMR in blue. The jacket is printed at intervals with a unique descending length marking starting at 1000 feet and ending at zero per spool and at 8200 feet to zero per reel Offers (EIA/TIA 568A) Comm. Building telecommunications wiring standards
Warranty	15 year	15 year
Price	Twisted Pair—$91.75 per 1000 feet	Twisted Pair—$1,095.00 per 1000 feet

Manufacturer	NORDX/CDT	NORDX/CDT
Cable Types	Twisted Pair, Fiber Optic	Twisted Pair, Fiber Optic
Coaxial	N/A	N/A
Twisted Pair	Data Grade Riser (DGR) 25 Pair cable: Category 5 CMR rated, made up of 24 AWG copper thermoplastic insulated conductors that are assembled into one group of 25 pairs. The cable core is enclosed with ALVYN sheath consisting of a dielectric core wrap and a corrugated 0.2mm aluminum shield which is bonded to an outer PVC jacket. Meet and exceed TIA/EIA-568-A NEXT PowerSum requirements.	Modular Patch/Line cords: Cat 5, 24 /AWG stranded or solid copper conductors. Exceed TIA/EIA-568-A Cat 5 performance. Available in both configurations: T568A (ISDN) or T569B.
Fiber Optic		
Comments	Offers Category 5 CMR in Gray color. Available in 8200 feet standard master reel or custom length.	Offers Cat 5 CMR rated in 6 pantone colors with variable length 4, 7, 10, 15, and 25 feet
Warranty	15 year	15 year
Price	Twisted Pair—$1,150.00 per 1000 feet	Twisted Pair—$4.50 per foot

N/A—Not applicable   INA—Information not available

Bridges ∎

Manufacturer	Accton Technology	Annexus Data Systems	Annexus Data Systems
Model	EtherBridge-L Part# EN2011-1	R33A+	R338
Processor	80C 186 running at 16MHz	486	486
LAN/WAN Connections	L to L	L to W	L to W
Memory	RAM: 512K EPROM: 64K	1MB	1MB
Protocols	Transparent to upper level protocols. Bridges at data link layer.	WAN: Proprietary LAN: All Ethernet, 802.1d Spanning Tree	WAN: Proprietary LAN: All Ethernet, 802.1d Spanning Tree
Interface	IEEE802.3 Ethernet	IEEE 802.3, Ethernet	IEEE 802.3, Ethernet
Ports (Number and Type)	2 AUI/BNC ports	1 LAN, 1 WAN Fully integrated V.34 modem, AUI/ BNC/ 100BASE-T	1 LAN, 1 WAN RS-232/ D89, AUI/ BNC/ 10BASE-T
LED\	Per port: Link, Forwarding, Collision. For unit: Power, System diag.	Link, Send, Receive, Power, Collision	Link, Send, Receive, Power, Collision
Network Management	N/A	SNMP, MIBII, Bridge MIB	SNMP, MIBII, Bridge MIB
Configuration Management	Transparent to all NOS	Via 3.5" Risk	Via 3.5" Risk
Bandwidth	10Mbps	LAN: 10Mbps WAN: 115Kbps	LAN: 10Mbps WAN: 115Kbps
Power	100-2440 V 50/60Hz up to 30W max	110/220 VAC, 50/60Hz	110/220 VAC, 50/60Hz
Speed/Throughput	Filtering rate: 12,000pps Forwarding Rate: 10,000pps	115.2Kbps with 4:1 Compression	115.2Kbps
Comments/Options	Plug and play installation. Self learns network addresses.	Auto dial on power up, address filtering, et al.	Auto dial on power up, address filtering, DSU/CSU, ISDN, et al.
Warranty	3 year	1 year	1 year
Price	$799	$1,595	$1,295

Manufacturer	Asante Tech	Ascend
Model	Asante' Fast 10/100 Bridge	MAX 4002/4004
Processor	Custom ASIC	Intel i960
LAN/WAN Connections	L to W	4MB
Memory	N/A	L to W
Protocols	Protocol Independent	WAN: PPP, HDLC, SLIP, Frame Relay LAN: IP, IPX, Transparent Bridging
Interface	IEEE 802.3u and 802.3	Ethernet, Serial
Ports (Number and Type)	2 (100BASE-TX, 10BASE-T and AUI)	T1/ PRI, Serial v35, Serial RS449
LED\	Activity, Forwarding, Traffic, Error Detection, Link Integrity, Transmit Status	Link, Integrity, Traffic, Power
Network Management	None	SNMP, MIB2,
Configuration Management	N/A	TelNet, VT100
Bandwidth	10/100	10Mbps
Power	100/240 volts, 50/60Hz	90-240VAC, 47-63Hz
Speed/Throughput	14,8080	56Kbps-2.048Mbps

N/A—Not applicable   INA—Information not available

Table Continues →

■ Bridges

Manufacturer	Asante Tech	Ascend
Comments/Options	Also includes Nway auto-negotiation to determine 10Mbps or 100Mbps operation automatically	MP and MP+ allows up to 6 channels aggregated together
Warranty	Lifetime	1 year
Price	$995	$11,000/$15,500

Manufacturer	D-Link	D-Link	Develcon
Model	DI-11201	DI-1140	120
Processor	RISC CPU		68000
LAN/WAN Connections	L to WAN	L to W	L to L
Memory	INA	INA	1MB
Protocols	WAN: PPP IEEE 802.1D	WAN: PPP IEEE 802.1D	LAN: IEEE-1d
Interface	IEEE 802.3, Ethernet	IEEE 802.3, Ethernet	IEEE 802.3, Ethernet
Ports (Number and Type)	UTP/BNC/AUI for LAN port. RS-232 for WAN port.	UTP/BNC/AUI for LAN port. RS-232 for WAN port.	AUI/BNC, 10BASE-T up to 2 ports
LED\	Link, TX, RX, State, Collision	Link, TX, RX, State, Collision	LAN, Power
Network Management	SNMP, MIBII, Bridge MIB	SNMP, MIBII, Bridge MIB	SNMP, MIBII, Bridge MIB, Enterprise, Extension
Configuration Management	TCP/IP, NetWare	TCP/IP, NetWare	TelNet, Out of Band, SNMP
Bandwidth	10Mbps	10Mbps	10Mbps
Power	Internal, Universal, Power Supply	Internal, Universal, Power, Supply	90/250 Volts, 50/60Hz
Speed/Throughput	Up to 76.8Kbps	Up to 2.048Mbps	LAN speed
Comments/Options		WAN ports are user selectable	
Warranty	1 year	1 year	Lifetime
Price	$1,595	$3,095	INA

Manufacturer	Develcon	Farallon	Fore Systems
Model	3000	Fast Starlet 10/100 Bridge	PowerHub 4000
Processor	68302	FASTLAN	R3071@40MHz
LAN/WAN Connections	L to L; L to W	L to L	L to L
Memory	1MB	128K	4MB
Protocols	WAN: Frame Relay, LAPB, ISDN LAN: IEEE-1d	CSMA/CD 802.3 Ethernet	LAN: IEEE 802.1d
Interface	IEEE 802.3, Ethernet	802.3 Ethernet	IEEE 802.3 Ethernet FDDI-x379.5 ATM- 003, D53
Ports (Number and Type)	AUI/BNC, 10BASE-T-LAN, v.35, RS232, v.11, ISDN BRI, DSU/CSU—WAN up to 3 ports	2 Etherwane 10BASE-T ports and 1 AUI port	10BASE-T—up to 12; 100BPX, 100BTX—up to 2 SM, MM, MIC, FDDI—(2)
LED\	LAN, WAN, Power	6 Etherwave LEDs for link, transmit, receive, and collision	Ethernet: LNK, A/R, C/X FDDI: W.S.X; S,W,R ATM: X, R, L
Network Management	SNMP, MIBII, Bridge MIB, Enterprise, Extension	N/A	SNMP Agent with MIB II, Ethernet MIB, Bridge MIB (RFC), Foreview Agent with Forethought
Configuration Management	TelNet, Out of Band, SNMP	N/A	TCP/IP, NetWare, AppleTalk
Bandwidth	10M-LAN 1.5M-WAN	10Mbps/100Mbps	Increments of 10Mbps

N/A—Not applicable   INA—Information not available

Bridges ■

Manufacturer	Develcon	Farallon	Fore Systems
Power	90/250 Volts, 50/60Hz	110-250V	100/250 Volts, 50/60MHz, 48VOC
Speed/Throughput	9.6Kbps—1.544Mbps	Wirespeed, forwarding, full 10BASE-T throughput, and 256K of buffering	400Mbps
Comments/Options	Optional Compression	The bridge module slides into the fast starlet hub. No configuration required or software to install	Multi-port LAN Bridge, Ethernet, FDDI, ATM
Warranty	Lifetime	1 year	1 year
Price	INA	INA	$6,950+

Manufacturer	Fore Systems	Fore Systems	GDC
Model	PowerHub 6000	PowerHub 7000	TPP
Processor	R3071@40MHz	R3071@40MHz	Risc i960
LAN/WAN Connections	L to L	L to L	L to L; L to W
Memory	4MB	2-8MB	8MB
Protocols	LAN: IEEE 802.1d	LAN: IEEE 802.1d	WAN: Frame Relay, TI, FTI LAN: 802.1d Spanning Tree
Interface	IEEE 802.3 Ethernet FDDI-x379.5 ATM- 003, D53	IEEE 802.3 Ethernet FDDI-x379.5 ATM—003, D53	IEEE 802.3 Ethernet
Ports (Number and Type)	6 independent MOD ports, 48 10BASE-T ports, 2 100BT/100BX ports	240 Ethernet segments 16 FDDI Rings	10BASE-T up to 16ports
LED\	Ethernet: LNK, A/R, C/X FDDI: W.S.X; S,W,R ATM: X, R, L	Ethernet: LNK, A/R, C/X FDDI: W.S.X; S,W,R ATM: X, R, L	INA
Network Management	SNMP Agent with MIB II, Ethernet MIB, Bridge MIB (RFC), Foreview Agent with Forethought	SNMP Agent with MIB II, Ethernet MIB, Bridge MIB (RFC), Foreview Agent with Forethought	SNMP, MIB
Configuration Management	TCP/IP, NetWare, AppleTalk	TCP/IP, NetWare, Appletalk	INA
Bandwidth	Increments of 10Mbps	Increments of 10Mbps	10Mbps
Power	100/250 Volts, 50/60MHz, 48VOC	100/250 Volts, 50/60MHz, 48VOC	100 VAC to 240 VAC, -48VDC
Speed/Throughput	600Mbps	700Mbps	9.6Kbps-2.048Mbps
Comments/Options	Multi-port LAN Bridge, Ethernet, FDDI, ATM	Hot swappable	Bridge module is integral to the TMS 3000 PlatForm, supports voice/data/LAN
Warranty	1 year	1 year	1 year
Price	$8,950+	$9,950+	INA

Manufacturer	LANcity	LANcity	LANcity
Model	LCP	LCw	LCb
Processor	IDT 3041	IDT 3051	IDT 3051
LAN/WAN Connections	L to L	L to L	L to W
Memory	1MB	1MB	4MB
Protocols	SNMP, Bootp, TFTP, 802.1d	SNMP, Bootp, TFTP, 802.1d	SNMP, Bootp, TFTP, 802.1d
Interface	IEEE 802.3	IEEE 802.3	IEEE 802.3
Ports (Number and Type)	AUI, 10BASE-T, F	AUI, 10BASE-T, F	AUI, F

N/A—Not applicable   INA—Information not available

Table Continues →

■ Bridges

Manufacturer	LANcity	LANcity	LANcity
LED\	Link, Power, Ethernet, Cable, Tx, Sync	Link, Power, Ethernet, Cable, Tx, Sync	Link, Power, Ethernet, Cable, Tx, Sync
Network Management	SNMP, MIBII, Bridge MIB, CATV MIB	SNMP, MIBII, Bridge MIB, CATV MIB	SNMP, MIBII, Bridge MIB, CATV MIB
Configuration Management	Remote FTP, Bootp	Remote FTP, Bootp	Remote FTP, Bootp
Bandwidth	10Mbps	10Mbps	10Mbps
Power	88-264 VAC, 47-63Hz	88-264 VAC, 47-63Hz	88-264 VAC, 47-63Hz
Speed/Throughput	10Mbps	10Mbps	10Mbps
Comments/Options	App/Top Independent, Plug and Play	App/Top Independent, Plug and Play	App/Top Independent, Plug and Play
Warranty	1 year	1 year	1 year
Price	$595	$1,495	$2,095

Manufacturer	LANcity	LANcity	LANTRONIX
Model	LCh	LCe	LB2
Processor	IDT 3051	IDT 3081	68020
LAN/WAN Connections	L to W	L to W	L to L
Memory	4MB	4MB	1MB
Protocols	SNMP, Bootp, TFTP, 802.1d	SNMP, Bootp, TFTP, 802.1d	All
Interface	IEEE 802.3	IEEE 802.3	1EEE 802.3 Ethernet
Ports (Number and Type)	AUI, F	AUI, F	AUI-2
LED\	Link, Power, Ethernet, Cable, Tx, Sync	Link, Power, Ethernet, Cable, Tx, Sync	Power, Port, Activity, Serial Activity
Network Management	SNMP, MIBII, Bridge MIB, CATV MIB	SNMP, MIBII, Bridge MIB, CATV MIB	SNMP, MIB II, Bridge MIB, Ethernet MIB
Configuration Management	Remote FTP, Bootp	Remote FTP, Bootp	TCP/IP, NetWare, AppleTalk, DECNet, Console
Bandwith	10Mbps	10Mbps	20Mbps
Power	88-264 VAC, 47-63Hz	88-264 VAC, 47-63Hz	95-250 VAC, 50
Speed/Throughput	10Mbps	10Mbps	10Mbps
Comments/Options	App/Top Independent, Plug and Play	App/Top Independent, Plug and Play, 2Ch, 2RU	
Warranty	1 year	1 year	5 year
Price	INA	INA	$1,695

Manufacturer	Larson, Inc.	PairGain Technologies
Model	EtherSpan	Campus Rex
Processor	RISC	Motorola 683oz.
LAN/WAN Connections	L to L; L to W	L to L
Memory	1MB	1MB
Protocols	Self Learning per 802.3; Spanning Tree per 802.1(d) PPP per 1638, RFC 1220	Spanning Tree, HDLC, PPP
Interface	IEEE 802.3, Ethernet	10BASE-T
Ports (Number and Type)	LAN Port, 10BASE-T, DTE, HSSI or HUD; WAN: HSD/HSSI	1-HDSL port 1-10BASE-T port

N/A—Not applicable   INA—Information not available

Bridges ∎

Manufacturer	Larson, Inc.	PairGain Technologies
LED\	Power, Status, XMTLAN, RCV LAN, XMT WAN, RCV WAN, Test	Link
Network Management	SNMP, MIB II, Bridge MIB (RFC),	SNMP
Configuration Management	SLIP, VT100 Terminal, SNMP	Console out of band
Bandwith	10Mbps	384Kbps, TI 768Kbps, EI
Power	DC 48 volts with adapter	110/220 AC
Speed/Throughput	10Mbps	6000pps
Comments/Options	WAN port supports up to 10Mbps on Ethernet wire speed	
Warranty	2 year	3 year
Price	$3,700	$695

Manufacturer	Pinnacle Communications, Inc.	Pivotal Networking, Inc.	Pivotal Networking, Inc.
Model	5051	Pivotal 2000	Pivotal 1610/1680
Processor	INA	Intel i960	Motorola 68 EN 360 at 33MHz
LAN/WAN Connections	L to L	L to W	L to W
Memory	INA	1-2MB flash memory, 2-4MB EDO DRAM	1MB flash memory, 2-4MB EDO DRAM
Protocols	IEEE 802.3 MAC Layer Operation	IP, IP Multicast, RSVP, IPX, bridging (IP/IPX/ AppleTalk/XNS/DEC), RFC 1490, PPP, BACP, ISDN	IP, IP Multicast, RSVP, IPX, bridging (IP/IPX/ AppleTalk/XNS/DEC), RFC 1490, PPP, BACP, ISDN
Interface	D Bridge 802.1 Ethernet 802.3	INA	IP RIP, IPX RIP
Ports (Number and Type)	AUI, BNC, Fiber 2 ports	1 Ethernet 10BASE-T (LAN) 2/4 Serial ports (WAN)	1 (for 1610) or 8 (for 1680) Ethernet 10BASE-T ports
LED\	Traffic, reject, power	System status LED, Link, XMT, Receiving	System status LED, Link, XMT, Receiving
Network Management	SNMP, MIB II	SNMP, IP, GUI, SNMP Manager	SNMP, IP, GUI, SNMP Manager
Configuration Management	INA	INA	INA
Bandwidth	10Mbps	INA	INA
Power	Universal 100/250 VAC 50/60Hz	100/250V, 50/60Hz	Table-mount 9V AC transformer
Speed/Throughput	INA	INA	Up to T1/E1
Comments/Options	Filtering rate: 14880 pps one way, 29,760 aggregate forwarding rate: 10,000pps	Spanning Tree Protocol, Data prioritization, Data compression (Stacker Size), Multimedia	Spanning Tree Protocol, Data prioritization, Data compression (Stacker Size), Multimedia
Warranty	3 year	5 year	5 year
Price	$1,265 to $1,597	$1,495 and $2,495(1680)	$1,495 and $2,495(1680)

Manufacturer	RAD Data Communications	RAD Data Communications	Ragula Systems
Model	TRE Family/ MBE Family	Trimbridge-16/ Trimbridge-10	#90001
Processor	68302	80286	AM29200
LAN/WAN Connections	L to L; L to W	L to L; L to W	L to L
Memory	0.5MB	0.5MB	2MB

N/A—Not applicable   INA—Information not available

Table Continues →

■ Bridges

Manufacturer	RAD Data Communications	RAD Data Communications	Ragula Systems
Protocols	WAN: Proprietary SLIP, CSLIP, PPP, Frame Relay, X.25, ISDN, 4-Wire	WAN: Transparent Bridging	IP, IEEE 802.1d
Interface	IEEE 802.5 Token Ring/ ISEEE 802.3 Ethernet	IEEE 802.5 Token Ring/ ISEEE 802.3 Ethernet	1EEE 802.3 Ethernet, 802.12 100VG
Ports (Number and Type)	1 Token-Ring Port; 1-8 WAN ports	1 Main Link, 1 Back-up: STP/UTP (T 16)/ AUI, BNC, TUP (T 10)	AUI, BNC, 10BASE-T, 100VG
LED\	LAN and LINKS: TX, RX, Err. STATUS: Ready, Power, 4/16M, Main	Link Integrity, Power, Rdy, Overflow	LINK, Activity, Power
Network Management	SNMP, MIB II, Bridge, Token-Ring, Private MB	SNMP, MIB II, Bridge, Private MB	SNMP, MIBII, Bridge MIB, 100VG
Configuration Management	Transparent and IP, IPX	INA	TCP/IP, NetWare
Bandwidth	4/16M-Token-ring; up to TI Rates for WAN	LAN—10Mbps, WAN-p to E1 Speed	100Mbps
Power	100-220 VAC, 47-63Hz, 10 VA max.	100-220 VAC, 47-63Hz	100-250, 50/60Hz
Speed/Throughput	1.2Kbps-115.22K Async 0-1.536M-Sync	Up to E1	INA
Comments/Options	Available with 1-8 Link Modules	Highs speed compression, masking, Back-up	10/100 Speed Matching Bridge, STP
Warranty	1 year	1 year	3 year
Price	$1,450–$4,000	$1,900–$3,495	$1,899

Manufacturer	South Hills Datacomm	Telco Systems	TTI Wireless
Model	33563	Series 3000 and 4000	TTI 200TSE 4MB
Processor	MC68302	MC68000/MC68030	486/66
LAN/WAN Connections	L to W	L to L; L to W	L to L; L to W
Memory	1 Byte	2MB/4MB	1MB
Protocols	IP, IPX, RIP, DECNet, XNS, OSI	All	WAN: HALC LAN: 802.3, 802.5
Interface	LAN: 802.3, WAN: V.35	IEEE 802.3	802.3 Ethernet 802.5 Token-Ring
Ports (Number and Type)	(1) AUI, (1) BNC, 1DB-9M, DB-25F	AUI/ BNC	AUI, BNC, 10BASE-T
LED	Power, Link, LAN, Link2	Link Integrity	Power, Link, Integrity
Network Management	Optional	SNMP	SNMP, MIBII, V1V2
Configuration Management	Telnet Terminal	N/A	TelNet Terminal keyboard
Bandwith	10Mbps	10Mbps	Up to 155Mbps
Power	110/250 V, 50/60Hz	61/100 watts	110/220VAC, 50/60Hz
Speed/Throughput	INA	INA	INA
Comments/Options	Also available in dual link. Remote Ethernet Bridge.		
Warranty	2 year	INA	INA
Price	INA	INA	INA

N/A—Not applicable   INA—Information not available

Bridges ■

Manufacturer	UB Networks	UB Networks	UB Networks
Model	GeoLink/LA	GeoLink/LF	Token Ring Bridge/Switch
Processor	Intel 960 Risc	Intel 960 Risc	Intel 960 Risc
LAN/WAN Connections	L to L	L to L	L to L
Memory	1MB	1MB	1MB
Protocols	IEEE 802.3 Ethernet + ATM Lade & UNI	IEEE 802.3 Ethernet to FDDI	TCP/IP, IPX/SPX, AppleTalk, DEC, XNS, IP
Interface	LAN to ATM bridging	LAN-to-FDDI bridging	LAN-to-RMS Bus connectivity—ATM, FDDI Ethernet
Ports (Number and Type)	1-Plus Bus connection 1—155Mbps ATM uplink	1-Plus Bus connection 1—100Mbps ATM FDDI connection	2 LAN ports HUB dependent for WAN ports
LED\	Port status indicator	Port status indicator	Port status
Network Management	Integrated in chassis hub for mgt.	Integrated in chassis hub for mgt.	SNMP-Integrated in chassis hub for mgt.
Configuration Management	UB Networks TelNet Net Director	UB Networks TelNet Net Director	UB Networks TelNet Net Director
Bandwidth	155Mbps	100Mbps	32Mbps Token Ring $(&) 320Mbps Bus
Power	GeoLAN 100 A	FDDI	Integrated into hub
Speed/Throughput	155Mbps	100Mbps	32-320Mbps
Comments/Options	GeoLAN 100 and GEO LAN 500; ATM-uplink capability	FDDI uplink for GEOLAN 100 and GEOLAN 500 chassis hub	FDDI uplink for GEOLAN 100 and GEOLAN 500 chassis hub
Warranty	1 year	1 year	1 year
Price	INA	INA	INA

Manufacturer	UB Networks
Model	Ethernet Bridge/ Router
Processor	Intel 960
LAN/WAN Connections	L to L
Memory	1MB
Protocols	TCP/IP, IPX/SPX, AppleTalk, DEC, XNS, IP
Interface	LAN-to-FDToken Ring to RMS Bus connectivity-ATM, FDDI Token Ring,
Ports (Number and Type)	2 LAN ports HUB dependent for WAN ports
LED\	Port status
Network Management	SNMP-integrated in chassis hub for mgt.
Configuration Management	UB Networks TelNet Net Director
Bandwidth	20Mbps Ethernet and 320Mbps Bus
Power	Integrated into hub
Speed/Throughput	32-320Mbps
Comments/Options	FDDI uplink for GEOLAN 100 and GEOLAN 500 chassis hub
Warranty	1 year
Price	INA

N/A—Not applicable   INA—Information not available

E n d ■

■ Ethernet Hubs

Manufacturer	3Com Corp.	3Com Corp.	3Com Corp.
Model	Office Connect HUB 8/ TPO	Office Connect HUB 8/ TPC	Office Connect HUB 8/ TPM
Total Ports:	8	9	9
Port Types:	8 UTP	1 BNC, 8 UTP	1 BNC, 8 UTP
LEDs	Alert, Power, Packet, Collision, Port Status	Alert, Power, Collision, Port Status, Network, Utilization	Alert, Power, Collision, Port Status, Network, Utilization
Polarity	Auto-detect, auto-correct	Auto-detect, auto-correct	Auto-detect, auto-correct
Bandwidth	10Mbps	10Mbps	10Mbps
Stacking	Clippable up to 4	Clippable up to 4	Clippable up to 4
Form Factor	Desktop, wall mount	Desktop, wall mount	Desktop, wall mount
Comments	Noiseless (no fan)	Noiseless (no fan)	SNMP Full RMON Configuration Mgt. Noiseless (no fan)
Warranty	Lifetime, incl. Power adapter	Lifetime, incl. Power adapter	Lifetime, incl. Power adapter
Price	$229	$279	$749

Manufacturer	3COM Corp.	Accton Technology	Accton Technology
Model	Link Builder FMS II (12) port TP HUB	EtherHub-8s Part# EN2040	EtherHub-16s Part# EH2041s
Total Ports:	13	8	16
Port Types:	(1) AUI, (12) UTP	(1) BNC, (8) UTP	1 BNC, 16 UTP
LEDs	Link, Partition, Power, Traffic, Collision, Mgmt	Power, Overall Activity, Collision, Link/Transmit, Activity/Receive, Partition	Power, Overall Activity, Collision, Link/Transmit, Activity/Receive, Partition
Polarity	Auto-correct	Auto-detect, auto-correct	Auto-detect, auto-correct
Bandwidth	10Mbps	10Mbps	10Mbps
Stacking	Up to 8 hubs	Up to 3	Up to 3
Form Factor	Desktop, 19" rack	Desktop,wall mount (Installation kit included)	Desktop, rack mount
Comments	AUI, BNC, 10BaseFB (optional)	Extra uplink port for chaining to additional hubs. SmartWatch monitoring display. BNC connector included.	Extra uplink port for chaining to additional hubs.
Warranty	Lifetime	Lifetime	Lifetime
Price	$879	$149	$349

Manufacturer	Accton Technology	Accton Technology	Accton Technology
Model	EtherHub-16i	Venus Part# EH2044s	EtherHub-16mi
Total Ports:	16	5	16
Port Types:	1 BNC, 16 UTP, 1 FlexBus (Expansion Connector)	5 UTP	1 BNC, 16 UTP, 1 FlexBus (Expansion Connector)
LEDs	Collision, Link, Transmit, Receive, Segment, Utilization, Partition	Power, Overall Activity, Collision, Link/Transmit, Activity/Receive, Partition	Collision, Link, Transmit, Receive, Segment, Utilization, Partition
Polarity	Auto-detect, auto-correct	Auto-detect, auto-correct	Auto-detect, auto-correct
Bandwidth	Up to 30Mbps	10Mbps	Up to 30Mbps
Stacking	Up to 10	Up to 3	Up to 10
Form Factor	Desktop, rack mount	Desktop, wall mount (Installation Kit Included)	Desktop, rack mount

N/A—Not applicable   INA—Information not available

Ethernet Hubs ■

Manufacturer	Accton Technology	Accton Technology	Accton Technology
Comments	SNMP Ready. Use with EH1502. Automatic HUB ID and termination within stack. Hub level segmentation (up to 3 segments).	5 port unit. Includes AC adapter. Extra uplink port for chaining to additional hubs.	SNMP Ready. Use with EH1502. Automatic HUB ID and termination within stack. Includes ACC/View Management software.
Warranty	Lifetime	Lifetime	Lifetime
Price	$699	$99	$1,199

Manufacturer	AccuLan	AccuLan	AccuLan
Model	AL-HUB12S/	AL-HUB24M	AL-HUB16L/AL-HUB24L
Total Ports:	14	26	18/26
Port Types:	(1) AUI, (1)BNC, (12)UTP	(1) AUI, (1)BNC, (24)UTP, RS232	(1) AUI, (1)BNC, (16)UTP/ (1) AUI, (1)BNC, (24)UTP
LEDs	UTP Ports: Link/Partition (bicolor), Power, Collision.	UTP Ports: Link/Partition (bicolor), Power, Collision, (8)Mgt, Status	Power, Collision, Port Link Status
Polarity	Auto-detect, auto-correct	Auto-detect, auto-correct	Auto-detect, auto-correct
Bandwidth	10Mbps	10Mbps	10Mbps
Stacking	Up to 120 Ports	Up to 120 Ports	Cascade
Form Factor	Desktop, rack mount, wall mount	Desktop, rack mount, wall mount	Desktop, rack mount, wall mount
Comments	SNMP slave when connected to AL-HUB24M.	In-band or out-of-band mgt.	Only 0.9" high
Warranty	5 year	5 year	5 year
Price	$475	$1,769	$385/$585

Manufacturer	AccuLan	AccuLan
Model	AL-HUB8L/AL-HUB12L	AL-HUB24S
Total Ports:	9/14	26
Port Types:	(1)BNC, (8)UTP/ (1) AUI, (1)BNC, (12)UTP	(1) AUI, (1)BNC, (24)UTP, RS232
LEDs	Power, Collision, Port Link Status	UTP Ports: Link/Partition (bicolor), Link, Collision
Polarity	Auto-detect, auto-correct	Auto-detect, auto-correct
Bandwidth	10Mbps	10Mbps
Stacking	N/A	Up to 120 Ports
Form Factor	Desktop, rack mount, wall mount	Desktop, rack mount, wall mount
Comments	Only 0.9" high	SNMP slave when connected to AL-HUB24M
Warranty	5 year	5 year
Price	$179/$331	$979

Manufacturer	Addtron	Addtron	Addtron
Model	UTP 16IL/UTP16A	UTP12M	UTP12D
Total Ports:	18	14	14
Port Types:	(1)AUI, (1)BNC, (16)UTP	(1)AUI, (1)BNC, (12)UTP	(1)AUI, (1)BNC, (12)UTP
LEDs	Power, Collision, Activity, Link	Power, Fault, Collision, Hub IO, Activity	Power, Fault, Collision, Hub IO, Activity
Polarity	Auto-correct, auto-detect	Auto-correct, auto-detect	Auto-correct, auto-detect
Bandwidth	10Mbps	10Mbps	10Mbps
Stacking	Up to 6 hubs	N/A	Up to 5 hubs

N/A—Not applicable   INA—Information not available

Table Continues →

■ Ethernet Hubs

Manufacturer	**Addtron**	**Addtron**	**Addtron**
Form Factor	Desktop (IL) rack (A)	Rack	Rack
Comments	CE, UL, CSA certified	Software included	CE, UL CSA certified
Warranty	1 year-limited	1 year-limited	1 year-limited
Price	$249 (IL) $399 (A)	$695	$595

Manufacturer	**Addtron**	**Addtron**	**Addtron**
Model	UTP 4/L	AEF-8TX/AEF-12TX	UTP85L
Total Ports:	5	9/13	10
Port Types:	(1) BNC, (4) UTP	8 UTP, 1 Uplink/ 12 UTP, 1 Uplink	(1) AUI, (1) BNC, (8) UTP
LEDs	Power, Collision, Link/TX	Power, Activity, Link	Power/Activity, Link/TX
Polarity	Auto-correct, auto-detect	Auto-detect, auto-correct	Auto-correct, auto-detect
Bandwidth	10Mbps	100Mbps	10Mbps
Stacking	Up to 6 hubs	Up to 1 hub	Up to 6 hubs
Form Factor	Desktop	Rack	Desktop
Comments	CE Certified, UL, CSA	CE, UL, CSA Certified	CE Certified, UL, CSA
Warranty	1 year limited	1 year limited	1 year limited
Price	$99	$999/ $1,299	$129

Manufacturer	**Allied Telesyn**	**Allied Telesyn**	**Allied Telesyn**
Model	TurboStack Hub Series	3600 Hub Series	3100 Hub Series
Total Ports:	Available with 6, 8, 12, and 24 ports	Available with 6, 8, 12, and 24 ports	Available 24 or 48 ports
Port Types:	(1)AUI, (8)BNC, (12 or 24)UTP, (6 or 12)Fiber	(1)AUI, (8)BNC, (12 or 24)UTP, (6)Fiber	(1)AUI, (1)BNC, (24 or 48)UTP
LEDs	Power, Master, Fault, Activity, Collision, Link (UTP & Fiber), Partition, Port On-line, Receive	Power, Master, Fault, Activity, Collision, Link (UTP & Fiber), Partition, Port On-line, Receive	Link, Receive, Partition, Status, Bridge-port status, Transmit, Power Activity, Fault
Polarity	SNMP agent, Local ASCII Terminal, TelNet	SNMP agent, Local, ASCII, Terminal, TelNet	SNMP agent, Local ASCII Terminal, TelNet
Bandwidth	10Mbps	10Mbps	10Mbps
Stacking	Up to 8 hubs or seven hubs and one switch	Up to 8 hubs, or 7 hubs and 1 switch	Up to 2 hubs
Form Factor	19" rack mount or tabletop	19" rack mount or tabletop	19" rack mount or tabletop
Comments	TurboStack hubs can store up to 300 MAC addresses per unit and offer network security through intrusion support. Backbone connector user configurable with Fiber, BNC or RJ-45 connectors.	The Hubs are equipped with SNMP redundancy, built-in TelNet, software downloading, and hot swappability. Backbone connector user configurable with Fiber, BNC or RJ-45 connectors.	Provides a network solution for small-to-medium workgroups. Provides security (intrusion and eavesdropping), and hub segmentation. Can be used as managed or unmanaged hubs.
Warranty	Lifetime (fans, power supplies 1 year)	Lifetime (fans, power supplies 1 year)	Lifetime (fans, power supplies 1 year)
Price	$1,295–$4,155	$895–$2,495	$1,700–$2,700

N/A—Not applicable   INA–Information not available

Ethemet Hubs ■

Manufacturer	BASS MICRO	BASS MICRO	Asante' Technologies
Model	807-16, 807-17	807-35, 807-36	AsanteHub 1016-IQ
Total Ports:	5/9/18	13/26	18
Port Types:	5 UTP/1 BNC, 9 UTP/1 AUI, 1 BNC, 16 UTP	1 AUI, 1 BNC, 12 UTP/ 2 AUI, 1 BNC, 24 UTP	1 AUI, 1 BNC, 16 UTP
LEDs	Power, Link, Activity	Power, Link/ Partitioning, Collision, Receive	Link, Integrity per port, Partition per port, Power, and Collision
Polarity	Auto-correct, auto-detect	Auto-correct, auto-detect	Auto-detect, auto-correct
Bandwidth	10Mbps	10Mbps	10Mbps
Stacking	N/A	N/A	Uplink port
Form Factor	Desktop, wall mount	Desktop, rack mount	Desktop, rack mount
Comments	Auto-partitioning	Media auto-sensing on AUI/BNC port; auto-partitioning.	Approx. 5 pounds
Warranty	3 year	3 year	Lifetime
Price	$75 (807-16) $149 (807-17)	$215 (807-35) $345 (807-36)	$899

Manufacturer	Asante' Technologies, Inc.	Asante' Technologies	Asante' Technologies
Model	Asante' NetStacker	Asante' Hub 2072	Asante' Plug and Play Ethernet Hubs
Total Ports:	12-24	12-72	Hub/6=6, Hub/8=8, Hub/12=12, Hub/24=24
Port Types:	(1)AUI, (10)BNC, (12-24)UTP, (6-12)Fiber	(1)AUI, (10)BNC, (12-72)UTP, (6-12)Fiber	(1)AUI, (6)BNC/ (1)AUI, (1)BNC, (8)UTP/ (1)AUI, (1)BNC, (12)UTP/ (1)AUI, (24)UTP
LEDs	Link, Integrity, Partition, Power, Traffic, Stations, Collision, Polarity	Link, Integrity, Partition, Power, Traffic, Stations, Collision, Polarity	Link, Status, Traffic, Power, and Collision (collision on BNC Hub/6 only)
Polarity	Yes	Yes	INA
Bandwidth	10Mbps	10Mbps	10Mbps
Stacking	Stacks 3 high	No	INA
Form Factor	Desktop, rack	Chassis	All desktop or rack
Comments	Weight: chassis 15 pounds Repeater Modules: single=2l pounds, double=4 pounds	Chassis: 20 pounds; Modules: single=2 pounds, double=4 pounds	8.6 x 5.3 x 1.3" 4.5 pounds Hubs 8, 12, & 24- port #1 is wired for in and out (1)RJ45 connector only. Hub/12 also supports (1) RJ21
Warranty	Lifetime	Lifetime	Lifetime
Price	$1,999	Chassis=$1,099 Modules vary	(10BASE-T) $149 (100BASE-T) S895

Manufacturer	CELAN Technology	CELAN Technology	CELAN Technology
Model	EHUB-16A	EHUB-16N/ EHUB-16M/ EHUB-16i	EHUB-9A
Total Ports:	18	18	9
Port Types:	(1)AUI, (1)BNC, (16)UTP	(1)AUI, (1)BNC, (16)UTP	(1)BNC, (8)UTP
LEDs	Power, Link, Activity/Partition, Collision	Power, Link, Activity/Partition, Collision	Link, Power, Activity/ Partition

N/A—Not applicable   INA—Information not available

Table Continues →

■ Ethernet Hubs

Manufacturer	CELAN Technology	CELAN Technology	CELAN Technology
Polarity	Port-16 Switch	Port-16 Switch	Port-8 Switch
Bandwidth	10Mbps	10Mbps	10Mbps
Stacking	-N/A	Up to 4 Hubs	N/A
Form Factor	Rack	Rack	Desktop
Comments		16N—Standard 16M—SNMP 16I—Intelligent models available	
Warranty	1 year	1 year	1 year
Price	$295	16N—$520/ 16M—$699/ 16I—$1040/	$159

Manufacturer	CELAN Technology	CNET Technology Inc.	CNET Technology Inc.
Model	EHUB-8A	CN8900TPC/ CN89110TPC	CN8816TPC/ CN8020
Total Ports:	8	12	17/220
Port Types:	8 UTP	(1)BNC, (12)UTP/ (1)AUI, (12)UTP	16-RJ-45/1 BNC. (8016) 18-RJ-45/1 BNC/1 AUI (8020)
LEDs	Link, Power, Activity/ Partition	Link, Partition, Power, Traffic, Collision	Link, Partition, Power, Traffic, Collision
Polarity	Port-8 Switch	Auto-detect, auto-correct	Auto-detect, auto-correct
Bandwidth	10Mbps	10Mbps	10Mbps
Stacking	N/A	Up to 7	Up to 7
Form Factor	Desktop	Stack	Desktop, rack
Comments		Managed hub	
Warranty	1 year	5 year	5 year
Price	$149	$679/$899	$359/$599

Manufacturer	CNET Technology Inc.	CNET Technology Inc.	CNET Technology Inc.
Model	CN8810/ CN8000TPC	PowerSwitch CNSH-40/ CNSH-80	CNSH-40/CNSH—80
Total Ports:	10/12	4/8	4/8
Port Types:	(1)BNC, (10)UTP	(2)BNC, (4)UTP/ (1)AUI (1)BNC, (8)UTP	(4) UTP/(1)AUI, (1)BNC, (6)UTP
LEDs	Link, Partition, Power, Traffic, Collision	29/22	Link, Partition, Power, Traffic, Collision
Polarity	Auto-detect, auto-correct	Auto-detect, auto-correct	Auto-detect, auto-correct
Bandwidth	10Mbps	40Mbps/ 80Mbps	Full duplex 20Mbps
Stacking	Up to 7	29	Up to 7
Form Factor	Desktop, rack mount	Desktop, rack mount	Desktop, rack
Comments	Mini-hub/ concentrator	Fast wirespeed	Cut-thru tech 14.5 ms latency
Warranty	5 year	3 year	5 year
Price	$179/$299	$728/$1,398	$898/$1,798

Manufacturer	Cray Communications	Cray Communications	D-Link
Model	SH-0508/SH-0516	SH-1550/SH-1510	DE-809TC
Total Ports:	10/19	19/20	9
Port Types:	(1)BNC, (8)UTP,(1)Daisy chain/ (1)AUI, (1)BNC, (16) UTP, (1)Daisy chain	(1) BNV, (16) UTP, (1)Flex Bus IN, (1)Flex Bus Out, (1)Serial Port (1510 only)	1 BNC, 8 UTP

N/A—Not applicable   INA—Information not available

Ethernet Hubs ■

Manufacturer	Cray Communications	Cray Communications	D-Link
LEDs	Power, CPU, Network, Utilization, Link, Traffic/Status, Partition, Collision	Power, CPU, Interhub, Isolated, Terminator, SNMP, Alert, Jabber, Utilization, Collision, Link/Traffic, Partition	Link, Partition, Power, Traffic, Collision
Polarity	Auto-detect, auto-correct	Auto-detect, auto-correct	N/A
Bandwidth	10Mbps	10Mbps	10Mbps
Stacking	Up to 5 hubs	Up to 10 hubs	
Form Factor	Desktop, wall mount, 19"	Desktop, rack mount (19"), wall mount	Desktop, wall mount
Comments		Unique port-intrusion and port-eavesdropping security featured STD. SNMP Manageable. Optional AUI and Fiber ports.	9 UTP only available
Warranty	1 year	1 year	Lifetime
Price	$275/$525	$1,325/$1,715	$199

Manufacturer	D-Link	Develcon	Develcon
Model	DE-805TP	2712-02-0	2712-03-0/2724-03-00
Total Ports:	5	13	13/26
Port Types:	5 UTP	1 AUI, 12 UTP	1 AUI, 12 UTP/ 2 AUI, 24 UTP
LEDs	Link, Transit, Power	Port: Link Integrity, Partition Unit: Power, Traffic, Jabber, Collision	Port: Link Integrity, Partition Unit: Power, Traffic, Jabber, Collision
Polarity	None	Auto-detect	Auto-detect
Bandwidth	10Mbps	10Mbps	10Mbps
Stacking	N/A	Up to 20 Units, any mix of 12/24	
Form Factor	Desktop	19" rack mount with removable tabs	19" rack mount with removable tabs
Comments		SNMP Management available; optional BNC and Fiber ports. UTP port#1 has MDI/MDIX switch.	SNMP Management available; optional BNC and Fiber ports. UTP port#1 has MDI/MDIX switch.
Warranty	Lifetime	Lifetime	Lifetime
Price	$99	$1,010	$1,085/$1,635

Manufacturer	Develcon	Digi International	Digi International
Model	2724-02-00	Digi 4510//Digi 4511	Digi 4710H-8// Digi 4711H-8
Total Ports:	26	24 plus 2 Uplink slots	8
Port Types:	2 AUI, 24 UTP	(24) or (26) UTP with (2) AUI, BNC, or Fiber (ST or SMA) uplink modules	(8) UTP link ports, with optional AUI, BNC, or Fiber
LEDs	Port: Link Integrity, Partition Unit: Power, Traffic, Jabber, Collision	Link, Receive, Partition	Link/ Receive, Polarity, Partition, Power, Collision
Polarity	Auto-detect	24 ports MDI with 2 selectable MDI/MDIX uplink port modules	Auto-correct; auto-detect
Bandwidth	10Mbps	10Mbps	10Mbps
Stacking	Up to 20 Units, any mix of 12/24	Up to 10 units	Cascadable, not stackable
Form Factor	19" rack mount with removable tabs	Rack mount or desktop	Desktop and rack mount

N/A—Not applicable   INA—Information not available

Table Continues →

■ Ethernet Hubs

Manufacturer	Develcon	Digi International	Digi International
Comments	SNMP Management available; optional BNC and Fiber ports. UTP port#1 has MDI/MDIX switch.	SNMP MIB-II manageable over either IPX or IP network protocols, as well as out-of-band management application. Provides port pairing redundant links	4711H comes with Fast Manage, a graphical management tool; modular network uplink.
Warranty	Lifetime	5 year	5 year
Price	$1,560	$1,199 (4510) $1,699 [4511(mngd)]	$199// $474 (4711H)

Manufacturer	Digi International	Digi International
Model	Digi 510H//Digi 910H	Digi 4720H-4//Digi 4730H-4
Total Ports:	5/9	4
Port Types:	5 BNC// 1 BNC, 8 UTP	4 BNC (4720H); 4 Fiber (4730H); optional for 4720H
LEDs	Power, Polarity, Collision, Receiving, BNC cascade port status transmit	Link/Receive, Polarity, Partition, Power, Collision
Polarity	Auto-correct; auto detect	Auto-correct; auto-detect
Bandwidth	10Mbps	10Mbps
Stacking	Cascadable,not stackable	Cascadable, not stackable
Form Factor	Desktop, wall mount	Desktop, rack mount
Comments	Stack design; one port can be used for uplink	Optional AUI, BNC, UTP, and Fiber ports; modular network uplink
Warranty	5 year	5 year
Price	$99 (510H)//$910H (910H)	$795//$7,495 (4730H)

Manufacturer	EFA Corporation	Farallon
Model	EFA300-I	Ether 10-T Starlet/4
Total Ports:	9	5
Port Types:	8 RJ; 1 BNC	(1)BNC, (4)UTP
LEDs	Link, Collision, Power, Traffic	Power, Link/Port, Transmit/Port, Collision
Polarity	Auto-detect, auto-correct	Auto-detect, auto-correct
Bandwidth	10Mbps	10Mbps
Stacking	Up to 5 hubs	
Form Factor	Desktop	Wall or desktop mount
Comments		
Warranty	Lifetime	Lifetime
Price	$150	$119

Manufacturer	Farallon	Farallon	Fibronics
Model	Ether 10-T Starlet/10	Ether 10-T Starlet/18	FER2061
Total Ports:	10	18	16=uplink
Port Types:	(1)AUI, (1)BNC, (8)UTP	(1)AUI, (1)BNC, (16)UTP	INA
LEDs	Power, Link/Port, Transmit/Port, Collision	Power, Collision, Activity, BNC & AUI Uplink, Link/Port, Receive/Port	Per port status, and activity and global set-up
Polarity	Auto-detect, auto-correct	Auto-detect, auto-correct	Auto-detect
Bandwidth	10Mbps	10Mbps	10Mbps

N/A—Not applicable   INA—Information not available

Ethernet Hubs ■

Manufacturer	Farallon	Farallon	Fibronics
Stacking	N/A	No	Up to 5
Form Factor	Wall or desktop mount	19" rack	Desktop, rack mount
Comments		Built-in Universal Power supply	N/A
Warranty	Lifetime	Lifetime	3 year
Price	$149	$455	$1,190

Manufacturer	Hewlett-Packard	Hewlett-Packard	Hewlett-Packard
Model	AdvanceStack 10 Base-T Hub-8U	AdvanceStack 10 Base-T Hub-8E	AdvanceStack 10 Base-T Hub-12
Total Ports:	8 ports + 1 transceiver	8 RJ-45 ports, 1 BNC port, 1 Daisychain port	14 (12 ports + 1 BNC + 1 transceiver)
Port Types:	INA	INA	INA
LEDs	Power, Activity, Collision, AUI/Xcvr, per port status	Activity, Collision, per port partition status, per port link/activity	INA
Polarity	Auto-detect, auto correct	Auto-detect, auto-correct	INA
Bandwidth	10Mbps	10Mbps	10- to 100Mbps
Stacking	INA	INA	INA
Form Factor	Desktop, wall, wiring closet	Desktop, wall, wiring closet	INA
Comments	Economical, upgradeable, Ethernet hub that's designed for small standalone and branch office networks.	Entry level hub for small workgroups	Also supports FDDI & 100Mbps Ethernet LAN types
Warranty	Lifetime Limited	Lifetime Limited	Lifetime Limited
Price	$299 w/ SNMP bundle $599	$199	$849

Manufacturer	Hewlett-Packard	Hewlett-Packard	Hewlett-Packard
Model	AdvanceStack 10 Base-T Hub-16U	AdvanceStack 10 Base-T Hub-48	AdvanceStack 10 Base-T Hub-24
Total Ports:	16 ports + 1 transceiver	48	26 (24 ports + 1 BNC + 1 transceiver)
Port Types:	INA	INA	INA
LEDs	Power, Activity, Collision, AUI/Xcvr, per port status	INA	INA
Polarity	Auto-detect, auto-correct for VTP ports	INA	INA
Bandwidth	10Mbps	10- to 100Mbps	10- to 100Mbps
Stacking	INA	INA	INA
Form Factor	Rack-mountable, wall, or any horozontal surface	INA	INA
Comments	Economical choice in upgradeable hubs for small standalone and branch office networks	Also supports 100Mbps Ethernets	Also supports FDDI & 100Mbps Ethernet LAN types
Warranty	Lifetime limited	Lifetime limited	Lifetime limited
Price	$579 w/ SNMP bundle $999	$2,739	$1,459

N/A—Not applicable   INA—Information not available

Table Continues →

■ Ethernet Hubs

Manufacturer	IBM	IBM	IBM
Model	8224-001,002	8222-008	8222-016
Total Ports:	17	9	16
Port Types:	Includes redundant links between 10BASE-T port pairs via IBM MIB extensions	Eight 10BASE-T ports One BNC port.	Sixteen 10BASE-T ports. One BNC port
LEDs	Link, Partition, Management, Power, Collision	Link, Partition, Activity, Power, Collision	Link, Partition, Activity, Power, Collision
Polarity	Auto-detect, auto-correct	Auto-detect, auto-correct	Auto-detect, auto-correct
Bandwidth	10Mbps	10Mbps	10Mbps
Stacking	Up to 10 hubs	Cascading	Cascading
Form Factor	Rack mount, desktop	Desktop, wall mount	Desktop, wall mount
Comments	Model 002-SNMP management segmentation		
Warranty	1 year	1 year	1 year
Price	$895 for 001 $1,395 for 002	$299	$575

Manufacturer	Fibronics	Intellicom	Intellicom
Model	GigaHub	Quick-Net TP-406	Quick-Net TP-426/ SNMP
Total Ports:	432 ports	6	6
Port Types:	Up to (48)AUI, 96(BNC), (432)UTP, (96)Fiber	6 BNC	6 BNC
LEDs	Full information on LCD and LED	Link, Collision,	Link, Integrity, Collision
Polarity	Auto-detect	Auto-correct, auto-detect	Auto-detect, auto-correct
Bandwidth	10Mbps/100Mbps	10Mbps	10Mbps
Stacking	N/A, modular hub	Up to 4 hubs	Up to 4 hubs
Form Factor	Rack mount, 19" 9U high	Hub card	Internal hub card
Comments	The unit can be configured automatically to be a member in one of 8 segments with dual homing option. 20km over fiber optic when full duplex in use.		Windows SNMP Management
Warranty	3 year	3 year	3 year
Price	$7,290+	$225	$275

Manufacturer	Intellicom	Intellicom	Intellicom
Model	506/LE //512/LE	Quick-Net TP-426/ HMI	SP-612/B SP-612/M
Total Ports:	7 //13	6	13
Port Types:	(1)AUI, (6)UTP// (1)AUI, (12)UTP	6 UTP	1 AUI, 12 UTP
LEDs	Link, Receive, Transmit	Link, Integrity, Collision	Link, Power, Collision, Jabbering, Receive
Polarity	Auto-detect, auto-correct	Auto-detect, auto-correct	Auto-correct, (SP612/B also has Auto-detect)
Bandwidth	10Mbps	10Mbps	10Mbps
Stacking	Standalone	Up to 4	Up to 3

N/A—Not applicable   INA—Information not available

Ethernet Hubs ■

Manufacturer	Intellicom	Intellicom	Intellicom
Form Factor	Internal hub card	Internal hub card	Desktop, rack
Comments	Novell compatible	Novell Network compatible	SP612 Router Model Available; optional BNC and Fiber ports.
Warranty	3 year	3 year	3 year
Price	$139//$285	$275	$569/$899

Manufacturer	Intellicom	Intellicom	Kingston Technology Corp.
Model	SP-624/B SP-624/M	SP612/R	KNE-16TP/WG
Total Ports:	25	13	18
Port Types:	(1)AUI, (24)UTP	(1)AUI, (12)UTP	(1)AUI, (1)BNC, (16)UTP
LEDs	Link, Power, Receive, Collision, Jabbering	Link, Power, Receive, Jabbering	Bi-color LED Link, Activity, Power, Collision, Jabber Lock
Polarity	Auto-detect, auto-correct	Auto-detect, auto-correct	Auto-detect, auto-correct
Bandwidth	10Mbps	10Mbps	10Mbps
Stacking	Up to 2	Up to 2 24 ports	N/A
Form Factor	Desktop, rack	Desktop, rack	Desktop, wall mount
Comments	(624/M includes SNMP, TelNet, UT100); optional BNC and Fiber ports.	Stacks with SP612/B bars hub; optional BNC and Fiber ports.	Small form factor with rugged all steel construction and built-in crossover port
Warranty	3 year	3 year	Limited lifetime
Price	$950/$1,275	$1,495	$295

Manufacturer	Kingston Technology Co.	Kingston Technology Co.
Model	KNE-8TP/S	KNE-8TP/WG
Total Ports:	11	9
Port Types:	(1)BNC, (8)UTP, (2)Stacking ports	(1)BNC, (8)UTP
LEDs	Bi-color LED Link, Activity, Power, Collision, Jabber Lock	Bi-color LED Link, Activity, Power, Collision, Jabber Lock
Polarity	Auto-detect, auto-correct	Auto-detect, auto-correct
Bandwidth	10Mbps	10Mbps
Stacking	Up to 4	N/A
Form Factor	Desktop, wall mount	Desktop, wall mount
Comments	Small form factor with rugged all steel construction. Stackable up to 4 units for single logical 32 port repeater.	Small form factor with rugged all steel construction. Stackable up to 4 units for single logical 32 port repeater.
Warranty	Limited lifetime	Lifetime
Price	$165	$140

Manufacturer	KTI Networks	KTI Networks
Model	KH-18M	KH-9M
Total Ports:	18	9
Port Types:	(1)AUI, (1)BNC, (16)UTP	(1)AUI, (1)BNC, (8)UTP
LEDs	Link, Partition, Power, Collision	Link, Power, Partition, Collision
Polarity	Auto-detect, auto-correct	Auto-detect, auto-correct

N/A—Not applicable   INA—Information not available

Table Continues →

■ Ethernet Hubs

Manufacturer	KTI Networks	KTI Networks
Bandwidth	10Mbps	10Mbps
Stacking	N/A	N/A
Form Factor	Desktop, rack	Desktop
Comments		
Warranty	3 year	3 year
Price	$289	$129

Manufacturer	KTI Networks	KTI Networks	KTI Networks
Model	HUB-2000	KH-10M	KH-5MB
Total Ports:	18	10	5
Port Types:	(1)AUI, (1)BNC, (16)UTP	(1)AUI, (1)BNC, (8)UTP	(1)BNC, (4)UTP
LEDs	Link, Partition, Power, Collision	Link, Power, Collision	Link, Partition, Power, Collision
Polarity	Auto-detect, auto-correct	Auto-detect, auto-correct	Auto-detect, auto-correct
Bandwidth	10Mbps	10Mbps	10Mbps
Stacking	Up to 5	N/A	N/A
Form Factor	Desktop, rack	Desktop	Desktop
Comments	SNMP Manageable		
Warranty	3 year	3 year	3 year
Price	$459	$149	$909

Manufacturer	LanOptics	LanOptics
Model	StackNetPro	StarNet
Total Ports:	144	288
Port Types:	INA	INA
BNC	Ethernet (1 port), 8 port module	Ethernet (1 port), 8 port module
UTP	12,24 TR and Ethernet, (8) 3270, (8, 16) 5250	12,24 TR and Ethernet, (8) 3270, (8, 16) 5250
FIBER	Ethernet 1, 4 TR 4	Ethernet 1, 4 TR 4
Other		
LEDs	Status, collision, isolate (Ethernet), 4/16, status, isolate (Token Ring)	Status, collision, isolate (Ethernet), 4/16, status, isolate (Token Ring)
Polarity	Auto-detect, Auto-correct	Auto-detect, Auto-correct
Bandwidth	Ethernet—10Mbps Token Ring—4/16Mbps	Ethernet—10Mbps Token Ring—4/16Mbps
Stacking	Up to 6 hubs	Up to 6 hubs
Form Factor	Stackable, rack-mountable	Stackable, rack-mountable
Comments		
Warranty	3 year	3 year
Price	$800+	$2,500+

Manufacturer	Lanart	Lanart	Lanart
Model	EFM 0830/ EFM 1630	ETH nn2x	ETM nn3x
Total Ports:	9/17	9, 13, 17, or 25	18, 26, 50
Port Types:	(1)AUI, (8)Fiber/ (1)AUI, (16)Fiber	(1)AUI, (1)BNC, (8-24)UTP, (4-9) Fiber	(1)AUI, (1)BNC, (16-48)UTP, (1) Fiber

N/A—Not applicable   INA—Information not available

Ethernet Hubs ■

Manufacturer	Lanart	Lanart	Lanart
LEDs	Link, Integrity, Partition, Power, Traffic, Stations, Collision, Polarity	OK, Link Fail, Partitioned, Activity, Collisions	LED display for all
Polarity	N/A	Auto-detect, auto-correct	Auto-detect, auto-correct
Bandwidth	10Mbps	10Mbps	10Mbps
Stacking	1	Up to 30	Up to 2
Form Factor	Stackable, rack mount	Desktop, rack mount	Stackable, rack mount
Comments	SNMP Manageable	Unmanageable	SNMP Managed
Warranty	5 year	5 year	5 year
Price	$2,795+	$249	$1,295

Manufacturer	LANart	LANart
Model	EFH nn 2x	ETM 0850/ETM 1650
Total Ports:	5 or 9	9/17
Port Types:	(4)Fiber and (1)AUI, BNC, or Fiber/ (8)Fiber, and (1)AUI, BNC, or Fiber	(1)AUI, (8)UTP/(1)AUI, (16)UTP
LEDs	OK Link, Fail, Partitioned, Activity, Collisions	LED display for all
Polarity	Auto-detect, auto-correct	Auto-detect, auto-correct
Bandwidth	10Mbps	10Mbps
Stacking	Up to 30	Up to 30
Form Factor	Desktop, rack mount	Stackable, rack mount
Comments	Unmanaged	SNMP Managed
Warranty	5 year	5 year
Price	$1375+	$799 (0850) $1,199 (1650)

Manufacturer	LANcast	LANcast
Model	5000	4410/4411/4412
Total Ports:	Up to 264 Ethernet or 132 Token Ring	12
Port Types:	N/A	(1)AUI, (1)BNC, (12)UTP, (1)Fiber
LEDs	Power, Link, Activity, Partition	Power, Collision, SNMP, Link/ Activity, Partition
Polarity	Auto-detect, Auto-correct	Auto-detect, Auto-correct
Bandwidth	10Mbps/16Mbps	10Mbps
Stacking	N/A	Up to 5 hubs
Form Factor	Modular Chassis Based	Desktop, rack mount
Comments	12-slot case allows up to 11 Ethernet or Token Ring Modules to combined	Available in basic, client, and master versions
Warranty	3 year	3 year
Price	From $2,695	$1,060–$1,500

Manufacturer	LANcast	LANcast	LANcast
Model	4395	4397	4490
Total Ports:	8	16	8
Port Types:	(1)AUI, (1)BNC, (8)UTP	(1)AUI, (1)BNC, (16)UTP	1
LEDs	Power, Collision, Link/Activity, Partition	Power, Collision, Link/Activity, Partition	Power, Collision, Activity, Link, Partition
Polarity	Auto-detect, auto-correct	Auto-detect, auto-correct	Auto-detect, auto-correct

N/A—Not applicable   INA—Information not available

Table Continues →

■ Ethernet Hubs

Manufacturer	LANcast	LANcast	LANcast
Bandwidth	10Mbps	10Mbps	10Mbps
Stacking	N/A	N/A	INA
Form Factor	Desktop	Desktop	Desktop
Comments	Complete internal network management functions	Complete internal network management functions	Switch-selectable AUI/BNC for additional network interconnection
Warranty	3 year	3 year	3 year
Price	$254	$480	$165

Manufacturer	Lancast	Lancast	Landings Technology
Model	4392	4399	5 Port Hub/ 8 Port TC Hub/ 8 Port TCA Hub
Total Ports:	12	8	5/8/8
Port Types:	(2)AUI, (1)BNC, (12)UTP	8 Fiber	(5)UTP/(1)BNC, (8)UTP/ (1)AUI, (1)BNC, (8)UTP
LEDs	Power, SNMP, Collision, Activity, Partition, Link	Power, Collision, SNMP, Load/ Activity, Partition	Link, Collision, Partition, Activity, Power
Polarity	Auto-detect, auto-correct	Auto-detect, auto-correct	Auto-detect, auto-correct
Bandwidth	10Mbps	10Mbps	10Mbps
Stacking	N/A	Up to 4 hubs	N/A
Form Factor	Desktop, rack	Desktop, rack	Desktop
Comments	Management upgrade available, accommodates Cascaded bus or daisy-chain topologies	Manageable through LANWARE or any other SNMP-based software	
Warranty	3 year	3 year	Lifetime
Price	$696–$1,296	$2,517–$3,500	$95/$119/$139

Manufacturer	Landings Technology	Landings Technology	Linksys
Model	16 Port TCA Hub	16 Port TCA RM Hub	5 port Ethernet workgroup hub
Total Ports:	16	16	6
Port Types:	1 AUI, 1 BNC, 16 UTP	1 AUI, 1 BNC, 16 UTP	6 UTP
LEDs	Link, Collision, Partition, Activity, Power	Link, Collision, Partition, Activity, Power, Jabber, Uplink,	Act/RX, Link/TX, Collision, Power, Status
Polarity	Auto-detect, auto-correct	Auto-detect, auto-correct	N/A
Bandwidth	10Mbps	10Mbps	10Mbps
Stacking	N/A	N/A	Cascadeable
Form Factor	Desktop	Rack mount	Desktop
Comments	Crossover Port	Crossover Port	
Warranty	Lifetime	Lifetime	3 year
Price	$245	$295	$129

Manufacturer	Linksys	Linksys	MaxTech
Model	10 Port Ethernet Workgroup Hub	Ethernet 16 Port Workgroup Hub	HX-5
Total Ports:	10	16	6
Port Types:	(1)BNC, (9)UTP	(1)AUI, (1)BNC, (16)UTP	5 UTP, 1 Daisy Chain
LEDs	Link/TX, Power, RX/Act, Collision, BNC	Power, Jabber, Collision, Link/RX	Link, Collision, Power, Receive

N/A—Not applicable   INA—Information not available

Ethernet Hubs ■

Manufacturer	Linksys	Linksys	MaxTech
Polarity	N/A	N/A	Yes
Bandwidth	10Mbps	10Mbps	10Mbps
Stacking	Cascadable	Cascadeable	No
Form Factor	Desktop, rack	Desktop, rack	Mini-desk, wall, or top mount
Comments			Compact 5 port mini hub
Warranty	3 year	3 year	5 year
Price	$169	$499	$99

Manufacturer	Microdyne Corp	NHC	NHC
Model	Eagle MicroHub	TokenEase 10-Port Active HUB	TokenEase 8-port UTP HUB/ 16-port UTP HUB
Total Ports:	8 port/ 12 port/ 24 port	10	8/ 16
Port Types:	(8)UTP or (8)Fiber/ (12)AUI, BNC, UTP, or Fiber/ (24) AUI, BNC, UTP, or Fiber	10 UTP	8 UTP/ 16 UTP
LEDs	Link integrity, Data integrity	Link, Status, Power, Speed, Integrity	Link
Polarity	Auto partitioning	INA	INA
Bandwidth	10Mbps 10BASE-T	4 or 16M	4 or 16M
Stacking	No	INA	INA
Form Factor	Rack mount on 24 port	Rack	Desktop
Comments	N/A	Trunk, Routing, Switches, no external routing	Trunk, Routing, Switches, no external routing. Up to 550 ft. per lobe.
Warranty	3 year	5 year	5 year
Price	$160/$230/$400	$1,695	$550/$1,100

Manufacturer	NHC	NHC
Model	Twinstar III	TokenEase Stackhubble
Total Ports:	7 or 14	16
Port Types:	(7) or (14) UTP	16 UTP
LEDs	Power, Parity, Polarity, Sync	Link, Status, Power, Speed, Integrity
Polarity	INA	INA
Bandwidth	10Mbps	4 or 16M
Stacking	INA	Up to 16 hubs
Form Factor	Rack or desktop	Rack or desktop
Comments	Repeater technology AS/400	Option RS232 or SNMP Mgt repeater tech
Warranty	5 year	5 year
Price	$545 to $995	$1,895

Manufacturer	Pinacl Communications	Pinacl Communications
Model	5080 A/B/F/T	5040 S
Total Ports:	9	5
Port Types:	(1)AUI, (1)BNC, (8) or (9)UTP, (1)Fiber	(1)AUI, (4)UTP

N/A—Not applicable   INA—Information not available

Table Continues →

■ Ethernet Hubs

Manufacturer	Pinacl Communications	Pinacl Communications
LEDs	Power, Receive Activity, Link	TX, RX, Link, Power, Collision, F1Fo error, Manchester Encoder Error, and Partitions
Polarity	Auto-detect	Auto-detect
Bandwidth	10Mbps	10Mbps
Stacking	N/A	Up to 20 hubs (100 ports)
Form Factor	Desktop, bracket for wall mount	Desktop, bracket for wall mount
Comments		
Warranty	3 year	3 year
Price	$235 to $299	$160

Manufacturer	Pinacl Communications	Pinacl Communications	Pinacl Communications
Model	5016S/SF	5031 A/B/F/SNMP	5032 A/B/F/SNMP
Total Ports:	18	25	11
Port Types:	(1)AUI, (1)BNC, (16)UTP	(1)AUI, (1)BNC, (24)UTP, (1)Fiber	(1)AUI, (1)BNC, (2)UTP,(8) or (9)Fiber
LEDs	Power, Collision, Link, Partition, Data, Polarity, Enabled Port	Power, Collision, Management, Link, Partition, Data, Polarity, Enabled Port	Power, Collision, Management, Link, Partition, Data, Polarity, Port Enabled
Polarity	Auto-detect	Auto-detect, auto-correct	Auto-detect, auto-correct
Bandwidth	10Mbps	10Mbps	10Mbps
Stacking	Up to 6 Hubs (108 ports)	Up to 3 hubs (75 pounds)	Up to 3 hubs (33 ports)
Form Factor	Rackmount, desktop	Rackmount, desktop	Rackmount, desktop
Comments	Optional fiber port	Optional AUI, BNC or Fiber, Optional SNMP, Optional Integral Bridge	Optional SNMP, optional Integrated Bridge, optional AUI, BNC, or Fiber port
Warranty	3 year	3 year	3 year
Price	$499 to $699	$1,499+	$2,399

Manufacturer	Pivotal Networking	Plexcom, Inc.	Plexcom, Inc.
Model	Pivotal 1000	H8025SX	8025SX
Total Ports:	8	25	13
Port Types:	INA	(1)AUI, (1)BNC, (24)UTP, (1)Fiber, (4)Backplane	(1)AUI, (1)BNC, (12)UTP, (1)Fiber, (4)Backplane
LEDs	3/port. Link, transmit, receive	Link, RD, Partition, Enable/Disable, Collision	Link, RD, Partition, Enable/Disable, Collision
Polarity	N/A	Auto-correct	Auto-correct
Bandwidth	7x10Mbps + 1 x 20Mbps full duplex	10Mbps	10Mbps
Stacking	Standalone	1, 2 , 5, 7 per Chassis	1, 2, 4, 10, 14 per Chassis
Form Factor	6"Dx10"X1.8"H	Chassis Module	Chassis Module
Comments	Low cost, high performance, unmanaged 8-port 10BASE-T switching hub.	On Board SNMP Agent with RMON, Security and Net Fault Correction	On Board SNMP Agent with RMON, Security and Net Fault Correction
Warranty	5 year	1 year	1 year
Price	$1,095	$2,555	$1,595

N/A—Not applicable   INA—Information not available

Ethernet Hubs ■

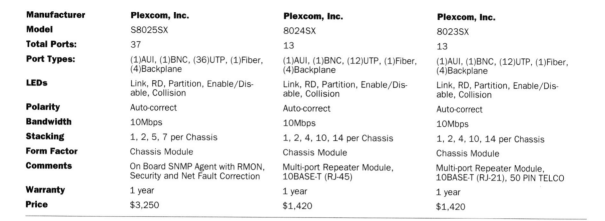

Manufacturer	Plexcom, Inc.	Plexcom, Inc.	Plexcom, Inc.
Model	S8025SX	8024SX	8023SX
Total Ports:	37	13	13
Port Types:	(1)AUI, (1)BNC, (36)UTP, (1)Fiber, (4)Backplane	(1)AUI, (1)BNC, (12)UTP, (1)Fiber, (4)Backplane	(1)AUI, (1)BNC, (12)UTP, (1)Fiber, (4)Backplane
LEDs	Link, RD, Partition, Enable/Disable, Collision	Link, RD, Partition, Enable/Disable, Collision	Link, RD, Partition, Enable/Disable, Collision
Polarity	Auto-correct	Auto-correct	Auto-correct
Bandwidth	10Mbps	10Mbps	10Mbps
Stacking	1, 2, 5, 7 per Chassis	1, 2, 4, 10, 14 per Chassis	1, 2, 4, 10, 14 per Chassis
Form Factor	Chassis Module	Chassis Module	Chassis Module
Comments	On Board SNMP Agent with RMON, Security and Net Fault Correction	Multi-port Repeater Module, 10BASE-T (RJ-45)	Multi-port Repeater Module, 10BASE-T (RJ-21), 50 PIN TELCO
Warranty	1 year	1 year	1 year
Price	$3,250	$1,420	$1,420

Manufacturer	Plexcom, Inc.	Plexcom, Inc.	Plexcom, Inc.
Model	8012SX	8026SX	PLEXSTACK 4000
Total Ports:	7	13	13, 26, 39
Port Types:	(1)AUI; (1)BNC; (1)UTP; (1, 2, 4, or 6)Fiber, (4)Backplane	(1)AUI, (12)BNC, (1)UTP, (1)Fiber, (4)Backplane	(1)AUI, (1)BNC, (12)UTP, (1)Fiber/(2)AUI, (2)BNC, (24)UTP, (2)Fiber/(3)AUI, (3)BNC, (36)UTP, (3)Fiber
LEDs	Link, RD, Partition, Enable/Disable, Collision	Link, RD, Partition, Enable/Disable, Collision	Link, RD, Partition, Enable/Disable, Collision
Polarity	N/A	Auto-correct	Auto-correct
Bandwidth	10Mbps	10Mbps	10Mbps
Stacking	1, 2, 4, 10, 14 per Chassis	1, 2, 4, 10, 14 per Chassis	Up to 8 Hubs
Form Factor	Chassis Module	Chassis Module	Rack or standalone
Comments	Multi-port Repeater Module, 10BaseFL(ST) Link redundancy	Multi-port Repeater Module, 10BASE-T (RJ-45)	On Board SNMP Agent with RMON, Security and Net Fault Correction; ASYNC Monitor Single Segment
Warranty	1 year	1 year	5 year
Price	$945–$1,800	$1,420	$800–$3,195

Manufacturer	Plexcom, Inc.	Plexcom, Inc.
Model	PLEXSTACK 4100	PLEXSTACK 4400
Total Ports:	13, 26, 39	8, 12, 16
Port Types:	(1)AUI, (1)BNC, (12)UTP, (1)Fiber/(2)AUI, (2)BNC, (24)UTP, (2)Fiber/(3)AUI, (3)BNC, (36)UTP, (3)Fiber	(1)AUI, (1)BNC, (8)UTP, (1)Fiber/(1)AUI, (1)BNC, (12)UTP, (1)Fiber/(1)AUI, (1)BNC, (16)UTP, (1)Fiber
LEDs	Link, RD, Partition, Enable/Disable, Collision	Link, RD, Partition, Enable/Disable, Collision
Polarity	Auto-correct	Auto-correct
Bandwidth	40Mbps	10Mbps
Stacking	Up to 8 Hubs	Standalone
Form Factor	Rack or standalone	Rack or standalone
Comments	On Board SNMP Agent with RMON, Security and Net Fault Correction; ASYNC Monitor Quad Segment	Multi-port repeater HUB 10BASE-T
Warranty	5 year	5 year
Price	$1,095–$3520	$299–$935

N/A—Not applicable   INA—Information not available

Table Continues →

■ Ethernet Hubs

Manufacturer	Plexcom, Inc.	Protec Microsystems	Protec Microsystems
Model	PLEXSTACK 4206	Hub-16E	Hub-8E
Total Ports:	7	18	9
Port Types:	(1)AUI, (1)BNC, (1)UTP, (7)Fiber	(1)AUI, (1)BNC, (16)UTP,	(1)BNC, (8)UTP,
LEDs	Link, RD, Partition, Enable/Disable, Collision	Link, Activity, Partition, Collision, Power	Power, Activity, Link, Partition, Collision
Polarity	Port Redundancy	Auto-detect, auto-correct	Auto-detect, auto-correct
Bandwidth	10Mbps	10Mbps	10Mbps
Stacking	Up to 8 hubs	Cascadable	Cascadable
Form Factor	Rack or standalone	Desktop, rack	Desktop
Comments	On board SNMP Agent with RMON, Security, and Net Fault Correction; ASYNC Monitor Single segment	Uplink switch to cascade unit	Uplink switch to cascade unit
Warranty	1 year	5 year	5 year
Price	$1,695–$2,395	$484	$218

Manufacturer	RAD Data Communications	Silcom Technology	Sonic Systems
Model	RADring Hub	MaxSTAC	IntelliStack 16I Base Hub
Total Ports:	Up to 80 per chassis	16	17
Port Types:	Up to 10 AUI, up to 80 BNC, up to 40 Fiber	16 UTP, 2 Fiber	(1)AUI, (1)BNC, (16)UTP
LEDs	Link, Integrity, Partition, Power, Traffic, Stations, Collision, Polarity	(4) Lobe line states: Active, Non-active, Speed, Lockout, and Mgt. Lockout. (5) Additional monitor data integrity, Line speed, RI/RO Cable integrity, and Power	Power, Activity, Collision, Base, Flash, Link, Port Activity
Polarity	Auto-detect, auto-correct	Speed lockout	Auto-detect; Auto-correct
Bandwidth	10 MB 802.3 16/4 MB 802.5	4/16Mbps Token Ring	10Mbps
Stacking	254 Devices per Segment/Ridge	Up to 16 Hubs	Stackable
Form Factor	Rack	Stackable or rackable	INA
Comments	2 Models	Combines error-recovery and fault-isolation technologies with signal retiming and regeneration on every port. SNMP optional.	Family of SNMP manageable, stackable, Ethernet Hubs which allows for a flexible and expandable network
Warranty	1 year	5 years	Lifetime
Price	$700 (Basic chassis)	$1,699	$1,299

Manufacturer	Sonic Systems	Sonic Systems	Standard Microsystems Corp.
Model	StarBase T/16, StarBase T/9, HubLite	IntelliStack 16 Expansion Hub	Elite 3812TP
Total Ports:	18/9/5	17	14
Port Types:	1 BNC	(1)AUI, (1)BNC, (16)UTP	12 UTP, 2 optional
LEDs	Link, Activity, Power, Collision	Power, Activity, Collision, Base, Link, Port Activity	Link integrity, Power, NMM, Segments, Source (traffic), Partition
Polarity	Auto-detect; auto-correct	Auto-detect; auto-correct	Automatic polarity detection and correction
Bandwidth	10Mbps	10Mbps	10Mbps
Stacking	Standalone	Stackable	Up to 8 hubs
Form Factor	Desktop	Desktop	Desktop, rack

N/A—Not applicable   INA—Information not available

Ethernet Hubs ■

Manufacturer	Sonic Systems	Sonic Systems	Standard Microsystems Corp.
Comments	Cat.3 UTP; Cat.5 UTP	Allows stacking of up to five hubs to create one logical hub with 85 ports	Manageable with optional NMM. Supports data path redundancy. Supports 2 Slide-in modules that have either a BNC, AUI, RJ-45, or Fiber ST port.
Warranty	Lifetime	Lifetime	3 year
Price	$429/$229/$149	$999	$899

Manufacturer	Standard Microsystems Corp.	Standard Microsystems Corp.	Standard Microsystems Corp.
Model	Ether EZ Hub 5T	Ether Ez Hub 16TC	Elite 3512TP
Total Ports:	5	18	14
Port Types:	5 UTP	(1)AUI, (1)BNC, (16)UTP,	1 AUI, 12 UTP, 1 AUI/BNC switchable
LEDs	Power, Utilization 40%, Collision, Link-Rx partition	Power, CPU, Utilization 70, Collision 70, Link/Traffic, Partition	Power, NMM, Collision, Link, Source/Partition.
Polarity	Auto-detect, auto-correct	Auto-detect, auto-correct	
Bandwidth	10Mbps	10Mbps	10Mbps
Stacking	INA	INA	No
Form Factor	Desktop	Desktop, rack	Desktop, rack
Comments	Ether EZ 8 port Hub model available.		Available in TELCO model with 1 AUI and 1 switchable AUI/BNC port. Manageable with optional NMM.
Warranty	Lifetime on unit, 5 years on power supply	Lifetime on unit, 5 years on power supply	3 year
Price	$125 5–port Hub/ $239 8-Port Hub	$449	$699

Manufacturer	Standard Microsystems Corp.	Standard Microsystems Corp.
Model	TigerHub TP6	TigerHub TP12
Total Ports:	7	14
Port Types:	1 AUI, 6 UTP	1 AUI, 1 BNC, 12 UTP
LEDs	Power, Collision, Link, Source, Partition	INA
Polarity	Auto-detect, auto-correct	INA
Bandwidth	10Mbps	10Mbps
Stacking	INA	INA
Form Factor	Desktop	Desktop, rack
Comments		
Warranty	3 year	3 year
Price	$225	$499

Manufacturer	Standard Microsystems Corp.	Standard Microsystems Corp.	South Hills Datacomm
Model	TigerStack 3328T	TigerStack 3312TCT	37641
Total Ports:	28	14	26
Port Types:	28 UTP	1 AUI, 1 BNC, 12 UTP, 2 Fiber	INA
LEDs	Link Integrity, Partition, Segmentation, Power, NMM, Traffic (Source), Collision	Link Integrity, Partition, Segmentation, Power, NMM, Source (Traffic), Collision	Link Integrity, Partition, Power, Traffic, Jabber, Collision
Polarity	Auto-detect, auto-correct	Auto-detect, auto-correct	Auto-detect, auto-correct

N/A—Not applicable   INA—Information not available

Table Continues →

■ Ethernet Hubs

Manufacturer	Standard Microsystems Corp.	Standard Microsystems Corp.	South Hills Datacomm
Bandwidth	10Mbps	10Mbps	10Mbps
Stacking	Up to 8 Hubs	Up to 8 hubs	Up to 20 hubs
Form Factor	Desktop, rack	Desktop, rack	Desktop, Rack
Comments	Other models available: TigerStack 3314T, 3326TC, 3306BC, 3306FC	3328Telco. Price range $699-$2169.	12 port also available
Warranty	Limited lifetime on unit, 5 years on power supply & fan	Limited lifetime on unit, 5 years on power supply & fan	2 year
Price	$1,089	$699	$1,560

Manufacturer	TrendWare	TrendWare
Model	TE-500/TE-900	TE-910, TE 1420, TE-182, TE-2620
Total Ports:	5/9	9, 14, 18, 26
Port Types:	5 UTP/9 UTP	(1)AUI, (1)BNC, (8)/(12)/(16)/ (24)UTP
LEDs	Power, Link-Receive, Collision	Power, Collision, Link/Receive, Jabber
Polarity	Auto Partition	Auto Partition
Bandwidth	10Mbps	10Mbps
Stacking	Up to 4 Hubs using UTP cable	Up to 30 Hubs in 1 segment using 10Base 2 thin coax cable
Form Factor	Desktop, wall mount (TE-900 only)	Desktop, rack mount (except TE-910). Wall mount (TE-910 only).
Comments	Port No. 1 has Up-Link function	TE-1820 and TE-2620 Port No. 1 has Up-Link function
Warranty	5 year	5 year
Price	$119–$199	$189–$499

Manufacturer	UB Networks	UB Networks	UB Networks
Model	Port Mobile Ethernet Concentrator	ASM 320/ ASM324	ASM 410// ASM 420
Total Ports:	24	12\24	10\20
Port Types:	(24) UTP	12 UTP/ 24 UTP	10 UTP/ 20 UTP
LEDs	Port status	Port status	Port status
Polarity	Auto-correct	Auto-detect, auto-correct	INA
Bandwidth	10Mbps per segment; up to 12 segments available	10Mbps	8Mbps or 16Mbps per port
Stacking	12 modules per GEOLAN/500	GEOLAN/100—11 GEOLAN/500—12	INA
Form Factor	GEOLAN/500 chassis hub module	Chassis-hub module	Integrated into GEOLAN/100 or GEOLAN/500 chassis
Comments	Allows each port to be switched; Punch Block	66-B Block	
Warranty	1 year	1 year	1 year
Price	$180 per port	$1,295 (320) $2,250 (324)	$1,150 (410) $2,795 (420)

N/A—Not applicable   INA—Information not available

Ethernet Hubs ■

Manufacturer	UNICOM	UNICOM	UNICOM
Model	Dyna-Net/4	Dyna-Net/12	Dyna-Net/8
Total Ports:	5	14	9
Port Types:	5 UTP	1 AUI, 1 BNC, 12 UTP	1 BNC, 8 UTP
LEDs	Power, Collision, UTP(4), hub port	Power, UTP(12), Coax, AUI, Reset	Power, UTP(8), Coax, Collision
Polarity	Auto-detect, auto-correct	Auto-detect, auto-correct	Auto-detect, auto-correct
Bandwidth	10Mbps	10Mbps	10Mbps
Stacking	N/A	N/A	N/A
Form Factor	Desktop	Rack	Desktop
Comments			
Warranty	5 year	5 year	5 year
Price	$114	$279	$169

Manufacturer	UNICOM	UNICOM	UNICOM
Model	Dyna-FL/4	Dyna-FL/1	Dyna-Net/16
Total Ports:	7	4	18
Port Types:	(1)AUI, (1)BNC, (1)UTP, (4)Fiber	(1)AUI, (1)BNC, (1)UTP, (1)Fiber	1 AUI, 1 BNC, 16 UTP
LEDs	Power, LMON(4), XMT(4), RCV(4), COL(4), AUI, COL, BNC, Link/RCV	Power, Collision, Link, TP RCV, JAB, AUI, BNC, LMON, XMT, RCV	Power, UTP(16), COL, AUI, Coax
Polarity	Auto-detect, auto-correct	Auto-detect, auto-correct	Auto-detect, auto-correct
Bandwidth	10Mbps	10Mbps	10Mbps
Stacking	N/A	N/A	N/A
Form Factor	Desktop	Desktop	Rack
Comments			
Warranty	5 year	5 year	5 year
Price	$899	$449	$339

Manufacturer	Whitaker Xyplex	Whitaker Xyplex	Whittaker Xyplex
Model	Network 9000/Hub	3020/3030 10Base-T Non-Managed Hubs	3130/3140 10BASE-T Managed Hubs
Total Ports:	24 Port per module	16	24
Port Types:	AUI, BNC, UTP	AUI, BNC, UTP	AUI, BNC, UTP
LEDs	Status LEDs Power system LED	Port status	Port status
Polarity	INA	INA	INA
Bandwidth	G-bps 10BASE-T	10Mbps, 10BASE-T	10Mbps
Stacking	Not stackable	Up to 30 units	Up to two hubs can be stacked
Form Factor	Chassis based with add-on modular. Rack mount	Stackable	Stackable
Comments	3, 6, or 15 slots are available. Access servers & ISDN PRI modules are optional as well as ATM.		Access Security and Eavesunp Security expansion unit is available
Warranty	3 year	3 year	3 year
Price	$3,685–$100,000	$545–$745	$1,445–$1,795

N/A—Not applicable   INA—Information not available

End ■

■ Fast Ethernet Hubs

Manufacturer	3Com Corp	Accton Technology	AccuLan
Model	Superstack II Hub 100	Fast Ethernet Hub-8s	AL-HUB12TX/ AL-HUB12T4
Ethernet Type	100BASE-TX, 100BASE-T$, 100BASE-FX	100BASE-TX	100BASE-TX (12TX) 100BASE-T (12T4)
Ports: Total	12	8	15
Port Types	TX, FX, T4=12 RJ45	8 UTP	(12)UTP, (1)UTP Fast Uplink, (2)Stacking
LEDs	INA	Power, Overall Activity, Collision, Link/ Transmit, Activity/ Receive, Partition	Link, Partition, Power, Activity, Collision
Polarity	Auto-detect, Auto-correct	Auto-detect, auto-correct	Auto-detect; auto-correct
Bandwidth	6-100Mbps	100Mbps	100Mbps
Stacking	Up to 8 units	Up to 2	Up to 5 hubs
Form Factor	Stackable desktop	Desktop or wall mount (Installation kit included)	Desktop, rack mount, wall mount
Comments		8 port, 100Mbps easy to install unit. Extra uplink port for chaining to an additional hub.	Only 0.9" high
Warranty	1 year	Lifetime	5 year
Price	$2,899	$1,595	$1,595

Manufacturer	ALFA NETCOM	ALFA NETCOM
Model	A4106 100VG-AnyLAN	A4112 100VG-AnyLAN
Ethernet Type	100VG-AnyLAN	100VG AnyLAN
Ports: Total	(7) RJ-46	(7) RJ-46
Port Types	100VGAnyLAN	100VGAnyLAN
LEDs	Uplink, Activity, Port: Link	Uplink, Activity, Port: Link
Polarity	7	13
Bandwidth	100Mbps	100Mbps
Stacking	No	No
Form Factor	Desktop	Desktop
Comments	Plug and play workgroup solution	Plug and play workgroup solution
Warranty	3 year	3 year
Price	$645	$1,095

Manufacturer	ALFA NETCOM	Asante' Technologies	Asante' Technologies
Model	A5112 Fast Ethernet	Asante' Plug and Play 100TX	Fast 100TX Hub/ Fast 100 TX/FX Hub
Ethernet Type	100BASE-TX	100BASE-TX	100BASE-TX
Ports: Total	12	6 and 12	8 or 12
Port Types:	(12) RJ-45	Hub 6=6 100BASE-TX RJ45/ Hub 12=12 100BASE-TX RJ45 ports	TX/Hub=12 100BASE-TX RJ45/ TX/FX Hub=8 100BASE-TX RJ45 ports. TX/FX Hub=1 Both hubs: 1 configurable as a 100BASE-TX uplink port
LEDs	Port: Link, Partition, Collision	LEDS indicating Link, Integrity per port, Partition per port, Power, Collision	LEDS indicating Link, Integrity per port, Partition per port, Power, Collision

N/A—Not applicable   INA—Information not available

Fast Ethernet Hubs ■

Manufacturer	**ALFA NETCOM**	**Asante' Technologies**	**Asante' Technologies**
Polarity	MDI-X	Auto-detect	Auto-correct; auto-correct
Bandwidth	100Mbps	100Mbps	100Mbps
Stacking	Yes	Stacks	Stacks 15 high
Form Factor	Desktop	Desktop, Rack	Desktop, Rack
Comments	Plug and play workgroup solution	Weigh 6 pounds	Weigh 6 pounds
Warranty	3 year	Lifetime	Lifetime
Price	$1,645	$1,095(Hub/6)/ $1,775	$1,995

Manufacturer	**BASS MICRO**	**BASS Micro**	**Bay Networks, Inc.**
Model	807-60	807-29	100BASE-T Stackable Hub
Ethernet Type	100BASE-TX	100BASE-TX	100BASE-TX; 100BASE- FX
Ports: Total	13	8	12—24 RJ-45 100BASE-TX 1—100BASE-FX
Port Types	12 RJ-45 ports for 100BASE-TX & 1 uplink port for easy hub to hub cascading	8 RJ-45 ports for 100BASE-TX & 1 uplink port for easy hub to hub cascading	12—24 RJ-45 100BASE-TX ports; 1 SC-type multimode fiber connector
LEDs	1 LED for Collision 2 LEDS/Port for Receive and Link	Power, Collision, Partition, RX, Link, Traffic	Port, media adapter, collision, data utilization, link status, redundant power status, expansion slot status
Polarity	Auto-correct; auto-detect	Auto-correct; auto-detect	Auto-detect, auto-correct
Bandwidth	100Mbps	100Mbps	100Mbps
Stacking	Up to 4 hubs	N/A	Up to 6 hubs–total 144 ports
Form Factor	Desktop, 19" EIA enclosure	Desktop, 19" EIA enclosure	Desktop, rack
Comments			Each 100Base-T Hub features 12 RJ-45 ports, 12 additional ports can be added through expansion slots
Warranty	3 year	3 year	1 year
Price	$995	$550	$2,375 and up

Manufacturer	**Cabletron Systems**	**Cabletron Systems**	**Canary**
Model	Workgroups SmartSwitch (7C04-R)	SmartSwitch 10/100	CFX-1422
Ethernet Type	100BASE-TX or FX	100BASE-TX or FX	INA
Ports: Total	30	16 (14 10 Mbps ports, 2 100Mbps ports)	13
Port Types	RJ-45, SC, Multi-mode fiber, single-mode fiber, TP, 10BASE-T, 100BASE-FX	RJ-45, SC, Multi-mode fiber, single-mode fiber, TP, 10BASE-T, 100BASE-FX	1 BNC, 12 Fiber
LEDs	Operational speed, port activity, status	Operational speed, port activity, status	Power, Collision, Link, Activity, Partition
Polarity	Auto-detect, auto-correct	Auto-detect, auto-correct	Auto-detect; auto-correct
Bandwith	10-100Mbps	10-100Mbps	100Mbps
Stacking	INA	INA	Up to 5 Hubs
Form Factor	Rack	Desktop	Rack mount
Comments	Embedded virtual routing, broadcast storm protection	Embedded virtual routing, broadcast storm protection	
Warranty	90 days	90 days	2 year
Price	$48,500	$7,995	$5,499

N/A—Not applicable   INA—Information not available

Table Continues →

■ Fast Ethernet Hubs

Manufacturer	Canary	Canary
Model	CTX-1421	CTX-1440
Ethernet Type	100BASE-T4	100BASE-T4
Ports: Total	13	12
Port Types	1 UTP, 12 FX/SC	12 UTP
LEDs	Power, Link, Collision, Activity, Partition	Power, Collision, Link, Partition, Activity
Polarity	Auto-detect, auto-correct	Auto-detect, auto-correct
Bandwidth	100Mbps	100Mbps
Stacking	Up to 5 hubs	Up to 5 hubs
Form Factor	Rack mount	Rack mount
Comments	Available	
Warranty	2 year	2 year
Price	$5,499	$1,649

Manufacturer	Canary	Canary	Canary
Model	CTX-1441	CT4-1482/ CT4-1483	CT4-1480
Ethernet Type	100BASE-TX	100BASE-T4	100BASE-T4
Ports: Total	13	13	12
Port Types	12 UTP, 1 FX/SC	1 (1483) UTP, 1 (1482) FX/ST, 12 T4	12 T4
LEDs	Power, Collision, Link, Partition, Activity	Power, Collision, Link, Activity, Partition	Power, Collision, Partition, Link, Activity
Polarity	Auto-detect, auto-correct	Auto-detect, auto-correct	Auto-detect, auto-correct
Bandwidth	100Mbps	100Mbps	100Mbps
Stacking	Up to 5 hubs	Up to 5 hubs	Up to 5 hubs
Form Factor	Rack mount	Rack mount	Rack mount
Comments		Available	Available
Warranty	2 year	2 year	2 year
Price	$1,649	$1,899(1482)/$1,789	$1,649

Manufacturer	Canary	CELAN Technology	CNet Technology
Model	CT4-1481	EHUB-100/ EHUB-100plus	CNFh-1200
Ethernet Type	100BASE-TX	100BASE-TX	100BASE-TX
Ports: Total	13	8	12
Port Types	1 FX/SC, 12 T4	8 100BASE-TX	12 UTP
LEDs	Power, Collision, Partition, Link, Activity	Link, Activity, Power	Link, Integrity, Partition, Power, Collision, Receive
Polarity	Auto-detect, auto-correct	INA	Auto-detect, auto-correct
Bandwidth	100Mbps	100Mbps	100Mbps
Stacking	Up to 5 hubs	EHUB-100plus capable up to 3 hubs	Up to 2
Form Factor	Rack mount	Rack mount	Rack mount
Comments	Available		
Warranty	2 year	1 year	Lifetime
Price	$1,649	$1,275/$1,575	$1,788

N/A—Not applicable   INA—Information not available

Fast Ethernet Hubs ■

Manufacturer	CNet Technology Inc.	CNet Technology Inc.	Fibronics
Model	PowerSwitch CNSH-1080/ CNSH-1080i	PowerSwitch CNSH-600/CNSH-600i	GigaHub
Ports: Total	8	6	432 ports
Port Types	1 AUI, 8 UTP, 1 SNMP (1080I)	1 AUI, 6 UTP, 1 SNMP (600I only)	Up to 48 AUI, up to 96 BNC, up to 432 UTP, up to 96 Fiber, singlemode fiberoptic
LEDs	25/26	19/20	Full information on LCD and LED
Polarity	Auto-detect, auto-correct	Auto-detect, auto-correct	Auto-detect
Bandwidth	260Mbps	600Mbps	10Mbps/100Mbps
Stacking	29	29	N/A, modular hub
Form Factor	Rack	Rack	Rack mount, 19" 9U high
Comments	Store and forward		The unit can be configured automatically to be a member in one of 8 segments with dual homing option. 20km over fiber optic when full duplex in use.
Warranty	3 year	3 year	3 year
Price	$2,688/$2,888	$3,688/$3,888	$7,290+

Manufacturer	Hewlett-Packard	Hewlett-Packard	Hewlett-Packard
Model	AdanceStack 100VG Hub-7m	AdvanceStack Hub-7E	AdvanceStack 100VG Hub-14
Ethernet Type	100VG	100VG-AnyLAN	100VG-AnyLAN
Ports: Total	7	6	14
Port Types	5 UTP,2 RJ45	6 UTP	INA
LEDs	Power, Fault, expansion slot, console, security, transceiver slot, activity, uplink, cascade, bride, and perport status	Power, Activity, Collision	Power, Fault, Expansion slot, Console, Security, Transceiver slot, activity, uplink, cascade, bride, and per port status
Polarity	INA	INA	INA
Bandwith	100Mbps	100Mbps	10-100Mbps
Stacking	INA	INA	INA
Form Factor	INA	INA	INA
Comments	Also supports Token Ring	Cost effective, high-speed solution for small standalone workgroups running Ethernet or Token-Ring	Also supports Token-Ring and Ethernet
Warranty	5 year on-site	Lifetime limited	Lifetime limited
Price	$2,100	$999	$2,159

Manufacturer	IBM	IBM	Intel Corporation
Model	8223	8225: 001,002,003	Express Stackable Hub
Ethernet Type	INA	INA	100BASE–TX
Ports: Total	8	12	12
Port Types	8 UTP	12 UTP. One feature port: 100 fiber, 10/100 switch	12 UTP
LEDs	Link, Partition, Utilization %. Collision %, Power	Link, Partition, Power, Collision rate, Utilization rate, filtering rate, forwarding rare	Utilization, link, activity, managed, partitioned, power
Polarity	Auto-detect, Auto-correct	Auto-detect, auto-correct	INA
Bandwith	100Mbps	100Mbps	100Mbps

N/A—Not applicable   INA—Information not available

Table Continues →

■ Fast Ethernet Hubs

Manufacturer	IBM	IBM	Intel Corporation
Stacking	INA	Up to 6 hubs	6-high
Form Factor	Desktop, wall mount	Rack mount, desktop	INA
Comments		001–unmanaged; 002–SNMP Mgmt. 003–SNMP & RMON	205 meter network diameter. Switchless. Class 1
Warranty	1 year	1 year	1 year
Price	$1,595	001—$2,895 002—$3,995 003—$4,495	$2,395

Manufacturer	LANcast	Linksys
Model	6490	Enterprise Etherfast 100BASE-TX Hub
Ethernet Type	100BASE–TX	100BASE–TX
Ports: Total	8	13
Port Types	8 UTP	13 UTP
LEDs	Link/Activity, Partition, Collision, Power	Link, RX, Activity, Power, Collision
Polarity	Auto-detect, auto-correct	N/A
Bandwidth	100Mbps	100Mbps
Stacking	Up to 9 hubs	N/A
Form Factor	Desktop, rack	Desktop, rack
Comments	Continuous monitoring of each port	
Warranty	3 year	3 year
Price	$1,450	$1,799

Manufacturer	MaxTech	Microdyne Corp	Network Peripherals
Model	FHX-8100	Eagle Century Hub	NuHub FE-5108
Ethernet Type	100BASE–TX	100BASE–TX	100BASE–TX
Ports: Total	8	6 port 12 port	8
Port Types	8 UTP, 1 Daisy chain port	6 and 12 Fiber, uplink available	8 UTP
LEDs	Link/ Traffic, Partition Collision Power, Utilization, Collision tracking	26 leds indicating Link Integrity, Power, Partition, Collision	Power, Link, RX, Partition, Collision
Polarity	Auto-detect, auto-correct	Nway Auto-integration	Auto-correct; auto-detect
Bandwidth	100Mbps	100Mbps (100BASE-TX)	100Mbps
Stacking	Up to 6 units	Available on 12-port	No limit using FE-200TT Product
Form Factor	Desktop	Rack mount	Rack/tabletop
Comments		Management module available	
Warranty	5 year	1 year	1 year
Price	$1,399	6 port=$1,139 12 port=$1,749	$1,195

Manufacturer	PLEXCOM, Inc.	Ragula Systems	Ragula Systems
Model	PLEXSTACK 4600	Workgroup Hub	Mini Hub
Ethernet Type	100BASE–TX	100BASEVG–Anylan	100BASEVG–Anylan
Ports: Total	8, 12	22+2 uplink	6+1 uplink
Port Types	8,12 100BASETX UTP, Cascade	24 UTP	7 UTP

N/A—Not applicable　INA—Information not available

Fast Ethernet Hubs ■

Manufacturer	PLEXCOM, Inc.	Ragula Systems	Ragula Systems
LEDs	Link, RD, Partition, Collision	Link, Fault, Activity Power	Link, Polarity, Power, Fault
Polarity	Auto-correct	Auto-correct; auto-detect	Auto-correct; auto-detect
Bandwidth	100Mbps	100Mbps	100Mbps
Stacking	Up to 2 Hubs	Cascade down three levels. Up to 1024 nodes.	Cascade down three levels. Up to 1024 nodes.
Form Factor	Rack or standalone	Rack	Desktop
Comments	Multi-port repeater 100BaseTX		
Warranty	1 year	5 year	5 year
Price	$800-$3,195	$2,869	$995

Manufacturer	Ragula Systems	Standard Microsystems Corp.	Syskonnect, Inc.
Model	Multimedia Hub	Tiger-Hub 100 5108TX/ Tiger-Hub 100 5116TX	SnapHub 8020
Ethernet Type	100VG–Anylan	100BASE-TX	100BASE–TX
Ports: Total	10 + 1 Uplink	8/16	12
Port Types	11 UTP	8/16 UTP	12 UTP
LEDs	Link, Fault, Activity, Power	Power, Collision, Link, Integrity/Receive, Disabled	Power on, Collision, Link, Receive, Partition
Polarity	Auto-correct; auto-detect	INA	N/A
Bandwidth	100Mbps	100Mbps	100Mbps
Stacking	Cascade down three levels. Up to 1024 nodes.	INA	Up to 5
Form Factor	Rack	Desktop	Desktop, rack
Comments			
Warranty	5 year	3 year	2 year
Price	$1,550	$1,595	$1,695

Manufacturer	TrendWare	TrendWare
Model	TE100-H8+/ TE100-H12+	TE-100/H12
Ethernet Type	100BASE–TX	100BASE–TX
Ports: Total	8/12	12
Port Types	8/12 UTP	12 (UTP/STP) Fast Ethernet
LEDs	Power, Collision, Link, and Partition	Power, Collision, Link, and Partition.
Polarity	Auto-partition	Auto-partition
Bandwidth	100Mbps	100Mbps
Stacking	Up to 5 Hubs	Up to 2 Hubs
Form Factor	Desktop, rack	Desktop, rack
Comments		Dual cooling fans
Warranty	5 year	5 year
Price	$1,499–$1,999	$1,999

N/A—Not applicable   INA—Information not available

End ■

■ Other Hubs

Manufacturer	3Com	3Com	Addtron
Model	Oncore Integrated System	LinkBuilder FDDI hub	MAU1
Hardware Protocol	The system's three backplanes support shared and switched Ethernet, Token Ring, FDDI shared and switchecd interfaces, ATM cell switching, integration of LAN/WAN, routing services and dial-in LAN access. Ethernet (shared, switched)	FDDI	MAU
Total Ports:	INA	24	10
Port Types:	9 AUI; 9 BNC; 10 fiber; 36 Telco connect	8 UTP; 4 fiber; 6 STP; 2 SC + 5 port UTP	8 AMP Data Connector
LEDs	Power supplies; per port/connection	Status Ledsnext to ports	N/A
Polarity	Auto-sensing	Auto-detect, auto-correct	INA
Bandwidth	11 Gigabits	10-100Mbps	INA
Stacking	7, 10, and 17-slot hub chassis models	INA	INA
Form Factor	Modular design hubs for core (data center) or edge (work group)	Desktop	INA
Comments	Power management; fault tolerant; no single point of failure; investment protection. All Oncore hub slots are available for "payload"		
Warranty	1 year; extended available	1 year	1 year
Price	Starting at $3,995	Starting at $9,495	INA

Manufacturer	ALFA NETCOM	ALFA NETCOM	ALFA NETCOM
Model	A2000	A2002	A2012
Hardware Protocol	FDDI	FDDI	FDDI
Total Ports:	8	8	8
Port Types:	(8) MIC, RS-232	(8) RJ-45, RS-232	(2) MIC, (6) RJ-45, RS-232
LEDs	Port, Ring, OP, Wrap A, Wrap B	Port, Ring, OP, Wrap A, Wrap B	Port, Ring, OP, Wrap A, Wrap B
Polarity	INA	INA	INA
Bandwith	100Mbps	100Mbps	100Mbps
Stacking	INA	INA	INA
Form Factor	Rack/desktop	Rack/desktop	Rack/desktop
Comments	Plug and Play workgroup solutions	Plug and Play workgroup solutions	Plug and Play workgroup solutions
Warranty	3 year	3 year	3 year
Price	$6,000	$4,500	$5,000

Manufacturer	ALFA NETCOM	ATTO Technology	D-Link
Model	A2012	ATTO TechnologyAccelNet	DE-812TP+
Hardware Protocol	FDDI	SCSI	Multiprocessor Hubs/ UnMngd
Total Ports:	8	4	14 (12 port unmanaged hub)
Port Types:	(2) MIC, (6) RJ-45, RS-232	4 SCSI	1 AUI, 1 BNC, 12 UTP
LEDs	Port, Ring, OP, Wrap A, Wrap B	Fault, online, Activity	Link, Integrity, Partition, Traffic, Stations, Collision, Polarity
Polarity	INA	INA	INA

N/A—Not applicable   INA—Information not available

Other Hubs ■

Manufacturer	**ALFA NETCOM**	**ATTO Technology**	**D-Link**
Bandwidth	100Mbps	160Mbps	INA
Stacking	INA	Up to 4 hubs	INA
Form Factor	Rack/desktop	Desktop, 5-1/4 19" rack	Desktop, rack
Comments	Plug and Play workgroup solutions	Delivers sustained data transfer rates up to 20Mbps; up to 20 times faster than Ethernet	INA
Warranty	3 year	1 year	Lifetime
Price	$5,000	2 port—$9,999 3 port—$10,899 4 port—$11,799	$385

Manufacturer	**D-Link**	**D-Link**	**Farallon**
Model	DE-816TP/ DE-824TP	DE-2200L 12-port HubU/ bridge-built	PhoneNET Star Controller/12
Hardware Protocol	Multiprocessor Hubs/UnMngd	Multiprocessor Hubs/UnMngd	LocalTalk
Total Ports:	18/26	15	12
Port Types:	1 AUI, 1 BNC, 16 UTP/ 1 AUI, 1 BNC, 24 UTP	1 AUI, 1 BNC, 12 UTP,1 RS-232	12 UTP
LEDs	Link, Integrity, Partition, Traffic, Stations, Collision, Polarity	Link, Integrity, Partition, Traffic, Stations, Collision, Polarity, and Utilization	Power, Signal fragments, Port jamming, Management bus-traffic, Selfdiagnostics, Master/Slave configuration
Polarity	INA	INA	LocaTalk is not polarity sensitive.
Bandwidth	INA	INA	1Mbps
Stacking	INA	Up to 5	Rack mount
Form Factor	Desktop, rack	Desktop, rack	Desktop, rack
Comments	INA	Built-in local bridge	
Warranty	Lifetime	1 year	1 year
Price	$479/$625	$1,695	$995

Manufacturer	**Farallon**	**Fibronics**	**Gandalf Canada Ltd.**
Model	PhoneNET StarController/24	GigaHub	Xpress Stack
Hardware Protocol	LocalTalk	Multiprocessor Hubs/UnMngd	ISDN
Total Ports:	24	432 Ethernet; 144 Token Ring ; 120 Switches; 108 FDDI	Up to 8
Port Types:	24 UTP	4 AUI, 8 BNC, 12-36 UTP, 8-12 Fiber, Singlemode	1 AUI, 8 ISDN BR I, 1 ISDN PR I
LEDs	Power, Signal fragments, Port jamming, Management bus-traffic, Selfdiagnostics, Master/Slave configuration	Link, Collision, Fault, Wrap, Receive transmit	Run, Fault, Carrier, LAN, Collision, Power
Polarity	LocaTalk is not polarity sensitive.	Auto-detect	Auto-correct
Bandwidth	1Mbps	12Gbps Aggregate	Up to 100Mbps
Stacking	Rack mount	Modular	Configuration dependent
Form Factor	Desktop, rack	Rack	Desktop
Comments		XH150 12slots XH152 4 slots	BRI or PRI models available
Warranty	1 year	2 year	1 year
Price	$1,595	Starts at $3,590	$6,995

N/A—Not applicable   INA—Information not available

Table Continues →

■ Other Hubs

Manufacturer	Gandalf Canada Ltd.	Gandalf Canada Ltd.	IBM
Model	Xpressway	Xpress Stack	8230–3/13/213
Hardware Protocol	Multiprocessor Hubs/UnMngd	ISDN	Token Ring
Total Ports:	Up to 143	Up to 8	2–92 ports
Port Types:	Up to 11 AUI, 132 BNC, 132 UTP, 66 Fiber	1 AUI, 8 ISDN BR I, 1 ISDN PR I	2–92RJ–45 ports; fiber RI/RO; UTP cat 3,4,5 STP
LEDs	Run, Fault, Carrier, LAN, Collision, Power	Run, Fault, Carrier, LAN, Collision, Power	Power, wrap state, 8230 status, insertion state, plus 2 char. LCD diagnostic
Polarity	Auto-correct	Auto-correct	Auto speed detect
Bandwith	Up to 100Mbps	Up to 100Mbps	4-16Mbps
Stacking	N/A	Configuration dependent	INA
Form Factor	Modular	Desktop	Stackable rack
Comments	Up to 74 other ports	BRI or PRI models available	PLL, fault tolerant, Intelligent SNMP & CMOL management
Warranty	1 year	1 year	1 year
Price	Starts at $15,900	$6,995	$2,630–$3,500

Manufacturer	IBM	IBM	IBM
Model	8230-04	8238	8226-001
Hardware Protocol	Token Ring	Token Ring	Token Ring
Total Ports:	16 ports	16-128	8-RJ-45
Port Types:	Fiber RI/RO; UTP cat 3,4,5 STP	16-128 RJ-45ports; fiber RI-RO modules; RS-232 (mgmt)	8 UTP
LEDs	Power, wrap state, 8230 status, insertion state, plus 2 char. LCD diagnostic	INA	Active (8)
Polarity	Auto speed detect	INA	INA
Bandwith	4-16Mbps	4-16Mbps	4-16Mbps
Stacking	INA	Up to 8 hubs. Desktop, rack	Desktop
Form Factor	Stackable rack	8-stackable, active, passive management units-hot swap fault tolerant	INA
Comments	PLL, fault tolerant, Intelligent SNMP & CMOL management		
Warranty	1 year	1 year	1 year
Price	$2,695–$2,995	$1,885–$5,665	$545

Manufacturer	IBM	IBM	KTI Networks
Model	8228-001	8228-001	DP 1012
Hardware Protocol	Token Ring	Token Ring	100 VG Any LAN
Total Ports:	8-RJ-45	8-ICS	12
Port Types:	8 UTP	8 UTP	12 UTP
LEDs	Active (8)	INA	Power, Traffic, Cascading, Training, Security Violation
Polarity	INA	INA	INA
Bandwith	4-16Mbps	4-16Mbps	100Mbps
Stacking	INA	Up to 32 via RI/RO	INA
Form Factor	Desktop	Desktop, rack	Desktop, rack

N/A—Not applicable   INA—Information not available

Other Hubs ■

Manufacturer	IBM	IBM	KTI Networks
Comments			100 VG Any LAN
Warranty	1 year	1 year	2 year
Price	$545	$545	$1,699

Manufacturer	Madge Networks	Madge Networks	NHC
Model	Smart CAU Smart CAM	Smart RAM	TokenEase 10-port Active hub
Hardware Protocol	MAU	MAU	Token Ring
Total Ports:	20-80	20	10
Port Types:	20-80 UTP, STP 20-80	20 UTP, STP 20	10 UTP
LEDs	Power, LCD, 4/16Mbps Fault, Disabled} per node	Power, LCD, 4/16Mbps Fault, Disabled} per node	Link, Status, Power, Speed, Integrity
Polarity	Auto-Speed Detection	Auto-Speed Detection	INA
Bandwidth	4/16Mbps	4/16Mbps	4 or 16Mbps
Stacking	Up to 4 CAMS per CAU (or MAU)	Up to 4 CAMS (for 60 nodes)	INA
Form Factor	Rack	Rack	Rack
Comments	Replacement for IBM CAU		Trunk, Routing, Switches, no external routing
Warranty	1 year	1 year	5 year
Price	$2,995 (single)	$3,700 (single)	$1,695

Manufacturer	NHC	NHC	NHC
Model	Twinstar III	Eagle Microhub	TokenEase 8-port UTP hub/16-port UTP hub
Hardware Protocol	Token Ring	Token Ring	Token Ring
Total Ports:	7 or 14	8 port/12 port/24 port	8/16
Port Types:	(7) or (14) UTP	8 UTP or 8 fiber; 12 AUI, BNC, UTP, or fiber; 24 AUI, BNC, UTP, or fiber	8UTP/16UTP
LEDs	Power, Parity, Polarity, Sync	Link integrity, Data integrity	Link, Status, Power, Speed, Integrity
Polarity	INA	Auto-partitioning	INA
Bandwidth	10Mbps	10Mbps, 10BASE-T	4 or 16Mbps
Stacking	INA	INA	INA
Form Factor	Rack or desktop	Rack mount on 24 port	Desktop
Comments	Repeater technology AS/400		Trunk, routing, switches, no external routing. Up to 550 ft. per lobe
Warranty	5 year	3 year	5 year
Price	$545–$995	$160/$230/$400	$550/$1,100

Manufacturer	NHC	Performance Technologies	Performance Technologies
Model	TokenEase Stackhubble	PT-UME610-10533	PT-UME610-10534
Hardware Protocol	Token Ring	FDDI	FDDI
Total Ports:	16	4	4
Port Types:	16 UTP	4 FDDI MIC	4 Port "ST" Connectors
LEDs	Link, Status, Speed, Power, Integrity	Master, Power, Fault, Integrity	Master, Power, Fault, Integrity

N/A—Not applicable   INA—Information not available

Table Continues →

■ Other Hubs

Manufacturer	NHC	Performance Technologies	Performance Technologies
Polarity	INA	N/A	N/A
Bandwidth	4 or 16 hubs	100Mbps	100Mbps
Stacking	Up to 16 hubs	Up to 5 connectors, 20 ports total	Up to 5 connectors, 20 ports total
Form Factor	Rack or desktop	VME-6U	VME-6U
Comments	Option RS232 or SNMP Mgt. Repeater tech	Comes with single or dual attach topologies	Supports triple fault tolerant alternative path FDDI
Warranty	5 year	1 year	1 year
Price	$1,895	$4,695	$4,695

Manufacturer	Performance Technologies	Plexcom, Inc.	Plexcom Inc.
Model	PT-UME610-10536	8035SX TOKEN RING ACTIVE MAU	8035SX-M TOKEN RING ACTIVE MAU
Hardware Protocol	FDDI	MAU	MAU
Total Ports:	4	14	14
Port Types:	4 FDDI UTP Connectors	(12) LOBE + RI + RO, (1)Fiber, (4) BACKPLANE ACTIVE RETIMING	(12) LOBE + RI + RO, (1)Fiber, (4) BACKPLANE ACTIVE RETIMING
LEDs	Master, Power, Fault, Integrity	Inserted, Enabled, Disabled, Beacon, Speed verification	Inserted, Enabled, Disabled, Beacon, Speed verification
Polarity	N/A	Auto-Polarity	Auto-Polarity, Counter rotating
Bandwidth	100Mbps	4- or 16Mbps	4- or 16Mbps
Stacking	Up to 5 connectors, 20 ports total	1,2,4,10,14 per chassis	1,2,4,10,14 per chassis
Form Factor	6U-VME	Chassis module	Chassis module
Comments	Works with single or dual attach topologies. Supports triple fault tolerant alternative path FDDI.	Anti-beacon protection, speed authentication, counter rotation	SNMP agent with RMON, anti-beacon protection, speed authentication
Warranty	1 year	1 year	1 year
Price	$2,895	$1,510	$2,600

Manufacturer	Plexcom Inc.	Plexcom, Inc.	Plexcom Inc.
Model	P8035SX W/PP500 TOKEN RING ACTIVE MAU	8034, Token Ring Passive Mau	832S, XFiber Optic TR Mau
Hardware Protocol	MAU	MAU	MAU
Total Ports:	14	14	8
Port Types:	(12) LOBE + RI + RO, (1)Fiber, ACTIVE RETIMING, PASSIVE NO POWER	12 Lobe, Ring In + Ring Out	2 RJ-45, RI + RO; 1,2,4,6,802.5J (ST); 4 Backplane Active Retiming
LEDs	Inserted, Enabled, Disabled, Beacon, Speed verification	Inserted, Enabled, Disabled	Inserted, Enabled, Disabled, Beacon, Speed verification
Polarity	Auto-Polarity	Auto-Polarity	Auto-Polarity, Counter rotating
Bandwidth	4- or 16Mbps	4- or 16Mbps	4- or 16Mbps
Stacking	1,2,4,10,14 per chassis	1,2,4,10,14 per chassis	1,2,4,10,14 per chassis
Form Factor	Chassis module	Chassis module	Chassis module
Comments	Anti-beacon protection, speed authentication, passive back-up	RJ-45 Ports, Counter rotating	802.5J NIC, 802.5J MAU, Fiber Optic RI + RO, Counter rotating
Warranty	1 year	1 year	1 year
Price	$2,105	$945	$945–$1,660

N/A—Not applicable   INA—Information not available

Other Hubs ■

Manufacturer	RAD DATA Communications	RAD DATA Communications	RAD DATA Communications
Model	FDX-100 FDDI/Ethernet Hub	S-TAU Smart Trunk Access Unit	F-TAU Fiber Trunk Access Unit
Hardware Protocol	Multiprocessor Hubs/UnMngd	MAU	MAU
Total Ports:	20	10	10
Port Types:	4 UTP, 20 Fiber FDDI—inclu. MIC STL, STM, 1 STP, STS 2 STP, UTP—A FDDI to Ethernet switch module is available.	8 Lobe, Z/RI/RO, RI/RO 2, Copper repeaters, Fiber repeaters	8 Lobe, RI/RO 2, UTP/IDC, Copper repeaters, Fiber repeaters
LEDs	70	Link Integrity & Power for repeater & Fault modules	Link Integrity & Power for repeater & Fault modules
Polarity	N/A	Auto-detect	Auto-detect
Bandwidth	100MB/200MB	16/4Mbps	16/4Mbps
Stacking	20	254 devices per ring	254 devices per ring
Form Factor	Desktop, rack	Rack	Rack
Comments		3 models	4 models
Warranty	1 year	1 year	1 year
Price	Starts at $1,100	Basic model $450	Basic model $3,200

Manufacturer	RNS	RNS	RNS
Model	NetExpander NX-6+2	NetExpander NX-8F	NetExpander NX-8UTP
Total Ports:	8	8	8
Port Types:	6 UTP, 2 Ffiber	8 Ffiber, 1 DIN, 1RS-232C	8 UTP, 1 DIN, 1RS-232C
LEDs	Link, Power	Power, Link- 1.8	Power, Link- 1.-8
Polarity	N/A	N/A	N/A
Bandwidth	100Mbps FDDI	100Mbps FDDI	100Mbps FDDI
Stacking	Up to 5 hubs	Up to 5 hubs	UP to 5 hubs
Form Factor	Desktop, 19" rack	Desktop, 19" rack	Desktop, 19" rack
Comments	SNMP MIBII, SMT 7.3	SNMP MIBII, SMT 7.3	SNMP MIBII, SMT 7.3
Warranty	1 year	1 year	1 year
Price	$5,515	$7,875	$4,725

Manufacturer	Silcom Technology	Silcom Technology	Standard Microsystems Corp.
Model	MaxSTAC	MaxMAU-U MaxMAU-S	Elite Stack 4016 RC (token ring MAU)
Hardware Protocol	Token Ring	MAU	MAU
Total Ports:	16	8	16
Port Types:	16 UTP, 2 fiber	8+ RI/RO	16 UTP
LEDs	(4) lobe line states: active, non-active, speed, lockout, and mgt. Lockout. (5) additional monitor data integrity, line speed, RI/RO cable integrity and power	Port status, Reset confirmation	Power, RMM, RI, RO, OBM>Transmit & Receive, Inserted/Locked
Polarity	Speed lockout	N/A	INA
Bandwidth	4/16Mbps Token Ring	4/16Mbps Token Ring	4/16Mbps
Stacking	Up to 16 hubs	N/A	Up to 8 MAU's
Form Factor	Stackable or rackable	Rackable/wall mount	Desktop, rack

N/A—Not applicable   INA—Information not available

Table Continues →

■ Other Hubs

Manufacturer	Silcom Technology	Silcom Technology	Standard Microsystems Corp.
Comments	Combines error-recovery and fault-isolation technologies with signal retiming and regeneration on every port. SNMP optional.	Compact one inch depth, passive UTP MAU, compatible with IBM's 8228 MAUs	Manageable via optional Ring Management Module
Warranty	5 year	3 year	3 year
Price	$1,699	$495/$509	$1,199

Manufacturer	Standard Microsystems Corp.	UB Networks	UB Networks
Model	Elite Stack 4008DC	GEOLAN/100	GEOLAN/500
Hardware Protocol	MAU	Multiprocessor Hubs/ UnMngd	Multiprocessor Hubs/ UnMngd
Total Ports:	8	264	312
Port Types:	8 Ports STP	AUI, BNC, UTP, Fiber, ATM and FDDI uplinks available	AUI, BNC, UTP, Fiber, Internal ATM, switching fabric, ATM and FDDI uplinks
LEDs	Power, RMM, RI, RO, OBM>Transmit & Receive, Inserted/Locked	Each module has status links that vary in functionality	Each module has status links that vary in functionality
Polarity	INA	Auto-detect, auto-correct	Auto-detect, auto-correct
Bandwidth	4/16Mbps	390Mbps total chassis can be more depending on switch technology	20 + Gbps of chassis bandwidth; more with switching
Stacking	Up to 8 MAU's	Up to 11 slots per chassis hub	2 center switching slots and 12 technology slots
Form Factor	Desktop, rack	Chassis	Chassis
Comments	Manageable via optional Ring Management Module	Chassis-based hub supporting multiple technologies	Chassis-based hub supporting multiple technologies
Warranty	3 year	1 year	1 year
Price	$799	Starts at $300/port	Starts at $500/port

Manufacturer	Whittaker-Xyplex
Model	3350 FDDI Concentraror
Hardware Protocol	FDDI
Total Ports:	1 port per module
Port Types:	1 UTP
LEDs	Power, Ring Up, Warp/Thru A/B port station
Polarity	INA
Bandwidth	100Mbps
Stacking	INA
Form Factor	Stackable
Comments	INA
Warranty	3 year
Price	$5,995-$9,750

N/A—Not applicable   INA—Information not available

End ■

Network Interface Cards ■

Manufacturer	3Com Corp.	3Com Corp.	3Com Corp.
Model	ATMLink Adapter Family	Fast EtherLink XL #3C905	Fast EtherLink XL #3C900
Network Interface Standards Supported	155Mbps ATM	10BASE-T, 10BASE2, 10BASE5, 100BASE-T, TX, T4	10BASE-T, 10BASE2, 10BASE5
Hardware Protocol	INA	Ethernet/Fast Ethernet	Ethernet
Connectors	Duplex SC	AUI, BNC, UTP, RJ-45	AUI, BNC, UTP, RJ-45
LAN Drivers	SBUS: Solaris, SunOS PCI: NetWare 4.x, Windows NT	NetWare, NDIS, ODI	NetWare, NDIS, ODI
Bus Width	32	32	32
On-board/Buffer RAM	N/A	8K	8K
PC Bus Interface	SBUS, PCI	PCI	PCI
LED Indicators	N/A	LEDs indicate Ethernet/Fast Ethernet modes. Activity	Link integrity with 10BASE-T hubs
Comments	SNMP Management	Parallel tasking for throughput	Parallel tasking for throughput
Warranty	Lifetime	Lifetime	Lifetime
Price	$1,495	$195+	$149

Manufacturer	3Com Corp.	Accton Technology	Accton Technology
Model	Token Link III Family	EtherPair-16	EtherCoax-16
Network Interface Standards Supported	16/4 Mbps Token Ring	Ethernet 10BASE-T	Ethernet 10BASE2
Hardware Protocol	INA	Ethernet	Ethernet
Connectors	DB-9, RJ-45	UTP-RJ45	BNC
LAN Drivers	3Com, TCP, OSI, NFS, OS.2, NetWare, Windows NT and 95, Vines	NetWare 2.X, 3.X, 4.X, Microsoft LAN Mgr, Windows for Workgroups 3.X, Windows NT 3.X, Windows 95, Wollongong Pathway Access, FTP PC/TCP, NCSA, TCP/IP, Sun PC-NFS, Banyan Vines, IBM LAN Server, SCO UNIX, Unixware, SunSoft Solaris	NetWare 2.X, 3.X, 4.X, Microsoft LAN Mgr, Windows for Workgroups 3.X, Windows NT 3.X, Windows 95, Wollongong Pathway Access, FTP PC/TCP, NCSA, TCP/IP, Sun PC-NFS, Banyan Vines, IBM LAN Server, SCO UNIX, Unixware, SunSoft Solaris
Bus Width	16/32bit	16 bit	16 bit
On-board/Buffer RAM	N/A	16K	16K
PC Bus Interface	EISA/ISA/PCMCIA	ISA	ISA
LED Indicators	N/A	Transmit, Receive, Link	Transmit, Receive
Comments	SNMP management, compatible with IBM applications	Built-in multi-packet accelerator (MPX2), NE2000 compatible, full duplex, plug and play (designed for Windows 95), 1 step installation unit	Built-in multi-packet accelerator (MPX2), NE2000 compatible, full duplex, plug and play (designed for Windows 95), 1 step installation unit
Warranty	Lifetime	Limited lifetime	Limited lifetime
Price	$255+	$75	$75

Manufacturer	Accton Technology	Accton Technology	Accton Technology
Model	EtherCombo-16 (EN1660)	EtherCombo-32 (EN1200)	EtherDuo-PCI
Network Interface Standards Supported	Ethernet 10BASE-T, 10BASE2, 10BASE5	Ethernet 10BASE-T, 10BASE2, 10BASE5	Ethernet 10BASE-T, 10BASE2
Hardware Protocol	Ethernet	Ethernet	Ethernet

N/A—Not applicable   INA—Information not available

Table Continues →

■ Network Interface Cards

Manufacturer	Accton Technology	Accton Technology	Accton Technology
Connectors	AUI, BNC, UTP-RJ45	AUI, BNC, UTP-RJ45	BNC, UTP-RJ45
LAN Drivers	NetWare, Microsoft LAN Mgr, Windows for Workgroups, Windows NT, Windows 95, Pathway Access, FTP PC/TCP, NCSA, TCP/IP, Sun PC-NFS, Vines, IBM LAN Server, SCO UNIX, Unixware, SunSoft Solaris	NetWare, Microsoft LAN Mgr, Windows for Workgroups, Windows NT, Windows 95, Pathway Access, FTP PC/TCP, NCSA, TCP/IP, Sun PC-NFS, Vines, IBM LAN Server, SCO UNIX, Unixware, SunSoft Solaris	NetWare, Microsoft LAN Mgr, Windows for Workgroups, Windows NT, Windows 95, Pathway Access, FTP PC/TCP, NCSA, TCP/IP, Sun PC-NFS, Vines, IBM LAN Server, SCO UNIX, Unixware, SunSoft Solaris
Bus Width	16 bit	32 bit	32 bit
On-board/Buffer RAM	16K	16K	N/A
PC Bus Interface	ISA	EISA	PCI
LED Indicators	Transmit, Receive, Link	Transmit, Receive, Link	Transmit, Receive, Link
Comments	Built-in multi-packet accelerator (MPX2), NE2000 compatible, full duplex, plug and play (designed for Windows 95), 1 step installation unit	Installation and diagnostic utilities included, socket for boot ROM, bus mastering, software configurable	Installation and diagnostic utilities included, socket for boot ROM, bus mastering, software configurable
Warranty	Limited lifetime	Limited lifetime	Limited lifetime
Price	$85	$249	$119

Manufacturer	Accton Technology	Accton Technology	Accton Technology
Model	EtherFastTX	FastEtherPairTX	EtherPair-PCMCA (EN2216-1)
Network Interface Standards Supported	Ethernet 10BASE-T, 10BASE2, Fast Ethernet 10BASE-T	Ethernet 10BASE-T, 10BASE2, 10BASE5	Ethernet 10BASE-T, 10BASE2, 10BASE5
Hardware Protocol	Ethernet/Fast Ethernet	Ethernet	Ethernet
Connectors	BNC, (2 UTP-RJ45 1-10Mbps, 1-100Mbps)	AUI, BNC, UTP-RJ45	AUI, BNC, UTP-RJ45
LAN Drivers	NetWare 2.X, 3.X, 4.X, Microsoft LAN Mgr, Windows for Workgroups 3.X, Windows NT 3.X, Windows 95, Wollongong Pathway Access, FTP PC/TCP, NCSA, TCP/IP, Sun PC-NFS, Banyan Vines, IBM LAN Server, SCO UNIX, Unixware, SunSoft Solaris	NetWare 2.X, 3.X, 4.X, Microsoft LAN Mgr, Windows for Workgroups 3.X, Windows NT 3.X, Windows 95, Wollongong Pathway Access, FTP PC/TCP, NCSA, TCP/IP, Sun PC-NFS, Banyan Vines, SCO UNIX, Unixware, SunSoft Solaris	NetWare 2.X, 3.X, 4.X, Microsoft LAN Mgr, Windows for Workgroups 3.X, Windows NT 3.X, Windows 95, Wollongong Pathway Access, FTP PC/TCP, NCSA, TCP/IP, Sun PC-NFS, Banyan Vines, IBM LAN Server, SCO UNIX, Unixware, SunSoft Solaris
Bus Width	32 bit	32 bit	16 bit
On-board/Buffer RAM	N/A	N/A	32K
PC Bus Interface	PCI	PCI	PCMCIA
LED Indicators	Transmit, Receive, Link, 100Mbps	Transmit, Receive, Link, 100Mbps	Transmit, Receive, Link
Comments	Full Duplex, 1 step installation utility, bus mastering, software configurable, automatically detects media type	Full Duplex, 1 step installation utility, bus mastering, software configurable, automatically detects media type	Built-in multi-packet accelerator (MPX2), NE2000 compatible, full duplex, plug and play (designed for Windows 95), 1 step installation unit
Warranty	Limited lifetime	Limited lifetime	Limited lifetime
Price	$159	$159	$139

Manufacturer	Accton Technology	Accton Technology	Accton Technology
Model	EtherPair-PCMCA (EN2216-2)	Ethernet + Fax/Modem Multi-Function PC Card (EN2218-1)	Ethernet + Fax/Modem Multi-Function PC Card (EN2218-2)
Network Interface Standards Supported	Ethernet 10BASE-T, 10BASE2	Ethernet 10BASE-T	Ethernet 10BASE-T, 10BASE2

N/A—Not applicable   INA—Information not available

Network Interface Cards ■

Manufacturer	Accton Technology	Accton Technology	Accton Technology
Hardware Protocol	Ethernet	Ethernet	Ethernet
Connectors	BNC, UTP-RJ45	UTP-RJ45, RJ-11 telephone jack	UTP-RJ45, RJ-11 telephone jack
LAN Drivers	NetWare 2.X, 3.X, 4.X, Microsoft LAN Mgr, Windows for Work-groups 3.X, Windows NT 3.X, Win-dows 95, Wollongong Pathway Access, FTP PC/TCP, NCSA, TCP/IP, Sun PC-NFS, Banyan Vines, IBM LAN Server, SCO UNIX, Unix-ware, SunSoft Solaris	NetWare 2.X, 3.X, 4.X, Microsoft LAN Mgr, Windows for Work-groups 3.X, Windows NT 3.X, Win-dows 95, Wollongong Pathway Access, FTP PC/TCP, NCSA, TCP/IP, Sun PC-NFS, Banyan Vines, IBM LAN Server, SCO UNIX, Unix-ware, SunSoft Solaris	NetWare 2.X, 3.X, 4.X, Microsoft LAN Mgr, Windows for Work-groups 3.X, Windows NT 3.X, Win-dows 95, Wollongong Pathway Access, FTP PC/TCP, NCSA, TCP/IP, Sun PC-NFS, Banyan Vines, IBM LAN Server, SCO UNIX, Unix-ware, SunSoft Solaris
Bus Width	16 bit	16 bit	16 bit
On-board/Buffer RAM	32K	32K	32K
PC Bus Interface	PCMCIA	PCMCIA	PCMCIA
LED Indicators	Transmit, Receive, Link	Transmit, Receive, Link	N/A
Comments	Built-in multi-packet accelerator (MPX2), NE2000 compatible, full duplex, plug and play (designed for Windows 95), 1 step installation unit	Combination 14.4 S/R Fax/Modem+Ethernet PC Card, sup-ports simultaneous LAN+ modem operation. 1 step installation utility	Combination 14.4 S/R Fax/Modem+Ethernet PC Card, sup-ports simultaneous LAN+ modem operation. 1 step installation utility
Warranty	Limited lifetime	5 year	5 year
Price	$149	$379	$399

Manufacturer	Accton Technology	Accton Technology
Model	Ethernet + Fax/Modem Multi-Function PC Card (EN2218-3)	Ethernet + Fax/Modem Multi-Function PC Card (EN2218-4)
Network Interface Standards Supported	Ethernet 10BASE-T	Ethernet 10BASE-T, 10BASE2
Hardware Protocol	Ethernet	Ethernet
Connectors	UTP-RJ45, RJ-11 telephone jack	UTP-RJ45, RJ-11 telephone jack
LAN Drivers	NetWare 2.X, 3.X, 4.X, Microsoft LAN Mgr, Windows for Workgroups 3.X, Windows NT 3.X, Windows 95, Wollongong Pathway Access, FTP PC/TCP, NCSA, TCP/IP, Sun PC-NFS, Banyan Vines, IBM LAN Server, SCO UNIX, Unixware, SunSoft Solaris	NetWare 2.X, 3.X, 4.X, Microsoft LAN Mgr, Windows for Workgroups 3.X, Windows NT 3.X, Windows 95, Wollongong Pathway Access, FTP PC/TCP, NCSA, TCP/IP, Sun PC-NFS, Banyan Vines, IBM LAN Server, SCO UNIX, Unixware, SunSoft Solaris
Bus Width	16 bit	16 bit
On-board/Buffer RAM	32K	32K
PC Bus Interface	PCMCIA	PCMCIA
LED Indicators	N/A	N/A
Comments	Combination 28.8 S/R Fax/Modem + Ethernet PC Card, supports simultaneous LAN+ modem operation. 1 step installation utility.	Combination 28.8 S/R Fax/Modem + Ethernet PC Card, supports simultaneous LAN+ modem operation. 1 step installation utility.
Warranty	5 year	5 year
Price	$529	$579

Manufacturer	AccuLAN	AccuLAN
Model	AL-NE-2/100IT	AccuQuick 4Plus1 AL-NE 2000E2A
Network Interface Standards Supported	Ethernet 10BASE-T, 100 BASE-TX	Ethernet 10 BASE-T, 10 BASE2, 10 BASE-S option
Hardware Protocol	Ethernet	Ethernet
Connectors	UTP: RJ-45	BNC, UTP, RJ-45 (AUI option)

N/A—Not applicable   INA—Information not available

Table Continues →

■ Network Interface Cards

Manufacturer	AccuLAN	AccuLAN
LAN Drivers	IPX, ODI, NOIS, TCP/IP	INA
Bus Width	16/8	16/8 bit
On-board/Buffer RAM	128K	16K
PC Bus Interface	ISA	ISA
LED Indicators	Link,Receive, Collision	Link, Receive, Collision
Comments	Full duplex	New APX parallel processing 300, BNC allowable. AUI kit available.
Warranty	5 year	5 year
Price	$363	$54

Manufacturer	AccuLAN	AccuLAN
Model	AccuQuick PCI AL-NET 5000 PSA	AL-NEPCM 2
Network Interface Standards Supported	Ethernet 10BASE-T, 100 BASE 2	Ethernet 10 BASE-T, 10 BASE-2
Hardware Protocol	Ethernet	Ethernet
Connectors	UTP: RJ-45, BNC, AUI Optional.	BNC, UTP, RJ-45
LAN Drivers	IPX, ODI, NOIS, TCP/IP	IPX, ODI, NOIS, TCP/IP
Bus Width	32 bit	32 bit
On-board/Buffer RAM	16K	16K
PC Bus Interface	PCI	PCMCIA
LED Indicators	Data, Receive, Collision	Data, Receive, Collision
Comments	New APX parallel processing 300m BNC allowable AUI kit available	
Warranty	5 year	5 year
Price	$129	$239

Manufacturer	Allied Telesyn Intl.	Allied Telesyn Intl.	Allied Telesyn Intl.
Model	AT-2000T Plus/AT-2000U Plus	AT-1500T PnP AT-1500BT PnP AT-1500AT PnP AT-1500FT PnP	AT-1700T Plus AT-1700BT Plus AT-1700AT Plus AT-1700FT Plus
Network Interface Standards Supported	10BASE-T/10BASE-T, 5, 2	10BASE-T/10BASE-T 2 10BASE-T 5 10BASE-T, FL	10BASE-T 10BASE-T, 2 10BASE-T, 5 10BASE-T, FL
Hardware Protocol	Ethernet	Ethernet	Ethernet
Connectors	UTP RJ-45/UTP RJ-45, BNC, AUI	UTP RJ-45, UTP RJ-45, BNC, UTP RJ-45, AUI, UTP RJ-45, Fiber Optic ST	UTP RJ-45, UTP RJ-45, BNC, UTP RJ-45, AUI, UTP RJ-45, Fiber Optic ST
LAN Drivers	NDIS, ODI, IPX, UNIX, packet driver	NDIS, ODI, IPX, UNIX, packet driver	NDIS, ODI, IPX, UNIX, packet driver
Bus Width	16-bit	16-bit	16-bit
On-board/Buffer RAM	16K	Bus mastering DMA	32K
PC Bus Interface	ISA	ISA	ISA
LED Indicators	Link	Link, Transmit, Receive, Collision	Link, Transmit, Receive, Collision

N/A—Not applicable   INA—Information not available

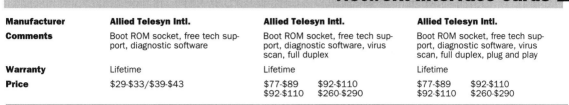

Network Interface Cards ■

Manufacturer	Allied Telesyn Intl.	Allied Telesyn Intl.	Allied Telesyn Intl.
Comments	Boot ROM socket, free tech support, diagnostic software	Boot ROM socket, free tech support, diagnostic software, virus scan, full duplex	Boot ROM socket, free tech support, diagnostic software, virus scan, full duplex, plug and play
Warranty	Lifetime	Lifetime	Lifetime
Price	$29-$33/$39-$43	$77-$89 $92-$110 $92-$110 $260-$290	$77-$89 $92-$110 $92-$110 $260-$290

Manufacturer	Allied Telesyn Intl.	Allied Telesyn Intl.	Antares Microsystems
Model	AT-2450T AT-2450BT AT-2450A AT-2450FT	AT-2560TX 10/100	Sbus Ethernet Products
Network Interface Standards Supported	10BASE-T, 10BASE-T, 2 10BASE-T 5,10BASE-T, FL	10BASE-T, 10BASE-TX	Ethernet 10BASE-T, 10BASE2, 10BASE5, 100BASE-TX, MII
Hardware Protocol	Ethernet	Fast Ethernet	Ethernet
Connectors	UTP RJ-45, UTP RJ-45, BNC, UTP RJ-45, AUI, UTP RJ-45, Fiber Optic ST	UTP RJ-45x	BNC, RJ-45, AUI, MII
LAN Drivers	NDIS, ODI, IPX, UNIX, packet driver	NDIS, ODI, UNIX	Solaris 1 & Solaris 2
Bus Width	32-bit	32-bit	32 bits
On-board/Buffer RAM	Bus mastering	Bus mastering	64 Bytes
PC Bus Interface	PCI	PCI	SBus
LED Indicators	Link, Transmit, Receive, Collision	Activity, Link, Speed	None
Comments	Boot ROM socket, free tech support, diagnostic software, virus scan, full duplex, plug and play	BootROM socket, free tech support, diagnostic software, virus scan, full duplex, plug and play	Plug and play installation
Warranty	Lifetime	Lifetime	1 year
Price	$106–$130, $116–$129 $116–$129,$299–$349	$149–$169	$325–$995

Manufacturer	Artisoft, Inc.	Artisoft, Inc.	Asante Technologies, Inc.
Model	Node Runner Pro Combo Adapter	Node Runner Pro UTP Adapter	Asante' Fast 10/100 Adapter (For PCI "PC Edition")
Network Interface Standards Supported	10BASE-T, 10BASE2	10BASE-T	10BASE-T, 100BASE-T
Hardware Protocol	Ethernet	Ethernet	INA
Connectors	RJ45, BNC	RJ45	RJ-45
LAN Drivers	DOS/Windows 3.X, IBM OS/2, Novell NetWare, Windows NT3.1 and 3.5, Windows 95, SCO UNIX, Lantastic v.6.0 and Lantastic Power Suite v.6.1	DOS/Windows 3.X, IBM OS/2, Novell NetWare, Windows NT3.1 and 3.5, Windows 95, SCO UNIX, Lantastic v.6.0 and Lantastic Power Suite v.6.1	ODI, NDIS 2.0, 3.0
Bus Width	16/8	16/8	32
On-board/Buffer RAM	32K	32K	None
PC Bus Interface	ISA	ISA	PCI

N/A—Not applicable   INA—Information not available

Table Continues →

■ Network Interface Cards

Manufacturer	Artisoft, Inc.	Artisoft, Inc.	Asante Technologies, Inc.
LED Indicators	Yes	Yes	10Mbps operation, 100Mbps operation, Link, Integrity, and Data link
Comments			Also includes Nway auto-negotiation to determine 10Mbps or 100Mbps operation automatically
Warranty	5 year limited free, limited tech support	5 year limited free, limited tech support	Lifetime/free tech support
Price	$109	$99	$159

Manufacturer	CeLan Technology	CeLan Technology
Model	EPCI-Plus	EFAST NIC
Network Interface Standards Supported	Ethernet 10BASE-T, 10BASE2	Ethernet 10BASE-T, 100BASE-TX
Hardware Protocol	Ethernet	Ethernet
Connectors	BNC, RJ-45	RJ-45
LAN Drivers	IPX, ODI, NDIS, Fast, Packet	IPX, ODI, NDIS, Fast, Packet
Bus Width	32 bit, PCI	32 bit
On-board/Buffer RAM		
PC Bus Interface	PCI	PCI
LED Indicators	Data, Link, Receive	Data, Link, Receive
Comments	Configuration and diagnostic software included	Configuration and diagnostic software included
Warranty	Lifetime	Lifetime
Price	$89	$175

Manufacturer	CeLan Technology	CeLan Technology	CeLan Technology
Model	E2000C	E2000T	ENE/2C
Network Interface Standards Supported	Ethernet 10BASE-T, 10BASE2	Ethernet 10BASE-T	Ethernet 10BASE-T, 10BASE2
Hardware Protocol	Ethernet	Ethernet	Ethernet
Connectors	BNC, RJ-45	RJ-45	BNC, RJ-45
LAN Drivers	IPX, ODI, NDIS, Fast, Packet	IPX, ODI, NDIS, Fast, Packet	IPX, ODI, NDIS, Fast, Packet
Bus Width	16/8 bit	16/8 bit	16 bit
On-board/Buffer RAM	16K	16K	
PC Bus Interface	ISA	ISA	MCA
LED Indicators	Data, Link, Receive	Data, Link, Receive	Data, Link, Receive
Comments	Configuration and diagnostic software included	Configuration and diagnostic software included	Configuration and diagnostic software included
Warranty	Lifetime	Lifetime	Lifetime
Price	$49	$59	$199

N/A—Not applicable   INA—Information not available

Network Interface Cards ■

Manufacturer	CeLan Technology	CeLan Technology
Model	EMAC IIC	EMAC LCBT
Network Interface Standards Supported	Ethernet: 10BASE-T, 10BASE2, 10BASE5	Ethernet 10BASE-T, 10BASE2
Hardware Protocol	Ethernet	Ethernet
Connectors	BNC, RJ45, AUI	BNC, RJ45
LAN Drivers	AppleTalk	AppleTalk
Bus Width	16 bit	16 Bit
On-board/Buffer RAM		
PC Bus Interface	NUBus	PDS
LED Indicators		Data, Link, Receive
Comments		
Warranty	Lifetime	Lifetime
Price	$99	$99

Manufacturer	Cogent Data Tech	Cogent Data Tech	Cogent Data Tech
Model	EM525, EM525 C	EM110 T4 ISA, EM110 T4 C ISA	EM110 TX ISA EM110 TX C ISA
Network Interface Standards Supported	10BASE-T, 10BASE-T, 10BASE2, 10BASE5	10BASE-T, 100BaseT4, 10BASE-T, 10BASE2, 100BASET4	10BASE-T, 100BASE-TX, 10BASE-T, 10BASE2, 100BASE-TX
Hardware Protocol	Ethernet	Ethernet, Fast Ethernet	Ethernet, Fast Ethernet
Connectors	RJ-45, BNC, AUI	RJ-45, BNC	RJ-45, BNC
LAN Drivers	DOS ODI, NDIS 2.0 for DOS and OS/2, Windows95, Windows NT, NEXTSTEP	DOS ODI, NetWare server, Windows for Workgroups, Windows95, Windows NT	DOS ODI, NetWare server, Windows for Workgroups, Windows95, Windows NT
Bus Width	16 bit	16 bit	16 bit
On-board/Buffer RAM	64Kbps	128Kbps	128Kbps
PC Bus Interface	ISA	ISA	ISA
LED Indicators	Activity, Link Integrity	Activity, Link Integrity	Activity, Link Integrity
Comments	Boot ROM socket	CAT 3 support for 100Mbps, 10/100 auto-sensing, BNC for 10Mbps (on TX C ISA)	CAT 3 support for 100Mbps, 10/100 auto-sensing, BNC for 10Mbps (on TX C ISA)
Warranty	Lifetime	Lifetime	Lifetime
Price	$110/$124	$229/$259	$229/$259

Manufacturer	Cogent Data Tech	Cogent Data Tech	Cogent Data Tech
Model	EM110 T4 EISA EM110 T4 C EISA	EM100 TX EISA EM100 TX ISA	EM110 TX EISA EM110 TX C EISA
Network Interface Standards Supported	10BASE-T, 100BASE-T4 10BASE-T, 10BASE2, 100BaseT4	100BASE-TX	10BASE-T, 100BASE-TX 10BASE-T, 10BASE2, 100BASE-TX
Hardware Protocol	Ethernet, Fast Ethernet	Fast Ethernet	Ethernet, Fast Ethernet
Connectors	RJ-45, BNC	RJ-45	RJ-45, BNC
LAN Drivers	DOS ODI, NetWare server, Windows for Workgroups, Windows 95, Windows NT	DOS ODI, NetWare server, Windows for Workgroups, Windows 95, Windows NT	DOS ODI, NetWare server, Windows for Workgroups, Windows 95, Windows NT
Bus Width	32 bit	32 bit, 16 bit	32 bit

N/A—Not applicable　INA—Information not available

Table Continues →

■ Network Interface Cards

Manufacturer	**Cogent Data Tech**	**Cogent Data Tech**	**Cogent Data Tech**
On-board/Buffer RAM	128Kbps	128Kbps	128Kbps
PC Bus Interface	EISA	EISA, ISA	EISA
LED Indicators	Activity, Link Integrity	Activity, Link Integrity	Activity, Link Integrity
Comments	CAT 3 support for 100Mbps, 10/100 Auto-sensing, BNC for 10Mbps (on TX C EISA)	Low cost 100Mbps only	10/100 Auto-sensing, BNC for 10Mbps (on TX C EISA)
Warranty	Lifetime	Lifetime	Lifetime
Price	$298/$329	$249/198	$298/$329

Manufacturer	**Cogent Data Tech**	**Cogent Data Tech**	**Cogent Data Tech**
Model	EM935 EISA XL	EM110 T4 PCI, EM110 T4 C PCI	EM100 FX ST PCI, EM100 FX SC PCI
Network Interface Standards Supported	10BASE-T, 10BASE2, 10BASE5	10BASE-T, 100BaseT4, 10BASE-T, 10BASE2, 100BASE-T4	100BASE-TX
Hardware Protocol	Ethernet	Ethernet, Fast Ethernet	Fast Ethernet
Connectors	RJ-45, BNC, AUI	RJ-45 RJ-45, BNC	RJ-45
LAN Drivers	DOS ODI, NDIS 2.0 for DOS and OS/2, Windows 95, Windows NT, NEXTSTEP	DOS ODI, NetWare server, Windows for Workgroups, Windows 95, Windows NT for Intel, DEC Alpha and MIPS, NDIS 2.0 for DOS and OS/2, NEXTSTEP, SCO UNIX	DOS ODI, NetWare server, Windows for Workgroups, Windows 95, Windows NT for Intel, DEC Alpha and MIPS, NDIS 2.0 for DOS and OS/2, NEXTSTEP, SCO UNIX
Bus Width	32 bit	32 bit	32 bit
On-board/Buffer RAM	Bus master	6K FIFO	6K FIFO
PC Bus Interface	EISA	PCI	PCI
LED Indicators	Activity, Link Integrity	Activity, Link Integrity	Activity, Link Integrity
Comments	EISA Burst mode (32MB/sec.) support	10/100 auto-sensing, BNC for 10Mbps (on T4 C PCI)	Supports up to 2 km; runs in full duplex
Warranty	Lifetime	Lifetime	Lifetime
Price	$398	$198/$239	$698

Manufacturer	**Cogent Data Tech**	**Cogent Data Tech**	**Cogent Data Tech**
Model	EM110 TX PCI, EM110 TX C PCI	EM960 PCI, EM960 C PCI	EM964 PCI TP, EM964 BNC
Network Interface Standards Supported	10BASE-T, 100BASE-TX, 10BASE-T, 10BASE2, 100BASE-TX	10BASE-T, 10BASE2,	10BASE-T, 10BASE2,
Hardware Protocol	Ethernet, Fast Ethernet	Ethernet	Ethernet
Connectors	RJ-45, RJ-45, BNC	RJ-45, RJ-45, BNC	RJ-45 (qty. 4), BNC (qty.4)
LAN Drivers	DOS ODI, NetWare server, Windows for Workgroups, Windows 95, Windows NT for Intel, DEC Alpha and MIPS, NDIS 2.0 for DOS and OS/2, NEXTSTEP, SCO UNIX, Solaris	DOS ODI, NetWare server, Windows for Workgroups, Windows 95, Windows NT for Intel, DEC Alpha and MIPS, NDIS 2.0 for DOS and OS/2, NEXTSTEP, SCO UNIX, Solaris	DOS ODI, NetWare server, Windows for Workgroups, Windows 95, Windows NT for Intel, DEC Alpha and MIPS, NDIS 2.0 for DOS and OS/2
Bus Width	32 bit	32 bit	32 bit
On-board/Buffer RAM	6K FIFO	512 Bytes	4K FIFO
PC Bus Interface	PCI	PCI	PCI

N/A—Not applicable   INA—Information not available

Network Interface Cards ∎

Manufacturer	Cogent Data Tech	Cogent Data Tech	Cogent Data Tech
LED Indicators	Activity, Link Integrity	Activity, Link Integrity	Activity (4), Link Integrity (4)
Comments	Full duplex, 10/100 auto-sensing, BNC support for 10Mbps (on T4 C PCI)	Full duplex, BNC support on 960-C model	Supports up to four segments, full duplex
Warranty	Lifetime	Lifetime	Lifetime
Price	$189, $239	$119, $139	$498, $598

Manufacturer	Cogent Data Tech	Cogent Data Tech
Model	EM100 TX PCI	EM440 T4 PCI, EM440 TX PCI
Network Interface Standards Supported	100BASE-TX	10BASE-T, 100BASE-TX, 10BASE-T, 10BASE2, 100BASE-TX
Hardware Protocol	Fast Ethernet	Ethernet, Fast Ethernet
Connectors	RJ-45	RJ-45
LAN Drivers	DOS ODI, NetWare server, Windows for Workgroups, Windows 95, Windows NT for Intel, DEC Alpha and MIPS, NDIS 2.0 for DOS and OS/2, NEXTSTEP, SCO UNIX, Solaris	DOS ODI, NetWare server, Windows for Workgroups, Windows 95, Windows NT for Intel, DEC Alpha and MIPS, NDIS 2.0 for DOS and OS/2
Bus Width	32 bit	32 bit
On-board/Buffer RAM	6K FIFO	24K FIFO
PC Bus Interface	PCI	PCI
LED Indicators	Activity, Link Integrity	Activity (4), Link Integrity (4)
Comments	Low cost 100Mbps only	10/100 Auto-sensing, supports up to 4 segments, CAT 3 Support for 1 (T4), full duplex (TX)
Warranty	Lifetime	Lifetime
Price	$165	$998

Manufacturer	Compaq	Compaq
Model	Netelligent 10BASE-T ISA UTP Controller	Netelligent 10BASE-T/2 ISA UTP Coax Controller
Network Interface Standards Supported	10BASE-T	10BASE-T, 10BASE2
Hardware Protocol	802.3	802.3, Ethernet
Connectors	RJ-45	RJ-45, BNC
LAN Drivers	ODI Server, client, NDIS 2.X, 3.X, Banyan	ODI Server, client, NDIS 2.X, 3.X, Banyan
Bus Width	16	16
On-board/Buffer RAM	Internal to chipset	Internal to chipset
PC Bus Interface	ISA	ISA
LED Indicators	Link, Network Activity	Link, Network Activity
Comments	Bus mastering, plug and play, full duplex, NE-2100 compatibility, configuration/diagnostic utility	Bus mastering, plug and play, full duplex, NE-2100 compatibility, configuration/diagnostic utility
Warranty	3 year	3 year
Price	$71, $382 (6 pack), $2,786 (50 pack)	$92, $511 (6 pack), $3,912 (50 pack)

N/A—Not applicable   INA—Information not available   **Table Continues →**

■ Network Interface Cards

Manufacturer	Compaq	Compaq	Compaq
Model	Netwlligent 10BASE-T ISA UTP Controller	Netwlligent 10/100 PCI UTP Controller	4/16 TR PCI UTP/STP
Network Interface Standards Supported	10BASE-T	10BASE-T, 100BASE-TX	802.3 and 802.5
Hardware Protocol	802.3	802.3	Token Ring
Connectors	RJ-45	RJ-45	Rj-45 and DB-9
LAN Drivers	ODI Server, clientNDIS 2.X, 3.X, Banyan, SCOUNIX	ODI Server, clientNDIS 2.X, 3.X, Banyan, SCOUNIX	DOS ODI Client, NetWare, NDIS, LLC, and many others.
Bus Width	32	32	32 bit
On-board/Buffer RAM	Internal to chipset	Internal to chipset	128K
PC Bus Interface	PCI	PCI	PCI specification 2.0
LED Indicators	Link, network activity	Link, network activity, network speed	2-activity and insertion
Comments	Bus mastering, plug and play, full duplex, diagnostic utility	Bus mastering, plug and play, full duplex, configuration/diagnostic utility, auto-negotiating	Scaleable Clock Architecture™, 32-bit bus mastering. Other similar models available.
Warranty	3 year	3 year	3 year
Price	$119, $543 (6 pack), $4,950 (50 pack)	$159, $894 (6 pack), $6,950 (50 pack)	$284 (single)

Manufacturer	Danya Communications	Danya Communications	Danya Communications
Model	DanyaPort E/SE, E/LC, EII	DanyaPort E/si30, DanyaPort CS	BlueStreak 10/100 NuBus
Network Interface Standards Supported	Ethernet 10BASE-T, 2, 5	Ethernet 10BASE-T, 2, 5	Ethernet 10BASE-T, Fast Ethernet 100BASE-TX
Hardware Protocol	Ethernet	Ethernet	Ethernet/Fast Ethernet
Connectors	RJ-45, AUI, BNC	RJ-45, AUI, BNC	RJ-45 only, on both sides
LAN Drivers	DanyaPort drivers, AppleTalk, IPX	DanyaPort drivers, AppleTalk, IPX, IP	AppleTalk and Blue Streak drivers, IPX, TCP/IP
Bus Width	16 bit, 32 bit	32 bit	32 bit
On-board/Buffer RAM	32K, 64K	32K, 64K	128K
PC Bus Interface	Mac PDS, PDS slot (Mac), NuBus (Mac)	PDS slot (Mac), Mac Communications Slot	NuBus
LED Indicators	Data link	Data link	Data link
Comments			
Warranty	Lifetime	Lifetime	Lifetime
Price	$138–$209 $85–$209 $96–$209	$138–$209 $75–$99	$298–$399

Manufacturer	Danya Communications	Danya Communications	Digi International, Inc.
Model	BlueStreak 10/100 PCI	BlueStreak 10/100 LC	DataFire U, DataFire S/T
Network Interface Standards Supported	Ethernet 10BASE-T, Fast Ethernet 100BaseT	Ethernet 10BASE-T, Fast Ethernet 100BaseT	ISDN
Hardware Protocol	Ethernet/Fast Ethernet	Ethernet/Fast Ethernet	Ethernet, ISDN
Connectors	RJ-45 only, on both	RJ-45 only, on both	RJ45

N/A—Not applicable   INA—Information not available

Network Interface Cards ■

Manufacturer	Danya Communications	Danya Communications	Digi International, Inc.
LAN Drivers	NDIS, ODI, AppleTalk and Blue Streak drivers, IPX, IP	AppleTalk and Blue Streak drivers, IPX, IP	WAN: ODI, NDIS
Bus Width	32 bit	32 bit	8 bit
On-board/Buffer RAM	Bus mastering 4K	128K	256K
PC Bus Interface	PCI-Bus mastering	PDS slot (Mac)	ISA, EISA
LED Indicators	Data link	Data link	Internal LEDs, Sync, Receive, Transmit
Comments			
Warranty	Lifetime	Lifetime	5 year
Price	$194–$259	$261–$349	INA

Manufacturer	Digital Equipment Corp.	Digital Equipment Corp.
Model	DEC FDDI controller/EISA MMF Model	DEC FDDI controller/EISA UTP Model
Network Interface Standards Supported	(ANSI X3T9.5, PMD, SMT V.7.3)	(ANSI X3T9.5, PMD, SMT V.7.3)
Hardware Protocol	FDDI	FDDI
Connectors	2 MIC; 1 RJ12 connector for optical bypass relay	2 UTP (RJ-45)
LAN Drivers	ODI, NDIS 2, NDIS 3, NetWare, Windows, LAN Mgr., LAN Server, PATHWORKS, Banyan Vines Client, UNIX	ODI, NDIS 2, NDIS 3, NetWare, Windows, LAN Mgr., LAN Server, PATHWORKS, Banyan Vines Client, UNIX
Bus Width	32 bit	32 bit
On-board/Buffer RAM	1MB	1MB
PC Bus Interface	EISA	EISA
LED Indicators	Data link and port status	Data link and port status
Comments	On-Board CPU; supports Alpha, Intel, MIPS, and PowerPC platforms, full duplex capability extends bandwidth to 200Mbps	On-Board CPU; supports Alpha, Intel, MIPS, and PowerPC platforms, full duplex capability extends bandwidth to 200Mbps
Warranty	Lifetime	Lifetime
Price	$2,500	$1,500

Manufacturer	Digital Equipment Corp.	Digital Equipment Corp.
Model	EtherWORKS 3 Turbo TP	EtherWORKS
Network Interface Standards Supported	10BASE-T	10BASE-T
Hardware Protocol	Ethernet	Ethernet
Connectors	TP (RJ-45)	TP (RJ-45)
LAN Drivers	ODI, NDIS 2, NDIS 3,native DLL, packet driver, NetWare, Windows, LAN Mgr., LAN Server, PATHWORKS, Banyan Vines Client, UNIX, MOP/RPL Remote Boot	ODI, NDIS 2, NDIS 3, native DLL, NetWare, Windows, LAN Mgr., LAN Server, PATHWORKS, Banyan Vines Client, UNIX, MOP/RPL Remote Boot
Bus Width	16	32
On-board/Buffer RAM	128K	2 x 256 FIFOs
PC Bus Interface	ISA	PCI
LED Indicators	Twisted pair link, network activity	Link, Connection, Transmit, Receive
Comments	Includes EZWORKS for installation Other models available	Supports Alpha, Intel, MIPS, and Power PC platforms
Warranty	Lifetime	Lifetime
Price	$119 (single), $535 (5 pack), $2,529 (20 pack)	Unavailable

N/A—Not applicable   INA—Information not available

Table Continues →

■ Network Interface Cards

Manufacturer	Efficient Networks, Inc.	Efficient Networks, Inc.	Efficient Networks, Inc.
Model	ENI-100s	ENI-155p	ENI-155e, ENI-100e
Network Interface Standards Supported	ATM	ATM	ATM
Hardware Protocol	ATM	ATM	ATM
Connectors	MMF	MMF, UTP-5	MMF, UTP-5 (100e) MMF only
LAN Drivers	SunOS, Solaris	Windows NT, Novell NetWare	Windows NT, Novell NetWare
Bus Width	32 bit	32 bit	32 bit
On-board/Buffer RAM	512K	512K or 2MB	512K or 2MB/ (100e) 512K only
PC Bus Interface	SBus	PCIBus	EISABus
LED Indicators	Physical data link	Physical data link	Physical data link
Comments	Signaling, LANE, ILMI, 1577, tested interoperability	Signaling, LANE, ILMI, 1577, tested interoperability	Signaling, LANE, ILMI, 1577, tested interoperability
Warranty	1 year (hardware), 90 days (software)	1 year (hardware), 90 days (software)	1 year (hardware), 90 days (software)
Price	$995+	INA	INA

Manufacturer	Efficient Networks, Inc.	Efficient Networks, Inc.
Model	ENI-25p	ENI-155's
Network Interface Standards Supported	ATM	ATM
Hardware Protocol	ATM	ATM
Connectors	UTP-3, 4, or 5	MMF, UTP-5
LAN Drivers	Windows NT, Windows 95	SunOS, Solaris
Bus Width	32 bit	32 bit
On-board/Buffer RAM	None	512K or 2MB
PC Bus Interface	PCIBus	SBus
LED Indicators	Physical data link	Physical data link
Comments	Signaling, LANE	Signaling, LANE, ILMI, 1577, tested interoperability
Warranty	1 year (hardware), 90 days (software)	1 year (hardware), 90 days (software)
Price	$249	$995

Manufacturer	Farallon	Farallon
Model	EtherWave LC card	Fast Ether TX-10/100 PCI card & Fast EtherTX-10/100 NuBus Card
Network Interface Standards Supported	10BASE-T Ethernet	Ethernet and Fast Ethernet
Hardware Protocol	Ethernet TCP/IP. Novell IPX/SPX, IEEE 802.3	Ethernet and Fast Ethernet
Connectors	2 RJ-45 10BASE-T ports	RJ 45
LAN Drivers	Mac OS	ODI, Mac OS, NOIS 2.0 & 3.0 Ethernet
Bus Width	16 bit	32 bit
On-board/Buffer RAM	64K	64K
PC Bus Interface	ISA/EISA	PCI/NuBus

N/A—Not applicable   INA—Information not available

Network Interface Cards ■

Manufacturer	Farallon	Farallon
LED Indicators	4 (one received and link per port)	10Mbps and 100Mbps Link, Network Activity
Comments	Daisy chainable 10BASE-T	Works in Power Macintoshes and Intel PC's Autosenses between 10 BASE-T and 100BASE-T
Warranty	Lifetime	Lifetime
Price	$189	$199 $319

Manufacturer	Farallon	Farallon
Model	EtherMac-TP NuBus Card & EtherMac TN NuBus Card.	EtherMac-TP NuBusCard & EtherMac LC-TP LC/PDS Card
Network Interface Standards Supported	Ethernet 10 BASE-T Ethernet	Ethernet 10BASE-T
Hardware Protocol	Ethernet	Ethernet
Connectors	RJ-45, AUI BNC, AUI	RJ-45, AUI RJ-45
LAN Drivers	Mac OS	Mac OS Mac OS, ODI & NDIS
Bus Width	32 bit	32 bit 16 bit
On-board/Buffer RAM	64K	64K
PC Bus Interface	NuBus	NuBus LC/PDS
LED Indicators	Link N/A	Link
Comments		
Warranty	Lifetime	Lifetime
Price	$112 $122	$112 $95

Manufacturer	Farallon	Farallon
Model	EtherMac Lan/Modem PC Card & EtherMac LC/PDS Card.	EtherMac PC card for Powerbook (10BASE-T/Thinnet) & EtherMac PC card for Powerbook (10 BASE-T)
Network Interface Standards Supported	Ethernet 10BASE T Ethernet 10BASE-2	10 BASE-T AND 10 BASE-2 Appletalk, NetWare, A/UX, Timbuktu, Mac SNMP, Mactop
Hardware Protocol	Ethernet	Ethernet: CSMA-CD. IEEE 802.3 compliant
Connectors	RJ-45 BNC, AUI	10BASE-T, 10BASE-2 10BASE-T
LAN Drivers	Mac OS, ODI & NOIS Mac OS	Mac OS, ODI & NOIS Mac OS, ODI & NOIS
Bus Width	16 bit	16 bit
On-board/Buffer RAM	64K	16K
PC Bus Interface	PC MCIA LC/PDS	Type II PC card (version 2.1 compliant) Type II PC card (PCMIA)
LED Indicators	Link, Activity N/A	3 (Power, Collision, Transmit) N/A
Comments	Combination Ethernet and 2f.f modem PC card	
Warranty	Lifetime	Lifetime
Price	$499 $115	$199 $169

N/A—Not applicable   INA—Information not available

Table Continues →

■ Network Interface Cards

Manufacturer	**Farallon**	**Farallon**
Model	EtherWave PowerBook PC card & EtherWave NuBus card.	EtherWave ISA card
Network Interface Standards Supported	10 BASE-T 10 BASE-T Ethernet	Ethernet 10 BASE-T, CSMA-CD-IEEE 802.3 compliant
Hardware Protocol	Ethernet: CSMA/CD-IEEE 802.3 compliant Ethernet	Ethernet
Connectors	2 RJ-45 10 BASE_T ports	2 RJ-45 10 BASE-T port
LAN Drivers	Mac OS, NOIS & DDI Apple or Farallon Ethernet Drives	NDIS and ODI
Bus Width	16 bit 32 bit	16 bit
On-board/Buffer RAM	16K 64K	8K
PC Bus Interface	PC Card-Type II NuBus	ISA
LED Indicators	One Receive and Link per port; one Collision, one Transmit, one Power test One Receive and Link per port; one Collision, one Transmit	One Receive and Link per port; one Collision, one Transmit
Comments	Daisy-chainable 10 BASE-T	Daisy-chainable 10 BASE-T
Warranty	Lifetime	Lifetime
Price	$169 $189	$139

Manufacturer	**IBM**	**IBM**
Model	Ethernet Credit Card	EtherJet ISA
Network Interface Standards Supported	Ethernet 10BASE-T, 10BASE2	Ethernet 10BASE-T, 10BASE2, 10BASE5
Hardware Protocol	INA	INA
Connectors	BNC, RJ-45	AUI, BNC, RJ-45
LAN Drivers	IPX, ODI, NDIS, Windows 95, Windows NT	IPX, ODI, NDIS, Windows 95, Windows NT
Bus Width	16	16
On-board/Buffer RAM	16K	4K
PC Bus Interface	PCMIA (PC Card)	ISA/EISA
LED Indicators	Link, Activity	Link, Activity
Comments	Other Ethernet cards available	LAN client DOS memory reduction software full duplex, plug and play.
Warranty	Lifetime	Lifetime
Price	$159 10BASE-T $205 10BASE2	$135

Manufacturer	**IBM**	**IBM**
Model	100/10 Ethernet PCI	100/10 Ethernet ISA
Network Interface Standards Supported	Ethernet 10BASE-T, 100BASE-TX	Ethernet 10BASE-T, 100BASE-TX
Hardware Protocol	INA	INA
Connectors	RJ-45	RJ-45

N/A—Not applicable   INA—Information not available

Network Interface Cards ∎

Manufacturer	IBM	IBM
LAN Drivers	IPX, ODI, NDIS, Windows 95, Windows NT	IPX, ODI, NDIS, Windows 95, Windows NT
Bus Width	32	16
On-board/Buffer RAM	N/A	5K
PC Bus Interface	PCI	ISA/EISA
LED Indicators	Link, Activity, 100Mbps	Link, Activity, 100Mbps
Comments	Auto-sense and select speed, full duplex, plug and play	Auto-sense and set speed, full duplex
Warranty	Limited lifetime	Limited lifetime
Price	$199	$199

Manufacturer	IBM	IBM
Model	EtherJet Wake-On LAN	EtherJet 10BASE-T ISA
Network Interface Standards Supported	Ethernet 10BASE-T	Ethernet 10BASE-T
Hardware Protocol	INA	INA
Connectors	RJ-45	RJ-45
LAN Drivers	IPX, ODI, NDIS, Windows 95, Windows NT	IPX, ODI, NDIS, Windows 95, Windows NT
Bus Width	16	16
On-board/Buffer RAM	4K	4K
PC Bus Interface	ISA/EISA	ISA/EISA
LED Indicators	Link, Activity	Link, Activity
Comments	DOS memory reduction software full duplex, plug-n-play. Wake-on LAN capability.	LAN client DOS memory reduction software full duplex, plug-n-play
Warranty	Limited lifetime	Limited lifetime
Price	$120	$110

Manufacturer	IBM	IBM
Model	Auto 16/4 ISA	Turbo 16/4 Token Ring ISA
Network Interface Standards Supported	Token Ring 16/4	Token Ring 16/4
Hardware Protocol	INA	INA
Connectors	STP, UTP, RJ-45, 9-pin	STP, UTP, RJ-45, 9-pin
LAN Drivers	IPX, ODI, NDIS, Windows 95, Windows NT	IPX, ODI, NDIS, Windows 95, Windows NT
Bus Width	8/16	16
On-board/Buffer RAM	64K	64K
PC Bus Interface	ISA	ISA/EISA
LED Indicators	(2) adapter & ring status	(2) adapter & ring status
Comments	Auto ring speed select, RPL included, auto media select	Auto ring speed select, RPL included, auto media select, plug and play, 8 interrupts and 768 I/O ports
Warranty	Lifetime	Lifetime
Price	$265	$265

N/A—Not applicable   INA—Information not available

Table Continues →

ZIFF-DAVIS PRESS

■ Network Interface Cards

Manufacturer	IBM	IBM
Model	Auto Wake ISA Adapter	PCI Token Ring Adapter
Network Interface Standards Supported	Token Ring 16/4	Token Ring 16/4
Hardware Protocol	INA	INA
Connectors	STP, UTP, RJ-45, 9-pin	STP, UTP, RJ-45, 9-pin
LAN Drivers	IPX, ODI, NDIS, Windows 95, Windows NT	IPX, ODI, NDIS, Windows 95, Windows NT
Bus Width	16	32
On-board/Buffer RAM	64K	32K Flash EPROM 512 byte FIFO
PC Bus Interface	ISA	ISA/EISA
LED Indicators	(2) adapter & ring status	(2) adapter & ring status
Comments	Network manager can start PC from network management workstation.	Auto ring speed select, RPL included, auto media select, plug-n-play, 8 interrupts and 768 I/O ports
Warranty	Lifetime	Lifetime
Price	$305	$350

Manufacturer	IBM	IBM	IBM
Model	Auto 16/4 Credit Card	Auto LAN Streamer PCI	Triple Auto LAN Streamer PCI
Network Interface Standards Supported	Token Ring 16/4	Token Ring 16/4	Token Ring 16/4
Hardware Protocol	INA	INA	INA
Connectors	PCMCIA type 2	STP, UTP, RJ-45	STP, UTP, RJ-45
LAN Drivers	IPX, ODI, NDIS, Windows 95, Windows NT	IPX, ODI, NDIS, Windows 95, Windows NT	IPX, ODI, NDIS, Windows 95, Windows NT
Bus Width	16	32	32
On-board/Buffer RAM	INA	32K Flash EPROM 256 byte FIFO	32K Flash EPROM 256 byte FIFO
PC Bus Interface	PCMCIA type 2	PCI	PCI
LED Indicators	No	(2) adapter & ring status	(2) adapter & ring status
Comments	Auto ring speed select, RPL included, auto media select	Auto ring speed select, RPL included, auto media select, plug and play, auto full duplex	Auto ring speed select, RPL included, auto media select, plug and play, auto full duplex
Warranty	Lifetime	Lifetime	Lifetime
Price	$435	$360	$1,115

Manufacturer	Intel Corp.	Intel Corp.
Model	Ether Express™ Pro/100 ISA	Ether Express™ Pro/100
Network Interface Standards Supported	10BASE-T, 100BASE-TX	10BASE-T, 100BASE-TX
Hardware Protocol	Ethernet	Ethernet
Connectors	RJ-45	RJ-45
LAN Drivers	All standard NOS, OS, including UNIX, packet, et al.	All standard NOS, OS, including UNIX, packet, et al.
Bus Width	16	32-bit bus master

N/A—Not applicable   INA—Information not available

Network Interface Cards ■

Manufacturer	Intel Corp.	Intel Corp.
On-board/Buffer RAM	8K	16K
PC Bus Interface	ISA	EISA
LED Indicators	Data, Link, Activity, 100MB	Data, Link, Activity @10 Data, Link, Activity,@100
Comments	Install and diagnostic software included	Install and diagnostic software included
Warranty	Limited lifetime	Limited lifetime
Price	$199 (single) $179 (20 pack)	$299 (single)

Manufacturer	Intel Corp.	Intel Corp.
Model	Ether Express™ Pro/100 SMART	Ether Express™ Pro/100 B
Network Interface Standards Supported	10BASE-T, 100BASE-TX	10BASE-T, 100BASE-TX
Hardware Protocol	Ethernet	Ethernet
Connectors	RJ-45	RJ-45
LAN Drivers	NetWare Server, DOS OPI, Microsoft NT, NetWare MSL	All standard NOS, OS, including UNIX, packet, et al.
Bus Width	32-bit bus master	32-bit bus master
On-board/Buffer RAM	2MB	6K
PC Bus Interface	PCI	PCI
LED Indicators	Data, Link, Activity @10 Data, Link, Activity,@100	Data, Link, Activity,@100
Comments	Diagnostic software included	
Warranty	Limited lifetime	Limited lifetime
Price	$895	$169 (single) $149 (20 pack)

Manufacturer	Kingston Technology, Corp.	Kingston Technology, Corp.	Kingston Technology, Corp.
Model	KNE2000TLC KNE2021LC	KNE20T KNE20BT	KNE40T KNE40BT
Network Interface Standards Supported	10BASE-T or 10BASE-T2	10BASE-T or 10BASE-T/2	10BASE-T or 10BASE-T/2
Hardware Protocol	Ethernet	Ethernet	Ethernet
Connectors	RJ-45 or RJ45 and BNC	RJ-45 or RJ45 and BNC	RJ-45 or RJ45 and BNC
LAN Drivers	ODI, NDIS2, NDIS3, Packet Drives, SCO MDI/LLI	ODI, NDIS2, NDIS3, Packet Drives, SCO MDI/LLI	ODI, NDIS2, NDIS3, Packet Drives, SCO MDI/LLI
Bus Width	16 bit	16 bit	32 bit
On-board/Buffer RAM	32K	32K	DMA
PC Bus Interface	ISA	PnP ISA	PCI
LED Indicators	Link, Activity	Link, Activity	Link, Activity
Comments	QSTART, autoconfiguration and diagnostic program	QSTART, autoconfiguration and diagnostic program	QSTART, autoconfiguration and diagnostic program
Warranty	Lifetime	Lifetime	Lifetime
Price	$45+	$65+	$99+

N/A—Not applicable   INA—Information not available

Table Continues →

■ Network Interface Cards

Manufacturer	Kingston Technology Co.	Kingston Technology Co.	LANART
Model	KNE-PCM/T KNE-PCM/M	KNE-100TX	EFA-0101-ST
Network Interface Standards Supported	10BASE-T or 10BASE-T/2	Fast Ethernet 100BASE-TX Ethernet 10BASE-T	10BASE-FL Ethernet
Hardware Protocol	Ethernet	Ethernet/Fast Ethernet	Ethernet 802.3
Connectors	RJ-45 or RJ-45 and BNC	RJ-45	ST, SMA, SC
LAN Drivers	ODI, NDIS2, NDIS3, Packet Drives, SCO MDI/LLI	ODI, NDIS2, NDIS3, Packet Drives, SCO MDI/LLI	IPX, ODI, NDIS, IP
Bus Width	16 bit	32 bit	8/16 bit
On-board/Buffer RAM		DMA	
PC Bus Interface	PC Card	PC Card	ISA
LED Indicators	Link, Activity	Link, Activity	Link, XMIT/Receive, Collision
Comments	System soft socket and card ser- vices included for capability	Qstart, autoconfiguration and diag- nostic program	Patented Linkalert provides 100% Link Fault Isolation and Detection
Warranty	Lifetime	Lifetime	5 year
Price	$139+	$139	$299

Manufacturer	LANCAST	LANCAST	LANCAST
Model	EZ Link 4109	EZ Link 4216	Fast Link 6110
Network Interface Standards Supported	IEEE 802.3 10BASE-T and 10BASE2	IEEE 802.3 10BASE-T, 10BASE2, and 10BASE5	IEEE 802.3 10BASE-T, IEEE 802.3a 100BASE-TX
Hardware Protocol	Ethernet	Ethernet	Ethernet
Connectors	RJ45, BNC	RJ45, BNC, AUI	UTP
LAN Drivers	NetWare, Windows, LAN Manager, OS/2, Vines, SCO, UNIX, LAN Server, DEC Pathworks, NE2000 Compatible	NetWare, Windows, LAN Manager, OS/2, Vines, SCO, UNIX, LAN Server, DEC Pathworks, NE2000 Compatible	NetWare, Windows, OS/2, Vines, SCO, UNIX, LAN Server, DEC Path- works, and DDI, NDIS and UI compliant
Bus Width	16 bit	16 bit	32 bit
On-board/Buffer RAM	8K	8K	4K
PC Bus Interface	PCMCIA	ISA	PCI
LED Indicators	Link, Traffic	Link, Traffic	Transmit, Receive
Comments			Autosensing detector for 10- and 100Mbps operation
Warranty	3 year	3 year	3 year
Price	$159–$179	$59–$79	$199

Manufacturer	LANCAST	LANCAST
Model	Fast Link 6111	Fast Link 6112
Network Interface Standards Supported	IEEE 802.3 10BASE-T, IEEE 802.3a 100BASE-FX	IEEE 802.3 10BASE-T, IEEE 802.3a 100BASE-FX
Hardware Protocol	Ethernet	Ethernet
Connectors	SC and ST for multi-mode; SC for single mode	RJ45
LAN Drivers	NetWare, Windows, OS/2, Vines, SCO, UNIX, LAN Server, DEC Pathworks, and DDI, NDIS and UI compliant	NetWare, Windows, OS/2, Vines, SCO, UNIX, LAN Server, DEC Pathworks, and DDI, NDIS and UI compliant

N/A—Not applicable   INA—Information not available

Network Interface Cards ■

Manufacturer	LANCAST	LANCAST
Bus Width	32 bit	32 bit
On-board/Buffer RAM	4K	4K
PC Bus Interface	PCI	PCI
LED Indicators	Transmit, Receive	Activity, Link
Comments	Multi-mode and singlemode versions available	
Warranty	3 year	3 year
Price	$399–$1,950	$225

Manufacturer	Landings Technology	Landings Technology
Model	ISA NS 2000/ ISA PnP 2000	ISA PnP 2100
Network Interface Standards Supported	Ethernet 10BASE-T, 10BASE2,	Ethernet 10BASE-T, 10BASE2,
Hardware Protocol	Ethernet	Ethernet
Connectors	RJ45, BNC	RJ45, BNC
LAN Drivers	IPX, ODI, NDIS, Packet driver	IPX, ODI, NDIS, Packet driver
Bus Width	16/8 bit	16/8 bit
On-board/Buffer RAM	16K	N/A
PC Bus Interface	ISA	ISA
LED Indicators	Data link, Collision	Data link, Collision
Comments	NE2000 compatible, software configuration, diagnostic software, boot ROM option, Windows 95 plug and play (ISA PnP only), National Semiconductor (ISI NS only)	NE2100 compatible, includes configuration and diagnostic software, boot ROM option, Windows 95 plug and play, Bus mastered
Warranty	Lifetime	Lifetime
Price	$28–32 (ISA NS)/ $32–34 (ISA PnP)	$55–$67

Manufacturer	Landings Technology	Landings Technology
Model	ISA NS 2000 Jumpered	VESA 2100
Network Interface Standards Supported	Ethernet 10BASE-T, 10BASE2, 10BASE2	Ethernet 10BASE-T, 10BASE2,
Hardware Protocol	Ethernet	Ethernet
Connectors	RJ45/BNC/AUI Combo	RJ45, BNC
LAN Drivers	IPX, ODI, NDIS, Packet driver	IPX, ODI, NDIS, Packet driver
Bus Width	16/8 bit	32 bit
On-board/Buffer RAM	16K	N/A
PC Bus Interface	ISA	VESA
LED Indicators	Data link, Collision	Data link, Collision
Comments	Jumpered or jumperless operation, NE2000 compatible, includes configuration and diagnostic software	NE2100 compatible, includes configuration and diagnostic software, boot ROM option, bus mastered
Warranty	Lifetime	Lifetime
Price	$45	$79–$95

N/A—Not applicable   INA—Information not available

Table Continues →

■ Network Interface Cards

Manufacturer	Landings Technology	Landings Technology	Landings Technology
Model	PCI 10	PCI 10	PCMCIA
Network Interface Standards Supported	Ethernet 10BASE-T, 10BASE2,	Ethernet 100BASE-T	Ethernet 10BASE-T, 10BASE2,
Hardware Protocol	Ethernet	Ethernet	Ethernet
Connectors	RJ45, BNC	RJ45	RJ45, BNC
LAN Drivers	IPX, ODI, NDIS, Packet Driver	IPX, ODI, NDIS, Packet Driver	IPX, ODI, NDIS, Packet Driver
Bus Width	32 bit	32 bit	N/A
On-board/Buffer RAM	N/A	N/A	16K
PC Bus Interface	PCI	PCI	PCMCIA II
LED Indicators	Data link, Collision	Data link, Collision	Data link
Comments	Includes configuration and diagnostic software, bus mastered, DEC chip, full duplex	Auto-negotiation, speed selection, supports full duplex, multi-thread operation	NE 2000 compatible, supports Card and Socket services and "hot swap," software configuration, diagnostic software
Warranty	Lifetime	Lifetime	Lifetime
Price	$59–$65	$129	$138

Manufacturer	Landings Technology	Madge Networks
Model	Pocket	Smart 16/4 Fiber AT Ringnode (#52-09)
Network Interface Standards Supported	Ethernet 10BASE-T, 10BASE2,	Token Ring 16/4Mbps IEEE 802.5j
Hardware Protocol	Ethernet	Token Ring (FIBER)
Connectors	RJ45, BNC	ST (Bayonet) Connectors
LAN Drivers	IPX, ODI, NDIS, Packet driver	IPX, ODI, NDIS2, NDIS3, LCC, TCP/IP, NetBios
Bus Width	N/A	8/16 ISA
On-board/Buffer RAM	32K	256K
PC Bus Interface	Parallel port	ISA
LED Indicators	Data link	N/A
Comments	Supports EPP, uni- and bidirectional modes, software configuration, external power supply	Data, security, and long transmission capability for ISA bus
Warranty	Lifetime	Lifetime
Price	$119	INA

Manufacturer	Madge Networks	Madge Networks	Madge Networks
Model	Smart 16/4 Fiber PCI Ringnode (#51-09)	Blue+ 16/4 ISA(#62-03)	Smart 16/4 EISA Ringnode (#52-08)
Network Interface Standards Supported	Token Ring 16/4Mbps, IEEE 802.5j	Token Ring 16/4Mbps, IEEE 802.5j	Token Ring 16/4Mbps, IEEE 802.5j
Hardware Protocol	Token Ring (FIBER)	Token Ring	Token Ring
Connectors	ST (Bayonet) Connectors	UTP: RJ-45-STP: 9-pin D	UTP: RJ-45-STP: 9-pin D
LAN Drivers	IPX, ODI, NDIS2, NDIS3, LCC, TCP/IP, NetBios	IPX, ODI, NDIS2, NDIS3, LCC, TCP/IP, NetBios	IPX, ODI, NDIS2, NDIS3, LCC, TCP/IP, NetBios
Bus Width	32 bit	16 bit	32 bit
On-board/Buffer RAM	512K	256K	256K

N/A—Not applicable   INA—Information not available

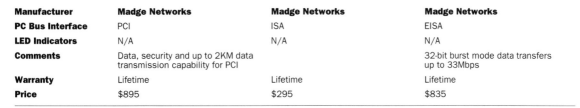

Network Interface Cards ■

Manufacturer	Madge Networks	Madge Networks	Madge Networks
PC Bus Interface	PCI	ISA	EISA
LED Indicators	N/A	N/A	N/A
Comments	Data, security and up to 2KM data transmission capability for PCI		32-bit burst mode data transfers up to 33Mbps
Warranty	Lifetime	Lifetime	Lifetime
Price	$895	$295	$835

Manufacturer	Madge Networks	Madge Networks	Madge Networks
Model	Smart 16/4 AT Plus Ringnode (#52-03)	Smart 16/4 MC32 Ringnode (#54-09)	Smart 16/4 MC32 Ringnode (#54-08)
Network Interface Standards Supported	Token Ring 16/4Mbps, IEEE 802.5j	Token Ring 16/4Mbps, IEEE 802.5 standard	Token Ring 16/4Mbps, IEEE 802.5 standard
Hardware Protocol	Token Ring	Token Ring	Token Ring
Connectors	UTP: RJ-45-STP: 9-pin D	UTP: RJ-45-STP: 9-pin D	UTP: RJ-45-STP: 9-pin D
LAN Drivers	IPX, ODI, NDIS2, NDIS3, LCC, TCP/IP, NetBios	IPX, ODI, NDIS2, NDIS3, LCC, TCP/IP, NetBios	IPX, ODI, NDIS2, NDIS3, LCC, TCP/IP, NetBios
Bus Width	16 bit	32 bit	16/32 bit
On-board/Buffer RAM	512K	256K	256K
PC Bus Interface	ISA	MCA	MCA
LED Indicators	N/A	N/A	N/A
Comments	Up to seven protocols can be downloaded simultaneously to the card	40Mbps streaming data transfers from PC RAM to adapter	Up to five protocols can be down-loaded concurrently to the adapter
Warranty	Lifetime	Lifetime	Lifetime
Price	$595	$835	$555

Manufacturer	Madge Networks	Madge Networks	Madge Networks
Model	Smart 16/4 PCMCIA Ringnode (#20-00)	Smart 16/4 PCMCIA Ringnode (#51-02)	Smart 16/4 ISA Client PnP Ringnode (#22-04)
Network Interface Standards Supported	Token Ring 16/4Mbps, IEEE 802.5 standard	Token Ring 16/4Mbps, IEEE 802.5 standard	Token Ring 16/4Mbps, IEEE 802.5 standard
Hardware Protocol	Token Ring	Token Ring	Token Ring
Connectors	UTP: RJ-45-STP: 9-pin D	UTP: RJ-45-STP: 9-pin D	UTP: RJ-45-STP: 9-pin D
LAN Drivers	IPX, ODI, NDIS2, NDIS3, LCC, TCP/IP, NetBios	IPX, ODI, NDIS2, NDIS3, LCC, TCP/IP, NetBios	IPX, ODI, NDIS2, NDIS3, LCC, TCP/IP, NetBios
Bus Width	16 bit	32 bit	16bit
On-board/Buffer RAM	512K	512K	128K
PC Bus Interface	PCMCIA	PCI	ISA
LED Indicators	N/A	N/A	N/A
Comments	Host memory efficient; combined IPX + TCP/IP protocol stack in 12K	132Mbps bursting data transfer	
Warranty	Lifetime	Lifetime	Lifetime
Price	$480	$435	$295

N/A—Not applicable   INA—Information not available

Table Continues →

■ Network Interface Cards

Manufacturer	Madge Networks	MagicRAM, Inc.	Microdyne Corp
Model	Smart 16/4 Fiber AT Ringnode (#52-09)	Ethernet PC Card P/N 933819	Eagle EP2000T plus, Eagle EP2000 plus
Network Interface Standards Supported	Token Ring 16/4Mbps IEEE 802.5j	10BASE-T & 10BASE2	Ethernet 10BASE-T/ 10BASE5, 10BASE2
Hardware Protocol	Token Ring (FIBER)	Ethernet	Ethernet
Connectors	ST (Bayonet) Connectors	RJ-45 and BNC	RJ-45, AUI, BNC
LAN Drivers	IPX, ODI, NDIS2, NDIS3, LCC, TCP/IP, NetBios	ODI, NDIS, and packet drivers	ODI, NetWare, ODI, NetWare, NDIS, Packet Drives (2000+)
Bus Width	8/16 ISA	16-bit	16 bit
On-board/Buffer RAM	256K	16K	16K or 64K
PC Bus Interface	ISA	PCMCIA	ISA
LED Indicators	N/A	Data traffic and link status	Polarity and link status
Comments	Data, security and long transmission capability for ISA bus	NE2000 compatible	Jumperless configuration
Warranty	Lifetime	Lifetime	Lifetime
Price	$995	$99	$74 $84

Manufacturer	Microdyne Corp	Microdyne Corp	Microdyne Corp
Model	NE10/100 PCI	NE 2000 plus 3 NE 2000 plus 3V	NE 2500T Plus, NE 2500 Plus
Network Interface Standards Supported	Ethernet 10BASE-T, 100BASE-TX	Ethernet 10BASE-T 10BASE2, 10BASE5	Ethernet 10BASE-T (2500T+), 10BASE2, 10BASE-T (2500+)
Hardware Protocol	Ethernet	Ethernet	Ethernet
Connectors	RJ-45	RJ-45, AUI, BNC	RJ-45, BNC
LAN Drivers	NDIS2, NDIS3, ODI Client, ODI Server	NDIS, ODI, NetWare	NDIS, ODI, NetWare, Packet Drivers
Bus Width	32-bit bus master	8/16 bit	16-bit bus master
On-board/Buffer RAM		16K or 64K	
PC Bus Interface	PCI	ISA/EISA	ISA/EISA
LED Indicators	Link Integrity, Traffic	Polarity and Link Status	4 LED's programmable
Comments	NWAY Auto negotiation, full duplex, plug and play	Jumperless configuration, the NE2000 plus 3V also includes ROMSHIELD PROM	Full duplex fast frame exchange, plug and play, DMI
Warranty	Lifetime	Lifetime	Lifetime
Price	$161	$107 (Plus 3V) $119 (3V)	$109 $119

Manufacturer	Microdyne Corp	Microdyne Corp	Microdyne Corp
Model	NE10/100 ISA	NE 2000T plus NE 2000 plus	NE 2000T NE 2000
Network Interface Standards Supported	Ethernet 10BASE-T, 100BASE-TX	Ethernet 10BASE-T (2000T)/ 10BASE2, 10BASE5 (2000)	Ethernet 10BASE-T (2000T)/ 10BASE2, 10BASE5 (2000)
Hardware Protocol	Ethernet	Ethernet	Ethernet
Connectors	RJ-45	RJ-45, AUI, BNC	RJ-45, AUI, BNC
LAN Drivers	NDIS2, NDIS3, ODI Client, ODI Server, packet driver, IPX	NDIS, ODI, NetWare	NDIS, ODI, NetWare

N/A—Not applicable   INA—Information not available

Network Interface Cards ■

Manufacturer	Microdyne Corp	Microdyne Corp	Microdyne Corp
Bus Width	16 bit	8/16 bit	16 bit
On-board/Buffer RAM	8K	16K or 64K	16K
PC Bus Interface	ISA	ISA/EISA	ISA/EISA
LED Indicators	Link Integrity, Traffic	Link Status	Link Status
Comments	Full duplex, NWAY autonegotiation, full duplex, plug and play		
Warranty	Lifetime	Lifetime	Lifetime
Price	$185	$87 $96	$116

Manufacturer	Microdyne Corp	Microdyne Corp
Model	NE 5500T Plus, NE 5500 Plus	NE 3300, NE 3200 Plus, NE 3200 with TPA
Network Interface Standards Supported	Ethernet 10BASE-T (5500T+)/ 10BASE2, 10BASE-T	Ethernet 10BASE-T 10BASE2, 10BASE5
Hardware Protocol	Ethernet	Ethernet
Connectors	RJ-45, BNC	RJ-45, AUI, BNC
LAN Drivers	NDIS, ODI, NetWare, Packet Drivers	NDIS, ODI, NetWare, Packet Drivers
Bus Width	32-bit bus master	32 bit (NE3300)/ 32-bit bus master
On-board/Buffer RAM		32K (3300) 48K
PC Bus Interface	PCI	PCI
LED Indicators	3 LED's programmable	Link Status
Comments	Full duplex fast frame exchange, plug and play, CE certified	Software selectable jumperless configuration (3300). Intelligent server card on-board processors.
Warranty	Lifetime	1 year (3300) Lifetime
Price	$108 $119	$249/$546/$544

Manufacturer	Microdyne Corp	Microdyne Corp	Microdyne Corp
Model	Eagle 3210T Eagle 3210	NE 3200	NE4200 PCMCIA
Network Interface Standards Supported	Ethernet 10BASE-T (3210T)/ 10BASE2, 10BASE5	10BASE2, 10BASE5	10BASE-T, 10BASE2
Hardware Protocol	Ethernet	Ethernet	Ethernet
Connectors	RJ-45, AUI, BNC	AUI, BNC	RJ-45, BNC
LAN Drivers	NDIS, ODI, NetWare	NDIS, ODI	NDIS, ODI, NetWare
Bus Width	32-bit EISA, 32 bit	32-bit bus master	
On-board/Buffer RAM	32K	48K	16K
PC Bus Interface	EISA	EISA	PCMCIA Release 2, type 2
LED Indicators	Link Status	Link Status	Power, Data link, Transmission, Receiver, Jabber

N/A—Not applicable   INA—Information not available

Table Continues →

■ Network Interface Cards

Manufacturer	Microdyne Corp	Microdyne Corp	Microdyne Corp
Comments		Intelligent server card on-board processors	Dual media PCMCIA Adapter
Warranty	Lifetime	Lifetime	Lifetime
Price	$154 $164	$530	$179

Manufacturer	Mitron Computer, Inc.	Mitron Computer, Inc.	Mitron Computer, Inc.
Model	F10/100TX	LX-2100	LX-2100P
Network Interface Standards Supported	10BASE-T	10BASE-T/10BASE2	10BASE-T/10BASE2
Hardware Protocol	Ethernet	Ethernet	Ethernet
Connectors	RJ45	BNC/RJ45	BNC/RJ45
LAN Drivers			NE-2000 compatible
Bus Width	32 bit	16 bit	32 bit
On-board/Buffer RAM			
PC Bus Interface	PCI	ISA	PCI
LED Indicators	Link, Collision	Link, Collision	Link, Collision
Comments	100Mbps		
Warranty	Lifetime	Lifetime	Lifetime
Price	$299	$89	$149

Manufacturer	Mitron Computer, Inc.	Mitron Computer, Inc.	Motorola ISG
Model	E-3200P	E-2000	BitSURFR PC
Network Interface Standards Supported	10BASE-T/10BASE2	10BASE-T/10BASE2	None
Hardware Protocol	Ethernet	Ethernet	
Connectors	BNC/RJ45	BNC/RJ45	2-RJ11 1-RJ45
LAN Drivers	NE-2000 compatible	NE-2000 compatible	None
Bus Width	32 bit	16 bit	8 bit 16K
On-board/Buffer RAM			
PC Bus Interface	PCI	ISA	ISA
LED Indicators	Link, Collision	Link, Collision	None
Comments			None
Warranty	Lifetime	Lifetime	5 year
Price	$89	$59	$375

Manufacturer	Multi-Tech Systems, Inc.	RNS (formerly Rockwell Network Systems)	RNS (formerly Rockwell Network Systems)
Model	EN301 CT 16C	RNS 2300-TX	RNS 2340-TX
Network Interface Standards Supported	10BASE-T or Thinnet	10BASE-T, 100BASE-TX	10BASE-T, 100BASE-TX
Hardware Protocol	INA	Ethernet	Ethernet

N/A—Not applicable   INA—Information not available

Network Interface Cards ■

Manufacturer	Multi-Tech Systems, Inc.	RNS (formerly Rockwell Network Systems)	RNS (formerly Rockwell Network Systems)
Connectors	RJ-45, BNC	RJ-45	RJ-45
LAN Drivers	NetWare, Windows, Windows NT, NDIS compatible networks, SunSolaris	NetWare, Windows NT, Windows 95, OS/2, Windows for Workgroups	NetWare, Windows NT, Windows 95, OS/2, Windows for Workgroups
Bus Width	16	32 bit	32 bit
On-board/Buffer RAM	16K	6K	24K
PC Bus Interface	ISA	PCI	PCI
LED Indicators	Link, Receive, Polarity, Transmit	Network functions/Operation	Data link
Comments	Diagnostic software included; software programmable	Wide variety of drives, no hardware adaptation	Provides 4 fast Ethernet connections using one PCI slot
Warranty	2 year	3 year	3 year
Price	$159	$245	$1,195

Manufacturer	RNS (formerly Rockwell Network Systems)	RNS (formerly Rockwell Network Systems)	RNS (formerly Rockwell Network Systems)
Model	RNS-2350TX	CMC-1156	ENP-10 Series
Network Interface Standards Supported	10BASE-TX, 100BASE-TX	ANSI X3T9.5	10BASE-T
Hardware Protocol	Ethernet	FDDI	Ethernet
Connectors	RJ-45	ST	AUI
LAN Drivers	ODI, NDIS, DCO UNIX, Solaris	SunOS, VxWork, OS/9, PSOST, LynxD	SunOS
Bus Width	32 bit	32 bit	32 bit
On-board/Buffer RAM	128K	512K	128-512K
PC Bus Interface	PMC	VME	VME
LED Indicators	Network connectivity	Run/Fail	Data link/Receive
Comments		On-board, RISC processor frees host CPU	
Warranty	2 year	1 year	2 year
Price	$445	$5,995	$1,805–$2,195

Manufacturer	RNS (formerly Rockwell Network Systems)	RNS (formerly Rockwell Network Systems)	RNS (formerly Rockwell Network Systems)
Model	CMC-130	RNS-2250TX	RNS 1250 Series
Network Interface Standards Supported	10BASE-T	INA	ANSI X3T9.5
Hardware Protocol	Ethernet	FDDI	FDDI
Connectors	AUI	RJ-45, SC	ST, MIC, RJ-45
LAN Drivers	SunOS	ODI, NDIS, DCO UNIX, Solaris + other	HP-RT, Solaris, HP-UX, OG-UX; PLUS 3rd party drives (VxWorks, psost, VRTX, SunOS)
Bus Width	32 bit	32 bit	32 bit
On-board/Buffer RAM	128K	128K	128K
PC Bus Interface	VME	PMC	VME
LED Indicators	Data link/Error	Network connectivity	Run/Fail

N/A—Not applicable   INA—Information not available

Table Continues →

■ Network Interface Cards

Manufacturer	RNS (formerly Rockwell Network Systems)	RNS (formerly Rockwell Network Systems)	RNS (formerly Rockwell Network Systems)
Comments	On-board, processor frees host CPU	Only dual PMC on the market (their claim)	Optimizes throughput
Warranty	2 year	2 year	1 year
Price	INA	$1,495–$1,995	$4,495–$4,995

Manufacturer	RNS (formerly Rockwell Network Systems)	SilCom Technologies
Model	RNS 2200 Series	TR Direct/16
Network Interface Standards Supported	ANSI XT312	4/16Mbps Token Ring IEEE 802.5
Hardware Protocol	FDDI	Token Ring
Connectors	ST, MIC, RJ-45	RJ-45, DB-9
LAN Drivers	ODI, NDIS, NetWare, Windows 95, Windows NT, Windows for Workgroups, Solaris, SCO UNIX, OS/2, AIX, PowerMAC	IPX, ODI, NDIS
Bus Width	32 bit	16 bit
On-board/Buffer RAM	128K	128K DRAM
PC Bus Interface	PCI	ISA
LED Indicators	Error, Data link	N/A
Comments		Early Token Release (ETR), to increase network speed; bus mastered DMA allows data to be entered directly into system memory
Warranty	3 year	3 year
Price	$795–$1,695	$295; $195 ea. for pack of 50 NICs

Manufacturer	SMC	SMC
Model	Ether Power 10/100	Ether 10/100
Network Interface Standards Supported	IEEE 802.3, ISO/IEC 8802-3, PCI 2.0	IEEE 802.3, ISO/IEC 8802-3
Hardware Protocol	Fast Ethernet	Fast Ethernet
Connectors	100BASE-TX: RJ-45, DB-9, 10BASE-T: RJ-45	100BASE-TX: RJ-45, DB-9, 10BASE-T: RJ-45
LAN Drivers	NetWare, Windows (95, for Workgroups, NT, 3.x) Banyan Vines, DEC Pathworks, IBM LAN Server	NetWare, Windows (95, for Workgroups, NT, 3.x) Banyan Vines, DEC Pathworks, IBM LAN Server
Bus Width	32	32-bit EISA
On-board/Buffer RAM	INA	128K
PC Bus Interface	PCI	EISA, I/O or DMA Type C
LED Indicators	Network Activity, Link Integrity	Network Activity, Link Integrity
Comments	SMC EZStart	SMC EZStart
Warranty	Lifetime	Lifetime
Price	$142 per unit based on quantity purchased	$259 per unit based on quantity purchased

Manufacturer	SMC	SMC
Model	Ether Power[2]	Ether EZ
Network Interface Standards Supported	IEEE 802.3, ISO/IEC 8802-3, PCI 2.0, PCI-to-PCI bridge specification	IEEE 802.3, ISO/IEC 8802-3, ISA PnP spec v1.01a

N/A—Not applicable   INA—Information not available

Network Interface Cards ■

Manufacturer	SMC	SMC
Hardware Protocol	Ethernet	Ethernet
Connectors	RJ-45	RJ-45, BNC, AUI
LAN Drivers	NetWare, Windows (95, for Workgroups, NT, 3.x) Banyan Vines, DEC Pathworks, IBM LAN Server	NetWare, Windows (95, for Workgroups, NT, 3.x) Banyan Vines, DEC Pathworks, IBM LAN Server, LANtastic, UNIX
Bus Width	32	16
On-board/Buffer RAM	INA	8K
PC Bus Interface	PCI	ISA
LED Indicators	Network Activity, Link Integrity	Network Activity, Link Integrity
Comments	SMC EZStart	SMC EZStart
Warranty	Lifetime	Lifetime
Price	$286	$66–$99

Manufacturer	SMC	SMC
Model	Ether Power	TokenCard Elite
Network Interface Standards Supported	IEEE 802.3 Ethernet, ISO/IEC 8802-3	IEEE 802.2 LLC NetBIOS
Hardware Protocol	Ethernet	Token Ring
Connectors	RJ-45, BNC, AUI	DB-9, RJ-45
LAN Drivers	NetWare, Windows (95, for Workgroups, NT, 3.x) Banyan Vines, DEC Pathworks, IBM LAN Server, AppleTalk	NetWare, Windows, IBM LAN Server and IBM PC LAN, DEC, NDIS
Bus Width	32	8/16
On-board/Buffer RAM	INA	64K
PC Bus Interface	PCI	ISA/EISA
LED Indicators	Network Activity, Link Integrity	Ring Insertion Loopback test
Comments	SMC EZStart	SMC EZStart
Warranty	Lifetime	Lifetime
Price	$101–$150	$199

Manufacturer	SMC	SMC
Model	TokenCard Elite/A	TokenCard Elite Master 32
Network Interface Standards Supported	IEEE 802.5, 802.2, ISO/IEC 8802-5	IEEE 802.5, 802.2, ISO/IEC 8802-5, Token Ring
Hardware Protocol	Token Ring	Token Ring
Connectors	DB-9, RJ-45	DB-9, RJ-45
LAN Drivers	NetWare, Windows, IBM LAN Server and IBM PC LAN, DEC, NDIS	NetWare, Windows, IBM LAN Server and IBM PC LAN, DEC, NDIS
Bus Width	8/16	32
On-board/Buffer RAM	64K	128K
PC Bus Interface	ISA/EISA	EISA
LED Indicators	Ring Insertion Loopback test	Ring Insertion Loopback test
Comments	SMC EZStart	SMC EZStart
Warranty	Lifetime	Lifetime
Price	$199	$379

N/A—Not applicable   INA—Information not available

Table Continues →

■ Network Interface Cards

Manufacturer	SMC	SMC
Model	Ether EZ PC Card	Ether EZ PC Card + Modem
Network Interface Standards Supported	IEEE 802.3 Ethernet, ISO/IEC 8802-3, PC Card standard, PMCI-A TypeII	IEEE 802.3 Ethernet, ISO/IEC 8802-3, PC Card standard, PMCI-A TypeII
Hardware Protocol	Ethernet	Ethernet
Connectors	RJ-45, BNC	RJ-45, BNC, RJ-11
LAN Drivers	NetWare, Windows (95, for Workgroups, NT, 3.x) Banyan Vines, DEC Pathworks, IBM LAN Server, AppleTalk	NetWare, Windows (95, for Workgroups, NT, 3.x) Banyan Vines, DEC Pathworks, IBM LAN Server, AppleTalk
Bus Width	68-pin PCMCIA	68-pin PCMCIA
On-board/Buffer RAM	4K	4K
PC Bus Interface	PCIPCMCIA	PCIPCMCIA
LED Indicators	Network Activity, Link Integrity	Network Activity, Link Integrity
Comments	SMC EZStart	SMC EZStart
Warranty	Limited lifetime	Limited lifetime
Price	$145–$200	$500–$540

Manufacturer	SMC	SMC
Model	ATMPower 155	ATMPower 155
Network Interface Standards Supported	Sonet/SDH STS-3c/STM-1 (155, 52 Mbps)	Sonet/SDH STS-3c/STM-1 (155, 52 Mbps)
Hardware Protocol	ATM	ATM
Connectors	RJ-45, SC-type optical	RJ-45, SC-type optical
LAN Drivers	SunOS/Solaris	NetWare, Windows
Bus Width	32 bit	32 bit
On-board/Buffer RAM	512K/2MB	512K/2MB
PC Bus Interface	SBUS	PCI/EISA
LED Indicators	Sonet/SDH format signal	Sonet/SDH format signal
Comments	SMC EZ Configuration management	SMC EZ Configuration management
Warranty	5 year	5 year
Price	$1,150–$2,000	$1,150–$2,000

Manufacturer	South Hills Datacomm	South Hills Datacomm
Model	37702	37707
Network Interface Standards Supported	10BASE-T, 10BASE2	10BASE-T, 10BASE2, 10BASE5
Hardware Protocol	Ethernet	Ethernet
Connectors	BNC, RJ-45	BNC, RJ-45, AUI
LAN Drivers	IBM LAN Server, Novell, Microsoft	IBM LAN Server, Novell, Microsoft
Bus Width	8/16 bits	32 bits
On-board/Buffer RAM	16K	Ind. xmit. rec. 256-bytes
PC Bus Interface	ISA	PCI
LED Indicators	Data link	Data link

N/A—Not applicable   INA—Information not available

Network Interface Cards ■

Manufacturer	South Hills Datacomm		South Hills Datacomm
Comments	Available in 5 and 20		Available MCA, EISA, VESA
Warranty	2 year		5 year
Price	$69		$249

Manufacturer	TrendWare	TrendWare	TrendWare
Model	TE-16CAT	TE-16PNP	TE-MC
Network Interface Standards Supported	Ethernet 10BASE-T, 10BASE2, 10BASE5	Ethernet 10BASE-T, 10BASE2	Ethernet 10BASE-T, 10BASE2,
Hardware Protocol	Ethernet	Ethernet	Ethernet
Connectors	BNC, RJ-45, AUI	BNC, RJ-45	BNC, RJ-45, AUI
LAN Drivers	IPX, ODI, NDIS	IPX, ODI, NDIS	IPX, ODI, NDIS
Bus Width	16/8 bit	16/8 bit	32 bit
On-board/Buffer RAM	16K	16K	N/A
PC Bus Interface	ISA	ISA	Micro Channel
LED Indicators	Power, Link,Receive, Collision, Jabber	Power, Transmit, Link, Receive	Power, Link, Transmit, Receive, Collision, Jabber
Comments	Diagnostic software included, jumperless, software configuration	Windows 95 plug andplay, software configurable	Diagnostic software included, jumperless, software configuration
Warranty	5 year	5 year	5 year
Price	$89	$79	$199

Manufacturer	TrendWare	TrendWare	TrendWare
Model	TE-16PCI	TE-100/PCI	TE-16XP/CT
Network Interface Standards Supported	Ethernet 10BASE-T, 10BASE2	100 BaseTX Fast Ethernet, 10BASE-T, Ethernet	Ethernet 10BASE-T, 10BASE2
Hardware Protocol	Ethernet	Ethernet, Fast Ethernet	Ethernet
Connectors	BNC, RJ-45	UTP, ODI, NDIS	BNC, RJ-45
LAN Drivers	IPX, ODI, NDIS	IPX, ODI, NDIS	IPX, ODI, NDIS
Bus Width	32 bit	32 bit	16/8 bit
On-board/Buffer RAM	N/A	N/A	16K
PC Bus Interface	PCI	PCI	ISA
LED Indicators	Power, Transmit, Receive, Link	Power, Transmit, Link, Receive, Collision	Power, Transmit, Link, Receive
Comments	PCI Bus Master, 100% plug and play	10/100Mbps Auto-Sense	Diagnostic software included, jumperless, switchless
Warranty	5 year	5 year	5 year
Price	$199	$199	$69

N/A—Not applicable   INA—Information not available

Table Continues →

■ Network Interface Cards

Manufacturer	Xircom, Inc.	Xircom, Inc.	Xircom, Inc.
Model	CreditCard Ethernet + Modem 28.8	CardBus Token Ring Adapter IIps	CreditCard Ethernet + Modem 33.6
Network Interface Standards Supported	Ethernet 10BASE-T, 10BASE2	16/4Mbps Token Ring	Ethernet 10BASE-T, 10BASE2
Hardware Protocol	Ethernet	Token Ring	Ethernet
Connectors	UTP (RJ-45), RJ-11	STP (9-pin), UTP (RJ-45)	UTP (RJ-45), RJ-11, BNC
LAN Drivers	ODI, NDIS-DOS, NDIS-OS/2, packet	Novell NetWare, Windows NT, Windows 95, LAN Mgr, LANtastic, Banyan VINES, DEC PATHWORKS, ODI, NDIS2, NDIS3, packet	ODI, NDIS-DOS, NDIS-OS/2, packet
Bus Width	8 bit	16 bit	8 bit
On-board/Buffer RAM	32K	128K RAM packet buffer	32K
PC Bus Interface	PCMCIA	PCMCIA	PCMCIA
LED Indicators	Ethernet: Link integrity, LAN activity Modem: Modem Activity, Carrier detect, Digital line alert	Power on, Ring insertion, 16Mbps indication	Ethernet: Link integrity, LAN activity Modem: Modem Activity, Carrier detect, Digital line alert
Comments	High-speed Ethernet and V.34 fax modem in a single card; digital line protection, cellular-capable	Windows 3.1x installation program and diagnostic test program included	Includes 33.6Kbps modem; simultaneous LAN and modem operational; digital line protection, cellular-capable
Warranty	Limited lifetime, hardware Two year, software	Limited lifetime, hardware	Lifetime
Price	$489	$439 (STP) $459 (STP and UTP)	$449–$489

Repeaters ■

Manufacturer	Addtron	Addtron	Addtron
Model	E-MPR4	E-MPR4/F2	E-MPR5
Speed	10Mbps	10Mbps	10Mbps
Distance	500m for AUI 185m for BNC 100m for 10BASE-T	100m for ST Fiber Optic	500m for AUI 185m for BNC 100m for 10BASE-T
Connectors	4-AUI/BNC 2-Spare Port Option	4-AUI/BNC 2-FOIRL Fiber Optic with ST	1-AUI, 2-BNC, 2-10Base-T
LEDs	Power, Jabber, Collision, Activity, Receive	Power, Jabber, Collision, Activity, Receive	Power, Collision, Activity, Receive, Link
Switches	Power	Power	Terminator
Size	16.9x 8.2 x 1.6"	16.9 x 8.2 x 1.6"	7.5 x 4.5 x 1.27"
Weight	4 lbs. (1.818 Kg)	4 lbs. (1.818 Kg)	.818 Kg or 1.8 lbs.
Comments	Connects up to 4 to 6 combinations of either 10BASE2, 10BASE5, and/or FOIRL	Connects up to 4 to 6 combinations of either 10BASE2, 10BASE5, and/or FOIRL	Connects up to 5 combinations of either 10BASE2, 10BASE5, and 10BASE-T-segments
Warranty	1 year limited	1 year limited	1 year limited
Price	$499	$729	$279

Manufacturer	Asante' Technologies, INC.	Asante' Technologies	Asante' Technologies
Model	Net Extender -FN Net Extender-AUI	NetExtender-FN	NetExtender-AUI
Speed	10Mbps	10Mbps	10Mbps
Distance	INA	INA	INA
Connectors	4 RJ45, and either 1-AAUI(FN) or 1-AUI(AUI)	4 RJ45, 1AAUI	4 RJ45, 1AUI
LEDs	Link, Integrity	Link, Integrity	Link, Integrity
Switches	INA	INA	INA
Size	3.6" x 1 x 1.75"	3.6" x 1 x 1.75"	3.6" x 1 x 1.75"
Weight	6 ozs.	6 ozs.	6 ozs.
Comments	FN model is attached with AAUI cable; AUI model is attached by DB-15 cable	AAUI Hub with (4) RJ45 ports, attached AAUI cable	AUI Hub with (4) RJ45 ports, attached DB-15 AUI cable
Warranty	Lifetime	Lifetime	Lifetime
Price	$179/$199	$179	$179

Manufacturer	Canary	Canary	Canary
Model	CR-2001	CR-2002	CR-2003
Speed	10Mbps	10Mbps	10Mbps
Distance	500 M Thick on each side	500 M on thick 185 M on thin	185 M of thin on each side
Connectors	(2)D-Type	(2)D-Type, BNC	2-BNC
LEDs	Power, Collision, Partition, Activity, Link	Power, Collision, Partition, Activity, Link	Power, Collision, Partition, Activity, Link
Switches	INA	INA	INA
Size	3(h) x 11.9(w) x 18.5cm	3(h) x 11.9(w) x 18.5cm	3(h) x 11.9(w) x 18.5cm
Weight	82 ozs.	82 ozs.	82 ozs.

N/A—Not applicable   INA—Information not available

Table Continues →

■ Repeaters

Manufacturer	Canary	Canary	Canary
Comments	Thick-Thick, fully compliant with 1EEE 802.3 Standards	Thick-Thin, fully compliant with 1EEE 802.3 Standards	Thick-Thin, fully compliant with 1EEE 802.3 Standards
Warranty	2 year	2 year	2 year
Price	$439	$459	$479

Manufacturer	Canary	Canary	Canary
Model	CR-2004	CR-2005	CR-2006
Speed	10Mbps	10Mbps	10Mbps
Distance	500 M on thick, 2 Km on fiber optic	185 M on thin 2 Km onfiber optic	100 M on UTP 2 Km on fiber optic
Connectors	D-Type SMA, or ST	BNC, SMA or ST Type	RJ45, SMA or ST Type
LEDs	Power, Collision, Partition, Link, Activity	Power, Collision, Partition, Link, Activity	Power, Collision, Partition, Link, Activity
Switches	INA	INA	INA
Size	3(h) x 11.9(w) x 18.5cm	3(h) x 11.9(w) x 18.5cm	3(h) x 11.9(w) x 18.5cm
Weight	82 ozs.	82 ozs.	82 ozs.
Comments	Thick-FO, SMA, or ST fully compliant with IEEE 802.3 standards	Thin-FO, SMA or ST Type, fully compliant with IEEE 802.3 standards	UTP-FO, SMA or ST Type, fully compliant with IEEE 802.3 standards
Warranty	2 year	2 year	2 year
Price	$599	$654	$499

Manufacturer	Canary	Canary	Canary
Model	CR-2007	CR-2008	CR-2009
Speed	10Mbps	10Mbps	10Mbps
Distance	2Km	185M on thin 100M on UTP	500M on thick 100M on UTP
Connectors	2-SMA or ST	BNC, RJ45	D-Type, RJ45
LEDs	Power, Collision, Partition, Activity, Link	Power, Collision, Partition, Activity, Link	Power, Collision, Link, Activity, Link
Switches	INA	INA	INA
Size	3(h) x 11.9(w) x 18.5cm	3(h) x 11.9(w) x 18.5cm	3(h) x 11.9(w) x 18.5cm
Weight	82 ozs.	82 ozs.	82 ozs.
Comments	FO-FO SMA/SMA, SMA/ST, ST/ST, Type IEEE 802.3 standards	Thin-UTP, Fully compliant with IEEE 802.3 standards	Thick-UTP, Fully compliant with IEEE 802.3 standards
Warranty	2 year	2 year	2 year
Price	$699	$379	$349

Manufacturer	Canary	CELAN Technology	CELAN Technology
Model	CTX-8016	EMRT-2	EMRT-4
Speed	100Mbps	10Mbps	10Mbps
Distance	100M	BNC-185M Max. AUI-500M Max.	BNC-185M Max. AUI-500M Max.
Connectors	8-RJ45	BNC-10BASE2 AUI-10BASE5	BNC-10BASE2 AUI-10BASE5
LEDs	Power, Collision, Partition, Link, Activity	Power, Link, Send/Receive	Power, Link, Send/Receive

N/A—Not applicable   INA—Information not available

Repeaters ■

Manufacturer	Canary	CELAN Technology	CELAN Technology
Switches	INA	INA	INA
Size	4.4) x 43.7(w) x 20.6 cm	24(h) x 15(w) x 4cm	24(h) x 15(w) x 8cm
Comments	100BaseTX, 8 ports, half-duplex, Class II, Rack Mount		
Warranty	2 year	1 year	1 year
Price	$1,299	$299	$650

Manufacturer	CNET Technologies	CNET Technologies	Cogent Data Technologies
Model	CN 4020 ERP	CN 8900 BNC	S-1200 T4 S-1200 TX
Speed	10Mbps	10Mbps	100Mbps (Fast Ethernet)
Distance	INA	INA	100 meters (node to repair)
Connectors	2-BNC, 2-AUI	8-BNC, 1-AUI	12-RJ45
LEDs	Yes	Yes	Power, Collision, Activity, Link, Partition
Switches	10	10	INA
Size	135 x 190 x 32 mm	425 x 210 x44.5 mm	1.75 x 16.94 x 8.42"
Weight	INA	INA	5 lbs., 4 ozs.
Comments		The 8900BNC is a SNMP-able repeater.	Stackable up to 5. Port 12 acts as an MDI/MDI-X Uplink.
Warranty	Lifetime	Lifetime	5 year
Price	$388	$998	$1,998–$2,098

Manufacturer	Cogent Data Technologies	D-Link	Digi International
Model	S-800 FX ST/ S-800 FX SC	DE-802/ DE-804	Digi 4200R Repeaters
Speed	100Mbps	10Mbps	10Mbps
Distance	137 M	600 ft. using thin coax	UTP-100 M; 10BASE2-185 M; Multi-mode Fiber-2 Km; Single-mode Fiber- up to 10 Km
Connectors	12-RJ45	2-BNC + 2-AUI/ 4-BNC + 4-AUI	AUI, IEEE 802.3
LEDs	Power, Collision, Activity, Link, Partition	Collision, Link, TX, Receive, Power	Power, Collision, Receive, Fault (Link also on Fiber module 4241R)
Switches	INA	INA	N/A
Size	1.75 x 16.94 x 8.42 in	10.5 x 8.5 x 2.5	1.75(H) x 6(W) x 5"
Weight	5 lbs., 4 ozs.	5-5.3 lbs.	1.41 lbs.
Comments	Stackable up to 5. Port 12 acts as an MDI/MDI-X Uplink.		Automatic port partitioning and reconnection of segmented ports.
Warranty	5 years	1 year	5 year
Price	$3,998	$565/ $725 (DE-804)	$314 (4201R)/ $399 (4221R)/ $375 (4231)/ $535 (4241)

Manufacturer	EFA Corp	Fibronics	Fibronics
Model	EFA 350	FR9230	FR9234
Speed	19Mbps	16- or 4Mbps	16- or 4Mbps
Distance	607 ft. before repeaters at 10Mbps	3000 M in main ring, using fiber optic 109 M lobe length	109 M on main ring UTP to 9230 109 M lobe length

N/A—Not applicable   INA—Information not available

Table Continues →

■ Repeaters

Manufacturer	EFA Corp	Fibronics	Fibronics
Connectors	2-BNC 1-AUI	4-ST for F/O, 32-RJ45 for UTP	2-Uplink UTP RJ45 for UTP
LEDs	Power, Traffic, Collision, Jabber, Partition	Channel Status, Fault, Data Rate, Test, Power	Channel Status, Fault, Test Power
Switches	None	None	None
Size	4.25 x 3.25 x 1"	6.7 x 43 x 33 cm	6.7 x 43 x 33 cm
Weight	.33 Kg	3 Kg	3 Kg
Comments	Stackable	Modular RI/RO for UTP/STP/FO, 32 ports for lobe for which 16 of them can be extended by FR9234, Ring Integrity Monitoring and automatic reconfiguration.	Extensions to the FR9230 allowing distribution of the Ring in the building, Monitoring and automatic reconfiguration.
Warranty	Lifetime	3 year	3 year
Price	$170	$3,200	$1,800+

Manufacturer	KTI Networks	LANCAST	LANCAST
Model	KR-5M	4373	4230
Speed	10Mbps	10Mbps	10Mbps
Distance	100 M for 10 Base-T 195 M for 10 Base-2	185 M over thinnet (BNC); 50 M over AUI	2 Km over Fiber Optics; 185 M over thinnet (BNC); 100 M over 10BASE-T; 50 M over AUI
Connectors	2-NC, 2-UTP 1-AUI	4-BNC, 1-AUI	SMA, ST, BNC, RG-58, RJ45, 15-pinD
LEDs	Collision, Partition, Link	Power, Collision, Activity, Partition	Power, Link, Activity, Partition, Collision,
Switches	INA	INA	INA
Size	19.4 x 11.6 x 2.6 cm	6.7 x 1.67 x 8.875"	6.7 x 1.75(h) x 7.15(l)"
Weight	1.1 Kg	3 lbs.	3 lbs.
Comments		Internal Auto-Switching 110/220V power supply	Automatic partitioning/ re-enable for each port
Warranty	3 year	3 year	3 year
Price	$299	$370	$195–$400

Manufacturer	LANART	LANCAST	Lantronix
Model	ECROX00	4372	LMR4TA
Speed	10Mbps	10Mbps	Ethernet IEEE 802.3 10Mbps
Distance	100 M-UTP 185 M-BNC 2 Km-Fiber	50 M over AUI, 185 M over BNC	100 M
Connectors	AUI, BNC, UTP, Fiber	BNC	4 RJ45 Female
LEDs	Power, Activity, Collisions	Power, Activity, Collision, Local, Partition,	Power, Collision, Link
Switches	SQE, Linknet	INA	None
Size	8.25 x 1.75 x 6"	8" x 1.7(h) x 17"(l)	21 x 13.5 x 7.5cm
Weight	4 lbs.	4 lbs.	.5 Kg
Comments		Available in 4-port and 8 port versions	
Warranty	5 year	3 year	5 year
Price	$395+	$1,595–$1,675	$125

N/A—Not applicable   INA—Information not available

Repeaters ■

Manufacturer	Lantronix	NHC	NHC
Model	LMR8TA	TokenEase Repeater/ TokenEase Dual Fiber Repeater	TokenEase Jitter Beater
Speed	Ethernet IEEE 802.3 10Mbps	4- or 16 Mbps	4- or 16Mbps
Distance	100 M- RJ45 500 M- AUI 185 M- BNC	2100 M at 16 M in main ring length via fiber 380 M via UTP (Rptr).// 2500 M at 16 M in main ring length via fiber (Dual Fiber)	INA
Connectors	8 RJ45 Female 1 Auto-selectable BNC/AUI	RJ45, Fiber ST	RJ45
LEDs	Link, Activity	Fault, lookback, link status	Excess, Jitter
Switches	None	Speed, Test, Integrity	INA
Size	36 x 17 x 7.5cm	1.72(H) x 9(D) x 19"/ 1.69 x 6.5 x 19"	1.69(H) x 6.5(D) x 19"
Weight	2.6 Kg	1.4 Kg/3 Kg	3 Kg
Comments		Single token ring repeater// Dual token ring repeater. Backup path.	Jitter, Attenuator
Warranty	5 year	5 year	5 year
Price	$195	$1,300–$1,700// $3,000	$2,250

Manufacturer	NHC	NHC	Plexcom, Inc.
Model	CityLAN 16	CityLAN 100	8012SX
Speed	4- or 16Mbps	100Mbps FDDI	10Mbps
Distance	40 Km in main ring length via singlemode fiber	Up to 40 Km via single mode fiber	3 Km (fiber) 185 M Thin Coax 100 M UTP/STP 50 M AUI
Connectors	Fiber ST, RJ45	Fiber-Mic, ST, SC, FC	ST, BNC, RJ45, D15
LEDs	INA	Alarm, Line, State	Link, Redundancy, Enable/Disable, Collision
Switches	INA	INA	Link Redundancy
Size	INA	1.75 x 6.7(D) x 19"(W)	1in x 9in x 12in
Weight	INA	INA	3 lbs.
Comments	Long distance Token Ring	RS232 Management- auto dial alarms	Ethernet Fiber Optic 10Base-FL/ Floral Repeater
Warranty	2 year	2 year	1 year
Price	$3,995	$6,165	$1,200

Manufacturer	Plexcom, Inc.	RAD Data Communications	SilCom
Model	8032SX	AMC-101	TR/ Repeater
Speed	4- or 16Mbps	51\100\155Mbps	4- or 16Mbps Token Ring
Distance	3 Km (fiber) 100 UTO/STP	5 Km/3Mi- Multi-media 20 Km/ 12Mi- Singlemode 40 Km\24Mi- Singlemode Laser	660' on trunk lengths, 1000' on lobe lengths- CAT 5 UTP, 16Mbps; 1260' trunk, 1900' lobe- IBM Type 1 STP, 16Mbps
Connectors	ST, RJ45	Duplex SE, ST, STP-Type1, UTP-CAT5	IBM (RI/RO) RJ45 (RI/RO)

N/A—Not applicable   INA—Information not available

Table Continues →

■ Repeaters

Manufacturer	Plexcom, Inc.	RAD Data Communications	SilCom
LEDs	Link, Redundancy, Enable/Disable,	Fault, Wrap, Module, Signal, Power	Power, Insertion signal detect, Lobe mode, RI&RO Quality, Fault, RI&RO UTP Media, trunk mode, loopback
Switches	Speed, R1/R0 or 802.5J	Interfaces	Single/dual, RO&RI UTP or STP, Speed, Lobe or Trunk, Auto Loopback,
Size	1 x 9 x 12"	1.8 x 8.5 x 9.5"	2.5(H) x 6.7(W) x 6.3"
Weight	3 lbs.	1.1 Kg/2.8 lbs.	3 lbs.
Comments	Token Ring Fiber Optic 802.5J and R1/R0 Counter Rotating Repeater	Interchange modules supports OC-1, OC-3 FDDI & 100BaseT, Ethernet, Token Ring	Extends backbone and lobe lengths; automatic loopback in case of signal or power failure
Warranty	1 year	1 year	5 year
Price	$1,170	$1,050 Base Unit $500–$1,300 modules	$995

Manufacturer	TTI Wireless	UB Networks	UB Networks
Model	TTI 200TSE 4Mb	GeoStax/E 16port	GeoStax/ E24 port
Speed	2Mbps 4Mbps	4Mbps	4Mbps
Distance	30 miles	Extended repeater architecture allows for up to 250 ft b/tn stacks	Ethernet
Connectors	AUI, BNC, 10BASE-T	AUI, 10BASE-T, 10BASE2, 10BASEFL	AUI, 10BASE-T, 10BASE2, 10BASEFL
LEDs	Power, Link, Integrity	Link, Activity, Collision, Power, Management	Link, Activity, Collision, Power, Management
Switches			Port assignment button
Size	17.5 x 5.5 x 19"	1.75 x 17(W) x 8.4(L)"	1.75 x 17(W) x 8.4(L)"
Weight	INA	4.1 lbs.	< 6 lbs.
Comments	Units are rack mountable	10 stack units for 160 ports, full management	Segmentable, 5 stack units for 120 ports, full management
Warranty	1 year	Limited lifetime	year
Price	INA	$1,150	$1,495

Manufacturer	UB Networks	UB Networks	UB Networks
Model	GeoStax IE- Micro	GeoStax IT	GeoStax/ FE
Speed	10Mbps	4- or 16Mbps	100Mbps
Distance	Ethernet	Token Ring	100 M UTP and 412 M
Connectors	AUI, 10BASE-T, 10BASE2	RJ45	100BASE-TX, FX
LEDs	Link, Activity, Power	Link, Activity, Power,	Link, Activity, Power
Switches	INA	INA	INA
Size	1.4 x 7 x 5"	1.75(H) x 17.25(W) x 11.75"	1.75(H) x 17(W) x 13.65"
Weight	<5 lbs.	<9 lbs.	6.65 lbs.
Comments	Provides simple to use unmanaged 10Base connectivity	Provides up to 132 ports of intelligent token ring connectivity	Provides GeoLink/XFE technology to greatly extend Hub cable distance. Dual Power.
Warranty	3 year	3 year	1 year
Price	$245	$2,895	$2,995

N/A—Not applicable   INA—Information not available

Repeaters ■

Manufacturer	UB Networks	UB Networks	UB Networks
Model	GeoStax/ FE Micro	GeoStax 1E-Micro	GeoStax 1T
Speed	100Mbps	10Mbps	4- or 16Mbps
Distance	100M UTP and 412 meter fiber	Standard Ethernet	Standard Token Ring
Connectors	100BASE-TX, FX	10BASE-T, AUI, 10BASE2	RJ45
LEDs	Link, Activity, Power	Link, Activity, Power	Link, Activity, Power
Switches	INA	INA	INA
Size	1.75(H) x 17(W) x 13.65"	1.4 x 7 x 5	1.75 x 17.25 x 11.75
Weight	6.65 lbs.	<5 lbs.	<9 lbs.
Comments	Provides GeoLink/XFE technology to greatly extend Hub cable distance. Dual Power.	Provides unmanaged 10BASE-T connectivity	Provides up to 132 ports of intelligent token ring connectivity
Warranty	1 year	3 year	3 year
Price	$1,795	$1,245	$2,895

■ Routers

Manufacturer	3Com Corp	3Com Corp	Accton Technology
Model	Netbuilder II	Super Stack II Netbuilder	Compass EZrouter Part# BR2400
Protocols Supported	AppleTalk, Vines, OSI, IP, IPX, XNS, SUA, APPN	AppleTalk, Vines, OSI, IP, IPX, XNS, SUA, APPN	TCP/IP, IPX/SPX, NetBIOS
Routing Protocol Used	Iso, IS-IS, OSPF, X.25, SMDS, PPP, RIP, Frame Relay	Iso, IS-IS, OSPF, X.25, SMDS, PPP, RIP, Frame Relay	IP, TCP, RIP, ARP, Proxy, RIP, ICMP, BOOTP, TFTP, DHCP, SNMP, NetBIOS, IPX WAN2 Type20
LAN Media Supported	Ethernet Token Ring, ATM, FDDI, Fast Ethernet,	Ethernet Token Ring,	Ethernet (RJ-45, AUI)
WAN Media Supported	V.35, RS232, RS449, ISDN PRI, Switched 56, channelized E1 or T1	V.35, RS232, RS449, ISDN PRI	Sync. Leased line, Sync. Switched Connection, IDSN, Frame Relay
Max. # of LAN Ports	49	1	1
Max. # of WAN Ports	21	3	2
Management Platforms	HP OpenView, Transcend	HP OpenView, Transcend	SNMP MIBII
Security Features	IP packet filtering	IP packet filtering	IP packet filtering, IPX, RIP/SAP filtering
Power Supply	4 Slot-40-120 VAC, 476Hz 2.3A; 8 Slot- 90-120 VAC, 4763Hz, 4.1 A; 8 slot extended-90-132 VAC, 4673 Hz, 6.2	90-132 VAC, 47-63Hz, 10A	Auto-switching 100-12- or 200-240VAC, 47-63Hz
Enclosure	INA	12(W) x 1.7(H) x 17.3"	11.93 x 9.64 x 2.83" Rack mountable (kit sold separately)
Comments	This multiprotocol router is available in three different chassis sizes.	This multiprotocol router is available in 17 different models.	A variety of configurations are offered depending on LAN/WAN specification.
Warranty	1 year	1 year	1 year
Price	$12,000–$115,000	$1,595–$4,295	$2,229–$2,599

Manufacturer	ADC Kentrox	ADC Kentrox	Annexus Data Systems
Model	PACESETTER U	PACESETTER S21	R44A Remote Bridge/Router
Protocols Supported	IP, IPX	IP, IPX	IP, IPX Bridges
Routing Protocol Used	RIP, RIP-II, IP Translate (unique)	RIP, RIP-II, IP Translate (unique)	RIP
LAN Media Supported	Ethernet	Ethernet	Ethernet
WAN Media Supported	ISDN BRI U (embedded NT-1), V.35 to 2.048 Mb/s, RS-232 to 115.2 kb/s, Frame Relay, X.25	ISDN BRI S/T, X.21 to 2.048 Mb/s, RS-232 to 115.2 kb/s, Frame Relay, X.25	Fully integrated V.34 modem
Max. # of LAN Ports	1	1	1
Max. # of WAN Ports	3	3	1
Management Platforms	Telnet, SNMP MIB-II, Enterprise MIB	Telnet, SNMP MIB-II, Enterprise MIB	Ang Snap
Security Features	PAP/CHAP, IP packet filtering, Radius, Supervisor 2 levels of password	PAP/CHAP, IP packet filtering, Radius, Supervisor 2 levels of password	IP/IPX Packet filter
Power Supply	INA	INA	110-220 VAC, 50/60Hz
Enclosure	INA	INA	15 x 14.5 x 3.5"
Comments	INA	INA	Includes Dial on demand and IPX spoofing to reduce line charges

N/A—Not applicable   INA—Information not available

Routers

Manufacturer	ADC Kentrox	ADC Kentrox	Annexus Data Systems
Warranty	INA	INA	1 year
Price	$1,195	$1,195	$1,795

Manufacturer	Annexus Data Systems	Annexus Data Systems	Annexus Data Systems
Model	R44S Remote Bridge/Router	R44A+ Remote Bridge/Router	R445 Remote Bridge/Router
Protocols Supported	INA	Routes IP, IPX; Bridges all others	Routes IP, IPX; Bridges all others
Routing Protocol Used	RIP	RIP	RIP
LAN Media Supported	Ethernet	Ethernet	Ethernet
WAN Media Supported	T-!, Fractional TI, DOS, V.35	Fully integrated V.34 modem	T1, Fractional T1, DDS, V.35
Max. # of LAN Ports	1	1	1
Max. # of WAN Ports	1	1	1
Management Platforms	Ang Snap	SNMP	SNMP
Security Features	IP/IPX Packet filter	IP/IPX Packet filtering	IP/IPX Packet filtering
Power Supply	110-220 VAC. 50/60Hz	110-220 VAC, 50/60Hz	110-220 VAC, 50/60Hz
Enclosure	15 x 14.5 x 3.5"	15(D) x 14.5(W) x 3.5"	15(D) x 14.5(W) x 3.5"
Comments		IPX spoofing to reduce line changes	56K-1.5M, interface cable (V.35) included
Warranty	1 year	1 year	1 year
Price	$2,395	$1,795	$2,395

Manufacturer	APT Communications	APT Communications	APT Communications
Model	ComTalk HF	ComTalk H100	ComTalf HX/Remotes
Protocols Supported	AppleTalk, TCP/IP	Apple Talk, TCP/IP	AppleTalk, TCP/IP, IPX
Routing Protocol Used	RTMP, RIP	RTMP, RIP	RTMP, RIP, RIP/SAP
LAN Media Supported	Ethernet Local Talk	Ethernet Local Talk	Ethernet
WAN Media Supported	N/A	N/A	V.35 or RS232 Sync.
Max. # of LAN Ports	4	8	8
Max. # of WAN Ports	N/A	N/A	6
Management Platforms	Macintosh (Proprietary) and SNMP	Macintosh (Proprietary); SNMP	Macintosh (Proprietary); SNMP
Security Features	Zone, Network Device Hiders	AppleTalk, 80np and Device filters	AppleTalk, IPX and IP filters
Power Supply	External AC Adapter 12 VAC	110-240 VAC Universal, Auto-sensing	110-240 VAC Universal, Auto-sensing
Enclosure	1.65 x 8.4 x 9.5" Rack mount option	5.75 x 9 x 17" Rack mount option	5.75 x 9 x 17" Rack mount option
Comments	Available with Optional AppleTalk to IP Gateway	Modular expandable to 2 Ethernet, 6 LocalTalk	Modular expandable
Warranty	2 year	2 year	2 year
Price	$1,500	$2,500	$2,500

N/A—Not applicable   INA—Information not available

Table Continues →

■ Routers

Manufacturer	APT Communications	Ascend Communications	Bay Networks, Inc.
Model	ComTalk H200	Pipeline 130	Backbone Link Node
Protocols Supported	AppleTalk, TCP/IP, IPX	IP/IPX	AppleTalk, Vines, DECNet, IPX, SNA, TCP/IP, XNS
Routing Protocol Used	RTMP, RIP, RIP/SAP	RIP v1 and v2	IS-IS, OSDF, RIP, PPP, RIP-2
LAN Media Supported	Ethernet	Ethernet	ATM UNI, Ethernet, 100BASE-T, FDDI, Token Ring
WAN Media Supported	N/A	T1, Frame Relay, PPP, MP, MP+, SW56, DDS56	ATM, CBR/UBR, frame Relay, ISDN PRI, SMDS, Sonet
Max. # of LAN Ports	8	1	16
Max. # of WAN Ports	N/A	1	32
Management Platforms	Macintosh (Proprietary); SNMP	TelNet, SNMP, Syslog, Ascend Remote Management	SunNet, NetView, HP OpenView
Security Features	AppleTalk, JPX, IP filters	Call back, packet filtering, Ascend secure access firewall	Router firewall, encryption
Power Supply	110-240 VAC Universal, Auto-sensing	90-130VAC, 0.4A 22-24 VAC, 0.2A 47-63Hz	100-120VAC at 10A, 200-240VAC, at 5A min.
Enclosure	5.75 x 9 x 17" Rack mount option	22 x 15.7 x 3.2cm	8.7 x 19 x 19.7"
Comments	Dual Ethernet ports, WAN and LocalTalk options	3 models available	
Warranty	2 year	1 year	3 months
Price	$2,500	$1,895–$1,995	$26,000+

Manufacturer	Bay Networks, Inc.	Bay Networks, Inc.	Bay Networks, Inc.
Model	Backbone Concentrator Node	Access Node	Access Stack Node
Protocols Supported	AppleTalk, Vines, DECNet, IPX, SNA, TCP/IP, XNS	AppleTalk, Vines, DECNet, IPX, OSI, IP, XNS	AppleTalk, Vines, DECNet, IPX, SNA, IP, XNS, TCP/IP
Routing Protocol Used	IS-IS, OSDF, RIP, PPP, RIP-2	IS-IS, OSDF, RIP, PPP, RIP-2	IS-IS, OSDF, RIP, PPP, RIP-2
LAN Media Supported	ATM UNI, Ethernet, 100BASE-T, FDDI, Token Ring	Ethernet, Token Ring	ATM UNI, Ethernet, 10BASE-T, FDDI, Token Ring
WAN Media Supported	ATM, CBR/UBR, frame Relay, ISDN PRI, SMDS, Sonet	ATM, Frame Relay, ISDN PRI, SMDS, PPP, HDLC,	HDLC, PPP, Frame Relay, SMDS, x.25, ATM DXI, ISDN, BRI and PRI
Max. # of LAN Ports	56	2	24
Max. # of WAN Ports	104	3	40
Management Platforms	SunNet, NetView, HP OpenView	SunNet, NetView, HP OpenView	SunNet, NetView, HP OpenView
Security Features	Router firewall, encryption	Router firewall, encryption	Router firewall, encryption
Power Supply	200-240VAC, at 13A min.	100-120VAC at 10A, 200-240VAC, at 5amin.	100/240VAC, at 4.04 max.
Enclosure	24.4 x 19 x 19.7"	7.3 x 17.5 x 9.15" tabletop/rack mount	4.33 x 17.5 x 17" tabletop/rack mount
Comments			
Warranty	3 months	3 months	3 months
Price	$28,000+	$2,195+	$5,650

N/A—Not applicable   INA—Information not available

Routers ■

Manufacturer	Cisco Systems	Cisco Systems	Cisco
Model	CPA1120	CPA1140	Cisco 7206 High-End Multi-protocol Router
Protocols Supported	IP, IPX	IP, IPX, AppleTalk	AppleTalk, Vines, DECnet, IPX, SNA, NetWare, OSI, TCP/IP, XNS, et. al.
Routing Protocol Used	RIP, I6RP	RIP, I6RP	ISO, IS-IS, OSPF, PPP, RIP, PPP, NLSP, APPN, BGP, SLIP, ES-IP, PIM, RIP 2, et. al.
LAN Media Supported	Ethernet, Token Ring	Ethernet, Token Ring	Ethernet, FDDI, Token Ring
WAN Media Supported	RS232, Fractional TI, TI, DSX-3, RS-422, V.35, x.21, Frame Relay, PPP	RS232, Fractional TI, TI, DSX-3, RS-422, V.35, x.21, X.25, Frame Relay, PPP	Frame Relay (DS-1), Serial, X.25, SMDS
Max. # of LAN Ports	INA	INA	48
Max. # of WAN Ports	12 (6 adapters)	12 (6 adapters)	24
Management Platforms	INA	INA	HP OpenView, IBM NetView 6000, SunNet Manager/Solstice HTML-based management
Security Features	Access lists	Access lists	IP packet filtering, TCP/IP Header Compression, Internet Firewall capability
Power Supply	INA	INA	Link and payload compression 100-240VAC, 48-60Hz
Enclosure	INA	INA	5.25(H) x 16.8(W) x 17"
Comments	This product resides in the network operating system (NOS), therefore it is a function of NOS support.	This product resides in the network operating system (NOS), therefore it is a function of NOS support.	High density with multi-layer LAN switches. HTML-based management tool to simplify router configuration. Other routers available at www.cisco.com/warp/ public/
Warranty	1 year	1 year	90 days
Price	INA	INA	$11,700

Manufacturer	Cisco	Cray Communications	Crosscom
Model	Cisco 7513 High-End Multi-protocol Router	MR-1010/ MR-1110	XL Series
Protocols Supported	AppleTalk, Vines, DECnet, IPX, SNA, NetWare, OSI, TCP/IP, XNS, et. al.	Route: IP, IPX Bridge: All others	TCP/IP, IPX/ SPX, DECNET, XS, SNA
Routing Protocol Used	ISO, IS-IS, OSPF, PPP, RIP, PPP, NLSP, APPN, BGP, SLIP, ES-IP, PIM, RIP 2, et. al.	RIP, Static	RIP, OSPF
LAN Media Supported	Ethernet, FDDI, Token Ring, ATM, IBM Channel Attach	Ethernet (AUI, 10BASE-T)	Ethernet, Token Ring
WAN Media Supported	ATM, Frame Relay, Serial, X.25, SMDS, ISDN, Sonet, T1, E1, T3,DS-3, et al	V.11(X.21), V.24(RS232), V.35, V.36, EIA530, T1, Fractional T1, E1, Frame Relay, Dedicated Link (LAPB, PPP)	RS-232, V.35, TI, FTI, Frame Relay, ATM
Max. # of LAN Ports	176	1/8	1 to 32
Max. # of WAN Ports	88	2	1 to 32
Management Platforms	HP OpenView, IBM NetView 6000, SunNet Manager/Solstice HTML-based management	VT100 (Console) Telnet, HP OpenView, IBM Netview 6000, Sun Net Manager, Castle Rock SNMP	HP OpenView

N/A—Not applicable   INA—Information not available

Table Continues →

■ Routers

Manufacturer	Cisco	Cray Communications	Crosscom
Security Features	IP packet filtering, TCP/IP Header Compression, Internet Firewall capability	IP Packet Filing	Smart filters
Power Supply	Link and payload compression 100-240VAC, 48-60Hz	110VAC-240VAC, 47 to 63Hz., Class I, 70Watts	100VAC to 240VAC
Enclosure	33.75(H) x 17.5(W) x 22"	9.5 D x 118 W x 28"	XL80-21.5 x 17.5 x 11.8" XL20-7.3 x 17.6 x 11.5"
Comments	Supports Distributed switching and NetFlow switching, enabling performance to scale to more than 1 million pps. Other routers available at www.cisco.com/warp/ public/	Adaptive Data Compression on links to 128K, Spanning Tree Bridging, RIP/SAP Spoofing. (The 1110 also has integral 7 port 10BASE-T Hub)	Modular Platform accepts routing, LAN switching and ATM switching
Warranty	90 days	1 year	1 year
Price	$28,000	$1,495/$1,795	INA

Manufacturer	D-Link	Develcon	Develcon
Model	DI-1150	Orbitor 4000	Orbitor 3000
Protocols Supported	IP and IPX	TCP/IP, IPX/SPX	TCP/IP, IPX/SPX
Routing Protocol Used	RIP, SAP	RIP	RIP
LAN Media Supported	Ethernet	Ethernet	Ethernet
WAN Media Supported	RS-232, RS-449/422, V.35	v.35, v11, Frame Relay, Fractional T1, T1, E1	RS232, v.35, ISDN BRI, DSU/CSU, x.25, ppp, Frame Relay, Fractional T1, T1,
Max. # of LAN Ports	1	1	1
Max. # of WAN Ports	2	2	2
Management Platforms	HP Openview, SunNet	NMC Vision	NMC Vision
Security Features	INA	INA	Protocol filtering, MAC filtering
Power Supply	Internal Universal Power supply	Universal	Universal
Enclosure	17.5 x 8.5 x 1.75" 19" rack mountable	2 x 10 x 14.5"	2" x 10' x 14.5"
Comments		Bridge Router, Frame Relay, Central site	Bridge Router, Multipurpose, remote office
Warranty	1 year	Lifetime	Lifetime
Price	$1,495	INA	$1,395

Manufacturer	Develcon	Digi International	Digital Equipment
Model	Orbitor 1000	Refoura	RouteAbout Access Family
Protocols Supported	TCP/IP, IPX/SPX	IP, IPX/SPX, Bridging	IP, IPX, AppleTalk, DECnet, OSI, DLSw, SDLC relay, Vines
Routing Protocol Used	RIP	Rip	OSPF, RIP, EGP, BGP4, Integrated IS-IS
LAN Media Supported	Ethernet	Ethernet	Ethernet, Token Ring
WAN Media Supported	ISDN BRI, ppp,	RS-232, V.35, T-I, X.21	RS232, V.35, X.21, RS422/423, PPP, Frame Relay, X.25, ISDN/BRI
Max. # of LAN Ports	None (PC BUS)	1	1
Max. # of WAN Ports	1 (BRI)	6	2

N/A—Not applicable   INA—Information not available

Routers ■

Manufacturer	Develcon	Digi International	Digital Equipment
Management Platforms	NMC Vision	N/A	Console/Telnet out-of-band, clearVISN Router Manager
Security Features	MAC filtering	IP filtering	IP packet filtering
Power Supply	None	Universal 90-265VAC @60 Watts	Universal, 5W
Enclosure	PC Half card	8.5(L) x 7.5(W) x 2"	12.25 x 1.25 x 4.4"
Comments	Protocol Spoofing. Provides automatic ISDM Call Management.	Bridge/Router supports 2BRi, 2 Async, 2 Sync for bridging/routing	Available as a standalone or DEChub modules
Warranty	Lifetime	2 year	1 year
Price	$595	$1,499	$1,950–$2,950

Manufacturer	Digital Equipment	Digital Equipment	Digital Equipment
Model	RouteAbout Central	DECNIS 500/ DECNIS 600	DECbrouter 90 Series
Protocols Supported	IP, IPX, AppleTalk, DECnet, OSI, DLSw, SDLC relay, Vines	IP, IPX, AppleTalk, DECnet, OSI	IP, IPX, AppleTalk, DECnet, OSI, DLSw, SDLC relay, Vines, RFC1490, XNS
Routing Protocol Used	OSPF, RIP, EGP, BGP4, Integrated IS-IS	OSPF, RIP, EGP, BGP4, Integrated IS-IS	OSPF, RIP, EGP, BGP4, Integrated IS-IS, IGRP, EIGRP
LAN Media Supported	Ethernet	Ethernet, FDDI, ATM	Ethernet
WAN Media Supported	RS232, V.35, X.21, RS422/423, PPP, Frame Relay, X.25	RS232, V.35, X.21, RS422/423, PPP, Frame Relay, X.25, SMDS/ DXI, ATM	RS232, V.35, X.21, RS422/423, PPP, Frame Relay, X.25, SMDS, BRI
Max. # of LAN Ports	2	500: 4/ 600: 14	1
Max. # of WAN Ports	8	16/ 56	2
Management Platforms	Console/Telnet out-of-band, clearVISN Router Manager	Console/Telnet out-of-band, clearVISN Router Manager	Console/Telnet out-of-band, clearVISN Router Manager, Ciscoworks
Security Features	IP packet filtering	IP packet filtering, secure firewall	IP packet filtering
Power Supply	Universal, 33.5W	Universal, 287-600W	Universal, 9W
Enclosure	17.5 x 1.75 x 6"	8.5 x 19 x 13.97" 21.82 x 19 x 18.61"	12.25 x 1.25 x 4.4"
Comments	Available as a standalone or DEChub modules	Modular backbone platforms supporting network interface cards	Available as a standalone or DEChub module, runs Cisco IOS softwares
Warranty	1 year	1 year	1 year
Price	$7,950–$8,950	$6,600/ $13,900	$3,490–$4,050

Manufacturer	Emerging Technologies, Inc.	Emulex Network Systems	Engage Communication, Inc.
Model	NET/ROUTE	DL220I Multi-protocol Router	IP Express
Protocols Supported	TCP/IP, IPX/SPX	TCP/IP, IPX/SPX, AppleTalk	TCP/IP
Routing Protocol Used	RIP, EGP, BGP4, OSPF, R1P2	(TCP/IP)—ICMP, ARP, RIP, OSPF, EGP, UDP, FTP, IPCP (IPX)—NLSP, RIP, SAP, CIPX (AppleTalk)—RTMP, AARP, ATCP, AURP	RIP, ICMP, UDP, RTMP
LAN Media Supported	Ethernet, FDDI, Fast Ethernet	Ethernet, Token Ring, Arcnet, FDDI, Fast Ethernet, ATM	Ethernet, 10BASE2 and 10BASE-T

N/A—Not applicable   INA—Information not available

Table Continues →

■ Routers

Manufacturer	Emerging Technologies, Inc.	Emulex Network Systems	Engage Communication, Inc.
WAN Media Supported	RS-232, v.35, x.21, Frame Relay, T1, 56K, Fractional T1	RS232C (V.24/V.28), RS422, (V.11), X.21, T-1, Fractional T-1, Frame Relay, X.25	RS-232, V.35, T1, Fractional T-1, E-1, T-3, Frame Relay, X. 25 Micro-wave
Max. # of LAN Ports	4	16	1
Max. # of WAN Ports	8	32	3
Management Platforms	SNMP	HP Open View, Netview, Sun Net Manager	SNMP
Security Features	IP Firewall, WAN filtering	IP/IPX SAP filtering	IP packet filtering
Power Supply	STD US and European	None (PC/Server-based solution)	INA
Enclosure	MiniTower-PC	Standard ISA/EISA PC/Server bus slot	1.75 x 7 x 10" Rack mountable
Comments	UNIX OS with source Pentium processor	NetWare Server based bridge/router solution. Comes pre-bundled with MPR V3.1 software.	Internal FracT1 and T1 DSU/CSU
Warranty	1 year	3 year	1 year
Price	$2,395	$1,795 (2 ports)	$995

Manufacturer	Engage Communication, Inc.	Fore Systems	Fore Systems
Model	Express Router	PowerHub 4000// PowerHub 6000	PowerHub 7000
Protocols Supported	TCP/IP, Novell IPX, AppleTalk	ID, IPX, ID Multicast, AppleTalk, DECNET	ID, IPX, ID Multicast, AppleTalk, DECNET
Routing Protocol Used	RIP, ICMP, UDP, RTMP, DDP, ZIP, NBP, ATP, ADSP, AEP	RIP, OSPF	RIP, OSPF
LAN Media Supported	Ethernet, 10BASE2 and 10BASE-T	Ethernet, Fast Ethernet, FDDI, ATM	Ethernet, Fast Ethernet, FDDI, ATM
WAN Media Supported	RS-232, V.35, T1, Fractional T-1, E-1, T-3, Frame Relay, X. 25 Micro-wave	DS-3	DS-3
Max. # of LAN Ports	1	14 (4000) 50 (6000)	240
Max. # of WAN Ports	3	1	1
Management Platforms	SNMP	HP Open View, IBM, Netview 6000, Sun net Manager	HP Open View, IBM, Netview 6000, Sun net Manager
Security Features	IP packet filtering	L2: post and racket filtering L3: post and ID racket filtering	L2: post and racket filtering L3: post and ID racket filtering
Power Supply		100/250 V, 50/60MHz, 48VDC	100/250 V, 50/60MHz, 48VDC
Enclosure	1.75 x 7 x 10" Rack mountable	3.8 x 17 x 16" (4000) 5.25 x 17 x 17.5" (6000)	5.25 x 17 x 17" (5 slot) Rack mountable
Comments	Internal FracT1 and T1 DSU/CSU	Multi-protocol switch	Modular multi-protocol, redundant PLS
Warranty	1 year	1 year	1 year
Price	$1,595	$6,950 (4000) $8,950 (6000)	INA

Manufacturer	GDC	Hewlett Packard	Hewlett-Packard
Model	OPP	AdvancedStack Router 210	AdvancedStack Router 430
Protocols Supported	TCP/IP, IPX/ SPX	AppleTalk, ARP, TCP/IP, IPX/SPX, DECNet, XNS	AppleTalk, ARP, TCP/IP, IPX/SPX, DECNet, XNS
Routing Protocol Used	RIP, OSPF	RIP, OSPF, EGP, RMTP	RIP, OSPF, EGP, RMTP

N/A—Not applicable   INA—Information not available

Routers ∎

Manufacturer	GDC	Hewlett Packard	Hewlett-Packard
LAN Media Supported	Ethernet	Ethernet, 100VG	Ethernet
WAN Media Supported	RS-232, V.35, TI, FTI, Frame Relay	RS-232, V.35, T-1, Fractional T-1, E-1, Frame Relay, x.25, SMDS, x.21, ISDN, PPP	RS-232, V.35, T-1, Fractional T-1, E-1, Frame Relay, x.25, SMDS, x.21, ISDN, PPP
Max. # of LAN Ports	2	1	1
Max. # of WAN Ports	1	1	3
Management Platforms	HP OpenView	HP OpenView	HP OpenView
Security Features	Smart filters	INA	INA
Power Supply	100/117VAC, 48VDC 220VAC, 240VAC	INA	INA
Enclosure	16 slot—7 x 19 x 12" 10 slot—9 x 13.5 x 11.5"	INA	INA
Comments	Bridge/Router module is integral to the OCM, that supports Voice/Data/LAN	Available with 10BASE-T SNMP module, 100VG SNMP module	Supports SNMP Other AdvancedStack Router Models available
Warranty	1 year	3 year on site	3 year on site
Price	Varies	$1,999	$3,299

Manufacturer	Hewlett-Packard	Hewlett-Packard	Hypercom Network Systems
Model	AdvancedStack Router 480	AdvancedStack Router 480	IEN 5000
Protocols Supported	AppleTalk, ARP, TCP/IP, IPX/SPX, DECNet, XNS	AppleTalk, ARP, TCP/IP, IPX/SPX, DECNet, XNS	AppleTalk, IP/IPX, DECNET, SNA, BSC, Burroughs, X.25, TCP/IP
Routing Protocol Used	RIP, OSPF, EGP, RMTP	RIP, OSPF, EGP, RMTP	RIP, OSPF, NLSP, RIP/IPX
LAN Media Supported	Ethernet, FDDI	Token Ring, FDDI	Ethernet, Token Ring
WAN Media Supported	RS-232, V.35, T-1, Fractional T-1, E-1, Frame Relay, x.25, SMDS, x.21, ISDN, PPP	RS-232, V.35, T-1, Fractional T-1, E-1, Frame Relay, x.25, SMDS, x.21, ISDN, PPP	RS-232, V.25 Frame Relay, RFC1490 IISDN,
Max. # of LAN Ports	5	1	Typical configuration: 14
Max. # of WAN Ports	0	1	2
Management Platforms	HP OpenView	HP OpenView	HP OPEN VIEW, SUN NET, NETVIEW FOR AIX, SNMP
Security Features	INA	INA	Protocol\Port Priorities filtering, Security MGT System
Power Supply	INA	INA	AC: 110 or 220 V, 90-130 or 185-225 VAC Dual
Enclosure	INA	INA	19(w) x 5 1/8 x 21 7/8" Rackmount
Comments	Supports SNMP Other AdvancedStack Router Models available	Supports SNMP Other AdvancedStack Router Models available	16-Slot chassis is expandable, parallel processing architecture
Warranty	3 year on site	3 year on site	1 year
Price	$12,500	$2,999	$7,000–$14,500

N/A—Not applicable   INA—Information not available

Table Continues →

■ Routers

Manufacturer	Hypercom Network Systems	Hypercom Network Systems (FRAD)	Hypercom Network Systems
Model	IEN 3000	IEN 500	IEN 1000
Protocols Supported	AppleTalk, IP/IPX, DECNET, SNA, BSC, Burroughs, X.25, TCP/IP	SNA, BSC, X.25, Burroughs Poll Select	SNA, BSC, X.25, Burroughs Poll Select, IPX/PX, AppleTalk
Routing Protocol Used	RIP, OSPF, NLSP, RIP/IPX	INA	RIP, OSPF, NLSP, RIP-IPX
LAN Media Supported	Ethernet, Token Ring	INA	Ethernet, Token Ring
WAN Media Supported	RS-232, V.25 Frame Relay, RFC1490 IISDN,	TI, FTI, X.25, Frame Relay, RFC 1490, ISDN, RS-232, V.35	TI, FTI, X.25, Frame Relay, RFC 1490, ISDN, RS-232, V.35
Max. # of LAN Ports	Typical configuration: 4	0	1
Max. # of WAN Ports	2	2	1
Management Platforms	HP OPEN VIEW, SUN NET, NET-VIEW FOR AIX, SNMP	HP OPEN VIEW, SUN NET, NET-VIEW FOR AIX, SNMP	HP OPEN VIEW, SUN NET, NET-VIEW FOR AIX, SNMP
Security Features	Protocol\Port Priorities filtering, Security MGT System	Protocol\Port Priorities filtering	Protocol\Port Priorities filtering, Security MST filtering
Power Supply	AC: 110 or 220 V, 90-130 or 185-225 VAC Dual	AC: 110 or 220 V, 90-130 or 185-225 VAC Dual	AC: 110 or 220 V, 90-130 or 185-225 VAC Dual
Enclosure	10 7/8(w) x 5 1/8 x 17"	8 _(w) x 2(h) x 14 1/2" Standalone	19(w) x 1.72(h) x 12.5" Rackmount
Comments	6-slot chassis, parallel processing architecture	Mono fraud cases, migration to frame relay	Combines FRAD, HUB, MAN, Router, CSU/DSU modem, data comprehension/encryption in one unit
Warranty	1 year	1 year	1 year
Price	$5,400–$9,500	$1,000–$1,700	$1,750–$4,500

Manufacturer	Intellicom	Intellicom	LanOptics (OEM from Cisco)
Model	OS9000 Firewall Hub/Router	Hub/Router SP612/R	AccessPro
Protocols Supported	IP/IPX, TCP/IP	IP/IPX, TCP/IP	All Cisco IOS supported protocols
Routing Protocol Used	RIP	RIP	All Cisco IOS supported protocols
LAN Media Supported	Ethernet	Ethernet	Ethernet, Token Ring
WAN Media Supported	RS232, X.25	RS232, X.25	RS-232, RS-449, RS-530, V.35, X.21, HDLC, PPP, Frame Relay, Dial on demand, SDMS
Max. # of LAN Ports	Up to 100	13	1
Max. # of WAN Ports	1	1	3
Management Platforms	HP Openview, SNMP, TelNet TFTP, VT100	HP OpenView, SNMP, TelNet TFTP, VT100	HP OpenView, AIX, SunNet Manager
Security Features	IP packet filtering, data encryption, IP/IPX tunneling	INA	N/A
Power Supply	100-250 VAC	100-250 VAC	N/A
Enclosure	17.5 x 17.25 x 3.5" 19" rack mount kit	2.25 x 8.5 x 7.5" (Rack mount kit included)	Integrated in 19" StackNetPro
Comments	Support up to 7LAN segments	Stackable hub/router part of SP600 Series	AccessPro router integrated into StackNetPro base unit for a one box remote office solution. Includes 24 port hub

N/A—Not applicable   INA—Information not available

Routers

Manufacturer	Intellicom	Intellicom	LanOptics (OEM from Cisco)
Warranty	3 year	3 year	1 year
Price	$3750+	$1,495	$5,045+

Manufacturer	Motorola	Motorola	Multi-Tech
Model	6520 MPRouter	6560 MPRouter PLus	MTASR3
Protocols Supported	AppleTalk, TCP/IP, TelNet, ISDN, Frame Relay, X.25, Voice Relay, PPP, et. al.	AppleTalk, TCP/IP, TelNet, ISDN, Frame Relay, X.25, Voice Relay, PPP, plus many more	TCP/IP, IPX/SPX, and bridging all others
Routing Protocol Used	OSPF/RIP, IP, IPX AppleTalk AOON	OSPF/RIP, IP, IPX AppleTalk AOON	RIP
LAN Media Supported	Ethernet, Token Ring	Ethernet, Token Ring	Ethernet
WAN Media Supported	RS-232, V.35, V.36, V.11, SMDS, ISDN, Frame Relay, X.25	RS-232, V.35, V.36, V.11, SMDS, ISDN, Frame Relay, X.25	RS232, V32, V35, ISDN
Max. # of LAN Ports	2	2	1
Max. # of WAN Ports	18	18	3
Management Platforms	HP OpenView, SunNet Manager, Netview	HP OpenView	Windows, SNMP, Multi-Tech Software
Security Features	INA	INA	PPP/CHAP
Power Supply	90-132 VAC/ 180-264 VAC, 48-63Hz	90-132 VAC/ 180-264 VAC, 48-63 Hz	115V or 240 V option 47 to 63Hz
Enclosure	17.8(H) x 10(W) x 16.8"	17.8(H) x 10(W) x 16.8"	Standalone
Comments	Standalone or rackmount	Standalone or rackmount	Also Bridges
Warranty	INA	INA	2 year
Price	$2,995	$5,995	$1,599

Manufacturer	Multi-Tech	N.E.T.	Network Express, Inc.
Model	RouteFinder100 MTSARI-100	LAN/WAN Exchange (LWX) Module	NE7000
Protocols Supported	TCP/IP, IPX/SPX, and bridging all others	IPX, IP, SNA, DECnet, AppleTalk, Appollo, Domain, and Vines ISO/CLNS, XNS	TCP/ IP, IPX/ SPX
Routing Protocol Used	INA	IGRP, OSPF, RIP, BGP, EGP, ISO, CLNS, GDP, and IDP	RIP
LAN Media Supported	Ethernet	Ethernet, Token Ring (with optional interface), IEEE 822.3 15 Pin AUI, IEEE 802.5, 9 Pin	Ethernet
WAN Media Supported	RS232, V32, V35, ISDN	Fractional TI, TI, EI, T3, E3, DSX-3, INT-422, RS422/449, V.35, x.25, Frame Relay	RS-232, V.35, T-1, FT1, Frame relay, X.25
Max. # of LAN Ports	1	Up to 42 LAN ports	2
Max. # of WAN Ports	1	Up to 336 WAN ports	184
Management Platforms	Windows, SNMP, Multi-Tech Software	SNMP; TelNet; NetOpen/Series 5000	SNMP, Proprietary, TelNet
Security Features	INA	2-level password	IP and IPX filters PAP, CHAP, CLIP, Radius, Taloas, ACE
Power Supply	115V or 240 V option 47 to 63Hz	Universal 90 VAC-240 VAC	Dual 356W, 50 or 60HZ, Hot Swappable
Enclosure	1.625 x 6 x 9" 2 lbs.	Varies, depends in IDNX in which used	7 x 19 x 18"

N/A—Not applicable   INA—Information not available

Table Continues →

■ Routers

Manufacturer	Multi-Tech	N.E.T.	Network Express, Inc.
Comments	Also Bridges	LWX is fully integrated WAN Router based on Cisco IOS software	Also available in smaller platforms with fewer slots for hardware cards
Warranty	2 year	1 year	1 year + optional extension
Price	$999	$5,750	$4,500–$40,000

Manufacturer	Penril Datability Networks	Pivotal Networking	Pivotal Networking
Model	Access Beyond multiprotocol router	Pivotal 2000	Pivotal 1610/ Pivotal 1680
Protocols Supported	TCP/IP, IPX/SPX, AppleTalk, DEC-NET	IP, IP Multicast, RSVP (ReSerVation Protocol), IPX, bridging, (IP/ IPX/ AppleTalk/ XNS/DEC/), Multi-protocol over frame relay (RFC 1490), PPP	IP, IP Multicast, RSVP, IPX, bridging, Multiprotocol over frame relay (RFC 1490), PPP, BACP (Bandwidth Allocation Control Protocol), Q.931/ Q.921 ISDN signaling
Routing Protocol Used	RIP, OSPF, EGP	IP RIP, IPX RIP	IP RIP, IPX RIP
LAN Media Supported	Ethernet	10BASE-T Ethernet	10BASE-T Ethernet
WAN Media Supported	RS-232, V.35, T1, E1, Frac-T1, Frame Relay, X,25	RS232, V.35, 56/64Kbps DDS, or TI/FTI, Frame Relay	RS232, V.35, 56/64Kbps DDS, or TI/FTI, Frame Relay
Max. # of LAN Ports	2	1	1 (for 1610)/ 8 (for 1680)
Max. # of WAN Ports	4	4 serial (frame relay or PPP leased line)	1 ISDN 1 serial, or 2 serial (frame relay or PPP leased line)
Management Platforms	Windows SNMP	SNMP Agent, standard and proprietary MIBs, Windows 95/NT based PvtView, compatible with generic SNMP Network Management Stations	SNMP Agent, standard and proprietary MIBs, Windows 95/NT based PvtView, compatible with generic SNMP Network Management Stations
Security Features	IP packet filtering	Firewall (packet filtering), Packet capturing and decoding (for packets such as those filtered due to security reasons), DES encryption	Firewall (packet filtering), Packet capturing and decoding (for packets such as those filtered due to security reasons), DES encryption
Power Supply	Universal, 110-240 VAC 50-60Hz	Universal 100/250 V, 50/60Hz	Table-mount 9V AC transformer
Enclosure	1.74 x 14.2 x 10.27"	Standalone, dimension: 15 x 8 x 2.7"	Standalone:12 x 9 x 1.5"/ 17 x 9 x 1.5"(1680)
Comments	Modular LAN/WAN interface modules for integrated CSU/DSU, ISDN, or Modems	Makes a complete LAN/WAN solution for small offices when ordered with the built-in 8-port switching hub, DSU/CSU	Complete LAN/WAN solution for small offices when ordered with the built-in 28.8 modem, 8-port switching hub, DSU/DCU
Warranty	1 year	5 year	5 year
Price	$1,395	$2,495 (DSU/CSU and multimedia separate)	$1,495 (1610)/$2,495 (1680)

Manufacturer	Proteon, Inc.	Proteon, Inc.	Proteon, Inc
Model	Globtrotter 60 and 62	Globetrotter 70 and 72	RBX 200/205/250
Protocols Supported	60: IP 62: IP, IPX, AT	70=IP 72=IP, IPX, AppleTalk	IP, IPX, AppleTalk, DECNet, Vines, DLSW
Routing Protocol Used	RIP, PPP	RIP, PPP, MPP	RIP, OSPF, EG-P, BGP-4, MOSPF, DVMRP
LAN Media Supported	Ethernet	Ethernet	Ethernet and Token Ring
WAN Media Supported	RS-232, v.35, x.21, up to T1/El Speeds	ISDN BRI	RS-232, V.35, x.21 (ISDN BRI on 205 also)
Max. # of LAN Ports	1	1	200 and 205 have 1; 250 has 2

N/A—Not applicable   INA—Information not available

Routers

Manufacturer	Proteon, Inc.	Proteon, Inc.	Proteon, Inc
Max. # of WAN Ports	1	1	200=2 205=3 250=4
Management Platforms	HP OpenView, SunNet, IBM, other SNMP	HP OpenView, SunNet, IBM, other SNMP	HP OpenView, SunNet, IBM other SNMP
Security Features	IP antispoofing, PAP, CHAP for async	Caller ID, PAP, CHAP	IP antispoofing
Power Supply	Universal 90VAC to 264VAC, 47-63Hz.	Universal 90VAC to 264VAC, 47-63Hz.	100 to 250 VAC, 50 to 60Hz
Enclosure	7.25 x 6.38 x 1.25"	7.25 x 6.38 x 1.25"	200/205 = 17.25 x 10 x 1.75" 250 = 17.3 x 12 x 3.4"
Comments	60 is an IP router; 62 is a bridge/router	70 is an IP Router 72 is a bridge/router	Multiprotocol Bridge/Routers
Warranty	1 year	1 year	1 year
Price	60=$795 62=$995	70=$995 72=$1,195	205/205=$1,900–$3,400 250=$3,800–$5,000

Manufacturer	Proteon, Inc.	RAD Data Communications	RNS
Model	CNX 600	WEB Ranger Access Router	NetHopper: NH-BRI Series; NH-Euro Series
Protocols Supported	DLSW, IPX, NLSP, Vines, TCPIP, PDP, SDLC, AppleTalk, DECNet	IP, IPX	TCP/IP IPX
Routing Protocol Used	OSPF, MOSPF, RIP, BGD, EGP, IS-IS, DNMRP	RIP	RIP
LAN Media Supported	Ethernet, Token Ring, FDDI	Ethernet	Ethernet
WAN Media Supported	RS232, V.35, TI/E1, Frame Relay, X. 21, X25, 6.073, HSSI	RS-232, V.35, Frame Relay, ISDN, up to T-1 Rates	ISDN BRI Analog Optional
Max. # of LAN Ports	20	1	1
Max. # of WAN Ports	20	1	3
Management Platforms	HP Open View	PC/Windows IBM Netview 6000	Any SNMP Mgr
Security Features	Radius, PAP/CHAP, IP packet filtering	PAP, CHAP, Firewall, Protocol/Frame filters	IP filtering, PAP, CHAP, Radius, SecurID
Power Supply	Dual Power Supply	Universal 100-230 VAC 49-63Hz, 10 VAC	250 VAC, 50Hz 2 Amps
Enclosure	Includes Bandwidth Reservation System	1.8(IU) x 9.6 x 8.5" 19" rack mountable	Desktop
Comments	27.4 x 42.7 x 42.7 cm	Designed for Branch/Home Internet Access; Plug-and-Play Installation; WAN Interfaced	Optional internal NT-1 Optional internal V.54 modem
Warranty	1 year	1 year	2 year hardware 90 days software
Price	$1,650	$890	INA

Manufacturer	RNS	South Hills Datacom	Symplex Communications
Model	NetHopper NH-Sync+	36805	Direct Route DR-1/PR-1
Protocols Supported	TCP/IP IPX	TCP/IP, IPX, Vines, IBM SNA, DEC LAT	Routed: IP+IPX Bridged: All Others
Routing Protocol Used	RIP	IP RIP, IPX RIP, SPF	RIP, RIP2
LAN Media Supported	Ethernet	Ethernet	Ethernet: AUI/ 10BASE-T

N/A—Not applicable   INA—Information not available

Table Continues →

■ Routers

Manufacturer	RNS	South Hills Datacom	Symplex Communications
WAN Media Supported	v.35, x.21	V.35 up to 1.544 MBPS, RS232	PR1, RS232, v.35, x.21
Max. # of LAN Ports	1	(1)RJ-45	2
Max. # of WAN Ports	1	(1)V.35, 1-RS-232 (backup)	3
Management Platforms	Any SNMP Mgr	Supports major management platforms	Async Console, Telnet, SNMP, DR Manager
Security Features	IP filtering, PAP, CHAP, Radius, SecurID	IP packet filtering	PAP, CHAP, Caller ID, RAD145, Talas, Extensive filtering systems
Power Supply	250 VAC, 50Hz 2 Amps	Internal auto-switching, 80-240VAC 50-60 Hz	100-240 VAC
Enclosure	Desktop	8(W) x 2.5(H) x 14.5"	2.6(L) x 13(W) x 2.6"
Comments		Also available in dual link and with internal CSU/DSUs. Other models available.	ISDN Alternative to Leased-Line routers; provides 4Mbps WAN Bandwidth over ISDN lines
Warranty	2 year hardware 90 days software	2 years	1 year
Price	$2,195	$2,295	DR-1EPD $4,499 DR-1EPC $4,995 (Integrated)

Manufacturer	Symplex Communications	Symplex Communications	Telebit Corporation
Model	Direct Route DR-1/BR-1	Direct Route RO-1	NetBlazer STI
Protocols Supported	Routed: IP+IPX Bridged: All Others	Routed: IP+IPX Bridged: All Others	AppleTalk, TCP/IP, IPX + NetBEUI
Routing Protocol Used	RIP, RIP2	RIP, RIP2	IPX-RIP, IP-RIP, IPX-SAP, AppleTalk AARP
LAN Media Supported	Ethernet: AUI/ 10BASE-T	Ethernet: AUI/ 10BASE-T	Ethernet, Token Ring
WAN Media Supported	4 BRI/ S or U RS232, v.35, x.21	(1) ISDN BRI	RS-232, RS-530, X.21, RS-449, V.35, TI, EI, ISDN (BRI+ PRI), Frame Relay, SLO564
Max. # of LAN Ports	1	2	3
Max. # of WAN Ports	6	1	32
Management Platforms	Async Console, Telnet, SNMP, DR Manager	Async Console, Telnet, SNMP, DR Manager	SNMP manageable
Security Features	PAP, CHAP, Caller ID, RAD145, Talas, Extensive filtering systems	PAP, CHAP, Caller ID, RAD145, Talas, Extensive filtering systems	Radius, PAP/CHAP, SecurID, Kerberos, ID/password, dial back, cryptographic, handshake, IP and IPX filtering, and AppleTalk zone filtering
Power Supply	100-240 VAC	100-240 VAC	90 to 132 VAC/ 180 to 240 VAC, auto-selecting input. 47 to 63Hz
Enclosure	2.6(L) x 13(W) x 2.6"	2.6(L) x 13(W) x 2.6"	4.3 x 16.3 x 15.5"
Comments	ISDN Alternative to Leased-Line routers; provides 4Mbps WAN Bandwidth over ISDN lines	ISDN Alternative to Leased-Line routers; provides 4Mbps WAN Bandwidth over ISDN lines	The NetBlazer Sti comes with an Ethernet port, and 3 expansion slots
Warranty	1 year	1 year	1 year—hardware 90 days—software
Price	DR- I E S/T $2,999 DR-I E4 $3,799	$599+	$3,199

N/A—Not applicable   INA—Information not available

Routers ■

Manufacturer	Telebit Corporation	Telebit Corporation	Triticom
Model	NetBlazer PN family	NetBlazer LS family	BRouteIT!
Protocols Supported	AppleTalk, TCP/IP, IPX + NetBEUI	AppleTalk, TCP/IP, IPX + NetBEUI	IP, IPX
Routing Protocol Used	IPX-RIP, IP-RIP, IPX-SAP, AppleTalk AARP	IPX-RIP, IP-RIP, IPX-SAP, AppleTalk AARP	RIP
LAN Media Supported	Ethernet	Ethernet, LocalTalk	Ethernet
WAN Media Supported	RS-232 (X.21, RS-449, V.35, are options on PN4)	RS-232 (X.21, RS-449, V.35, on 2 port and V.34 versions)	RS-232, Frame Relay, ISDN
Max. # of LAN Ports	1	2	2
Max. # of WAN Ports	2-4	2	1
Management Platforms	SNMP manageable	SNMP manageable	Any SNMP Mgr.
Security Features	Radius, PAP/CHAP, SecurID, Kerberos, ID/password, dial back, cryptographic, handshake, IP and IPX filtering, and AppleTalk zone filtering	IP packet filtering	Station filters
Power Supply	25 Watts AC	100 to 250 VAC, 50/60Hz, 9A auto-ranging	INA
Enclosure	2.4 x 8.5 x 13"	2.4 x 8.5 x 13"	Software only
Comments	6 models	LS2-port- 2async/ sync ports; LSISDN-BRI port- async/sync ports	
Warranty	1 year—hardware 90 days—software	1 year—hardware 90 days—software	60 days
Price	$1,849–$2,149	$899–$1,399	$345

Manufacturer	Webster Communications Corp.	Whittaker Xyplex	Whittaker Xyplex
Model	MultiPort/LT	Route Runner	Network 3000 Brand of File Router
Protocols Supported	AppleTalk, TCP/IP, DEC NET, ARAP	IP, IPX, AppleTalk, TCP/I P	IP, IPX, AppleTalk, DECNet, OSI, TCP/IP, NetBios, NetBEUI
Routing Protocol Used	RTMP	RIP, IGP,EGP, RIP2	RIP, OSPF, IGP, EGP, IS-IS
LAN Media Supported	Local talk, Ethernet	Ethernet	Ethernet
WAN Media Supported	RS-232	Frame relay, ISDNBRI, R5232, v.35, E1, X.25, Async	Frame relay, x.25, ISDN,TI/EI, RS232, V.35, ISDN BRI, Asynch
Max. # of LAN Ports	5	1LAN	2
Max. # of WAN Ports	4	1 WAN 2 WAN (ISDN Model)	2
Management Platforms	SNMP, Proprietary	HP Open View UNIX and Windows, Sun Net	HP Open View UNIX and Windows, Sun Net
Security Features	Zone hiding, device filtering	IP packet filtering	Filtering, perplex password protection, dial back, Kerbens 4 and 5, secure ID, Rading
Power Supply	120/240 Volt 20 Watt, 50/60Hz	100-240 VAC, 50/60Hz 25 W(max), 85 BTU/hr., .7A(Max) @ 120 V, .3 A(max) @220V	100-240 VAC, 50/60Hz 65 W(max), 221 BTU/hr., 1.58A(Max) @ 120 V, .85 A(max) @220V
Enclosure	9.7 x 9.7 x 2.4"	.4.1 x 23.3 x 19.5 cm	Model
Comments	Combined Router, Rework Access Server, Network Modem Server	ISDN and Synchronic models available	8-port async model is also available
Warranty	1 year	3 year	3 year
Price	$1,995	$1,395–$1,495	$1,995–$4,795

N/A—Not applicable   INA—Information not available

End ■

■ Switches

Manufacturer	3COM Corp.	3COM Corp.	3COM Corp.
Model	Linkswitch 2200	Lanplex 2500	Lanplex 6004
Type	Ethernet, FDDI	Ethernet, Fast Ethernet, FDDI, ATM OC-3	Ethernet, Token Ring, FDDI, 100Mbps Ethernet
Ports	16 Switched Ethernet(RJ-45) and 1 FDDI (DAS)	16 Ethernet, 2 FDDI/TP-DOI, 2 Fast Ethernet, 2 ATM	48 Ethernet, 18 Fast Ethernet, 24TR, 6FDDI
Speed	10Mbps/100Mbps	10Mbps/100Mbps ATM (OC-3 155Mbps)	10Mbps/100Mbps 4Mbps/16Mbps
LEDs	Ports: Link, Error System: Run, Power, Over Temp, DIAG	Port Linkstate Up = Green Down = Red	Link, Error, Power, Fault
Software	SNMP Agent, Terminal Telnet, RLOGIN	SNMP Agents, ASCII Terminal Connection FTP Soft Down Loads	Telnet, SNMP, Console/Terminal Agent Amon, TCP/IP, IPX and AppleTalk Routing, VLAN, Auto-Cast, Routing, Filtering and Firewall
Chassis	Stackable	Modular, rack mountable	Rack
Packet Forward Techniques	Store & Forward	Store & Forward	Store & Forward
Comments	Stackable Ethernet with FDDI connectivity; uses 3COM's ISE chip		Software functionality including integrated routing, VLAN support, Multicast services, and network management with embedded RMON
Warranty	1 year	1 year	1 year
Price	$7,995	$6,095	$13,300

Manufacturer	3COM Corp.	3COM Corp.	3COM Corp.
Model	Cell Plex 7000	Lanplex 6012	Super Stack LinkSwitch 1000
Type	ATM	Ethernet, Token Ring, FDDI, 100Mbps Ethernet	Ethernet/Fast Ethernet or ATM
Ports	OC-3C-155 ATM-16 ports	176 Ethernet, 66 Fast Ethernet, 88TR, 22FDDI	(12 or 24) Ethernet RJ45 (1 or 2) Fast Ethernet RJ45
Speed	155Mbps	10Mbps/100Mbps 4Mbps/16Mbps	10Mbps/100Mbps
LEDs	Ports: Links, Status, Collision, Fail, Activity, Power	Link, Error, Power, Fault	Status, Activity, Power, Management
Software	UWI 3.0+1.1 IISP, SVC/PVC,	Telnet, SNMP, Console/Terminal Agent Amon, TCP/IP, IPX and AppleTalk Routing, VLAN, AutoCast, Routing, Filtering and Firewall	SNMP, RMON, Terminal, Smart Agent, Telnet
Chassis	Tabletop 43 lbs.	Rack	Rack/tabletop
Packet Forwarding Technique	Store & Forward	Store & Forward	Store & Forward
Comments	Expandable to 32 OC-3c ports. Ethernet and Fast Ethernet modules are available.	Software functionality including integrated routing, VLAN Support, Multicast Services, and Network Management with embedded RMON	High Performance PACE Multimedia onboard RMON ATM module SUPERSTACK
Warranty	1 year	1 year	1 year
Price	$15,200	$24,400	$3,975 12 ports $4,975 24 ports

N/A—Not applicable   INA—Information not available

Switches ■

Manufacturer	3 COM Corp.	Accton Technology	Accton Technology
Model	Super Stack LinkSwitch 3000	SwitchHub-8s Part# EH2002	SwitchHub-8se Part# EH2005-TX
Type	Fast Ethernet Switch	Ethernet	Ethernet/Fast Ethernet
Ports	8 Fast Ethernet RJ45 6 (5x Fiber, 1 x RJ45)	8	8
Speed	100Mbps	10Mbps	10/100Mbps
LEDs	Status, Activity, Power, Management	Port, Link, Collision, TX, RX, Half/Full duplex, Port Bandwidth Utilization	Port, Link, TX, RX, Half/Full duplex, Port, Bandwidth Utilization
Software	SNMP, RMON, Terminal, Smart Agent, Telnet	N/A	N/A
Chassis	Rack/tabletop	Rack mountable or Desktop	Rack mountable or desktop
Packet Forwarding Technique	Store & Forward	Cut-through	Cut-through
Comments	High Performance PACE Multimedia onboard RMON ATM module SUPERSTACK.	Up to 80Mbps total bandwidth. Cut-through switching scheme. 4K addresses/port, plug and play installation.	Up to 260Mbps total bandwidth. 5-10BASE-T, 1-10Mbps combo, 2-100Mbps. 4K address/port. Half/Full duplex operation.
Warranty	1 year	3 year	3 year
Price	$7,995	$1,695	$2,599

Manufacturer	Accton Technology	Alfa Netcom	Alfa Netcom
Model	Fast SwitchHub-2se Part#EH3001-TX	A5304	A5308
Type	Ethernet/Fast Ethernet	Ethernet	Ethernet
Ports	2	(4) RJ45 Ethernet	(8) RJ45 Ethernet
Speed	10/100Mbps	10Mbps	10Mbps
LEDs	Port, Link, TX, RX, Half/Full duplex, Port, Bandwidth	Ports: Link, Receive, Collision	Ports: Link, Receive, Collision
Software	N/A	No	No
Chassis	Rack mountable or desktop	Rack/desktop 7.5 lbs.	Rack/desktop 8 lbs.
Packet Forwarding Technique	Store & Forward, Cut-through, and Modified Cut-through	Cut-through	Cut-through
Comments	Up to 200Mbps total bandwidth. 2-10/100 ports. Useful as 10-100 bridge or to extend limited Fast Ethernet segment.	Plug and play workgroup solution	Plug and play workgroup solution
Warranty	Limited lifetime	3 year	3 year
Price	$1,249	$945	$1,495

Manufacturer	Allied Telesyn International	Asante' Technologies, Inc.
Model	AT-4016TR AT-4016F	5216XP
Type	Ethernet to ATM	Ethernet/Fast Ethernet
Ports	16 10BASE-T(for TR) or 16 10BASE-FL(for F), & 1 155Mbps OC-3c ATM	(16) 10BASE-T, (2) Expansion slots
Speed	10Mbps	10/100Mbps
LEDs	Front: Ports link, Receive, Collision, ATM Online, Sync, LOS, Alarms, segments, Power present and fail, Internal and Loop	Power, Error, Link, Data, Collision, Utilization

N/A—Not applicable   INA—Information not available

Table Continues →

■ Switches

Manufacturer	Allied Telesyn International	Asante' Technologies, Inc.
Software	SNMP agent, Local ASCII terminal, Telnet, LAN emulation client	Asante' View, SNMP Agent, RMON, TelNet and Terminal support
Chassis	Rack or tabletop	Desktop/rack 17.25 x 14.10 x 1.70"
Packet Forwarding Technique	Store & Forward and cut-through	Store & Forward and cut-through
Comments	Ethernet to ATM access switch with support for 2048 MAC addresses and 64 virtual LANs	Modules for both 100BASE-TX, FX, FDDI single attach, FDDI Dual attach
Warranty	1 year	3 year
Price	$12,320(TR) $17,230(F)	$6,995

Manufacturer	Asante' Technologies	Asante' Technologies	Asante' Technologies
Model	Ready Switch 5104	Ready Switch 5104 fx	5216 Switch
Type	Ethernet/Fast Ethernet	Ethernet/Fast Ethernet	Ethernet/Fast Ethernet
Ports	4 switched RJ-45 and (1) 100BASE-TX port	4 switched RJ-45 and (1) 100BASE-FX port	(16) 10BASE-T, (2) 10BASE-TX
Speed	10/100Mbps	10/100Mbps	10/100Mbps
LEDs	Power, Fault, Link, Collision, Utilization	Power, Fault, Link, Collision, Utilization	Power, Error, Link, Data, Collision, Utilization
Software	SNMP, TelNet management support	SNMP, TelNet, management support,	Asante' View, SNMP Agent, RMNO, TelNet and Terminal support
Chassis	Desktop/rack 10 lbs.	Desktop/rack 10 lbs.	Desktop/rack 17.25 x 14.10 x 1.70"
Packet Forwarding Technique	Store & Forward	Store & Forward	Store & Forward, Cut-through
Comments	Flash memory for future upgrades, spanning tree, dynamically allocated buffers	Flash memory for future upgrades, spanning tree, dynamically allocated buffers	VLAN by port, MAC & IP, 9 groups of RMON, Dynamic port buffering, port mirroring, redundant power ready
Warranty	Lifetime	Lifetime	3 year
Price	$2,195	$2,495	$5,595

Manufacturer	Asarte Fiber Networks, Inc.	Asarte Fiber Networks, Inc.	BASS MICRO
Model	STAR*SWITCH Model PCS-1620	STAR*SWITCH Model 7200	807-61
Type	Single mode Optical Cross-Connect	Multimode Optical Cross-Connect	Ethernet/Fast Ethernet
Ports	Up to 16 Input x 16 Output	Up to 72 Input x 72 Output	4 RJ-45 10BASE-T 1 RJ-45 100BASE-TX
Speed	50 ms (avg.)	Less than 150 ms	10Mbps/100Mbps
LEDs	System OK, Check System, System Down	System OK, Check System, System Down	Power, Collision, Link Activity, System status, Jabber, and Partition protection
Software	DOS, Windows, Line Terminal Control, SNMP MIB	DOS, Windows, Line Terminal Control, SNMP MIB	SNMP manageable, Ethernet MIB, and Bridge MIB
Chassis	Rack/tabletop 105 lbs.	Rack/tabletop 130 lbs.	Tabletop
Packet Forwarding Technique	Protocol Transparent	Protocol Transparent	Store & Forward

N/A—Not applicable   INA—Information not available

Switches ∎

Manufacturer	**Asarte Fiber Networks, Inc.**	**Asarte Fiber Networks, Inc.**	**BASS MICRO**
Comments	Complete photonic connectivity, protocol transparency, multiple wavelength/bidirectional through-out, full media speed connectivity. Cable management, disaster recovery and test access.	Complete photonic connectivity, protocol transparency, multiple wavelength/bidirectional through-out, full media speed connectivity. Cable management, disaster recovery, and test access.	All ports support full-duplex, store and forward Ethernet packet. Switching, spanning, tree algorithm, RS-232 for remote console
Warranty	1 year	1 year	INA
Price	$24,500–$63,200	$23,600–$93,600	INA

Manufacturer	**D-Link**	**D-Link**	**D-Link**
Model	DES-604/ DES-608	DES-2205	DES-2208
Type	Ethernet	Ethernet/Fast Ethernet	Ethernet/Fast Ethernet
Ports	4 RJ-45 (604)/ 8 RJ-45 (608)	(4) RJ-45 (1) Fast Ethernet	(6) RJ-45 (2) Fast Ethernet (optional)
Speed	10Mbps	10Mbps/100Mbps	10Mbps/10Mbps
LEDs	Ports: Link, Receiver, Collision, Network, Load, Fault, Power	Ports: Link, Receiver, Collision, Network, Load, Fault, Power	Ports: Link, Receiver, Collision, Network, Load, Fault, Power, Utilization
Software	Not Manageable	D-View	MIDII SNMP
Chassis	Rack/tabletop	Rack/tabletop	Rack/tabletop
Packet Forwarding Technique	Store & Forward	Store & Forward	Store & Forward
Comments	Both store-and-forward and cut-through	Full duplex, store-and-forward, fixed 4+1	Full duplex, store-and-forward, cut-through, Option 6+2
Warranty	1 year	1 year	1 year
Price	$795/ $1,590 (608)	$1,795	$1,995

Manufacturer	**D-Link**	**Develcon**	**Develcon**
Model	DES-Pro16	7508SND	7516BND
Type	Ethernet/Fast Ethernet	Ethernet	Ethernet
Ports	(16) RJ-45 (2) Fast Ethernet	8-10Mbps, RJ-45	16-10Mbps RJ-45, optional 100MbpsTX
Speed	10Mbps/100Mbps	10Mbps	10Mbps
LEDs	Ports: Link, Receivers, Collision, Network, Load, Fault, Power	Power, Port Activity, TBST	Uplink, Power, TBST, Port Activity
Software	MIBII SNMP	TelNet, BOOTP/TFTP, SNMP, Flash ROM, STP	TelNet, XMODEM/TFTP, SNMP, Flash Rom, STP
Chassis	Rack/tabletop	Tabletop	Rack-mount kit included 10 lbs.
Packet Forwarding Technique	Store & Forward	Store & Forward	Store & Forward
Comments	100M full duplex, store-and-forward, cut-through, Option 16+2	User configurable Multiple logical Bridge Entities, Virtual LAN. Buffers up to 400 frames per port, store and forward, aggregate address table of 16,000 entries	Full 16 segment port mirroring permits RMON/Protocol Analyzer traffic analysis, store-and-forward, aggregate address table of 16,000 entries
Warranty	1 year	Lifetime	Lifetime
Price	$7,150	$1,599	$3,995

N/A—Not applicable   INA—Information not available

Table Continues →

■ Switches

Manufacturer	Develcon	Digi International	Digi International
Model	7516TND	Right Switch SE-6	Right Switch SE-4
Type	Ethernet, Fast Ethernet	Ethernet	Ethernet
Ports	16-10Mbps RJ-45, 1-1-1-1-100Mbps RJ-45	6	4
Speed	Uplink, Power, TBST, Port Activity	10Mbps	10Mbps
LEDs	Uplink, Power, TBST, Port Activity	Link	Link
Software	TelNet, XMODEM/TFTP, SNMP, Flash Rom, STP	SNMP MTB-II Agent 802.1d Spanning Tree Filtering Supports Novell Netware, Windows NT, SCO UNIX, and UNIXware	SNMP MTB-II Agent 802.1d Spanning Tree Filtering Supports Novell Netware, Windows NT, SCO UNIX, and UNIXware
Chassis	Rack-mount kit included 10 lbs.	No chassis— Installed in PCI bus of server	No chassis—Installed in PCI bus of server
Packet Forwarding Technique	Store & Forward	Store & Forward	Store & Forward
Comments	Full 16-segment port mirroring permits RMON/Protocol Analyzer traffic analysis, store-and-forward, aggregate address table of 16,000 entries.	Server-based LAN switch provides direct connection from switched Ethernet segments to PCI bus operating at 1Gbps, thereby increasing bandwidth and reducing latency to server.	EISA compatible server-based LAN switch available on the market.
Warranty	Lifetime	5 year 30 day money-back guarantee	5 year 30 day money-back guarantee
Price	$4,495	$2,595	$1,695

Manufacturer	Fibronics
Model	AX7008
Type	ATM Switch
Ports	8 OC-3
Speed	155Mbps 5Glops Fabric
LEDs	INA
Software	SNMP Telnet
Chassis	Rack/tabletop
Packet Forwarding Technique	Distributed output bufferingStore & Forward
Comments	Optional backbone switch provides 32000 VCC, and 64000 multicasts
Warranty	3 year
Price	$27,000

Manufacturer	Fibronics	Fibronics	Fore Systems
Model	FX8616	FX8618	Power Hub 4000// Power Hub 6000
Type	Ethernet/Fast Ethernet	Ethernet/Fast Ethernet/FDDI	Ethernet, Fast Ethernet, FDDI, ATM
Ports	16 RJ45 Ethernet, 2 Fast Ethernet or FDDI	12 ST FOIRL	12 Ethernet segments and 1 Fast Ethernet, 1 FDDI or 1 ATM/(6000) up to 48 Ethernet segments
Speed	10/100 or 125	10/100 or 125	10Mbps/100Mbps/155Mbps
LEDs	Power, Fault, System Load, Boot IP, outband, Service Link, Data, Collision	Power, Fault, System Load, Boot IP, outband, Service Link, Data, Collision	Ethernet: LNK, A/R, C/X FDDI: W.S.X; S,W,R ATM: X, R, L

N/A—Not applicable   INA—Information not available

Switches ■

Manufacturer	Fibronics	Fibronics	Fore Systems
Software	SNMP, SMT 7.3, IEEE802.1D	SNMP, SMT 7.3, IEEE802.1D	SNMP Agent with MIB II, Ethernet MIB, Bridge MIB, ForeView management teaching forethought
Chassis	13 x 43 x 43cm 12Kg	13 x 43 x 43cm 12Kg	Rack/tabletop 18 lbs.
Packet Forwarding Technique	Store & Forward	Store & Forward	Store & Forward
Comments	The unit has two high speed slots for Fast Ethernet or FDD.	The unit has two high speed slots for Fast Ethernet or FDD.	Complete Bridging, value-added network management
Warranty	1 year	1 year	1 year
Price	$5,990	$11,995	$6,950+// $8,950+

Manufacturer	Fore Systems	Intellicom	Ipsilon
Model	Power Hub 7000	Officestak 5000 Multi-segment switching Hub	IP Switch ATM 1600
Type	Ethernet, Fast Ethernet, FDDI, ATM	Ethernet/Fast Ethernet	IP Switch
Ports	48 Fast Ethernet ports, 240 Ethernet segments, 456 Ethernet ports/ could include 16 FDDI Rings, 80 FDDI ports, 2 ATM uplinks	Up to 48 switched Ethernet ports; 104 hub/repeater ports	16 OC-3
Speed	10Mbps/100mbps/155Mbps	10/100Mbps	155Mbps
LEDs	Ethernet: LNK, A/R, C/X FDDI: W.S.X; S,W,R ATM: X, R, L	Link, Receive, Collision, Power	Running light; Failure light; Power, Link, Collision, Transmit, Activity
Software	SNMP Agent with MIB II, Ethernet MIB, Bridge MIB, ForeView management teaching forethought	OfficeView, SNMP, VT100, TelNet, TFTP, HPOpenview	GSMP
Chassis	Rack 55 lbs.	Rack mount, stackable	Rack
Packet Forwarding Technique	Store & Forward	Store & Forward	Store & Forward, Cut-through
Comments	Expandable chassis supports 5-20 lbs.	Expands to support up to 104 hub/repeater ports, or up to 48 switched ports	Provides routing capabilities with 2.5 million pps performance
Warranty	1 year	3 year	90 days plus 30 transit allowance.
Price	$9,950+	$2,500+	Starting at $40,000

Manufacturer	LANART	LANCAST	LANCAST
Model	ETS-0630 Ethernet Switch	6600	5608
Type	Ethernet/Fast Ethernet	Ethernet/Fast Ethernet	Ethernet
Ports	6 RJ-45 Ethernet, 1 Fast Ethernet	(6) RJ-45 Ethernet, (1) Fast Ethernet	(7) RJ-45 Ethernet; (1) selectable RJ-45 or AUI Ethernet
Speed	(6) 10Mbps (1) 100Mbps	10Mbps/100Mbps	10Mbps
LEDs	LCD displays all statistics	Power, Error, Alert	Power, Activity, Test
Software	SNMP, TelNet, TFTP, Rs232, Front Panel LCD Display	LANWARE, SNMP, Agent	LANWARE, SNMP, Agent
Chassis	Standalone rack/tabletop 7 lbs.	Rack/tabletop	Rack/tabletop
Packet Forwarding Technique	Store & Forward	Store & Forward	Store & Forward

N/A—Not applicable   INA—Information not available

Table Continues →

■ Switches

Manufacturer	LANART	LANCAST	LANCAST
Comments	Spinning-tree bridge with 100Mbps uplink and modules for AUI, BNC, & Fiber	100Mbps uplink port supports either 100BASE-TX or 100BASE-FX virtual LAN support.	Optional redundant power supply. Filtering and forwarding at sustained wire speed.
Warranty	5 year	3 year	3 year
Price	$2,995+	$3,400	$1,990-$2,100

Manufacturer	LANtronix	LANtronix	Linksys
Model	LSB4	LSW8	Etherfast 5 Port 10/100 BaseTX, Switching Hub
Type	Ethernet	Ethernet/Fast Ethernet	Fast Ethernet
Ports	(4) AUI Ether	(6) RJ-45 on AUI Ethernet (2) Fast Ethernet	4RJ-45 Ethernet, 1 Fast Ethernet
Speed	10Mbps	10Mbps/100Mbps	10/100Mbps
LEDs	Ports, Power, Serial, Port ACT	Unit: SNMP, Power, MGMT, Fault, Port: Link, Collision, ACT, Flow Control	Link, Collision, Activity
Software	BRCON (UNIX, NOVELL, Macintosh); TelNet	ONMP (Uses HPOpeview) SNMP, TelNet	Terminal Agent
Chassis	Tabletop	Rack/tabletop	Rack, tabletop
Packet Forwarding Technique	Store & Forward	Store & Forward	Store & Forward
Comments	Wirespeed workgroup switch with 4 full Ethernet segments, 4k addresses, custom filter.	Wirespeed Ethernet switch with RJ-45 on AUI ports; 2 optional 100Mbps ports for 100BASE-TX or 100BASE-FX adapters; rack on tabletop option.	Offers power and speed of 100Mbps networking, while providing backward compatibility with existing 10Mbps network equipment.
Warranty	5 year	1 year	3 year
Price	Starts at $1,995	Starts at $2,995	$1,899

Manufacturer	Madge Networks	Microdyne Corporation	Nashoba Networks
Model	Smart Ringswitch	Eagle Switch 4+100 & Eagle Switch 4x4	Concord
Type	Token-Ring	Ethernet/Fast Ethernet	Token-Ring Switch
Ports	8-12 UTP TR, 8-12 Fiber TR, 2FDDI, 2ATM ISS	(4) 10BASE-T, (1) 100BASE-TX & (4) 10BASE-T, (4) 100BASE-TX	(8) RJ-45, (2) Fast Ethernet
Speed	4/16/100/155	10Mbps/100Mbps	4/16 Token Ring 100Mbps FDDI
LEDs	LCD Panel, Power LED, Port Status	Dynamic port buffering	Ring Status, Port Activity, Speed, System Status, Power
Software	Trueview windows (HP/OVWIN, UNIX, Audioable Q4) NetView 6000, SNMP, TelNet	INA	Source Route, Transparent, SRT, Spanning Tree, NetBIOS, SNMP, RMON
Chassis	Rack	Standalone	19" rack mount or tabletop
Packet Forwarding Technique	Cut-through	Store & Forward	Store & Forward
Comments	3-slot chassis cut thru TR Switch highest thruput switch on market, optimized for TR Backbone use non-blocking	NWAY autonegotiation automatically determines best speed; DMI support SNMP agent; full duplex	Optical FDDI Uplink supports for translational switching
Warranty	1 year	1 year	1 year
Price	$9,950 (8 port copper)	$2,149/ $2,899	$1,500/port

N/A—Not applicable   INA—Information not available

Switches ■

Manufacturer	Network Peripherals	Network Peripherals	Network Peripherals
Model	NuSwitch FE-101	NuSwitch FE-105	NuSwitch FE-106
Type	Ethernet/Fast Ethernet	Ethernet/Fast Ethernet	Ethernet/Fast Ethernet
Ports	(1) RJ-45 Ethernet, (1) RJ-45 fast Ethernet	(5) RJ-45 Ethernet, (1) RJ-45 fast Ethernet	(5) RJ-45 Ethernet, (1) RJ-45 fast Ethernet
Speed	10/20/100/200Mbps	10/20/100/200Mbps	10/20/100/200Mbps
LEDs	Status, Link, TX/RX, Collision, System Status, Activity	Status, Link, TX/RX, Collision, System Status, Activity	Status, Link, TX/RX, Collision, System Status, Activity
Software	Unmanageable	Unmanageable	SNMP, Port, Mirroring, TelNet, TFTP
Chassis	Rack/tabletop	Rack/tabletop	Rack/tabletop
Packet Forwarding Technique	Store & Forward	Store & Forward	Store & Forward
Comments	Provides wire-speed filtering and forwarding.	Provides wire-speed filtering and forwarding.	Provides wire-speed filtering and forwarding.
Warranty	1 year	1 year	1 year
Price	$695	$1,695	$2,995

Manufacturer	Nbase Communications
Model	NH2012 megaSwitch II
Type	Ethernet/Fast Ethernet Switch w/very high speed uplinks
Ports	ATM and Gigabit Ethernet uplinks (Q4/96), Expandable to 12 FE ports
Speed	Dual speed 10/100 Ethernet/Fast Ethernet Switch with high speed uplinks (ATM, Gigabit Ethernet)
LEDs	TX, RX, Collisions, Half/Full duplex, Link
Software	Supported by MegaVision, Nbase SNMP graphical application (Windows/UNIX) and HP OV
Chassis	Rack/tabletop 19"
Packet Forwarding Technique	Store & Forward
Comments	
Warranty	1 year
Price	$7,960 for base unit

Manufacturer	Network Peripherals	Network Peripherals	Network Peripherals
Model	NuSwitch FE-210	NuSwitch FE-224c	NuSwitch FE-506
Type	Ethernet/Fast Ethernet	Ethernet/Fast Ethernet	Ethernet/Fast Ethernet
Ports	(10) RJ-45 Ethernet, (2) RJ-45 Fast Ethernet	(24) RJ-45 Ethernet, (2) RJ-45 Fast Ethernet	(6) RJ-45 Ethernet, (5) RJ-45 Fast Ethernet
Speed	10/20/100/200Mbps	10/20/100/200Mbps	10/100Mbps
LEDs	Status, Link, TX/RX, Collision, System Status, Activity, VLAN	Status, Link, TX/RX, Collision, System Status, Activity, VLAN	Status, Link, TX/RX, Collision, System Status, Activity
Software	SNMP, Port Mirroring, VLAN, TFTP, Spanning Tree	SNMP, Port Mirroring, VLAN, TFTP, Spanning Tree	SNMP, Port Mirroring, TFTP, Spanning Tree
Chassis	Rack/tabletop	Rack/tabletop	Rack/tabletop
Packet Forwarding Technique	Store & Forward	Store & Forward	Store & Forward

N/A—Not applicable   INA—Information not available

Table Continues →

■ Switches

Manufacturer	Network Peripherals	Network Peripherals	Network Peripherals
Comments	Provides wire-speed filtering and forwarding. Also provides Power Link feature for 400Mbps trunk connection.	Provides wire-speed filtering and forwarding	Provides wire-speed filtering and forwarding
Warranty	1 year	1 year	1 year
Price	$3,995	$2,995	$4,995

Manufacturer	Network Peripherals	Network Peripherals	Network Peripherals
Model	NuSwitch FE-512	NuSwitch FE-200TT	NuSwitch FE-200TF
Type	Ethernet/Fast Ethernet	Fast Ethernet	Fast Ethernet
Ports	(12) RJ-45 Ethernet, (5) RJ-45 Fast Ethernet	(2) RJ-45 Fast Ethernet	(1) RJ-45 Fast Ethernet, (1) Fiber ST Fast Ethernet
Speed	10/100Mbps	100/200Mbps	100/200Mbps
LEDs	Status, Link, TX/RX, Collision, System Status, Activity	Status, Link, TX/RX, Collision, System Status, Activity	Status, Link, TX/RX, Collision, System Status, Activity
Software	SNMP, Port Mirroring, TelNet, TFTP	Unmanageable	Unmanageable
Chassis	Rack/tabletop	Rack/tabletop	Rack/tabletop
Packet Forwarding Technique	Store & Forward	Store & Forward	Store & Forward
Comments	Provides wire-speed filtering and forwarding	Provides wire-speed filtering and forwarding	Provides wire-speed filtering and forwarding
Warranty	1 year	1 year	1 year
Price	$5,995	$995	$1,995

Manufacturer	Network Peripherals	Network Peripherals	Network Peripherals
Model	NuSwitch FE-600	NuSwitch FE-1200	NuSwitch FD-212F
Type	Fast Ethernet	Fast Ethernet	Ethernet/Fast Ethernet
Ports	(6) RJ-45 Fast Ethernet	(12) RJ-45 Fast Ethernet	(1) RJ-45 Ethernet, (2) Fiber MIC FDDI
Speed	100/200Mbps	100/200Mbps	10/100Mbps
LEDs	Status, Link, TX/RX, Collision, System Status, Activity	Status, Link, TX/RX, Collision, System Status, Activity, VLAN	Status, Link, TX/RX, Collision, System Status, Activity, VLAN
Software	Unmanageable	SNMP, Port, Mirroring, VLAN, TFTP, Spanning Tree	SNMP, Port, Mirroring, VLAN, TFTP
Chassis	Rack/tabletop	Rack/tabletop	Rack/tabletop
Packet Forwarding Technique	Store & Forward	Store & Forward	Store & Forward
Comments	Provides wire-speed filtering and forwarding	Provides wire-speed filtering and forwarding. Also provides Power Link feature for 800Mbps Trunk connection.	Provides wire-speed filtering and forwarding. Also has 4 port concentrator module.
Warranty	1 year	1 year	1 year
Price	$3,995	$8,995	$9,595

Manufacturer	Network Peripherals	Network Peripherals	Network Peripherals
Model	NuSwitch FD-212	NuSwitch FD-212AF	NuSwitch FD-112A
Type	Ethernet/FDDI	Ethernet/FDDI	Ethernet/FDDI
Ports	(5) RJ-45 Ethernet, (2) RJ-45 FDDI	(1) RJ-45 Ethernet, (2) Fiber MIC FDDI	(10) RJ-45 Ethernet, (1) RJ-45 FDDI
Speed	10/100Mbps	10/100Mbps	10/100Mbps

N/A—Not applicable   INA—Information not available

Switches ■

Manufacturer	**Network Peripherals**	**Network Peripherals**	**Network Peripherals**
LEDs	Status, Link, TX/RX, Collision, System Status, Activity, VLAN	Status, Link, TX/RX, Collision, System Status, Activity	Activity, Link, Collision, TX/RX, Status, System Status
Software	SNMP, Port, Mirroring, VLAN, TFTP	SNMP, TelNet, TFTP	SNMP, TelNet, TFTP
Chassis	Rack/tabletop	Rack/tabletop	Rack/tabletop
Packet Forwarding Technique	Store & Forward	Store & Forward	Store & Forward
Comments	Provides wire-speed filtering and forwarding. Also has optional 4 port concentrator module.	Provides wire-speed filtering and forwarding. Also has optional 4 port concentrator module.	Provides wire-speed filtering and forwarding. Also has optional 4 port concentrator module.
Warranty	1 year	1 year	1 year
Price	$8,495	$8,995	$7,495

Manufacturer	**NHC**	**NHC**	**NHC**
Model	Switchex	STAKIT	SHARE-IT
Type	Protocol - Independent	Protocol - Independent	Protocol - Independent
Ports	48 x 48 (48 IN, 48 OUT)	2 RJ45 In 12 RJ45 Out	24 RJ45 In 48 RJ45 Out
Speed	Up to 100Mbps	Up to 100Mbps	Up to 100Mpbs
LEDs	Transmit, Received, Fault, Memory	Transmit, Received, Fault, Memory	Transmit, Received, Fault, Memory
Software	VCCS - Windows VCCS - DOS	VCCS - Windows VCCS - DOS Terminal Emulation	VCCS - Windows VCCS - DOS
Chassis	RACK	RACK	RACK
Packet Forwarding Technique	INA	INA	INA
Comments	Moves, adds, changes, remote site , WAN DSS sharing	Resource sharing LAN Diagnostics Equipment sharing Timer	Lan Probe sharing Connection sheet Scenario Time programming
Warranty	2 year	2 year	2 year
Price	$5,920	$1,655	$3,460

Manufacturer	**Performance Technologies**	**Plaintree Systems**	**Plaintree Systems**
Model	Nebula 2000/ Nebula 2001	Waveswitch 100-FL	Waveswitch 4800
Type	Ethernet	Ethernet/Fast Ethernet	Fast Ethernet
Ports	(8) RJ-45 Ethernet (1) WAN, (1) Conine xxx, (1) Trace/ LAN Analyzer	(12) 10BASE-FL, (2) High Speed	(8) 100Mbps
Speed	10/20Mbps	10/100Mbps	100Mbps
LEDs	Ports: Link, Receive, Transmit, Collision Other: Power, Ready	Ports: Error, Link, Data, Collision	INA
Software	Stargazer, SSNMP MII, Network Mgt, Local ACSI Terminal Agent, TelNet, MIB for Sunnet Mgt, HPOpenview	SNMP Agent, Waveview	SNMP Agent, Waveview
Chassis	Rack/tabletop 10-11 lbs.	Rack/freestanding 27 lbs.	Freestanding
Packet Forwarding Technique	Store & Forward	Store & Forward	Store & Forward, Cut-through

N/A—Not applicable   INA—Information not available

Table Continues →

■ Switches

Manufacturer	Performance Technologies	Plaintree Systems	Plaintree Systems
Comments	2000–With PTI's StarGazer GUI, Nebula gives users the ability to selectively filter unwanted traffic, create firewalls, broadcast groups, virtual switch groups and control broadcast storms.	12 10BASE-FL ports for fiber-optic cable; adds advantages of security and noise immunity of fiber.	800Mbps full duplex, non-blocking bandwidth, 8 100Mbps slots for "mix and match" FastLink or Vrouter virtual routing modules, 4096 addresses, full RMON, and N+1 redundant power
Warranty	3 year	1 year	1 year
Price	INA	$9,995	$29,995

Manufacturer	Plaintree Systems	Plaintree Switch	Plaintree Systems
Model	Waveswitch 100-16	WaveSwitch 100-8	WaveSwitch 4+1
Type	Ethernet/Fast Ethernet	Ethernet/Fast Ethernet	Ethernet/Fast Ethernet
Ports	(16) 10BASE-T, (2) High Speed	(8) 10BASE-T, (2) High Speed	(4) 10BASE-T, (1) 100BASE-TX or FX
Speed	10/100Mbps	10/100Mbps	10/100Mbps
LEDs	Ports: Error, Link, Data, Collision	Ports: Error, Link, Data, Collision	Ports, Error, Load, Power
Software	SNMP Agent, Waveview	SNMP Agent, Waveview	SNMP Agent, Waveview
Chassis	Rack/freestanding	Rack/freestanding 27 lbs.	Rack/freestanding 10 lbs.
Packet Forwarding Technique	Store & Forward	Store & Forward	Store & Forward
Comments		Maximizes bandwidth availablity, and increases network efficiency and performance.	Designed for wire speed, low latency and low cost boost bandwidth availability and network efficiency.
Warranty	1 year	1 year	1 year
Price	$5,295 (pre-configured 16 ports w/4 100BASE-TX)	$4,995 (pre-configured 8 ports w/4 100BASE-TX)	$1,995(TX)/$2,295(FX)

Manufacturer	Plaintree Systems	Plaintree Systems	Plaintree Systems
Model	WaveSwitch 4+4	WaveSwitch 1216	Waveswitch 1018
Type	Ethernet/Fast Ethernet	Ethernet/Fast Ethernet	Ethernet/Fast Ethernet
Ports	(4) 10BASE-T, (4) Shared 100BASE-TX	(16) Ethernet/(2) Fast Link	(16) Ethernet/(2) Fixed full duplex 100BASE-TX
Speed	10/100Mbps	10/100Mbps	10Mbps/100Mbps
LEDs	Ports, Error, Load, Power	Power, Error, Ports, Load	Ports, Power, Error, Load
Software	SNMP Agent, Waveview	SNMP Agent, Waveview,	SNMP Agent, Waveview
Chassis	Rack/freestanding 10 lbs.	Rack/freestanding 20 lbs.	Rack/freestanding 12 Pounds
Packet Forwarding Technique	Store & Forward	Store & Forward, Cut-through	Store & Forward, Cut-through
Comments	Provides new levels of performance demanded by quick response, data-intensive applications.	Full duplex operation on all ports 4096 addresses, positive filtering, full RMON, VLANS, SmartVips, Vrouter & 536, 070.pps forwarding capability	1024 addresses. Positive filtering, Full RMNO, Virtual LANs, Smart VIPS & 536,000 pps forwarding capability.
Warranty	1 year	1 year	1 year
Price	$2,495	$5,995	INA

N/A—Not applicable   INA—Information not available

Switches ■

Manufacturer	Plexcom, Inc.	Plexcom, Inc.	Plexcom, Inc.
Model	5016	5012FL	5106
Type	Ethernet, Fast Ethernet FDDI	Ethernet, Fast Ethernet FDDI	Ethernet, Fast Ethernet
Ports	(24) 10BASE-T, (4) AUI, (8) 100BASE-TX, (10) VG AnyLAN, (2) 100BASE-FX, 2 FDDI SAS, 2 DAS, (4) 100M Fiber Optic Ethernet	10BASE-FL Fiber Optics; (8) 10BASE-T, (4) AUI, (8) 100BASE-TX, (10) 100VG AnyLAN, (2) 100BASE-FX, 2 FDDI SAS, 2 DAS, (4) 100M Fiber Optic Ethernet	(6) 10BASE-T (1) 100BASE-TX (1) 100BASE-FX
Speed	560Mbps	520Mbps	160Mbps
LEDs	Link, RxD, Enable/Disable, Error, Load	Link, RxD, Enable/Disable, Error, Load	Link, RxD, Enable/Disable, Error, Load
Software	TFTP Telnet	TFTP Telnet	TFTP Telnet
Chassis	Rack mount or standalone	Rack mount or standalone	Rack mount or standalone
Packet Forwarding Technique	Store & Forward	Store & Forward	Store & Forward
Comments	Spanning Tree, singlemode and multimode fiber, two expansion slots, SNMP Agent	Spanning Tree, singlemode and multimode fiber, two expansion slots, SNMP Agent	Spanning Tree, one expansion slot
Warranty	1 year	1 year	1 year
Price	$4,895	$9,995	$2,495–$3,495

Manufacturer	Standard Microsystems Corp.	Standard Microsystems Corp.	Syskonnect
Model	EZ Switch	Tiger Switch XFE	SnapSwitch 6020
Type	Ethernet	Ethernet/Fast Ethernet	Ethernet
Ports	(5) RJ-45 (1) Combo RJ-45, BNC, AUI	(16) RJ-45 Ethernet (1) Fast Ethernet	(16) RJ-45 Ethernet
Speed	10Mbps	10Mbps/100Mbps	10Mbps
LEDs	Ports: Link, full duplex, Transmit, Receive, Collision%, Utilization%, Forward%, Filter%, Demo, Diagnostic, Full/Half duplex, CPU, Status	Power, Test, Ports: Link	3 status lights, power good, test and uplink. On each port a multi-colored LED.
Software	EZ Watch LED panel displays above mentioned LED's, to monitor system performance	SNMP Agent	None
Chassis	Rackmount/tabletop	Rack/tabletop 10 lbs.	Rack/tabletop
Packet Forwarding Technique	Cut-through	Store & Forward	Cut-through
Comments	Each port supports full/half duplex independently	Manageable via SNMP using an SNMP based network manager, or in-band via TelNet, or out-of-band via serial console port	FDDI DAS option, 100BASE-TX uplink, full SNMP support, Spanning Tree protocol
Warranty	3 year	1 year	2 year
Price	$1,199	$3,390	$3,495

Manufacturer	TRENDware	TRENDware	TRENDware
Model	TE100-S26 TE100-S55	TE-5040 TE-5080	TE-100/S14
Type	Ethernet/Fast Ethernet	Ethernet	Ethernet/Fast Ethernet

N/A—Not applicable   INA—Information not available   **Table Continues →**

■ Switches

Manufacturer	TRENDware	TRENDware	TRENDware
Ports	6 RJ-45, 2 Fast Ethernet 5 Ethernet/Fast Ethernet Auto-Sensing	4 RJ-45/ 8 RJ-45	4RJ45 Ethernet 1 Fast Ethernet
Speed	10Mbps/100Mbps	10Mbps	10Mbps/100Mbps
LEDs	Power, Activity, Collision, System Status	Power, Activity, Collision, System Status	Power, Activity, Collision, System Status
Software	N/A	N/A	N/A
Chassis	Rack/tabletop 10 lbs.	Rack/tabletop 10 lbs.	Rack/tabletop 10 lbs.
Packet Forwarding Technique	Store & Forward	Store & Forward	Store & Forward
Comments			One RS-232 port allowing local terminal access to comprehensive setup and management functions
Warranty	5 year	5 year	5 year
Price	$2,999	$699–$1,399	$1,999

Manufacturer	UB Networks	UB Networks	UB Networks
Model	GeoRim/E	GeoRim/EDT	GeoRim/T
Type	Ethernet	Ethernet	Token Ring
Ports	(12) RJ45, AUI, BNC or Fiber (1) ATM, FDDI, 100BASE-T, Uplink	(16) RJ-45 Ethernet (1) 100BASE-TX Uplink	(8) RJ-45
Speed	10Mbps	10Mbps	4/16Mbps
LEDs	Link, Activity, LCD management readout, Power	Link, Activity, Power	Link, duplex, Activity, Power, test condition
Software	SNMP Agent, downloadable firmware	SNMP Agent, downloadable firmware	SNMP Agent
Chassis	Rack/stackable	Desktop/rack	Rack/stackable
Packet Forwarding Technique	Store & Forward	Store & Forward	Store & Forward, Cut-through
Comments	Modular and fault tolerant design; choice of high speed uplinks	Provides low cost dedicated 10Mbps to desktop connections and 100Mbps uplinks	Provides 8-12 Token Ring switch ports, with adaptive switching technology. High speed uplinks are also available.
Warranty	3 year	1 year	1 year
Price	$5,995	$3,195	$5,600

Manufacturer	UB Networks	UB Networks	UB Networks
Model	GeoSwitch/155	CenterSwitch	Dragon Switch 16 port
Type	ATM	Ethernet	Ethernet
Ports	(2) Ethernet (4-16) OC3	(12) 10BASE-T intergrated switching ports	(16) 10BASE-T
Speed	155Mbps	10Mbps	10Mbps
LEDs	Link, power, activity	Status lamps for ports	Port Status
Software	SNMP Agent, LAN Emulation, ID over ATM, IISP	Managed through chassis system RMON, 6MNP	Managed through Hub SNMP
Chassis	Rack/stackable	Chassis module	Chassis module Rack/module
Packet Forwarding Technique	N/A	Store & Forward	Store & Forward

N/A—Not applicable   INA—Information not available

Switches ■

Manufacturer	UB Networks	UB Networks	UB Networks
Comments	Provides up to 16 155Mbps ATM ports for workgroup or campus connectivity. Fully ATM UNI 3.0/ 3.1 compliant.	Max of 2 modules supported	Switched 10BASE-T ports for Geo LAN/100 and GEO LAN/500 chassis HUB provides 160Mbps bandwidth.
Warranty	1 year	1 year	1 year
Price	$15,920	$11,995	$13,200

Manufacturer	UB Networks	US ROBOTICS
Model	Dragon Switch 8 port	TotalSwitch
Type	Ethernet	Ethernet/Fast Ethernet, upgradable to ATM
Ports	(8) 10BASE-T	6 to 32 Ethernet, 2 to 8 Fast Ethernet
Speed	10Mbps	10/100Mbps per port 1.2 Gbps backbone
LEDs	Port Status	Link, Receive, Transmit, Collision, Duplex
Software	Managed through Hub SNMP	SNMP, 802. 1D Spanning Tree, VLANS, TelNet, ASCII menu
Chassis	Chassis module Rack/module	4 useable slots, rack/wall and tabletop mount 19 lbs.
Packet Forwarding Technique	Store & Forward	INA
Comments: (25 words)	Switched 10BASE-T ports for Geo LAN/100 and GEO LAN/500 chassis HUB provides 80Mbps bandwidth	Modular chassis supports customprogrammable Switched LAN cards for 10BASE-T, 10BASE2, 10BASE-FL, 100BASE-TX, and 100BASE-FX
Warranty	1 year	3 year
Price	$7,995	$1,995 for 8 10BASE-T ports, $175 for add. ports $6,280 for 24 10BASE-T and 2 100BASE-T ports

Manufacturer	Whitetree, Inc.	Whitetree, Inc.	Whittaker Xyplex
Model	WS2500	WS3000	600 Series LAN Switching CAR DS xxx for Network 9000 HUB
Type	ATM	Switched Ethernet/ATM	Ethernet/Fast Ethernet
Ports	(12) ATM25, (2) Network option slots	(12) Either Ethernet or ATM25, (2) Network Option slots	20 10BASE-T, 12 10BASE-FL, 2 100BASE-TX, 2 100BASE-FX
Speed	25Mbps/ATM155/Ethernet 100Mbps	10Mbps or 25Mbps; ATM 55/ 100Mbps	(20)10BASE-T, (20) 10BASE-FL, (12) 100BASE-TX,
LEDs	Ports: mode indicator alternate Ethernet AUI Unit level; system status, PCMCIA slot status, mgmt. Activity, serial activity	Ports: mode indicator alternate Ethernet AUI Unit level; system status, PCMCIA slot status, mgmt. Activity, serial activity	Run, Console, Memory card activity, Port status activity
Software	SNMP v1 Agent, Whitetree Wmlock element management utility for windows/ATM forum LAN emulation	SNMP v1 Agent, Whitetree Wmlock element management utility for windows/ATM forum LAN emulation	LAN Switching Software, RMON, SNMP
Chassis	Tabletop/19" rack	Tabletop/19" rack	Modular chassis 21 lbs.
Packet Forwarding Technique	Store & Forward, Cut-through	Store & Forward, Cut-through	Store & Forward
Comments	Low-cost ATM 25 connectivity for the workgroup. Two network option slots for modules supporting ATM155 or 100BASE-TX	Automatically mixes and matches any combination of 12 Ethernet and ATM ports. With stacking Bus module, can connect up to 12 switches to provide 144 desktop ports	Hot-swappable 24 LAN ports supported throughout
Warranty	1 year	1 year	3 year
Price	$6,995	$7,795	$2,495–$3,995

N/A—Not applicable   INA—Information not available

Table Continues →

■ Switches

Manufacturer	Whittaker Xyplex	XLNT Designs, Inc	XLNT Designs, Inc
Model	SX6660 Family of Ethernet Workgroup Switches	QuikEther	QuikEther-16
Type	Ethernet	Ethernet	Ethernet
Ports	16 10BASE-T; 12 10BASE-FL, 2 FDDI, 2 100BASE-FX, 8 100BASE-TX	8 10BASE-T	16 10BASE-T Ethernet Ports
Speed	10/100Mbps	10/20Mbps full duplex	10/20Mbps full duplex
LEDs	Front panel LED's: Power, System error and System load, Link, Data	Ports: Port Status, Transmit, Collision, Receive, Link, Full duplex	Ports: Port Status, Transmit, Collision, Receive, Link, Full duplex
Software	RMON, SNMP, switching software	SNMP, MIB II, Etherlike MIB, Bridge MIB, XLNT Designs Private MIB, Spanning Tree	SNMP, MIB II, Etherlike MIB, Bridge MIB, XLNT Designs Private MIB, Spanning Tree
Chassis	Stackable 27 lbs.	Rack/tabletop	Rack/tabletop 23 lbs.
Packet Forwarding Technique	Store & Forward	Cut-through, Store & Forward	Cut-through, Store & Forward
Comments	Store-and-forward architecture; fixed configuration with 2 slots for higher speed interface module; can stack 2 switches.	All QuickEther components can be combined to expand to over 80 Ethernet ports, multiple FDDI rings, and Mult. 100Mbps Ethernet	Can be combined with other QuikStack units for multiple LAN technologies in one stack
Warranty	3 year	1 year	1 year
Price	$6,295	$3,500	$6,400

Manufacturer	XLNT Designs,Inc	XLNT Designs, Inc.	XLNT Designs, Inc.
Model	QuikFDDI+	QuikFDDI+4	QuikEther 100/8
Type	Ethernet/FDDI	Ethernet/FDDI	Ethernet/Fast Ethernet
Ports	8 10BASE-T Ethernet ports, 1 FDDI DAS	8 10BASE-T Ethernet ports, 1 FDDI DAS, 4 FDDI Concentrator	8 Distributed 100Mbps Repeater ports
Speed	10Mbps/100Mbps	10Mbps/100Mbps	10Mbps/100Mbps
LEDs	Ports: Port Status, Transmit, Collision, Receive, Link, Full duplex	Ports: Port Status, Transmit, Collision, Receive, Link, Full duplex	Ports: Port Status, Transmit, Collision, Receive, Link, Full duplex
Software	SNMP, MIB II, Bridge MIB, XLNT Designs Private MIB, Spanning Tree	SNMP, MIB II, Bridge MIB, Spanning Tree	SNMP, MIB II, Bridge MIB, XLNT Private MIB, Spanning Tree
Chassis	Rack/tabletop 26 lbs.	Rack/tabletop 26 lbs.	Rack/tabletop 26 lbs.
Packet Forwarding Technique	Cut-through, Store & Forward	Cut-through, Store & Forward	Cut-through, Store & Forward
Comments	All QuikFDDI+ components can be combined with other QuikStack units.	Expandable to 80 Ethernet potrs supporting multiple FDDI rings and 100Mbps Ethernet	Combine with other QuikStak units for multiple LAN technologies in one stack.
Warranty	1 year	1 year	1 year
Price	$9,999	$12,500	$5,600

N/A—Not applicable   INA—Information not available

Switches ■

Manufacturer	**XLNT Designs, Inc.**	**XLNT Designs**
Model	QuikEther100	QuikEther100F+4
Type	Ethernet/Fast Ethernet	Ethernet/Fast Ethernet
Ports	810BASE-T Ethernet 2 100Mbsp Fast Ethernet	810BASE-T Ethernet 1 100Mbps Fast Ethernet Fiber Port, 4 distributed 100Mbps repeater ports
Speed	10/100Mbps Full duplex	10/100Mbps Full duplex
LEDs	Ports: Port Status, Transmit, Collision, Receive, Link, Full duplex	Ports: Port Status, Transmit, Collision, Receive, Link, Full duplex
Software	SNMP, MIB II, Bridge MIB, XLNT Private MIB, Spanning Tree	SNMP, MIB II, Bridge MIB, XLNT Private MIB, Spanning Tree
Chassis	Rack/tabletop 26 lbs.	Rack/tabletop 26 lbs.
Packet Forwarding Technique	Cut-through, Store & Forward	Cut-through, Store & Forward
Comments	Combine with other QuikStak units for multiple LAN technologies in one stack.	Combine with other units for multiple LAN technologies in one stack.
Warranty	1 year	1 year
Price	$5,600	$5,600

N/A—Not applicable   INA—Information not available

E n d ■

■ Terminal Emulation

Manufacturer	Attachmate	Attachmate
Model	KEA 420 for Windows v.4.22/ v.4.23 for Windows 95 & NT/ KEA! 340 for Windows/ V.4.23 for Windows 95 & NT	RALLY! For AS/400 v.2.2
System/Software Requirements	386 or higher, Win 3.1	PC, Win 3.1
Host Platform	VMS/ UNIX	OS/400
Terminals Emulated	vt340, VT420- vt52	IBM 3179-2, 3477-FC
Other Emulation	ANSI, 401x. Tetronix	Printers emulated: IBM 3812, 5219, 5224/25
Protocol/ Connectivity Support	Telnet, Lat Serial, TAPI NetWare for DEC Access	Asynchronous, Ethernet, T02.2 LUC, LU7 console, SNA server, NetWare for SAA, SDLC/Synchronous, TCP/IP with TN5250, TCP/IP with AnyNet, Token Ring and Twinaxle
File Transfer Protocols	x, y, z modem FTP, Super Kermit, ASCII	Standard Client access formats
Other Features	OLE 2.0 support Client/Server tools support, remote access, automation capabilities, keyboard remapping	MS office compatibility
Comments		
Warranty/Upgrades	Trade ups and upgrades available	60 days free support, upgrade programs available
Price	$245/$245/$395/$395	$165

Manufacturer	Attachmate	Attachmate
Model	EXTRA! Personal Client 6.1	EXTRA! X v 3.0
System/Software Requirements	386/486 PC, Windows 3.x, Windows 95, Windows NT	486 PC or higher, Windows 3.x, Windows 95, Windows NT
Host Platform	All mainframe, AS/400, DEC VAX, UNIX Server or Alpha AXP platforms	UNIX, VMS, OpenVMS
Terminals Emulated	All IBM 3270 LU2 display terminals, models 2-5, 5250 models, VT models	X Terminal vt 420
Other Emulation	IBM LU1, and LU3 printer terminals 52xx models, VT/ UNIX	Any X based terminal emulator can be used via EXTRA! X
Protocol/ Connectivity Support	Coax, TN3270 direct, NCIA, TCP/IP, IPX/SPX, Net-BIOS, IEEE, 802.2, Virtual 802.2 or APPC, TN3270	TCP/IP, Telnet
File Transfer Protocols	IND$FILE, DISOSS, FTP, FT/Express, AS/400 SQL, FTP, Kermit, Z model, FTP	N/A
Other Features	Operating system auto-sensing, intelligent navigation, bookmarks and page events, OLE 2.0 automation and linking, and DB Query	Full X 11R6 Compliance, fully configurable MultiInstance support, localized versions, multivisual support font aliasing, drag and drop keymap editor
Comments		It is a PC-X server with terminal emulation capabilities.
Warranty/Upgrades	60 days free support, upgrade programs available	Trade ups and upgrades available
Price	$425	$425 (Windows) $395 (Windows NT or Windows 95)

Manufacturer	Distinct Corp.	FutureSoft
Model	Distinct® IntelliTerm™	The DynaComm Connectivity Series
System/Software Requirements	486, PC, Windows 3.X, NT, 95	Windows 3.1, 95, & NT
Host Platform	UNIX, MVS, VM, VMS, ASCII	HP/UX, MVS, VM, UNIX, AS/400, System 3X
Terminals Emulated	IBM 3270, 5250, DEC N52 through N420	Dec VT100, VT220, VT340, ADDS VP, IBM 3278, 3279, 5250, HP700/94 Tandem 6530, VT-420, VT-510
Other Emulation	3179G Veetor Graphics and 3279 536	IBM 3287

N/A—Not applicable   INA—Information not available

Terminal Emulation ■

Manufacturer	Distinct Corp.	FutureSoft
Protocol/ Connectivity Support	TN 3270, TN5250, TelNet, TCP/IP	Telnet, TN3270, SDCC, Coax (COT, DFT), ADLC, XADLC, IPS/SPX, TC/IP, VINES, NetBios, SPP, 802.2, SDLC
File Transfer Protocols	VM/CMS, MVS/TSO and Music/SP file transfer	X,Y, and Z mode, Kermit, INCC, IND$FILE, Tandem IXF
Other Features	Keyboard mapping, toolbar customization, VBA advanced scripting and macrolanguage, DDE, HUAP, EHUAOI, with Visual Basic	Keyboard mapping, toolbar customization, OLE 2.0, automation and linking software management tool, Internet tools, et. al.
Comments		Single instance multisession. 350+Command and function script languages.
Warranty/Upgrades	90 day, subscription programs available	Yes
Price	INA	Call for pricing

Manufacturer	IBM	IGEL LLC
Model	IBM Personal Communications AS/400 & 3270 Version 4.1	Ethermulation
System/Software Requirements	386 or higher	486 PC, Windows 3.11, Windows 95, NT
Host Platform	MVS, VM	Any UNIX Host
Terminals Emulated	IBM 327x (models 2, 3, 4, 5), TN3270, IBM 5250, TN5250	ANSI-ISO, IBM SCO-ANSI VT200/100
Other Emulation	Printer Emulation: IBM 3287, TN3287, 3812	Printing from UNIX to Windows, Windows to UNIX
Protocol/ Connectivity Support	SNA, TCP/IP, IPX/SPX	TCP/IP
File Transfer Protocols	SDLC, ISDN, IDLC, COAXx, Twinax, DFT, FDDI, X.25, Async, Hayes AutoSync, SNA over ASYNC, APPN End Node, LU2 over APPC, Win APPC, FMI on NT SNA Server	INA
Other Features	API support, host graphics support, customizable iconic toolbar, graphical keyboard and color remapping, 3-D hot spots, record and play back	Keyboard, happling, NFS, print utilities, easy set up
Comments	Includes multiprotocol support that enables SNA applications over TCP/IP and sockets applications over SNA. Includes response time monitor.	
Warranty/Upgrades	30 day, upgrade programs available	1 year for media; 1 year upgrade free
Price	$329 and $279 for additional license	$349

Manufacturer	Microcom, Inc.	NCD Software Corporation	NCD Software Corporation
Model	Carbon Copy Remote Control Software	PC-Xware Suite for Windows 95 and Windows NT	PC-Xware Suite for Windows
System/Software Requirements	386 or better, Windows for Workgroups, Windows 95, DOS 5.0, Windows 3.1,	386/486 PC, Windows 95/NT, 8MB memory (Win95), 16MB memory (NT)	366 PC, Windows 3.1, 8MB memory (NT)
Host Platform	Windows and DOS	UNIX	UNIX
Terminals Emulated	VT100, VT52 ANSI, TTY	UNIX workstations, X terminals	UNIX workstations, X terminals
Other Emulation		IBM 3270, 5250, VT 320, 220, 132, 131, 100, 52, HP, Wyse, ANSI	IBM 3270, 5250, VT 320, 220, 132, 131, 100, 52, HP, Wyse, ANSI
Protocol/ Connectivity Support	Async, NCSIANSI, INT14	Telnet, TCP/IP, DECnet, TN3270	Telnet, TCP/IP, DECnet, TN3270
File Transfer Protocols	X, Y, Z Modem, Kermit, ASCII	FTP, NFS	FTP, NFS

N/A—Not applicable   INA—Information not available

Table Continues →

Terminal Emulation

Manufacturer	Microcom, Inc.	NCD Software Corporation	NCD Software Corporation
Other Features	Scroll-back buffer, redefinable keymap. Translate table selectable fonts and colors. Configurable toolbar, status bar.	Automatic script generator, dynamix data exchange, EHLLAPI, full color-editing	Full-color editing
Comments			
Warranty/Upgrades	Upgrade program; 60 day money-back guarantee	30 days on media only	30 days on media only
Price	$99	$545	$545

Manufacturer	Serengeti Systems	Serengeti Systems	South Hills Datacomm
Model	3780 Link	BSCLIB	36322
System/Software Requirements	DOS, Windows 3.X, 95, NT, OS/2, UNIX, AIX, Solaris	DOS, Windows 3.X, 95, NT, OS/2, UNIX, AIX, Solaris	MS or PC DOS 3.3
Host Platform	Numerous	Numerous	ISA or MCA bus
Terminals Emulated	ICM 2780, 3780	ICM 2780, 3780	IBM 5251-11, 5291, 5292-1, 3180
Other Emulation	N/A	N/A	INA
Protocol/ Connectivity Support	Bisync (BSC)	Bisync (BSC)	5250 Twinax via DB15 male
File Transfer Protocols	Built-in	Built-in	Only on the remote terminal emulation packages
Other Features	Standalone IBM 2780/3780 RTE terminal emulation	Point-to-point and multi-point BSC protocol API	ISA bus card has built in balun for UTP connection
Comments			Also available in remote emulation packages
Warranty/Upgrades	INA	INA	1 year
Price	$395	$395	$745

Manufacturer	Wall Data Inc.	Zephyr Development Corporation
Model	Mac Rumba for the Mainframe	3270 Windows 3.1, Windows 95 or NT
System/Software Requirements	Mac OS System 7.0 or later	MVS, VM, IMS, CICS
Host Platform	VM/CMS, MVS/TSO,CICS, and OS/400	IBM 3278, 3279, 3179G, 319G, 3472G, 32795G
Terminals Emulated	3278/79 display terminals (models 1-5); LU Type 2	IBM 3287, LUI and 3
Other Emulation	3287 printers with 3287 printer panel	TN3270 (TCP/IP), IPX/SPX, 802.2 and COAX DFT
Protocol/ Connectivity Support	TCP/IP, SNA, SAA/IPX	INDS File
File Transfer Protocols	IND$FILE (Mainframe) PC Support (AS/400) FTP (Both)	HLLAPI, custom keyboard mapping. Macros, cut and paste, security, file server installation et. al.
Other Features	Copy and paste to Mac applications using the clipboard; On-line help; Keyboard remapping, configurable on-screen keypads; keystroke recording and playback; multiple language support; and IBM 3287 printer support	Corporate licenses available
Comments	A single user application for Apple Macintosh PCs, providing a direct connection to Mainframes via standard SNA, TCP/IP, or NetWare (with AppleTalk) networks.	One year free upgrades and technical support
Warranty/Upgrades	Unlimited phone support; Upgrades available	INA
Price	$125–$275	$95–$195

N/A—Not applicable   INA—Information not available

Transceivers ■

Manufacturer	3COM	3COM	3 COM
Model	ISOLAN TR	ISOLAN Fiber	ISOLAN COAX
Interface	10BASE-T	10BASE-FL	10Based/ 10BASE5
Connectors	RJ-45, AUI	ST, D-type (AUI)	BNC\ ATR, N Series
LEDs	Transmit, Receive, Polarity, Link Test	Transmit, Receive, Link OK/Loss of Light, Collision	Power from DTE
Enclosure	Plastic 2 ozs.	Plastic 2.5 ozs.	Metal, 6 ozs.
Comments	Supports extended distances up to 150m	Supports all major fiber types	
Warranty	1 year	1 year	1 year
Price	$88	$395	$165

Manufacturer	Addtron	Addtron	Addtron
Model	ET-10CIB	ET-10TIB	ET-10FI/ ET-10FL
Interface	10BASE5, 10BASE2	10BASE5, 10BASE-T	AUI, FOIRL/ AUI, 10BASE-FL
Connectors	AUI, BNC with T-Connector	AUI, 10BASE-T	AUI, FOIRL/ AUI, 10BASE-FL
LEDs	Power	Power, Receive, Link, Transmit, Polarity, Collision	Receive, Link, Transmit, Collision
Enclosure	Metal, 8 ozs.	Metal, 8 ozs.	Metal, 8 ozs.
Comments	Full complement of diagnostic LED indicators; switch-selectable SQE function	Full complement of diagnostic LED indicators; switch-selectable SQE function	Full complement of diagnostic LED indicators; switch-selectable function
Warranty	1 year limited	1 year limited	1 year limited
Price	$35	$35	$189/ $199

Manufacturer	Addtron	Addtron	Asante' Technologies
Model	ET-10CIN	ET-10CIT	FNTKA
Interface	AUI, BNC with pre-cut Nseries Connector	AUI, BNC with Piercing Tap Connector	
Connectors	AUI, BNC with pre-cut Nseries Connector	AUI, BNC with Piercing Tap Connector	AUI, AAUI
LEDs	Power	Power	
Enclosure	Metal, 8 ozs.	Metal, 8 ozs.	4 x 2.5 x 8" 3.5 ozs.
Comments	Full complement of diagnostic LED indicators; switch-selectable function	Full complement of diagnostic LED indicators; switch-selectable function	
Warranty	1 year limited	1 year limited	Lifetime
Price	$65	$65	$89

Manufacturer	Asante' Technologies	Asante' Technologies	Asante' Technologies
Model	FN10TA	FNTNA	FN 10T/TN
Interface	10BASE-T	10BASE2	10BASE2
Connectors	RJ-45, AAUI	BNC, AAUI	RJ45, BNC, AAUI

N/A—Not applicable   INA—Information not available

Table Continues →

◼ Transceivers

Manufacturer	Asante' Technologies	Asante' Technologies	Asante' Technologies
LEDs	Link	Power	Power, Link
Enclosure	3.5 x 1 x 1.6 3.5 ozs.	1.25 x 3.5 x .8" 3.5 ozs.	3.5 x 1 x 1.6 3.5 ozs.
Comments		Self terminating	Auto sensing
Warranty	Lifetime	Lifetime	Lifetime
Price	$35	$52	$115

Manufacturer	Asante' Technologies	Canary	Canary
Model	FNBNC	MTX-1070	MBX-1020
Interface	10BASE2	10BASE-T	10BASE2
Connectors	AAUI	RJ-45, D-Type	BNC, D-Type
LEDs	Power	Power, SQE, Link, Transmit, Receive, Collision, Receive polarity	Power, SQE
Enclosure	3.5 x 1 x 1.6" 3.5 ozs.	Metal/aluminum, 5 ozs.	Metal/aluminum, 5 ozs.
Comments		Ethernet IEEE 802.3 10BASE-T compliant	Ethernet IEEE 802.3 10BASE2 compliant
Warranty	Lifetime	2 year	2 year
Price	$59	$39	$49

Manufacturer	Canary	Canary	Canary
Model	MFZ-1060	CFX-1071-SM	CFX-1073/ CFX-1074
Interface	10BaseFL	MII	MII
Connectors	ST/SMA, D-Type	FO(SC-Type)	FO(ST-Type)
LEDs	Power, Link, Transmit, Receive, Collision, Full duplex	Power, Receive, Link, Full duplex, Collision, 100Mbps	Power, Receive, Link, Full duplex, Collision, 100Mbps
Enclosure	Metal/aluminum, 5 ozs.	Metal/aluminum, 8 ozs.	Metal/aluminum, 8 ozs.
Comments	Ethernet IEEE 802.3 10BASE-FL compliant	100BASE-FX/MII, SC-Type, full or half duplex, single mode, 15Km	100BASE-FX/MII, ST-Type, full or half duplex, single mode, 15Km
Warranty	2 year	2 year	2 year
Price	$199	$2,695	$459–$499

Manufacturer	Canary	Canary	Digi International, Inc.
Model	CT4-1030/ CTX-1070	CFX-1071/ CFX-1072	Digi 02F
Interface	MII	MII	10BASE-FL
Connectors	RJ-45	FO (SC-Type)	AUI/ST
LEDs	Power, Link, Activity(CT4 only), and Transmit, Receive, Collision, Auto-polarity, Full duplex(CTX only)	Power, Transmit, Receive, Link, Full duplex, Collision, 100Mbps	Power, Link, Transmit, Receive, Collision
Enclosure	Metal/aluminum, 8 ozs.	Metal/aluminum, 8 ozs.	Metal
Comments	100BASE-U/MII(CT4), 100BASE-TX/MII(CTX), ST-Type, full or half duplex, 100m	100BASE-FX/ MII, SC-Type, full or half duplex, multi mode, 2Km(1071), 500m(1072)	Link disable
Warranty	2 year	2 year	5 year
Price	$389	$499(1071)–$459	$199

N/A—Not applicable   INA—Information not available

Transceivers

Manufacturer	**Digi International, Inc.**	**D-Link**	**D-Link**
Model	Digi 100TX/FX	DE-850	DE-851
Interface	100BASE-T/F	Piercing Tap, Thick, Ethernet	BNC Ethernet
Connectors	MII to RJ45/SC and ST	Piercing Tap, Thick Ethernet	BNC, AUI
LEDs	Transmit, Receive, Collision, Link, Power, Full or half duplex.	Collision, Jabber, TX, RX	Collision, Jabber, TX, RX
Enclosure	Metal,1.2 lbs.	Metal	Plastic
Comments	Link disable		
Warranty	5 year	1 year	1 year
Price	TX= $395 FX= $575	$160	$85

Manufacturer	**D-Link**	**D-Link**	**D-Link**
Model	DE-852	DE-853	DE-854
Interface	N-Series Ethernet	UTP Ethernet	Fiber Optic
Connectors	N-Series, AUI	RJ-45, AUI	ST, AUI
LEDs	Collision, Jabber, TX, RX	Collision, Jabber, TX, RX	Collision, Jabber, TX, RX
Enclosure	Metal	Plastic	Plastic
Comments			
Warranty	1 year	1 year	1 year
Price	$160	$85	$395

Manufacturer	**D-Link**	**ETA Corp.**	**ETA Corp.**
Model	DE-855	EFA 400	EFA 410
Interface	BNC to UTP	10BASE2	10BASE-T
Connectors	BNC, RJ-45	BNC	RJ-45
LEDs	Collision, Jabber, TX, RX	Power	Power, Receive, Link, Transmit, Collision, Polarity
Enclosure	Plastic	Metal, 3 oz.	Metal, 3 ozs.
Comments			
Warranty	1 year	Lifetime	Lifetime
Price	$250	$32	$32

Manufacturer	**Farallon**	**Farallon**	**Ferroalloy**
Model	Etherwave AUI Transceivers	Etherwave AAUI Transceivers	Etherwave AUI Transceivers
Interface	AUI 10BASE-T	Apple AUI connection (AAUI) 10BASE-T	AUI Transceivers
Connectors	2 RJ - 45 10BASE-T ports	2 RJ - 45 10BASE-T ports	2 RJ-45 10 BASE-T ports
LEDs	7 (1 Receive and Link per port, 1 Collision, 1 Transmit, 1 Power/ test)	7 (1 Receive and Link per port, 1 Collision, 1 Transmit, 1 Power/ test)	7 (1 Receive and Link per port, 1 Collision, 1 Transmit, 1 Power/ tool
Enclosure	Metal	Metal	Metal
Comments			
Warranty	Lifetime	Lifetime	Lifetime
Price	$109	$99	$109

N/A—Not applicable   INA—Information not available

Table Continues →

■ Transceivers

Manufacturer	Ferroalloy	KTI	LANART
Model	Etherwave AAUI Transceivers	PE-300C	EXC0013/ ECR012E
Interface	Apple AUI connection (AAUI) 10BASE- T	10BASE-T 10BASE-2	10BASE-T/ 10BASE2
Connectors	2 RJ-45 10BASE- T ports	RJ45, BNC	AUI to UTP
LEDs	7 (1 Receive and Link per port, 1 Collision, 1 Transmit, 1 Power/ tool	Link, Activity	Power, Link, Transmit, Receive, Collision, SQE, Full duplex
Enclosure	Metal	Metal, 8 ozs.	Metal, 3.5 ozs.
Comments			LINKALENT signal provides 100% fault protection and isolation.
Warranty	Lifetime	5 year	5 year
Price	$99	$139	$55/ $59

Manufacturer	LANART	LANCAST	LANCAST
Model	EFT1101-ST	4304	6211
Interface	10BASE-FL	10BASE2, 10BASE5	100BASE-FX
Connectors	AUI to ST	Vampire, N-Series, BNC	SC, ST, MII
LEDs	Power, Link, Transmit, Receive, Collision, SQE, Full duplex	Power, SQE	Power, Link, Transmit, Receive, Collision
Enclosure	Metal, 3.5 ozs.	Metal, 8 ozs.	Metal, 3.5 ozs.
Comments		User selectable SQE variety of interchangeable network taps for flexibility	Half and full duplex operation. Multimode and singlemode versions.
Warranty	5 year	3 year	3 year
Price	$215	$180	$1,995-$4,398

Manufacturer	LANCAST	LANCAST	LANCAST
Model	4320	4321	6214
Interface	10BASE-T	10BASE2	100BaseTX
Connectors	RJ-45, DB ISP	BNC, DB ISP	RJ-45, MII
LEDs	Link, Collision, Receive, Transmit, Polarity, Power	Jabber, Collision, Receive, Transmit, Power	Power, Link, Transmit, Receive, Collision
Enclosure	Metal, 1 ozs.	Metal, 1 ozs.	Metal, 3.5 ozs.
Comments	Locking posts for direct connection to use DTE or AUI cable	Locking posts for direct connection to use DTE or AUI cable	Half and full duplexing operation. Autosensing 10/100Mbps
Warranty	3 year	3 year	3 year
Price	$46	$46	$320

Manufacturer	Lantronix	Lantronix	Lantronix
Model	LTX-T	LTX-2	LTX-5
Interface	10BASE-T	10BASE2	10BASE5
Connectors	RJ-45, AUI	BNC, AUI	AUI
LEDs	Collision, Transmit, Receiving, Jabber, Polarity, Link	Activity, Power	Transmit, Collision, Receive, Heartbeat (SQE), Power
Enclosure	Metal	Metal	Metal

N/A—Not applicable   INA—Information not available

Transcevers ■

Manufacturer	Lantronix	Lantronix	Lantronix
Comments	Polarity correcting, selectable heartbeat	Selectable heartbeat	Selectable heartbeat, selectable linktest, selectable TX/RX thresholds
Warranty	5 year	5 year	5 year
Price	$79	$79	$159

Manufacturer	Lantronix	Lantronix	Lantronix
Model	LTX-FL	LTX-TA	LTX-2A
Interface	10BASE-FL	10BASE-T	10BASE2
Connectors	Dual ST, AUI	RJ-45	BNC
LEDs	Power, Receive, Transmit, Link	Power, Good link	Power
Enclosure	Metal	Metal	Metal
Comments	Selectable heartbeat	Selectable heartbeat, Twisted Pair polarity connection	Selectable heartbeat
Warranty	5 year	5 year	5 year
Price	$249	$39	$39

Manufacturer	Landings Technology	Landings Technology	Linksys
Model	Transceiver Series	Fiber Transceivers	Ethernet Workgroup Hub with Mac Transceiver
Interface	10BASE-T, 10BASE2, 10BASE5	10BASE5 FL	10BASE-T
Connectors	RJ-45, BNC, AUI	ST, AUI	RJ-45
LEDs	Link, Collision, Power	Tx, Rx, Collision, Power	Power, link, AAUI, TX, RX, collision
Enclosure	Metal, 6 ozs.	Metal, 8 ozs.	Plastic
Comments	AUI/BNC or AUI/UTP	Collision detection, jabber protection, data loopback, auto-partition	Transforms fleet of PCs and/or Mac computers into a high performance Workgroup
Warranty	Lifetime	Lifetime	1 year
Price	$36	$195	$139

Manufacturer	Linksys	Pinacl Communications	Pinacl Communications
Model	Mac Combo Transceiver	2227	2212 ST/SMA
Interface	10BASE-T Thin Coax	AAUI to RJ45/BNC	AUI to Fiber
Connectors	RJ-45, BNC	AAUI, RJ45, BNC	AUI, ST/SMA
LEDs	Power, TX	Link, TX, RX, Collision	Link, Jabber, Transmit, Receive, Collision, Power
Enclosure	Plastic	Metal	Metal
Comments			
Warranty	1 year	3 year	3 year
Price	$69	$69	$229

Manufacturer	Pinacl Communications	Pinacl Communications	Pinacl Communications
Model	2216	2213-ST?SMA	2214
Interface	AUI to ThinNet (BNC)	10BASE-T to 10BASE-FL	10BASE-T to 10BaseZ
Connectors	AUI, BNC	RJ45, ST/SMA	RJ45, BNC

N/A—Not applicable   INA—Information not available

Table Continues →

■ Transceivers

Manufacturer	Pinacl Communications	Pinacl Communications	Pinacl Communications
LEDs	Collision, Jabber, Power, Transmit, SQE, Receive	Power, Data, Collision, Jabber, Link, Fiber link	Jabber, Polarity, UTP, Collision, Link, BNC collision, BNC receive, UTP Recover, Power
Enclosure	Metal	Metal	Metal
Comments			
Warranty	3 year	3 year	3 year
Price	$56	$369	$219

Manufacturer	Pinacl Communications	Plexcom, Inc.	Plexcom, Inc.
Model	2215	8058	8080
Interface	AUI to 10BASE-T	AUI-10BASE2	AUI-10BASE-FL
Connectors	AUI, RJ45	BNC (10BASE2) D15 (AUI)	ST (10BASE-FL) D15 (AUI)
LEDs	Collision, Power, Polarity, Transmit, SQE, Receive, Link	Link, Tx, Rx, Collision, Jabber, Power	Link, Tx, Rx, Collision, Jabber, Power
Enclosure	Metal	Metal, 4 ozs.	Metal, 4 ozs.
Comments		Compact, direct attachable unit, built-in "T" connector	Compact, direct attachable unit multimode
Warranty	3 year	1 year	1 year
Price	$50	$110	$425

Manufacturer	Plexcom, Inc.	Plexcom, Inc.	RAD DATA COMMUNICATIONS
Model	8080	8054S	M-TFC
Interface	AUI-10BASE-FL	AUI-10BASE-T	STP-TYPE 1 SM/MM
Connectors	ST (10BASE-FL) D15 (AUI)	RJ-45 (10BASE-T) D15 (AUI)	DB-9 Male ST, FC
LEDs	Link, Tx, Rx, Collision, Jabber, Power	Link, Tx, Rx, Collision, Jabber, Power	Power, Fault
Enclosure	Metal, 4 ozs.	Metal, 8 ozs.	Metal
Comments	Half/Full duplex direct attachable unit, singlemode	Compact, direct attachable unit	Miniature, single or multimode fiber
Warranty	1 year	1 year	1 year
Price	$750	$30	$250–$600

Manufacturer	RAD DATA COMMUNICATIONS	Standard Microsystems Corp.	TRENDware
Model	M-EFC	3402TP/ 3402BNC/ 3402F	TE-TT, TE-T2, TE-T5P, TE-TP
Interface	802.3 AUI 10BASE-FL, SM\MM	10BASE-T 10BASE2 10BASE-FL	10BASE-T, 10BASE2, 10BASE5, 10BASE-TL
Connectors	DB-15 Male ST, FC	RJ45 BNC ST	RJ-45, BNC, Piercing Tap, ST FOIRL, AUI
LEDs	Link, Power, TX, RX	Power, Link, Transmit, Receive, Collision, SQE	Power, Transmit, Link, Receive, Collision, Jabber
Enclosure	Plastic	Aluminum, 0.25 lbs.	Plastic, 2 ozs.

N/A—Not applicable   INA—Information not available

Transceivers ▪

Manufacturer	RAD DATA COMMUNICATIONS	Standard Microsystems Corp.	TRENDware
Comments	Miniature, singlemode or multi-mode fiber. Self-powered from AUI interface		
Warranty	1 year	3 year	5 year
Price	$250–$600	$99 (3402TP) $149 (3402BNC) $399 (3402F)	$49–$269

Manufacturer	UNICOM	UNICOM	UNICOM
Model	10BASE-T Transceiver	Trans-One	Trans-2/5
Interface	10BASE-T	10BASE-T	10BASE-2
Connectors	NA	NA	NA
LEDs	Power/TX, LINK/RCV, Collision, Jabber	Power/TX, LINK/RCV, Collision, Jabber	Power
Enclosure	94VO	94VO	94VO
Comments			
Warranty	5 year	5 year	5 year
Price	$39	$25	$50

Manufacturer	UNICOM	UNICOM	UNICOM
Model	MacTrans-10T	MacTrans-2/5	Trans-FL
Interface	10BASE-T	10BASE2	10BASE-FL
Connectors	NA	NA	NA
LEDs	Power/TX, Link/RCV, Collision, Jabber	Power	Power, Collision, XMT, LMON, Jabber, RCV
Enclosure	94VO	Aluminum	Aluminum
Comments			
Warranty	5 year	5 year	5 year
Price	$50	$50	$189

N/A—Not applicable   INA—Information not available

End ▪

■ WAN Links

Manufacturer	ADC Kentrox	ADC Kentrox
Model	DataSMART Sport T1 DSU/CSU	DataSMART T1/FT1 Single-Port IDSU
General Description	Has embedded SNMP and an auto-configuration feature, expedites installation. Designed to reduce on-site support for growing high-density sites, such as central offices, corporate and government networks, data centers, and Internet service provider networks.	The DataSMART T1/FT1 Single-Port IDSU connects routers or other CPE to T1/FT1 networks. In addition to T1/FT1, the DataSMART supports Frame Relay, SMDS DXI and ATM FUNI.
Performance Features	Enables attached routers, bridges, codecs to operate at all fractional speeds up to full T1 rates, 1.544Mbps	The DataSMAMRT IDSU can be used as a high-speed line driver across private facilities, converting a data signal to a 4-wire T1 format, and then extending the signal out to 6000 feet. It operates at T1 fractional data rates between 56Kbps and 1.536Mbps, Nx56 or Nx64Kbps
Connectivity Features	Selectable V.35, EIA-530 or RS-449 data ports, DB-15 network interface. Compatible with Frame Relay, ATM DXI, SMDS DXI and clear T1.	Selectble V.35 or EIA-530 data ports, DB-15P network interface. Compatible with Frame Relay, SMDS DXI and ATM FUNI.
Physical Features(20 words max)	12-slot shelf: 17(W) x 7(H) x 12"(D), 24/48 VDC dual power inputs	Standalone: 8(W) x 1.93(H) x 11.25"(D), 12-Slot Chassis: 17(W) x 17(H) x12"(D), Plug-in: 2 lbs. 5 ozs.
Comments		
Warranty	5 year	5 year
Price	$2,995	$1,495

Manufacturer	ADC Kentrox	ADC Kentrox
Model	D-SERV T1/FT1 DSU/SCU	D-SERV 56/64 Multirate Data Service Unit
General Description	The D-SERV is a single port DSU combined with CSU functionality. The D-SERV supports T1/FT1 services including Frame Relay, and frame-based services including SMDS and ATM.	The D-SERV 56/64 provides access to SDMS, Frame Relay and ATM. It is a multirate DDS DSU/CSU that connects any DDS corporate application and is ideal for interconnecting LANS, Internet access, and remote PCs to local hosts.
Performance Features	The D-SERV can be used as a high-speed line driver across private facilities, converting a data signal to a 4-wire T1 format, and then extending the signal out to 600 feet. It operates at T1 fractional data rates between 56Kbps and 1.536Mbps, Nx56 or Nx64Kbps.	Provides termination for DDS at 64,56,19.2,9.6,4.8 and 2.4Kbps. Synchronous rate adaption allows legacy equipment operating at 38.4,19.2, or 9.6 to transmit over a 56K facility. Asychronous rate adaption allows for 57.6,38.4,19.2 and 9.6Kbps DTE equipment to run over a 56K line.
Connectivity Features	Single V.35 data port interface to a router. The T1 facility connects to the D-SERV network port using a network interface cable with modular jacks.	Selectable V.35 or EIA-232 data ports. RJ48S network interface. Operates at T1 fractional data rates between 56Kbps and 1.536Mbps.
Physical Features	Weight: 2.5 lbs., 8(W) x 1.93(H) x 11.25"(D)	Standalone: 3.5 lbs., 6.8(W) x 1.3(H) x 8.9"(D) 12-slot chassis: 17(W) x 7(H) x 12"(D) Plug-in: 2 lbs.
Comments		
Warranty	5 year	5 year
Price	$1,345	$495

Manufacturer	Ascend	Ascend
Model	2000	MAX 1800
General Description	Provides LAN to WAN connectivity with flexible WAN S/W	Provides LAN to WAN connectivity with flexible WAN S/W
Performance Features	Operates with the LAN protocols and WAN protocols to provide dynamic bandwidth for end-to-end connections	Operates with the LAN protocols and WAN protocols to provide dynamic bandwidth for end-to-end connections
Connectivity Features	(1) PRI/ T1/ E1, also (1) serial (RS 449 or V.35)	(1) Ethernet with a serial port and (8) BRI ports
Physical Features	1.75 x 17 x 12" 90-240 VAC 47 to 63Hz	1.75 x 17 x 12" 90-240 VAC 47 to 63Hz

N/A—Not applicable   INA—Information not available

WAN Links ■

Manufacturer	Ascend	Ascend
Comments	Same software features as rest of MAX family	Same software features as rest of MAX family
Warranty	1 year	1 year
Price	$6,500	$6,400

Manufacturer	Ascend	Ascend
Model	Max 200Plus	4002/4004
General Description	Provides WAN connectivity to small LAN networks	Provides LAN to WAN connectivity with flexible WAN feature sets
Performance Features	Operates with the network protocols and WAN protocols to efficiently provide bandwidth on demand connectors	Operates with the LAN protocols and WAN protocols to provide bandwidth for end-to-end connections
Connectivity Features	(1) Ethernet and (8) analog modems, or up to 4 ISDN BRI	Supports up to (4) PRI/ T1/ E1, and (1) Serial (v.35, RS449)
Physical Features(20 words max)	2 x 17 x 12" 90 to 240 VAC 47 to 63Hz	3 x 17 x 12" 90 to 240 VAC 47 to 63Hz
Comments	Same software features as the rest of the MAX family	Same software features as the rest of the MAX family
Warranty	1 year	1 year
Price	$2,400	$11,000

Manufacturer	Astrocom	Astrocom
Model	WanMaster	WANMaster BR/
General Description	Modular new TI, fractional TI CSU/DSU with embedded SNMP support. Easy to install and upgrade.	Full-featured terminal adapter for Basic Rate ISDN that enables users to more fully and easily optimize the switched public features of ISDN
Performance Features	DSO channels may be non-contiguous.	Excellent for ride conferencing, LAN interconnect, Internet access, telecommuting. Front panel keypad makes installation easy. Call-screening enhances network security, speed dial, and multiple profile storage.
Connectivity Features	(1) or (2) user ports, choice of V.35 or EIA 530. Optional Ethernet port, second TI port foor routine back-up, video re-routing, or TI failover standby.	(2) user ports, V.35 or RS-232 or EIA530. Optional POTs port. Intergrated NTI (U Interface).
Physical Features	Small footprint 3.1 x 7.9 x 9.9" 3.2 lbs. 110/220 V	7.6 x 2.25 x 9.5" 3.4 lbs.
Comments	Part of a new generation of advanced WAN products geared toward Internet and other applications using TI.	Second in the WANMaster family of high performance WAN products.
Warranty	5 year, free overnight replacement in USA; free 7-day, 24-hour tech support.	5 year, free overnight replacement in USA; free 7-day, 24-hour tech support.
Price	$1,695	$695

Manufacturer	Astrocom	Astrocom
Model	NX6456	Rack 64
General Description	TI Multiplexer CSU/DSU, simple to install, used to fractionalize TI within an organiation. Excellent for videoconferencing.	Compact card rack CSU/DSU for 56/64Kbps DDS, perfect for Internet service providers and other organizations with many sites.
Performance Features	Tolerates jitter and wander 350% better than industry standards. Front panel LCD for configuration terminal menus for monitoring.	Optional control card provides configuration and monitoring via terminal menus. Built in tests and LEDs enhance diagnostic and monitoring. Mid-plane power supply provides redundancy and fault tolerance.

N/A—Not applicable   INA—Information not available

Table Continues →

■ WAN Links

Manufacturer	Astrocom	Astrocom
Connectivity Features	2 or 4 user ports, choice of V.35 or RS449. Users may assign any number of contiguous or alternating DSO's to each port (max 24).	Single user port choice of V.35 or RS232. Rate adaption, async to sync conversion, support for Switched 56 available.
Physical Features	Rack mountable (hardware included) 3.5 x 17.5 x 13.6" 18 lbs., fully loaded	3.5 (H) x 19"(W) rack chassis holds up to (16) 2364 cards. 110/220V -48V available
Comments	Optional DSX/DSI for drop and insert allows users to combine video, voice, and data on a single TI line.	Cards are hot swappable.
Warranty	5 year, free overnight replacement in USA; free 7-day, 24-hour tech support.	5 year, free overnight replacement in USA; free 7-day, 24-hour tech support.
Price	$2,695–$3,395	$395 rack chassis w/ power supply $195 control card $495 each 2364 rack card

Manufacturer	Astrocom	Astrocom
Model	2364	NX1
General Description	CSU/DSU for 56Kbps DDS and 64Kbps clear channel. Compatible with frame relay networks. Used by Internet subscribers.	TI, fractional TI CSU/DSU simple to install, well suited for Internet, video conferencing and other WAN applications.
Performance Features	Front panel LEDs indicate unit conditions and alarms. Built-in test generators make diagnostics easy. Dip switches on bottom for configuration.	Front panel push button configuration or terminal menu control
Connectivity Features	Supports one V.35 or RS232 user port (both interfaces supplied on the auto-sensing unit). Supports rate adaption and async to sync conversion and anti-streaming.	Single DTE interface, choice of V.35 or RS449
Physical Features	1.62 x 7.3 x 6.6" 21 lbs.	Low Profile 1.75" high, includes brackets and screws for rack mounting 110/220 VAC -48V available
Comments	Popular unit for branch offices	Optional DSX/DSI for drop and insert applications, to combine voice, and data
Warranty	5 year, free overnight replacement in USA; free 7-day, 24-hour tech support.	5 year, free overnight replacement in USA; free 7-day, 24-hour tech support.
Price	$520	$1,795–$2,695

Manufacturer	HT Communications	Laser Communications, Inc.
Model	Pro[TM]4501-C and Pro[TM]5501-C	OmniBeam 4000
General Description	ISA bus PC Card DSU/CSU. COM port addressable and compatible with most common communications software. Models support 56Kbps leased lines or frame relay for Internet access.	The advanced modular design, low power output and field adjustable optics make the OB4000 a safe, versatile, and reliable networking. No frequency licensing required.
Performance Features	COM port rate up to 57.6Kbps Asynchronous. Frame Relay version supports Async, SLIP, and PPP data.	Supports high-speed communications of 34Mbps to 155Mbps, which includes protocols such as E3, T3, SonetV, ATM52, 100BASE-VO, Fast Ethernet, FDDI, OC3/Sonet5/ ATMS.
Connectivity Features	ISA PC Card Bus for CPE and 4-wire digital RJ-48S for WAN (CSU).	Interface is 1330nm. Multimode fiber between 34Mhz and 155Mhz. Usually connected to a hub, switch, or connector.
Physical Features	Mini-ISA Card	20 x 5 x 6" (weatherproof) Remote power supply-supplied 24 VAC 2.5 AM Power Supply
Comments	Ideal for dedicated Internet access via 56Kbps digital leased line or via 56Kbps frame relay	Part of complete line of laser-optic communicating equipment for interbuilding connectivity
Warranty	5 year	2 year
Price	$395+	$17,995

N/A—Not applicable   INA—Information not available

WAN Links ■

Manufacturer	**Microwave Bypass Systems, Inc.**	**Motorola**
Model	Etherwave LAN Radio	925 AccessWay™ System
General Description	Point-to-point microwave system for connecting LAN's, telephone systems or video systems	It is a solution for modem pool applications ranging from a local network to a service provider that requires 50,000 central site modems. The 925 can serve as the centralized hub-based access system for a range of businesses.
Performance Features	Highly reliable transmission of Ethernet, TI-DS-3, or video over distances up to 20 miles.	Uses T1, PRI or other high-speed lines for voice, video, and data applications. The 925 consolidates LAN connections, PBX connections, and more into different segments of a T1 line. Can drop and insert DSO' between T1 lines.
Connectivity Features	Industry standard connections to LANs, telephone, and video systems.	The connections to the LAN can use T1 lines, V.34 Dual Hybrid modems and multiprotocol LAN access servers. TCP/IP, IPX, and a variety of other protocols are supported.
Physical Features	All units rack mountable	19 or 23" rack
Comments	Complete installation, licensing, and maintenance service available	The system is a basic communications server and a remote access and wide area networking system, linking corporate sites with data, voice, and video communications across high-speed lines.
Warranty	1 year, parts and labor	2 years (hardware) 90 days (software)
Price	Equipment only from $20,000	24 port begins at $27,995 Custom systems available

Manufacturer	**Niwot Networks, Inc.**	**Patton Electronics Co.**
Model	Niw RAS Kit	Model 2066RC
General Description	RAS driver for use with Microsoft Windows NT, plus high-speed communications board	V.35 to X.21 Interface Converter rack card
Performance Features	NT based router replacement. Internet and Intranet dial-ip and leased access above 64Kbps	Supports synchronous data rates up to 2.048Mbps; (2) 16-bit elastic buffers ensure data integrity.
Connectivity Features	V.35, RS449 for Switched 56, ISDN and PRI, leased lines 56Kbps-7Mbps	Transparent to protocol
Physical Features	ISA bus master communication board and cable	Fits in Patton's 3.5" high rack chassis. Hot swappable front/rear cards. AC and DC power supplies available.
Comments	Passed Microsoft conformance tests and received Certificate of Conformance, V.25 bis sync dialing	DCE/DTE switchable; rack chassis sold separately; (2) UD-26 connectors.
Warranty	1 year	1 year
Price	$995	$695 (card only)

Manufacturer	**Patton Electronics Co.**	**Patton Electronics Co.**
Model	Model 2065RC	Model 2040
General Description	RS-232 to X.21 Interface Converter rack card	V.35 to HSSI
Performance Features	Supports synchronous data rates up to 128Kbps; (2) 16-bit elastic buffers ensure data integrity.	Supports synchronous data rates to 10Mbps; passes data, control lines, and two loopback modes.
Connectivity Features	Transparent to protocol	Transparent to protocol
Physical Features	Fits in Patton's 3.5" high rack chassis. Hot swappable front/rear cards; AC and DC power supplies available.	M/34 and SCCI (HD-50) Connectors, with intergral 6ft. cable.
Comments	DCE/DTE switchable; rack chassis sold separately; (2) UD-26 connectors.	Available in DTE-DCE or DCE to DTE versions
Warranty	1 year	1 year
Price	$595 (card only)	$895

N/A—Not applicable   INA—Information not available

Table Continues →

■ WAN Links

Manufacturer	Patton Electronics, Co.	Patton Electronics, Co.
Model	Model 2022	Model 2015/ Model 2014
General Description	RS-232 to CCITT V.36 (RS-449) interface converter	RS-449/422 to V.35 interface converter (2015); RS-530 to V.35 interface converter (2014)
Performance Features	Supports synchronous data to 200Kbps; passes all necessary data, clocking, and control signals.	Supports synchronous data to 2.048Mbps; passes all necessary data, clocking, and control signals.
Connectivity Features	Transparent to protocol	Transparent to protocol
Physical Features	Built into 6' interface cable; RS-232 (DB-25), CCITT V.36 (RS-449) (DB-37)	Built into 6' interface cable; RS-449/422 (DB-37), V.35 (M/34) [2015] RS-530 (DB-25), V.35 (M/34) interface converter [2014]
Comments	No AC power or batteries required; DCE/DTE switchable.	No AC power or batteries required; various DCE/DTE combinations available.
Warranty	1 year	1 year
Price	$195	$119

Manufacturer	Patton Electronics, Co.	Patton Electronics, Co.
Model	Model 2021	Model 2020
General Description	RS-232 to X.21 interface converter	RS-232 to V.35 interface converter
Performance Features	Supports synchronous data to 200Kbps; passes all necessary data, clocking, and control signals.	Supports synchronous data to 384Kbps; passes all necessary data, clocking, and control signals.
Connectivity Features	Transparent to protocol	Transparent to protocol
Physical Features	Built into 6' interface cable; RS-232 (DB-25), X.21 (DB-15)	Built into 6' interface cable; RS-232 (DB-25), V.35 (M/34) or RS-530 (DB-25); rack card available.
Comments	No AC power or batteries required; DCE/DTE switchable.	No AC power or batteries required; DCE/DTE switchable.
Warranty	1 year	1 year
Price	$295	$295

Manufacturer	Patton Electronics	Patton Electronics
Model	Model 2500 Series	Model 2450
General Description	Dedicated All rate (64Kbps) Switched-56 CSU/DSU	56/64Kbps DDS/Clear Channel CSU/DSU
Performance Features	V.54; V.52 diagnostic rate adaptation to 64Kbps, Anti-Streaming and Auto EQ; 9 LED indicators	V.54, V.52 diagnostics; distances to 3.4 miles over two pair; internal, external, or receive recover clock; six LED indicators
Connectivity Features	4 wire operation; ATiT 62310 compliant RS-232 control port, V.35 & RS-232 DTE ports	Compatible with 56Kbps DDS or 64Kbps Clear channel circuits (synchronous)
Physical Features	Standalone and rack mount versions available; internal AC or DC power supply	Available with RS-232 (DB25) or V.35 (M/34) interface; 1.65(H) x 4.18(W) x 3.96"; external AC power
Comments	All rate, switched-56 or combination models available (standalone)	Smallest 56/64Kbps CSU/DSU currently on the market (their words)
Warranty	1 year	1 year
Price	$520–$620	$349–$375

N/A—Not applicable   INA—Information not available

WAN Links ■

Manufacturer	Performance Technologies	Performance Technologies
Model	PT-VME151A PT-VME161 (SBC/Communications Controllers)	PT-PCI370 Primary Rate ISDN Communications Controller
General Description	A 68040 based VMEbus platform designed to offer maximum communications configurability. Featuring up to 64MB of on-board memory, it functions as a communications subsystem	It is an intelligent 1 or 2 port, T1/ E1 primary rate ISDN communications interface
Performance Features	Using the EPAK extension interface, it supports 10BASE-T Ethernet and up to 16 ports of (56Kbps/ port) sync/async local or WAN communications	It is built around the 4.5 MIPs QUICC communications controller and includes a 128K Flash PROM for program storage. Relegates most of the ISDN communications related processing.
Connectivity Features	Interfaces with the VMEbus using the 60 MBPS VME64 mode. All WAN connections are provided using industry standard interfaces.	The board is available with either RJ-45 or coaxial connectors. Secondary overvoltage protection, at 100 (T1), 120 or 75 (E1) Ohms
Physical Features	234(W) x 160mm(D), front panel = 20.3mm	10.5 x 15.5 cm, PCI bus short slot
Comments	It processes communications protocols independently. Other models available	Designed as a fully programmable sub-system, its on-board intelligence and 4MB DRAM array allow the product to off-load much of the low level communications activities. Other models available
Warranty	Not available	Not available
Price	$2,595/ $4,090	$2,245

Manufacturer	Renex, Co.	Renex, Co.
Model	TMS-5	RPad-2
General Description	A turn-key solution that supports up to 64 simul. users (32 can be async connects). Supports multiple simul. hosts connections:SNA/SDLC, X.25, Token Ring and Ethernet. These include IBM mainframe, AS/400, LAN Servers, and async hosts.	Provides complete connectivity from PCs (and ASCII terminals) to IBM 3270, midrange systems and ASCII hosts over X.25 networks. Offers remote connectivity for variable applications through one convenient hardware platform.
Performance Features	Enables devices to perform at their rated local outputs: Token Ring, 16Mbps, Ethernet 10Mbps, Sync 128Kbps, Async 57.6K	Supports multiple, simultaneous host connections: SNA/SDLC, X.25/QLLC, ASCII Host. User connections direct, dial-in X.25. Opt. Token Ring, supports up to 64 LC's with speeds up to 128Kbps.
Connectivity Features	4 Sync (RS232, V.35) SNA/SDLC config. (3270 or 5250) PU types 1, 2 and 2.1 LU 1, 2, 3, 4, 6.2 and 7 X.25/ QLLC up to 64 LC's LAN—Token Ring or Ethernet	X.25/HDLC host & terminal PAD HDLC/LAPB link level, modulo 8 or 128 operations SNA/SDLC PU types 1, 2 and 2.1 LU 1, 2, 3, 4, 6.2 and 7 Token Ring IEEE 802.5 & 802.2, Modulo 128
Physical Features	8.5(H) x 16.5(D) x 19" 4 Sync ports, up to 32 user ports, X.25 (RS-232, V.35), LAN—Token Ring or Ethernet	Rack mount panel, four sync DB-25 8.5(H) x 16.5(D) x 19", 25 lbs., Voltage 110-220 VAC, up to 32 async ports. Opt. V.35 & Token Ring, DB-9
Comments	The TM-5 is a part of a complete line of remote access products. It is the first product to combine dial-in access to both IBM hosts and LAN-based file servers.	Model is part of a complete line of remote access products for IBM connectivity over LAN/WAN networks.
Warranty	90 days	90 days
Price	Compact unit starts at $5,995	Rpad-2 with 8 x .25 Lcs starts at $8,495

Manufacturer	Sealevel Systems, Inc.	Simpact, Inc.
Model	Route 56™	Freeway 1000
General Description	Single channel synchronous WAN adapter for Internet and other wide area network applications. High speed (10Mbps) link ideal for transmission of data intensive images (digital video and audio, X-rays, et. al.)	Modular data communication servers that allow companies to integrate proprietary and legacy WAN applications onto the open systems corporate network.

N/A—Not applicable   INA—Information not available

Table Continues →

■ WAN Links

Manufacturer	**Sealevel Systems, Inc.**	**Simpact, Inc.**
Performance Features	On-board Zilog Z16C32 serial communications controller with built-in DMA controller and 256K of on board RAM and 32 byte FIFO buffer. Software selectable IRQ and memory range.	Users of DEC, IBM, Sun, or HP systems can access any number of WANs, data feeds, or mission-critical services. Supports up to 4 to 8 high speed ports.
Connectivity Features	Supports PPP, Frame Relay, X.25, HDLC, SDLC, and MIL-STD-1554B protocols. Supports multiple electrical interface standards, including RS-232, RS-422/485/449, EIA-530, V.35 X.21. Two or four wire operation in RS-485 mode.	LAN interface: TCP/IP, and FTP Electrical interfaces: EIA-232, 449, 485, 530, 562, V.35, ISO-4903 (V.11), Mil-188
Physical Features	ISA bus with external DB-25 connector. Board dimensions are 8.4 x 4.8".	Rack mountable 6.25(H) x 16.35(W) x 16.75" 21 lbs.
Comments	Route 56 ™ is one of the Advanced Communication Board family of synchronous communication boards. The ACB family includes the one and two channel boards in all standard electrical interfaces.	Freeway can easily handle primary and consolidated financial needs, military satellite communications, process control monitoring, telecommunications, and device specific, real-time applications.
Warranty	1 year	1 year
Price	$569	$5,500

Manufacturer	**Simpact, Inc.**	**Telco Systems**
Model	Freeway 2000/ 4000	Series 500M Optimizer
General Description	Modular data communication servers that allow companies to integrate proprietary and legacy WAN applications onto the open systems corporate network.	Significantly increases the throughput of WAN lines. Reduces the cost of internetworking by reducing the amount of bandwidth required to transport LAN traffic over WAN links.
Performance Features	Users of DEC, IBM, Sun, or HP systems can access any number of WANs, data feeds, or mission-critical services. Supports up to 8 to 64 high speed ports.	Supports up to 256Kbps WAN speed (1) input port; (1) output port; oOperates in Hardware compression Mode, Software compression mode, CISCO compression mode.
Connectivity Features	LAN interface: TCP/IP, and FTP Electrical interfaces: EIA-232, 449, 530, V.35, ISO-4903 (V.11), Mil-188	Interfaces: V.35, RS-449, EIA-530, X.21, RS232C; ConsolePort: RS232C (DB9); Compatible with all HDLC/SDLC Framed data.
Physical Features	Rack mountable (2000) 6.9(H) x 19(W) x 19.46" 38.14 lbs./ (4000) 10.5(H) x 19(W) x 19.46" 46.9 lbs.	8(L) x17(W) x 2" 5 lbs.
Comments	Freeway can easily handle primary and consolidated financial needs, military satellite communications, process control monitoring, telecommunications, and device specific, real-time applications.	Part of the Optimizer complete family of data compression products, for point-to-point and multi-point networks.
Warranty	1 year	1 year 24-hour support hotline spare in air service
Price	$5,500	$3,495

Manufacturer	**Telco Systems**	**Telco Systems**
Model	Series 5000 Frame Relay Optimizer	Series 5000 LAN/WAN Optimizer
General Description	A high performance data compressor that increases the throughput of transmission circuits in frame relay networks. It is ideally suited for multi-point, packet-switched environments requiring high levels of cost-effective throughput and performance.	Significantly increases the throughput of Wide Area Network lines. A high performance, synchronous network data compressor ideally suited for network enviroments where high line speed support and high performance compression is required.
Performance Features	Supports WAN speeds up to TI/EI 2.048Mbps (1) input port; (1) output port: (1) console port; optional redundant link pass-through features for internetworking integrity.	Supports WAN speeds up to TI/EI 2.048Mbps (1 or 2) input ports; (1) output port: (1) console port; optional redundant link pass-through features for internetworking integrity.

N/A—Not applicable   INA—Information not available

WAN Links ■

Manufacturer	Telco Systems	Telco Systems
Connectivity Features	Interfaces: DTE: V.35, RS-449, EIA-530, X.21; DCE: V.35, RS-449, EIA-530, X.21, RS232C; ConsolePort: RS232C (DB9); Compatible with all HDLC/SDLC Framed data	Interfaces: DTE: V.35, RS-449, EIA-530, X.21; DCE: V.35, RS-449, EIA-530, X.21, RS232C; ConsolePort: RS232C (DB9); Compatible with all HDLC/SDLC Framed data
Physical Features	17(L) x 17(W) x 2" 16 lbs. Tabletop, 19" rack mount; Optional intelligent front panel	17(L) x 17(W) x 2" 16 lbs. Tabletop, 19" rack mount; Optional intelligent front panel
Comments	Part of the optimizer complete family of data compression products, for point to point and multi-point networks	Part of the optimizer complete family of data compression products, for point to point and multi-point networks
Warranty	1 year; 24-hour support hotline spare in air service	1 year; 24-hour support hotline spare in air service
Price	$5,900+	$4,900+

Manufacturer	UB Networks	Verlink, Corp.
Model	GeoStax/ Remote	AS56plus (centum series)
General Description	Provides cost-effective solution for connecting small branch offices to enterprise networks. Supports a variety of WAN options.	Fully featured DDS, FT1, or T1 DSU/CSU in one package. Supports a single data port connection. Management/ configuration provided by either ASCII terminal SLIP SNMP or front panel controls with LCD display.
Performance Features	Includes bandwidth optimization features for improved performance. Supports B 10Mbps Ethernet connection + 1 WAN connection.	Supports DDS data speeds of 2400, 4800, 9600, 19.2Kbps, 56Kbps, or 64Kbps clear channel capability In TI: mode supports NX24 DS0's. (56Kbps or 64Kbps) up to 1.536Mbps
Connectivity Features	8 10BASE-T ports, SNMP managed, RS-232, V.35, RS422, X.21 + ISDN WAN options; TCP/IP, IP + AppleTalk support	Connects to either a North American DDS format (AMI/ 8825 Bipolar) facility. In FTI/TI mode supports either D4-SF or ESF framing formats.
Physical Features	LED indicators for light + activity Size: 10.5 x 1.75 x 6.5" 110 + 220 V power available	8.35(W) x 1.75(H) x 10" 7 lbs. 90-230 VAC, 47-63Hz Optional 19" Rack-mount kit
Comments	GeoStax/ Remote is a part of an entire line of workgroup connectivity products for LAN and enterprise environments.	Model is a part of a complete line of DSU/ CSUs for connections to the North American Digital Network.
Warranty	1 year	5 year
Price	$2,795–$3,395	$1,395

Manufacturer	Verlink, Corp.	Xircom Systems Division
Model	AS2200 with SNMP	MPM-4/ MPM-8
General Description	Fully featured integrated DSU/CSU (IDCSU) supporting a single data port (V.35 or RS449) enabling high-speed data applications to connect to a T1 Facility	MultiPort Modem remote access server card providing direct telephone line connection for up to 8 users; combines with remote access software to extend networks for remote users and servers.
Performance Features	Takes advantage of the Fractional TI, or Full TI bandwidth (64Kbps to 15336Mbps): (n x 64Kbps)	Integrated V.34 modems for connection speeds up to 28.8Kbps; V.42 and MNP-2-4 error correction, V.42bis and MNP 5 data compression.
Connectivity Features	Connects to a North American TI facility with either a B8Z5 or AMI (RTZ) format. ESF or D4 super-framing formats.	Supports Novell Netware Connect, Novell MultiProtocol Router, and Microsoft NT RAS software using PPP compliant software; supports popular remote control, security, and modem pooling software packages.
Physical Features	Mounts in a dual-line shelf 17.25(W) x 1.75(H) x 10" Voltage 110-115VAC or -48VDC	Full-sized ISA bus card; four or eight RJ-11 connectors; up to 8 cards per server supported.

N/A—Not applicable   INA—Information not available

Table Continues →

■ WAN Links

Manufacturer	**Verlink, Corp.**	**Xircom Systems Division**
Comments	Model AS2200 is part of a complete line of WAN access solutions using Fractional TI or TI Facilities.	Part of Netaccess Open Remote Server product family of analog and ISDN connectivity products
Warranty	5 year	5 year (hardware) 90 days (software)
Price	$2,995 (Dual Line Shelf)	$1,699(MPM-4), $2,999(MPM-8)

Manufacturer	**Xircom Systems Division**
Model	MCI-2, MCI-8, MCI-23
General Description	MultiChannel ISDN remote access server cards for single or quad BRI (MCI-2, MCI-8) and single PRI (MCI-23) applications for Novell and Microsoft servers.
Performance Features	On-board processor to offload communications tasks from server; B channel bit rates up to 64Kbps supported.
Connectivity Features	Supports Novell Netware Connect, Novell MultiProtocol Router, and Microsoft NT RAS software using PPP compliant software; supports popular remote control and remote access software.
Physical Features	Full-sized ISA bus card (MCI is half-sized); four or eight RJ-11 connectors; one or four RJ-45 connections with S/T interface (MCI-2, MCI-8); one RJ-45 connection to CSU (MCI-23); up to 2 cards per server supported.
Comments	Part of Netaccess Open Remote Server product family of analog and ISDN connectivity products
Warranty	5 year (hardware) 90 days (software)
Price	$499 $2,499 $3,195

N/A—Not applicable   INA—Information not available

End ■

Wireless LAN Systems ■

Manufacturer	AMP Inc.	Aironet
Model	AMP Wireless Access Point	Arlan 630-900
Description	2.4GHz wireless, Ethernet access point	900Mhz wireless, ethernet access point
Wireless Medium/ Modulation Technique	Frequency hopping spread spectrum radio	Direct sequence spread spectrum radio
Frequency and Channels	2.4-2.4835GHz (Country specific)	902-928Mhz (fcc, Canada)/ 12 channels
Data Rate per Channel (Min/Max)	1.6Mbps	215Kbps/860Kbps (fcc,Canada)
CPU	Intel 486 25/33Mhz	25MHz Motorola 68360
Directional Range	Up to 500 ft. indoors Up to 1000 ft. outdoors	6 miles
Wired LAN Protocol	IEEE 802.3 Ethernet	IEEE802.3 CSMA/CD and Ethernet Blue Book
Wired LAN Connections	10BASE-T	10BASE2, 10BASE5, 10BASE-T
Wired LAN Speed	10Mbps	10Mbps
Users per Access Points	255	2048
SNMP Compliance	MIBII (RFC1213), IEEE 802.1d Bridge MIB (RFC1443), and Proxim Enterprise MIB	MIB I, MIB II, and ARLAN Enterprise MIB
Data Security, Integrity, and User Privilege	Frequency hopping spreading over 16 Domains, over 2 million security ID choices.	Direct sequence spreading with over 16 million System ID choices, password protected
Dimensions	9 x 7(W) x 3"(H)	7.8 x 5.9 x 1.9"
Power supply	85-264 VAC, 50/60Hz, 24VDC	90-260 VAC, 50/60Hz
Comments	Ceiling mountable, DC powered for easy installation for most effective coverage.	Intelligent packet filtering by network address, protocol, or packet content
Warranty	1 year	1 year parts and labor returned to factory
Price	$2,199	$2,595

Manufacturer	C-Spec	C-Spec
Model	IP Router RF+	IP Router 2.4 G
Description	OverLAN Wireless Bridge, 2.4GHz	OverLAN Wireless Bridge, 2.4GHz
Wireless Medium/ Modulation Technique	Direct radio Sequencing	Direct radio Sequencing
Frequency and Channels	2.4GHz	2.4GHz
Data Rate per Channel (Min/Max)	10Mbps over 5 channels	1.8/2Mbps over 5 channels
CPU	386/40 Intel	386/40 Intel
Directional Range	10 miles	10 miles
Wired LAN Protocol	IEEE 802.3	IEEE 802.3
Wired LAN Connections	BNC/AUI/10BASE-T	BNC/AUI/10BASE-T
Wired LAN Speed	10/100Mbps	10Mbps
Users per Access Points	INA	50
SNMP Compliance	SNMP manageable	SNMP manageable
Data Security, Integrity, and User Privilege	Direct sequencing and DES encryption	Direct sequencing and DES encryption

N/A—Not applicable   INA—Information not available

Table Continues →

■ Wireless LAN Systems

Manufacturer	C-Spec	C-Spec
Dimensions	3.25 x 13.5(L) x 11.8"(W)	3.25 x 13.5(L) x 11.8"(W)
Power supply	110-120 VAC	110-120 VAC
Comments	Point-to-point and multi-point	Point-to-point and multi-point
Warranty	1 year cross ship	1 year cross ship
Price	$8,000–$10,000	$3,995

Manufacturer	C-Spec	C-Spec
Model	OverLAN Wireless Bridge/IP Router	OverLAN Roaming Bridge
Description	915Mhz wireless bridge/IP Router	915Mhz Access Point
Wireless Medium/ Modulation Technique	Direct sequencing spread spectrum radio	Direct sequencing spread spectrum radio
Frequency and Channels	902-928Mhz (FCC, Canada)	902-928MHz
Data Rate per Channel (Min/Max)	1.8/2Mbps over 1 channel	1.8/2Mbps over 1 channel
CPU	386/40 Intel	386/40 Intel
Directional Range	10 miles	1000'
Wired LAN Protocol	IEEE 802.3	IEEE 802.3
Wired LAN Connections	10BASE2, 10BASE5, 10BASE-T	BNC/AUI/10BASE-T
Wired LAN Speed	10Mbps	10Mbps
Users per Access Points	50 avg.	50 avg.
SNMP Compliance	SNMP manageable	SNMP manageable
Data Security, Integrity, and User Privilege	Direct sequencing and DES Encryption standard	Direct sequencing and optional DES eEncryption
Dimensions	3.25 x 13.5(L) x 11.8"(W)	3.25 x 13.5(L) x 11.8"(W)
Power supply	110-120 VAC/60Hz	110-120 VAC/60Hz
Comments	Point-to-point and multi-point plug and play	Point-to-point and multi-point
Warranty	1 year cross ship	1 year cross ship
Price	$3,995	$2,495

Manufacturer	Digital Equipment Corp.	Digital Equipment Corp.
Model	RoamAbout Access Point (DEIAP-AA)	RoamAbout 915MHz DS/PC Card (DEINA.**)
Description	A wireless LAN switch equipped with a PCMCIA card slot to support multiple wireless PC cards	A wireless LAN adapter that uses direct sequence (DS) spread spectrum radio technology in the 915Mhz frequency band
Wireless Medium/ Modulation Technique	Either direct sequence (DS) or frequency hopping (FS) spread spectrum	Direct sequence (DS) spread spectrum/ DQPSK, DBPSK
Frequency and Channels	915MHz frequency band w/ DS-1 Channel. 2.4GHz frequency band w/ DS 3 Channel. 2.4GHz frequency band w/ FH-15 Channels.	915MHz frequency band with Direct Sequence-1 Channel
Data Rate per Channel	2Mbps (DSSS) 1.6Mbps (FH)	2Mbps
CPU	25MHZ Motorola 68360	N/A
Directional Range	Approx. 800 feet in an open environment. 300-400 feet within a building w/ drywalls, cubicles, etc.	Approx. 800 feet in an open environment. 300-400 feet within a building w/ drywalls, cubicles, etc.

N/A—Not applicable   INA—Information not available

Wireless LAN Systems ■

Manufacturer	Digital Equipment Corp.	Digital Equipment Corp.
Wired LAN protocol	IEEE 802.3 CSMA/CD and Ethernet Blue Book	N/A
Wired LAN connections	10BASE2/T (also DEChub 90, MultiSwitch 900, and Digital's stackable Hub product line)	N/A
Wired LAN speed	10Mbps	N/A
Users per access points	Unlimited	N/A
SNMP compliance	SNMP Management, MIB II, Bridge MIB, Ethernet MIB, Digital ELAN and PCOM MIB Extension, SNMP MIBS for WaveLAN and WaveLAN Roaming for DS versions, Proxim MIB	N/A
Data Security, Integrity, and User Privilege	Over 65K network IDs. DES encrypted versions available.(DS) Software encryption through 15 channels,and 16 domains per network (FH)	Available with over 65K network IDs
Dimensions	1.25 x 10.75 x 5"	4.7 x 2.6 x0 6"
Power supply	16 watts	Sleep mode: 36mA Receive mode: 300mA Transmit mode: 600mA
Comments	Allows portable and desktops with similar wireless PC CARDS TO WIRELESSLY CONNECT TO A WIRED Ethernet LAN	Available in North America only Plus standard PCMCIA Card
Warranty	1 year	1 year
Price	$1,795	$695

Manufacturer	Digital Equipment Corp.	Digital Equipment Corp.
Model	RoamAbout 2.4GHz DS/PC Card (DEIWB.**)	RoamAbout 2.4GHz FH/PC Card (DEIRB.**)
Description	A wireless LAN adapter that uses direct sequence (DS) spread spectrum radio technology in the 915MHz.frequency band. Available worldwide.	A wireless LAN adapter that uses direct sequence (DS) spread spectrum radio technology in the 915MHz.frequency band. Available worldwide.
Wireless Medium/ Modulation Technique	Direct sequence (DS) spread spectrum/ DQPSK, DBPSK	Frequency hopping spread spectrum/ 2GFSK, 4GFSK
Frequency and Channels	2.4GHz frequency band with Direct Sequence-8 Channels	2.4GHz frequency band with Direct Sequence-15 Channels
Data Rate per Channel (Min/Max)	2Mbps	1.6Mbps
CPU	N/A	N/A
Directional Range	Approximately 800 feet in an open environment. Typically 300-400 feet within a building w/ drywalls, cubicles, etc.	Approximately 800 feet in an open environment. Typically 300-400 feet within a building w/ drywalls, cubicles, etc.
Wired LAN protocol	N/A	N/A
Wired LAN connections	N/A	N/A
Wired LAN speed	N/A	N/A
Users per access points	N/A	N/A
SNMP compliance	N/A	N/A
Data Security, Integrity, and User Privilege	Available with over 65K network IDs. DES encrypted versions available.	Software encryption through 15 channels, 16 domains per network, and over 1M encryption ID choices per domain.
Dimensions	4.7 x 2.6 x 0 6" Plus standard PCMCIA Card	3.5 x 2.25 x 5" Plus standard PCMCIA Card
Power supply	Sleep mode: 30mA Receive mode: 340mA Transmit mode: 390mA	Sleep mode: 5mA Receive mode: 125mA Transmit mode: 225mA

N/A—Not applicable   INA—Information not available

Table Continues →

ZIFF·DAVIS PRESS

■ Wireless LAN Systems

Manufacturer	Digital Equipment Corp.	Digital Equipment Corp.
Comments		
Warranty	1 year	1 year
Price	$695	$695

Manufacturer	Laser Communications Inc.	Laser Communications, Inc.	Laser Communications, Inc.
Model	LACE	OMNIBEAM 2000	OMNIBEAM 4000
Description	IR Point-to-point	IR Point-to-point	IR Point-to-point
Wireless Medium/ Modulation Technique	FM	FM	AM
Frequency and Channels	820 nm IR	820 nm	820 nm
Data Rate per Channel (Min/Max)	Up to 16Mbps	Up to 16Mbps	34 to 155Mbps
CPU	INA	INA	INA
Directional Range	1 KM	1.2 KM	1.2 KM
Wired LAN Protocol	802.3 and 802.5J	802.3 and 802.5J	Clear Channel
Wired LAN Connections	10BASE5/FOIRL/FIBER	FOIRL/FIBER	INA
Wired LAN Speed	10- or 16Mbps	10- or 16Mbps	INA
Users per Access Points	N/A	N/A	N/A
SNMP Compliance	N/A	N/A	N/A
Data Security, Integrity, and User Privilege	Supports encrypted data, laser transmission is inherently secure	Supports encrypted data, laser transmission is inherently secure	Supports encrypted data, laser transmission is inherently secure
Dimensions	20(L) x 5 (W) x 6"	25(L) x 7.5 (W) x 6"	25(L) x 7.5 (W) x 6"
Power supply	100/220 VAC, 50/60Hz	100/220 VAC, 50/60Hz	100/220 VAC, 50/60Hz
Comments			
Warranty	2 year	2 year	2 year
Price	$11,995	$13,995	$17,995

Manufacturer	Lucent Technologies	Lucent Technologies
Model	Wave Point	Wave LAN ISA
Description	902MHz/2.4GHz/Ethernet Access Point	902MHz/2.4-2.487GHz/Network Interface Card
Wireless Medium/ Modulation Technique	Direct sequence spread spectrum radio	Direct sequence spread spectrum radio
Frequency and Channels	902-928MHz, 2.4-2.484GHZ, 2.487-2.5GHz/8 Channels	902-928MHz, 2.4-2.484GHZ, 2.487-2.5GHz/8 Channels
Data Rate per Channel (Min/Max)	2Mbps	2Mbps
CPU	Intel 80 x 86	None
Directional Range	2-25 miles	5-25 miles
Wired LAN protocol	Wired protocol IEEE 802.3 Wireless protocol CSMA/CD	Wired IEEE 802.3 CSMA/CD Wireless protocol CSMA/CA
Wired LAN connections	10BASE2, 10BASE5, 10BASE-T	N/A
Wired LAN speed	10Mbps	N/A

N/A—Not applicable   INA—Information not available

Wireless LAN Systems ■

Manufacturer	Lucent Technologies	Lucent Technologies
Users per access points	Unlimited	N/A
SNMP compliance	MIB I, MIB II, and other Wave LAN MIBs'	N/A
Data Security, Integrity, and User Privilege	Optional encryption chip, direct sequence spreading with 56-BIT key	Optional encryption chip, direct sequence spreading with 56-BIT key
Dimensions	7 x 14 x 1.6"	Half-s ISA card
Power supply	Output 25dbm at 902MHz Input 15dbm at 2.4GHz	Power consumption 325Mw average
Comments	Available with Wave Around roaming software and site survey diagnostic tools	Available with site survey diagnostic tools
Warranty	Returned to factory one year parts and labor	Returned to factory one year parts and labor
Price	$1,995	$695

Manufacturer	Lucent Technologies	Microwave Bypass Systems	Proxim, Inc.
Model	Wave LAN PCMCIA	Etherwave LAN Radio	Range LAN PCMCIA
Description	902MHz/2.4GHz/Network Interface Card	Point-to-point microwave system for connecting LANs TI-DS-3, and video systems	2.4 6Hz Wireless Ethernet Adapter
Wireless Medium/ Modulation Technique	Direct sequence spread spectrum radio	FM	Frequency Hopping Spread Spectrum Radio
Frequency and Channels	902-928MHz, 2.4-2.484GHZ 8 Channels	21.2-23.6GHz	2.4-2.485/6Hz/15 Channels
Data Rate per Channel (Min/Max)	2Mbps	T1, Ethernet, DS-3	1.6Mbps
CPU	None	N/A	INA
Directional Range	5-25 miles	Up to 20 miles	3 miles
Wired LAN protocol	Wired IEEE 802.3 CSMA/CD Wireless IEEE 802.3 CSMA/CA	802.3	IEEE 802.3
Wired LAN connections	N/A	All networks	10BASE2, 10BASE5, 10BASE-T
Wired LAN speed	N/A	10Mbps	10Mbps
Users per access points	N/A	N/A	No theoretical limit
SNMP compliance	N/A	MIB II	MIB II (RFC 1213), IEEE 802.1d Bridge (RFC 1493), Proxim Enterprise MIB
Data Security, Integrity, and User Privilege	Optional encryption chip, direct sequence spreading with 56-BIT key	N/A	15 Frequency Hopping Channels and 16 million possible encryption ID choices
Dimensions	3.4 x 2.1 x 0.2"	18 x 3 x 11"	PC Card
Power supply	Power consumption 325Mw average	120 VAC	Mobile Computer
Comments	Available with Wave Around roaming software and site survey diagnostic tools	Complete installation and licensing available	
Warranty	Returned to factory 1 year parts and labor	1 year	1 year
Price	$695	Starts at $20,000	$695

N/A—Not applicable   INA—Information not available

Table Continues →

■ Wireless LAN Systems

Manufacturer	Proxim, Inc.	PRXM, Inc.
Model	Range LAN2 ISA	Range LAN2 Access Point
Description.	2.4 6Hz wireless Ethernet adapter	2.4Ghz wireless Ethernet access point
Wireless Medium/ Modulation Technique	Frequency hopping spread spectrum radio	Frequency hopping spread spectrum radio
Frequency and Channels	2.4-2.485/6Hz/15 Channels	2.4-2.485GHz
Data Rate per Channel (Min/Max)	1.6Mbps	1.6Mbps
CPU	INA	INA
Directional Range	3 miles	Up to 1000 ft. Unlimited through roaming
Wired LAN protocol	IEEE 802.3	IEEE 802.3
Wired LAN connections	10BASE2, 10BASE5, 10BASE-T	10BASE2, 10BASE5, 10BASE10
Wired LAN speed	10Mbps	10Mbps
Users per access points	No theoretical limit	No theoretical limit
SNMP compliance	MIB II (RFC 1213), IEEE 802.1d Bridge (RFC 1493), Proxim Enterprise MIB	MIB II (RFC1213), IEEE 802.1d Bridge (RFC 1493), Proxim Enterprise MIB
Data Security, Integrity, and User Privilege	15 frequency hopping channels and 16 million possible encryption ID choices	15 frequency hopping channels and 16 million possible encryption ID choices
Dimensions	INA	3.4 x 9.75 x 14.75"
Power supply	PC	110 Volts
Comments	Card for PC XT/AT bus computers	
Warranty	1 year	1 year
Price	$595	$1,895

Manufacturer	RDC Communications	SilCom Technology
Model	PortLAN	FreespaceTurbo
Description	2.4-2.5GHz Wireless LAN, Ethernet access point	Wireless building-to-building link that uses laser technology to provide protocol independent, wire-speed LAN connectivity. Supports all high-performance topologies.
Wireless Medium/ Modulation Technique	Frequency hopping spread spectrum	Laser (IR)
Frequency and Channels	2.4-2.483GHz	1300 nm
Data Rate per Channel (Min/Max)	1Mbps	Up to 155Mbps
CPU	68302	N/A
Directional Range	2500 ft.	1000 ft.
Wired LAN Protocol	Centrally coordinated multiple access points	Protocol independent; supports T3, FDDI, Fast Ethernet, ATM (to 155Mbps)
Wired LAN Connections	10BASE2, 10BASE3	Multimode fiber
Wired LAN Speed	10Mbps	Up to 155Mbps
Users per Access Points	10-100	N/A
SNMP Compliance	Yes	N/A

N/A—Not applicable   INA—Information not available

Wireless LAN Systems ■

Manufacturer	RDC Communications	SilCom Technology
Data Security, Integrity, and User Privilege	User authentication, data scrambling	Laser data transmission
Dimensions	4.53 x 3.15 x .78" User unit radio	Head Unit: 16.5(L) x 6(H) x 7"(W) Diagnostics Unit: 10(L) x 8(H) x 6"
Power supply	INA	120 VAC 60Hz 240 VAC 50Hz
Comments	App. 10% of typical portable computer battery	Building-to-building link
Warranty	1 year	1 year
Price	$649 (ISA)/$695 (PCMCIA)/ $1,995 (Turnkey AP)	$18,995

Manufacturer	SilCom Technology	SilCom Technology
Model	FreespaceLite	Freespace SkyVoice
Description	Building-to-building short range laser link. Designed to connect Ethernet LANs.	Uses laser technology to consolidate wire-speed Ethernet data transmissions, and as many as four voice channels.
Wireless Medium/ Modulation Technique	Laser (IR)	Laser (IR)
Frequency and Channels	790 nm	790 nm fiber optic ST connector
Data Rate per Channel (Min/Max)	10Mbps (half or full duplex)	10Mbps (half or full duplex)
CPU	N/A	N/A
Directional Range	500 ft.	1000 ft.
Wired LAN Protocol	Ethernet (half or full duplex)	Ethernet
Wired LAN Connections	Ethernet 10BASE5 (AUI)	Ethernet 10BASE-FL, 10BASE-FOIRL and up to 4 T1, or E1 channels
Wired LAN Speed	10Mbps	10Mbps
Users per Access Points	N/A	N/A
SNMP Compliance	N/A	N/A
Data Security, Integrity, and User Privilege	Laser data transmission	Laser data transmission
Dimensions	16.5(L) x 6(H) x 7"(W)	1.75(L) x 12(D) x 17"(W)
Power supply	Via AUI port; 12-volt supply	115 VAC 60Hz 200-250 VAC 50Hz
Comments	Building-to-building link	
Warranty	1 year	1 year
Price	$7,995	$24,155

Manufacturer	SilCom Technology	South Hills Datacomm
Model	Freespace	38451
Description	Wireless building-to-building link that uses laser technology to provide protocol independent, wire-speed LAN connectivity.	2.4-2.4835Ghz. Wireless Ethernet Bridge
Wireless Medium/ Modulation Technique	Laser (IR)	Frequency Hopping Spread Spectrum

N/A—Not applicable   INA—Information not available

Table Continues →

ZIFF-DAVIS PRESS

■ Wireless LAN Systems

Manufacturer	SilCom Technology	South Hills Datacomm
Frequency and Channels	830nm	2.4-2.4835Ghz./17 channels
Data Rate per Channel (Min/Max)	Up to 20Mbps	3Mbps with auto-fallback to 2Mbps & 1Mbps
CPU	N/A	25Mhz Motorola 68360
Directional Range	1000 ft.	Up to 5 miles
Wired LAN Protocol	Protocol independent up to 20Mbps	Transparent to Network Protocol
Wired LAN Connections	TI, EI, Ethernet, Token Ring	10BASE-T
Wired LAN Speed	Up to 20Mbps	10Mbps
Users per Access Points	N/A	256
SNMP Compliance	N/A	MIB II, Bridge MIB, Radio MIB
Data Security, Integrity, and User Privilege	Laser data transmission	17 Channel Frequency Hopping Technology
Dimensions	Head Unit: 16.5(L) x 6(H) x 7"(W) Diagnostics Unit: 10(L) x 8(H) x 6"	5.1" X 3.4" x 1.2"
Power supply	120 VAC 60Hz 240 VAC 50Hz	7.5 watts
Comments		
Warranty	1 year	1 year
Price	$14,995	$1,690–$2,000

Manufacturer	South Hills Datacomm	South Hills Datacomm
Model	38454	38453
Description	2.4-2.4835Ghz Wireless Ethernet access point	2.4-2.4835Ghz Wireless station adapter
Wireless Medium/ Modulation Technique	Frequency hopping spread spectrum	Frequency hopping spread spectrum
Frequency and Channels	2.4-2.4835Ghz./17 channels	2.4-2.4835Ghz./17 channels
Data Rate per Channel (Min/Max)	3Mbps with auto-fallback to 2Mbps & 1Mbps	3Mbps with auto-fallback to 2Mbps & 1Mbps
CPU	25Mhz Motorola 68360	25Mhz Motorola 68360
Directional Range	Up to 5 miles	Up to 5 miles
Wired LAN protocol	Transparent to Network Protocol	Transparent to Network Protocol
Wired LAN connections	10BASE-T	10BASE-T
Wired LAN speed	10Mbps	10Mbps
Users per access points	256	N/A
SNMP compliance	MIB I & II, Bridge MIB, Private MIB	MIB I & II, & Arlan Enterprise MIB
Data Security, Integrity, and User Privilege	17-channel frequency hopping technology	17-channel frequency hopping technology
Dimensions	5.1 X 3.4 x 1.2"	5.1 X 3.4 x 1.2"
Power supply	7.5 watts	7.5 watts
Comments		
Warranty	1 year	1 year
Price	$1,100–$1,300	$515–$700

N/A—Not applicable   INA—Information not available

Wireless LAN Systems ■

Manufacturer	Southwest Microwave, Inc.	Spectrix
Model	875 LAN-HD/ 950 LAN-HD	SpectrixLite
Description	23GHz microwave point-to-point Ethernet radio	Wireless network, Ethernet access point
Wireless Medium/ Modulation Technique	FM	Diffuse infrared
Frequency and Channels	21.2-23.6GHz 48 licensed channels	850m (IR)
Data Rate per Channel (Min/Max)	10Mbps or 10Mbps + TI's	4Mbps
CPU	N/A	N/A
Directional Range	Up to 3 miles line of site. Up to 10 miles typically line of site (950 LAN-HD)	50 ft.
Wired LAN protocol	IE802.3	Ethernet capable
Wired LAN connections	10BASE5, 10BASE2, 10BASE-T Fiber	10BASE-T
Wired LAN speed	10- or 20Mbps	4Mbps
Users per access points	Point- to- point	1000'
SNMP compliance	MIB II	Planned
Data Security, Integrity, and User Privilege	23GHz microwave- narrow bandwidth	Network management security by password; access security by authorization; physical security by infrared.
Dimensions	Interface: 3.5(H) x 13.75(W) x 13.5" Radio weight: 7 lbs. (875)/ 20 lbs. (950)	3 x 6 x 1" 6 ozs.
Power supply	110 VAC 15 VDC output	<300M-1.5
Comments		
Warranty	2 year	1 year
Price	$11,990	$500/node

Manufacturer	TTI Wireless	Wave Access Inc.
Model	TTI 200 TSE 4Mb	Jaguar™ PC132
Description	400Mhz wireless bridge 2.48Hz	3.2Mbps wireless PC Card Adapter
Wireless Medium/ Modulation Technique	Direct sequence and frequency hopping	Frequency hopping spread spectrum radio
Frequency and Channels	2.4 to 2.48, and 902-928	2400-2483MHz
Data Rate per Channel (Min/Max)	2Mbps	3.2Mbps 1Mbps and 2Mbps
CPU	486/66	16MHz ARM-6
Directional Range	30 miles	10 miles
Wired LAN Protocol	802.3 Ethernet 802.5 Token Ring	N/A
Wired LAN Connections	AUI, BNC, 10BASE-T	10BASE2
Wired LAN Speed	10Mbps full duplex	INA
Users per Access Points	5000	62

N/A—Not applicable   INA—Information not available

Table Continues →

■ Wireless LAN Systems

Manufacturer	TTI Wireless	Wave Access Inc.
SNMP Compliance	MIB1, MPBII, VI, V2	MIB II and Jaguar™ proprietary MIB
Data Security, Integrity, and User Privilege	Direct sequence, DOS/AES, network ID, encryption	Frequency hopping spreading with 8K system ID choices, associate process
Dimensions	6.5 x 5.5 x 1.5"	5.4 x 2.1" one-piece PC Card Type II w/integrated dual antenna system
Power supply	90-260VAC	Laptop
Comments		Also available in OEM and private label models. Fully supported automatic optimized load balancing.
Warranty	1 year	1 year
Price	INA	$595

Manufacturer	Wave Access Inc.	Wi-LAN, Inc.
Model	Jaguar™ AP132	Hopper Plus
Description	3.2Mbps wireless Ethernet Access point	Wireless Ethernet Bridge
Wireless Medium/ Modulation Technique	Frequency hopping spread spectrum radio	Direct sequence spread spectrum radio
Frequency and Channels	2400-2483MHz	902-928Mhz FCC & Industry Canada
Data Rate per Channel (Min/Max)	Mbps and 3.2Mbps. 1Mbps and 2Mbps	1.5Mbps
CPU	26Mhz ARM-6	16MHz Analog Devices 2101 DSP
Directional Range	10 miles	6 miles (rural); 2 miles urban
Wired LAN Protocol	IEEE 802.3 CSMA/CD	IEEE 802.3 CSMA/CD (Ethernet)
Wired LAN Connections	10BASE2	10BASE2, 10BASE-T
Wired LAN Speed	10Mbps	10Mbps
Users per Access Points	62	50
SNMP Compliance	MIB II and Jaguar™ proprietary MIB	INA
Data Security, Integrity, and User Privilege	Frequency hopping spreading with 8K system ID choices, associate process	DSSS with unique spreading codes, irregular transmission of data packets and optional factory set Access code.
Dimensions	5.4 x 2.1" one-piece PC Card Type II w/integrated dual antenna system	33 x 8 x 21 cm
Power supply	Laptop	Zone 110 VAC max.
Comments	Also available in OEM and private label models. Fully supported automatic optimized load balancing.	13 x 3.2 x 8.3"
Warranty	1 year	1 year
Price	$1,295	INA

N/A—Not applicable   INA—Information not available

End ■

Gateways ■

Manufacturer	Nitwot Networks, Inc.	Nitwot Networks, Inc.
Model	DFT	Express
Operating Systems	DOS, Windows	MAC OS
Desktop/Clients Supported	DOS, Windows batch files	MAC
Mgmt. Software	No	No
Connection Protocols:	WAN- V.35, RS232, RS449, EIA530, HDLC	WAN- V.35, RS232, RS449, EIA530, HDLC
Management Support	No	No
Management Port Interface	No	No
Line Speed Support	56Kbps-4Mbps	56Kbps-4Mbps
Storage Media	N/A	N/A
Dimensions	Full-size ISA board	Full-size ISA board
Protocols	Local- IPX, TCP/IP WAN- HDLC Reliable	Local-AppleTalk, EtherTalk, TCP/IP WAN- HDLC Reliable
Comments	Compressed file transfer	Compressed file transfer, shares NIWOTSD transport with Alanas, Adobe Virtual Network
Warranty	1 year	1 year
Price	$895	$1,895

Manufacturer	Polaris Communications, Inc.	Renex Corp.
Model	System 2000	Multi-Tech
Operating Systems	Windows NT & NetWare	RN108
Desktop/Clients Supported	All 3270 or TN3270 clients	Netware, TCP/IP
Mgmt. Software	OS dependent	Windows 3.1, Windows 95, Windows NT, DOS, PPP
Connection Protocols:	Ethernet, Fast Ethernet, Token Ring or FDDI	Multi-Tech Windows
Management Support	Local monitor or LAN user	Ethernet 8-32, RS232 Aasync
Management Port Interface	DB9 or LAN	DOS and Windows management software
Line Speed Support	Ethernet or FDDI 100 Mbps Token Ring 16 Mbps	Over LAN, or Directive on PC
Storage Media	Hard disk, 3.5" floppy, CD ROM	Up to 115.2 Kbps
Dimensions	24.5"H x 9.0"W x 23.0"D	3.5" floppy
Protocols	TCP/IP, IPX/SPX, AppleTalk, Banyan Vines, Named Pipes, RAS	TCP/IP, IPXSPX PPP
Comments	ESCON host attachment, or Bus/Tag or both	Dial-in remote control, remote node, opt. internal modems
Warranty	1 year	2 year
Price	$19,000	$2,099

Manufacturer	South Hills Datacomm	Webster
Model	37110	MultiPort/LT
Operating Systems	Novell NetWare, Banyan VINES LAN, IBM NETBIOS	MacOS, UNIX
Desktop/Clients Supported	INA	MacIntosh

N/A—Not applicable   INA—Information not available

Table Continues →

■ Gateways

Manufacturer	**South Hills Datacomm**	**Webster**
Mgmt. Software	MS or PC DOS 3.3 or later	Multiport manager, MacOS, mgcc (both provided)
Connection Protocols:	5250 Twinax via DB15M ISA bus card has built in balun for UTP SDLC via RS-232M on Remote Gateway card	(1) Ethernet (AUI, Thin, TwP), (4) RS-422 high-speed serial ports
Management Support	API support IBM v2.1	In band, MultiPort manager (Mac), mgccc (UNIX), mgcmd (UNIX), telnet, SNMP
Management Port Interface	N/A	Out of band, Async serial port (MD-8)
Line Speed Support	9600 bps supporting up to 16 node sessions 56Kbps supports up to 64 sessions (Remote Gateway packages only)	2.4-57. 6Kbps serial 230Kbps LocalTalk
Storage Media	ISA or MCA bus	Code and config stored in on-board FLASH, software upgradeable
Dimensions	N/A	9.7w, 9.7d, 2.4"h 4.6 lbs.
Protocols	SDLC on remote Gateway	Appletalk, TCP/IP, DECnet, IPTalk, MacIP, ARA, PortShare Pro
Comments	Available in a remote Gateway package. Dedicated 286 or faster machine as the Gateway-server. Dedicated 386 or higher for remote Gateways.	Any of the four LocalTalk ports can alternately be hooked to modem for Apple Remote Access (ARA) dial-in and/or PortShare Pro Dial-out serving.
Warranty	1 year	1 year (90 day overnight replacement)
Price	$2,495	$1,995

Manufacturer	**Whittaker Xyplex**
Model	6025 X.25 Gateway
Operating Systems	NetWare, DOS and OS/2
Desktop/Clients Supported	MacIrma Mainframe Irma, DOS/Irma Windows
Mgmt. Software	Max Server Software with Gateway Image (ver. 1.2 or later)
Connection Protocols:	(1) Ethernet AUI (1) X.25 (V.35, RS-423, RS-232, or X.21)
Management Support	Sample control port software, Telnet, local ASCII Management port
Management Port Interface	Asynchronous serial port, 8-pin RJ-45 connector Operates from 75Bps 38.4Kbps w/modem control signals
Line Speed Support	9.6-64Kbps
Storage Media	3.5" disk drive
Dimensions	(H) 1.75 x (D) 12 x (W) 19" 19 lbs.
Protocols	Appletalk, TCP/IP, IPX
Comments	PPP, SLIP + CSLIP support offered
Warranty	3 years
Price	$3,995 $4,995 for card for network

N/A—Not applicable   INA—Information not available

Multiplexors ◼

Manufacturer	**ADC Kentrox**	**ADC Kentrox**
Model	DataSMART E1 MAX Dual Port Multimedia Access Multiplexer	DataSMART T1 MAX Quad-Port Add/Drop Multimedia Access Multiplexer
Number of Channels	Two data ports, plus one voice for enterprise networks	Four data ports, plus one voice for enterprise networks
Type of Media Supported	Data, voice, video	Data, voice, video
Communication Format	Serial, digital	Serial, digital
Protocol/ Multiplexing Technique	INA	TDM
Sub-channel data rate	INA	56K to 1.536Mbps
Composite Link Rate (Kbps)	2.048Mbps	1.544Mbps
Composite Link Interface	E1/FE1	T1/FT1
Additional Features	Built-in SNMP agent, Ethernet option, installation utility, program data ports, diagnostics and status	Built-in SNMP agent, Ethernet option, installation utility, program data ports, diagnostics and status
Dimensions	43.2(W) x 5.4(H) x 29.2cm(L), desktop or rack mount	17(W) x 2.12(H) x 11.5"(L), desktop or rack mount
Comments		
Warranty	5 year	5 year
Price	$3,995	INA

Manufacturer	**ADC Kentrox**	**ADC Kentrox**
Model	DataSMART T1 MAX Dual-Port Add/Drop Multimedia Access Multiplexer	DataSMART Add/Drop DSU/CSU
Number of Channels	Two data ports, plus one voice for enterprise networks	One or two data ports, plus a T1 add/drop
Type of Media Supported	Data, voice, video	Data, voice, video
Communication Format	Serial, digital	Serial, digital
Protocol/ Multiplexing Technique	TDM	TDM
Sub-channel data rate	56K to 1.536Mbps	56K to 1.536Mbps
Composite Link Rate	1.544Mbps	1.544 Mbps
Composite Link Interface	T1/TF1	INA
Additional Features	Built-in SNMP agent, Ethernet option, installation utility, program data ports, diagnostics and status	SNMP traps, Telnet capabilities
Dimensions	17(W) x2.12(H) x 11.5"(L), desktop or rack mount	8.35(W) x 3.58(H) x 11.25"(L), desktop or rack mount
Comments		
Warranty	5 year	5 year
Price	$2,995	$1,995

Manufacturer	**ADC Kentrox**	**ADC Kentrox**	**ADC Kentrox**
Model	AAC-1 ATM Access Concentrators	AAC-3 ATM Access Concentrators	DataSMART E1 MAX Quad-Port Add/Drop Multimedia Access Multiplexer

N/A—Not applicable   INA—Information not available

Table Continues →

■ Multiplexors

Manufacturer	ADC Kentrox	ADC Kentrox	ADC Kentrox
Number of Channels	3	Up to 28	Four data ports, plus one voice for enterprise networks
Type of Media Supported	Voice, video, data	Voice, video, data	Data, voice, video
Communication Format	Sync, HDLC, CBR, Frame Relay, SMDS	Sync, HDLC, CBR, Frame Relay, SMDS	Serial, digital
Protocol/ Multiplexing Technique	ATM	ATM	INA
Sub-channel data rate	56K to 2Mbps	56K to 155Mbps	INA
Composite Link Rate	1.5/ Mbps	45/155 Mbps	2.048Mbps
Composite Link Interface	T1/E1	T3/E3/OC-3	E1/FE1
Additional Features	Video dial, in-band SNMP, passwords, multi-protocol, modular	Ethernet, in-band SNMP, passwords, multi-protocol, modular	Built-in SNMP agent, Ethernet option, installation utility, program data ports, diagnostics and status
Dimensions	1.7 x 11.8 .17", 19" rack mount kit inc.	7 x 16.7 x 17.7"	43.2(W) x 5.4(H) x 29.2 cm(L), desktop or rack mount
Comments			
Warranty	2 year	2 year	5 year
Price	$5,000 and up	$10–$50,000	$4,995

Manufacturer	ASCEND	ASCEND
Model	MB+ Multiband Plus	MB-VSX Multiband VSX
Number of Channels	7, 8, 24, 48	8, 24
Type of Media Supported	Data	Data
Communication Format	Sync	Sync
Protocol/ Multiplexing Technique	TOM	TOM
Sub-channel data rate	INA	INA
Composite Link Rate	56K-3.0M	56K-1.5M
Composite Link Interface	56K-3.0M	56K-1.5M
Additional Features	In board remote mgt. AIM/bonding Network diagnostics statistics Asci; download configurable RS366, x 21, dialing Password security	In board remote mgt. AIM/bonding Network diagnostics statistics Asci; download configurable RS366, x.21, dialing Password security
Dimensions	1.75(H) x 17(W) x 12"(D)	1.75(H) x 12.63(W) x 12.25"(D)
Comments	Main applications are videoconferencing and dial data backup/overflow.	Main applications are videoconferencing and dial data backup.
Warranty	1 year	1 year
Price	$7,000–$10,000	$1,195–$7,195

N/A—Not applicable   INA—Information not available

Multiplexors ■

Manufacturer	Astrocom	Cray Communications	General Data Communications
Model	ASIMES 3/ ASIMES 7	TIE-6/ TIE-12/ TIE-24	OCM-1000
Number of Channels	3/7	Up to 30/ Up to 60/ Up to 120	Up to 60
Type of Media Supported	Data	Voice, data, video	Voice, data, video, LAN
Communication Format	Async	Async, sync, analog, digital,	Sync, async
Protocol/ Multiplexing Technique	STM	TDM	TDM, packet
Sub-Channel Data Rate	19.2Kbps	50bps to 1.536Mbps	300bps-1.9Mbps
Composite Link Rate	1.2, 2.4, 4.8, 9.6, 19.2, and 38.4Kbps	1.544Mbps	9.6K-2.048Mbps
Composite Link Interface	57.6Kbps, RS232/ 134.4Kbps, RS232	DS-1	V.24, RS232, V.35, X.21, V.11, RS422, TI, EI
Additional Features	Supports full duplex modems operating at the above listed speeds Diagnostic Password, command made lock-out	Integral ESF/CSU VT100 or SNMP management PCM/ADPCM Voice Local/Remote loops Password access	Integral Power PC-based management Data compression Optional redundant power and logic 2 composite links
Dimensions	2.25 x 10.75 x 10", 6 lbs. 2.75 x 12 x 12", 7 lbs.	17(D) x 17(W) x 5.25" (TIE-6) 17(D) x 17(W) x 10.5 (TIE-12) 17(D) x 17(W) x 21 (TIE-24) 19" rack-mount kit	9 x 13.5 x 11.5"
Comments	115/230 VAC power	Remote inbound management, unmanned alarm call. Drop and insert.	Shelf 7 x 19 x 12" optional integral TI CSU
Warranty	2 year; 24x7 free tech support	Lifetime	1 year
Price	$640// $975	$3200// $4600// $5100	$1,995+

Manufacturer	HT Communications	HT Communications	Lanart
Model	Pro™ 4100 Series (P4102-64, P4102-128, P4104-64, P4104-128)	Centra™ Series T3000 and Centra™ Series T4000	ETP 8201
Number of Channels	2, 4	1 to 48	8
Type of Media Supported	Data	Voice, data, video	802.3 Ethernet
Communication Format	Sync, async	Sync	Async
Protocol/ Multiplexing Technique	Time Division Multiplexing (TDM)	Byte-Interrelated Time Division Multiplexing (TDM)	TDM
Sub-channel Data Rate rate	75bps to 38.4Kbps asynchronous and 2.4Kbps to 128Kbps synchronous	2.4 Kbps to 1526Kbps synchronous	10Mbps Ethernet
Composite Link Rate	Up to 128Kbps Synchronous	DSI or DSK-1 electrical	120Mbps
Composite Link Interface	EIA-232 or V.35	Dual T1's in a single chassis (48 DSO's) on T3000 and T4000	Fiber via ST connector

---

N/A—Not applicable   INA—Information not available   **Table Continues →**

■ Multiplexors

Manufacturer	HT Communications	HT Communications	Lanart
Additional Features	Synchronous and asynchronous data can be supported on the same unit Low multiplexing overhead to maximize user data rates All user ports support EIA-232 and V.35 electrical interfaces Configuration can be downloaded to remote units. Integral test pattern generator For use with local and remote loop back tests	Drop and insert and Dual drop and-insert supported on T4000 Optional load sharing power redundancy on T3000 & T4000 Optical TI logic/CSU redundancy on T4000 Remote dial-in diagnostics supported on T4000 Easy VT100 network management on T4000 Dip-switch configuration on T3000	8 RJ45 1 PR ST Supports 8 Ethernet Over single pair of power Data encryption
Dimensions	11(L) x 8.5(W) x 2.4"	20(L) x 19(W) x 7" (Standalone or rack mount in same chassis)	INA
Comments	Available with 115 VAC or 230 VAC power options. Lifeboat Spares overnight replacement program available.	Lifeboat Spares overnight replacement program available	Link LEDs for each Ethernet
Warranty	5 year	5 year	5 year
Price	$745+	$3,900+	$1,995

Manufacturer	Larscom, Inc.	Larscom, Inc.
Model	Orion 4000 Broadband Access Multiplexer	Orion 4000/5 Broadband Access Multiplexer
Number of Channels	Up to 88 T1's, up to 3 T3', up to2 OC3c's	Up to 32 T1's, up to 3 T3', up to2 OC3c's
Type of Media Supported	Voice, video, data	Voice, video, data
Communication Format	Async, sync	Async, sync
Protocol/ Multiplexing Technique	TDM, ATM	TDM, ATM
Sub-channel Data Rate	T1 (1.54Mbps)	T1 (1.54Mbps)
Composite Link Rate	Up to 52Mbps (HSSI); up to 12Mbps (V.35/EIA 530)	Up to 52Mbps (HSSI); up to 12Mbps (V.35/EIA 530)
Composite Link Interface	INA	INA
Additional Features	Simultaneously supports circuit (TDM) and cell (ATM) traffic Manageable locally and remotely via SNMP, Telnet, RS232 M13 multiplexing and crossconnect capabilities Supports NxT1 and NxE1 links via inverse multiplexing HSSI and V.35/EIA530 DTE interfaces Supports T1, E1, Fractional E3, and OC3c ATM	Simultaneously supports circuit (TDM) and cell (ATM) traffic Manageable locally and remotely via SNMP, Telnet, RS232 M13 multiplexing and crossconnect capabilities Supports NxT1 and NxE1 links via inverse multiplexing HSSI and V.35/EIA530 DTE interfaces Supports T1, E1, Fractional E3, and OC3c ATM
Dimensions	21(H) x 17(W) x 13" 19" or 23" rack-mount kit included	7(H) x 17(W) x 13" 19" or 23" rack-mount kit included
Comments	The Orlon 4000 Is a broadband access multiplexer that can simultaneously support both cell and circuit traffic.	The Orlon 4000 Is a broadband access multiplexer that can simultaneously support both cell and circuit traffic.
Warranty	2 year	2 year
Price	$8,550+	$6,550+

N/A—Not applicable   INA—Information not available

Multiplexors ■

Manufacturer	Larscom, Inc.	Larscom, Inc.
Model	Mega-T Multiple T1 Inverse Multiplexer	Mega-T241 Multiple T1 Inverse Multiplexer
Number of Channels	Up to 4 T1's for aggregate bandwidth up to 6.112 Mbps	One E1, two T1's
Type of Media Supported	Video, data	Video, data
Communication Format	Async, sync	Async, sync
Protocol/ Multiplexing Technique	TDM	TDM
Sub-channel Data Rate	T1 (1.344 or 1.536Mbps)	T1 (1.344 or 1.536Mbps)
Composite Link Rate	Up to 52Mbps (HSSI); up to 12Mbps (V.35/EIA 530)	2.048Mbps (E1)
Composite Link Interface	INA	INA
Additional Features	Manageable locally and remotely via SNMP and RS232/SLIP Automatic fallback to lower T1 increment in the event of line failure; optional restoral. Optional built-in CSU's Upgradeable from 2 to 4 ports via software download Complete visibility of T1 and DTE channel performance	Manageable locally and remotely via SNMP and RS232/SLIP Propagation of E1 alarm signaling Automatic alarm reporting, including dial-out Downloadable software for easy upgrades
Dimensions	1.75(H) x 17(W) x 12" 19" or 23" rack-mount kit included	1.75(H) x 17(W) x 12" 19" or 23" rack-mount kit included
Comments	Mega-T employs inverse multi-plexing to create a multi-Mbps single virtual channel across multiple T1's, for applications needing > T1 bandwidth without the expense of a T3.	Mega-T241 provides completely transparent inverse-multiplexing of an E1 signal over 2 T1 circuits, for an effective transport of international data traffic across a T1 network.
Warranty	2 year	2 year
Price	$8,550+	$6,550+

Manufacturer	Larscom, Inc.	Larscom, Inc.
Model	Orion 200/400/800	Access-T 100, 200, 400 & 1500
Number of Channels	2, 4, 8	1, 2, 4, 30
Type of Media Supported	Voice, data, video	Voice, data, video
Communication Format	Sync	Sync
Protocol/ Multiplexing Technique	TDM	TDM
Sub-channel Data Rate	56/64Kbps	56/64Kbps
Composite Link Rate	1.536Mbps	1.536Mbps
Composite Link Interface	1.536Mbps	1.536Mbps
Additional Features	E1-to-T1 conversion LAN-to-LAN connection; LAN/WAN interconnection Performance monitoring Local and remote management Transcode alarms between E1 & T1	Drop and insert LAN interconnection Performance monitoring Local and remote management
Dimensions	1.75 or 3.5 x 17 x 11.22"	1.75 or 3.5 x 17 x 11.22"

N/A—Not applicable   INA—Information not available

Table Continues →

■ Multiplexors

Manufacturer	Larscom, Inc.	Larscom, Inc.
Comments	Video teleconferencing. Downloadable software for upgrades. CAD/CAM applications and other high speed networks.	Combines the features of a multiplexor, a DSU and a CSU. SNMP management via internal agent.
Warranty	2 year	2 year
Price	$4,995+	$1,895+

Manufacturer	Multi-Tech	Multi-Tech
Model	MMV808C/V MMV161C/V MMV3232C	DT101
Number of Channels	8, 16, 32 async data 1 sync data & 2 voice	3
Type of Media Supported	Data, voice	1 data, 2 voice
Communication Format	INA	Async, sync
Protocol/ Multiplexing Technique	APSM	APSM
Sub-channel Data Rate	300-19.2Kbps	600bps-128Kbps
Composite Link Rate	128Kbps sync	128Kbps sync
Composite Link Interface	V.24/RS232, V.35	V.24/RS232, V.35
Additional Features	Hardware, software, flow control Pass EIA Feature on channels Diagnostic capabilities Dual composite links	Hardware, software, flow control Pass EIA Feature on channels Diagnostic capabilities
Dimensions	INA	INA
Comments	Supports Internal CSU/DSU	Supports FXS, FXO, and E&M voice interfaces
Warranty	2 year	2 year
Price	$745+	$1,199+

Manufacturer	Multi-Tech	Multi-Tech
Model	MMH904Ca MMH908Ca	LT101
Number of Channels	4/8	2
Type of Media Supported	Data	1 data, 1 voice
Communication Format	Async, sync	Sync
Protocol/ Multiplexing Technique	STM	APSM
Sub-channel Data Rate	150bps-38.4Kbps	600bps-128Kbps
Composite Link Rate	128K sync 57.6K async	128K sync
Composite Link Interface	V.24/RS232, V.35	V.24/RS232, V.35
Additional Features	Hardware, software, flow control Pass EIA feature on channels Diagnostic capabilities	Hardware, software, flow control Pass EIA feature on channels Diagnostic capabilities

N/A—Not applicable   INA—Information not available

Multiplexors ■

Manufacturer	Multi-Tech	Multi-Tech
Dimensions	INA	INA
Comments	Supports internal CSU/DSU, V.34 modem, ISDN TA	Supports FXS, FXO, and E&M voice interfaces, supports 10BASE-T and A interfaces
Warranty	2 year	2 year
Price	$1,299–$2,349	$1,349–$1,659

Manufacturer	N.E.T.	N.E.T.
Model	IDNX/90 Multiservice Bandwidth Mgr.	IDNX/20 Multiservice Bandwidth Mgr.
Number of Channels	Up to 96 E1/T1; 4 or 6 E3/T3; up to 372 data ports; up to 2000 voice ports	Up to 15 E1/T1; up to 88 data ports; up to 480 voice ports
Type of Media Supported	Voice, video, data, Internetworking	Voice, video, data, Internetworking
Communication Format	Sync, async, LAN, frame relay, digital voice, analog voice, fax, voice band data, video	Sync, async, LAN, frame relay, digital voice, analog voice, fax, voice band data, video
Protocol/ Multiplexing Technique	Packet/Frame/Circuit TDM	Packet/Frame/Circuit TDM
Sub-channel Data Rate	75Kbps to 3Mbps	75Kbps to 3Mbps
Composite Link Rate	Up to T3/E3	Up to T1/E1
Composite Link Interface	DSX-1, G.703, DSX-1, G.703 NRZ(RS-530, X.21, V.36) DSX-3, INT-422, RS-422/499 V.35	DSX-1, G.703, DSX-1, G.703 NRZ(RS-530, X.21, V.36) DSX-3, INT-422, RS-422/499 V.35
Additional Features	Optional Software NetOpen/5000—Management of physical circuits Optional Software NetOpen Circuit Manager—Mgt. Of connections and acct Optional Software FrameXpress Node Mgr.—Configuration and monitor of FR Virtual Circuits via SNMP Optional Software FrameXpress Accountant—Usage accounting for FR circuits Optional hardware LAN Internetworking Router, Frame Relay, ISDN modules can be added to all units.	Optional Software NetOpen/5000—Management of physical circuits Optional Software NetOpen Circuit Manager—Mgt. Of connections and acct Optional Software FrameXpress Node Mgr.—Configuration and monitor of FR Virtual Circuits via SNMP Optional Software FrameXpress Accountant—Usage accounting for FR circuits Optional hardware LAN Internetworking Router, Frame Relay, ISDN modules can be added to all units.
Dimensions	67.6 x 22.1 x 32.5" (HWD)	24.5. x 17.2 x 21.5" (HWD)
Comments	Designed for multimegabit voice and data T3, T1, E3 and E1 environments	For bringing power and functionality of IDNX networking to smaller locations within a large complex network.
Warranty	1 year	1 year
Price	$70,500+	$17,000+

Manufacturer	N.E.T.	N.E.T.
Model	IDNX/20-S Multiservice Bandwidth Mgr.	IDNX/Micro 20 Multiservice Bandwidth Mgr.
Number of Channels	Up to 15 E1/T1; up to 76 data ports; up to 480 voice ports	Up to 7 E1/T1; up to 28 data ports; up to 420 voice ports
Type of Media Supported	Voice, Video, Data, Internetworking	Voice, Video, Data, Internetworking
Communication Format	Sync, async, LAN, frame relay, digital voice, analog voice, fax, voice band data, video	Sync, async, LAN, frame relay, digital voice, analog voice, fax, voice band data, video
Protocol/ Multiplexing Technique	Packet/Frame/Circuit TDM	Packet/Frame/Circuit TDM

N/A—Not applicable   INA—Information not available

Table Continues →

■ Multiplexors

Manufacturer	N.E.T.	N.E.T.
Sub-channel Data Rate	75Kbps to 3Mbps	75Kbps to 3Mbps
Composite Link Rate	Up to T1/E1	Up to T1/E1
Composite Link Interface	DSX-1, G.703, DSX-1, G.703 NRZ(RS-530, X.21, V.36) DSX-3, INT-422, RS-422/499 V.35	DSX-1, G.703, DSX-1, G.703 NRZ(RS-530, X.21, V.36) DSX-3, INT-422, RS-422/499 V.35
Additional Features	Optional Software NetOpen/5000—Management of physical circuits Optional Software NetOpen Circuit Manager—Mgt. Of connections and acct Optional Software FrameXpress Node Mgr.—Configuration and monitor of FR Virtual Circuits via SNMP Optional Software FrameXpress Accountant—Usage accounting for FR circuits Optional hardware LAN Internetworking Router, Frame Relay, ISDN modules can be added to all units.	Optional Software NetOpen/5000—Management of physical circuits Optional Software NetOpen Circuit Manager—Mgt. Of connections and acct Optional Software FrameXpress Node Mgr.—Configuration and monitor of FR Virtual Circuits via SNMP Optional Software FrameXpress Accountant—Usage accounting for FR circuits Optional hardware LAN Internetworking Router, Frame Relay, ISDN modules can be added to all units.
Dimensions	24.5. x 17.2 x 21.5" (HWD)	10.5 x 17 x 15" (HWD)
Comments	For low volume networks and for adding peripheral networks	For entry level networks and for providing access to complex IDNX backbone networks for smaller sites
Warranty	1 year	1 year
Price	$16,000–$21,000	$9,400 to $18,800

Manufacturer	Nuera Communications Inc.	Nuera Communications Inc.
Model	Access Plus F100	Access Plus 100/ Access Plus 200
Number of Channels	30 voice; 16 data	30 voice; 16 data
Type of Media Supported	Voice, data, fax, and video	Voice, data, fax, and video
Communication Format	Async, bisync, SNA, transparent	Async, sync, SNA, transparent
Protocol/ Multiplexing Technique	(STM) Frame Relay	TDM & STM
Sub-channel Data Rate	1.2-256Kbps	1.2-2Mbps
Composite Link Rate	9.6-2Mbps	9.6K-2Mbps
Composite Link Interface	V.35; RS422	V.35; RS422, DSX-1, G.704
Additional Features	4 trunks Full voice switching T1/E1 voice interface Built in T1/E1, CSU/NTU F/R switching	N x64Kbps data channels Quad-trunk capacity Drop-insert capability T1/E1 voice interface Built in T1/E1, CSU ISDN & CCS support
Dimensions	5.25(H) x 17.6(W) x 18"(D)	5.25(H) x 17.6(W) x 18"(D)
Comments	E/C to 45 msec, code download, DC power	Built-in echo cancellation to 45 msec, code download, DC power
Warranty	1 year	1 year
Price	$4,250	$2,750/ $4,050

N/A—Not applicable   INA—Information not available

Multiplexors ■

Manufacturer	Nuera Communications Inc.	Nuera Communications Inc.
Model	CS 8000	CS 4100
Number of Channels	8 voice; 20 data	4 voice; 1 data
Type of Media Supported	Voice, data, fax, and video	Voice, data
Communication Format	Async, sync, SNA, transparent	Async, sync
Protocol/ Multiplexing Technique	TDM	TDM
Sub-channel Data Rate	1.2-1.5Mbps	4.8-64Mbps
Composite Link Rate	56K-T1	38.4K-2Mbps
Composite Link Interface	V.35; RS422, DSX-1	V.35; RS422
Additional Features	Built-in T1 CSU Drop-insert T1 capable Software controllable	Voice compression 5.3K-24K Modem & fax transparency FXO/FXS, E&M voice Built in diagnostic capabilities Password secured access
Dimensions	5.25(H) x 16.75(W) x 15.4"(D)	3.5(H) x 15.2(W) x 12.2"(D)
Comments		
Warranty	1 year	1 year
Price	$2,750	$4,500

Manufacturer	Patton Electronics	Patton Electronics
Model	354\358	3022/3032
Number of Channels	4/8	2
Type of Media Supported	Data	Data
Communication Format	Async	Async
Protocol/ Multiplexing Technique	TDM	STM
Sub-channel Data Rate	9.6Kbps	38.4Kbps/57.6Kbps
Composite Link Rate	38.4Kbps/76.8Kbps	38.4Kbps/115.2Kbps
Composite Link Interface	Proprietary, 1 mile over 4 wires	INA
Additional Features	Built-in short range modem No switches or straps Line test/loopback test LED indicators Low profile enclosures	Plugs directly into modem Uses at command set Hardware (RTS/CTS) or Software (X/on/X-off) Flow control supported
Dimensions	11.25(W) x 9.5(L) x 1.625"	INA
Comments	Modular connectors(RJ-45); connects to RS-232 or RS-422 sub-channels	CD activation of data mode
Warranty	1 year	1 year
Price	$250–$450	$199\ $249

N/A—Not applicable   INA—Information not available

Table Continues →

■ Multiplexors

Manufacturer	RAD Data Communications	RAD Data Communications
Model	FLM-12	FLM-3
Number of Channels	12	48
Type of Media Supported	Data	Data
Communication Format	Async	Async
Protocol/ Multiplexing Technique	TDM	High bit oversampling
Sub-channel Data Rate	19.2Kbps	38.4Kbps
Composite Link Rate	1.2288Mbps	10Mbps
Composite Link Interface	EIA RS-232-C/ CCITT V.24	EIA RS-232-C/ CCITT V.24
Additional Features	Integral modem Compatible with FLM-1 1.6km (1 mile) range 4 wire phone line RJ-45 connectors	Double fiber optic SMA or ST 4km (2.5 mile) range
Dimensions	7.4 x 4.5 x 1.3"	8.5 x 19 x 1.7"
Comments	Other models available	Other models available
Warranty	1 year	1 year
Price	INA	INA

Manufacturer	RAD Data Communications	RAD Data Communications
Model	Megaplex 2000	Megaplex 2100
Number of Channels	40 high-speed data circuits, 100 RS-232 data circuits, or 40 voice circuits	40 high-speed data circuits, 100 RS-232 data circuits, or 40 voice circuits
Type of Media Supported	Data, voice fax, and LAN over E1/T1 lines	Data, voice fax, and LAN over E1/T1 lines
Communication Format	Asynch, synch	Asynch, synch
Protocol/ Multiplexing Technique	Time division BYTE interleaved	Time division BYTE interleaved
Sub-channel Data Rate	RS-232 data channels/ 1,200-19,200bps/ High speed 56-1989Kbps	
Composite Link Rate	T1 1544Mbps/ E1 2048Mbps/ Fiber 2048Mbps	T1 1544Mbps/ E1 2048Mbps/ Fiber 2048Mbps
Composite Link Interface	T1, E1 & Fiber	T1, E1 & Fiber
Additional Features	Single or dual T1 or E1 main lines 27 different I/O modules Up to 62 time slots Built in Ethernet or Token Ring Bridges Optional redundancy on links control circuitry and power supply	Single or dual T1 or E1 main lines 27 different I/O modules Up to 62 time slots Two management platforms: Radview-PC (Windows-PC), Radview-HPOV (UNIX) Optional redundancy on links control circuitry and power supply
Dimensions	INA	INA
Comments	Remote management via TSO, supervisory port or in-band control channel	Remote management via TSO, supervisory port or in-band control channel
Warranty	1 year	1 year
Price	$4,800	$3,200

N/A—Not applicable   INA—Information not available

Multiplexors ■

Manufacturer	RAD Data Communications	South Hills Datacomm
Model	STM-2/ STM-4	32495
Number of Channels	4	8
Type of Media Supported	Data	Data
Communication Format	Async, internal timing/ Async	Data ports: Asynchronous Composite: Synchronous
Protocol/ Multiplexing Technique	STM	STM
Sub-channel Data Rate	19.2Kbps	Up to 19.2Kbps
Composite Link Rate	19.2Kbps	Up to 19.2Kbps
Composite Link Interface	V.24/ RS-232-c	RS-232, DB-25F
Additional Features	Non-volatile RAM Hardware/software flow-control RJ-45 Built-in diagnostics Command port any channel	Composite port available with V.35 V.35 port supports speeds up to 64Kbps Also 4 & 16 port models available All data ports are RJ-45 Option package for port contention, flow control, usage
Dimensions	.9 x 2.1 x 4.3"/ 1.7 x 8.5 x 9.5"	9.7(W) x 2.5(L) x 10.1"(D)
Comments	Other models available	Adapters for DTE & DCE DB-25 ports
Warranty	1 year	2 year
Price	INA	$1,295

N/A—Not applicable   INA—Information not available

End ■

■ Converters

Manufacturer	Canary	Canary	Canary
Model	CC-2000	CC-2001	CC-2002
From	UTP	BNC	UTP
To	BNC	FO (SMA/ST)	FO (SMA/ST)
LED	Power, Jabber, Link, Collision, Activity, Auto polarity	Power, Jabber, Link, Collision, Activity, Auto polarity	Power, Jabber, Link, Collision, Activity, Auto polarity
Comments	Flexibility to change media or extend segments	Flexibility to change media or extend segments	Flexibility to change media or extend segments
Warranty	2 year	2 year	2 year
Price	$285	$439	$399

Manufacturer	Canary	Canary	Canary
Model	CC-2003	CFT-2131	CFT-2132
From	AUI	UTP	UTP
To	AUI	FO (SC-Type)	FO (ST-Type)
LED	Power, Jabber, Link, Collision, Activity, Auto polarity	Transmit, Receive, Link, Collision, Full duplex	Transmit, Receive, Link, Collision, Full duplex
Comments	Flexibility to change media, extend segments	100Base-TX/FX 2 ports, SC-type multimode, 2Km	100Base-TX/FX 2 ports, ST-type multimode, 2Km
Warranty	2 year	2 year	2 year
Price	$259	$799	$799

Manufacturer	Canary	Kingston Technological Co.	Kingston Technological Co.
Model	CFT-2131-SM	KNE-TRN/T	KNE-TRN/2
From	UTP	AUI	AUI
To	FO (SC-Type)	RJ-45	BNC
LED	Power, Transmit, Receive, Link, Collision, Full duplex, 100Mbps	Receive, Transmit, Collision, Power	Receive, Transmit, Collision, Power
Comments	100BASE-TX/FX 2 ports, SC-Type, Singlemode, 15K		
Warranty	2 year	Lifetime	Lifetime
Price	$3,395	$31	$31

Manufacturer	LANART	LANCAST	LANCAST
Model	EXC0013/ ECR102E	6318	4318
From	UTP	100BaseTX	TP
To	FO (ST)/ BNC	100BaseFX	Fiber Optic, BNC, AUI
LED	Receive, Transmit, Collision, Power	Power, Link, Receive,	Power, Collision, Activity
Comments	Supports full media distances 100M(UTP), 2KM(FO)	Allows transparent integration of TX and FX Fast Ethernet segments	All signal activity and collision data is reliably translated.
Warranty	5 year	3 year	3 year
Price	$249 $229	$190–$2,250	$195–$379

N/A—Not applicable   INA—Information not available

Converters ■

Manufacturer	LANCAST	LANCAST	Lantronix
Model	4318-13	6348	LTX-C
From	BNC	Half duplex 100BASE-TX	UTP
To	Fiber Optic	Full duplex 100BASE-FX	AUI
LED	Power, Collision, Activity	Power, Link, Receive	Power, Collision, Transmit, Receive, Jabber, Polarity, Good Link
Comments	All signal activity and collision data is reliably translated.	Virtually eliminates the 200M collision domain. Features 1 megabyte buffer memory.	Can be mated with transceiver for conversion to 10BASE2, 10BASE_T, 10bASE-FL
Warranty	3 year	3 year	5 year
Price	$379	$950–$2,950	$189

Manufacturer	Pinacl Communications	Pinacl Communications	Plexcom, Inc.
Model	502-AIF/ 502-BIF	502-B/13	8052
From	AUI/ BNC	BNC	10BASE2
To	Fiber Optic	BNC	10BASE-T
LED	PSUI, PSU2, Power, Data, Collision, Position 1, Position 2, Link	PSU 1, PSU 2, power, data, collision, position 1, position 2	Link, TX, RX, Collision, Power
Comments	Dual PSU Options	Dual PSU option	
Warranty	3 year	3 year	1 year
Price	$599/ $629	$579	$425

Manufacturer	RAD Data Communications	RAD Data Communications	RAD Data Communications
Model	RIC-24/35	RIC-232/530	MIC Family
From	RS-232/V.24	RS-232/V.24	V.24/RS-232, V.35, RS-530, V.36/RS-449, X.21
To	V.35	RS 530	V.24/RS-232, V.35, RS-530, V.36/RS-449, X.21
LED	TD1, RD1, TD2, RD2, Clock, Power	Power, TD, RD	None
Comments	DCE/DTE Switch for both interfaces	RS-232 to RS-422, RS-423, or MIL-188-114	Individual models will convert any interface to any interface, 6ft. cable length, Most units to 2Mbps
Warranty	1 year	1 year	1 year
Price	$325	$325	$70–$405

Manufacturer	RAD DATA Communications	RAD DATA Communications	RAD DATA Communications
Model	UCI Universal Interface Converter	AMC-101 ATM Media Converter	FMC-101 Fiber Optic Media Converter
From	(Several) v.24, v.35, v.36, v.21	SC/MM/, ST/MM, ST/SM, UTP, STP, ST/SM/Laser	ST-Multimode 850NM & 1300 NM
To	(Several) G.703	SC/MM, ST/MM, ST/SM, UTP, STP, ST/SM/Laser	ST-Singlemode 1300 NM LED & Laser
LED	TD-1, TD-2, RD-1, RD-2, Power	Fault, Wrap, Signal, Power	MM-IN, MM-OUT, SM-IN, SM-Out, Power, Local, Loop, RMT Loop
Comments	Interfaces are replaceable modules; speeds up to 2.045Mbps	Interchangeable modules, in repeater and transparency modes	Transparent conversion from multimode to single mode fiber optics, with speeds up to 155Mbps

N/A—Not applicable   INA—Information not available

Table Continues →

■ Converters

Manufacturer	RAD DATA Communications	RAD DATA Communications	RAD DATA Communications
Warranty	1 year	1 year	1 year
Price	$700 Base unit $125 540 Interface modules	$1,050 Base unit $500–$1300 Modules	$2,500–$3,300

Manufacturer	South Hills Datacomm	South Hills Datacomm	South Hills Datacomm
Model	33371	36670	33405
From	UTP	10BASE-T	10BASE-2
To	BNC	BNC, RJ45, AUI	BNC, AUI
LED	Power, Jabber, Activity, Collision	Power, Receive, Transmit, Jabber, Polarity, Collision, SQE	Power, SQE
Comments			
Warranty	1 year		
Price	$230–$280	$70–$90	$75–$120

Manufacturer	South Hills Datacomm	South Hills Datacomm	South Hills Datacomm
Model	33406	33407	37104
From	10BASE-FI	10BASE-FL	UTP
To	ST, AUI	SMA, AUI	ST Fiber
LED	Power, Link, Receive, Transmit, Jabber, Collision,	Power, Link, Receive, Transmit, Jabber, Collision,	Power, Link, Port Activity, Jabber, Collision,
Comments			
Warranty			1 year
Price	$255–$300	$245–$300	$330–$430

Manufacturer	TRENDware	UNICOM
Model	TE-TC	XTEND-2/T
From	UTP	BNC
To	BNC	UTP
LED	Receive, Data link, Collision, Jabber, Power	Power, Link, UTP PLR, UTP RCV, UTP COL, CX COL, CX RCV
Comments	Also acts as an Ethernet repeater	
Warranty	5 year	5 year
Price	$199	$145

Manufacturer	UNICOM	UNICOM
Model	XTEND-T/T	XTEND-T/FL
From	UTP	UTP
To	UTP	ST
LED	Power, Link (2), COL (2), RCV(2)	LMON, COL, XMT, Power, RCV, Jabber, Link
Comments		
Warranty	5 year	5 year
Price	$147	$289

N/A—Not applicable   INA—Information not available

End ■

6 NETWORK OPERATING SYSTEMS

NETWORK OPERATING SYSTEMS (NOS) are the software infrastructure that allow computers on a network to
communicate with one another. A key difference between
UNIX and PC computing platforms is that UNIX operating
systems include sophisticated built-in networking capabilities. In the PC environment, robust networking capabilities
usually require a separate network operating system working
with existing computer operating systems. However, this is
changing as PC operating systems such as Microsoft's Windows products add more native network capabilities. Costs,
sharing needs, scalability, and your existing computing equipment are some key factors that will guide your decision on
which NOS to choose.

NETWORK OPERATING SYSTEMS

Server-Based and Peer-Based Solutions

Network operating systems are designed for either server-based or peer-to-peer connectivity. The server-based model requires computers dedicated to providing network services; the peer-to-peer (peer, for short) model provides station-to-station sharing of information and resources. The server-based network model is widely used, even for networks of just ten workstations. UNIX networking, which is technically a peer-to-peer system, is often functionally implemented as server-based by dedicating machines to providing network services. Server-based network operating systems allow the implementation of client/server applications, creating a powerful network environment. In a peer-to-peer network environment, the NOS is generally transparent, simply providing access to other machines and their resources. Historically, these products were layered on top of DOS, which limited what they could do. Many of the new peer NOSs don't have such limitations. Peer-to-peer's low cost and ready availability as part of many operating systems make it an attractive way to start a small network or create a small workgroup within the framework of a larger system.

A network operating system's scalability is also an important consideration. Peer networks tend to be less scalable than server-based systems because of the processing power drain on workstations that are also providing network services. It helps to keep peer workgroups small and limit the amount of traffic, but it's difficult to get consistent performance. Server-based systems provide more consistent performance as the number of users increases. In addition, server-based systems can handle thousands of workstations efficiently and economically.

Computing Platform

Networking is usually done with existing computers. If you primarily have UNIX computers, it doesn't make much sense to consider a PC-based NOS like Novell's NetWare. Even when companies migrate to another computing platform, the change is usually gradual. It's important to find a balance between implementing new equipment, and possibly a new NOS, and integrating existing computers. A good choice in NOS may be dictated by the industry you're in. For instance, in the financial industry, UNIX systems are typically used for mission critical functions. This means that it's usually best to use UNIX-compatible applications. This is not to say that PC-based networking cannot support mission critical applications. Your unique computing demands may steer you towards one computing platform over another. Creating a mission critical computer environment means creating a reliable network system that is secure and highly available (minimal network downtime). This is also referred to as fault tolerance.

NETWORK OPERATING SYSTEMS

Peer and server NOSs support varying degrees of network fault tolerance. For example, server-based NetWare can manage disk drive mirroring. If one drive fails, the other takes over automatically without interruption to the users or server activity. It makes sense to build this type of fault tolerance into a server because the server is providing so many critical functions. It's also easier to have the management feature for disk drive mirroring built into the NOS than to try to integrate another application that performs this function.

Hardware Requirements

There are certain hardware requirements associated with the network operating system you choose. For instance, peer-to-peer networks require less hardware investment than server-based systems. If you create a high-speed (100 Mbps) network, you'll need specialized hardware and an NOS that can provide that level of performance. Installation, setup, and user disruption can add significantly to the purchase costs of network equipment, including network operating system software. In general, for small network environments using just basic services, peer-to-peer NOSs cost less to buy and maintain. However, as the network grows and service demands increase, a server-based solution can become more cost effective even though your initial cash outlay may be higher. Ongoing maintenance costs (upgrades, repairs, downtime, and so on) are a large part of network expenses. Choosing an NOS that will easily scale to changing needs will help minimize these costs.

Major PC-Based Network Operating Systems

There are a number of good choices in PC network operating systems. Novell's NetWare dominates this market because of its long history, but there are viable challengers and peer-to-peer alternatives to consider, each with their own distinct advantages. The major PC network operating systems under server-based and peer-to-peer categories are listed here:

Server-Based	**Peer-to-Peer**
High performance, scalable, client/server functions	Basic services, low cost, easy to install and use
NetWare	LANtastic
Windows NT Server	Windows 95, WFW
VINES	Apple Talk
OS/2 WarpServer	
Apple Share	

NETWORK OPERATING SYSTEMS

NetWare

NetWare, from Novell Inc., is by far the most popular network operating system, with about 60 percent of the PC LAN market. Novell began networking PCs in the late 1980s and is a pioneer in the field. But NetWare's success is not just due to its early entry into the market. The product has evolved into a robust and affordable NOS for small to large businesses.

NetWare is available today as two versions, 3.*X* and 4.*X*. The installed base is predominantly version 3.*X*, a solid and proven NOS that has been in the market for some time. Most network software products for the PC support version 3.*X*. In addition, there is a broad base of knowledge on NetWare 3.*X*, so it's easy to get help from programmers and network engineers. The largest certification program for network engineering is provided by Novell (for the designation of a Certified Network Engineer, or CNE) specifically for NetWare networking.

Besides providing fast and efficient core network services such as print and file sharing, NetWare 3.*X* provides extensive server and network management, fault-tolerant storage support including full server redundancy (SFTIII), a long list of client operating system support, and incredible scalability that cost effectively serves from ten to thousands of users.

NetWare 4.*X*, introduced in 1994, offers improved management features such as global naming and active security. It also provides extensive connectivity features. NetWare 4.*X* works well in small network environments but its management capabilities make it well-suited for managing large network environments, too.

Hoping to leverage its reputation as the leading server-based NOS provider, Novell entered the peer-to-peer networking market with a product called NetwareLite, later to become known as Personal NetWare (with major changes). This product, which runs under Novell DOS 7, was similar to LANtastic but could not shake Artisoft's dominance in the peer NOS market. Then came the built-in peer networking capabilities of Microsoft's Windows products, intensifying the competition in the peer market. Novell has changed focus back to continuing NetWare's success as a very scalable server-based product.

Windows NT Server

Microsoft introduced Windows NT Server as a PC network operating system in the same class as UNIX. Its 32-bit multitasking OS can run programs from other operating systems like DOS, OS/2, and others. Like UNIX, Windows NT Server incorporates powerful network capabilities that you manage through a user-friendly interface. Ease of management is a big plus for this operating system, which can manage huge amounts of disk capacity. In addition, it includes a tool to simplify migrating from

NETWORK OPERATING SYSTEMS

NetWare to NT. Although not yet as scalable in numbers of clients as Net-Ware and without the NetWare's huge list of compatible software, NT's market presence is building up steam. It stands to make a significant impact on NOS market share, including that of the UNIX market. Microsoft offers a well-integrated application suite for NT called Microsoft Back Office that includes network management, mainframe/midrange connections, and a client/server database.

VINES
Banyan's VINES is a powerful PC NOS that serves large network installations well. It is based on an AT&T UNIX operating system. Banyan has not made the same commitment to marketing as Microsoft and Novell, and the result has been a good product without a lot of market share. Now, both Microsoft and Novell have robust product offerings that can compete well in Banyan's space.

VINE's uniqueness has been its speedy and seamless communication capabilities between remote servers, mainframes, and minicomputers. Its advanced connectivity and robust features made VINES a solid choice for PC-based large business networking. In addition, VINES is known for pioneering the network-wide, directory-based services. Street talk, VINES' network directory service, has allowed VINES to effectively manage very large multiple server networks that were beyond the abilities of NetWare before 4.1 and still beyond NT.

OS/2 Warp Server and LAN Server
IBM came out with LAN Server to provide an OS/2-based network server environment. LAN Server can also be run on an IBM AS/400 to provide AS/400 and PC connectivity. It offers an "entry-level" version designed for networks with fewer than 100 users and an advanced version for groups of up to 1,000. OS/2 Warp Server is an enhanced version of LAN Server designed for the newer OS/2, OS/2 Warp, as the host platform. OS/2 Warp Server is feature rich and can communicate with other major NOSs from Novell and Microsoft. This is a solid product that compares well to Windows NT and will compete in that market space.

LANtastic
Artisoft's LANtastic has been a popular peer network solution for PCs since it began offering low-cost peer networking for DOS machines. When Windows came onto the scene and began incorporating peer networking capabilities, LANtastic continued to build better features and simple integration of many O/S types into their networking scheme. You can buy LANtastic modules to create a hybrid of server-based and peer network functions. With Window for Workgroups (WFW) and Windows 95

NETWORK OPERATING SYSTEMS

becoming the predominant installed base of PC operating systems, the
need for third-party peer networking software is decreasing. Artisoft continues to enhance LANtastic and the product often comes out on top in
peer NOS comparisons. But like most peer NOSs, it is not very scalable
and performance is heavily affected as users and network traffic increases.

Windows 95 and Window for Workgroups

Windows 95 and Window for Workgroups include peer networking capabilities. Windows for Workgroups (WFW) serves an installed base of 386
and 486 PCs with less than 8MB of RAM and is an adjunct to PCs running DOS. WFW does a good job of providing basic print and file services
for this aging class of machines. Windows 95 is a step up from WFW, providing true 32-bit multiprocessing. New PCs are usually shipped with an
operating system, which currently is Windows 95. The networking features are richer in Windows 95 and integration with existing NetWare
LANs is seamless. Microsoft Office, an application suite for Windows 95,
includes groupware tools such as e-mail and scheduling. Setting up Windows 95 for networking is highly automated.

Apple Share and Apple Talk

AppleTalk is a peer-based NOS for Apple computers. Because of the
growth in heterogeneous networking and performance advantages of
server-based computing, Apple came out with Apple Share—a server-
based solution that offers more client operating system support (DOS
and Windows in addition to Macintosh), better performance, and more
scalability than Apple Talk. Its market is Macintosh-dominant environments that need mostly Mac connections but also need to be able to incorporate other PC clients such as Windows machines.

■ PC Network Operating System Assessment

Key Features	Apple Share	OS/2 WARP Server	LANtastic
Manufacturer	Apple Computer	IBM	Artisoft
General Description	Server-based system for Macintosh dominated environments	Server-based system operating on OS/2 (WARP) computers	Peer-to-peer based system for sharing wide range of PC compatible computers
Primary Hardware Platform	Apple Computers	PC Compatibles	PC Compatibles
Application Availability	Provides seamless connectivity and is designed to be transparent to all Mac applications	Wide support for IBM applications but limited library of client/server applications available	This NOS simply provides connectivity, not client server applications. Supports most DOS and Windows applications.
User Base	Slight growth Apple computer shipments have been slipping some but the huge installed base continues to network existing machines.	Shrinking OS/2 is losing market share to other operating systems. In addition, companies will often incorporate OS/2 workstation connections as part of another NOS.	Flat With peer-to-peer networking capability being built into most OS software sold today, the need for a third party solution such as LANtastic shrinks, even though LANtastic usually compares favorably.
GENERAL FEATURES:			
Hardware Requirements	Very Small	Small	Very Small
# of Clients Supported	Small	Small to Medium	Small
Overall Network Speed	Slow	Medium	Slow
Ease of Install/ Administration	High	Medium	High
Supported Applications	N/A	Limited	N/A
Heterogeneous Net Support	Low	Medium to High	Low
Install and Maintenance Costs	Low	Low to Medium	Low
Price Structure	Not Available	Warp Server 4.X Base $629 5 User $229 10 User $439 50 User $1,959	LANtastic ver 7.X 2 User base $349 2-10 User $499 Unlimited $999 LANtastic for Windows 95 2 User base $349 10 User $899

Key Features	NetWare	UNIX	VINES
Manufacturer	Novell, Inc.	Many systems manufacturers	Banyan, Inc.
General Description	Popular NOS that can fit small to large PC-based networking situations	Networking capabilities are built into UNIX operating systems.	Very capable NOS for PC compatible computers
Primary Hardware Platform	PC Compatible	UNIX (mostly Motorola-based processor computers)	PC Compatible
Application Availability	High	High	Low
User Base	Growing NetWare continues to be used for its reasonable costs, performance, and scalability.	Flat to Growing Some UNIX OS are thriving and machine connectivity continues. Windows NT may impact growth.	Flat to Declining VINES has a loyal user base and sites tend to be large. However, VINES is usually passed over for other NOS's in new installations.

N/A—Not applicable   INA—Information not available

PC Network Operating System Assessment ■

Key Features	NetWare	UNIX	VINES
GENERAL FEATURES:			
Hardware Requirements	Medium to High	Medium	Medium to High
# of Clients Supported	High	Medium to High	High
Overall Network Speed	High	High	Medium to High
Ease of Install/ Administration	Low to Medium	Medium to High	Medium to High
Supported Applications	High	High	Low
Heterogeneous Net Support	High	High	Low
Installation and Maintenance Costs	Low to High	Medium to High	Medium to High
Price Samples	NetWare 3.X 10 User $2,495 25 User $3,695 NetWare 4.X 100 User $6,995	Examples: Solaris 2.5 (Intel or Sparc CPU) Server $1,295 Per Client $795 HP-UX v10.X, Series 700 8 Users $1,250 32 Users $4,900	VINES 6.X 10 Users $2,995 50 Users $7,895 100 Users $9,995 250 Users $14,995 500 Users $27,995 1000 Users $49,995

Key Features	Windows 95x	Windows NT	WFW
General Description	This OS has built-in peer-to-peer networking capabilities and hooks for linking to NetWare networks. Workgroup networking.	High performance OS bridging PC and UNIX performance and network capabilities.	Another Windows OS with built in peer-to-peer network capabilities for workgroup networking
Primary Hardware Platform	PC Compatible	PC Compatible	PC Compatible
Application Availability	High (transparent)	Medium and growing rapidly	Medium (transparent) but Windows 95 now standard
User Base	Growing Windows 95 is growing primarily as an OS. NOS growth is in small workgroup applications.	Growing Windows NT is a very capable PC-based OS which provides UNIX like performance and characteristics.	Shrinking Windows 95 has quickly become the standard PC OS, but Windows NT Workstation 4.0 may become the business PC preference in the near future.
GENERAL FEATURES:			
Hardware Requirements	Low	High	Low
# of Clients Supported	Low	Medium	Low
Overall Network Speed	Low	Medium to High	Low
Ease of Install/ Administration	High	Medium	Low
Supported Applications	High (transparent)	Medium (growing rapidly)	High (transparent)
Heterogeneous Net Support	Low (only through NetWare)	Medium to High	Low
Install and Maintenance Costs	Low	Medium to High	Low
Price Structure	Single license $179 Volume discounts available	Windows NT Server O/S $699 Client license $39.95 Volume discounts available	WFW $149 WFW 1 user license pack $129 Volume discounts available

N/A—Not applicable   INA—Information not available   **End** ■

PC Network Operating System Comparison

	Novell NetWare	Microsoft Windows NT	IBM LAN Server
TYPE			
Server-based	Y	Y	Y
Peer-to-Peer			
System Standards			
POSIX 1003.1	N	Y	N
Networking			
TCP/IP	Y	Y	Y
IPX/SPX (Novell)	Y	Y	N
ATM	Third-party	Third-party	Third-party
NetBeui	Y	Y	Y
SMB	N	Y	N
SYSTEMS AND NETWORK MGMT.			
SNMP	Y	Y	N
Built-in Mgt. Tools	Y	Y	Y
DESKTOP COMPATIBILITY			
DOS	Y	Y	Y
Windows 3.x	Y	Y	Y
Windows 95	Y	Y	Y
Windows NT	Y	Y	Y
Macintosh	Y	Y	Optional
OS/2 1.3 & 2.x	Y	Y	Y
OS/2 Warp	N	N	Y
UNIX	Y	Y	N
HIGH AVAILABILITY			
Local Server Mirroring	Y	Y	Y
Remote Server Mirroring	Y	N	N
Storage Clustering			
Replicating File Syst.	N	N	N
Clustering	N	Y	N
Software Disk RAID	N	N	N
Software Mirroring	Y	Y	Y
HARDWARE PLATFORMS			
Intel	Y	Y	Y
RISC	N	Alpha; MIPS	N
Network Scalability			
Range of Users	5 to 1000s	5 to 1000s	Up to 1000
Network Directory Svc	Y	Y	Y

Y—Existing feature   Third-party—Definite third-party supplier   N—No announced plans

PC Network Operating System Comparison ■

	Banyan VINES	Apple Apple Share	Artisoft LANtastic
TYPE			
Server-based	Y	Y	
Peer-to-Peer			Y
System Standards			
POSIX 1003.1	N	N	N
Networking			
TCP/IP	Y	Y	Y
IPX/SPX (Novell)	N	Y	N
ATM	Third-party	Third-party	Third-party
NetBeui	Y	N	N
SMB	N	N	N
SYSTEMS AND NETWORK MGMT.			
SNMP	N	N	N
Built-in Mgt. Tools	Y	Y	Y
DESKTOP COMPATIBILITY			
DOS	Y	Y	Y
Windows 3.x	Y	Y	Y
Windows 95	Y	Y	Y
Windows NT	Y	N	N
Macintosh	Y	Y	N
OS/2 1.3 & 2.x	Y	N	Y
OS/2 Warp	Y	N	N
UNIX	Y	N	N
HIGH AVAILABILITY			
Local Server Mirroring	Y	N	N
Remote Server Mirroring	N	N	N
Storage Clustering			
Replicating File Syst.	N	N	N
Clustering	N	N	N
Software Disk RAID	N	N	N
Software Mirroring	Y	N	N
HARDWARE PLATFORMS			
Intel	Y	Y	Y
RISC	N	N	N
Network Scalability			
Range of Users	100 to 1000s	Up to 250	2 to 500
Network Directory Svc	Y	N	N

Y—Existing feature   Third-party—Definite third-party supplier   N—No announced plans   **E n d ■**

■ UNIX Operating Systems Comparison

System Standards	SunSoft Solaris 2.4	HP HP-UX 10	IBM AIX 4.1	Digital OSF/1 3.2
POSIX 1003.1	Y	Y	Y	Y
POSIX 1003.2	Y	Y	Y	Y
POSIX 1003.1B	Y	Y	Y	Y
XPG3 Base	Y	Y	Y	Y
XPG4 Base	Y	Y	Planned	Y
SVID 3	Y	Y	N	Y
SPEC 1170	Planned	Planned	Planned	Planned
Networking				
TCP/IP	Y	Y	Y	Y
SPX/IPX (Novell)	Y	Y	Y	Y
LAN Manager	Third-party	Y	Planned	Third-party
Ethernet	Y	Y	Y	Y
FastEthernet	Y	N	N	Planned
100VG any LAN	Third-party	Y	N	N
ATM	Y	Y	Third-party	Y
Software router	Y	Y	Y	Y
56KB direct interface	Y	Y	Planned	Y/A
Systems and Network Mgmt.				
SNMP	Y	Y	Y	Y
CMIS-CMIP	Y	Y	Y	Y
Distributed Computing				
ONC-NFS	Y	Y	Y	Y
ONC-RPC	Y	Y	Y	Y
NFS-Diskless	Y	Y	Y	Planned
DCE	Y	Y	Y	Y
AFS	Third-party	Third-party	Y	Third-party
CORBA	Y	Y	Y	Y
OpenStep	Y	N	N	Planned
Taligent	N	Planned	Planned	N
User Interfaces				
X11 R5 or R6	Y	Y	Y	Y
Motif 1.1 or 1.2	Y	Y	Y	Y
Common Desktop Environment	Y	Y	Y	Y
High Availability				
CPU clustering	Y	Y	Y	Y
Journaled file system	Y	Y	Y	Y
Dynamic FS resizing	Y	Y	Y	Y
Mirroring-striping	Y	Y	Y	Y
Hardware Platforms				
RISC	SPARC PowerPC	PA-RISC	PowerPC; Power	Alpha
Intel	Y	N	N	N

Y—Existing feature   Third-party—Definite third-party supplier   Planned—There by end of 1995   N—No announced plans

UNIX Operating Systems Comparison ◼

System Standards	SCO OpenServer	Microsoft Windows NT	SCO UnixWare 2
POSIX 1003.1	Y	Y	Y
POSIX 1003.2	Y	N	Planned
POSIX 1003.1B	Y	N	N
XPG3 Base	Y	N	Y
XPG4 Base	Y	N	Y
SVID 3	Y	N	Y
SPEC 1170	Planned	N	Planned
Networking			
TCP/IP	Y	Y	Y
SPX/IPX (Novell)	Y	Y	Y
LAN Manager	Y	Y	Third-party
Ethernet	Y	Y	Y
FastEthernet	Y	N	Third-party
100VG any LAN	Y	N	Third-party
ATM	Y	Third-party	Third-party
Software router	Y	N	Y
56KB direct interface	Third-party	N	N
Systems and Network Mgmt.			
SNMP	Y	Y	Y
CMIS-CMIP	Y	N	Third-party
Distributed Computing			
ONC-NFS	Y	Third-party	Y
ONC-RPC	Y	Third-party	Y
NFS-Diskless	Y	N	N
DCE	Y	Y	Third-party
AFS	Planned	Third-party	Third-party
CORBA	Planned	N	N
OpenStep	N	N	N
Taligent	N	N	N
User Interfaces			
X11 R5 or R6	Y	Third-party	Y
Motif 1.1 or 1.2	Y	N	Y
Common Desktop Environment	Third-party	N	Third-party
High Availability			
CPU clustering	Third-party	N	Planned
Journaled file system	Y	N	Y
Dynamic FS resizing	Planned	N	Y
Mirroring-striping	Y	N	Y
Hardware Platforms			
RISC	Planned	Alpha; MIPS	N
Intel	Third-party OEMs	Y	Y

Y—Existing feature   Third-party—Definite third-party supplier   Planned—There by end of 1995   N—No announced plans   **E n d** ◼

7 MANAGEMENT TOOLS

ONCE YOU INSTALL A network, you need to manage it. To keep your network up and running, you need to manage security, user access, directory changes, network connections, disk drives, and network software, among other things. For many people, the management tools embedded in network operating system software are enough to do the job. Some NOSs, like NetWare 4.*X*, even have built-in utilities for managing large networks. If you have a larger installation, managing the network and related equipment may exceed the capabilities or effectiveness of the NOS. In this case you'll probably want to buy additional management tools. Third-party management tools can provide specialized functions and more robust capabilities than most NOSs. Some of these programs function across multiple operating systems and computing platforms to provide enterprise-wide management. In many cases, these tools are designed to work with information provided by other network hardware and software.

MANAGEMENT TOOLS

Types of Management Tools

Traditional management functions fall under two categories: network management and systems management. Network management involves monitoring, reporting, and tuning the connectivity aspects of the network. Systems management focuses on aspects of server and workstation systems such as disk management, CPU analysis, and so on. These two categories are beginning to merge as products evolve to provide both network and systems management services. The third major management category is storage management. Storage management functions often fall under systems management. Many network and systems management products provide ways to plug in storage tools such as backup. However, network administrators often pieced together storage management by using a suite of individual software products. Table 7.1 shows how management functions are grouped.

It's difficult to compare management tools because many products offer so many different functions. Products like Hewlett-Packard's Open-View and Computer Associate's Unicenter provide features in all of these categories—licensing and metering, equipment inventory, software distribution, network monitoring, and storage management—and are really both network and systems management products. This book lists such products in the category in which they fit best. For example, HP Openview is under network management and CA Unicenter is under systems management. Again, there are more and more "management suite" products that include both network and systems management tools. These products provide a management framework that can accommodate more specific "snap-in" tools and utilities so network administration can operate from a single administrative console and interface.

Necessary Hardware

You need more than software to gather network information for management purposes. Network information often comes from network hardware components such as hubs and routers specially designed to collect and pass on information about network traffic, performance, and so on.

■ Table 7.1   Management and Control Functions

NETWORK	SYSTEMS	STORAGE
Events and alerts	Software	Storage access
Communications	Assets	Capacity/disk repositories
Connectivity/traffic	Configuration	Data protection (backup and archive, disaster Recovery)

MANAGEMENT TOOLS

Network hardware that can collect information about network traffic and the like can usually report on its own. Network management software then takes this information and incorporates it into a single database for integrated analysis and presentation. If you're a network administrator, you benefit from having information taken from various sources at all levels of the network (cable traffic, server activity, and so forth). It's also easier to gather information and perform reporting, since you can use a common interface rather than multiple programs from different vendors. Tools like cable testers and protocol analyzers are also used to manage networks, as discussed in Chapter 12.

Information Sharing Standards

The standard network management protocol (SNMP) was established to let people share information collected from various sources and products. It's easy to integrate various pieces of equipment that can read and report using the SNMP format. This creates an open systems environment in which you can mix and match various products instead of sticking with a single vendor and a proprietary architecture. Network management hardware and software products must be compatible with this standard. The Data Management Task Force (DMTF) standard is a sublayer standard that defines the organization and reporting of Management Information Bases (MIB), databases of the logical names of all network resources. Standards like DMTF make it easier for vendors to produce SNMP-compatible products.

The Common Management Information Protocol (CMIP) is another standard designed to improve management communications and take the place of SNMP. Although a number of products by major vendors support this standard, SNMP continues to be the open systems standard, leaving the future of CIMP uncertain.

Inventory and License Management

Maintaining and tracking software licenses can be a chore. Without the proper tools, companies may overbuy, underutilize their resources, or put themselves legally at risk by not being in compliance with software licenses. Some software applications enable you to monitor usage and license compliance. But it's inconvenient to use separate tools for each application. There are now products that specifically monitor and control the licensing of many applications. The benefits can be significant. You can reduce costs by buying just what you need while still complying to avoid possible penalties for software piracy. Usage monitoring and reporting are valuable for planning purchases, training, and justifying software expenditures.

MANAGEMENT TOOLS

| Compatibility | | | | | |

| Performance | Reliability | **Manageability** | **Scalability** | **Flexibility** | Value |

Operating system and network compatibility determine whether a product is suitable for enterprise use. For instance, a product that runs on Net-Ware may only track NetWare-based software. This may be fine if the enterprise is all NetWare, but cumbersome if you must also track other environments such as Windows NT. Consider what NOS environments you wish to incorporate. In some cases, you may be forced to run separate license management applications on different platforms.

Good compatibility also means an open architecture in database compatibility and integration with other applications. This may include database links to other applications, SNMP reporting, and so on.

| Metering Capability | | | | | |

| **Performance** | Reliability | **Manageability** | Scalability | Flexibility | Value |

Metering is measuring and controlling software usage based on its license. Some products only meter applications installed on servers while others manage workstation installations as well. Software is licensed in a number of different ways and not all products can be licensed in the same manner. Look for a number of different metering methods. The most common method today is for concurrent use, meaning one license can be shared but not at the same time. Metering consists of tracking the number of concurrent users so the administrator can buy enough licenses without having to buy everyone a license. Another consideration is how the software handles product "suites" in which multiple applications are sold under one license. Metering features might also include proactively freeing licenses by sending a message to users who may have just left an application open, recognizing that a license is no longer in use if a workstation freezes or reboots, and providing waiting lists for users who want to use an application, notifying them when it's available.

| Alerts and Reporting | | | | | |

| Performance | Reliability | **Manageability** | Scalability | Flexibility | Value |

Alerts and reporting are important management tools. Monitoring reports should handle at least a month's usage, with reports that show not only license violations but also underutilization of existing licenses. Some products recommend how to reorganize licenses as well as how many new

MANAGEMENT TOOLS

licenses to buy. Alerts (pager or console) indicate usage limits reached or exceeded, and license expirations.

Application Library					
Performance	Reliability	**Manageability**	Scalability	Flexibility	Value

When your network is loaded with software, it's important to have a product that can identify and log applications in the management database. First, look for the library of applications the product contains for the applications you want to monitor and manage. These are applications that the software can detect automatically. Second, look for a product that makes it easy to manually log applications that are not included in the default database.

Network Management

Network management is by far the largest management tool product classification. Many network management applications include systems management functions. Their main purpose is to simplify network management and provide capabilities that are not built into network operating systems. Many network utilities assist in network management in some way, but in this book the term "network management software" refers to products that act as the main console for network management.

Scope of Function					
Performance	Reliability	Manageability	**Scalability**	**Flexibility**	**Value**

You need to determine what will be managed—a department, site, or the entire network enterprise. Site-based network management is not necessarily less complicated than enterprise management. Individual sites may be managed in gory detail with little done to manage remote sites of a network enterprise. Some products are specifically geared towards one or the other.

Compatibility					
Performance	Reliability	**Manageability**	Scalability	Flexibility	**Value**

Compatibility with operating systems and other applications is extremely important. First you must decide what computer platform and operating system the network will be managed from. Then you must consider what network and operating systems this application needs to manage.

MANAGEMENT TOOLS

Compatibility with other equipment is important and unfortunately not as simple as some make it out to be. Even SNMP-compliant products may be difficult to integrate into a network management application. The vendor should have a list of compatible products. In addition, the application should be able to autodetect equipment on the list and let you add equipment references manually. Good compatibility contributes to the product's ability to scale upwards as your network and management needs grow.

Policy and Alert Settings

Performance	Reliability	Manageability	Scalability	Flexibility	Value

Network management software should not only monitor and report but also take action when necessary. The software should be able to carry out instructions—such as paging the administrator, shutting down servers, and rerouting network traffic—when certain events occur. The network administrator presets what actions are taken by setting "policies." Policy settings are a powerful network management tool because they provide preventative and automated network maintenance. Alerts may be an e-mail, a pop-up window on the administrator console, a page, or another form of notification. Alerts may need to go out to more than one person or to a hierarchy of people based on response or nonresponse by those who are notified.

Reporting and Presentation

Performance	Reliability	Manageability	Scalability	**Flexibility**	Value

Ideally, a single application will meet all of your network management reporting needs. This arrangement simplifies your work and creates a centralized database for complete and integrated analysis. Reports should be flexible and customizable, with plenty of defaults to select from. This type of information is often used to make arguments for new equipment, so it's also important to have clear presentation graphics.

Administration Console

Performance	Reliability	**Manageability**	Scalability	**Flexibility**	Value

If you are moving to a centralized network application, the console layout and features are very important. Consoles should have a GUI interface and be able to take advantage of the viewing capabilities of large color monitors. Layered views of the network connections—views of different

MANAGEMENT TOOLS

network levels such as workgroups, departments, and entire buildings—also help you quickly identify connections. In addition, these layouts should indicate the faults and potential faults with appropriate alarms. A potential fault could be when a router reaches an upper threshold of traffic, increasing the likelihood of lockup or failure.

Electronic Software Distribution

As a network grows, it becomes more time consuming to distribute and install applications. Fortunately, there are now products that let you distribute (or retrieve) software over the network rather than physically going to remote stations to install it. (Don't confuse this with buying and downloading software from a vendor over the Internet or a BBS system.) These software distribution products may include features such as usage tracking to ensure that the company is in compliance with its software license agreement. Electronic software distribution appears in more and more systems management software products. However, a number of products still provide just software distribution for those who have not yet fully integrated their systems management environment.

Compatibility					
Performance	Reliability	Manageability	**Scalability**	**Flexibility**	Value

Your software distribution application will probably be designed to run from a single platform. This is fine for most people, but if you might migrate to another platform at some point, look for multiplatform support at the administration level. If your network incorporates a variety of workstation types and operating systems, the software should be able to distribute across a variety of environments. Most products support IPX/SPX and TCP/IP protocols and a variety of workstation operating systems.

Administrator and User Controls					
Performance	Reliability	**Manageability**	Scalability	**Flexibility**	Value

There are certain levels of control for both the administrator and the end user. Administrator controls for software distribution may include scheduling, forced delivery, undo, and others. The ability to run multiple distribution servers and perform simultaneous installations could be important when the task load is heavy. The ability to compress distributed files can save time and reduce network load. Options for the user may include postpone, reject, accept, and so on. Some products let the user lock certain directories from administrator intervention.

MANAGEMENT TOOLS

Systems Management

Because practical systems management is now part of network and operating system software, the value of third-party systems management software is its wealth of tools, its ability to handle large environments, and your ability to take preventative and corrective actions based on administrator-defined policies. This represents the high end of the systems management market. System hardware vendors are leading providers, so their products tend to be best at managing their own environments.

Sometimes network hardware ships with its own management utility. Administrators often use utilities from third-party vendors to fill in a specific gap left by the operating system's systems management function. Those using systems management applications, the software suites offered primarily by major systems vendors, tend to have large sites to manage and tend to manage in terms of the network enterprise. Because this software is much like a suite of products, it tends to perform some tasks better than others.

Breadth of Functions

| **Performance** | Reliability | **Manageability** | **Scalability** | Flexibility | Value |

Systems management applications (not utilities) are often measured by the breadth of functions they can perform. Some vendors incorporate many functions into one application while others offer "management suites" or software modules. Software modules are convenient because you can buy just the features you need and later add others that will integrate easily. They can even expand on systems management and manage things like backup, networking, and so on all under one console. Systems management functions include system monitoring, hardware and software inventorying, software distribution and metering, remote management, and others. If you're managing a network enterprise rather than a single site, you may need special features that enable you to manage WAN links, remote servers, and so forth.

Compatibility

| Performance | Reliability | **Manageability** | **Scalability** | **Flexibility** | Value |

Compatibility with operating systems, network operating systems, and communications protocols is important. First you have to choose the hardware and operating system of the management platform—often consistent with the console's operating system. When you choose the network operating system and communications protocols, you must also consider the different

MANAGEMENT TOOLS

types of client servers and workstations that will be managed under the new software.

If you plan to install systems management software to manage a homogeneous local network, compatibility isn't a big issue. But systems management software is often used for larger sites that are managing a heterogeneous environment.

Policy Actions and Alerts

Performance	Reliability	**Manageability**	Scalability	Flexibility	**Value**

Like network management, systems management continues to evolve towards "expert systems" capabilities. This simply means that the software can take action automatically when an event occurs. Actions are based on predefined policies set by the administrator. Alerts are also an important part of systems management that enable the administrator to focus more on resolving problems and less on finding them.

Systems management is often referred to as desktop management. Policies not only standardize how things are done but also handle repetitive tasks, leaving the administrator free to handle other tasks.

Administration Console

Performance	Reliability	**Manageability**	Scalability	Flexibility	**Value**

The criteria you use to choose a systems management console are similar to those you use for network management. Console layout should be clear and comfortable. Layered views of systems should indicate the faults and potential faults with appropriate alarms. It's good to be able to customize the interface so you can have easy access to the functions you need. How additional products are integrated into the console may also be an important consideration. You should spend some time testing interfaces to find one you are comfortable with. The same product may have different interfaces depending on the operating system of the administration console.

Application Support

Performance	Reliability	Manageability	Scalability	**Flexibility**	**Value**

Some systems management products are "complete" solutions with many built-in functions. Others are more modular, allowing you to buy just the functions you need. Either type may also let you integrate other

MANAGEMENT TOOLS

applications, still using the systems management console as the point of management. Application support often means integrating SNMP data from other sources.

■ Inventory Management Tools

Manufacturer	**Blue Ocean Software, Inc.**	**Seagate**
Model	Track-It! v.2.0 for Windows	Seagate LAN Directory
Description	Automatically tracks all hardware and software on any type of LAN, as well as on standalone PCs	32-bit automated asset management application which simplifies the collection, tracking, and reporting of networked/standalone PC's hardware/software inventory
Administrator O/S	Windows 3.1, Windows 95, Windows NT, or DOS	Windows 3.1, Windows 95, Windows NT, DOS
Server O/S	DOS, Windows 3.1, Windows 95, Windows NT, OS/2, and System 7 (Mac)	Windows 95, Windows NT, DOS
NOS Support	Any NOS supporting file and record looking	Windows 95, Windows NT, Novell NetWare, Banyan VINES, Microsoft LAN manager, Microsoft Windows for Workgroups, IBM LAN server, AT&T StarLAN, DEC pathworks, and more
Inventory Methods	LAN inventory Standalone inventory Manual inventories Supports DOS, Windows, Windows 95, Windows NT, and O/S2 auditing	Inventories over 300 hardware and 6,700 software applications Rapid hardware-software scans with optional time constraints Change tracking with alerts and reporting Multiple database merging capabilities Merge data from multiple server sites Integrates with Seagate WinINSTALL to generate lists for WinINSTALL distribution of software packages out to PCs
Administration Features	Includes modules for inventory, help desk, purchasing, training, and library Includes graphical, SAC-based report writer, customizable reports, and 30 graphs Open database format Several user-definable fields	32-bit application ODBC level 2 SQL database Available in both as a point and suite solution Custom report writer Requires no TSR's
Comments	Can be customized to recognize noncommercial proprietary software	
Warranty/Support	30-day free tech support	30-day money-back guarantee. Free unlimited support to registered users.
Price	$395 for 100 PCs	$595 for initial 50 users $495 for additional 100 users

Manufacturer	**Tally Systems Corporation**
Model	NETCENSUS
Description	Automatic hardware and software inventory for all your PCs, either networked or standalone. Servers as well.
Administrator O/S	Windows 3.1, Windows 95, Windows NT
Server O/S	DOS, Windows 3.1, Windows 95, Windows NT, OS/2 and Mac
NOS Support	NOS independent-any NOS. Supporting file sharing and record locking (i.e., Novell NetWare, Banyan, LAN manager, LAN server, Windows NT Server)
Inventory Methods	Quiet mode Patented census recognition technology Provides detailed reports for analysis Scheduled inventories Provides an audit of registered DMI information
Administration Features	Product recognition library updated every 60 days. Extensive hardware recognition PCs, add-on drives, communications cards, processes, peripherals, etc. Automatic software serial recognition: Manufacturer, name, version, serial numbers. Multiuser reports and tables. Integration with help desk. Enhanced output formats: SMS, CSV.
Comments	Can be customized to add local products, integration with SMS
Warranty/Support	1 year free tech support
Price	$12 per PC for 1,000 PCs

N/A—Not applicable   INA—Information not available

End ■

License Management Tools ■

Manufacturer	**Attachmate**	**Multima Corp.**
Model	NetWizard 3.1	NetKeeper Express, version 5.1
Description	NetWizard is a comprehensive software management solution (inventory distribution, metering, remote control) for PC LANs and servers. It is scalable to any size network.	Automatically tracks hardware, software and configuration files on LANs, WANs, and on stand-alone computers. Administrator determines what will be audited.
Administrator O/S	Windows 3.1, Windows 95, Windows NT, Macintosh	Windows 3.1, Windows 95, Windows NT, DOS, OS/2
Workstation O/S support	DOS, Windows, Windows 95, Windows NT, Macintosh	Windows 3.1, Windows 95, Windows NT, IBM, Sun
Server O/S Support	NetWare, NT, UNIX, Windows	NetWare, NT, UNIX, Windows
NOS Support	NetWare, VINES, NTAS, LANMAN, others	Novell NetWare, Windows NT, Windows 95, OS/2, LAN Manager, Banyan VINES, Lantastic
License Models Supported	Nodelocked, per user, site, concurrent use, suite, time limited	PCT node or PCT site or per concurrent user
Administration Features	Remote control—NetWizard adminstrators can "take over" remote workstations, including full redirected video, keyboard I/O, and mouse I/O. Windows 95/NT policy management—Through NetWizard managers can centrally define, distribute, and implement Windows 95 and Windows NT policies.	Real-time integration into NetKeeper Help Desk Pro, NetKeeper Inventory, Bar Code software and Net-Keeper Purchase Order User scripted inventories to specify type of inventory Open database and architecture On-line help system
Comments	Modem connectivity between NetWizard components—using asynchronous dial-out via RAS or any compatible interface, NetWizard managers can communicate with remote nodes and remote nodes can communicate with the manager.	The program includes many standard reports. The program is designed to "learn" unlimited new PC types or software.
Warranty/Support	60 days free support	45 day
Price	$39 (1,000-nodes) to $59 (10-nodes)—per node cost	$225 (per 100 users/per server)

Manufacturer	**Network Analysis Center**
Model	WinMIND
Description	Data Network modeling, pricing, and performance analysis software capable of pricing, managing, and designing local access and wide area communication networks.
Administrator O/S	Windows 3.1, Windows 95, Windows NT, UNIX
Workstation O/S support	Windows 3.1, Windows 95, Windows NT, UNIX
Server O/S Support	Windows 3.1, Windows 95, Windows NT, UNIX
NOS Support	Any NOS
License Models Supported	Single copy or multi-user LAN version
Administration Features	Network modeling and pricing
Comments	
Warranty/Support	1 year update and 1 year support
Price	$41,000

N/A—Not applicable   INA—Information not available

Table Continues →

■ License Management Tools

Manufacturer	Seagate	Tally Systems Corporation
Model	Seagate Software Metering and Resource Tracking (SMART)	Centameter 2.6
Description	Ensures software usage conforms to license requirements, including variations in licensing methods, lack of license management and the open architecture of most networks	Comprehensive software license metering and monitoring
Administrator O/S	Windows 3.1, Windows 95, Windows NT, DOS	Windows 3.x, Windows 95, Windows NT
Workstation O/S support	Windows 95, Windows NT	DOS, Windows 3.x, Windows 95, Windows NT, OS/2 (under Windows OS/2)
Server O/S Support	DOS, Windows 95, Windows NT	Windows 3.x, Windows 95, Windows NT, OS/2 (under Windows OS/2)
NOS Support	Compatible with all major forms of network hardware approved by Novell including Ethernet, ARCNET, Star-LAND, and Token Ring licensing	All NOS supporting file sharing and record locking
License Models Supported	Node, concurrent-use over network or for host, site licenses, time-limited licenses, demo licenses, product grouping, license querying, usage-based license	Over network or concurrent use for Host, sire licenses, demo licenses, product grouping, license querying, usage-based licenses
Administration Features	Tracks real-time/historical usage. Records multiple application usage by same user. Provides reporting/ documentation. View, add, or release users currently using an application/suite. Notification when application/suite becomes available.	Intelligent agent. License sharing across locally connected servers. License allocation (by user group or machine). Trace Internet usage. Change back reports. Suite metering and monitoring. Querying. Active/passive metering. Inactivity reminders. Acert notification via e-mail.
Comments		Reports are SPA approved, SHS integration
Warranty/Support	30-day money-back guarantee. Free unlimited support to registered users.	1 year free tech support
Price	$495 for additional 100 users $995 per 250 users	$12 per PC for 1,000 PCs

---

Network Management Tools ■

Manufacturer	3Com/Axon	3Com/Axon
Model	Transcend Enterprise Manager for Unix	Transcend Enterprise Manager for Windows
Product Description	Transcend Enterprise Manager (TEM) provides integrated, end-to-end network management for all 3Com networking systems.	Transcend Enterprise Manager (TEM) provides integrated, end-to-end network management for all 3Com networking systems.
Operating Systems Support	SunOS, Sun Solaris, HP-UX, IBM AIX	Windows 3.1 or above, DOS 5.0 or above
Topology	Ethernet, Fast Ethernet, Token Ring, FDDI	Ethernet, Fast Ethernet, Token Ring, FDDI
Features	Configures, monitors and analyzes NICs, hubs, switches, and routers. Manages as a single system with graphical user interfaces.	Configures, monitors and analyzes NICs, hubs, switches, and routers. Manages as a single system with graphical user interfaces.
Hardware Requirements	SPARCstation IPX and above (SunNet Manager), HP OpenView, or IBM RISC System/6000-POWERstation/ 340 minimum (NetView for AIX). 48MB RAM minimum, 64MB RAM recommended. 450MB hard drive space. 256 color monitor, 1152x900 minimum.	IBM 486 PC or higher recommended. 8MB RAM; 16MB swap file recommended. 40MB minimum available disc space.
Comments	TEM resides on standard management platforms.	TEM resides on standard management platforms.
Warranty	INA	INA
Price	$9,495	$3,495

Manufacturer	3Com/Axon	3Com/Axon
Model	Transcend LANsentry	Transcend Enterprise Monitor
Product Description	A suite of RMON-based management applications available for both Unix and Windows	i960 processor-based Ethernet and Token Ring RMON probes
Operating Systems Support	SunOS, Sun Solaris, Hp-UX, IBM AIX	N/A
Topology	Ethernet, Fast Ethernet, Token Ring, FDDI	Ethernet, Fast Ethernet, Token Ring
Features	Delivers RMON-compliant performance monitoring, troubleshooting and protocol analysis. Segment-at-a-glance view shows all RMON statistics. Comprehensive set of easy-to-read protocol decodes with a conversation trace feature. Templates for quick filter set up; user-specifiable start and stop condition, alarm thresholds and triggers.	Supports all 9 RMON groups for Ethernet. Provides complete out-of-band, dial-back capabilities. When configured with 16MB, TEM is powerful enough extends beyond RMON by downloading additional modules including RMON2.
Hardware Requirements	Unix workstation with 24MB memory	INA
Comments		Dual-Port Ethernet version is available, including special switch monitor mode.
Warranty	INA	INA
Price	Windows $1,995 Unix $4,495	Transcend Enterprise monitors with 16MB start at $3,295

Manufacturer	3Com/Axon	3Com/Axon
Model	Transcend Traffix Manager	SuperStack II Enterprise Monitor
Product Description	A tool for collecting and interpreting RMON and RMON2 protocol and application statistics	Multi-port, i960 processor-based RMON and ROMON2 probe expandable to 128MB
Operating Systems Support	SunOS, Sun Solaris, HP-UX, IBM AIX	N/A
Topology	Ethernet, Fast Ethernet, Token Ring, FDDI	Ethernet, Fast Ethernet, Token Ring, FDDI

N/A—Not applicable   INA—Information not available

Table Continues →

Network Management Tools

Manufacturer	3Com/Axon	3Com/Axon
Features	Collects and interprets RMON and RMON2 protocol and application statistics. Provides complete end-to-end visualization of enterprise traffic for performance management, trend analysis and troubleshooting. Flexible groupings support network tuning. Relational database stores historical information for reporting and trend analysis.	Collects RMON and RMON2 statistics, maintaining separate tables for each segment. Simultaneously tracks traffic and trends on multiple segments. Dense multi-segment capability. Configured with extra memory to accommodate RMON2 data collection at the network and application layers.
Hardware Requirements	Unix station with 64MB. 200-500 disk space	INA
Comments		Simultaneously monitors multiple networks of multiple media types
Warranty	INA	INA
Price	Transcend Manager $7,995	SuperStack II Enterprise Monitor with 16MB and 4-port Ethernet module starts at $7,790

Manufacturer	Alexander LAN Inc.	Alexander LAN Inc.	Alexander LAN, Inc.
Model	Dexter 2.10	Edna 1.20	NetCheck 2.11
Product Description	Reports the events that led up to the crash	Automatically diagnoses and restarts a crashed NetWare server	Preempts NetWare file server crashes by trapping illegal memory overwrites
Operating Systems Support	NetWare 3.x-4.x	NetWare 3.x-4.x	NetWare 3.x-4.x
Topology	N/A	N/A	N/A
Features	Diagnoses sequence of events that brought the server down. Allows viewing of symbolic information normally hidden or encrypted by Novell. Process (thread) symbolic stack walking.	Restarts a crashed server. Reports the cause of the crash. Runs Vrepair. Saves all details concerning the state of the server when it crashed. Uses Windows work station to view crash file. E-mails all crash detail for remote support.	Prevents many server crashes caused by memory corruption. Moves all NLMs and Drivers to ring 3, without invoking performance hit on OS. Reports name, address, location of NLM or Driver which overwrote. Optionally protects OS memory so corruption is prevented. Integrates with Dexter to provide Symbolic information.
Hardware Requirements	INA	10MB on DOS partition, 1MB on file server	INA
Comments	Free technical support. Free maintenance upgrades.	Free technical support. Free maintenance upgrades.	Free technical support. Free maintenance upgrades.
Warranty	Unconditional money–back guarantee within 30 days	Unconditional money–back guarantee within 30 days	Unconditional money–back guarantee within 30 days
Price	INA	INA	INA

Manufacturer	AG Group	AG Group
Model	EtherPeek™	TokenPeek™
Product Description	Ethernet packet-level network traffic and protocol analyzer to troubleshoot and debug multi-protocol networks	Token Ring packet-level network traffic and protocol analyzer to troubleshoot and debug multi-protocol networks
Operating Systems Support	Macintosh System 7.1, Windows 3.1, Windows 95	Macintosh System 6.0.5
Topology	Ethernet (10/100)	Token Ring
Features	Locates hardware and software faults. Name-to-address mapping. Event trigger and filtering mechanism. Identifies routing and addressing problems. Decodes protocols.	Locates hardware and software faults. Name-to-address mapping. Event trigger and filtering mechanism. Identifies routing and addressing problems. Decodes protocols.

N/A—Not applicable   INA—Information not available

Network Management Tools ∎

Manufacturer	AG Group	AG Group
Hardware Requirements	Mac. 68030 25Mhz. 8MB RAM.	Mac SE/30
Comments	AG supported Ethernet interface	AG supported Token Ring interface
Warranty	90 days	90 days
Price	$995	$995

Manufacturer	AG Group	AG Group
Model	Skyline™	LocalPeek™
Product Description	Multi-segment Ethernet network: A traffic, archiving, alert, and analysis system for heterogeneous networks	LocalTalk packet-level network traffic and protocol analyzer to troubleshoot and debug multi-protocol networks
Operating Systems Support	Macintosh System 7.1	Macintosh System 6.0.5
Topology	Ethernet	LocalTalk
Features	Threshold violation alerts. Simultaneous monitoring of local and remote segments. Historical and real-time traffic analysis. Measures server and router performance. Quantifies Internet usage. Tracks peak traffic times and loads.	Locates hardware and software faults. Name-to-address mapping. Event trigger and filtering mechanism. Identifies routing and addressing problems. Decodes protocols.
Hardware Requirements	Mac. 68030 25MHz. 8MB RAM.	Mac SE/30
Comments	AG supported Ethernet interface	AG supported LocalTalk interface
Warranty	90 days	90 days
Price	$795	$395

Manufacturer	AG Group	AG Group
Model	NetMeter™	NetWatchman™
Product Description	Real-time multimedia network monitoring: displays specified live network traffic statistics from multiple Ethernet segments	AppleTalk network early-warning system: monitors and reports on all AppleTalk devices
Operating Systems Support	Macintosh System 7.1	Macintosh System 6.0.5
Topology	Ethernet	AppleTalk
Features	Simultaneously displays live network traffic statistics. Uses instruments, movies, sounds, speech or graphics. Simultaneously displays local and remote segments. Focuses on specific nodes, protocols, subprotocols, and conversations. Monitors IP, client/server, NBP, HTTP, et. al.	Logs irregular activity. Issues warnings based on specified alerts. Monitors changes in network status.
Hardware Requirements	Mac. 68030 25MHz	Mac SE/30
Comments	AG supported Ethernet interface	
Warranty	90 days	90 days
Price	$395	$295

N/A—Not applicable   INA—Information not available

Table Continues →

■ Network Management Tools

Manufacturer	AG Group	BMC
Model	Nok Nok A/S™	Neptune Pro
Product Description	AppleShare File Server Manager: remotely monitors and manages multiple AppleShare servers from any Mac on the network	Performance and optimization hardware for NetWare and Microsoft NT. Monitors, tracks and reports data that analyzes server performance.
Operating Systems Support	Macintosh 7	NetWare 3.1x and 4.1x, and NT 3.51
Topology	AppleShare	Ethernet
Features	Remote administration capabilities. Improves Apple-Share security. Identifies anonymous guest logins. Instant notification of connections. Auto-disconnect capabilities.	Concurrently monitors unlimited number of NetWare and NT servers. Graphically displays file server statistics in real-time. Viewing of the servers configuration data.
Hardware Requirements	AppleShare 3.0 on any MAC. 4MB RAM.	PC 486 or Pentium. 32MB RAM. 10MB disk space. Super VGA RAM.
Comments		
Warranty	90 day	90 day
Price	$249	$895+

Manufacturer	BindView Development Corporation	Bull Information Systems
Model	BindView/NOSadmin for NetWare 4	ISM/ Open Master-Trans Master
Product Description		Monitors and manages heterogeneous networks
Operating Systems Support	PC-Windows, O/S2, Windows NT, DOS, NetWare 3.x	Unix, AIX, Solaris, Integrity, Irix, HP-UX(96), NT(96)
Topology	Ethernet	Ethernet, Token Ring, FDDI, X25, DSA
Features	Security analysis & rights/trustee analysis. Hidden object, disk space, and Server/NLM analysis. NDS database reporting and partition/replica analysis. Spreadsheet and graphing capabilities. Baselining, exporting, and referencing facilities. Query and filtering capabilities.	Network monitoring and configuration. Independent from management protocol: supports SNMP, CMIP, X25, FDDI-SMT, DSA, SNA, legacy protocols. Integrates 3rd party applications.
Hardware Requirements	INA	128MB RAM. 2GB Disk. 17" monitor.
Comments	Schedules reports during off-peak hours	Network management runs on Unix. Includes enterprise management
Warranty	1 year	2 year
Price	$695 (Console) $2,995 (5 user console pack) $595 (Single server license) $2,795 (5 server license pack) $695 (Single tree license) $1,195 (100 user object license)	$10,000+

Manufacturer	Cabletron Systems	Cinco Networks, Inc.
Model	SPECTRUM Enterprise Manager	NetXRay
Product Description	Enterprise Management Platform—Client/Server distributed architecture	Windows 95/NT 32-bit software protocol analyzer
Operating Systems Support	Unix, IBM AIX, SGI IRIX, and WindowsNT	Windows 95, Windows NT
Topology	Supports standards based management of LAN, WAN, PBX, SNA	Ethernet (10/100), Token Ring, FDDI, 100VG AnyLan

N/A—Not applicable   INA—Information not available

Network Management Tools ■

Manufacturer	**Cabletron Systems**		**Cinco Networks, Inc.**
Features	Multi-vendor, multi-protocol network management. Alarm suppression/fault isolation through use of inductive Modeling Technology. Client/server architecture. True distributed capability fault tolerance.		Full Windows95/NT GUI. High performance packet capture. Custom decodes available. Data export.
Hardware Requirements	Minimum requirements include 96MB RAM for server/ 64MB RAM for graph. Contact local representative form more details.		PC 486 or higher, 12+MB RAM. 640 x 480, 16-color monitor. NDIS 3.1 32-bit driver.
Comments	Integrated 3rd party application support for network, systems and applications management. Cabletron resells BMC Software's PATROL and Matrix's Win-Watch for tightly integrated systems and applications management.		Available in single segment or multi-segment versions
Warranty	90 day		1 year
Price	Base price is $15,000		$995

Manufacturer	**Concord Communication**		**Concord Communication**
Model	Network Health- WebLink		Network Health- Frame Relay
Product Description	WebLink is a Web–viewing system allowing Intranet access of Concord's network performance reports.		Allows users to analyze individual Frame Relay circuits and identify cause of traffic congestion
Operating Systems Support	Solaris 1.1.2 (SunOS 4.1.4), Solaris 2.4 (SunOS 5.4), Solaris 2.5 (SunOS 5.5), HP-UX 9.5 or 9.7		Solaris 1.1.2 (SunOS 4.1.4), Solaris 2.4 (SunOS 5.4), Solaris 2.5 (SunOS 5.5), HP-UX 9.5 or 9.7
Topology	Ethernet, Token Ring, FDDI, CDDI		Ethernet, Token Ring, FDDI, CDDI
Features	System includes WebServer scheduling, HTML conversion software, and built-in security. Snapshot view of network traffic. Automates service level reporting and domain management. Automated reporting and analysis.		Implements SmartScan Technology that collects data on individual Frame Relay PVCs. Homogenizes data and produces color reports. Automated reporting. Designed specifically for Frame Relay networks.
Hardware Requirements	Sun SPARCstation or HP-UX workstation		Sun SPARCstation or HP-UX workstation
Comments			
Warranty	6 month, includes updates and phone support		6 month, includes updates and phone support
Price	$10,000		$8,995

Manufacturer	**Concord Communication**		**Concord Communication**
Model	Network Health- Spectrum		Network Health- Bay Dialogs
Product Description	Multi-level integration of Concord's Network Health and Cabltron's SPECTRUM Manager		Automated reporting is integrated with Bay Network's RMON-RMON2 analysis of their Advanced Analyzer.
Operating Systems Support	Solaris 1.1.2 (SunOS 4.1.4), Solaris 2.4 (SunOS 5.4), Solaris 2.5 (SunOS 5.5), HP-UX 9.5 or 9.7		Solaris 1.1.2 (SunOS 4.1.4), Solaris 2.4 (SunOS 5.4), Solaris 2.5 (SunOS 5.5), HP-UX 9.5 or 9.7
Topology	Ethernet, Token Ring, FDDI, CDDI		Ethernet, Token Ring, FDDI, CDDI
Features	Launch Network Health from SPECTRUM and click on events on the SPECTRUM map. Captures names of managed devices used by SPECTRUM. Automated reporting and analysis.		Analyzes network layer traffic to identify users, departments, and locations. Allows network managers to redeploy network resources. Provides cost allocation or "charge back" information. Automated reporting and analysis.
Hardware Requirements	Sun SPARCstation or HP-UX workstation		Sun SPARCstation or HP-UX workstation
Comments			
Warranty	6 month, includes updates and phone support		6 month, includes updates and phone support
Price	$6,995		$14,995 for 25 interfaces

N/A—Not applicable   INA—Information not available

Table Continues →

■ Network Management Tools

Manufacturer	Concord Communication	Cylink
Model	Network Health-2.5	Securemanager
Product Description	Automated performance reporting and analysis software for enterprise-wide networks	Security management certificate authority, management of security device VPN
Operating Systems Support	Solaris 1.1.2 (SunOS 4.1.4), Solaris 2.4 (SunOS 5.4), Solaris 2.5 (SunOS 5.5, HP-UX 9.5 or 9.7	Solaris 2.4 or Solaris 2.5
Topology	Ethernet, Token Ring, FDDI, CDDI	SUN Sparc dependent-ALL
Features	Distributed data collection. Exception reporting. Domain reporting.	Advanced security policy control. Drag and drop. SNMP based. Hierarchy of maps. Scalable to thousands of devices. Configuration management and monitoring of security devices.
Hardware Requirements	Sun SPARCstation or HP-UX workstation	SUN Sparc 5 or better. 64MB RAM. 500MB disk. Color monitor.
Comments		
Warranty	INA	90 day
Price	$9,995	$10,000

Manufacturer	Digital Equipment Corporation	Fotec
Model	clearVISN network management applications	Fodoc/Wiredoc
Product Description	Network management suite of applications: stack manager (all stackables); VLAN manager (all chassis); VLAN manager (VLANs on switches/DEChub 900); recovery manager (backup/restore); RMON manager (Ethernet, Token Ring, FDDI, WAN); clearVISN router manager (Digital, Cisco, Bay, 3Com)	Cable plant management software for fiber optics/copper wire networks
Operating Systems Support	Windows 95, Windows NT on Intel, Alpha and Unix	DOS
Topology	Ethernet, Token Ring, FDDI	All
Features	Policy–based network management. Distributed intelligent agents. Common installation, registration, user interface. Multivendor legacy management.	Tracks all fiber, cable, connection, hardware. Reports on cables connections and paths. Stores ten million datapoints.
Hardware Requirements	Intel PC-80486, 66MHz or higher. IBM-compatible PC. Color VGA or SVGA monitor. Minimum 16MB RAM. CD-ROM drive. Minimum 25MB of disk space. 16-bit Ethernet NIC.	PC 386. 4MB RAM. 4MB hard drive.
Comments		Help installer manage connections. Written specifically for fiber optic cable. Can test data on each individual fiber. Can help create parts lists.
Warranty	90 day	1 year
Price	Stack Manager-$495 MultiChassis Manager-$995 VLAN Manager $1,495 Recovery Manager $495C RMON Manager $2,995 Router Manager $4,995	$500 Wiredoc is free w/Fodoc

N/A—Not applicable   INA—Information not available

Network Management Tools ■

Manufacturer	**Hewlett-Packard**	**Ipswitch, Inc.**
Model	HP OpenView-Network Node Manager, v.4.0	WhatsUp
Product Description	A family of products and solutions for managing networks, systems, applications and databases from the desktop PC to the mainframe. HP Network Node Manager is the "managing" application, designed to manage distributed, multivendor networks and systems, from workgroups and management domains to complete enterprises.	Graphical network monitoring tool for TCP/IP Networks. Monitors any device on the Internet, corporate intranet. Alerts the user via alarm, pager, or e-mail.
Operating Systems Support	HP—HP-UX 9.x, 10.01, 10.10 including X Windows and OSF/Motif or Sun—Solaris 2.3, or 2.4	Windows NT, Windows 3.51 or greater, Windows 95
Topology	Ethernet, Token Ring, others	All
Features	Hundreds of HP OpenView Solution Partner Applications for customizing management solutions. Scalable distributed architecture and dispersed collection stations. Continuous network device monitoring. Automated device discovery and layout. GUI with Pan and Zoom. Customizable toolbar, map and symbol menus. Event subsystem and filtering. Flat file database or relational, SQL database (Oracle or CA-Ingres).	Automatic detection and display of all connected network elements in a subset. Graphical map display and status of network elements. Continual connection confirmation.
Hardware Requirements	Bit mapped display or X-terminal color graphics:1024X768 minimum resolution; 6 color planes minimum (8 recommended). HP—HP 9000 servers and workstations. 64MB recommended (32MB min. for Entry Network Node Manager); 1.2GB free disk space: 85MB plus 120MB swap space LAN/Link for HP 9000 ARPA Services/9000. Sun—Sun SPARC stations 5, 10, 20, SPARCclassics and SunServer including multiprocessors (threads not supported). 64MB recommended (32MB minimum for Entry Network Node Manager;1.2GB free disk space: 130MB plus 120MB swap space	Intel 386, 486, or Pentium. Power PC. DEC Alpha.
Comments	The recommendations are the minimum requirements for managing a 2,500 node network. Management of larger networks require more RAM and swap space.	Monitors: hierarchical networks, "unmanageable" network devices, specific remote services, predefined services (WWW, SMTP, POP3, FTP, Telnet, or News); and hubs, hosts, servers, et. al.
Warranty	90 day	30-day money-back guarantee
Price	$15,995 license per user $4,995 license for Entry Node Mgr. $300 documentation $25 distribution media	$145

Manufacturer	**ISOTRO Network Management**	**Knozall Systems, Inc.**
Model	Net ID	NLMAuto 1.31F
Product Description	A multi-user database application so that network managers can manage IP addresses and domain names from anywhere on the network	Server task scheduler certified by Novell. Can load and unload NLMs, initiate NCF files, and command line inputs. Sends direct commands to server console.
Operating Systems Support	Windows 3.X, Windows 95, Windows NT, Solaris 2.4, HP-UX 10	DOS, Windows 3.x, Windows 95, NetWare 3.x or higher
Topology	TCP/IP Networks	Any IPX compatible
Features	Manage addresses and names for multiple class A, B, and C networks. Validation rules eliminate duplicate addresses and names. Eliminates subnet mask calculators and address plan errors.	Logically control tasks on a singer server. Unlimited jobs active concurrently. Control interactive tasks on up to 5 client workstations. Schedule jobs based on events as well as time. Launch job templates from any workstation command line.
Hardware Requirements	PC 386SX or higher. SPARC 5 or higher	PC 386 IBM or compatible. 256K RAM.

N/A—Not applicable   INA—Information not available

Table Continues →

■ Network Management Tools

Manufacturer	ISOTRO Network Management	Knozall Systems, Inc.
Comments	Download free evaluation copy from WWW.ISOTRO.COM	
Warranty	30 days	Unlimited tech support via phone or online free
Price	$9,500	$395

Manufacturer	Knozall Systems, Inc.	Knozall Systems, Inc.
Model	NLM Auto Professional 3	NL Merlin 3
Product Description	NLM that allows you to schedule and control local and remote server and workstations tasks	Can manage all servers and unlimited clients on LAN's and non-connected remote networks. Multi-threaded jobs and console commands. Schedule job based on value of identifiers. Background mode transfer files.
Operating Systems Support	DOS, Windows 3.x, Windows 95, NetWare 3.x or higher	DOS, Windows 3.x or higher, Windows 95, NetWare 3.x or higher
Topology	Any IPX compatible	Any IPX compatible
Features	Job scheduling on remote dial-up servers. Users can schedule jobs based on the condition of identifiers. Users can schedule jobs based on time since last run. Files can be transferred to workstations in background mode. Commands: Make directory on NetWare file server, modify file, purge, rename, remove directory, synchronize directory.	Write NLMerlin scripts-same power as intelligent NLM's you can run from any server. Use Basic or REXX. Control interactive tasks on unlimited servers and workstations. Schedule jobs based on events and time. Use with other network analysis and warning systems to automate responses. Transfer files in background mode. Run jobs or commands simultaneously. Manage jobs scheduling on remote dial-up servers.\nRecord the keystrokes of any job and paste. Help solve its own problems with the MDEBUG directory.
Hardware Requirements	INA	IBM PC or compatible 386 or higher. 360KB or server for administration. 174KB on target server. 4KB on each workstation used as a target agent.
Comments		
Warranty	Free unlimited tech support via phone or online	Free unlimited tech support via phone or online
Price	INA	$2,395 for one administration agent, 2 server agents and 20 client agents

Manufacturer	Knozall Systems, Inc.	Knozall Systems, Inc.
Model	File Auditor	ZipWiz 1
Product Description	Server-based tool that tracks all file and directory activity. The administrator may select the activity by file, directory, user, and specific action. Data selected is maintained in an Audit log file. Custom reports are generated from filters that the administrator selects.	PKZip compatible server compression utility
Operating Systems Support	DOS, Windows 3.x, Windows 95, NetWare 3.x or higher	DOS, Windows 3.x, Windows 95, NetWare 3.x or higher
Topology	Any IPX compatible	Any IPX compatible
Features	Monitor file activities. Monitor directory activities. Selectively block access to files. Initiate scripts in NLMAuto Prom. Notify individuals or groups of specified file activity. Include or exclude files, directories or users. Define maximum Audit log file size. Create custom reports based on all file and directory activity. Export report information to other applications.	Users at their workstations can unzip files that were compressed on the server files. Network administrators have the ability to set rules for file compression. ZipWiz will keep track of all the extended attributes of a file. Integrated with FileWizard 3's HSM capabilities. ZipWiz can migrate and compress files to another location. Retrieve and decompress are automatic as needed.
Hardware Requirements	IBM PC or compatible. 2MB RAM	IBM PC or compatible

N/A—Not applicable   INA—Information not available

Network Management Tools ■

Manufacturer	Knozall Systems, Inc.	Knozall Systems, Inc.
Comments		
Warranty	Free tech support via phone or online	Free tech support via phone or online
Price	$395/server	$395/server

Manufacturer	Knozall Systems, Inc.	Lanworks Technologies
Model	FileWizard 3	BootWare Manager
Product Description	Server space analysis and management tool with Windows front end, customizable HSM, PKZip compatible compression on the server. Network administrators can create management strategies to automatically carry out desired actions.	Boot file management software runs under Windows 3.1, Windows 95, or Windows NT
Operating Systems Support	DOS, Windows 3.x, Windows 95, NetWare 3.x or higher.	NetWare 3.x or higher
Topology	Any IPX compatible	Ethernet
Features	Reclaim unused, duplicate, outdated or wasted space. Customizable HSM. Utilize your currect hardware investment. Track the effectiveness of your HSM strategy. Stop space cell crisis.Graph and report flexibility. Records actions taken so users can access their files w/o supervisor.	Edit or update users bootfile. Search and sort by various parameters. Manage boot files across multiple servers. Diagnostics. IP number management. Drag and drop.
Hardware Requirements	NetWare 3.x or higher workstation. Windows 3.1 or higher. 2MB RAM.	Boot ROMs in workstations. Windows 3.1 or higher. 386 PC or higher. 4MB system memory. 5MB free hard disk space.
Comments		
Warranty	Free tech support via phone or online	90 day
Price	$695/server	$259

Manufacturer	Lanworks Technologies Inc.	Markham Computer Corp. Danware Data A/S	Microsoft Corporation
Model	BootWare	NetOp for Windows v5.2	Systems Management Server 1.2
Product Description	Boot ROMs enable PCs to boot from server rather than local drives	Remote control software	Enterprise level, centralized management of networked Windows-based systems. Scalable architecture with HW and SW inventory, and SW distribution.
Operating Systems Support	All with following protocols :NCP/ IPX, TCP/IP, RPL	Windows NT, Windows95, Windows 3.X, OS/2 (1.3 and higher), and DOS	MS-DOS, Windows, Win95/NT, OS/2, NetWare, Macintosh, LAN Manager, and others
Topology	Arcnet, Ethernet, Token-Ring, Fast Ethernet, Wireless	Ethernet, Token Ring	Ethernet, Token Ring, FDDI, ISDN, SNA, X.25, Async and Internet
Features	Multi-Protocol ROMs. Mcafee boot sector virus software embedded. Update, edit troubleshoot boot files centrally. Upgrade entire network in minutes.	Remotely accesses and controls screen, mouse, and keypad. Simultaneous viewing of multiple PCs and platform. File transfer and chat; also cross platform. Security maintained with multiple-level passwords and access confirmation/notification functions. Print redirection, remote boot, screen blanking, inactivity time-out, et. al.	Integrated multi-site administration. Drag and drop. Integration with network management consoles using SNMP trap forwarding of SMS events.

N/A—Not applicable   INA—Information not available

Table Continues →

■ Network Management Tools

Manufacturer	Lanworks Technologies Inc.	Markham Computer Corp. Danware Data A/S	Microsoft Corporation
Hardware Requirements	PC 486 (66MHz or higher). 32MB RAM. 50MB disk space. 17" monitor.	IBM PS/PC with an 80386 processor or higher	Pentium or RISC based processor supported by NT Server 3.51+. 32MB RAM min. 100MB free disk space on an NTFS partition. Access to any CD-ROM drive with Windows NT Server 3.51+. Microsoft SQL Server 6.0+.
Comments		NetBIOS, IPX/SPX, Asynchronous, ISDN, TCP/IP compatible	Integration modules available for HP OpenView, CA-Unicenter, Tivoli TME and Novadigm EDM from respective manufacturers
Warranty	90 day	60 day	INA
Price	$39	$295+ (For Guest/Host combo)	$925 per server + 5 managed clients; additional clients: $275 per 5 clients

Manufacturer	Multima Corporation	NBase Communications Inc.
Model	NetKeeper Configuration Manager version 5.1	Megavision
Product Description	A network management tool to create, modify or update workstation configurations remotely through the LAN. Automatically tracks hardware, software and configuration files on LANs, WANs as well as on stand-alone computers.	Work Group Management, Software for NBase MegaSwitch and MegaStack, family of Ethernet products
Operating Systems Support	Windows 3.1, Windows 95, Windows NT, IBM, Sun	MS Windows, Unix, MP Openview, SUN OS
Topology	Ethernet	Ethernet/Fast Ethernet (10- and 100MB)
Features	Automatically collects and creates a database of hardware and software configuration files. Creates a library of files such as autoexec.bat.config.sys.shell.efg.device drivers.network shells. User defined inventories of hardware, software, and configuration files. Tracks maintenance data.	Multi platform capability. Full SNMP. User friendly. Graphical User Interface running MS Windows. Unix.
Hardware Requirements	An IBM PC or compatible computer or an IBM Personal System/2 or compatible computer. PC DOS or MS DOS version 3.0 or higher (or equivalent). Windows 3.1 or above OS/2 2.0 or above. 6M RAM.	Windows version: IBM PC 486 DX or Compatible, 3.1, 95, NT—8MB RAM, Novell NMS—16MB RAM. Unix version, Sun-16 MB RAM + CG-3 W101 Graphics Adapter.
Comments	The program includes many standard reports; useful tool for disaster recovery.	
Warranty	45 day, free technical support for 6 months	1 year
Price	$499 (per 100 users/per server)	$495 and up

Manufacturer	NetPlus Software Inc.	NetSuite
Model	OnQueue and OnQueue-M	Professional Design
Product Description	Allows for offloading of jobs through distributed processing and task scheduling. Captures results to logfile and prioritizes task queues for selective servicing in single or multiple Novell server networks.	Intelligent physical network design, documentation, and asset management
Operating Systems Support	DOS, Windows, NetWare	Windows 3.1, Windows 95, Windows NT
Topology	Ethernet	Ethernet (10/100), Token Ring, FDDI, CDDI, ATM, WAN

N/A—Not applicable   INA—Information not available

Network Management Tools ■

Manufacturer	**NetPlus Software Inc.**	**NetSuite**
Features	Task examples include nightly virus scans, unattended backups, resource sharing, downsizing, data uploads/downloads, database searches, language compilations and links, mainframe style batch processing, scientific/statistical analyses, and more	Network design validation. Graphic drag and drop. Bills-of-materials. Over 2700 intelligent network devices in library. Network asset reporting, Import and Export; Network protocol advanced diagramming.
Hardware Requirements	PC 386 or faster	PC 486 (66MHz or higher). 16MB RAM. 25MB disk.
Comments	OnQueue-M users can also submit jobs involving data stored on one NetWare File Server with an application installed on the same or different NetWare File Server.	Product and device updates (100-300/mo.) via subscription
Warranty	90 day	30 day
Price	OnQueue—$495 OnQueue-M—$695	$795

Manufacturer	**NetSuite**	**Novell Inc.**
Model	Design View	ManageWise 2.1
Product Description	HTML Publisher for network designs and documentation	Manages the entire network through NetWare and Windows NT server management, network traffic analysis, desktop management, automated network inventory, remote control, virus protection, and software management
Operating Systems Support	Windows 3.1, Windows 95, Windows NT	Windows 3.1, Windows for Workgroups 3.11, Windows 95
Topology	Ethernet (10/100), Token Ring, FDDI, CDDI, ATM, WAN	Ethernet (10MB and 100MB)
Features	One button publishing of network designs to Intranet or Internet. Embedded device photographs. Multi-level diagrams with maps, floorplans.	Monitors and analyzes the network for network optimization. Decodes all major network protocols. Creates diagrams of the network configuration. Automatically collects desktop hardware and software inventory. Automatically detects network problems. Provides virus protection for the LAN. Central collection of real-time and long-term network performance trends. RMON compliant monitoring. SNMP-based communications.
Hardware Requirements	PC 486 (66MHz or higher). 16MB RAM. 5MB disk.	Intel1486 or Pentium microprocessor-based PC. 16MB RAM. 45MB RAM to 60MB free hard disk space.
Comments	Requires NetSuite	Integrates with Unix-based enterprise management consoles. An open solution with over 100 snap-in applications provided by third party vendors.
Warranty	30 day	90 day
Price	$295	ManageWise starts at $795 for a 5-user license

Manufacturer	**Optimal Networks**	**Plaintree Systems**
Model	Optimal Internet Monitor	WaveView
Product Description	A 32 bit Windows-based application that monitors Internet usage or a corporate LAN; summarizes the traffic in numerous displays, maps, and reports.	A graphical, SNMP compliant, switch management application
Operating Systems Support	Windows 3.1, Windows 95, Windows NT	HP OpenView for Windows, Novell, and Castle Rock's SNMP
Topology	Ethernet, Token Ring, FDDI	Ethernet, FDDI, VG
Features	Keeps track of Internet traffic. Real-time and historical views. View Internet.	SNMP compliant, MIB Browser. Auto-discovery—locates and identifies wavejumps. Alarms. Tool and screen tips. Front panel access. Control center

N/A—Not applicable   INA—Information not available

Table Continues →

■ Network Management Tools

Manufacturer	Optimal Networks		Plaintree Systems
Hardware Requirements	PC 486 100MHz or higher. 16 MB RAM. 15MB disk space. 17" monitor.		IBM PC or compatible with Intel 80386. 8MB RAM (16 rec.). 3MB HD. VG monitor.
Comments			Network connection with IP address, Winsock compatible TCP/IP protocol stack
Warranty	INA		INA
Price	$1,500		$1,195

Manufacturer	Plexcom, Inc.	Plexcom, Inc.	Performance Technologies Inc.
Model	PlexView 3.0	PlexView/ UX	StarGazer
Product Description	SNMP Network Management Application software for Windows 3.1, Windows 95, or Windows NT	SNMP Network management GUI that operates from HP OpenView or Sun Net Manager	Supports on-site and remote diagnostics, and on-line network traffic management with complete security using its simple drag and drop GUI interface
Operating Systems Support	Windows 3.1, Windows 95, or Windows NT	Sun OS, Solaris, HP-UX	Windows 3.1 or later, SUN O/S, Solaris 2.x
Topology	Ethernet, Token Ring	Ethernet, Token Ring	Ethernet
Features	SNMP compatible, MIB browser. RMON, and Private MIB support. Vendor specific GUIs. Multi-level security	GUI for Plexcom Intelligent LAN hub products. Per port statistics, activity status, security and control. Can operate as a stand-alone application	Supports Virtual Switch Groups and firewalls. Dynamic, 3-D graphic display real-time performance statistics. Extensive network configuration/traffic control and management features. Network diagramming/ topology at a glance. Filters IP, Novell™IPX and DECnet™ Appletalk™, and other protocols. SNMP I and II compatible.
Hardware Requirements	486DX-2 or better. 16MB RAM. 20MB hard disk.	Sun Sparc, HP 9000	Windows—386 or higher. 4MB of RAM. 5MB disk space (or) OSF/ Motif. 10MB swap space. 30MB disk space.
Comments	Compiles 3rd party MIBs	Integrates multi-vendor environments	
Warranty	1 year	1 year	1 year
Price	$1,195	$4,995	$695

Manufacturer	Preferred Systems, Inc.		Preferred Systems, Inc.
Model	AuditWare for NDS		DS Standard NDS Manager
Product Description	A Windows-based, advanced NDS reporting and security analysis tool. Using the reporting capabilities of AuditWare for NDS, network managers can generate comparison, analysis, security and documentation reports.		A Windows-based, off-line, NDS management tool. Using DS standard, network managers alter a back-end database, not the "live" network.
Operating Systems Support	Windows 3.1 and Windows 95		Windows 3.1 and Windows 95
Topology	Ethernet		Ethernet
Features	Time-line Reports. Security Management. NDS Analysis. Tree Documentation. Point-and-Click objects profile reports. Object list manager. Object rights expert. "The Assistant" Online Security Tutorial.		Off-line, Risk-free "Safety Net." Global Search-and-Replace.-Copy Object. Enhanced Reporting. Import. View Import/Export. Object Rights Expert. "The Assistant" online NetWare 4 and NDS Tutorial. Inherited property reporting.
Hardware Requirements	CPU 386/33 or higher. 8MB RAM or higher. 17MB hard disk space or higher.		CPU 386/33 or higher. 8MB RAM or higher. 17MB hard disk space or higher.

N/A—Not applicable   INA—Information not available

Network Management Tools ■

Manufacturer	Preferred Systems, Inc.		Preferred Systems, Inc.
Comments	True off-line reporting engine		
Warranty	30–day money-back guarantee		30-day money-back guarantee
Price	$695-$5,995		$695-$5,995

Manufacturer	RAD Network Devices Inc.	RAD Network Devices Inc.	Seagate
Model	Conkig Master	MultiVu 10V/WIN/6000	Seagate Desktop Management Suite
Product Description	SNMP Based Management	SNMP add-on software	Enables network/systems managers to perform automated asset management, software distribution, and remote administration from a single administrator's toolbar
Operating Systems Support	Windows 3.1, Windows 95, or Windows NT	Sun, IBM, Windows 3.1	Windows 3.1, Windows 95, Windows NT, DOS
Topology	Ethernet	Ethernet	Novell NetWare, Banyan VINES, Microsoft LAN manager, Windows NT, Windows for Workgroups, IBM LAN server, AT&T StarLAN, DEC Pathworks, Windows 95, and more
Features	Full SNMP management of RAD equipment	Full SNMP management of RAD equipment	Sold as point or suite solutions. Microsoft ODBC level 2 SQL database. Common automatic installation from a single CD ROM. GUI interfaces. Compatible with major network and desktop operating systems. Free StatRack monitoring tool.
Hardware Requirements	PC 386	INA	IBM PC, XT, PS.2 or compatible. Windows 3.1. 8MB of RAM.
Comments	All that is needed is a Windows PC with IP		
Warranty	1 year	1 year	30-day money back guarantee. Free unlimited support to registered users.
Price	$595	$995—$3,995	$1,495 for first 50 users $1,395 for each additional user

Manufacturer	SilCom Technology	Triticom
Model	TR\Tracer for Windows	MasteRMON
Product Description	Tracks all traffic on a workgroup or departmental Token Ring LAN for troubleshooting, evaluating, and planning	Distributed LAN traffic monitor
Operating Systems Support	Windows 3.1, Windows for Workgroups, Windows 95	Windows 3.1
Topology	Token Ring	Ethernet, Token Ring
Features	Alarms triggered when user thresholds are reached. Data and graphs can be exported into popular PC-based applications.	Monitors traffic levels. Creates reports. Alarm notification. Graphing capabilities.
Hardware Requirements	PC 486 (33MHz or higher). 8MB RAM. 8MB hard disk.	486 or higher. 8MB RAM.
Comments		
Warranty	30-day money-back guarantee	60 day
Price	$399	$595

N/A—Not applicable   INA—Information not available

Table Continues →

■ Network Management Tools

Manufacturer	Triticom	UB Networks
Model	DecodeRMON	Net Director Enterprise
Product Description	Distributed protocol analyzer	Management that includes FocusView graphical device applications for configuration, fault, and performance management
Operating Systems Support	Windows 3.1	HP OpenView and IBM NetView, SunOS, Solaris, HP-UX, OS/2, AIX
Topology	Ethernet, Token Ring	All topologies
Features	Captures and decodes traffic from RMON probe	Automatic discovery and mapping of Internet Protocol (IP) devices. Automatic mapping updating. Consistent graphical user interface.
Hardware Requirements	486 or higher. 8MB RAM.	SUN Sparcstation 5, HP9000 WkSt 715, RS 6000. 64MB RAM. 500MB hard drive min.
Comments		
Warranty	60 day	90 day
Price	$845	$5,995

Manufacturer	UB Networks	UB Networks	UB Networks
Model	Traffic Tuner	Net Director for Workgroups	EMPower Automated Device Management Module
Product Description	An intelligent application that provides advanced configuration and performance management of the Port Mobile Ethernet Concentrator Module for the GeoLAN/500 hub.	Workgroups suite of management applications that include FocusView graphical device applications for configuration, fault, and performance management	Designed to allow GeoLAN hubs to manage themselves and the network
Operating Systems Support	SunOS, Solaris, HP-UX, AIX	Windows for Workgroups 3.11, Windows 3.1, Windows 95	N/A
Topology	All topologies	All topologies	Ethernet, Token Ring, ATM, Fast Ethernet
Features	Automatic discovery and mapping of Internet Protocol (IP) devices. Automatic mapping updating. Consistent graphical user interface.	Small enterprise or department management up to 1000 nodes. Online NetAdvice. IP address management automates assignment and device configuration using BootP and TFTP.	Policy-based management. Event management system. In-hub event processing system allowing applications to respond in real-time to heal network. SNMP agent and manager runs on real-time.
Hardware Requirements		486 or Pentium, 33MHz or higher. 8MB RAM. 10MB hard disk.	
Comments		Net Director is scalable to support workgroup networks.	Allows network manager to proactively manage the network
Warranty	90 day	90 day	90 day
Price	$3,995	$2,449	$5,995–$7,995

Manufacturer	U.S.A. Communications	U.S.A. Communications Corporation
Model	Network/Sentry Plus	Teleboot TB-250/450
Product Description	Watchdog	It can remotely "reboot" any locked-up system via telephone or modem with complete security.
Operating Systems Support	DOS or as a DOS application running over Windows 95 and OS/2	All
Topology	IPX/SPX	All

N/A—Not applicable   INA—Information not available

Network Management Tools ■

Manufacturer	U.S.A. Communications	U.S.A. Communications Corporation
Features	Continuously monitors servers and "beeps" pager in case of a lock-up. Can notify pager when system is rebooted. Up to 3 pager numbers can be entered per device.	Access any of 5 outlets individually (TB-450 only). 10,000 combination security code. Reboot via telephone or modem. Designed to work even if the modem answers. Supports leading communication software.
Hardware Requirements	Any dedicated IBM PC, XT, AT or compatible with a network card installed. Any numeric or alpha pager.	INA
Comments	Versions available to monitor 5, 20 and "unlimited" number of devices	
Warranty	1 year	1 year
Price	$139 (5 server) $199 (20 server) $299 (Unlimited)	$249 $449

Manufacturer	Wandel & Goltermann, Inc.	Whittaker Xyplex
Model	WG DOMAIN™ Manager	Control Point
Product Description	Icon-based management software supplies centralized SNMP/RMON analysis tools for WG Domain Probes or any RMON-compliant agent	SNMP-based network management application that manage Xyplex's routers, access servers, et. al.
Operating Systems Support	SunOS, Solaris, SunNet, MS Windows 3.1, HP-UX, OpenView, IBM AIX, NetView, Unix	HP OpenView, Windows/ Unix, SunNet Manager/ SunOS and Solaris
Topology	Ethernet(10/100), Token Ring, FDDI/CDDI, and WAN	Ethernet
Features	Integrated scripting for unattended monitoring; Diagnostics with automated troubleshooting. Seven layered, color-coded protocol decode for all major protocol stacks. Includes accounting, long/short-term trend analysis, and client/server applications.	RMON support across a 9 group. SNMP compatible. Templates and aggregate feature. Fault tolerant capabilities. MIB I support. Remote configurations. Event notification on-screen, e-mail, pager, and fax.
Hardware Requirements	SPARCstation, AT&T GIS, RS6000, HP9000 with 24MB RAM or higher. 386/486 PC with 4MB RAM.	INA
Comments	Diagnostics architecture allows real-time isolation of problems	
Warranty	1 year	
Price	$2,995–$4,995	$4,995

N/A—Not applicable   INA—Information not available

End ■

■ Software Distribution Management Tools

Manufacturer	Attachmate	Computer Associates
Model	NetWizard 3.1	Unicenter software delivery option
O/S Compatibility	DOS, Windows 3.1, Windows for Wordgroups, Windows 95, Windows NT, Macintosh	Windows 95, Windows NT, Windows 3.x, PC-MS/DOS, OS/2, HP-UX, Sun-Solaris, IBM AIX, Novell NetWare
Network Compatibility	NetWare, LAN Manager, NT Advanced Server, Banyan VINES, LANtastic, others	Novell NetWare, LAN Manager, LANserver, LANtastic
Protocols Supported	TCP/IP, IPX, NetBIOS, NetBEUI, IPC	TCP/IP, IPP, IPX, NetBios, NETBEUI
Application Types	16-bit, 32-bit	16-bit, 32-bit
User Initiation	Yes	Yes
Remote administration	Yes	Scheduling, troubleshooting, inventory
Scheduling	Yes	Through calendars, predessors, resources, etc.
Undo	Multiple, on demand	Multiple, on demand, scheduled
Metering	Yes	Yes
License Management	Yes	Yes
Openfile Replacement	Yes	INA
Security Features	Workstation and manager limitations by user name, also encryption and password protection	NOS Authorization, policy based, user id/group
Other Features	Hardware/software inventory. Remote control. Automatic script generation.	Drag and drop user interface. Ability to "undo" multiple distributions on demand. Fully automates the delivery of software along with installation, activation, de-install, reconfiguration, software and inventory management.
Comments		
Warranty/Service	60 day free support	Unlimited
Price	$39 (1,000-nodes) to $59 (10-nodes)/per node	

Manufacturer	Interlink	Mcafee
Model	Harbor Distribution 4.1	Saber LAN Workstation 6.0/Software Distribution
O/S Compatibility	MUS/XA, MUS/ESA, OS/390, DOS, Windows 95	Windows 95, Windows NT, Windows 3.x, PC-MS/DOS, OS/s
Network Compatibility	DOS, Windows, Windows 95, NY, OS/2 Warp, AT &T, HP-UX, IBM AIX, Solaris, Sun OS, DEC UNIX, DG-UX, Novell NetWare, Banyan VINES, LAN Manager	Novell Netware, Windows NT
Protocols Supported	TCP/IP, APPC/LUG:2, 3270/HLLAPI, IPX, NETBIOS, ASYNC	TCP/IP, IPX
Application Types	32-bit	16-bit/32-bit
User Initiation	Yes	Yes
Remote Administration	Scheduling, administration	Attach to and control remote servers
Scheduling	Batch scripts	Batch Scripts
Undo	Multiple, on demand	Multiple, on demand
Metering	Yes	Yes
License Management	No	Yes

N/A—Not applicable   INA—Information not available

Software Distribution Management Tools ■

Manufacturer	Interlink	Mcafee
Openfile Replacement	Yes	Yes
Security Features	Integrated security	Standard operating system security and authorized file feature allows the administrator to authorize which files can be run from the server.
Other Features	Drag and drop. Fan out scheme.	Inventory integration allows distribution list creation based on hardware and software inventory Information. Many pre-packaged installation scripts Undo. Before and after snapshots of installs SNMP trap alerting. Crystal reports.
Comments		SPA uses inventory software to conduct license audits. Pricing included hardware and software inventory. Software metering, desktop management and menuing.
Warranty/Service	90 day tech phone support	30-day warranty; business hour support and 7 x 24 support options available.
Price	$30K site license available	100 user $6,200 500 user $30,200 1000 user $47,300

Manufacturer	Novell	Seagate
Model	NetWare Navigator 3.01	WinInstall 5.1
O/S Compatibility	PC-MS/DOS, Windows 3.X, Windows 95, OS/2	Windows 95, Windows NT, Windows 3.x, PC-MS/DOS
Network Compatibility	NetWare, LAN Manager, NT Advanced Server, Banyon VINES, LAN tastic, others	Novell NetWare, Banyan, DEC, Pathworks, LAN manager, LAN server, LANtastic
Protocols Supported	IPX	TCP/IP, IPC, Banyan, IPX, NetBIOS
Application Types	16-bit, 32-bit	16-bit, 32-bit
User Initiation	Yes	Yes
Remote administration	Scheduling	Scheduling, troubleshooting
Scheduling	Batch scripts	Batch scripts
Undo	Yes	Multiple, on demand
Metering	No	Yes
License Management	No	Yes
Openfile Replacement	No	Yes
Security Features	NOS authorization	NOS authorization
Other Features	Feedback to administrators. Multi-tiered distribution.	Drag-and-drop user interface. Ability to "undo" multiple distributions on demand.
Comments	Major new release planned Qt 1996	
Warranty/Service	90 day	3 year. Free phone support. Tech support via online access.
Price	$995 for 25 user version	$495 (50 seat license), $1,295 (1,250 seat license), site licensing available

N/A—Not applicable   INA—Information not available   **E n d** ■

■ Systems Management Tools

Manufacturer	Bull Information Systems	Compaq	Computer Associates
Model	ISM/Open Master- Operation Master	Compaq Insight Manager 3.0	CA-Unicenter TNG
Product Description	Software platform for management and monitoring of legacy and open systems	Compaq Insight Manager offers an in-depth view of event, configuration, and performance mgmt. of Compaq servers, desktops, portables and network devices from a Windows console.	Software for managing an entire enterprise—including the IT environment and business processes
Communication Protocols	TCP/IPX,X.25,FDDI	IP/IPX,PPP	INA
Server System Requirements	UNIX AIX, Solaris, Integrity, Irix, HP-UX(96), NT(96)	Compaq ProLiant, Pro Signia, 386 or higher, 512K RAM to load agents, 2MB disk, SNMP protocol	486/66 with 32MB RAM for NT, OS/2, Novell. All UNIX systems; 200-500MB HD.
Workstation Requirements	Requirements: 125MB RAM, 17" monitor, 2GB disk	386/25 or higher, 8 MB RAM (16 MB recommended) Windows NT 3.51, VGA, 8 MB disk space	Pentium 133, 32MB RAM, VGA, Windows NT 3.51
Features	OS monitoring and management. Applications and management. Console concentration and automation. Software distribution. Job scheduling. Backup/restore scheduling. Performance management. Fault management	Scalability: (32 bit-bit addressing, multi-threaded processing agents). Configuration mgmt.: reporting and maintenance, database export, version control, Fault Mgmt.: fault prediction, pre-failure warranty, event alerting, information, corrective actions, alphanumeric paging. Performance mgmt.: set and monitor controls, auto data collection. Remote mgmt.: remote diagnostics, system configuration.	End to End management—including systems, methods, databases, and applications. Business process views. Real World Interface—3-D animated representation of the entire IT environment. Object-oriented, multi-tiered architecture.
Comments	Includes enterprise management functions		
Warranty	2 year	90 day	Unlimited
Price	$10,000+	Included with purchase of Compaq Server	INA

Manufacturer	Cybermation	Cylink
Model	Enterprise Systems Platform (ESP)	SecureManager
Product Description	Complete family of mission-critical MVS-centric systems management products	Software for management monitoring, certificate authority, and security policy management
Communication Protocols	TCP/IP, APPC	TCP/IP
Server System Requirements	Any IBM/IBM compatible supporting MVS 4.3 or later	Sun Sparc St. with Solaris 2.4/2.5, 64MB RAM
Workstation Requirements	386 PC +	Sun Sparc St. with Solaris 2.4/2.5, 64MB RAM
Features	Complete job scheduling and workload management. Rerun/restart technology. Desktop scheduling. Remote systems communications. Uses GUI. Single point of control.	Certificate authority for digital certificates. Implements security policies for network devices. Manages, configures and monitors Cylink security products. Scalable to thousands of devices. Full audit trail. Audit/logs trail.
Comments	Provides enterprise-wide workload management from single point of control without a single point of failure	Management protocol—SNMP
Warranty	1 year	90 day
Price	$50,000–$800,000 (US)	$10,000

N/A—Not applicable   INA—Information not available

Systems Management Tools ■

Manufacturer	**Elegant**	**GD Associates Ltd.**
Model	InSpec	QMaster
Product Description	Security and system management software that audits and monitors UNIX systems	Integrated process and output management software
Communication Protocols	UUCP;	TCP/IP
Server System/DOS	Intel UNIX, SunOS, Solaris, HP-UX, AIX, SCO, Ultrix	NT 3.51-4.00, 386PC 16MB RAM
Workstation Requirements	X/Motif or Netscape	386 PC, Winsock
Features	Audits and monitors continuously. Executes corporate policy corrective actions. Internet enabled. Used by FM and outsourcing companies. Provides detailed diagnostic analyses, recommendations, graphs, and alerts.	Alerts: Notification through central console. Print spooling. Remote processing. Complete audit trail. Disaster recovery. Open client/server technology. Dynamic load leveling by machine/by device. Truly distributed control. Heterogeneous support UNIX, NT, PC.
Comments	For networked or remote systems. Shipped pre-configured.	
Warranty	Year-round support	90 day
Price	$3,000+	$4,950+

Manufacturer	**Heroix Corporation**	**INTRAK, INC**
Model	RoboMon V6.0	Server Trak v3 for NetWare
Product Description	Software solution that automatically detects and corrects system and operational problems before the system is affected	Software for local and/or centralized mgmt. Supports servers in real time.
Communication Protocols	TCP/IP,DEC Net	TCP/IPX
Server System Requirements	AIX, Digital UNIX, HP-UX, OpenVMS, Solaris, SunOS, or Windows NT	Novell NetWare 3.x, 4.x
Workstation Requirements	AIX, Digital UNIX, HP-UX, OpenVMS, Solaris, SunOS, or Windows NT	486 Windows 3.1, WFW, Windows 95, Windows NT
Features	Problem detection and correction. Enterprise-wide event management. Staff notification. Remote site management. Extensible, site-specific correction. Out-of-box operation. Automated corrective actions. Open architecture. Manage Windows NT, UNIX, and OpenVMS systems.	SNMP compatible. NDS compliant. Server performance monitoring. Out of band mgmt. Capability. Alerts and alert log. Direct link to paging products. Broadcasts to individual or groups.
Comments		Free product support
Warranty	30-day and guarantee of performance	60 day
Price	$300–$15,000 per license	(1) Server $249 (5) Servers $999 (10) Servers $1,499

Manufacturer	**INTRAK, INC**	**Knozall Systems, Inc.**
Model	Server Trak v2 for NetWare	File Wizard 3
Product Description	Software for local and/or remote management of servers	Designed so that network administrators can create automatic management strategies. Provides server space analysis with Windows front end, PKZip compatible server compression.
Communication Protocols	TCP/IPX	IPX/SPX
Server System Requirements	Novell NetWare 3.x, 4.x	Novell NetWare 3.x or higher, 2MB RAM

N/A—Not applicable   INA—Information not available

Table Continues →

■ Systems Management Tools

Manufacturer	INTRAK, INC	Knozall Systems, Inc.
Workstation Requirements	486 Windows 3.1, WFW, Windows 95, Windows NT	Windows 3.1 or higher 6MB RAM
Features	Archives over 80 graphable performance statistics and ratios. Graphs multiple servers on one screen. Retrieves and processes archived data at any workstation. Analyzes historical data up to one year. Projects trend lines up to one year	Reclaims unused, duplicated, and outdated space. Customizable HSM; Tracks the effectiveness of HSM strategy. Utilizes current hardware. Defines graphs by user, groups, directory, and volume. Aged and volume analysis graphs. Saves/restores file access dates.
Comments	Free product support	Works with Windows 95. User defined actions through FileWizard's scripting capability.
Warranty	60 days	Free unlimited tech support via phone or online
Price	(1) Server $649 (5) Servers $2,250 (10) Servers $1,499	$695/server

Manufacturer	McAfee	Novell Inc.	SCH Technologies
Model	SaberLAN Workstation 6.0/Desktop Management	ManageWise 2.1	SystemWatch
Product Description	Software for centralized maintenance of Windows, Windows 95, and Windows NT desktops	ManageWise manages the entire network through NetWare and Windows NT server mgmt., network traffic analysis, desktop mgmt., automated network inventory, remote control, virus protection, and software mgmt.	Provides scalable systems management services for heterogeneous UNIX networks
Communication Protocol	SNMP	SNMP, RMON	TCP/IP
Server System/DOS Win	200MB disk space. NetWare: 16MB RAM. WindowsWIN NT: 32MB RAM. 486 DX.	NetWare 3.11, NetWare 3.12, NetWare 4.1, NetWare SMP, NetWare/IP	SUN, HP, IBM or DEC Alpha 32MB Graphic Display Recommended (SUN Sparc2)
Workstation Requirements	Windows 95, 8MB RAM min, 486 DX	Intel 486 or Pentium microprocessor-based PC, 23 MB hard disk space	16MB
Features	Centrally controls the user's desktop; determines application visibility. Standardizes desktops across the network. Scripting language automates software distribution. Connects with Novell's NDS bindery, and WindowsWIN NT to restrict access to applications by user IDs and network groups	Central mgmt. of servers, desktops, and devices on the network. Automatic collection of desktop hardware and software inventory. Automatic detection of problems on servers, virus protection for the LAN. Remote control of desktops, remote mgmt. optimization, central collection of real-time and long term network optimization. Asset mgmt. with topology maps, inventories, and software/hardware discovery.	Client-centric design reduces traffic. Monitors and automatically restarts daemon processes. Monitors load average, CPU and memory utilization for each process. Tracks virtual memory consumption and triggers low SWAP-space alerts. Charts system loads, disk space consumption or application-specific data across the network.
Comments	Pricing includes: software distribution, hardware and software inventory, software metering, desktop management, and menuing.	ManagWise integrates with Unix-based enterprised management consoles and has over 100 snap-in applications provided by third party vendors.	Add-on modules available, such as TrendWatch and LogWatch
Warranty	30 day	90 day	30 day
Price	$6,200 (100 user), $30,200 (500 user), $47,300 (1000 user)	Starts at $795 for 5 user NetWare Server and $595 ManageWise Agent for Windows NT Server for each server copy	$590 per node

N/A—Not applicable   INA—Information not available

Systems Management Tools ■

Manufacturer	**Software Management Associates**	**Systemetrics, Inc.**
Model	OPCON/XPS	SENTRY
Product Description	Job scheduling software for heterogeneous networks	Software for monitoring system operation network-wide
Communication Protocol	TCP/IP	TCP/IP, NetBEUI, IPX/SPX, DECnet
Server System/DOS Win	Engine: Windows NT Agents: Windows NT, Windows 95, most UNIX systems, AS/400, OpenVMS, Unisys A Series	Windows 3.1/3.11, Windows NT, HP-UX, Sun OS/Solaris, IBM AIX, SCO UNIX, Digital UNIX, Open VMS
Workstation Requirements	Windows, Windows NT, Windows 95	Any Windows, UNIX or Open VMS system
Features	Calendar and event driven operation. Comprehensive security. Load and resource checking. Centralized or distributed management. Automatic restarts/recovery. Interface capabilities to other applications.	Provides notification of system crashes or loss of network connectivity. Monitors disk and file system utilization. Monitors system security, hardware, system performance, and processes in select configuration and environments. Automates response and recovery for specified events.
Comments		Worldwide distribution and support
Warranty	90 day	30 days with license. Renewal option.
Price	Starts at $7,500	$500–$50,000

N/A—Not applicable   INA—Information not available

End ■

CHAPTER

8 NETWORK APPLICATIONS

MOST NETWORKING EQUIPMENT DOESN'T directly involve users. It runs in the background, serving the files they need, managing their print requests, routing the messages they send, and so on. You usually make network purchases to solve the technical challenges of network administration. But network applications are the user's interface with the network, and determine their productivity to a great extent. This makes it more difficult to buy network applications, because they must meet both user needs and network administration needs.

NETWORK APPLICATIONS

THERE ARE COUNTLESS NETWORK applications designed to make businesses run smarter. This chapter introduces some of the core types of network applications designed to enhance group productivity.

Electronic Mail

Electronic mail is perhaps the first group productivity network application to become available (maybe second to print sharing). E-mail was once just a communications tool for internal networks, but its use has exploded due to Internet accessibility. Some companies even use the Internet as their internal e-mail system. The e-mail products covered in this buyer's guide are designed to provide e-mail services over an existing network system. Products that meet these criteria vary from basic e-mail utilities to full-featured e-mail packages that can handle graphics within the messages themselves. Groupware products are often based on an e-mail system but provide additional groupware functions such as whiteboards, file notations, and so on.

Administration Features

Performance   Reliability   **Manageability**   **Scalability**   Flexibility   Value

E-mail applications need to keep the directory of addresses current. Products should provide periodic updates automatically in addition to forced updates. You should also be able to selectively view directories based on criteria such as department or location.

Most products are compatible with many other e-mail systems. These e-mail gateways should be easy to manage with the administrator interface and should offer a choice of links (LAN-to-LAN, ISDN, leased lines, and so on) and communications protocols (IPX/SPX, TCP/IP, and so forth).

Look for reporting features such as connection logs and individual usage logs. These can be helpful in planning or adjusting network traffic. Error notifications should go to both the administrator and the sender. Some products notify the administrator of errors and also keep an error log on the server.

End User Features

Performance   Reliability   **Manageability**   Scalability   **Flexibility**   Value

Users like an easily accessible directory with multiple viewing options for group lookups as well. It's also important to be able to broadcast a single

NETWORK APPLICATIONS

message to a group of individuals. Message queuing and scheduling are standard now in most packages. Attachments are standard for e-mail packages, but attachment compression and encryption are not necessarily included. These features increase the speed and security of file transmissions. Being able to assign priorities to messages can get important messages handled more quickly. As multimedia files and PCs proliferate, there's an increasing demand for more elaborate messages that can include objects such as graphics. Products with these capabilities are emerging but are not yet in widespread use.

Message Storage

Performance	**Reliability**	**Manageability**	Scalability	Flexibility	Value

Messages are stored either on the server or the workstation. Storing messages on the server saves disk space because a broadcasted message is stored just once, with pointers to the recipients. In addition, messages are more likely to be backed up by the network backup system that's in place. The administrative functions here are similar to any database management, including the key issue of being able to administer the database while it is still open (as with compression, reindexing, or backup). Administrators may be limited in managing messages in the database. For instance, they may have limited rights to delete individual messages or old ones that could be archived.

Security

Performance	**Reliability**	Manageability	Scalability	Flexibility	Value

Security often involves standard password features that the administrator can alter. There may be encryption features for passwords, messages sent, messages stored, and/or attached documents. In most cases, you can turn some of these features on or off depending on user preferences or administration policy.

Mobile Client Features

Performance	Reliability	Manageability	Scalability	**Flexibility**	Value

Software packages vary in their support for remote access. Check the number of modems and simultaneous connections. Users accessing e-mail remotely have special needs such as being able to update the directory on

NETWORK APPLICATIONS

demand to their remote computer. Different applications let you do this in different ways. Remote users also appreciate prioritized messages for assessing importance and being able to download just the messages they want.

Desktop Video Conferencing

Is video conferencing a core network applications category? Maybe not just yet, but this technology is becoming affordable and will be a part of most networks in the near future. Not long ago, video conferencing systems were specialized telecommunications networks in their own right. These high-cost, proprietary systems were difficult to cost justify and use effectively. But now there are desktop video conferencing systems, generally PC-based systems using ISDN connections. The desktop systems complement rather than replace the video conference rooms of today.

Even a small desktop installation can put great demands on network resources such as storage and bandwidth. For this reason, you need to carefully consider how these applications might affect your network. Although these types of systems are still in their infancy (this is clear from their performance and image quality), they can meet basic needs, and their development is progressing quickly. Phone services through the Internet create an opportunity for these systems to proliferate even further, but there are still technical hurdles like adequate network bandwidth.

Video Coder/Decoder					
Performance	Reliability	Manageability	Scalability	**Flexibility**	Value

Video coder and decoder mechanisms are the engines of video conferencing systems. They handle the large data streams necessary for video and audio transmission. Compressing and decompressing data is a key task. Most systems adhere to a compression standard (ITU H.320) that lets them use other equipment using the same standard on the other end of the transmission (although other compatibility issues may be involved). You can implement coding and decoding as hardware or software; software is usually a bit slower but less expensive. A system should be able to accurately synchronize the audio and video signals; some products are better than others at this. The latency or delay in delivering signals is another consideration, but the network environment will affect this factor.

NETWORK APPLICATIONS

I/O Components					

Performance	Reliability	Manageability	Scalability	Flexibility	**Value**

Cameras and microphones supply the video and audio input into the conferencing system. Some conference systems may require specific devices and are more proprietary in nature. Image and sound quality usually depend more on the computer hardware and software, since they lag behind the camera component in image quality.

Audio/Video Quality					

Performance	Reliability	Manageability	Scalability	Flexibility	**Value**

The desktop systems have varying audio/video (A/V) quality and are all well below broadcast quality. Broadcast quality is about 30 frames per second (fps) whereas desktop video is often around 10 fps. But a clear picture can help make up for slower frames per second. Some systems sacrifice image quality to sustain fps rates when transmission loads increase. Transmission loads are greater when there are changes to the image. (For example, more information is transmitted during gesturing and other movements than during a relatively still head shot.)

Connections					

Performance	**Reliability**	Manageability	Scalability	Flexibility	Value

Most desktop systems use ISDN connections, but access to ISDN is still limited or even unavailable in some areas. Some systems use switched 56 Kbps lines.

Document Management

Document management can refer to anything from a basic O/S file manager to a complete imaging and document management system. In addition, document management products can perform many of the same functions as work flow and groupware products such as Lotus Notes. Network operating systems and word processing applications now offer excellent file organization and searching features, leaving little room for third-party applications in the low end of the market. Document management becomes more important as electronic documents switch from text files to files that incorporate dynamic links, embedded objects, and the like.

NETWORK APPLICATIONS

Document management is further complicated because there are now more sources of documents, including electronic mail and faxes.

Document management applications provide advanced document revision and authoring management for security and work flow beyond the capabilities provided in word processing applications. These applications are common in engineering firms where it's critical to have accurate and traceable documents. Businesses moving to electronic documentation also need to author, track, and manage documents and large databases of imaged files. Document management for this market is closely tied with the complete imaging solution and is more closely related to a database application. A third market is just now emerging: managing HTML documents on an Internet/intranet server.

Core Application					
Performance	Reliability	Manageability	**Scalability**	**Flexibility**	**Value**

There are many different types of document management software. Before you buy, you need to determine which core features you need. For example, an engineering company may need document control and work flow features. A law firm, on the other hand, may want access to imaged documents on an optical library.

Work Flow Features					
Performance	Reliability	**Manageability**	Scalability	Flexibility	Value

Work flow refers to the way in which people and resources interact to complete a task. For example, a request to attend a conference is initiated as a document. It then goes to a manager for approval, to accounting to get funded, and finally to a records archive that handles such requests. Some document management software performs all these tasks electronically over a network rather than using a paper-based system. Document management software of this type is sometimes called a "work flow application." These applications usually handle a variety of file types, such as drawings and spreadsheets. Work flow features might include authoring and revision control, notes, file or object attachments, forms, and various levels of security. Security is important when approval and signatures are needed. In an engineering setting, version control is critical to assure that the correct documents are used and changes can be traced. Editing and annotation of documents can take many forms, from simple notations to attaching audio or video objects.

NETWORK APPLICATIONS

Data Accessibility Features					
Performance	Reliability	**Manageability**	Scalability	Flexibility	Value

Document management can be much like database management. The terms "data input," "indexing," and "searching" commonly used for both. The first step is to get files into the system—either by scanning, electronic faxing, or importing files. Some products can automate this process with scripts and batch processing. Once they're in the system, documents must be indexed so they can be retrieved. The methods include manual entry, full text reading or scanning, bar code entry, and others. Most products offer more than one indexing method. Once indexed, documents can be searched for, usually in a variety of ways.

Compatibility					
Performance	Reliability	Manageability	**Scalability**	**Flexibility**	Value

Document management applications can usually handle a variety of file formats, such as text and graphics, from a number of different machine types. The software may organize information in a centralized database or multiple, distributed databases that act as one. Distributed databases offer more flexibility in configuration and help decrease network traffic by keeping resources closer to where they are needed.

Good compatibility also means flexible document and index data sharing. This includes integration with third-party applications for faxing and e-mail, the ability to import and export documents and index data in a number of different formats, and support for embedded files such as DDE and OLE.

Storage hardware support can be another important issue. As index files expand and the number of documents grows, it may be cost effective to move information to an optical jukebox. The software should be able to store on different mediums because your hardware requirements can change.

Internet Browsers

A browser provides a graphical user interface (GUI) to the Internet and intranet services. A single product—Netscape Communications' Netscape Navigator—currently dominates the market, but other products continue to struggle for share by offering unique features. Windows 95 includes built-in browser and Internet connection capabilities, which suggests a trend for operating system integration. Although browsers are not a

NETWORK APPLICATIONS

network application per se, they have quickly become an important network component, not only for Internet access but for using internal network applications that are built on the Web's design. Browsers are very inexpensive, and sometimes free, so price usually won't affect your decision about what to buy.

Standards					
Performance	**Reliability**	Manageability	Scalability	Flexibility	Value

Browsers provide an interface into the HTML standard, a document presentation standard that is consistent across all platforms. There are now three levels of the HTML standard and some products support the new standards sooner than others. The newer standards support more graphic options and can affect your view significantly. (You can use previous versions to read a Web page designed with the HTML 3.0 standard, but much of the formatting may be lost.) The appearance of an HTML document may vary slightly depending on the browser being used and more dramatically depending on the monitor being used.

User Interface					
Performance	Reliability	**Manageability**	Scalability	Flexibility	Value

The browsing options are fairly consistent in the various products. Products vary in the way they manage bookmarks, their support of multiple screen views, and their flexibility in controlling the images of the interface and HTML documents.

Speed					
Performance	Reliability	Manageability	Scalability	Flexibility	Value

Browsing speeds typically depend on the computer's processing power, the amount of RAM, the display adapter, and the speed of the Internet connection (modem speed, ISDN line, and so on). But browsers themselves can load a document more and less quickly, all other things being equal. However, this difference is often small.

Groupware/Scheduling

Almost everyone has heard of groupware, but the term is often misunderstood or simply used to refer to a single product, Lotus Notes. Actually,

NETWORK APPLICATIONS

groupware is a combination of communication tools such as messaging and scheduling that are tightly integrated to provide a collaborative work environment. These tools may address workgroups or an entire network enterprise.

Groupware Architecture					
Performance	Reliability	Manageability	**Scalability**	Flexibility	**Value**

There are essentially three approaches to groupware design: complete office automation, workgroup scheduling and messaging, and Internet/intranet-based groupware.

Complete office automation designs, like Lotus Notes, are intended to take over the desktop and handle everything the "group" needs—document creation and management, e-mail, scheduling, and so forth. These systems have well-integrated components and offer elaborate and cohesive work flow. But they require a large investment in development and training, making them an unlikely choice for most businesses of 200 or fewer employees.

An alternative approach is centered around e-mail and usually combines messaging, scheduling, and document management. These systems are not unlike a bulletin board system focusing on collaborative project and communication needs. Some provide links to other applications. These applications are easier to set up and are not as intrusive as the complete office design packages. They are usually quite scalable, serving small to large workgroups or network enterprises.

The third major approach to groupware involves using Internet/intranet technology to create a collaborative application. This approach is inexpensive, offers easy design, and flexibility in the groupware solution you would like to build. However, it can be somewhat limiting for a complete office automation design and may be lacking in some areas like security.

Computer Platform					
Performance	Reliability	Manageability	**Scalability**	**Flexibility**	Value

Your computing platform affects the type of groupware solution you choose. A PC environment may not be quite ready for the complete office automation approach to groupware. Although PC processing power is increasing, it is often expensive and somewhat cumbersome to set up full-blown groupware on this platform because of the necessary investments in server hardware. UNIX and Windows NT might be better platforms for this application.

NETWORK APPLICATIONS

Scheduling Features

Performance   Reliability   **Manageability**   Scalability   Flexibility   Value

Meeting and conference scheduling are a popular part of groupware solutions. Some applications provide these services exclusively. The programs must be able to identify "open space" for all potential attendees, reserve the space, and notify the relevant people. They may also reserve special equipment or services. Other powerful features are meeting RSVPs and taking actions based on RSVPs. You should also carefully check how remote users are integrated.

Work Flow Features

Performance   Reliability   **Manageability**   Scalability   Flexibility   Value

Work flow is often closely associated with document management, an application that is covered in more detail in Chapter 7. When evaluating work flow you should consider how information (most often documents) travels, what you can do to annotate the information, and how revision control and security are handled. Work flow features are usually centered around workgroups rather than a network enterprise.

The Impact on Work Environment

Performance   Reliability   Manageability   Scalability   Flexibility   **Value**

Groupware has the potential to completely change how things are done in an organization. Unavoidably, there will be some resistance to change; a good way to minimize this is to involve people in the planning and implementation process. Your users will need training and it will probably take some time before they completely understand and take full advantage of the new work flow setup. If you're considering groupware, determine whether it should enhance existing work flow or completely replace it. Good groupware won't fix a poor business organizational framework.

Fax Communications

Computer-based faxing using fax cards has raised faxing to a whole new level. Single-solution systems appear in many networks. But in a network environment it's difficult to manage and secure faxing and fax information with these solutions. For this reason, fax serving applications for the network have emerged to make it easier to administer the fax process.

NETWORK APPLICATIONS

These programs also allow you to make better use of corporate resources such as phone lines and fax cards.

Scope of Control					

Performance	Reliability	**Manageability**	**Scalability**	Flexibility	Value

The main thing to look at in fax software is its fax management features. If the software is to be implemented as a workgroup solution, scalability is not as critical a concern. Not many sites have implemented an enterprise fax solution, but including fax documents in the management of corporate information resources may require an enterprise approach. A good enterprise system will allow distributed actions (at the workgroup level) with centralized management and information cataloging (at the site or enterprise level). To decide on the scope of your fax solution, you must think about how faxes will be managed and who will manage them. Enterprise scalability may not be an issue today, but you need to consider how your fax solution will change if you move in that direction.

Price					

Performance	Reliability	Manageability	Scalability	Flexibility	**Value**

Obviously, price is a major factor when you're buying almost anything, but it can be tricky here. A low-cost solution may offer benefits over manual faxing but may not provide top-notch fax management capabilities. On the other hand, it can be difficult to justify the expense of a more sophisticated solution. The ideal solution is of course one that gets you in at entry level but can meet much larger needs if necessary.

Faults and Reporting					

Performance	**Reliability**	**Manageability**	Scalability	Flexibility	Value

Faxing is prone to error due to problem connections, busy lines, and network glitches. Although much of the communications issues are out of the sender's control, it's useful to have some level of fault tolerance. Some products can be configured to run on redundant servers and automatically fail over to working servers. Proprietary databases can make recovering data difficult in the case of file corruption. Also, it may be important to be able to do database maintenance such as compression or reindexing while the database is active.

NETWORK APPLICATIONS

Reporting is the other side of the error control issue. Detailed fax logs are pretty much standard, but different products may notify different people of errors and in different ways. The policies for alternative actions may be controlled by the user, the administrator, or both.

Establishing Priorities					
Performance	Reliability	**Manageability**	Scalability	Flexibility	Value

In a network setting, it is important to be able to set fax priorities according to company needs. You can do this at several levels. You can assign priority levels to certain departments in addition to individuals. For example, the accounting department may have a higher priority than the marketing department. But someone's high-priority marketing department fax may be queued ahead of an accounting department's low-priority fax. The politics of establishing priorities can be daunting, but the advantages of appropriate priority settings can be important if faxes are often backlogged.

User Interface					
Performance	Reliability	**Manageability**	Scalability	Flexibility	Value

There are no particular requirements for user interface, but it should be clear, easy to use, and customizable. It's good for users to be able to use their favorite word processor rather than type into the fax interface. Good products also make it easy to embed graphics and attach files. It's always wise to know something about your user's preferences and whether the product can accommodate them, instead of just focusing on the product's management features from the administrator's point of view.

■ E-mail Network Applications

Manufacturer	The ADM Group	Attachmate Corp
Model	QuickFlash 2.5	Emissary v.20
OS	Windows (all versions)	Windows 3.1, Windows 95, and Windows NT
RAM Requirements	1MB RAM, 6% resources	8MB/10MB disk space
Mail/Message Transport Agent	ADMport	SMTP/POP3
Communication Protocol	N/A	TCP/IP
Cross-platform Support	Windows	Windows only
Extensibility	Enterprise, Internet	Enterprise, Internet
User Interface	GUI	GUI
FEATURES		
Rules-Based Automation/ Customization	No	Yes
MIME Compliant	No	Yes
Remote Access	Yes	No
Group Scheduling	No	No
Message Encryption	No	No
Text Features	Yes	Spell checker, HTML support, text enhancements
Multiple Address Books	Yes	Yes
Message Logs	Inbound	No
OLE 2.0 Data Exchange	DDE only	No
Automated Messaging Features	Group distribution	Yes
Help Features	Online, hypertext	Online, printed
Searching Capabilities	No	Full text
Message Archiving	Manual	Yes
Comments	Sticky notes, phone message pad. Co-exists with large e-mail systems—good for real-time group support, call screening.	Import/export to EUDORA
Warranty	90 day	1 year
Pricing and Licensing	$15–$25 per user	$99 per user

Manufacturer	Banyan	Baranof Software
Model	Beyond Mail	MailCheck 3.0
OS	Windows 3.1, Windows 95, Windows NT, DOS, Mac, Unix, (HP-UX, Solaris)	Windows 3.x, Windows 95, Windows NT
RAM Requirements	INA	INA
Mail/Message Transport Agent	SMTP Intelligent Messaging	MAPI, MHS, SMTP, X.400
Communication Protocol	TCP/IP, VIP (Vines IP)	Compatible with any `protocol`
Cross-platform Support	Unix, Windows, DOS, Mac	Unix, Windows, DOS, and Mac

N/A—Not applicable   INA—Information not available

E-mail Network Applications ■

Manufacturer	**Banyan**	**Baranof Software**
Extensibility	Network Enterprise, Internet	Internet, Enterprise
User Interface	GUI	GUI
FEATURES		
Rules-Based Automation/ Customization	Yes	Yes
MIME Compliant	Yes	Yes
Remote Access	Yes	Yes
Group Scheduling	Yes	N/A
Message Encryption	Yes	N/A
Text Features	Rich text, spell checker, viewers	N/A
Multiple Address Books	Yes	N/A
Message Logs	Inbound, outbound	Inbound and outbound
OLE 2.0 Data Exchange	Yes	N/A
Automated Messaging Features	Filing, response, forward, sort, delete, filtering, work flow	N/A
Help Features	Online	Online
Searching Capabilities	Full text	N/A
Message Archiving	Yes	N/A
Comments	An SMTP/MIME gateway is required for field compatibility between Beyond Mail SMTP and Beyond Mail for Intelligent Messaging.	Dynamic monitoring, alerts, action commands, performance reporting, and enterprise management. Mailcheck can be used to monitor, manage, and report on any MAPI-compliant system. SNMP compatible.
Warranty	90 day	30 day unconditional
Pricing and Licensing	$45 (std) $85 (prof.) $132 (Remote Access)	$295 for base system $195 for additional licenses (volume discounts

Manufacturer	**Clarity Software**	**Control Data Systems**
Model	Compatibility Server	Mail*Hub 96
OS	UNIX, HP-UX, SunOS 4.1.3+, Solaris 2.x and others	HP-UX 9 and 10, Solaris 2.4 and 2.5, AIX 4.1.4, Solaris on Intel
RAM Requirements	16MB RAM	32MB plus directory space
Mail/Message Transport Agent	SMTP-supports all leading e-mail programs	SMTP/MIME, X.400/92
Communication Protocol	Protocol independent	TCP/IP, OSI TPO, OSI TP4
Cross-platform Support	All	Gateways for all LAN, IBM, and DEC mail systems
Extensibility	Enterprise, Internet Web	Enterprise, Global, Internet, ADMD
User Interface	GUI	GUI
FEATURES		
Rules-Based Automation/ Customization	Yes	Yes
MIME Compliant	Yes	Yes

N/A—Not applicable　INA—Information not available

Table Continues →

■ E-mail Network Applications

Manufacturer	Clarity Software	Control Data Systems
Remote Access	Yes	No
Group Scheduling	Yes	No
Message Encryption	Yes	Yes, X.509 compliant
Text Features	Platform independent	N/A
Multiple Address Books	Master	X.500 distributed directory
Message Logs	N/A	Multilevel logging
OLE 2.0 Data Exchange	Yes	Between like mail systems
Automated Messaging Features	N/A	Customizable filtering and response
Help Features	Online	Hypertext manuals and man pages
Searching Capabilities	INA	Full text and key word, optional
Message Archiving	N/A	Optional
Comments	Seamless hardware/software independence provides document image enrichment including HTML, PFD support. 1st platform independent, exchange of documents, images and web-based information.	Multiprotocol messaging backbone, based on X.400, SMTP/MIME, and X.500
Warranty	1 year	1 year service warranty
Pricing and Licensing	$10,000—1 time cost, no volume, user limitation	$40,000–$150,000 (depends on number of users and type of gateway)

Manufacturer	E-Mail, Inc.	ESKER, Inc.
Model	V.30	Tun Mail v.8.01
OS	HP 3000, MPEIX	Windows 3.x, Win 95
RAM Requirements	INA	4MCGS Win 3.x, 8MCGS Win 95
Mail/Message Transport Agent	SMTP, X.400, UUCP	SMTP/UUCP
Communication Protocol	INA	TCP/IP, UUCP
Cross-platform Support	HP3000	INA
Extensibility	LAN	LAN, WAN, Internet
User Interface	Terminal emulators	GUI
FEATURES		
Rules-Based Automation/ Customization	Yes	INA
MIME Compliant	Yes	Yes
Remote Access	Yes	Yes
Group Scheduling	No	No
Message Encryption	Yes	No
Text Features	Spell checker, templates, binary ASC files	OLE
Multiple Address Books	No	Yes
Message Logs	Inbound, outbound	In, out, folders

N/A—Not applicable   INA—Information not available

E-mail Network Applications ■

Manufacturer	E-Mail, Inc.	ESKER, Inc.
OLE 2.0 Data Exchange	INA	OLE 1.0
Automated Messaging Features	Forwarding, reply, file	Sort, forward, reply
Help Features	Online	Online help
Searching Capabilities	INA	Yes
Message Archiving	Yes	Yes
Comments	An SMTP gateway to AT&T mail included with fax, telex, postal, and EDI services	OLE, MIME, UUENCODE, Remote Max, Fax
Warranty	INA	Contact vendor
Pricing and Licensing	$3,000–$6,000	Contact vendor

Manufacturer	Fujitsu	Galacticomm
Model	TeamWare Messaging 5.0	Worldgroup 3.0
OS	Sun Solaris 2.4 or later, Windows NT 3.51 or later	Windows NT, Windows 95, DOS
RAM Requirements	16MB minimum	32MB RAM
Mail/Message Transport Agent	SMTP, X.400, MHS	ISDN/Modem, SMTP, POP3, IPX/SPX
Communication Protocol	TCP/IP, POP3	TCP/IP
Cross-platform Support	Windows 95, Windows NT, Windows 3.1, Unix, Macintosh, terminal, DOS	Windows, DOS, Unix
Extensibility	Department, Enterprise, Interanet, Internet	Intranet/Internet
User Interface	GUI, browser	GUI, A/A
FEATURES		
Rules-Based Automation/ Customization	Yes	No
MIME Compliant	Yes	Yes
Remote Access	Yes	Yes
Group Scheduling	Yes (optional)	No
Message Encryption	Yes	Yes
Text Features	RTF	Rich text format, spell checker
Multiple Address Books	Yes	Distribution lists, yes
Message Logs	Yes	Inbound, outbound
OLE 2.0 Data Exchange	No	No
Automated Messaging Features	File, fowarding, filtering, reply, sort	Filing, response, forwarding
Help Features	Online, context sensitive	Online
Searching Capabilities	Data range, subject, sender, sensitivity, size, recipient type, annotation	INA
Message Archiving	Yes	Yes

N/A—Not applicable　INA—Information not available

Table Continues →

■ E-mail Network Applications

Manufacturer	Fujitsu	Galacticomm
Comments	Also provides mailbox size restriction, multi-windowing, heirarchical folder structure, message retraction	
Warranty	Limited	30-day money-back guarantee
Pricing and Licensing	Base license: $495–$995 (including server software and 10-user license); $29–65 additional license per user	N/A

Manufacturer	Infinite Technologies	LAN-ACES, Inc.
Model	ExpressIT!	Office-Logic 3.0
OS	Any DOS-based NOS	Netware, Lantastic, Power LAN, LAN Manager, Invisible LAN, Windows NT, Windows 95, WFW, compatible NetBIOS networks
RAM Requirements	<2K	6K, as little as 0 bytes needed if UMB is available
Mail/Message Transport Agent	Connect^2, MHS, Global MAS	SMF, SMTP, Direct Delivery
Communication Protocol	N/A	IPX/SPX, TCP/IP, NetBIOS, NetBEUI
Cross-platform Support	Windows, DOS	DOS, Windows, Windows NT, Windows 95
Extensibility	INA	Network, Internet, Enterprise
User Interface	GUI	DOS TSR, 16bit GUI client, 32bit GUI client
FEATURES		
Rules-Based Automation/ Customization	No	Yes
MIME Compliant	With gateway	Yes
Remote Access	Yes	Yes
Group Scheduling	No	Yes
Message Encryption	No	Yes
Text Features	Spell checker	Spell checker
Multiple Address Books	Yes	Yes
Message Logs	Inbound, outbound	Configurable for full archiving
OLE 2.0 Data Exchange	No	Yes
Automated Messaging Features	Filing, response, forwarding	Auto reply, forwarding, filing, deleting
Help Features	Online	Online
Searching Capabilities	Full text	Full text including header information
Message Archiving	Yes	User definable
Comments	Gateways available for exstending e-mail to pagers, fax, printers, the Internet and more	No server required. Internet access via gateway. Faxing support for both outbound and viewing of inbound.
Warranty	2 year, free upgrade	1 year
Pricing and Licensing	$299 for 5 users and up	$495 (5 user), $1,995 (25), $4995 (100), $149 (remote)

N/A—Not applicable   INA—Information not available

E-mail Network Applications ■

Manufacturer	Lotus Development Corp.	Microsoft
Model	Notes 4.0	Exchange Server 4.0
OS	DOS, OS/2, Windows 95, NT and 3.0	MS Windows NT server
RAM Requirements	N/A	24MB RAM
Mail/Message Transport Agent	SMTP, X.400, MHS	X.4. SMTP
Communication Protocol	TCP/IP, Novell SPX, IBM SNA,	TCP/IP, IPX/SPX, NetBEAUI, Appletalk, Banyan
Cross-platform Support	DOS, Windows, Mac, UNIX, OS/2 Workplace Shell	Windows 3.x, Windows 95, Windows NT, DOS, Mac
Extensibility	LAN, WAN, Internet, intranets	LAN, WAN, Internet, intranets
User Interface	Winsock, MAPI	GUI clients and admin
FEATURES		
Rules-Based Automation/ Customization	Yes	Yes
MIME Compliant	Yes	Yes
Remote Access	Yes	Yes
Group Scheduling	Yes	Yes
Message Encryption	Yes	Yes
Text Features	Text enhancement, spell check, templates	Rich text, spell check, expiry
Multiple Address Books	Yes	Yes
Message Logs	In-bound, out-bound	In-bound, out-bound
OLE 2.0 Data Exchange	Yes	Yes
Automated Messaging Features	Filing, response, forwarding	Alerts, deletes, filing, response, forward OOF, grouping, sorting, filtering
Help Features	Online	Online and printed
Searching Capabilities	Full text	Messages
Message Archiving	Yes	Yes
Comments	Integrated group scheduling, Bulleting Boards, multiple log-ins, color highlighting, text editor ruler bar, fault tolerant directory propagation topology	Auto-recovery using transaction logs hot backup, automatic failover and load balancing, automatic directory replication, message tracking
Warranty		90 day
Pricing and Licensing	$55 client user	$54 client access license $529 server license

Manufacturer	Novell	Sound Ideas of America
Model	GroupWise 5	FineLine Message Manager
OS	Client: Mac, PowerMac, Unix (3 versions), Windows 3.x, Windows 95, Winodws NT Server: Netware, NLM, OS/2, Unix, WindowsNT	SCO, AIX, HP-UX
RAM Requirements	16MB RAM	250K and 3MB disk
Mail/Message Transport Agent	Proprietary through file services or TCP/IP; also accommodates MHS, SMTP, and x.400	Uses System Mail Program
Communication Protocol	Proprietary through file services (IPX/SPX) or TCP/IP; also accommodates MHS, POP3, NetBIOS, NetBEUI, SMTP and x.400	INA

N/A—Not applicable   INA—Information not available

Table Continues →

■ E-mail Network Applications

Manufacturer	Novell	Sound Ideas of America
Cross-platform Support	Same as OS	INA
Extensibility	Network enterprise (LAN/WAN), Internet/Intranet, remote access	LAN, Internet
User Interface	GUI, Web browser	Character
FEATURES		
Rules-Based Automation/ Customization	Yes	No
MIME Compliant	Yes	File attachments only
Remote Access	Yes	No
Group Scheduling	Yes	Yes
Message Encryption	INA	No
Text Features	Spell checker, thesaurus, rich text format	spell checker, full editor
Multiple Address Books	Yes	Yes
Message Logs	Complete inbound/outbound tracking	Inbound, outbound
OLE 2.0 Data Exchange	Yes	No
Automated Messaging Features	File, respond, forward, filter, sort, delegate, accept, decline, mark as private	File, forward, reply, print, delete, edit
Help Features	Online	Online and reference cards
Searching Capabilities	Database, full text and all post office data	Full text
Message Archiving	Yes	Yes
Comments	Calendaring/scheduling, conferencing, database management, open APIs	Supports fax and pager software. Character-to-system mail program.
Warranty	90 day when through Novell	Unlimited
Pricing and Licensing	$718 for 5 users, $32,625 for 250	$200, 5 users and up

N/A—Not applicable   INA—Information not available

Conferencing Network Applications ■

Manufacturer	Archtek	Cyber Access, Inc.
Model	2834 BMV	Broadcast Message System
General Description	Video conferencing using analog lines	Designed for businesses that need instant notification of emergencies
Server System Platforms/ Requirements	Netware, Windows NT OS/2	Windows 3.11, Windows NT and 95, AIX, Solaris, MP-RAS, HP-UX
Desktop Systems OS/Requirements	Hewlett-Packard EISA-bus card using NTSC, PAL and SECAM signal formats	Novell, Banyan, UNIX, Win 95 et al/ Winsock (for TCP/IP version)
Network configuration/ connectivity	N/A	LAN and TCP/IP
Necessary Hardware/ Software Components	Pentium TC 16MB RAM 120 MB Free HD Windows	NFS or TCP/IP, UnixUnix clients (TCP) require Motif 1.2
Compression Scheme(s)	BMP, PCX	
Administration Features	SNMP-based administration and configuration utility	
Video Features	Video call hold. Video call transfer. Do not disturb. Video broker's call. Video broadcast. Video on hold.	Targets individuals or groups. Same site or multi-site. Logs incoming and outgoing messages. Security. Messages announced immediately.
Comments		Spaded messages and a target button. Electronic sign-out board software is also available.
Warranty	5 year	30 day
Price	$439	$149–$23 for one year extra tech support/maintenance

Manufacturer	Intel	Intel
Model	Intel ProShare™ Video System 200	Intel Video Phone with ProShare™ technology
General Description	Fully integrated, standards-based video conferencing that operates over ISDN or LAN	H.324 standards-based consumer video phone software for PC OEM integration
Server System Platforms/ Requirements	N/A	N/A
Desktop Systems OS/Requirements	Intel 486, 66MHz PC with ISA bus, 16MB RAM, Windows 3.1 or Windows 95	Intel Pentium 133 or higher, 16MB RAM, 640 x 480 VGA with 256-color, Windows 95
Network Configuration/ Connectivity	Operates over ISDN and IPX or TCP/IP-based LANs.	N/A
Necessary Hardware/ Software components	Intel 486, 66MHz PC with ISA bus, 16MB RAM, Windows for Workgroups 3.11, Windows 3.1, and Windows 95	Intel Pentium 133 or higher, 16MB RAM, 640 x 480 VGA with 256-color, VFW YUV-12 compliant Video Conferencing card, 28.8 DSVD V.80 modem
Compression Scheme(s)	JPEG	H.263, G.723
Administration Features	LANDesk Conferencing Manager manages number of video/audio conferences permitted on LAN	N/A
Video Features	Standards-based video. Full screen display. Video mute. Variable-sized windows.	Two versions H.324 standard. Voice call first. Snap shot file transfer. Full duplex on Pentium 166MHz. Two video window sizes

N/A—Not applicable   INA—Information not available

Table Continues →

■ Conferencing Network Applications

Manufacturer	Intel	Intel
Comments	ProShare Video System is a unique T.120 multipoint A/V/D desktop system.	
Warranty	1 year	OEM specific
Price	$1,499	Adds $200 to final price of OEM SKU's Upgrades purchased from OEMs $300 or less

Manufacturer	Microsoft	Northern Telecom
Model	NetMeeting	Nortel's Multimedia Conferencing
General Description	Standards-based real-time voice communications with multipoint data conferencing	H.320 compliant desktop video conferencing with Whiteboarding, Applications Share, and File Transfer
Server System Platforms/ Requirements	N/A	N/A
Desktop Systems OS/Requirements	N/A	ISA bus card supporting NTSC and PAL video inputs with built-in ISDN terminal adapter
Network Configuration/ Connectivity	IP-based network connection. IPX-based network connection, or PSTN for point-to-point.	ISDN BRI line or standard digital phone interface
Necessary Hardware/ Software components	486/66 with 8MB required, Pentium recommended. Windows 95 (beta version for Windows NT 4.0. 14,400bps modem (minimum) or LAN (works best with a fast Internet connection). Sound card, speakers, and microphone recommended (required for real-time voice)	486 50MHz min, 12MB of RAM, Windows 3.1, 3.11 or 95, available ISA slot, 256 color VGA/SVGA monitor
Compression Scheme(s)	N/A	H.261
Administration Features	N/A	Software configuration utility for ISDN, I/O address, interrupts
Video Features	Standard-based (T.120, H.323) real-time voice communications multi-point data conferencing for application sharing, shared whiteboard, file transfer, chat	Scalable video window (up to full screen). Supports connection of external TV. Supports integration of Smart Technology's "Whiteboards." Screen-based telephony behind NT PBX.
Comments		Product can utilize the digital capabilities of the Northern Telecom phone system, eliminating the need for ISDN BRI
Warranty	N/A	1 year
Price	Free	$2,295+

Manufacturer	PictureTel	PictureTel
Model	LiveLAN 2.0	Live200P
General Description	LAN based video conferencing solution	Desktop video conferencing kit
Server System Platforms/ Requirements	N/A	N/A
Desktop Systems OS/Requirements	Windows 95	Windows 95
Network Configuration/ Connectivity	Network stacks supported: NetWare 3.11 or later IPX stack, MS Windows 95 IPX/SPX Protocol, FTP OnNet 1.2 or later TCP/IP stack	ISDN
Necessary Hardware/ Software components	Pentium Class PC with Win95: 16MB RAM, 15MB HD free space, 16-bit color driver support, 16-bit ISA/EISA slot (video/audio capture)	Pentium Class PC with PCI bus, Windows 95, 16MB RAM, 20MB hard disk space

N/A—Not applicable   INA—Information not available

Conferencing Network Applications ∎

Manufacturer	PictureTel	PictureTel
Compression Scheme(s)	H.261	System is fully H.320 compliant; it supports: video compression H.261 QCIF & FCIF (15 frames per second), audio compression G.711, G.722, G.728 & PT724 (PictureTel proprietary audio algorithm providing wide-band, 7KHz audio at only 24 Kbps)
Administration Features	Phonebook, Preferences, Diagnostic	Phonebook, Preferences, Diagnostic
Video Features	Video call transfer/forwarding, Dial out, Hang-up, Redial, Audio move	Full screen video
Comments	Next revision has Winsock 2 and H.323	Kit includes camera, speakers, microphone, video/audio capture card, documentation, software
Warranty	1 year	Hardware-1 year, Software-90 day
Price	$1,195-complete kit (includes camera, speakers, microphone, video/audio capture card, documentation, software)	$1,495

Manufacturer	PictureTel	PictureTel
Model	Live50	Live100
General Description	The PictureTel Live50 is a complete H.320 desktop video and data conferencing add-on solution for ISA (or EISA) bus PCs running Microsoft Windows 3.1 or Windows 95.	The PictureTel Live100 is a complete H.320 desktop video and data conferencing add-on solution for ISA (or EISA) bus PCs running Microsoft Windows 3.1 or Windows 95.
Server System Platforms/ Requirements	N/A	N/A
Desktop Systems OS/Requirements	Windows 95, Windows and Windows for Workgroups 3.1	Windows 95, Windows and Windows for Workgroups 3.1
Network Configuration/ Connectivity	Version 1.6, ISDN BRI S/T interface standard, supports 56Kbps-128Kbps; V.35/RS-449 w/RS-366 dialing and 4-wire SW56 interfaces are optional.	Version 1.6, ISDN BRI S/T interface standard, supports 56Kbps-128Kbps; V.35/RS-449 w/RS-366 dialing and 4-wire SW56 interfaces are optional.
Necessary Hardware/ Software components	PictureTel Live50, version 1.6: 386/25 or faster CPU, 8MB RAM, 20MB disk space, ISA or EISA bus, Microsoft Windows 3.1 or Windows 95, SVGA or VGA monitor	Version 1.6, system includes audio/video/ graphics, ISDN two board set, an adjustable color (Y/C) camera, a hands-free speakerphone, and much more.
Compression Scheme(s)	System is fully H.320 compliant and as such supports video compression H.261 QCIF and FCIF (15 frames per second), audio compression G.711, G.722, G.728 & PT724 (PictureTel proprietary audio algorithm providing wide-band, 7KHz audio at only 24Kbps)	System is fully H.320 compliant and as such supports video compression H.261 QCIF and FCIF (15 frames per second), audio compression G.711, G.722, G.728 & PT724 (PictureTel proprietary audio algorithm providing wide-band, 7KHz audio at only 24Kbps)
Administration Features	INA	INA
Video Features	INA	INA
Comments	Version 1.6 includes video/audio/ISDN board, color composite camera collaboration software and documentation.	
Warranty	1 year, return to factory, on hardware. 90 day on software.	1 year, return to factory, on hardware. 90 day on software.
Price	Starts at $2,495	Starts at $4,995

Manufacturer	RADVision	RADVision
Model	L2W-20/4E	VIU-10
General Description	LAN/WAN video conferencing gateway, supports 4 concurrent LAN/WAN calls (56k-384k) and multiple (configuration number) LAN/WAN calls.	Connects H.320 Room System to LAN

N/A—Not applicable   INA—Information not available

Table Continues →

■ Conferencing Network Applications

Manufacturer	RADVision	RADVision
Server System Platforms/ Requirements	N/A	N/A
Desktop Systems OS/Requirements	Any H323 system or RADVision VCP driver (Windows 95/3.11/NT + MS TCP/IP, Unix)	N/A
Network Configuration/ Connectivity	LAN: 4 10BASE-T connections WAN: 4 connections, ISDN/BRI or V.35 or X.21 (any combinations of 2 and 3)	LAN: 10BASE-T or AUI V.35 connection to the Room System
Necessary Hardware/ Software components	When configured with V.35 ports, Terminal Adapter or CSU/DSU or IMUX should be used	
Compression Scheme(s)	H.320, H323	H.320
Administration Features	SNMP management. Also includes H.323 Gatekeeper to control LAN bandwidth usage.	SNMP management
Video Features	Call Transfer Call Forward Broadcast	
Comments	WAN ports are ISDN/BRI or V.35. G.711/G.728 Audio Transcoder is optional.	The Room System must have V.35 connection
Warranty:	1 year	1 year
Price:	$5,950–$9,450	$3,450

Manufacturer	RADVision	Transformation Technologies, Inc
Model	VIC/MVIP	Wavephone for Windows
General Description	Connects PictureTel Live 100/50 to the LAN using the MVIP bus and RADVision's VCP protocol.	Software and hardware to provide full duplex voice conferencing across LANs
Server System Platforms/ Requirements	N/A	N/A
Desktop Systems OS/Requirements	Windows 3.11/95 (MS TCP/IP)	ISA Board Windows O/S
Network Configuration/ Connectivity	Any standard LAN network interface card	LAN connections through Windows
Necessary Hardware/ Software components	Free I/O address and IRQ on the ISA bus	PC 486 or higher, 4Mb RAM min, 16bit Ethernet NIC, Windows 3.11 or higher, TCP/IP stack
Compression Scheme(s)	H.320	Pcm and Adpcm voice compression
Administration Features	INA	INA
Video Features	Call Transfer Call Forward Broadcast	Audio only; video released in late '96
Comments		
Warranty	1 year	1 year
Price:	$695	$88

N/A—Not applicable   INA—Information not available

Conferencing Network Applications ■

Manufacturer	**White Pine Software**
Model	Enhanced CU-SeeMe
General Description	Real-time video conferencing software for person-to-person communicating or for group conferencing. Used over the Internet or any TCP/IP network
Server System Platforms/ Requirements	Windows NT, 95, 3.5.1 and higher, and Unix, 16 MB RAM min., 500K hard disk, 100MHz processor or faster
Desktop Systems OS/Requirements	Windows 3.1 or greater, or Windows 95, Macintosh 68020.030.040. Power Macintosh
Network Configuration/ Connectivity	Internet: 28.8K modem ISDN link or higher Intranet: TCP/IP
Necessary Hardware/ Software Components	14.4K+, SLIP/PPP compatible, camera with composite or S-video output, PC 486 or Pentium, recommended separate microphone or headset
Compression Scheme(s)	Audio-selectable compression algorithms with 100ms and 50ms sampling settings, 2.4 and 8.5 audio codecs to support 14.4K and 28.8K modem connections
Administration Features	Local Window Controls: microphone, video, status bar, and connection information.
Video Features	Viewing of up to 8 participant windows. Unlimited number for audio and talk window. Caller-ID message alert box for incoming connections. 24bit true color and 4bit greyscale reflector sites
Comments	Security password, caller ID, and other conference- and inbound-call security
Warranty	None
Price	$99

■ Document Management Network Applications

Manufacturer	Chrystal Software Inc.	Documentum, Inc.
Model	Astoria 1.1	EDMS (Enterprise Document Mgmt. System)
O/S Support	Windows NT, Sun Solaris	Windows NT, Windows 95, Macintosh, Unix, Sun, H.P., IBM
Network Support	TCP/IP	Unix, NT, TCP/IP, Web/Intranet
Features	Object management for documents and Web servers. Multilingual search on contact, context and attributes. Access, share and track documents, components and Web pages. Object-oriented database for maximum capacity and granularity. No set-up needed: Astoria is ready for production when installed.	Integrated workflow. Compound document management. Change and release control. Cross platform and cross database. Full text retrieval. Scalable for enterprise wide deployment.
Comments	Already integrated with leading document authoring tools	
Warranty	N/A	90-day, extended
Price	$42,500 10 seat system	$500—$1000/per user. Configuration and volume dependent.

Manufacturer	GD Associates Ltd.	Informative graphics Corporation
Model	Qdistrib	Myriad
O/S Support	PC MS Windows, Digital and Intel NT, Unix (16 O/S)	Windows (3x, NT, 95), DOS, Sun OS 4.1x, Solaris 2x, HP-UX, AIX, Macintosh
Network Support	Unix, Winsock	Myriad 2.2x: N/A Myriad 3.x: TCP/IP. Metbips
Features	Multiple destinations printer, font, internet, files. Parsing and partial file distribution. Keyword search. Compression/Encryption. Recipient and file profile definitions. Heterogeneous O/S support.	Views, redlines, and prints more than 100 file formats. Intelligent document API. Full pan and zoom. Bird's eye command. Layering and orientation. On-the-fly unzip. ISO 9000 stamping. Multiple documents (TIFF, PDF Postscript, fax), Internet support, Enhanced redlining, including notes, symbols, highlights, and more.
Comments	Document distribution for electronically routing reports throughout the network	
Warranty	90 day	90 day
Price	$15,000	$595–$795

Manufacturer	Inmagic, Inc.	Fujitsu
Model	DBIText WebServer	TeamWARE Library 5.0
O/S Support	Windows 3+, Windows 95, and Windows NT	Sun Solaris 2.4 or later, Windows NT 3.51 or later, Windows3.x and 95, Unix, Macintosh, terminal, DOS
Network Support	All	TCP/IP, NetBIOS, NetBEUI
Features	A text-centric document management system designed exclusively to manage HTML document text. DBMS and text-retrieval architecture allow for quick precise search, indexing and retrieval.	Client-server based, store any type of file (voice, video, image, etc.), full-text and profile searching (keyword, file type, date range), file locking, version control, revision history, hierarchical folder structure, multiple access rights, integrated with TeamWARE Mail and Forum and with popular productivity tools (save file to Library from within an application).
Comments		Also provides mailbox size restriction, maximum message size definition, multi-windowing, hierarchical folder structure, message annotation and reminder capability, message retraction
Warranty	N/A	Limited
Price	$5,000	Basic license: $150 per user

N/A—Not applicable   INA—Information not available

Document Management Network Applications ■

Manufacturer	Inmagic, Inc.	Salix Systems
Model	Inmagic DB/TextWorks	DocStor 2.2
O/S Support	PC Windows 3.X, Windows 95/NT	PC-Windows, Unix, HP-UX, Solaris, Sun OS
Network Support	NetWare	Any TCP/IP Network (Unix, Windows NT, Windows95, NetWare, WinSock, etc.)
Features	Unlimited length fields. Repeating fields. Rapid and precise searching. Integrated image management. Database linking. WYS/WYG report writing.	Customer-defined fields. Check out lock, File linking. Notes. Multiple-level security. File status query. Configurable audit trail. History query. Warnings. Version tracking. Configurable tool definitions. Responsible party notifications. Blocked action on files. Inherited security. Configurable hierarchy. Script language.
Comments	DB/TextWorks databases can be mounted on the Web using Inmagic's DB/Text Web Server.	Concurrent floating licenses. Manages any file format STAR-reseller program.
Warranty	N/A	30 day
Price	$795, single user $4,500, 10-user	$4,995

Manufacturer	Thunderstone Software	Uniplex Software
Model	TEXIS	onGO DMS
O/S Support	All Unix, Windows NT	MS Windows 3.1, Windows 95, Windows NT, HP/UX, Solaris, AIX, D6/UX, SCO Open Server
Network Support	Any TCP/IP	WINSOCK, TCP/IP
Features	Plug-in object drivers. 32-bit Opec. PDF, DBF file format support. Relevance ranking. Fully integrated SQL RDBMS. HTML file parsing. Variable sized document, records and objects. Automatic code generator.	Along with other corporate public and private documents, onGO DMS can contain and control Web Site documents, ensuring that corporate policies are applied to all company information.
Comments		Enterprise-wide system for managing the complete lifecycle of compound document projects
Warranty	1 year; 30-day money-back guarantee; tech support; "bug fixes" are lifetime	Free installation support for 30 days
Price	$4,395+; quantity discounts available	$650 per user

Manufacturer	Uniplex Software	Xerox Corp.
Model	onGO Office	Visual Recall 20
O/S Support	MS Windows 3.1, Windows 95, and Unix	MS Windows 3.1
Network Support	WinSock, TCP/IP	NetWare
Features	Enterprise-wide electronic mail, directory services, group and resource scheduling and calendaring system. Enterprise database is available to all users, from within mail, calendar, directory or external applications. Allows users to integrate their favorite desktop and client applications, such as cc:Mail, MS Mail, and WordPerfect.	Excepts Browser, highlights key points of document. Analyzes document repository contents through visualizations. Support for ODMA standard. High-performance searching. Real-time indexing over WANs.
Comments	It provides a communications backbone for any size organization.	Includes Xerox, TextBridge, OCR software
Warranty	Free installation support for 30 days	INA
Price	$350 per user	$395, client $695, server

N/A—Not applicable   INA—Information not available

End ■

Groupware Network Applications

Manufacturer Groupware	ADM Group	Attachmate
Model	Quick Flash 2.5	OpenMind 3.0
General Description	Groupware messaging system using graphic yellow sticky notes and phone message pads.	A client/server-based groupware application for collaborative workspaces. Combines group conferencing, document management, and electronic publishing.
General Applications	Messaging, e-mail	Conferencing, threaded discussions, Internet access, document management
Key Features	No passwords. Reads Novell. Sets common and private groups for distribution. Paging and screen capture annotation. Answering machine, Do Not Disturb, forwarding, DDE server.	Forum-style conferencing, integrated document management, workgroup- enhanced Internet access, e-mail, and netnews integration, full text searching, automatic notification, security, replication
Server OS Support	Windows compatible	Windows NT
Client OS Support	Any Windows	Windows, Windows NT, Mac
Communication Protocols	N/A	IPX/SPX, TCP/IP, NetBIOS/ NetBEUI, Banyan Vines IP, AppleTalk
Warranty	90 day	INA
Price	$345 (10 user), $449 (25 user)	Server + 5 clients free $75 (additional servers), $50 (additional clients)

Manufacturer Groupware	The Bristol Group	Crosswind Technologies, Inc.
Model	PowerBase II	Synchronize Groupware
General Description	PowerBase II is an Internet based contact manager accessible from any Web browser. Information is stored in a shared database and is password protected for security. PowerBase II integrates with e-mail and fax.	Synchronize is a scheduling, task and resource management tool designed for the corporate computing environment.
General Applications	Contact management, e-mail, fax, Internet contacts	Scheduling, task, resource management-email compliant
Key Features	Shared contact manager or intranet company database, accessible with any web browser, password security, e-mail/fax integration, text searching, customizable.	Groupware, scheduling, task management, resource scheduling
Server OS Support	Any	20 Unix platforms, Windows NT, Windows 3.1, Windows 95 ASCII X/11 motif
Client OS Support	Any desktop	Window, DOS, Macintosh
Communication Protocols	HTTP/ HTML	TCP/IP
Warranty	90 day	90 day
Price	Check with vendor	$100 per user

Manufacturer Groupware	Fujitsu	Galacticom
Model	TeamWARE Office 5.0	Worldgroup 3.0
General Description	TeamWARE office is browser-enabled Internet/Intranet group productivity software that provides a complete solution from workgroup to enterprise.	Launch plug-and-play client/server applications from your Web site. Includes customizable surveys, shared libraries, group messaging, SMTP Mail and Teleconference.

N/A—Not applicable   INA—Information not available

Groupware Network Applications ■

Manufacturer Groupware	Fujitsu	Galacticom
General Applications	Enterprise-wide E-mail, fax, group scheduling, document management, and discussion database. Also includes desktop imaging, collaborative workflow and real-time conferencing.	E-mail, messaging, teleconference, polling with shared whiteboard. Built-in Web server.
Key Features	Ready-to-run, remote connectivity, database replication, directory synchronization, X.500 DUA, connectors for MIME, X.500, MHS and others, API available, integrated with popular productivity tools.	Workgroup Internet access, remote connectiviy
Server OS Support	Windows NT, Solaris	Windows NT, Windows 95, DOS
Client OS Support	Windows 95, Windows NT, Windows 3.1, Unix, Macintosh, Terminal, DOS	Windows, DOS
Communication Protocols	GUI, browser	IPX/SPX, TCP/IP
Warranty	Limited	30 day money back guarantee
Price	$195–$369 per user for Office Suite	N/A

Manufacturer Groupware	IMB, Inc.	LAN-ACES, Inc.
Model	People-Planner Central	Office-Logic 3.0
General Description	A corporate-level reporting tool that consolidates productivity data for labor management analysis. Designed to highlight underperforming areas and to assess labor costs.	A complete groupware productivity solution with integrated DOS, Windows, Windows NT, Windows 95 support.
General Applications	Enterprise reporting tool	E-mail, scheduling, phone message center, real-time chat, fax view/send
Key Features	Can view information: for the entire chain, by region, district, store, department or job. Reports: daily sales, wage, wage costs, labor used, sales per hour, and average wage.	Intelligent e-mail routing, bulletin systems, group/personal scheduling, remote capabilities, phone message center, file/print queue manager, MAPI support, database/cardex, to-do lists, notepads, spell checker, non-intrusive notifications, in-out board, message tracking.
Server OS Support	Windows NT Server	Netware, LANtastic, Power LAN, LAN Manager, Invisible LAN, Windows NT, Windows 95, WFW, compatible NetBIOS networks
Client OS Support	Windows	DOS, Windows, Windows NT, Windows 95
Communication Protocols	Customer defined	IPX/SPX, NetBEUI, TCP/IP, NetBIOS
Warranty	30 day	
Price		$495 (5 user), $1,995 (25), $4,995 (100), $149 (remote)

Manufacturer Groupware	Lotus Development Corp.	Microsoft
Model	Notes 4.1	Exchange Server 4.0
General Description	A client/server platform for developing, and deploying groupware applications that help organizations communicate, collaborate & coordinate business processes within and beyond the organization.	MS Exchange is the messaging server with integrated groupware. It combines e-mail, group scheduling, electronic forms and groupware applications on a single platform that can be managed with a centralized administration program
General Applications	E-mail, messaging, enterprise mgmt.	E-mail, scheduling, BBS, tracking applications

N/A—Not applicable   INA—Information not available

Table Continues →

■ Groupware Network Applications

Manufacturer Groupware	Lotus Development Corp.		Microsoft
Key Features	Integrated Client/Server Messaging. Mobility using replication capabilities. With new intuitive tools such as Intelligent Agent. Internet Integration into Notes environment. Application Development and Programmability, Enterprise Management with enhanced administration and mgmt, increased server performance & greater scalability.		Universal Inbox, remote connectivity, replication, digital signatures and encryption, scheduling, forms design, BBS and tracking apps, X.400 and SMTP connectivity hotlinks to web, message tracking
Server OS Support	AIX, HP-UX, NetWare, OS/2, Solaris, Windows 95,NT		MS windows NT server
Client OS Support	AIX, HP-UX, OS/2, MAC, Solaris, Windows 3.0, Windows 95, Windows NT		Windows 3.x, 95, NT, DOS, Mac
Communication Protocols	AppleTalk, SPX, SPX II, Net Bios/Net BE UI, TCP/IP, VINES, X.PC, X.25, SNA		IPX/SPX, NetBEAUI, NetBIOS, Appletalk, Banyan Vines
Warranty	INA		90 day
Price	Notes Clients—$55–$275 Notes Servers—$2,995 + $275		$529

Manufacturer Groupware	Novell	SoftArc Inc.	TeleVell
Model	GroupWise 5	FirstClass 3.5	TeleSell
General Description	Novell's fifth generation messaging system, built on a scalable, proven architecture. It is a client/server cross-platform messaging and groupware product that allows users to access and manage e-mail, personal calendaring, group scheduling, tasks, voice mail, and faxes from within a Universal Mail Box.	A multi-platform, workgroup communication system. It integrates with replicable discussion databases, enterprise database access, remote access, forms processing, and online information support.	A networkable sales and support team automation. Nine modules are available to automate sales, marketing and customer support. Remote synchronization is also available.
General Applications	E-mail, fax, calendaring/scheduling, document management, workflow	Fax, e-mail, conferencing, Internet support	Sales tracking, customer support use, team automation.
Key Features	Conferencing, database access, document management, forms creation, Internet/ intranet access, open API's, remote support, shared folders, task management.	E-mail, conferencing, workgroup Internet access, file attachments, remote connectivity, complete security, full text searching, database access, real-time typed discussions, automatic notification, history tracking free upgrades	Fully relational contact data base, sales tracking, template letters, full page note taking, forecasting, report writing, product information, action item scheduling and more.
Server OS Support	NetWare, NLM, OS/2, UNIX (3 versions), Windows NT	Windows NT, Macintosh	Novell and all NetBIOS networks
Client OS Support	Macintosh, PowerMac, Unix, Win 3.x/95/NT	Windows, DOS, Macintosh	All Windows (95, NT, 3.1)
Communication Protocols	IPX.SPX, or TCP/IP; also accommodates MHS, POP3, NetBEUI, NetBIOS, SMTP, and x..400	IPX, TCP/IP, NetBIOS, AppleTalk	NetBIOS
Warranty	90 day	INA	INA
Price	$718 for 5 user license $32,635 for a 250 user license.	$495 (includes 5-user license)	$195–$1,495 depending on module

---

N/A—Not applicable   INA—Information not available

End ■

Scheduling Network Applications ■

Manufacturer	**Cross Wind Technologies**	**Fujitsu**
Model	Synchronize	TeamWARE Calendar 3.5
NOS	TCP/IP	OS/2, Windows NT, Netware, Solaris, HP-UX, UnixWare
Client OS	Windows, Vines, LANtastic	Windows 95, Windows NT, Windows 3.1
FEATURE SUMMARY		
Globally View Busy/ Available Slots	Yes	Yes
Administer Defined Workdays/Hours/ Holidays	Yes	Yes
View Group/ Individual Calendars	Yes	Yes
Sound Alarms	Yes	Yes
Auto-launch Programs	No	Yes (requires customization)
Attach Notes for Appointments	Yes	Yes
Finds Open-time for Participants	Yes	No
Conflict Notification	INA	Yes
Attendance Confirmation	Yes	Yes
Alerts to Changes	Yes	Yes
Allows Meeting and Appointment Searches	Yes	No
Remote Features	Yes	Remote viewing, remote editing
Template/Custom Reporting	No	No
Information Exchange	Import/export facility	No
Comments	Synchronize is designed for workgroups and enterprises from 5 to 50,000 users; it has a scalable, cross-platform, client/server design.	Allows both personal and resource calendars. Enterprise-wide scheduling capability.
Warranty	90 day	Limited
Price	$100 per user	$57–$88 per user

Manufacturer	**LAN-ACES, Inc.**	**ON Technology**
Model	Office-Logic 3.0	Meeting Maker XP
NOS	Netware, Lantastic, Power LAN, LAN Manager, Invisible LAN, Windows NT, Windows 95, WFW, compatible NetBIOS networks	Windows, Windows 95, Windows NT, Macintosh, Unix, PowerMac, OS/2, NLM
Client OS	DOS, Windows, Windows NT, Windows 95	Windows, Windows 95, Windows NT, Macintosh, Unix, PowerMac, OS/2, DOS
FEATURE SUMMARY		
Globally View Busy/ Available Slots	Yes	Yes
Administer Defined Workdays/Hours/ Holidays	Yes	Yes
View Group/ Individual Calendars	Yes	Yes

N/A—Not applicable   INA—Information not available

Table Continues →

■ Scheduling Network Applications

Manufacturer	LAN-ACES, Inc.	ON Technology
Sound Alarms	Yes	Yes
Auto-launch Programs	Yes	No
Attach Notes for Appointments	Yes	Yes
Finds Open-time for Participants	Yes	Yes
Conflict Notification	Yes	Yes
Attendance Confirmation	Yes	Yes
Alerts to Changes	Yes	Yes
Allows Meeting and Appointment Searches	Yes	Yes (by meeting title, agenda and notes)
Remote Features	Yes, bi-directional scheduler synchronization	Remote viewing and editing
Template/Custom Reporting	Yes	No
Information Exchange	PDA support, drag-and-drop (DDE)	PDA support, including 2-way sync with Newton
Comments	Features variable time-before-alarm settings, private appointments (encrypted), remote user in appointments, resource proxy, editable and deletable recurring appointments, multi-day continuous and non-continuous appointments.	
Warranty	INA	30 day
Price	$495 (5 user), $1,995 (25), $4,995 (100), $149 (remote)	$89 per user

Manufacturer	Russell Information Sciences	Sound Ideas of America
Model	Scheduler	FineLine Message Manager
NOS	TCP/IP, Netware, Vines, MS Winsock, PATHWORKS, AppleTalk/DECnet	TCP/IP compatible
Client OS	Windows 3.1, Windows 95, Windows NT, Macintosh, DOS, VT's (OpenVMS)	SCO, AIX, HP-UX
FEATURE SUMMARY		
Globally View Busy/ Available Slots	Yes	Yes
Administer Defined Workdays/Hours/ Holidays	Yes	Yes
View Group/ Individual Calendars	Yes	Yes
Sound Alarms	Yes	Yes
Auto-launch Programs	No	No
Attach Notes for Appointments	Yes	Yes
Finds Open-time for Participants	Yes	Yes
Conflict Notification	Yes	Yes
Attendance Confirmation	Yes	No

N/A—Not applicable   INA—Information not available

Scheduling Network Applications ■

Manufacturer	Russell Information Sciences	Sound Ideas of America
Alerts to Changes	Yes	No
Allows Meeting and Appointment Searches	Yes	No
Remote Features	Downloading, uploading, and calendar reconciliation between server and local clients	N/A
Template/Custom Reporting	No	Yes
Information Exchange	No	N/A
Comments	Real-time scheduling is supported cross-platform (servers and desktops). Additional administration client product manages multiple CM servers from single graphical desktop.	Character-based
Warranty	No	unlimited
Price	$49 a seat at 5,000 units	$200, 5 user and up

Manufacturer	Symantec	Symantec
Model	ACT! For Notes	ACT! For Windows
NOS	OS/2 Warp, NT	Netware, NT
Client OS	Windows 3.1, Windows 95, Windows NT	Windows 3.1, Windows 95, Windows NT
FEATURE SUMMARY		
Globally View Busy/ Available Slots	No	Yes
Administer Defined Workdays/Hours/ Holidays	No	No
View Group/ Individual Calendars	In task list format	Yes
Sound Alarms	Yes—through e-mail	Yes
Auto-launch Programs	Yes—Notes functionality	No
Attach Notes for Appointments	Yes	No
Finds Open-time for Participants	No	No
Conflict Notification	No	Yes
Attendance Confirmation	No	Sends e-mail to confirm
Alerts to Changes	Yes—unread marks	No
Allows Meeting and Appointment Searches	Yes	Yes
Remote Features	Via Notes replication	Yes
Template/Custom Reporting	Both	Both
Information Exchange	Data conversion from ACT!	DDE, defined import/export formats, PDA support
Comments	Also available for Newton & HP Palmtop	Also available for Newton & HP Palmtop
Warranty	60 day	90 day
Price	$249	$200

N/A—Not applicable   INA—Information not available

End ■

■ Network Browser Applications

Manufacturer	**Attachmate**	**Attachmate**
Model	Emissary Desktop 2.0	Emissary v.2.0
GENERAL		
Available On-line	Yes	Yes
Uninstall	Yes	Yes
WinSock	Yes	Yes
Claimed Level of HTML Support	3.0	3.0
Macro Support	Yes	Yes
Java Support	No	No
OS Support	No	Yes
BOOKMARKS		
Group Bookmarks	No	Yes
Import/Export	Yes/Yes	Yes/Yes
Save Formats (Images, HTML, Text)	Yes	Yes
MULTIMEDIA		
Integrated or Bundled AVI/MPEG	Yes/Yes	No/No
Integrated or Bundled QuickTime	No	No
Integrated or Bundled AU/IWAVE	Yes/Yes	Yes/Yes
Integrated or Bundled RA/WAV	Yes/Yes	Yes/Yes
Customizable MIME/Helper Support	Yes/Yes	Yes/Yes
PROPRIETARY EXTENSIONS		
Frames	Yes	Yes
Client-Side Image maps	Yes	Yes
Tables	Yes	Yes
Blinking Text	Yes	Yes
Body Image (Tilting)	No	No
Change Font Color	Yes	Yes
Static Backgrounds	Yes	No
Background Sound	Yes	No
Marquees	Yes	No
INTEGRATED TOOLS (E-mail, FTP, Gopher, Newsreader, Telnet)	E-mail, news, FTP, NFS, Telnet	E-mail, file manager, FTP, News Reader, Telnet
DOCUMENTATION (Online, Web-based, and/or Print)	Online, Web-based, text	On-line, printed
Comments		
Warranty	INA	INA
Price	$99	$99

N/A—Not applicable   INA—Information not available

Network Browser Applications ■

Manufacturer	CompuServ	FTP Software Inc.
Model	Mosaic in a Box for Windows 95	Explore Anywhere 2.0
GENERAL		
Available On-line	Yes	Yes
Uninstall	No	Yes
WinSock	Yes	Yes
Claimed Level of HTML Support	3.0	3.0
Macro Support	No	No
Java Support	No	No
OS Support	Windows 95, Windows 3.1x	Windows 95, Windows 3.1x, Windows NT
BOOKMARKS		
Group Bookmarks	Yes	Yes
Import/Export	Yes/Yes	No/No
Save Formats (Images, HTML, Text)	Save images and HTML	Yes
MULTIMEDIA		
Integrated or Bundled AVI/MPEG	Yes/Yes	No/No
Integrated or Bundled QuickTime	No	No
Integrated or Bundled AU/IWAVE	Yes/No	Yes/No
Integrated or Bundled RA/WAV	No/No	No/No
Customizable MIME/Helper Support	Yes/Yes	Yes
PROPRIETARY EXTENSIONS		
Frames	No	No
Client-Side Image maps	No	Yes
Tables	No	No
Blinking Text	No	No
Body Image (Tilting)	Yes	Yes
Change Font Color	No	Yes
Static Backgrounds	No	No
Background Sound	No	No
Marquees	No	No
INTEGRATED TOOLS (E-mail, FTP, Gopher, Newsreader, Telnet)	E-mail, FTP, Gopher, Newsreader	E-mail, FTP, Gopher, Newsreader, Telnet
DOCUMENTATION (Online, Web-based, and/or Print)	On-line, Web-based, text	On-line, Web-based, text
Comments		
Warranty	INA	INA
Price	$15	$199

N/A—Not applicable   INA—Information not available

Table Continues →

ZIFF-DAVIS PRESS

■ Network Browser Applications

Manufacturer	IBM	IBM
Model	WebExplorer 1.03	WebExplorer Mosaic 2.1
GENERAL		
Available On-line	Yes	No
Uninstall	No	No
WinSock	N/A	Yes
Claimed Level of HTML Support	2.0	3.0
Macro Support	No	No
Java Support	No	No
OS Support	OS/2	Windows 95, Windows 3.1x
BOOKMARKS		
Group Bookmarks	No	No
Import/Export	No/No	No/Yes
Save Formats (Images, HTML, Text)	Yes	Yes
MULTIMEDIA		
Integrated or Bundled AVI/MPEG	No/No	No/No
Integrated or Bundled QuickTime	No	No
Integrated or Bundled AU/IWAVE	No/No	Yes/No
Integrated or Bundled RA/WAV	No/No	No/No
Customizable MIME/Helper Support	Yes/Yes	Yes/Yes
PROPRIETARY EXTENSIONS		
Frames	No	No
Client-Side Image maps	No	Yes
Tables	Yes	Yes
Blinking Text	No	No
Body Image (Tilting)	Yes	Yes
Change Font Color	No	Yes
Static Backgrounds	No	No
Background Sound	No	No
Marquees	No	No
INTEGRATED TOOLS (E-mail, FTP, Gopher, Newsreader, Telnet)	E-mail, FTP, Gopher, Newsreader, Telnet	E-mail, FTP, Gopher, Newsreader, Telnet
DOCUMENTATION (Online, Web-based, and/or Print)	On-line, Web-based, text	On-line, Web-based, text
Comments		
Warranty	INA	
Price	Free	$39

N/A—Not applicable   INA—Information not available

Network Browser Applications ■

Manufacturer	Microsoft	Net Manage Inc.
Model	Microsoft Internet Explorer 2.0	Web Surfer 4.6
GENERAL		
Available On-line	Yes	Yes
Uninstall	Yes	No
WinSock	Yes	N/A
Claimed Level of HTML Support	3.0	3.0
Macro Support	No	No
Java Support	No	No
OS Support	Windows 95	Windows 3.1x
BOOKMARKS		
Group Bookmarks	Yes	Yes
Import/Export	Yes/Yes	Yes/Yes
Save Formats (Images, HTML, Text)	Yes	Yes
MULTIMEDIA		
Integrated or Bundled AVI/MPEG	Yes/No	Yes/No
Integrated or Bundled QuickTime	No	No
Integrated or Bundled AU/IWAVE	Yes/No	Yes/No
Integrated or Bundled RA/WAV	Yes/Yes	Yes/Yes
Customizable MIME/Helper Support	Yes/Yes	Yes/Yes
PROPRIETARY EXTENSIONS		
Frames	No	No
Client-Side Image maps	Yes	Yes
Tables	Yes	Yes
Blinking Text	No	No
Body Image (Tilting)	Yes	Yes
Change Font Color	Yes	No
Static Backgrounds	Yes	No
Background Sound	Yes	No
Marquees	Yes	No
INTEGRATED TOOLS (E-mail, FTP, Gopher, Newsreader, Telnet)	FTP, Gopher	E-mail, FTP, Gopher, Newsreader, Telnet
DOCUMENTATION (Online, Web-based, and/or Print)	On-line, Web-based	On-line, Web-based, text
Comments		
Warranty	INA	INA
Price	Free	Free

N/A—Not applicable   INA—Information not available

Table Continues →

Network Browser Applications

Manufacturer	Netscape Comm.	Oracle Corp.
Model	Netscape Navigator 2.0	Power Browser 0.9B
GENERAL		
Available On-line	Yes	Yes
Uninstall	Yes	No
WinSock	Yes	Yes
Claimed Level of HTML Support	3.0	2.0
Macro Support	No	Yes
Java Support	Yes	No
OS Support	Windows 95, Windows 3.1x, Windows NT	Windows 95, Windows 3.1x, Windows NT
BOOKMARKS		
Group Bookmarks	Yes	Yes
Import/Export	Yes/Yes	Yes/Yes
Save Formats (Images, HTML, Text)	Yes	Yes
MULTIMEDIA		
Integrated or Bundled AVI/MPEG	No/No	Yes/No
Integrated or Bundled QuickTime	No	No
Integrated or Bundled AU/IWAVE	Yes/No	No/No
Integrated or Bundled RA/WAV	No/Yes	No/No
Customizable MIME/Helper Support	Yes/Yes	Yes/Yes
PROPRIETARY EXTENSIONS		
Frames	Yes	No
Client-Side Image maps	Yes	Yes
Tables	Yes	Yes
Blinking Text	Yes	No
Body Image (Tilting)	Yes	Yes
Change Font Color	Yes	No
Static Backgrounds	No	No
Background Sound	No	No
Marquees	No	No
INTEGRATED TOOLS (E-mail, FTP, Gopher, Newsreader, Telnet)	E-mail, FTP, Gopher, Newsreader	None
DOCUMENTATION (Online, Web-based, and/or Print)	Web-based	Web-based
Comments		
Warranty	INA	INA
Price	$49	Free

N/A—Not applicable   INA—Information not available

Network Browser Applications ■

Manufacturer	Quarterdeck Corp.	Spyglass Inc.
Model	Quarterdeck Internet Suite 2.0	Spyglass Mosaic 2.1
GENERAL		
Available On-line	No	No
Uninstall	No	No
WinSock	Yes	Yes
Claimed Level of HTML Support	2.0	2.0
Macro Support	No	No
Java Support	No	No
OS Support	Windows 95, Windows 3.1x, Windows NT	Windows 95, Windows 3.1x, Windows NT
BOOKMARKS		
Group Bookmarks	Yes	No
Import/Export	Yes/Yes	No/Yes
Save Formats (Images, HTML, Text)	Yes	Yes
MULTIMEDIA		
Integrated or Bundled AVI/MPEG	No/No	No/No
Integrated or Bundled QuickTime	No	No
Integrated or Bundled AU/IWAVE	Yes/No	Yes/No
Integrated or Bundled RA/WAV	No/Yes	No/No
Customizable MIME/Helper Support	Yes/Yes	Yes/Yes
PROPRIETARY EXTENSIONS		
Frames	No	No
Client-Side Image maps	No	Yes
Tables	Yes	Yes
Blinking Text	No	No
Body Image (Tilting)	Yes	Yes
Change Font Color	No	Yes
Static Backgrounds	No	No
Background Sound	No	No
Marquees	No	No
INTEGRATED TOOLS (E-mail, FTP, Gopher, Newsreader, Telnet)	E-mail, FTP, Newsreader, Telnet	E-mail, FTP, Gooher, Newsreader, Telnet
DOCUMENTATION (Online, Web-based, and/or Print)	On-line, Web-based, text	On-line, varies, varies
Comments		
Warranty	INA	INA
Price	$60	Varies

N/A—Not applicable   INA—Information not available   **Table Continues →**

■ Network Browser Applications

Manufacturer	Symantec Corp	Traveling Software, Inc.
Model	Cyberjack Version 7.0 (for Windows 95 only)	Webfax
GENERAL		
Available On-line	Yes	Yes
Uninstall	Yes	Yes
WinSock	Uses Windows 95 stack	Yes
Claimed Level of HTML Support	3.0	3.0
Macro Support	No	Yes
Java Support	No	Class 1
OS Support	Windows 95 only	Windows 95
BOOKMARKS		
Group Bookmarks	Yes	N/A
Import/Export	Yes	N/A
Save Formats (Images, HTML, Text)	INA	N/A
MULTIMEDIA		
Integrated or Bundled AVI/MPEG	Yes through Windows 95 OLE 2.0	N/A
Integrated or Bundled QuickTime	No	N/A
Integrated or Bundled AU/IWAVE	No	N/A
Integrated or Bundled RA/WAV	Yes through Windows 95 OLE 2.0	N/A
Customizable MIME/Helper Support	No	N/A
PROPRIETARY EXTENSIONS		
Frames	No	Yes
Client-Side Image maps	Yes	Yes
Tables	Yes	Yes
Blinking Text	Yes	Yes
Body Image (Tilting)	No	Yes
Change Font Color	Yes	Yes
Static Backgrounds	No	Yes
Background Sound	No	Yes
Marquees	INA	Yes
INTEGRATED TOOLS (E-mail, FTP, Gopher, Newsreader, Telnet)	FTP, IRC, News, Gopher, Archie, Finger, Ping, Telnet	No
DOCUMENTATION (Online, Web-based, and/or Print)	On-line and manual	Yes
Comments	Includes image manager, ZIP manager, and Norton Anti Virus; automatic-update/upgrade; integrates with Netscape (eg. use Netscape to browse, and Cj FTP comes up if hit FTP site)	Off-line Web Browser; supports anything the browser supports.
Warranty	60-day money-back	30 day
Price	$79	$30

N/A—Not applicable   INA—Information not available

Network Browser Applications ■

Manufacturer	**University of Illinois**
Model	NCSA Mosaic 2.0
GENERAL	
Available On-line	Yes
Uninstall	Yes
WinSock	Yes
Claimed Level of HTML Support	2.0
Macro Support	No
Java Support	No
OS Support	Windows 95, Windows 3.1x, Windows NT
BOOKMARKS	
Group Bookmarks	Yes
Import/Export	Yes/Yes
Save Formats (Images, HTML, Text)	Yes
MULTIMEDIA	
Integrated or Bundled AVI/MPEG	No/No
Integrated or Bundled QuickTime	No
Integrated or Bundled AU/IWAVE	No/No
Integrated or Bundled RA/WAV	No/Yes
Customizable MIME/Helper Support	Yes/Yes
PROPRIETARY EXTENSIONS	
Frames	No
Client-Side Image maps	No
Tables	Yes
Blinking Text	No
Body Image (Tilting)	Yes
Change Font Color	Yes
Static Backgrounds	Yes
Background Sound	Yes
Marquees	No
INTEGRATED TOOLS (E-mail, FTP, Gopher, Newsreader, Telnet)	E-mail, FTP, Gopher, Newsreader
DOCUMENTATION (Online, Web-based, and/or Print)	On-line, Web-based, text
Comments	
Warranty	
Price	Free

N/A—Not applicable   INA—Information not available

End ■

■ Fax Communications Network Applications

Manufacturer	ArchTek	ArchTek
Model	2834BAV 2834BA 2834A	3334BR 3334BT
Server OS/NOS	Netware, NLM	Netware, NLM
Client OS	Windows, DOS	Windows, DOS
Max Fax/Modem Lines/Adapters	1	1
Configuration	Dedicated	Dedicated
Fax Hardware Compatibility	Class 0, 1 and 2 modems	Class 0, 1 and 2 modems
Nds Compliance	Yes	Yes
Security	No	No
SNMP Support	Yes	Yes
FEATURES		
Auto-redial/ scheduling	Yes	Yes
Inbound Notification	Yes	Yes
Inbound Routing	Yes	Yes
Fax Archives	Yes	Yes
Broadcasting	Yes	Yes
Integrates with E-mail	Yes	Yes
Comments	BAV: internal AT&T chip set with voice BA: internal AT&T chip set A: external AT&T chip set	Rockwell chip set, internal 33.6 TI chip set, internal 33.6
Warranty	5 year	5 year
Price	$239/$189/$219	$229

Manufacturer	The Bristol Group	Devcom Mid-America Inc.
Model	IsoFax	
Server OS/NOS	Sun, HP, IBM, Windows NT	All Unix- and MS NT- based
Client OS	Sun, HP, IBM, Windows, Windows NT, Windows 95	Windows, Windows 95,Windows NT, Macintosh, Unix
Max Fax/Modem Lines/Adapters	128	Unlimited
Configuration	Client/server	Non-dedicated server
Fax Hardware Compatibility	Check with vendor	Class 2 or 2.0 modems and serial ports
Nds Compliance	N/A	Yes
Security	Through O/S	Through Unix or NT
SNMP Support	No	Yes
FEATURES		
Auto-redial/ scheduling	Yes	Yes
Inbound Notification	Yes	Yes

N/A—Not applicable   INA—Information not available

Fax Communications Network Applications ■

Manufacturer	The Bristol Group	Devcom Mid-America Inc.
Inbound Routing	Yes	Yes
Fax Archives	Yes	Yes
Broadcasting	Yes	Yes
Integrates with E-mail	Yes	Yes
Comments		
Warranty	90 day	90 day
Price	Check with vendor	$1,200–$20,000

Manufacturer	ESKER, Inc.	Faximum Software, Inc.
Model	Tun Mail v.8.01	Faximum Client/ Server
Server OS/NOS	AIX, SLO, Sun, HP-UX	DG/UX, HP/UX 9.x and 10.x, AIX/6000, Linux, SCO Unix, Open Server, Sun Solaris 2.x, Sun OS 4.x
Client OS	Windows 3.x, Windows 95	All of the above including Windows 3.1, Windows 95, Windows NT; and any platform with a Web browser
Max Fax/Modem Lines/Adapters	1 modem on server	256
Configuration	Non-dedicated	Non-dedicated
Fax Hardware Compatibility	Fax modem on server TTY	Class 2 and 2.0 modems Terminal servers (with integral or external modems)
Nds Compliance	No	N/A
Security	Security in server configuration	Yes
SNMP Support	No	No
FEATURES		
Auto-redial/ scheduling	Yes, however configured	Yes (from last failed page)
Inbound Notification	Yes	Yes
Inbound Routing	No	Yes (DID, TSI, and others)
Fax Archives	Yes, in Tun Mail	Yes
Broadcasting	Yes	Yes
Integrates with E-mail	Yes	Yes
Comments		Least-cost routing, form overlays, command-line interface
Warranty	Contact vendor	90 day media
Price	Contact vendor	$495+

Manufacturer	Interstar Technologies	LAN-ACES, Inc.
Model	LightningFax 4.0	Office-Logic 3.0
Server OS/NOS	Windows NT	Netware, Lantastic, Power LAN, LAN Manager, Invisible LAN, Windows NT, Windows 95, WFW, compatible NetBIOS networks
Client OS	Windows 95, 3.11	DOS, Windows, Windows NT, Windows 95
Max Fax/Modem Lines/Adapters	720 lines per server	By gateway

N/A—Not applicable   INA—Information not available   **Table Continues →**

■ Fax Communications Network Applications

Manufacturer	**Interstar Technologies**	**LAN-ACES, Inc.**
Configuration	Dedicated recommended for higher volume, yet not obligatory	Built-in to e-mail interface
Fax Hardware Compatibility	GammaLink fax boards	By gateway
Nds Compliance	No	Yes
Security	Client/server	By gateway
SNMP Support	INA	By gateway
FEATURES		
Auto-redial/ scheduling	Yes	By gateway
Inbound Notification	Yes	Yes
Inbound Routing	Yes	Yes
Fax Archives	Yes	Yes
Broadcasting	Yes	Yes
Integrates with E-mail	No	Yes
Comments	To satisfy growing user needs for powerful, and intelligent faxing	The 5, 25, and 100 user units are "bumpable." Integrates with many fax gateways.
Warranty	N/A	INA
Price	$1,199	$495 (5 user), $1,995 (25), $4,995 (100), $149 (remote)

Manufacturer	**LanOptics**	**LANsource**
Model	NetXchange	FAXport
Server OS/NOS	Windows NT 3.51 or higher	Windows NT, Windows 95, DOS, NetWare, NLM
Client OS	Windows 3.11, Windows 95	Windows, Windows NT, Windows 95, DOS
Max Fax/Modem Lines/Adapters	24	32
Configuration	Dedicated PC fax machine	Dedicated or non-dedicated server PC
Fax Hardware Compatibility	Gamma Link, PureData	Class 2 modems, serial ports, fax boards
Nds Compliance	Yes	Yes
Security	Yes, via encryption	Through NetWare
SNMP Support	Yes	Yes
FEATURES		
Auto-redial/ scheduling	Yes	Yes
Inbound Notification	Yes	Yes
Inbound Routing	N/A	Yes
Fax Archives	N/A	Yes
Broadcasting	Yes	Yes
Integrates with E-mail	INA	Yes

N/A—Not applicable   INA—Information not available

Fax Communications Network Applications ■

Manufacturer	LanOptics	LANsource
Comments	NetXchange provides low-cost fax routing and delivery through the routing and delivery of faxes via the Internet.	Combines with WINport modem sharing for a complete data and fax communications server
Warranty	1 year	30 day
Price	$2,400–$20,000	Starts at $399

Manufacturer	SCH Technologies	Softlinx
Model	Merkur	Replix software, Faxcenter 1000 M/2, Replix IMG, Replix Enterprise Faxcenter (TI)
Server OS/NOS	INA	Unix (Sun OS, HP-UX, IBM AIX)
Client OS	Windows, Windows 95, Windows NT, DOS	Windows, NT, OS/2, Unix, X Motif, X terminals
Max Fax/Modem Lines/Adapters	Unlimited	Unlimited
Configuration	TCP/IP	Dedicated or non-dedicated Unix server
Fax Hardware Compatibility	Class 2 modems	Class 2 modems, Brooktrout (analog or digital)
Nds Compliance	No	No
Security	Yes	Yes
SNMP Support	Yes	No
FEATURES		
Auto-redial/ scheduling	Yes	Yes
Inbound Notification	Yes	Yes
Inbound Routing	Yes	Yes
Fax Archives	Yes	Yes
Broadcasting	Yes	Yes
Integrates with E-mail	Yes	Yes
Comments	Designed for integration with applications such as SAP R/3, Baan Triton, Uniplex, Applix, Word for Windows and others. Has unlimited fax line capability.	Offers scalable network fax management software and systems that support enterprise fax messaging needs over LAN, private WAN, or Intranet. Also: least-cost routing, direct inward dial, central administration, fault tolerance, e-mail and groupware integration.
Warranty	30 day	90 day software, 1 year hardware
Price	$590 per node (discounts available)	$2,399+ up

Manufacturer	Symantec Corp.	Teubner	V-Systems
Model	Winfax 4.15	Faxgate	VSI-FAX Gold Series
Server OS/NOS	Windows 95 and Windows 3.x	OS/2 Warp connect	Unix
Client OS	Windows 95 and Windows 3.x	Windows, Windows 95	Windows, Windows 95, Windows NT, Unix
Max Fax/Modem Lines/Adapters	16 lines per network segment	24	Unlimited
Configuration	Runs dedicated or non-dedicated	Dedicated PC	Non-dedicated
Fax Hardware Compatibility	Class 1, Class 2, CAS, Brooktrout, GammaLink	GammaLink-Brooktrout Faxboard	Multi-tech fax modem

N/A—Not applicable   INA—Information not available

Table Continues →

■ Fax Communications Network Applications

Manufacturer	Symantec Corp.	Teubner	V-Systems
Nds Compliance	No	Yes	INA
Security	No	Yes	Through Unix server
SNMP Support	No	No	INA
FEATURES			INA
Auto-redial/ scheduling	Yes	Yes	Yes
Inbound Notification	Yes	Yes	Yes
Inbound Routing	Yes, manual and DID	Yes	Yes
Fax Archives	Yes	Yes	Yes
Broadcasting	Yes	Yes	Yes
Integrates with E-mail	Tes, supports MAPI, VIM, MHS	Yes	Yes
Comments	Supports data comm. modem sharing through NCSI. New version available (7.5) with Internet fax capabilities designed to save on long distance rates.		
Warranty	60-day money-back	1 year software	90 day
Price	$399 starter pack (includes 1 server, 2 clients)	$2,950+	$995 = Unix server $99 = Windows clients

N/A—Not applicable   INA—Information not available

End ■

Modem Communications Network Applications ■

Manufacturer	Artisoft	Farallon
Model	INSYNC ModemShare™	Mac Netoia ISDN Modem
Server NOS	IPX/SPX, NetBEUI, or NetBIOS	Serial connection
Client OS	Windows 95, Windows, or DOS	MacOS System, System 7.1 or later
Max # of modems/ ports	16 at any server	1-ISDN
Interface	Transparent to user, utilized through other applications	Serial connection
Interaction with Other Applications	Yes, Internet Browsers, fax software, remote control software	Yes, AT commands and PPP client included
Supports Remote Access	Yes	Yes
Redirect COM Ports	Yes	N/A
Automatically Choose Available Resources	Yes	N/A
Que Jobs	Yes	N/A
Activity Logs	Yes	N/A
Central Mgt.	Yes	N/A
Display Active Usage	Yes	Yes
Comments	Allows every network user to share modems and phone lines for acces to desktop fax, Internet access programs, et. al.	ISDN terminal adapter for Macintosh with bundled Internet software
Warranty	90 day	1 year
Price	$129 (1 port), $229 (2), $429 (4), $729 (8)	$329

Manufacturer	Farallon	Microcom, Inc.
Model	Natoia PC Modem	ISPorte
Server NOS	Serial connection	N/A
Client OS	MS-DOS, or IBM PC 3.1 or later, Windows, Windows 95, Windows NT	N/A
Max # of Modems/ Ports	1-ISDN	64
Interface	Serial connection	RS-232
Interaction with Other Applications	Yes, AT commands and PPP client included	N/A
Supports Remote Access	Yes	Yes
Redirect COM Ports	N/A	N/A
Automatically Choose Available Resources	N/A	N/A
Que Jobs	N/A	N/A
Activity Logs	N/A	N/A
Central Mgt.	N/A	Yes
Display Active Usage	Yes	Yes
Comments	ISDN terminal adapter for PCs with bundled Internet software	64-port analog modem chassis with Essential Management. It is a rackmount product that can "front-end" a server product like Microcom's LANexpress.
Warranty	1 year	5 year
Price	$329	$250-300/port

N/A—Not applicable   INA—Information not available

Table Continues →

■ Modem Communications Network Applications

Manufacturer	Motorola	Symantec Corporation	Synergy Software
Model	925 AccessWay™ System by Lan-Rover/8E	pcANYWHERE32 v 7.5	Versa Term 5.0
Server NOS	IPX/IP, AppleTalk, PPP, Multilink PPP, Slip, NetBEUI, NetBios et al	Windows NT, NetWare, Banyan	any
Client OS	Windows, Windows 95, Windows NT 3.5, Windows for Workgroups, Macintosh, UNIX, also supports OS/2	Windows 95/NT	Macintosh
Max # of modems/ ports	Unlimited (scalable)	Supports multiple sessions, host supports multiple connections	N/A
Interface	Ethernet 10BASE-T, T/R, T-1, E1	Compatible with DOS, Win 3.x, Win 95, Win NT versions of product	Tool palette to hosts and Internet
Interaction with Other Applications	Yes, transparent	Yes	Yes, including Web browsers
Supports Remote Access	Yes	Remote control, file transfer	Yes
Redirect COM Ports	No	N/A	N/A
Automatically Choose Available Resources	No	N/A	N/A
Que Jobs	No	Can schedule multiple AutoXfer sessions	N/A
Activity Logs	Yes	Yes	Yes
Central Mgt.	Yes	Available through Norton Administrator Suite	N/A
Display Active Usage	Yes	N/A	Yes
Comments	Considered a basic communications and a sophisticated remote access and wide area networking system; it links corporate sites with data, voice and video communications	Security options. Integrated remote networking allows connections with RAS, NetWare Connect, Shiva LanRover or NetModem. OLE 2.0 capabilities. Internal or external help desk tool. Supports ISDN, TCP/IP.	TCP/IP network connections, and a graphical interface for mail, news, directory, Telnet, and FTP to exchange data with the Internet community
Warranty	2 year (hardware) 90 day (software)	60 day	90 day
Price	$27,995 (custom systems are available)	$149 (host/remote+cable) $1,199 (10 user pak)	$195

N/A—Not applicable   INA—Information not available

End ■

9 NETWORK UTILITIES

THE TERM "UTILITIES" OFTEN implies inexpensive add-on software for extending certain capabilities. Yet most of the products listed in this chapter are full-fledged network applications. They are grouped under utilities because they are not core network productivity applications but they are very important for keeping networks operable and accessible to users. For example, virus protection and security software don't in and of themselves make users more productive. They are, however, vital to keeping the network functioning and secure. Virus protection and security are both covered in this chapter. In addition, you'll learn about help desk software, which helps streamline and automate technical support for customers or internal network users. Network planning software, also covered in this chapter, can provide valuable assistance in making network plans, particularly for large networks.

NETWORK UTILITIES

Virus Protection

Computer viruses are those evil little programs that can infect files and applications, destroying data and causing other problems. They are created by computer hackers and can come into your network from any outside source such as a floppy disk, internetwork connection, or Internet connection. To clean files and destroy viruses you need special virus protection software that can scan the network to find and fix the problem. Viruses have become a big enough problem that network administrators cannot do without virus protection programs. Their implementation can vary and can affect your network's performance.

Scanning Methods					
Performance	Reliability	Manageability	**Scalability**	**Flexibility**	Value

Scanning for viruses happens either at the workstation or at the server. Often workstation-based products are used to scan file server drives. However, this method is not automated, nor is it complete if server bindery files or directory access is limited. Because server solutions tend to be robust, automated, and higher performance than workstation-based applications, they are the best solution for network protection.

Scanning for viruses is memory and processor intensive and can degrade network performance. Server-based software can take advantage of server performance (such as NLMs in the case of NetWare) in addition to minimizing network traffic if just server disk space is being scanned.

Whether you scan workstations is a matter of preference. Some people just scan servers continually because of the load TSRs place on workstations and the difficulty of managing so many stations. The theory is that if you run applications and use server storage almost exclusively, server protection will keep the network generally clean.

Scanning Features					
Performance	Reliability	**Manageability**	Scalability	**Flexibility**	Value

Finding virus strains is the most important part of virus protection. Virus types are distinguished by the way in which they infect systems. Some corrupt boot files, others corrupt macros, and there are many others. Your software will include a list of known viruses that it can recognize and immunize the system against.

NETWORK UTILITIES

Because scanning for viruses can place a load on the server and network bandwidth, virus software usually lets you choose whether to scan immediately, at scheduled times, or continually in the background. Most products scan disk boot sectors and partition tables in addition to system memory. You should also look for a program that can scan compressed files.

Antivirus software usually lets you choose what to do with infected files. For instance, you may want to move infected files to a certain location before cleaning them. Once you've scanned and cleaned files, some products enable you to inoculate the files to make them resistent to most viruses.

Administration Features

Performance | Reliability | **Manageability** | Scalability | **Flexibility** | Value

The configuration of your virus-protection program should be flexible. For instance, you should be able to set different policies on individual machines or groups of machines to match needs, minimize negative effects on network performance, and simplify administration.

Most virus protection programs have various methods of alerting administrators, including messages to the administrator's console and pager notification. Administrators may be able to set a policy to carry out certain actions in case of a viral attack, such as limiting server access or access to the infected directory. In some cases, you can automatically limit workstation or server access if virus protection policy is not followed.

Platform Support

Performance | Reliability | Manageability | **Scalability** | **Flexibility** | Value

It's crucial that the program support various computer platforms. If you are centrally managing virus protection from one server, the software must of course support that NOS. But suppose you add another network segment under a different NOS. Make sure the product will support the new platform so you don't have to learn a whole new package. Support for client operating systems should be broad if you plan to run the product at the workstations. Check that the TRS requirements won't place an undue burden on the workstations. Finally, be sure the program supports the communications protocols you are running.

NETWORK UTILITIES

Purchase Package					
Performance	Reliability	Manageability	Scalability	Flexibility	**Value**

The cost of most network antivirus applications is competitive. But make sure you consider what comes with the purchase. Often you'll get free virus list updates until another version release of the product or for a specific period of time. Find out the frequency of these list updates before buying. Access to list updates is usually provided by BBS or the Internet.

Help Desk

Help desk applications are specialized databases that provide both support information and inquiry tracking. They are a mainstay of modern technical support departments and are considered a mission critical network application in that environment. With help desk, technicians can quickly bring up information relevant to inquiries, maintain customer service accounts, and provide statistical reports on service department activities. These same functions can also be valuable to any organization that must provide help to a large number of users internally. Internal support with help desk software is more of a utility than a mission critical application.

Reference Information					
Performance	Reliability	Manageability	**Scalability**	Flexibility	**Value**

Reference information can come from a case history database created over time or from ready-made references, usually on CD-ROMs. Case history databases are built as real problem descriptions, with solutions entered and indexed into a database. This method requires speedy query systems to bring up relevant case histories. Sorting through cases to get the right information can be cumbersome. Ready-made references include a wealth of information and well-indexed topics, but cannot be customized as can case history databases. Many help desk products integrate both methods.

Customization					
Performance	Reliability	**Manageability**	Scalability	**Flexibility**	Value

Help desk software comes with a default database design that determines how information is stored and retrieved. Although the designs tend to be fairly complete, they always need some degree of customization. All

NETWORK UTILITIES

products allow user-defined fields, but the ones that let you change data table and form design give you additional flexibility while allowing you to retain the overall structure of the application. You should also be able to customize the user interface to highlight the most frequently used databases and queries, speeding up response times. In addition, you want to know whether the help desk application can incorporate other reference databases. For instance, the main database may be a case history database but the help desk application may also provide access to prepackaged CD-ROM references. Ideally, you could search for all references using the help desk's search functions.

Event and Client Management					
Performance	Reliability	**Manageability**	Scalability	Flexibility	Value

Building the help database involves tracking problems and their solutions. Tracking specific events includes opening a "case" on the problem, logging the various calls and actions in resolving the problem, and closing the case when the problem is resolved. Management features in the tracking process may include channeling problems to the appropriate expert, prioritizing events, escalating actions based on set conditions, and call management (including links to voice mail, reaching alternate technicians, and so on). Good event tracking makes it easier to figure out what has been done and what the next step should be. Client management involves not only tracking events by client but also keeping a record of equipment. This might include information such as equipment purchase (in-use) dates, office location, maintenance activity, service agreements, and so on.

Reporting					
Performance	Reliability	**Manageability**	Scalability	Flexibility	Value

Shop for a product with extensive reporting capabilities; most products offer over 50 predefined reports. Although these default reports should cover most of your reporting needs, it's nice to be able to customize reports, especially if database forms and/or tables have been customized. Reports should cover call activity, client profiles, technician activity, equipment inventories, and possibly other topics. These reports can help improve service by identifying consistent problems in equipment, can point out the need to train users in certain areas, can evaluate technician performance, and more. Reports can provide a lot of valuable data to improve many aspects of business performance.

NETWORK UTILITIES

Network Planning Software

Network planning often involves many software tools: a network analyzer or simulator to show performance and bottlenecks, a spreadsheet to inventory equipment and to calculate equipment costs, a word processor to describe the plan, and a graphics program to illustrate the necessary connections. Of course, a person must provide all the knowledge and expertise. The planner often puts together a variety of applications, in effect creating a custom network planning tool.

Dedicated network planning software is fairly new. Network graphing (or mapping) applications still make up a large part of the market. These are graphics applications with the clip art and features to put together nice network illustrations. In addition, some of these programs can track your network assets, including computers, hubs, and network cards. Some of the newer tools combine the capabilities of other applications to provide a single package for network planning from beginning to end. Only recently has network planning software gone beyond layout and inventory to providing real decision making assistance. Such products may correct you if you mismatch protocols, inform you if you fill available hub ports, let you select a real brand and model, and calculate equipment costs based on a price database. These high-level products are starting to provide real network expertise in addition to functional layout and design assistance.

Scope of Planning					
Performance	Reliability	Manageability	**Scalability**	**Flexibility**	**Value**

You should consider the scope of your planning needs when you evaluate network planning tools. If you still want to use your spreadsheets to create plans but need better physical mapping, there are tools that specialize in that area. If your plan is rather complete but you want to see a simulation of the plan in action, there is software to help you. A fully integrated planning tool may be complete for beginning-to-end planning, but it may sacrifice depth to provide a wide range of functions. The key components of complete network planning include a physical layout, reports on existing network activity, equipment lists and costs, growth plans, simulation, and budgeting.

NETWORK UTILITIES

Asset Inventory

Performance Reliability Manageability **Scalability** Flexibility Value

You need an inventory of network assets and business assets. Logging this information can be time consuming, particularly as changes occur and older assets are retired. A manual process may simply be too cumbersome for large networks. Some network planning software can automatically detect most equipment on the network. Products with this feature may allow the network administrator to run the process at scheduled intervals or whenever needed. If some equipment is not identified automatically, you can add it to the list manually. Elements of the asset inventory may vary, but it can be quite valuable to have information like purchase date, warranty information, cost, and so forth at your fingertips.

Graphics Capabilities

Performance Reliability **Manageability** Scalability **Flexibility** **Value**

Much of network planning focuses on the physical layout of the network. If you have a hierarchy of graphic layouts, you can get different views of the network, from workgroups to the enterprise. The more narrow your view of the network, the more information you should see. For instance, a workgroup view might include machine types, NICs, and other details; in an enterprise view, in contrast, you'll just see icons representing the connected workgroups.

Color can help make distinctions between protocols, NOSs, and the like. Many of these programs require at least a high-resolution 17-inch monitor to take advantage of the color and detail. You almost always need to annotate layouts that are created automatically, so look at the annotation features in addition to the flexibility of the automated settings. You should be able to save your views and settings for easy recall. Graphics are usually a key part of presenting network plans so also consider output options and printer support.

Program Integration

Performance Reliability **Manageability** Scalability **Flexibility** Value

Because most network planning is done with a number of different programs, you need to consider how this information will be combined for final output and how it will be managed over time. A fully integrated network planning package offers both the convenience of integrated functions

NETWORK UTILITIES

and the simplicity of using a single software application for everything. Even so, the program should be able to import and export information in various formats for use with other programs. When you use separate tools for planning, integration is even more important. For instance, you may use a help desk application to track assets but do cost planning on a spreadsheet. If you want to integrate the two, you not only need import/export compatibility but also a process for keeping both updated and accurate. SNMP may be an important part of integrating information with a network management application.

Network Security

Determining what additional security software you need, if any, means identifying points of exposure in your network. Network security means different things to different people. Network size, design, and information sensitivity all play a role in deciding how much security is enough. Network operating systems include built-in security features that are good at basic measures such as limiting access to information and resources. But even a small business network puts itself at risk when it connects to the Internet or other public and private networks. A typical single-server LAN in the private sector may find the NOS security tools enough. On the other hand, the same size LAN, with internetwork links, in a company doing strategic defense contract work, might need additional network security costing more than the entire LAN.

Security applications have quite a range of capabilities. Some are specialized monitoring and tracking tools, others provide data encryption between connections transparently to the user, and still others are designed to take over most security operations on the network. Hardware security solutions include network routers and computer systems that filter data packets according to administrator-set policies.

Limited User Access					
Performance	**Reliability**	Manageability	Scalability	Flexibility	Value

Limiting access is the most important and common form of security on any network. For example, NOS tools let you assign passwords and access rights to certain directories by user or groups of users. Network hardware, such as a router, can provide limited access through data packet filtering. To filter packets, you set a list of packet types to be included or excluded— that is, allowed or not allowed to be passed on. The term "firewalls" is often used to describe security products (hardware, software, or both) that protect network security from unwanted intrusions from outside sources such as the Internet or remote network links.

NETWORK UTILITIES

Third-party security software often enhances the NOS features for limiting access. For example, it may limit the hours a valid user can log in, preventing off-hour access. In addition, it may automatically disconnect idle connections in case someone left their station without logging off, helping to prevent unauthorized access by others. Such software may provide more security layers for remote access such as additional passwords, call-back verification (remote phone number is an approved source), and so forth.

Data Encryption					
Performance	**Reliability**	Manageability	Scalability	Flexibility	Value

Encryption means taking readable information such as a text file and coding it so it becomes unreadable to the naked eye. It is another layer of security beyond limited access. Encryption is often used to secure information that is en route to its destination. In this case, information is encrypted automatically when it is sent and is decoded when it arrives at the receiving station. Encryption is also used to protect information being stored off line—on tape or optical cartridges, for example. Encryption is sometimes an option in tape backup software, databases, or other software applications.

Monitoring and Reporting					
Performance	Reliability	**Manageability**	Scalability	Flexibility	Value

You should also consider the monitoring and reporting capabilities of security software products. These features are often used to maintain a history of network logins and activity of work sessions by workgroups, users, or other criteria. They provide a way of checking on employee activity, and may allow the administrator to set alerts based on certain events. For example, administrators may receive an alert that an account was locked due to a high number of unsuccessful logins. For users, it may provide warnings that certain actions are not permissible, and may indicate whom to see to get approved access. The product should be able to automatically address certain events and take specific action when specific events occur.

NETWORK UTILITIES

Product Integration					
Performance	Reliability	**Manageability**	**Scalability**	**Flexibility**	Value

Product integration refers to how the security product fits into the network. This includes the product's compatibility with various NOSs and communication protocols, and determines how scalable the product is to your network environment. It can also affect how the product is administered. (For example, does it centrally manage remote servers? Can it manage security across various computing platforms?) In addition, product integration refers to its integration with other security measures such as those in network operating systems, network routers, or network management applications. (Does it take over or enhance existing security policies? Does it integrate with network management applications and can it be controlled from that interface?)

If you understand the integration mechanics of security products you're considering, you can assess how security layers can affect existing work flow. Networking is about communicating and providing access to resources. You don't want extreme security measures to make it too difficult to get things done, and you don't want to spend too many administrative hours managing a complex security system. You must find a balance between security and accessibility that is appropriate for your work environment.

■ Help Desk Utilities

Manufacturer	Astea International, Inc.	Astea International, Inc.
Model	HEAT Premiere V2.11	HEAT for Windows Professional Edition V3.0
Product Description	A file-server based, user-customizable call logging and call tracking system designed to relieve support centers with lower call volume. Includes 70 pre-defined reports.	A complete, self-contained, problem resolution system operates in both file and client server environment. Links with other popular support tools like SYMON and Lotus Notes
OS Support	MS/DOS or PC/DOS 5.0 or later	MS/DOS or PC/DOS 5.0, Windows 3.x
NOS Support	Any NOS support file locking conventions of DOS 3.3	Any NOS support file locking conventions of DOS 3.3
Network Management Platform	None	Integrate to Microsoft SMS
Database Support	DBase, Microsoft Access	DBase, Gupta, Microsoft Access, Microsoft SQL Server, Oracle, Sybase, Sybase SQL Anywhere
Search	None	Keyword, CBR
Problems Resolution Tools	None	Auto-populate Auto-find E-mail linkage First level support Inference Third party knowledge bases
Features	100% user definable Add-on report writer Add-on knowledge bases Comprehensive call logging tools ODBC compliance	100% user definable Automatic ticket generation Automatic call escalation Calls on-hold Crystal Reports Pro File attachments HEAT alert ODBC compliance Link to other products MAPI/VIM integration Statistics monitor TAPI integration Ticket transfer
Hardware Requirements	PC 386 or higher 8MB RAM 40MB disk space on server 8-10MB disk space on workstation	PC 386 or higher 8MB RAM 40MB disk space on server 8-10MB disk space on workstation
Warranty	60-day money-back guarantee with license agreement	60-day money-back guarantee with license agreement
Price	$1,195 single user $5,195 5-user	$3,000 single user $40,000 unlimited user

Manufacturer	Astea International, Inc.	Blue Ocean Software, Inc.
Model	PowerHelp V2.2	Track-IT! Help Desk
Product Description	A comprehensive enterprise-wide solution that enables users to capture, analyze, route, and resolve customer calls in complex, high-volume support environment	Built-in support for automatic inventory of user configuration, end-user work order submission, e-mail, paging, knowledge base
OS Support	Window 3.x, Windows 95 or Windows NT	Windows 3.1, Windows 95, Windows NT, OS/2
NOS Support	Depends on database, includes Windows 3.x, Windows NT, and Unix	Netware, Windows NT, Pathworks, Banyan Vines, LAN Manager.
Network Management Platform	INA	Track IT! Product line
Database Support	Informix, Microsoft SQL Server, Oracle Sybase, Sybase SQL Anywhere (formerly Watcom)	Xbase
Search	Hypertext, Keyword, CBR	Full text, keyword, custom queries

N/A—Not applicable   INA—Information not available

Help Desk Utilities ■

Manufacturer	Astea International, Inc.	Blue Ocean Software, Inc.
Problems Resolution Tools	Case-based reasoning Linked Notes/Remarks/Multimedia Problem resolution and repair statistics Third party knowledge bases	Knowledge base, fuzzy text, diagnostics, e-mail links
Features	API Interface; Auto call escalation and notification; Case-based reasoning; Contract management; E-mail integration; Graphic statistical analysis; OBSA; Paging; Real-time online—Statistic; Web integration workflow	Automatically configures users' PC configuration. Includes modules for inventory, toning, and purchasing
Hardware Requirements	Pentium or higher 60MHz 16MB RAM(24 Recommended) 62MB disk space on server	PC 486 (66MHz or higher) 386 PC+ 4MB RAM 6MB disk space
Comments	Management reporting Multilingual Network mgmt. integration	Demo available at www.blueocean.com
Warranty	60 day MBG	30 day
Price	$40,000 10-user	$1,395 single user $995 40 users

Manufacturer	Computer Associates International, Inc.	Danaware Data A/S Markham Computer Corp
Model	CA-Unicenter Advanced Help Desk	NetOp for OS/2 v 5.2
Product Description	Designed to automate help-desk tasks completely, to reduce service time, to secure enterprise-wide resources and optimum organizations response to user requests	Remote control software that allows the user to access and control the screen remotely
OS Support	Windows 3.1x, Windows 95, Windows NT, AIX, HP-UX, Sun, and Silicon Graphics	OS/2, Windows NT, Windows 95, Windows 3.x, and DOS
NOS Support	Various UNIX	OS/2 LAN Server, Netware, Windows NT
Network Management Platform	OpenView, SunNet Manager, Netview Cabletron	N/A
Database Support	INA	N/A
Search	Stored queries, multiple field searches	N/A
Problems Resolution Tools	Automatic ticket generation, escalation, and notification. Service level agreements are tracked	Online, Set-Up Wizards
Features	Customizable and innovative interfaces. Automatic incident generation. Historical data inventory	Remotely accesses keyboard and mouse also. Simultaneous viewing of multiple PCs and platforms. File transfer and chat, also cross platform. Advanced Help Request feature permits user to request help from available help services/ providers
Hardware Requirements	PC 486MHz 16MB RAM, 5MB disk space	PC 1MB free disk
Comments Dele space above hd? did		
Warranty	Unlimited	60 day
Price	$2,000+ per server, $100 per workstation agents	$295+

Manufacturer	Fujitsu	Help Desk Tech Corp
Model	LiveHelp	helpSTAR
Product Description	A Windows remote support product that provides screen sharing and remote control capability	Automates the administration of end-user support and enhances the quality and reliability of service.

N/A—Not applicable   INA—Information not available

Table Continues →

■ Help Desk Utilities

Manufacturer	Fujitsu	Help Desk Tech Corp
OS Support	Windows 3.x, Windows 95, Windows NT	Windows 3.1, Windows 95, Windows NT
NOS Support	Netware	Netware, Windows NT
Network Management Platform	Interconnects Bridge/Router with recommended 56Kbps bandwidth	N/A
Database Support	Add-on-compatible product provides database support	Access 2.0
Search	INA	Full text
Problems Resolution Tools	Internet using TCP/IP	N/A
Features	Multiple Experts Screen transfers No knowledge of network addresses	Call logging/tracking. E-mail interface. Management reports. Builds a corporate knowledge. Reports historical performance. Snapshot reports.
Hardware Requirements	80386 or above 4MB RAM Video: VGA, Super VGA Modem: 9.6Kbps min. Disk storage: 4MB	PC 486 or higher 16MB RAM 5MB disk space
Comments		Download evaluation.www.helpstar.com
Warranty	90 day	INA
Price	$99 (single user) $175 (10 users)	$1,895 (single user) $13,995 (unlimited)

Manufacturer	McAfee	Magic Solutions
Model	VycorEnterprise v3.10	SupportMagic SQC
Product Description	A client/server help-desk solution that provides problem management, problem knowledge, and problem prevention	Designed to function as the central data repository for all enterprise support needs. Enterprise support data, network alerts and integrated voice technology, can all be managed from a single application.
OS Support	Windows 3.1, Windows 95, Windows NT	WFW 3.11, Windows NT 3.51, Windows 95, or Windows 3.1
NOS Support	Netware, Windows NT	Netware, Windows NT, Banyan Vines
Network Management Platform	INA	INA
Database Support	MS SQL Server, Sybase, Oracle	SQL, Oracle, Watcom, Sybase SQL Anywhere
Search	Keyword	SIR, Magic Search
Problems Resolution Tools	CBR with CasePoint, Knowledge-Pak Suite, decision tree with Expertise Viewer, Expert Link	Rule-based decision tree, problems resolutions, keyword
Features	Service level agreements. Problem prevention with SNMP and SMTP Listeners and Vycor beacon. Problem Empowerment with the SLW 6.0 integration. End-users can log a trouble ticket via e-mail or Rescue. Automatic ticket escalation. 72 customized notification events via e-mail, numeric paging, or text paging.	Problem resolution engine that searches the leading sources of support knowledge using artificial intelligence and neural networks. API for integration. Multiple support groups allow selective data segregation among multiple help desks on one database
Hardware Requirements	PC 486 (66MHz or higher) 16MB RAM 25MB disk space (wkst)	Server: Dedicated Windows NT server version 3.51, Pentium, 20MB free disk space on server, 32RAM Client: 14MB of free, 16MB RAM, 496/66 processor minimum
Comments		
Warranty	INA	1 year
Price	INA	$5,995 single user

N/A—Not applicable   INA—Information not available

Help Desk Utilities ■

Manufacturer	Magic Solutions	Multima Corporation
Model	Support Magic for Windows	NetKeeper Help Desk Pro version 5.1
Product Description	Integrated call tracking, problem management, and problem resolution help desk application. For small-to-mid-size internal help desks. Statistical Information Retrieval uses artificial intelligence and neural networks.	A multi-site, distributed help desk system to track and resolve service calls that contains a self-learning knowledge base.
OS Support	WFW 3.11, Windows NT 3.51, Windows 95, or Windows 3.1	Windows 3.1, Windows95, Windows NT, DOS
NOS Support	Netware, Windows NT, Banyan Vines	Netware, Windows NT, Windows 95, OS2, LAN Manager, Banyan Vines, LANtastic
Network Management Platform	INA	NetKeeper
Database Support	Btrieve	Clarion, ODBC, Oracle
Search	SIR, keyword	Keyword and full text
Problems Resolution Tools	SIR (Statistical Information Retrieval), Magic Tree (rules-based experts system Magic Search), Hypertext search, Ad Hoc Query by example	E-mail, Pager, Decision tree, FastSearch: text retrieval system and Solutions Keeper
Features	End-users can submit requests and receive answers via all popular e-mail packages. Customizable user interface. Intelligent rules-based escalation engine. Real-time system monitor. Perpetual calendar support and work system	Multi-site distributed load capabilities to track data from multiple help desks in multiple locations that allows staff to switch from site to site to pick up peak demands. Real time links to Inventory programs and other NetKeeper asset programs. Unique Solutions Keeper to solve service calls as they are logged. Priority and escalating priority notations.
Hardware Requirements	PC 486, 8MB of RAM, 25MB disk space, V6A Adapter Supported by Windows 3.1	IBM PC or compatible 10MB of hard-disk space for installation of entire Net-Keeper Asset Management series A super VGA monitor 6MB RAM
Comments		Supports both internal and external clients. Supports multimedia attachments to solutions
Warranty	1 year	90 day warranty (1 year tech. Support)
Price	$2,995	$1,095 single user $10,860 up to 16 users

Manufacturer	Platinum Technology, Inc. Answer System Laboratory	Professional Help Desk
Model	Apriori	PHD Solo PHD Premium PHD Enterprise
Product Description	It is specifically designed to provide dynamic support environments with leading-edge call tracking, workflow and workload management, with flexible reporting. Offers patented problem-resolution technology	Call-tracking management, problem management/resolution; Natural Intelligence suite includes Experience Based Reasoning™, PHDExpert™, Natural Language™, fuzzy logic, and other features
OS Support	Server: AIX, HP-UX, Windows NT Client: Windows 3.x, Windows 95, Windows NT, Motif, OpenLook, www/e-mail interface	Windows for Workgroups, Windows 95, Windows 3.1, Windows NT; OS/2
NOS Support	AIX, HP-UX, Windows NT (TCP/IP & Winsock communications)	Netware, Windows NT, Banyan Vines, LANtastic
Network Management Platform	HP OpenView	Netware, Windows NT, WFW, Pathworks, Banyan Vines, LANtastic
Database Support	Sybase, Oracle, native relational databases	ODBC compliant, SQL, Sybase, dBase, Oracle, Access, DB2, Paradox, Ingres
Search	Index search, natural language, keyword, full text, symptom	Full text, keyword, fuzzy logic
Problems Resolution Tools	Bubble-Up, Logical Filing, Qsearch, Symptom, Keyword, New Document List, cross reference	CBR, fuzzy logic, natural language, , web/e-mail link

N/A—Not applicable   INA—Information not available

Table Continues →

■ Help Desk Utilities

Manufacturer	Platinum Technology, Inc. Answer System Laboratory	Professional Help Desk
Features	Problem resolution technologies Central knowledge base Built-in call tracking Event triggers Groups technology (Custom Workflow Management)	Fuzzy logic. Case-based reasoning. E-mail, fax/pager, integration. Internet access. End-user access to problem resolution. Trouble tickets
Hardware Requirements	HP/9000, IBM RS/6000, or Sun systems	PC 486 (66MHz or higher)
Comments		Discounts for volume purchases
Warranty	Service: 12- and 24-hour hotline support options available. On-site assistance available from Enterprise Consulting Group.	90 day
Price	< $50,000	PHD Solo: $495 PHD Premium: $2,995PHD Enterprise: $4,995

Manufacturer	Quintus Corp	Software Artistry, Inc.	Televell
Model	CustomerQ 3.0	SA-Expertise	Telesell Customer Service
Product Description	Solutions for help desk and call centers serving critical line-of-business applications; for customer-driven enterprises embrace both internally and externally focused systems; includes call tracking, asset tracking, and solution management.	Suite of integrated Enterprise Support Management solutions that links SA-Expert Advisor at the help desk with network management and end-user empowerment tools	Integrates w/ Telesell sales automation system to provide sales and support automation
OS Support	Windows 95, Windows NT, Windows for Workgroups 3.11, any Web browser, Windows 3.1	Clients: Windows 3.x, Windows 95, Windows NT, OS/2 Servers: Windows NT, OS/2, HP-UX, Sun	Windows 3.1, Windows 95, Windows NT, DOS
NOS Support	NOS Independent (TCP/IP)	Netware, Windows NT	Novell, NetBios
Network Management Platform	Boole & Babbage, Command Post	HP OpenView, IBM NetView/AIX, SunNet Manager, Tivoli TME, Cabletron Spectrum, Boole and Babbage Command Post, CA-Unicenter	INA
Database Support	Oracle, Sybase, Informix	Oracle, Sybase, Informix, Microsoft SQLServer, DB2/2, DB2/6000	Btrieve, Dataflex
Search	Full text retrieval, document retrieval, keyword	Full text, keyword, concept matching	INA
Problems Resolution Tools	CBR, web/e-mail links, bookmarks	Adaptive learning, hypermedia decision trees, case-based reasoning, Hot News, Common Problems, Quick Solution, Error Messages	Online problem and answer categories
Features	Advanced reporting for managers. Fax-e-mail integration. Handles several calls simultaneously. Tracking of alerts. Pop-up calendars	Call- and problem-management capabilities. Linked to integrate the support center with network management, asset and change management	Full integration with Telesell sale database, RMA tracking, incident reports, online information, and more. Tracks support issues, RMA's, incident resolution, and more.
Hardware Requirements	PC 496 (66MHz or higher)	PC 486 66MHz 16MB RAM 10MB free disk	PC 486 66+ 8MB RAM 34MB disk space
Comments	Design tool allows changes to the applications without programming. WebQ, Quintus' Web interface provides universal client access to CustomerQ.		Desktop dialing, auto letter generation, task tracking
Warranty	90 day	1 year	INA
Price	$4,000 (per user) $20,000 (per server)	$3,500 (per user) $15,000+ (per server)	$195–$1,895 (depending on database)

N/A—Not applicable   INA—Information not available

End ■

Network Planning Utilities ■

Manufacturer	ImageNet Ltd.	Mcafee
Model	CANE (Computer-Aided Network Engineering)	SaberLan
General Description	Total network design software solution for planning, designing, documenting, analyzing, simulating, and maintaining a network.	Integrated Network Management; S/W metering, H/W and S/W inventory, S/W distribution and desktop management
Server Client OS	Windows NT 3.51+	NetWare 3.x, 4.1, Windows NT, 3.51, and 95
CPU	Pentium	Pentium 60MHz recommended
RAM	32MB	20-32MB
Free Disk Space	200MB	200-500MB
FEATURES		
Network Diagramming	Drag-and-drop network modeling, hierarchical design, object-oriented database that facilitates cookie-cutter designs.	Overall network planning and management with S/W metering, H/W and S/W Inventory, S/W distribution and desktop management
Physical Design Validation	Physical and protocol compatibility, vendor specific rules, end-user customizable rules. VLAN planning and validation.	INA
Network Topology Validation	Legacy LANs, common WANs, ATM, with the ability for end-users to add new network types. IP network planning and validation tool, including automatic IP address.	INA
Other Features	Impressive up-to-date network device and product library, event driven, process-oriented network simulation module, intelligent tool for linking between network configuration, comprehensive report capabilities	An integrated network management suite designed for both NetWare and NT environments. Software metering, hardware and software inventory, software distribution, desktop management, and storage management are all integrated under a common Windows 95, OLE-based console.
Comments	Subscriptions are available for quarterly updates of the network device and product library.	
Warranty	1 year	For as long as you are a valid license user
Price	$5,000–$20,000	INA

Manufacturer	Microsystems Engineering Co.	NetSuite
Model	SysDraw-The Network Illustrator	Professional Audit
General Description	Network design and documentation tool	Physical network discovery for network design and documentation maintenance
Server Client OS	Windows 3.1, Windows for Workgroups, Windows 95 and Windows NT	Windows 95, Windows NT
CPU	Pentium 486 50MHz	PC 486 (66MHz or higher)
RAM	8MB RAM	16MB
Free Disk Space	22MB	15MB
FEATURES		
Network Diagramming	Over 6000 exact replica device images, full drawing tool to modify existing devices; drag and drop	Object identification and mapping.
Physical Design Validation	N/A	Initial discovery of physical network using SNMP, Microsoft SMS import, Novell IPX import, HP OpenView for Windows import
Network Topology Validation	N/A	Ethernet (10/100), Token Ring, FDDI, CDDI, ATM
Other Features	Simulation, autodiscovery, database integration, drill-down to link multiple files, project management	Network document reconciliation
Comments	500 new images added to project quantity	
Warranty	N/A	30 day
Price	$399–$995	INA

N/A—Not applicable   INA—Information not available

Table Continues →

■ Network Planning Utilities

Manufacturer	NetSuite	NetSuite
Model	Professional Design	Design View
General Description	Intelligent physical network design, documentation, and asset management	HTML publisher for network designs and documentation
Server/Client OS	Windows 3.1, Windows 95, Windows NT	Windows 3.1, Windows 95, Windows NT
CPU	PC 486 (66MHz or higher)	PC 486 (66MHz or higher)
RAM	16MB	16MB RAM
Free Disk Space	25MB	5MB
FEATURES		
Network Diagramming	Network protocol advanced diagramming. Graphic drag-and-drop.	One button publishing of network designs to Intranet or Internet. Embedded device photographs. Multilevel diagrams with maps, floorplans.
Physical Design Validation	Network design validation	INA
Network Topology Validation	Ethernet (10/100), Token Ring, FDDI, CDDI, ATM, WAN	Ethernet (10/100), Token Ring, FDDI, CDDI, ATM, WAN
Other Features	Product and device updates (100-300/mo.) via subscription. Bills-of-materials. Over 2700 intelligent network devices in library. Network asset reporting. Import and export.	Requires NetSuite
Comments		
Warranty	30 day	30 day
Price	$795	$295

Manufacturer	Novell Inc.
Model	ManageWise 2.1
General Description	Intelligent integrated management system for planning, designing, and managing of PC-LAN environment
Server Client OS	NetWare 3.1x, NetWare 4.1
CPU	Server 386 or higher. Console 486 66mhz or Pentium.
RAM	Server 16MB additional Console 512K Conventional
Free Disk Space	Server 25MB; Console 50MB + 10-50MB for topology database
FEATURES	
Network Diagramming	INA
Physical Design validation	Protocols supported: IP, IPX DMI standard
Network topology Validation	Any protocol
Other Features	MS-Windows 95, Windows 3.1x, Windows for Workgroups 3.11 SNMP Based, MIB browser, NetWare and NT server management, server and desktop virus inventory, desktop management, desktop remote management, network planning, network analysis, traffic analysis, packet capture, NDS based application distribution, real time monitoring of server statistics, server configuration via Set Parameters, NW admin integration
Comments	Managewise is supported by over 100 third party snap-in-applications. Multilevel network with custom maps, drag-in-drop, floorplans, database schema extended via APIs and third party products.
Warranty	90 days
Price	Based on NetWare user count starting from $795 for five user version

---

N/A—Not applicable   INA—Information not available

End ■

Security Utilities ■

Manufacturer	Axent Technologies Inc.	Axent Technologies Inc.
Model	OmniGuardITA	OmniGuard Enterprise Access Control/Unix
General Description	Real-time security monitoring and anomaly detection	Central user administration with consistent security enhancement controls for Unix operating systems
CPU	INA	UNIX
OS	Sun OS, Solaris, HP-UX, Digital, Unix, AIX, NCR, SGI, Novell, Netware on various platforms	Sun OS, Solaris, HP-UX, Digital Unix, AIX, Silicon Graphics,
Management Platform	Novell NetWare, UNIX	Novell NetWare, UNIX
RAM	8MB	INA
Free Disk Space	1-8MB	INA
Topology	Ethernet, IPX, Token Ring	Ethernet, Token Ring
Protocols Supported	IPX/SPX, TCP/IP	TCP/IP
Data Encryption	No	No
Authentication	No	No
Auditing	Yes	Yes
Firewall	Works with firewalls	No
Features	Anomaly detection. Real-time intrusion detection. Real-time notification and/or action. Audit log reduction/Audit log analysis.	Single-administration GUI. Pro-active password controls. Password history. Time/day login restrictions. Password resets. Intruder lockout. Idle terminal locking. Login source restrictions.
Comments	Please call for complete platform information	Please call for complete platform support matrix
Warranty	1 year	1 year
Price and Licensing	$395–$3,995	$395–$3,995 per user

Manufacturer	Axent Technologies Inc.	Axent Technologies Inc.
Model	Omniguard Enterprise Access Control for PCs	OmniGuard/Enterprise SignOn
General Description	Central site administration PC DOS and Windows security product	Provides secure centralized administration and single-sign on to distributed network envionments
CPU	X386 or better	Intel 486 or better
OS	DOS, Windows 3X	NetWare and most Unix
Management Platform	Novell NetWare, UNIX	Novell NetWare, UNIX
RAM	75K	INA
Free Disk Space	INA	INA
Topology	Ethernet	Ethernet
Protocols Supported	IPX/SPX, TCP/IP	IPX/SPX, TCPIP
Data Encryption	DES	DES, office
Authentication	No	Yes
Auditing	Yes	Yes
Firewall	No	N/A
Features	Robust ISA (userid and password). Auditing. Discretionary access control (file encryption). Multi-user support. File storing. Guaranteed deletes. Central site administration. Idle terminal locking.	Centralized Adminstration. Single sign-on. Authentication.
Comments		In Beta at the time of this publication
Warranty	1 year	N/A
Price and Licensing	$195 per user	$200–$500 per user

N/A—Not applicable   INA—Information not available

T a b l e   C o n t i n u e s →

■ Security Utilities

Manufacturer	Axent Technologies Inc.	BrainTree Tech., Inc.
Model	Omniguard Enterprise Security Manager (ESM)	SQL<>SECURE Password Manager
General Description	Security management and administration framework utilizing a manager-agent architecture for implementing and auditing enterprise-wide security policies across heterogeneous computing environments.	A password management and analysis tool for multiple database instances; strengthens user authentication in client/server environments.
CPU	Netware 3.11 or better, HP-UX, Sun OS, Solaris, AIX, Ultrix	Sun, HP, IBM RS-6000, DEC, Sequent, Pyramid, NCR/AT&T, PCs, Macintosh
OS	Netware 3.11 or better, Windows 3.1, AT&T, Digital Unix, IBM-AIX, HP-UX, Sun OS, Solaris, AIX, Digital Ultrix, Silicon Graphics	Unix, Windows NT, Windows 95, Mac OS
Management Platform	NOS (Unix, VMS, Windows 3.1, Windows NT, Netware)	NOS
RAM	8-16MB	INA
Free Disk Space	1-18MB	INA
Topology		Ethernet, TCP/IP
Protocols Supported	IPX, TCP/IP, DECNet, CSPs of supported platforms	SQL*Net
Data Encryption	N/A	Proprietary
Authentication	Internal authentication available	Yes
Auditing	ESM can be used to perform security audits on a wide variety of systems	No
Firewall	ESM can be used to audit firewall systems but is not a firewall	No
Features	Cross platform. Enterprise wide. Security management framework. True client/server environment. API available. Graphical based, supports either Motif or Windows	Password synchronization. Password expirations enforced. Break-in detection and evasion. Application integration
Comments	Please contact for more detailed pricing and technical information	
Warranty	INA	30 day
Price and Licensing	$395–$995 per agent $1,995 per manager	$7,500 per database instance

Manufacturer	BrainTree Tech., Inc.	BrainTree Tech., Inc.
Model	SQL<>SECURE Policy Manager	SQL<>SECURE Audit Manager
General Description	A rules-based security review product for client/server RDBMS environments that provide policy definition, implementation, and enforcement.	An enterprise-wide client/server RDBMS auditing tool that utilizes a reporting GUI to manage and manipulate audit-trail data.
CPU	Sun, HP, IBM RS-6000, DEC, Sequent, Pyramid, NCR/AT&T, PCs, Macintosh	Sun, HP, IBM RS-6000, DEC, Sequent, Pyramid, NCR/AT&T, PCs, Macintosh
OS	Unix, Windows NT, Windows 95, Mac OS	Unix, Windows NT, Windows 95, Mac OS
Management Platform	NOS	NOS
RAM	N/A	N/A
Free Disk Space	N/A	N/A
Topology	Ethernet, TCP/IP	Ethernet, TCP/IP
Protocols Supported	SQL*Net	SQL*Net
Data Encryption	No	No
Authentication	No	No

N/A—Not applicable   INA—Information not available

Security Utilities ■

Manufacturer	BrainTree Tech., Inc.	BrainTree Tech., Inc.
Auditing	Yes	Yes
Firewall	No	No
Features		Row-value auditing and alerting. MS.Windows and Windows 95 GUI auditing. Client/server Oracle7 auditing. Data "drill-down" capability. Excess audit-trail data purging and deleting
Comments		
Warranty	30 day	30 day
Price and Licensing	$7,500 per database instance	$7,500 per database instance

Manufacturer	CheckPoint Software Technologies, Ltd.	Communication Devices Inc.
Model	FireWall-1 Version 2.1	Safeguard
General Description	Provides global, enterprise-wide secure connectivity services; protects organizations from internal and external unauthorized access.	Provides secure remote access to networks using DES encryption
CPU	Sun SPARC-based systems, Intel x86 or Pentium, HP PA 700/800	All
OS	Sun OS, Solaris, HP-UX, Windows NT, Windows 95	All
Management Platform	NOS	Proprietary
RAM	INA	INA
Free Disk Space	10MB	INA
Topology	Ethernet, FDDI, ADDI, TI, T3, 100BASE-T, ISDN	Dial-up network access
Protocols Supported	TCP/IP, SNMP, Telnet, FTP, NFS, SMTP mail, NNTP-news feeds	All
Data Encryption	RSA, DES	DES
Authentication	Login/ Password, S/key, SecureID, Bellcore	Yes
Auditing	Yes	Yes
Firewall	Yes	Yes
Features	Out-of-the-box support for over 120 applications, services and protocols. Authentication for remote and mobile users. Anti-spoofing. IP address translation. Encryption for VPNs	Session key authentication. Unique PC token. Full encryption option
Comments	Three different levels are available (up to 50, up to 250, and unlimited)	
Warranty	90 day (media only)	1 year
Price and Licensing	FW-1/50:$4,990 FW-1/250: $9,990 FW-1/Enterprise: $18,900	$30 per user

Manufacturer	Computer Associates International, Inc.	Cyberguard
Model	CA Unicenter TNG	Cyberguard Firewall
General Description	Software for managing and securing an entire enterprise including the IT environment and business processes.	Designed to prevent unauthorized Internet/ Intranet access or can be used to control access between any two networks
CPU	Intel: x486 66MHz Unix: varies platform to platform	Hardware/software/GUI solution. Runs on concurrent computer corp Night Hawk computer.
OS	Windows NT 3.51, Solaris 2.3, AIX, and other Unix	CX/SX secure UNIX
Management Platform	OpenView, SunNet Manager, Netview, Cabletron	N/A

N/A—Not applicable   INA—Information not available   **Table Continues** →

■ Security Utilities

Manufacturer	Computer Associates International, Inc.	Cyberguard
RAM	Intel: 32MB Unix: 32MB+	32MB
Free Disk Space	500MB, full installation	1GB hard disk
Topology	Ethernet, Token Ring, DECNet, et. al.	Ethernet
Protocols Supported	SNMP, TCP/IP, IPX/SPX, NetBIOS	TCP/IP
Data Encryption	DES	DES
Authentication	Yes	Yes
Auditing	Yes	Yes
Firewall	CA-Unicenter/ Network Security—option provided	Yes
Features	Policy-based administration Enterprise-wide security across all hardware platforms and operating systems. Advanced login and access controls. Calendar restrictions	Packet filtering. Application proxies. VPN. Strong authentication. Mandatory Access controls. GUI administration features. Remote administration support. High throughput and availability. Trusted O/S and networking product
Comments		Options include high performance web monitoring and filtering, Token Ring authentication and VPN. Evaluated by NCSC at B1
Warranty	Unlimited	1 year
Price and Licensing	Contact vendor	$24,995

Manufacturer	CyberSafe Corp.	CyberSafe Corp.
Model	CyberSafe SNAP (Simple Network Authentication Protocol)	CyberSafe Application Security ToolKit
General Description	Allows developers to secure applications with low bandwidth transfer requirements.	Allows developers to add CyberSafe Challenger security to in-house applications.
CPU	Sun OS 4.1x, Sun OS 5.3, 5.4; HP-UX 9.0; AIX 3.2.5; NEXTSTEP, NEXTSTEP for Intel; Sequent DYNIX/ptx 2.1; AT&T/NCR Unix; BSDi 1.1	Sun OS 4.1, Sun OS 5.3, 5.4; HP-UX 9.0; AIX 3.2.5; NEXTSTEP, NEXTSTEP for Intel; Sequent DYNIX/ptx 2.1; AT&T/NCR Unix; BSDi 1.1, MVS
OS	Windows 3.1, Windows for Workgroups 3.11	Windows 3.1, Windows for Workgroups 3.11
Management Platform	Windows NT 3.5	Windows NT 3.5
RAM		
Free Disk Space	2MB	2MB
Topology	Token Ring, Ethernet	Token Ring, Ethernet
Protocols Supported	All (transport independent)	All (transport independent)
Data Encryption	DES, MDS	DES, MDS variants, DES-Mac
Authentication	CyberSafe SNAP	Kerberos
Auditing	INA	INA
Firewall	INA	INA
Features	Secure authentication. Token-card authentication. Message integrity and privacy	Authenticating user identities. Mutual authentication between client and server. 20 C-callable generic functions provide name, buffer, credential, context, and message management. Message integrity and privacy.
Comments		
Warranty	90-day limited warranty for software and documentation	90-day limited warranty for software and documentation
Price and Licensing	$4,000 for authentication server $5,000 for ToolKit	$3,000 for ToolKit $295 for additional ToolKit

N/A—Not applicable   INA—Information not available

Security Utilities ■

Manufacturer	**CyberSafe Corp.**	**Cylink Corp.**
Model	CyberSafe Challenger	Secure Manager
General Description	Single sign-on authentication in a distributed, heterogeneous environment, including data, integrity, and encryption	Enterprise security, management for Cylink's Secure LAN and Secure WAN
CPU	Sun OS 4.1, Sun OS 5.3, 5.4; HP-UX 9.0; AIX 3.2.5; NEXTSTEP, NEXTSTEP for Intel; Sequent DYNIX/ptx 2.1; AT&T/NCR Unix; BSDi 1.1	Sun SPARC 5 or better
OS	Windows 3.1, Windows for Workgroups 3.11	Sun Solaris 2.4+
Management Platform	MS DOS 5.x or later, Windows NT 3.5	Integrates with HP OpenView
RAM	INA	64MB
Free Disk Space	10-15MB, + 1K per principal for KDCs	300MB
Topology	INA	Ethernet
Protocols Supported	All (transport independent)	SNMP v.1 Cylink Secure Extension
Data Encryption	DES, MD5, MD4	DES
Authentication	Kerberos	DSS certificates
Auditing	INA	Yes
Firewall	Can be used as a firewall	
Features	Single sign-on. Password checking. Token card integration. DCE interoperability. Fault tolerance and load balancing of the KDCs . Secured applications.	Enterprise security management. Graphical ability to control virtual secured networks. Scalable.
Comments	Fully documented and supported	
Warranty	90-day limited warranty for software and documentation	1 year
Price and Licensing	$60+ for desktop clients $120 for Unix clients	Call

Manufacturer	**Cylink Corp.**	**Cylink Corp.**
Model	Secure Domain Unit	SecureFrame Unit
General Description	Cryptographic firewall for use in both Internet and Intranet security applications	High-speed data encryption device for frame-relay-based public or private networks.
CPU	N/A	Standalone device
OS	N/A	N/A
Management Platform	HP OpenView	SPARC 5 or better, withSolaris 2.4 or better
RAM	N/A	N/A
Free Disk Space	N/A	N/A
Topology	Ethernet	Frame relay (V.35/X.21)
Protocols Supported	TCP/IP, Novell IPX, AppleTalk	Frame relay forum, ITU-T RFC1490 (FRF3) SNMP-1
Data Encryption	DES	DES, CEPA
Authentication	DSS certificates	Certificates with digital signature standard (DSS)
Auditing	Yes	Yes
Firewall	Yes	N/A
Features	Access control. Secure groups. VPNs. Security management.	Encryption up to 2.048. Transparent to users. SNMP-based network management. Fully automated Diffie-Hellman key management. Up to 1,024 virtual circuits

N/A—Not applicable   INA—Information not available

Table Continues →

■ Security Utilities

Manufacturer	Cylink Corp.	Cylink Corp.
Comments	Transparent data security	
Warranty	1 year	1 year
Price and Licensing	$9,500	$5,900

Manufacturer	Cylink Corp.	Cylink Corp.
Model	Secure Node S/W	Secure Traveler
General description	Provide end-to-end information security at the workstation level	Security agent for Windows and Macintosh.
CPU	IBM PC	Intel PC, Mac
OS	Windows 3.11, Windows 95, Windows NT	Windows 3.x, Windows 95, Windows NT, Mac
Management Platform	HP OpenView	N/A
RAM	N/A	8MB
Free Disk Space	N/A	600K
Topology	Any	N/A
Protocols Supported	TCP/IP	All
Data Encryption	DES	DES, EEPA
Authentication	DSS certificates	DSS, X.509
Auditing	No	N/A
Firewall	Yes	N/A
Features	Access control, Secure groups, VPNs, Security management	Authentication with X.509
Comments		
Warranty	1 year	1 year
Price and Licensing	INA	$295

Manufacturer	Cylink Corp.	Cylink Corp.
Model	Secure Data	Pocket Traveler
General Description	File encryption, directory encryption, digital signatures	RS-232 encryption with X.509 certificate authentication and DES encryption
CPU	Intel PC, Mac	Independent
OS	Windows 3.x, Windows 95, Windows NT, Mac	Independent
Management Platform	N/A	N/A
RAM	8MB	N/A
Free Disk Space	500K	N/A
Topology	N/A	RS-232 async/sync
Protocols Supported	N/A	IP, PPP, async/sync
Data Encryption	DES, CPPA	DES, CEPA
Authentication	DSS	DSS, X.509 certificate
Auditing	N/A	Yes, at SecureGate
Firewall	N/A	N/A

N/A—Not applicable   INA—Information not available

Security Utilities ■

Manufacturer	Cylink Corp.	Cylink Corp.
Features		Transparent authentication and date encryption for all modems
Comments		
Warranty	1 year	1 year
Price and Licensing	$95	$525

Manufacturer	Digital Pathways, Inc.	Digital Pathways, Inc.
Model	Defender Security Server	Software SecureNet Key
General Description	Authenticates users through a single security application for multiple network access connections. Compatible with leading servers, supports multiple, standards-based transport protocols.	Integrated into laptops or workstations located away from central sites to authenticate remote users. Pin and copy-protected, works with DPI and many third-party security systems.
CPU	Intel 486 DX2-66MHz or Pentium	Wintel PC, Macintosh, DOS, Windows, Windows 95, Mac OS 7.1
OS	Windows NT or Netware	Windows 95
Management Platform	Windows/Windows 95, Windows for Workstations	Windows 95
RAM	INA	INA
Free Disk Space	10MB	1.5MB
Topology	Ethernet	N/A
Protocols Supported	TCP/IP, IPX/SPX	N/A
Data Encryption	N/A	N/A
Authentication	Challenge/response, DES	One-time passwords, challenge/response, DES
Auditing	Yes, Windows Defender Management System	Yes, Windows Defender Management Software
Firewall	Yes, supports major firewall vendors	Yes
Features	Provides security for multiple wide area or remote access connections. Allows use of any wide area service, including dial-in, ISDN, frame relay, and ATM. Provides extended user authentication services for Internet business applications.	Available with a copy protected mechanism, with option to require the disk to be inserted in the floppy drive. Secret user information stored in a PIN-protected, encrypted file. Programmable using Windows Defender Management Software (WinDMS)
Comments		User authentication is handled automatically. Process requires user to click on the icon, and then enter the PIN.
Warranty	90-day extended warranty offered	1 year
Price and Licensing	INA	$40 per key

Manufacturer	Digital Pathways, Inc.	Digital Pathways, Inc.
Model	Windows Defender Management Software	Defender Series
General Description	Windows-based application for managing security for remote access applications.	Authenticates users with a two-factor challenge-response process; operates independently of hosts and protocols for protection in multiple OS environments.
CPU	Intel-based workstation	6-slot Defender chassis
OS	Windows 3.x, Windows 95	Embedded firmware
Management Platform	N/A	Optional-use WinDMS
RAM	8MB	N/A

N/A—Not applicable   INA—Information not available

Table Continues →

■ Security Utilities

Manufacturer	Digital Pathways, Inc.	Digital Pathways, Inc.
Free disk Space	10MB	N/A
Topology	Ethernet, Token Ring	N/A
Protocols Supported	TCP/IP, IPX/SPX	N/A
Data Encryption	N/A	N/A
Authentication	SecureNet Key, Password	N/A
Auditing	Yes, Defender Management System Reports	Two-factor, challenge/response, DES
Firewall	N/A	N/A
Features	Provides enterprise-wide or departmental management of Defended and other security systems. GUI. Manipulates critical user data to generate either pre-programmed or custom reports	Security for up to 48 communication ports and support up to 8,000 users. Host and protocol independent, supporting remote control, remote node and host access
Comments	System administrator can configure, add/modify/ delete users, collect audit data, and perform; provides intuitive tools	Protects geographically dispersed LANs, mainframes and minicomputers
Warranty	90 day	1 year
Price and Licensing	$1,595 (standalone price)	$9,955–$13,995

Manufacturer	FSA Corporation	IBM
Model	CIPHERLINK	Internet Connector Secured Network Gateway for AIX
General Description	Transparently encrypts all TCP/IP Netware traffic	IBM firewall, provides secure interface between internal, private network, and one or more nonsecure networks like Internet.
CPU	Windows 3.1, Windows 95, Windows NT, Unix, Macintosh software only	RS-6000
OS	N/A	AIX 4.1.4 or 4.2
Management Platform	NOS	TME10 Netview, others
RAM	1MB	32MB
Free Disk Space	3MB	500MB
Topology	INA	Ethernet, TR, ATM, FDDI
Protocols Supported	TCP/IP	TCP/IP
Data Encryption	(Shipped with) DES, TripleDES	DES, 40bit DES
Authentication	Yes	Password, Digital Pathways, SecureNet card or Security Dynamics' Secure ID
Auditing	N/A	Yes
Firewall	N/A	Yes
Features	Transparent encryption; fits between application and socket	Application Gateway Proxy. Alarm, with real-time notification. Filtering, such as IP source or destination address. Reporting. SOCKS server. Domain Name Server
Comments	Large-scale implementations; DES or Triple DES; can plug-and-play different encryptions.	Available worldwide; installation, support, emergency response service all available
Warranty	INA	Yes
Price and Licensing	$99 per user	$9,999 unlimited users

N/A—Not applicable   INA—Information not available

Security Utilities ∎

Manufacturer	Infinite Technologies	Intrusion Detection Inc.
Model	Guard IT!	Kane Security Analyst™ for Novell and for Windows NT
General Description	After a period of PC inactivity, Guard IT! prevents keyboard input until Netware password is entered.	Network security assessment tool that takes a snapshot of the entire network and reports security exposures.
CPU	DOS 3.0 or higher	Intel
OS	Netware 2.1x or higher	Windows 3.x, Windows 95, Windows NT 3.51 or later
Management Platform	N/A	Novell Netware 3.x, 4.x (NDS), Windows NT 3.51 or later
RAM	2.5K	8MB
Free Disk Space	200K	15MB
Topology	Any	All
Protocols Supported	Any	All
Data Encryption	INA	None
Authentication	Netware Bindery	None
Auditing	No	Yes
Firewall	No	No
Features	Smart password security for workstations. Background processes continue. Optional screen blanking. DOS and Windows versions included	Complete security assessment Does not affect production environment GUI front end. Password cracking against 20,000 words
Comments		Download free evaluation at htp://www.intrusion.com
Warranty	2 years free electronic upgrades	60-day limited
Price and Licensing	$149 per server	$495 per user

Manufacturer	Milkyway Network Corp.	NetLOCK
Model	Black Hole 3.0	NetLOCK™
General Description	Second-generation application level firewall supports VPN using Public Key Infrastructure implemented on the Internet	Authentication, encryption, and integrity pr network communications for LANs and WANs.
CPU	Sun SPARC 5 and up Pentium-based PC	INA
OS	Sun OS BSD	INA
Management Platform	Proprietary	INA
RAM	16MB	INA
Free Disk Space	500MB hard disk	INA
Topology	Ethernet, Token Ring	Topology independent
Protocols Supported	SMTP, Telnet, HTTP, Gopher, SNMP, IRP, NNTP, Real Audio, SSL, SHTTP	Protocol independent
Data Encryption	DES, RSA, CAST	Triple DES, DES, RC2, RC4, CXOR
Authentication	S-Key, Unix-like password, Enigma Logic, Cryptocard, Secure ID, Digital Pathways	RSA Certificates
Auditing	Yes	Yes
Firewall	Yes	Compatible with firewalls

N/A—Not applicable   INA—Information not available

Table Continues →

■ Security Utilities

Manufacturer	**Milkyway Network Corp.**	**NetLOCK**
Features	VPN support. Transparent mode. Full TCP and UDP support. Full authentication for all applications. One-step connection. Real-time Ethernet speed. GUI interface. Full network address translation. Ubiquitous monitoring of all access points	Transparent to end users. Multi-platform. Application independent. Selectable encryption algorithms. Configurable key lifetimes. Port filtering
Comments		Secures network communications within an organization and between the organization and its business partners
Warranty	N/A	90-day extended available
Price and Licensing	$2,950–$20,500 (unlimited users)	INA

Manufacturer	**NetPartners**	**Network-1 Software and Technology, Inc.**
Model	WebSENSE	FireWall/Plus
General Description	Internet screening system that functions with a control list of URL addresses to screen out sites deemed inappropriate for business use	Designed to filter more than 400 network protocols against Internet, Intranet, and LAN-to-LAN attacks.
CPU	Intel 486	Intel Pentium 100MHz standard
OS	Windows NT 3.5.1 or greater	MS-DOS, Windows NT
Management Platform	Windows NT	NOS
RAM	16MB	16MB disk standard, expandable to 128MB
Free Disk Space	3MB	500MB, expandable to 16GB
Topology	Ethernet, Token Ring, FDDI, ATM	Ethernet, Token Ring
Protocols Supported	TCP/IP	Over 400 network protocols including TCP/IP, AppleTalk, IP, IPX, DECNet, OSI, LAT, NetBEUI, et al
Data Encryption	No	Yes
Authentication	No	Yes
Auditing	Yes	Yes
Firewall	Yes	Yes
Features	26 categories of sites screening User defined InterNet access time Simple user Monitoring, logging, reporting activity Auto update of control list each night Supports wide range of TCP protocols	Multiprotocol support Frame, packet, and application-level filtering. Non-Unix based external routing, default configurations, instinctive GUI, transparency.
Comments		
Warranty	90 day	90 day
Price and Licensing	$495–$6,995	$3,995–$16,500 (including hardware and software)

Manufacturer	**On Technology Corp.**	**Ontrack DataRecovery, Inc.**
Model	On Guard	Ontrack Data Recovery for Netware
General Description	It is a NCSA certified firewall for IP and IPA networks	NLM data recovery and protection utilities for Netware 4.0
CPU	PC (486/66) or higher	As determined by NetWare
OS	Secure 32OS (proprietary)	Netware 3.1, 4.0, 4.1
Management Platform	Windows, Windows 95, Windows NT	NOS
RAM	4MB	Same as Netware

N/A—Not applicable   INA—Information not available

Security Utilities ■

Manufacturer	On Technology Corp.	Ontrack DataRecovery, Inc.
Free Disk Space	50MB	1.5MB
Topology	Ethernet	Ethernet
Protocols Supported	SNMP, IPX/SPX, TCP/IP, NetBIOS, Apple DDP	IPX/SPX
Data Encryption	No	No
Authentication	No	No
Auditing	Yes	No
Firewall	Yes	No
Features	Express Configuration Wizard. Packet and application layer screening. Unix-free. Hides addresses. Protects IP and IPX networks.	File recovery from corrupted Netware volumes. Complete NLM utilities. Data-protection features. Network management tools. Netware file system analysis and repair.
Comments	Free 30-day trial available	
Warranty	1 year	INA
Price and Licensing	$7,485 for 100 users	$495 (single user)

Manufacturer	OpenVision Technologies	OpenVision Technologies
Model	AXX/ON-Detective	AXX/ON-Authorize
General Description	Provides real-time authorization and access control for OpenVMS environments	Designed to enhance Unix access controls and to improve password policy management
CPU	VAX Systems	Unix-HP700 or 800 series workstation, IBM RS-6000, Sun 4 and Alpha workstations
OS	OpenVMS	Unix
Management Platform	OpenVMS/VAX 5.5+ OpenVMS/Alpha 6.0+	Solaris, AIX, HP-UX
RAM	INA	16K
Free Disk Space	INA	11MB
Topology	DECNet	TCP/IP
Protocols Supported	TCP/IP and DECNet	TCP/IP
Data Encryption	No	No
Authentication	No	No
Auditing	Yes	Yes
Firewall	No	No
Features	Real-time authorization and access control. Comprehensive monitoring of applications and information systems. Restricts user privileges. Provides a user help desk.	Will improve control of systems privileges, and control remote network access. Unix expertise is not required.
Comments		
Warranty	INA	INA
Price and Licensing	INA	INA

Manufacturer	OpenVision Technologies	OpenVision Technologies
Model	AXX/ON-SecureMax	AXX/ON-Authenticate
General Description	Performs security audits and manages security of large-scale distributed systems	Provides reduced sign-on, using Kerberos encryption technology to ensure identification
CPU	Windows: 486+, NIC or a dial-up connection Unix: HP700 or 800, IBM RS-6000, Sun 4 workstation, Alpha workstation	Windows: 486+, NIC or a dial-up connection Unix: HP700 or 800, IBM RS-6000, Sun 4 workstation, Alpha workstation

N/A—Not applicable   INA—Information not available

Table Continues →

■ Security Utilities

Manufacturer	OpenVision Technologies	OpenVision Technologies
OS	Windows NT 3.51+, Windows 95, Unix, and OpenVMS	Windows NT 3.51+, Windows 95, Unix, and OpenVMS
Management Platform	Windows NT, Windows 95, Solaris, AIX, HP-UX, Open-VMS	Windows NT, Windows 95, Solaris, AIX, HP-UX, Open-VMS
RAM	Windows: 16MB Unix: Console (motif)-8MB, Agent-16MB	Windows: 16MB Unix: 16MB
Free Disk Space	Windows: 3MB Unix: 6-9K	Windows: 3MB Unix: 16K
Topology	Ethernet	Ethernet
Protocols Supported	TCP/IP and DECNet	TCP/IP and DECNet
Data Encryption	Yes	DES(40bit and 56bit)
Authentication	Yes	Yes, Kerberos 5
Auditing	Yes (including Oracle and Sybase database checks)	Yes
Firewall	No	No
Features	Centralized security auditing. Can use pre-defined or created audit reports.	Reduces sign-on. Password management. Secured Telnet and FTP. Login control. Account management.
Comments	The Windows 95 Agent is not supported.	
Warranty	INA	INA
Price and Licensing	INA	INA

Manufacturer	PC Guardian	Personal Cipher Card Corp.
Model	Workstation Manager Plus	PCSS
General Description	Workstation control and security with centralized administration	Utilizes smart card as token to provide access to PC and network
CPU	286 or higher	PC compatible, running on DOS
OS	DOS, Windows 3.x, Windows 95	N/A
Management Platform	Novell Netware 3x, 4x	DOS, Novell, Banyan Vines
RAM	500K for install only	5K
Free Disk Space	3MB	2MB
Topology	Ethernet	Ethernet
Protocols Supported	Netware 3x, 4x	DES, batch encryption on PC
Data Encryption	Proprietary	No
Authentication	Network SOS	No
Auditing	Yes	Yes
Firewall	No	No
Features	Prevent execution of non-approved applications. Access control. Virus protection. Prevent copying of files. Single sign-on. Prevent changes to configuration files.	PIN-protected smart card. Executable file copy protection for virus prevention and licensed software. Network protected password and auto login.
Comments	Allows administrator to standardize and protect all workstations centrally.	
Warranty	90 day	INA
Price and Licensing	INA	$249 single user

N/A—Not applicable   INA—Information not available

Security Utilities ■

Manufacturer	**Platinum Technology**	**Premenos**
Model	AutoSecure Version 2.1	Templar
General Description	Provides computer security services which protect information and resources residing on enterprise computers	Software, services, and network solutions necessary to conduct EDI securely over TCP/IP networks like the Internet
CPU	Unix Workstation	IBM RS-6000, HP9000, PC, Sun SPARC
OS	Solaris, Sun OS, HP-UX, AIX	Unix, AIX, HP-UX, Sun Solaris, Windows 3.1x, Windows 95, Windows NT
Management Platform	N/A	INA
RAM	Workstation 32MB or more	32MB
Free Disk Space	50MB	500MB
Topology	Ethernet, Token Ring	Ethernet, Token Ring
Protocols Supported	TCP/IP	TCP/IP
Data Encryption	Proprietary data encryption algorithm	RSA, DES, RC2, RC4
Authentication	Inter-operates with a variety of authentication methods including Unix login and smart cards	Digital Signature
Auditing	Yes	Yes
Firewall	Soft Firewall	No
Features	File and program access control. Unix login control. Userid substitution control. Password quality management. Event notification. APIs.	Non-repudiation, tracking, Automatic notification of receipt, GUI
Comments		24-hour support, seven days a week
Warranty	1 year	1 year
Price and Licensing	Depends	$499+

Manufacturer	**Raptor Systems, Inc.**	**Secure Computing Corp.**
Model	Eagle 4.0	BorderWare Firewall Server 4.0
General Description	Application-level firewall that addresses the Five Domains of Security, including Internet, Intranet/LAN mobile PCs, remote sites and enterprise management	High-level security system that protects privacy and information from external Internet hackers, as well as corporate insiders.
CPU	SunSPARC 5 or better, HP PA workstation or server, Alpha workstation, Windows NT Workstation or server	Pentium, Intel CPU
OS	SunOS,Solaris, HP-UX Windows NT 3.51 and 4.0	Has its own OS
Management Platform	Raptor Security Management Console	Any that will run Netscape and JAVA
RAM	32MB	16MB min., 32MB rec
Free Disk Space	32MB	800K min.
Topology	Ethernet, Fast Ethernet, FDDI, Token Ring	Ethernet, Token Ring, FDDI, Fast Ethernet, WAN
Protocols Supported	TCP/IP	TCP/IP, UDP
Data Encryption	RSA, DES, Triple dES	DES 40bit, DES 56bit, Triple DES, RSA Bsafe
Authentication	TACACS, Radius, IETF IP Sec VPN, Digital Pathways, CrytoCard, SDI	Login/Password, Secure ID, Cryptocard, Enigma Logic, Digital Pathways
Auditing	Yes	Yes
Firewall	Yes	Yes

N/A—Not applicable   INA—Information not available

Table Continues →

■ Security Utilities

Manufacturer	Raptor Systems, Inc.	Secure Computing Corp.
Features	IPSec Virtual Private Networking support for interoperability across the VPN; Load balancing; Packet Filtering; Domain Name Service (DNS); IP Spoof Checking; GUI allows for remote management and configuration security; monitor provides 7 levels of alerts on suspicious activity in the network.	Java-based. Supports SSN and VPN. Web-based remote management. VPN encryption and authentication.
Comments	CyberPatrol URL blocker. enables organizations to deny access from a variety of URL's.	
Warranty	N/A	1 year
Price and Licensing	UNIX—$7,000+ for up to 50 NT—$6,500 + for up to 50 users	$4,000 for 25 users $15,000 for unlimited

Manufacturer	SecureNet Technologies	Technical Communications Corporation
Model	PC-Watchman ACS Plus	Cipher®
General Description	Provides effective security to individual terminals with network transparency. Passwords cannot be passed by booting to a floppy.	Encryption, authentication and firewall protection for Frame relay WANs operating at up to 2.048 Mbps
CPU	IBM PC compatible	N/A self contained unit that resides transparently on the network
OS	DOS, Windows 3.1x, Windows 95	N/A
Management Platform	Novell	Windows NT, UNIX
RAM	24K	N/A
Free Disk Space	1.2M	N/A
Topology	Any	Ethernet/Token Ring LANs to WAN
Protocols Supported	N/A	Frame relay
Data Encryption	Proprietary, DES	DES, TCC proprietary, exportable
Authentication	Yes	Yes
Auditing	Records user sign-ons, log-offs, and program executions including user names, program names and times is provided by an audit trail accessible only to the system administrator	Yes
Firewall	No	Yes
Features	Ability to administer discretionary controls to restrict access to unauthorized files, programs, subdirectories	Protocol sensitive frame relay security encryption, authentication and firewall. Support for 976 virtual circuits. Centralized management. U.S. and TCC proprietary algorithms FIPS 140-/FIPS 171 compliant.
Comments	Includes a secured "back door" that allows a security administrator access to a PC when the authorized operator is not available	
Warranty	90 day	15 month
Price and Licensing	$150, single user with 5-user minimum	N/A

Manufacturer	Technical Communications Corporation	Technical Communications Corporation
Model	Cipher X® 7300	Cipher® X 5000A/850
General Description	Link and packet encryption and authentication for voice, data, video, Frame relay, PPP, IP/IPX on basic and primary rate ISDN channels	Encryption, authentication and firewall protection for X.25 WANS. Also Link encryption up to 64bps.
CPU	N/A self contained unit that resides transparently on the network	N/A self contained unit that resides transparently on the network
OS	N/A	N/A

N/A—Not applicable   INA—Information not available

Security Utilities ■

Manufacturer	**Technical Communications Corporation**	**Technical Communications Corporation**
Management Platform	Windows NT, UNIX	Windows NT, UNIX
RAM	N/A	N/A
Free Disk Space	N/A	N/A
Topology	Ethernet LANs, WANs	Ethernet/Token Ring LANs to WAN
Protocols Supported	ISDN, operates transparently with all data protocols	X.25
Data Encryption	DES, TCC proprietary, exportable	DES, TCC proprietary, exportable
Authentication	Yes	Yes
Auditing	Yes	Yes
Firewall	Yes	Yes
Features	ISDN primary and basic rate interface. Encryption, authentication and firewall. Centralized management. Low throughput delay and overhead U.S. and TCC proprietary algorithms Windows-based user interface.	Protocol sensitive X.25 security. Support for 255 virtual circuits. Centralized management. U.S. and TCC proprietary algorithms.
Comments		
Warranty	15 month	15 month
Price and Licensing	N/A	N/A

Manufacturer	**Technical Communications Corporation**	**WRQ**
Model	Cipher X® 7200	Reflection Secure
General Description	Encryption, authentication and firewall protection for IP/IPX WANs/LANs operating at up to 10Mbps.	Reflection Secure delivers secure Telnet access with single Kerberos sign-on to multiple hosts; advanced options for security and configurations.
CPU	N/A self contained unit that resides transparently on the network	386 PC or higher
OS	N/A	Windows 3.1x, Windows for Workgroups
Management Platform	Windows NT, UNIX	Included client manager
RAM	N/A	6MB
Free Disk Space	N/A	500K
Topology	Ethernet LANs, WANs	N/A
Protocols Supported	IP, IPX	Runs over WinSock
Data Encryption	DES, TCC proprietary, exportable	DES
Authentication	Yes	Kerberos 5/DCE
Auditing	Yes	No
Firewall	Yes	No
Features	Protocol sensitive IP/IPX security. Centralized management. Support for 1024 virtual circuits. Low packet latency. U.S, and TCC proprietary algorithms. Up to 12 discretionary access groups. Selective filtering of transport layer protocols.	Single authentication. Single sign-on. Mutual Authentication
Comments		Windows 95, NT support in late 1996
Warranty	15 month	Contact vendor
Price and Licensing	N/A	$99 single user

N/A—Not applicable   INA—Information not available

Table Continues →

■ Security Utilities

Manufacturer	**Raptor Systems Inc.**	**Raptor Systems Inc.**
Model	Eagle Netwatch 1.1	Security Management Console
General description	Eagle Netwatch is a unique 3D visual, real-time monitor of network security activity	An enterprise security management platform. It allows users to assess the vulnerability of their networks, formulate, manage, and enforce security policy.
CPU	Sun SPARC 5 or better. Color monitor w/1280 x 1024 resolution/256 colors. Network interface card. DAT.	Sun SPARC 5 or better. Color monitor w/1280 x 1024 resolution/256 colors. Network interface card. DAT.
OS	Solaris 2.4	Solaris 2.4
Management Platform	Raptor Security Management	Raptor Security Management
RAM	32MB RAM	32MB RAM
Free Disk Space	1GB disk	1GB disk
Topology	Ethernet, Fast Ethernet, Token Ring, FDDI	Ethernet, Fast Ethernet, Token Ring, FDDI
Protocols Supported	IPX/SPX, TCP/IP	IPX/SPX, TCP/IP
Data Encryption	No	INA
Authentication	No	INA
Auditing	No	INA
Firewall	Yes	INA
Features	Centralized network security monitoring through 3-D visualization. Graphical visualization of logged session activity from several Eagle firewalls. Reporting and administration functionality, including 2-D and 3-D report printing.	Internet Scanner; Monitors and reports, in real-time, on security activity; displays activity in 3D visualization. GUI allows configuration and remote management of security. Provides 7 levels of alerts. Kills unauthorized processes on the firewall
Comments	Three viewing parameters available for display of security event information	Security software bundled with Eagle firewall. Monitors and manages system process events, such as file system and event logs.
Warranty	N/A	N/A
Price and LLicensing	$6,995	Depends on configuration

N/A—Not applicable   INA—Information not available

E n d ■

Virus Protection Utilities ■

Manufacturer	Cheyenne Software	Cheyenne Software
Model	Inoculan for NetWare	Anti-Virus Agents for Groupware
Product Description	Complete client/server network virus protection	Protects Lotus Notes, Microsoft Exchange server, and Novell Groupwise from viruses
OS Client Support	Win NT, 3.x, and DOS, Mac	N/A
NOS Support	NetWare 3.x and 4.x	NetWare, Windows NT, UNIX, OS/2
File Server Requirements	2MB RAM, 2MB disk space	Same as InocuLAN
Workstation Requirements	Windows NT: 16MB RAM/8MB disk, Windows 95 + 3.x: 8/6 DOS: 480K/2 Mac: System 6.02+	N/A
Install Created Rescue Disk by Default	Yes	N/A
Includes Native Uninstall Feature	No	N/A
Install Program Scans Memory Prior to Installation	Yes	N/A
Scans Boot Sector	Yes	N/A
Can Restore Master Boot Sector	Yes	N/A
Can Restore Partition Table	Yes	N/A
Scans Compressed Files	Yes (including Internet downloads)	Yes
Scans Memory	Yes	N/A
Can Schedule Automatic Scans	Yes	Yes
Reports Scan Results on Screen/ File Log	Yes (can be centralized)	Yes
Includes Inoculation Feature	Yes	Yes
Can Scan Inbound/ Outbound Files	Yes	Yes
Scans Files on Access	Yes (both server and client)	N/A
Detects/Removes Word Macro Viruses	Yes (proprietary macro virus analyze)	Yes
Monthly Updates	Yes (free and auto distribution)	Yes
Domain Management	Yes	Yes
Comments	100% NCSA certification. Languages: English, French, German, Japanese	Agents that work in conjunction with InocuLAN
Warranty	30-day money back, free support	30-day money back, free support
Price	$189	$995 ($495 with ARCserve)

N/A—Not applicable   INA—Information not available

Table Continues →

■ Virus Protection Utilities

	Cheyenne Software	ESaSS-ThunderBYTE International
Manufacturer	Cheyenne Software	ESaSS-ThunderBYTE International
Model	InocuLan 4.0 for Windows NT	ThunderBYTE Anti-Virus Utilities
Product Description	Complete client/server network virus protection. Carries the *Designed for BackOffice* logo and Windows NT Editors choice.	Five levels of virus protection including signature and heuristic scanning, generic decryption, integrity checking, plus active monitoring against ALL types of viruses
OS Client Support	Windows NT, Windows 95, Windows 3.x, and DOS, Mac	NT 3.51, Windows 95, Windows 3.x, and DOS
NOS Support	Windows NT 3.5x and 4.x (Intel, Alpha, MIPS, Power PC)	Network independent
File Server Requirements	16MB RAM, 8MB disk space	N/A
Workstation Requirements	Windows NT: 16 MB RAM/8 MB disk, Windows 95+3.x: 8/6, DOS: 480K/2, Mac: System 6.02 or above	DOS 3.0: 256K RAM, 1M storage. Windows 3.xx: 1M RAM, 1.5M storage. Windows 95: 4M RAM, 1M storage
Install Created Rescue Disk by Default	Yes	No
Includes Native Uninstall Feature	Yes	Windows 95 only
Install Program Scans Memory Prior to Installation	Yes	DOS only
Scans Boot Sector	Yes (automatic floppy disk sanning)	Yes
Can Restore Master Boot Sector	Yes	Yes
Can Restore Partition Table	Yes	Yes
Scans Compressed Files	Yes (including Internet downloads)	No
Scans Memory	Yes	Yes
Can Schedule Automatic Scans	Yes	Yes
Reports Scan Results on Screen/ File Log	Yes (including Internet downloads)	Yes
Includes Inoculation Feature	Yes	Yes
Can Scan Inbound/ Outbound Files	Yes	Yes
Scans Files on Access	Yes (Native NT Service)	Yes
Detects/Removes Word Macro Viruses	Yes (proprietary macro virus analyzer)	Yes
Monthly Updates	Yes (Free and auto distribution)	Bi-monthly
Domain Management	Yes	Separate network ddministrator package
Comments	100% NCSA certification. Languages: English, French, German, Japanese	English and French
Warranty	30-day money-back guarantee, free support	30 day
Price	$995 srp ($995 with Arcserve)	$100

N/A—Not applicable   INA—Information not available

Virus Protection Utilities ∎

Manufacturer	McAfee Associates	McAfee Associates
Model	Ontrack Virus Scan (2.2)	Ontrack NetShield (2.2)
Product Description	Advanced virus protection for DOS, OS/2, and Windows	NLM virus protection for file servers. Detects more than 95% of known viruses
OS Client Support	DOS, OS/2, and Windows	DOS, OS/2, and Windows
NOS Support	Netware 3.1x, 4.x, SFTIII	Netware 3.1x, 4.x, SFTIII
File Server Requirements	Netware for OS/2, Netware Lite, Artisoft Lantastic Version 6.0	At least 1MB
Workstation Requirements	DOS 3.x +, Windows 3.x+, Windows 95, OS2-2.1+, Windows NT 3.5	None, server-based
Install Created Rescue Disk by Default	No	No
Includes Native Uninstall Feature	No	No
Install Program Scans Memory Prior to Installation	Yes	Yes
Scans Boot Sector	Yes	No
Can Restore Master Boot Sector	Yes	No
Can Restore Partition Table	No	No
Scans Compressed Files	Yes	Yes
Scans Memory	Yes	No
Can Schedule Automatic Scans	Yes	Yes
Reports Scan Results on Screen/ File Log	Yes	Yes
Includes Inoculation Feature	Yes	Yes
Can Scan Inbound/ Outbound Files	Yes	Yes
Scans Files on Access	Yes	Yes
Detects/Removes Word Macro Viruses	Yes	Detection only
Monthly Updates	Yes	Yes
Domain Management	No	Yes
Comments	Version also available for Windows 95. Languages: English, French, German	English
Warranty	INA	INA
Price	$9,995 single user retail price	Multiple server pricing

---

N/A—Not applicable   INA—Information not available

Table Continues →

■ Virus Protection Utilities

Manufacturer	McAfee	Mcafee
Model	WebScan v 1.04	VirusScan
Product Description	Complete virus protection for web browsers and e-mail	Virus detection and removal software for multiple platforms
OS Client Support	Windows NT, Windows 95, Windows 3.1	Windows NT, Windows 95, Windows 3.x, DOS, OS/2, Mac, Solaris 2.4+
NOS Support	N/A	INA
File Server Requirements	N/A	3.5 or 5 depending on OS
Workstation Requirements	8MB disk space Modem 9600bps or greater Internet	
Install Created Rescue Disk by Default	N/A	Yes
Includes Native Uninstall Feature	Yes	Yes
Install Program Scans Memory Prior to Installation	N/A	Yes
Scans Boot Sector	N/A	Yes
Can Restore Master Boot Sector	N/A	Yes
Can Restore Partition Table	N/A	Yes
Scans Compressed Files	Yes	Yes
Scans Memory	N/A	Yes
Can Schedule Automatic Scans	N/A	Yes
Reports Scan Results on Screen/ File Log	Yes	Yes
Includes Inoculation Feature	N/A	Yes
Can Scan Inbound/ Outbound Files	No	Yes
Scans Files on Access	N/A	Yes
Detects/Removes Word Macro Viruses	Yes, detects	Yes
Monthly Updates	Yes	Yes
Domain Management	N/A	Yes
Comments	Scans zips, ARC, ARJ	English, French, German, Japanese, Dutch, Danish, Spanish, Italian
Warranty	1 upgrade, 1 year virus	Lifetime for licensed users
Price	$40	$65 per node

N/A—Not applicable   INA—Information not available

Virus Protection Utilities ■

Manufacturer	PC Guardian	Personal Cipher Card Corp.
Model	Workstation Manager Plus	PCSS
Product Description	Workstation control and security with built-in virus scanner and program approval function.	Prevents introduction and migration of virus by inhibiting all copying of exeecutables
OS Client Support	Windows 3.x, Windows 95, DOS	Windows 3.1, Windows 95, DOS
NOS Support	Netware 3.x, 4.x	Novell, Banyan Vines
File Server Requirements	Netware 3.x, 4.x	
Workstation Requirements	DOS 5.0, Windows, PC286 RAM 20K	2M disk, 5K TSR
Install Created Rescue Disk by Default	Yes	No
Includes Native Uninstall Feature	Yes	Yes
Install Program Scans Memory Prior to Installation	Yes	No
Scans Boot Sector	Yes	Yes
Can Restore Master Boot Sector	Yes	No
Can Restore Partition Table	Yes	No
Scans Compressed Files	Yes	No
Scans Memory	Yes	No
Can Schedule Automatic Scans	Yes	No
Reports Scan Results on Screen/ File Log	Yes	No
Includes Inoculation Feature	Yes	No
Can Scan Inbound/ Outbound Files	Yes	No
Scans Files on Access	Yes	No
Detects/Removes Word Macro Viruses	No	No
Monthly Updates	90 day	No
Domain Management	Yes	No
Comments	With central administration	Multi-language support
Warranty	First 90 days: all upgrades and tech support. After 90 days, 20% of unit price per year continues	
Price	INA	$249

N/A—Not applicable   INA—Information not available

Table Continues →

■ Virus Protection Utilities

Manufacturer	SecureNet Technologies	Stiller Research	TouchStone Software Corp.
Model	V-Net Gold with MACROBLASTER	Integrity Master	PC-cillin Enterprise Edition
Product Description	V-Net Gold software protects PCs that can be received via the Internet or floppy disks. V-Net Gold authorizes disks and programs, and automatically cleans "boot" viruses without user intervention.	Anti-virus and full data integrity protection; protects PCs from threats to programs and data.	An automated anti-virus program designed for Windows 95 and the Internet. It monitors online services, e-mail, floppy drives, shared folders and networks to protect against virus threats.
OS Client Support	DOS 2.11+, Windows 3.1x, Windows 95, Windows NT	DOS, Windows 3.x, Windows 95, OS/2	Windows 95
NOS Support	Novelle, Banyan, Windows NT, UNIX	All	Netware, Windows NT
File Server Requirements	System login script is required for network installations	Any	2MB disk space
Workstation Requirements	INA	400K free memory on any PC	Windows 95 with 4MB disk space
Install Created Rescue Disk by Default	Yes	Yes	Yes
Includes Native Uninstall Feature	Yes	Yes	Yes
Install Program Scans Memory Prior to Installation	Total hard disk and memory	No	Yes
Scans Boot Sector	Yes	Yes	Yes
Can Restore Master Boot Sector	Yes, automatically	Yes	Yes
Can Restore Partition Table	Yes, automatically	Yes	Yes
Scans Compressed Files	Yes	Yes (with add on)	Yes
Scans Memory	Yes	Yes	Yes
Can Schedule Automatic Scans	Yes	Yes	Yes
Reports Scan Results on Screen/ File Log	Yes	Yes	Yes
Includes Inoculation Feature	Yes	No	Yes
Can Scan Inbound/ Outbound Files	Yes	Yes	Yes
Scans Files on Access	Only first time, unless notified	No	Yes
Detects/Removes Word Macro Viruses	Yes	Yes	Yes
Monthly Updates	Yes	No	Yes
Domain Management	N/A	No	Yes
Comments	If virus reaches hard drive, isolates or eliminates infected files. It is compatible with any virus scanner, and can be used with multiple scanners.	Detects viral damage as well as infected files	
Warranty	1 year	60 day	Varies
Price	$132 for single user, with 5-user minimum; volume pricing available	$45 for single user; additional licenses range from $5 to $20	Varies per user

N/A—Not applicable   INA—Information not available

End ■

C H A P T E R

10 STORAGE HARDWARE

IF INFORMATION IS A company's most critical asset, the equipment that information is stored on is the second most critical asset. You can store digital information on basically three different mediums: hard disks, optical media, and tape. There is debate about which technology is best. All three have distinct characteristics that make them valuable in different environments and applications (See Table 10.1). This chapter covers storage products from all three technology types.

STORAGE HARDWARE

■ Table 10.1 Comparing Storage Media

	Hard Disk	Tape	Optical
Data access speed	Highest	Lowest	Lower
Capacity	Limited	Unlimited	Unlimited
Cost per megabyte	Highest*	Lowest	Lower
Most Popular Application	Primary online storage	Backup and archive of primary storage	Secondary storage and archive

* Hard drives can initially cost less than some tape and optical drives of similar capacity. However, the capacity of tape and optical is much higher if you consider multiple pieces of media. Removable media are inexpensive relative to hard disks.

CD-ROM Towers and Jukeboxes

CD-ROM has quickly become a popular format for storing and retrieving digital information. It is primarily used for software distribution, multimedia presentation, and storage of reference information. CD-ROM drives only read information from CDs, which hold approximately 650MB of information. Recordable CD drives can both read and write to CD and are covered in the "Optical Drives" section of this chapter.

One CD-ROM drive doesn't go too far on a network of even moderate size. The demand for reference information and new software installations usually keeps the drive busy and people waiting. In addition, swapping the necessary CDs becomes very disruptive. CD-ROM towers are cabinets that typically hold seven to ten CD-ROM drives, all active and accessible at once. If you use CD-ROM towers, there's less need to swap disks and more than one person at a time can be served.

Some network administrators build their own CD towers with existing equipment rather than purchasing a prepackaged unit. For those with a large library of CDs, CD-ROM jukeboxes (also known as "CD-ROM libraries") may be the answer. These units typically have one to four drives and keep 50 to 200 CDs accessible with a robotic arm that swaps CDs in and out of the drives. This setup provides "hands free" access to a much greater number of CDs than CD towers.

Number of Drives and Media

Performance	Reliability	Manageability	**Scalability**	**Flexibility**	**Value**

In CD-ROM towers, there are the same number of CDs loaded as there are drives to hold them. The number of drives in any one unit varies from approximately 5 to 100, but the typical number is under 10. This seems to match the typical controller and power supply capabilities and keeps the unit size manageable.

STORAGE HARDWARE

Most CD-ROM jukeboxes can have up to four drives. Multiple drives provide better performance because they allow you to serve more than one user at a time. Reliability also increases with the number of drives because the jukebox can continue using other drives while a failed drive is removed for repair. Having the right ratio of drives to media will help you get the optimum performance. If you have a small number of CDs that need frequent access, a CD tower or a jukebox with lots of drives will work best. If you have a large CD library with infrequent CD demands, the number of CD slots becomes more critical than the number of drives.

Drive Speed					
Performance	Reliability	Manageability	Scalability	Flexibility	Value

CD-ROM drives come in different speeds that measure how fast the disc rotates in operation. Popular speeds today are 6X and 8X, which are six and eight times faster than the original CD-ROM standard. A faster drive means faster access and transmission of information. The importance of drive speed is somewhat relative to the application. For example, speed may not be critical for software distribution but it can have a big impact on the performance of multimedia images and presentations. The type of CD-ROM drive will of course affect the performance of the tower or jukebox it is placed in.

CD Access Time					
Performance	Reliability	Manageability	Scalability	Flexibility	Value

In a CD tower, access to a CD is immediate if it is loaded in the drive and the drive is available. In a jukebox, you may have to wait for the machine's robotic arm to load the appropriate CD into a drive. This loading time is often referred to as "pick and place." Typical pick and place time is 8 to 20 seconds and depends on factors such as the number of media slots in the unit and the distance to the drive.

Network Connection					
Performance	Reliability	**Manageability**	Scalability	**Flexibility**	Value

In most cases, the CD-ROM tower or jukebox is connected to a server for network access. This makes sense because server access is already set up and a server can effectively manage the peripheral. However, some units are "direct attach"—they can plug right into the network, usually into a slot on the hub, where they appear as another network resource. This system has the advantage of not placing additional memory or computing overhead on a server. In addition, the resource is still available on the network if a server is down (except, of course, for anyone who requires the downed server for network access).

STORAGE HARDWARE

Modularity					
Performance	Reliability	**Manageability**	Scalability	**Flexibility**	Value

Modularity refers to how easy it is to custom fit the unit or units to your needs. This may include a feature like plug-and-play drives, where the necessary drive connections are made by a plug-like connector in the back of the drive. The chassis has a matched receiving end and the connection is made when the drive is slipped into the slot. For CD jukeboxes, modularity also refers to flexibility in the number of drives and media a unit can hold. Most jukeboxes have a fixed number of drive slots, but some can add additional drives in place of some media slots. In addition, in some cases you can load media using magazines rather than loading individual CDs. This gives you more flexibility in both organizing and transferring media into and out of the jukebox.

CD Management					
Performance	Reliability	**Manageability**	Scalability	Flexibility	**Value**

You can manage CDs in a tower through your NOS; this may be as simple as choosing a drive reference. But the user interface to the tower may be simply a choice in drives, requiring the drive to read the CD to see what is loaded. If the media title is not loaded in a drive, what happens? Media management software can help. In addition to informing you that this is the case, the system may send a message to the network administrator requesting that the appropriate CD be loaded. You might find this type of automation on a media management software utility that came with the unit or that you bought separately. Media management is particularly important for optical jukeboxes where the library is often large and the robotics need to know which slot holds which title. Chapter 11 covers media management software in more detail.

Disk Storage Subsystems

Hard disks are the primary medium for online data storage. Servers are usually sold with large hard disk repositories for data. In addition, servers can usually accommodate additional drives. Nevertheless, many network administrators buy external disk storage subsystems because they're easy to install and are preconfigured with power and controller requirements already met. They also don't crowd the server cabinet space and provide an efficient cabinet design to handle multiple drives.

Chassis Design					
Performance	**Reliability**	Manageability	**Scalability**	**Flexibility**	Value

When deciding on a disk storage subsystem you should consider the subsystem as a unit, not as individual drives. You can use the same chassis if

STORAGE HARDWARE

the drives fail or age and need updating over time, so it's important to get a suitable chassis. First determine how many drives the chassis can hold and the form factor of the drives ($3\frac{1}{2}$-inch drives, $5\frac{1}{4}$-inch drives, and so on). The chassis should accommodate a drive form factor that will be around for a while ($3\frac{1}{2}$-inch drives are most common today). You increase the expandability of the unit by choosing high-capacity drives and leaving extra slots open so you can add drives later. The chassis itself may be floor standing, a desktop unit, or a rack mountable unit.

Drive Capacity and Performance

Performance	Reliability	Manageability	**Scalability**	Flexibility	**Value**

Hard drive capacity and performance are key considerations when choosing a storage subsystem. You'll have better performance with fewer high-capacity drives rather than more lower capacity drives. In addition, choosing high-capacity drives may leave some space to add more drives later. Also take into account the average access speed of the drives. New $3\frac{1}{2}$-inch drives typically have access times in the 8 to 12 millisecond range, probably an unnoticeable difference in speed to the user for most applications. "Bulk disk drives" are larger format drives with very high capacities, but they have average access times in the 30 to 50 millisecond range. The cost per megabyte of storage is lower for bulk disk drives.

The hard-disk interface is an important part of the drive's performance. ESDI is an older standard and not widely supported today. IDE drives have a inherent limit of 540MB. This is exceeded with enhanced IDE drives, which actually mate 540 drives into multiples to achieve 1.2 and 1.6GB drives. Unfortunately, few NOSs support IDE drives on the server as they do not recognize the additional space. SCSI drives are widely supported by NOSs and have capacities in the 2 to 8GB range. In addition, the SCSI interface allows for more sophisticated drive access, including write queuing, read caching, and RAID. Within SCSI are several standards—each different and for the most part incapable of being mixed in the same subsystem. SCSI II is the most common but the newer Fast, Wide, and Fast and Wide form factors are widely available. The newest UltraSCSI is the cutting edge of disk systems. Each newer standard allows for faster access to data and higher throughput for the disk drives.

Supported Drivers

Performance	Reliability	Manageability	Scalability	**Flexibility**	Value

The drives in the subsystem should be widely accepted by systems they will be attached to. Ask the subsystem vendor for a list of supported drivers that enable compatibility with operating and network operating systems. You

STORAGE HARDWARE

should also look for an indication that the equipment is certified to work with the necessary network operating systems.

Modularity					
Performance	Reliability	**Manageability**	**Scalability**	**Flexibility**	Value

One aspect of modularity is how easy it is to change hard drives. A subsystem that lets you snap drives into place is more modular than one for which you need a screwdriver and rear access to hook or unhook drives from a controller. In addition, it's nice to be able to remove or add a drive without affecting the others; this is called "hot swapping." Being able to daisy chain a number of different units together easily can make expansion easier. This method may make expansion easier but it multiplies the fault intolerance by the number of drives in the daisy chain. Instead of a single point of failure with one isolated drive, the daisy chain creates as many points of failure as there are drives. If any one drive fails it brings down the whole chain, rendering all data useless, as if it were stored on a single volume or segment.

Optical Drives

Optical drives couple the advantages of removable media storage with performance relatively close to that of hard disks. A storage device with removable media offers "unlimited" capacity. Applications like graphics and CAD often require lots of disk space. With optical drives, you can simply purchase more cartridges for the same drive, keeping your cost per megabyte of storage below that of hard-disk drives. However, the access time for optical drives is about half that of hard-disk drives.

Unlike hard drives or tape drives, optical drives other than CD-ROM drives are not in wide use. Hard drives offer high performing online storage at a reasonable cost. Tape is the cheapest method for backing up the data on your hard drives. Optical drives fit somewhere in the middle. They are used as online storage for special applications such as CAD and graphics. In some cases, optical drives are used for backup and archiving because the media has a long life and the access is faster than tape; however, it's more expensive to do this than to use tape. Optical storage can also play a role in HSM (hierarchical storage management) when you use more than one storage hardware technology (more on HSM in Chapter 11).

Drive Type					
Performance	Reliability	Manageability	Scalability	**Flexibility**	**Value**

There are four basic optical drive types:

- Rewritable drives usually use magneto-optical technology and are therefore also referred to as MO drives. These drives can write, read, and overwrite optical media. They range in capacity from 230MB to over 4GB.

STORAGE HARDWARE

- WORM (Write Once, Read Many) drives can write and read media, but they cannot overwrite a piece of media once it has been written on. Capacities range from 1GB to 5GB. The standard form factor for these drives is now $5^1/4$-inch. WORM drives began disappearing as a product class with the introduction of multifunction drives.

- Multifunction drives can perform either like rewritable or like WORM drives, depending on the media you use. This gives them great flexibility and appeal if you're considering optical drives. You can use the rewritable functions for certain applications. But if you need permanent archives, you can use WORM media to create your permanent file records.

- CD recordable drives represent a very small piece of the market but have the potential to grow significantly. These drives have a storage capacity of 650MB and perform like WORM in that they can only write to a media that can never be overwritten (erasable versions are just coming to market). These drives are used primarily to prepare for the mass printing of CDs. Because of their low media cost (under $10) some companies use them for database file transfers, document archives, and internal publishing on CD-ROM.

Drive and Media Capacity					
Performance	Reliability	Manageability	**Scalability**	Flexibility	Value

Optical drives come in a range of capacities. Capacity is a function of both the drive and media. For small footprint ($3^1/2$-inch) MO drives, the typical capacity is 230MB. This makes them good for file archives but of limited use on the network. MO drives are really geared towards desktop users. The new $5^1/4$-inch drives have just climbed over 4GB, but the typical seller is the 2.6GB model—comparable to typical hard-drive capacities. These capacities make the drives usable for large capacity files and applications. Multifunction drives are only available in the $5^1/4$-inch format and have similar capacities to MO drives. CD recordable drives have remained at 650MB to adhere to the CD standard. Most optical drive and media capacities continue to increase at the same rate as the capacities of hard disks, with usually one capacity jump per year in one or more optical categories.

Supported Drivers and Software					
Performance	Reliability	Manageability	Scalability	**Flexibility**	Value

Software must be able to recognize a hardware device to use it. The software must have the appropriate "drivers," which are usually supplied by the hardware manufacturer. If you are using an application and you want to use an optical drive with it, check that the software can do so. Software vendors should supply you with a "device support" list.

STORAGE HARDWARE

MTBF and Duty Cycle					
Performance	**Reliability**	Manageability	Scalability	Flexibility	Value

Reliability is often measured by MTBF (Mean Time Between Failure). This number represents the typical number of hours the unit is powered up before a failure occurs. A 10^5 MTBF rating means the unit will typically experience a failure once in every 100,000 hours (or about eleven and a half years)! So why are the product warranties usually just a year? Because MTBF does not reflect the level of use the device is getting. In other words, I may have the unit on all day, but the drive may only be reading and writing for one hour. The actual drive use has a significant impact on the performance of the drive. Actual use is represented in percentage terms by "duty cycle." In the previous example, the duty cycle is 12.5 percent (1 divided by 8). Look for duty cycle numbers to put reliability in perspective. This number is also the mean, a mathematical variation on the average. If you had 100 drives running, one should fail every 2000 hours or every 81 days.

Tape Drives

Tape drives were once the main medium for storing digital information. Hard disks have long since taken over the task of online storage, but tape still provides a very important role in protecting company information. Tape is the medium of choice for backing up hard disks for the simple reason that is has the lowest cost per megabyte.

The choices in tape drives can be daunting. For example, minicartridge, a popular workstation backup choice, has over a dozen standards to choose from. Although there is a narrower range of choices for network backup, you still need to take into account the technological differences between the various tape drive standards. Because 90 percent of computer tape technology is used for hard drive backup, the rest of this section on tape drives focuses on this function. Most of the remaining 10 percent of tape usage is for data collection in scientific applications and for data archiving.

Technology Type					
Performance	**Reliability**	Manageability	**Scalability**	Flexibility	Value

The two most popular formats for UNIX and PC LAN network backup are 4mm (DAT) and 8mm. These numbers refer to the tape's width. Both of these technologies came from the audio and video markets and were adapted for computer data storage applications. Their popularity comes from their high capacity relative to unit costs. 4mm drives conform to an open standard (called DDS) that is licensed from Hewlett-Packard and Sony. 8mm is a proprietary design by Exabyte Corporation, which controls all manufacturing but sells to many companies who add value and relabel the product using their own name.

STORAGE HARDWARE

DLT is another tape technology growing in popularity for use in UNIX and PC network backup. It was originally developed by Digital Equipment Corporation for computer data storage and was sold to Quantum several years ago. This is a proprietary design that is relabeled and sold by other companies. DLT has superior performance and capacity statistics than 4mm and 8mm and also costs more.

Minicartridge drives have traditionally served the single workstation market. Now that capacities are over 3GB for high-end models, some people consider these drives an option for small LAN or workgroup backup. 3480/3490 is a traditional mainframe tape technology that is not commonly used for PC or UNIX backup.

Drive and Media Capacity					
Performance	Reliability	Manageability	**Scalability**	Flexibility	**Value**

If you're buying a tape drive for backup purposes, you need to determine how much data will be backed up. If the amount of hard disk data to be backed up exceeds the capacity of the drive, you'll need to use multiple cartridges to complete a backup. This may pose a problem if the backup is scheduled to run unattended overnight. Tape libraries can help address this issue (as discussed in the following section). The uncompressed capacity for 4mm drives is 4GB, for 8mm it's 7GB, and for DLT it's 10GB. Most drives include hardware data compression, which typically doubles their capacity. These capacities also assume use of the highest capacity tape cartridges. Don't forget that network storage capacity increases each year and your tape solution must keep up or you may have to install more. Either way, storage requirement planning is a good idea.

Backup Method					
Performance	Reliability	**Manageability**	Scalability	Flexibility	Value

Tape drives are capable of whatever backup method the compatible software specifies. But understanding how you will set up your backups may affect your choice in hardware. For instance, If you plan to do full backups of your servers every night, you'll need tape drives that can do so unattended. On the other hand, if you back up only files that have changed since the last full backup, you can probably get by with a lower capacity device. Backup methods vary and are ultimately controlled by your network backup software, which is discussed in Chapter 11.

Supported Drivers and Software					
Performance	Reliability	Manageability	Scalability	**Flexibility**	Value

STORAGE HARDWARE

It is important that the hardware is well supported by existing backup software. Major backup software supports a wide variety of drives so if you're using a popular software package, you probably won't have a problem. Either the hardware or software manufacturer should be able to tell you what you need to know in terms of compatibility.

MTBF and Duty Cycle

Performance	**Reliability**	Manageability	Scalability	Flexibility	Value

Reliability is often measured by MTBF (Mean Time Between Failure). This number represents the typical number of hours the unit is powered up before a failure occurs. A 10^5 MTBF rating means the unit will typically experience a failure once in every 100,000 hours (or about eleven and a half years!). So why are the product warranties usually just a year? Because MTBF does not reflect the level of use the device is getting. In other words, you may have the unit on all day, but the drive may only be reading and writing for one hour. The actual drive use has a significant impact on the performance of the drive. Actual use is represented in percentage terms by "duty cycle." In the previous example, the duty cycle is 12.5 percent (1 divided by 8). Look for duty cycle numbers to put reliability in perspective. This number is also the mean, a mathematical variation on the average. If you had 100 drives running, one should fail every 2000 hours or every 81 days.

Data Transfer Rate

Performance	Reliability	Manageability	Scalability	Flexibility	Value

Data transfer rate refers to the speed at which the drive can read and write data. This is a key performance indication. The faster the data transfer rate, the faster your backups and restores. For 4mm the uncompressed data transfer rate is 183 Kbps, for 8mm its about 250 Kbps, and for DLT its about 800 Kbps. But don't expect to get the same performance listed in the marketing literature because that presents the ideal transfer rate. To achieve this rate, the drive must stream constantly. In the real world, tape drives stop and start often because the data going to the drive can't keep up with the drive's capability. This means that the tape drive does not stream constantly. A slower drive streaming consistently can outperform a faster one that starts and stops constantly. Backup software and caching can play a role in optimizing transfer rates.

Tape Libraries and Optical Jukeboxes

Tape libraries and optical jukeboxes both have robotic mechanisms that pick and place media to and from the drives. This makes them similar to the CD-ROM jukeboxes discussed earlier in the chapter. One key advantage of robotic devices is that they automatically make media swaps,

STORAGE HARDWARE

so a single drive can serve many users and swap media without administrator intervention. Many of these devices offer a choice in drives and some even allow the administrator to use a mix of drive and media types.

The applications of tape libraries and optical jukeboxes are very similar. Both are designed to provide a large repository of data that is readily accessible. For optical jukeboxes, this data is often in the form of imaged documents stored electronically and accessible through a document retrieval system. Law firms are a target market for these devices because they create, store, and retrieve large amounts of documentation. Engineering firms may have large CAD files that need to be stored cost-effectively and whose file histories need to be easily accessible. Tape libraries also serve image storage and retrieval needs but performance is usually slower. Tape libraries are also well-suited for high-capacity, centralized backup, and data archives.

When choosing whether to get a tape library or optical jukebox, you need to decide how fast information needs to be updated or accessed. You also need to consider the attributes of optical and tape media. Typically, optical jukeboxes can retrieve information in less than a minute. Tape libraries usually take much longer—often in the neighborhood of five to ten minutes—because it takes time for the tape to load and get to the area containing the desired information. But tape is much less expensive than optical media.

In general, if you have low access needs you can probably get away with tape. If the system will be used heavily, however, you'll probably want optical. But the media capabilities will also play a role in your decision. If you need permanent records, you should use a medium such as WORM that cannot be altered once written to; tape would not be an option in this case. Permanence may be a requirement for a law firm archiving legal documents, and WORM is also a legally accepted form for permanent archives. But an engineering firm may be more concerned with media capacity being high enough to store a group of large files by project and may prefer the low cost and high capacity of tape.

Drive and Media Capacity					
Performance	Reliability	Manageability	**Scalability**	Flexibility	**Value**

You need to determine how many drives and media you need in a jukebox or library before you buy. Choosing a box with too few drives will create inaccessibility, but if the box has too many drives there may not be enough space for the necessary media. Multiple drives increase accessibility for the users and reduce downtime since the unit can continue operating should a drive fail. Administrators typically prefer a ratio of 1 to 10 for drives to media. This is higher (more drives) than most standard jukebox and library configurations.

STORAGE HARDWARE

Modularity

Performance	Reliability	**Manageability**	**Scalability**	**Flexibility**	Value

Modularity refers to how easy it is to custom fit the unit or units to your needs. This may include a feature like plug-and-play drives, where the necessary drive connections are made by a plug-like connector in the back of the drive. The chassis has a matched receiving end and the connection is made when the drive is slipped into the slot. For optical jukeboxes, modularity general refers to flexibility in the number of drives and media a unit can hold and how media is loaded and organized. Of course, the more drive and media options, the more modular the unit. Media loading can be cumbersome if they must be loaded one at a time. Some units use magazines that hold 10-50 pieces of media to load and unload media. This not only simplifies the actual loading process but it also provides a way to organize and store media effectively that is often shelved.

Network Connection

Performance	Reliability	**Manageability**	Scalability	**Flexibility**	Value

Libraries and jukeboxes are connected to the network in one of two ways: through a server or directly to the network (via hub or router). Direct network connections are easy to install and have a minimal impact on servers. In this case, the unit appears as a network resource. A catch is that this new resource might have more administrative requirements if not managed under a server.

Libraries and jukeboxes are more commonly attached to and accessible through the server. When you attach these devices to a server, access rights fall under current server management policy. In addition, the jukebox or library can use server memory or disk space for caching, storing the media database, and so on. However, server performance is often affected unless you add memory and/or make other improvements to the server.

Software Support

Performance	Reliability	Manageability	Scalability	**Flexibility**	Value

Libraries and jukeboxes are usually sold with media management software. This software lets you label and track media in the unit itself and determine what media or magazines have been removed. This tracking allows the users to pick appropriate resources; it also enables the unit to find the media's physical slot location and load it into an available drive. If you will use the library or jukebox with other applications—such as document management, archiving, and so on—be sure the drivers for that hardware are available for the software you plan to use.

STORAGE HARDWARE

Media Access Time					
Performance	Reliability	Manageability	Scalability	Flexibility	Value

With both libraries and jukeboxes, you have to wait for the machine's robotic arm to load the appropriate medium into a drive before using it (unless it happens to be loaded already). As mentioned, this loading time is often called "pick and place." Typical pick and place times are 8 to 20 seconds, depending on factors such as the number of media slots in the unit, their distance from the drive, and the number of drives. Once media is handed to the drive, the drive takes additional time to load the media and read media headers before information is available. In the case of tape, it takes more time to wind the tape to the location containing the desired information.

RAID

RAID (Redundant Array of Inexpensive Disks) subsystems add fault-tolerant features to standard disk subsystems. Fault tolerance means the ability to continue operation without interruption despite certain hardware failures. You can achieve fault tolerance with disk drives by always writing to two separate drives; this way if one drive fails, the other can continue operation without data loss. This is often referred to as "disk duplexing" or "disk mirroring." You can also stripe data across many drives. In this process, data streams are written across more than one drive. In the case of drive failure, the data can be reconstructed and the failed drive replaced without any downtime. In addition to providing fault tolerance, certain RAID methods can bring performance advantages.

RAID Level					
Performance	**Reliability**	Manageability	Scalability	**Flexibility**	**Value**

The RAID Advisory Board has established and standardized definitions for levels 0 through 5 of RAID. RAID levels 2 and 4 are seldom used because they are not considered practical solutions and are outperformed by RAID levels 3 and 5, respectively. Different vendors have introduced other RAID levels, but their definitions have not been standardized. For example, RAID 6 may refer to the use of two drives for redundancy, allowing two drives to fail before data is lost.

RAID 0

RAID 0 is not, strictly speaking, a RAID system, because it does not provide any redundancy. It distributes data across all drives in the array to improve performance. However, it can deliver higher performance only if tuned for specific applications and their I/O request characteristics.

STORAGE HARDWARE

RAID 1

RAID 1 is traditional disk mirroring. RAID 1 may provide performance improvement on read requests, because the controller can read from whichever drive is closest to the requested data. The cost of mirroring is twice that of single drives. To store four drives worth of data, eight drives are required. Mirroring can be implemented by hardware via the hard disk controller, or by software that will manage the multiple drives.

RAID 0+1

RAID 0+1 combines disk mirroring with disk striping. Some vendors call this RAID 1 for marketing purposes because they have combined the features of RAID 0 with mirroring to achieve better reliability and performance.

RAID 3

In RAID 3, user data is striped across a set of drives. A drive to hold parity data is added. Parity data (the combined binary value of the original striped data) is calculated dynamically as user data is written to the other drives. Segments are set small (bits or bytes) with respect to the average request size. The parity drive must be accessed for every write so write performance slows down. RAID 3 is best suited for use when large sequential read requests are the primary array activity. It is a poor solution for random access and small data segments. The cost of RAID 3 is the cost of the data drives plus one parity drive and a controller.

RAID 5

With RAID 5, user data is striped in large segment sizes and parity is computed and distributed evenly across all drives in the array. As a result, no single drive functions as a bottleneck to disk writes, as in RAID 3. Usually, one drive participates in any request, allowing several requests to be handled simultaneously from all drives in the array. Because the segments are large, insufficient data is received to enable parity to be calculated solely from the incoming data stream, as in RAID 3. Incoming data must be combined with existing parity data to recompute the new parity. Thus, each write request involves reading from two drives (old data, old parity) and writing on two drives (new data, new parity). This results in poorer write performance than the other RAID levels. RAID 5 is most appropriate in environments such as the office, transaction processing, and decision support that have small random I/O requests. The cost of RAID 5 includes the data drives plus one additional drive because parity is spread across all drives.

Modular Design					
Performance	Reliability	**Manageability**	Scalability	**Flexibility**	Value

RAID systems are designed to provide drive modularity. Although RAID subsystems often need drives that are matched (same manufacturer, same

STORAGE HARDWARE

model), replacing a bad drive is often easy. Not only is there no loss of data, but you can frequently swap out the drive without bringing the unit down (this is called a "hot swap").

Modularity also refers to the different types of RAID implementations possible with the same basic unit. Sometimes you'll need an extra drive to do this, but you can enable most of these changes through the management software for the device. The product design may also include options for easily replacing or adding other components such as power supply and controller, further increasing the unit's modularity and fault tolerance.

Redundant Components					
Performance	**Reliability**	Manageability	Scalability	Flexibility	Value

RAID is essentially defined by the use of redundant disk drives to create a fault-tolerant system. But drives are not the only thing that can fail. Some products also provide redundant power supplies, controllers, and other components to make an even more bulletproof storage device. Key to redundancy is the product's ability to convert over to the working components. In most cases, this is transparent to the user, even if it takes a matter of seconds to do so. The other issue surrounding component redundancy is the method by which administrators are notified of failures and corrective actions. This is initiated by hardware but managed by the RAID utility software, which is discussed in more depth in Chapter 11.

Bundled Software					
Performance	Reliability	**Manageability**	Scalability	Flexibility	Value

RAID can be implemented by the NOS such as Windows NT or Novell Netware or with vendor specific disk array controllers. The software solutions are included in the NOS but cannot mirror or stripe the nonnetwork partitions. Hardware-implemented RAID can mirror or stripe the whole data structure but are relatively expensive.

RAID devices are usually bundled with some form of software for managing and monitoring the activities of the device. There are also third-party products for doing so. They can perform such tasks as usage monitoring, performance tuning, failure alerts, system stress alerts, report logs, and so on. This software should be able to manage more than one device for expandability. If your RAID installation involves many units and your monitoring and performance management needs are significant, the software may play an important role in your decision. This software is discussed in more detail in Chapter 11.

CD Towers ■

Manufacturer	Advanced Media Services	ASM	ASM
Model	CD-ROM Network Towers	CD-ROM Tower	CD-ROM server
OS/NOS Compatibility	DOS, Windows, Windows 95, Macintosh, OS/2, and Unix clients	NetWare, Windows, NT, MS DOS, OS/2	NetWare, Windows, NT, MS DOS, OS/2
CD-ROM Drives	1–56	7	14
I/O Interface	SCSI-2	1 SCSI-2	2 SCSI-2
Controllers per Host System	4 max.	1	2
Redundant Components	Power, hot-swap drives	None	Power
Bundled Software	Preloaded CD server software for Novell, Windows NT, Vines, LAN Manager and all peer to peer Network OS's	None	None
Enclosure	Varies	398mm (D) x 180mm(W) x 330mm(H)	730mm (D) x 250mm(W) x 830mm(H)
Comments	Range of towers available, including plug-n-play network ready towers, standard towers with built-in servers, and rack mount towers	7–4x SCSI CD-ROM, SCSI adapter cables 6x and 8x	14 4xSCSI CD-ROM 2 SCSI adapter cables 6x and 8x available
Warranty	2 year	1 year	1 year
List Price	Varies	$1,599	$2,595

Manufacturer	CD International	CD International
Model	CDT 500	CDT 700
OS/NOS Compatibility	Windows NT, Novell, Unix	Windows NT, Novell, Unix
CD-ROM Drives	5	7
I/O Interface	1 SCSI-2	1 SCSI-2
Controllers per Host System	1	1
Redundant Components	None	None
Bundled Software	Optional Smart CD and CD Commander	Optional Smart CD and CD Commander
Enclosure	15"H x 9"W x 12"	18"H x 9"W x 13"
Comments	1GB hard disk cache	1GB hard disk cache
Warranty	1 year	1 year
List Price	$1,900	$2,500

Manufacturer	CeLAN Technology	Excel
Model	CDS 7000/ CDS7000R	7XT/7Rack
OS/NOS Compatibility	NetWare, Windows NT, MS-DOS, Unix	NetWare, OS/2, DOS, Windows 95, Windows 3.11, Windows NT and Unix
CD-ROM Drives	1–7	2–7
I/O Interface	1 SCSI-2	2 SCSI-I 50 Pin
Controllers per Host System	1	4 max.
Redundant Components	Power, hot-swap drives	None

N/A—Not applicable   INA—Information not available

Table Continues →

■ CD Towers

Manufacturer	CeLAN Technology	Excel
Bundled Software	CDS-View for NetWare, Windows NT	Options for Windows NT and NetWare compatible software
Enclosure	19"H x 8"W x 18" (7000) 2.5"H x 17"W x 8"(7000R)	13"H x 7"W x 15.25"D
Comments	Plug-n-play Firm Ware upgrade lockable cabinet (7000 only), rack mountable (7000R)	Tower or rack built with 4X, 6X or 8X CD-ROM drives. Optionally, towers can be assembled for direct attachment to the LAN. Locking door model available. Cable and terminator supplied.
Warranty	1 year	2 year
List Price	$1,449	$700–$3,700

Manufacturer	Excel	Excel
Model	14XT	28XT
OS/NOS Compatibility	NetWare, OS/2, DOS, Win95, 3.11, NT and Unix	NetWare, OS/2, DOS, Windows95, 3.11, NT and Unix
CD-ROM Drives	2–14	2–28
I/O Interface	4 SCSI-I 50 Pin	8 SCSI-I 50 Pin
Controllers per Host System	4 max.	4 max.
Redundant Components	None	None
Bundled Software	Various software NT and NetWare compatible (optional)	Various software NT and NetWare compatible (optional)
Enclosure	26"H x 9"W x 16"D	32.6"H x 22"W x 25"D
Comments	Towers built with 4X, 6X or 8X CD-ROM drives. Optionally, towers can be assembled for direct attachment to the LAN. Locking door model available. Cable and terminator supplied.	Towers built with 4X, 6X or 8X CD-ROM drives. Optionally, towers can be assembled for direct attachment to the LAN. Locking door model available. Cable and terminator supplied.
Warranty	2 year	2 year
List Price	$1,025–$7,150	$2,150–$15,000

Manufacturer	Luminex	Luminex
Model	LSX Tower	NetExpress Tower
OS/NOS Compatibility	NetWare, Windows NT Unix, LAN Manager, NFS, Appleshare	NetWare, Windows NT Unix, LAN Manager, NFS, Appleshare
CD-ROM Drives	4x, 6.7x 7–196 drives	4x, 6.7x 7
I/O Interface	1 SCSI per ID/7 drives	Ethernet, Token Ring
Controllers per Host System	1–4	1
Redundant Components	Hot swappable drives, modular cooling, power supply	Hot swappable drives, modular cooling, power supply
Bundled Software	Fire Series software	Fire Series software
Enclosure	INA	INA
Comments		
Warranty	3 year	3 year
List Price	Starting at $3,195	Starting at $3,195

N/A—Not applicable   INA—Information not available

CD Towers

Manufacturer	MDI	MDI	Meridian Data
Model	CD-Express Towers	CD-Express Cabinet	CD Net Integrated Systems
OS/NOS Compatibility	NetWare, Windows NT, DOS, OS/2, Mac	NetWare, Windows NT, DOS	NetWare, Windows NT, Vines
CD-ROM Drives	7–8	28–56	Up to 56 per server
I/O Interface	SCSI-2	SCSI-2	Embedded in server
Controllers per Host System	Unlimited—depends on server	Unlimited—depends on server	Embedded in server
Redundant Components	None	Dual power supply, hot-swap drives, hot-swap power	N/A
Bundled Software	SCSI Express option	SCSI Express	CD Net for NetWare, Windows NT, and Vines, CD Net Plus (peer-to-peer)
Enclosure	1.65"(H) x 5.82"(W) x 7.57"	INA	Min: 41cm H x 23cm W x 41cm D Max: 72cm H x 117cm W x 42cm D
Comments	Extender product allows up to 56 CD's on a single host adapter	Extender product allows up to 56 CD's on a single host adapter	
Warranty	1 year	1 year	1 year (extensions available)
List Price	$2,695–$5,095	$17,995–$49,995	Starts at $2,745

Manufacturer	Procom Technology	Procom Technology	Regal Electronics
Model	CD Tower-Rex	CD Force	CDC-4x
OS/NOS Compatibility	NetWare, OS/2, LanServer, Windows NT, Banyan Vines, Unix	NetWare, OS/2, LanServer, Windows NT, Banyan Vines, Unix	NetWare, Windows NT, Windows 3.1, Windows 95, OS/2, DOS, Unix, Mac
CD-ROM Drives	7–56	7–56	1 (5 disks)
I/O Interface	SCSI–2	SCSI-2	SCSI-2
Controllers per Host System	Variable	Variable	1
Redundant Components	Power, hot-swap drives, fans	Power, hot-swap drives, fans	None
Bundled Software	CD-ROM, CD-Net, Disc Serve, SCSI Express	MESA	Optional
Enclosure	77" X 25.25" x 36"	77" X 25.25" x 36"	6.9" x 3" x 9.6" (external)
Comments	Modular design	Modular design	256MB Buffer, 5 disks in _ ht slot, daisy chain up to 7 units from SCSI card
Warranty	1 year	1 year	1 year
List Price	$56,000	$56,000	$399 (internal) $459 (external)

Manufacturer	SMS Data Products Group	SMS Data Products Group
Model	S7007S	S7007NOV S7007NT S7007WEB
OS/NOS Compatibility	NetWare, Windows NT, MS-DOS, OS/2, Banyan Vines, and Unix	NetWare,Windows NT/ NetWare,Windows NT, MS-DOS, OS/2, Unix/ WEB, NetWare, Windows NT
CD-ROM Drives	1–7	1–7
I/O Interface	4 SCSI-2	4 SCSI-2
Controllers per Host System	1 or 2	1 or 2

N/A—Not applicable   INA—Information not available

Table Continues →

■ CD Towers

Manufacturer	SMS Data Products Group	SMS Data Products Group
Redundant Components	Power supplies (optional 2nd), fans, hot-swappable drive, and connectivity modules	Power supplies (optional 2nd), fans, hot-swappable drive, and connectivity modules
Bundled Software	Optional	CD-ROM networking with native or GUI interfaces providing multiple CD's as one drive letter and unlimited user licenses.
Enclosure	10.25"(W) x 20"(H) x 22"	10.25"(W) x 20"(H) x 22"
Comments	The S700 is a scalable, modular and upgradable system with plug and play network direct Ethernet and Token Ring connectivity modules for all environments, hot-swappable CD-ROM, CD-R and multi-disk changer drives. UL listed, CE compliant, FCC-B.	The S700 is a scalable, modular and upgradable system with plug and play network direct Ethernet and Token Ring connectivity modules for all environments, hot-swappable CD-ROM, CD-R and multi-disk changer drives. UL listed, CE compliant, FCC-B.
Warranty	3 year—advanced placement	3 year—advanced placement
List Price	$3,565	$4,589

Manufacturer	SMS Data Products Group	SMS Data Products Group
Model	S7000PT	1070TOWER Series
OS/NOS Compatibility	NetWare, Windows NT, MS-DOS, OS/2, Unix, and MAC	NetWare, Windows NT, MS-DOS, OS/2, Banyan Vines, and Unix
CD-ROM Drives	1–7	1–7
I/O Interface	2 SCSI-II	2 SCSI-II
Controllers per Host System	One host adapter supporting 7 drives as one SCSI Id or one host adapter supporting 49 drives.	1
Redundant Components	Power supplies (optional 2nd), fans, hot-swappable drive, and connectivity modules	None
Bundled Software	Optional	Optional
Enclosure	10.25"(W) x 20"(H) x 22"	7.5"(W) x 19.25"(H) x 11.7"
Comments	The S700 is a scalable, modular, and upgradable system with plug and play network direct Ethernet and Token Ring connectivity modules for all environments, hot-swappable CD-ROM, CD-R and multi-disk changer drives. UL listed, CE compliant, FCC-B.	Part of a Value Series of CD-ROM drive towers. Each tower is UL listed, CE compliant, FCC-B certified.
Warranty	3 year—advanced placement	1 year
List Price	$4,589	$841(T2), $1,683(T4), $1,986(T5), $2,309(T7)

Manufacturer	SMS Data Products Group	SMS Data Products Group	SMS Data Products Group
Model	3056S	S50196S	1070DPTOWER7S/ 1070DPTOWER7/ 1070DPTOWER4S/ 1070DPTOWER4
OS/NOS Compatibility	NetWare and Windows	NetWare and Windows	NetWare/Windows NT/NetWare/ Windows NT
CD-ROM Drives	56 drives	196	7/7 4/4
I/O Interface	SCSI-2 (quantity variable)	SCSI-2 (quantity variable)	2 SCSI-2
Controllers per Host System	Variable	Varaible	One host adapter supporting 7 drives as one SCSI Id, or one host supporting 49 drives
Redundant Components	Power supplies (optional 2nd), fans, and hot-swappable drives	Power supplies (optional 2nd), fans, and hot-swappable drives	Power supplies (optional 2nd), fans, hot-swappable drives, and connectivity modules
Bundled Software	CD-ROM networking with native or GUI interfaces providing multiple CD's as one drive letter and unlimited user licenses	CD-ROM networking with native or GUI interfaces providing multiple CD's as one drive letter and unlimited user licenses	CD-ROM networking with native or GUI interfaces providing multiple CD's as one drive letter and unlimited user licenses.

N/A—Not applicable   INA—Information not available

CD Towers

Manufacturer	SMS Data Products Group	SMS Data Products Group	SMS Data Products Group
Enclosure	24(W) x 77"(H) x 30"	INA	7.5"(W) x 19.25"(H) x 11.7"
Comments	The preconfigured Millenia 300 frame has 8 mounted S700 chassis with 56 standard CD-ROM drives. The frame is a network center grade 19" standard RETM configuration with positive ambient air filtration and cable management.	The Millenia 5000 frame model S50196 comes with 5 Millenia 5000 frame each with a door and 8 mounted S7000 chassis for a total of 196 standard CD-ROM drives.	The NETower is a plug and play network direct Ethernet (Token Ring available) tower for all major environments with a powerful yet quiet cooling fan and 4X or 6X CD-ROM drives. For information on networking features, www.sms.com
Warranty	3 year—advanced replacement	3 year—advanced replacement	1 year
List Price	$31,643	$104,840	$2,982/ $2,337

Manufacturer	Ten X Technology	Ten X Technology
Model	TenXpert-1System7p	DT40-115
OS/NOS Compatibility	NetWare, Windows NT, NFS, Windows 3.1, Windows 95, OS/2, Unix	Any compatible with the standard SCSI interface
CD-ROM Drives	Seven, 4X or 8X speed	seven, 8x speed
I/O Interface	2 SCSI-2 1 Ethernet twisted pair 1 Ethernet AUI	2 SCSI-2
Controllers per Host System	1 TenXpert-1 server with 1GB hard disk cache	1
Redundant Components	Hot-swap drives	Hot-swap drives
Bundled Software	No software needed. Tower is network ready.	None
Enclosure	21.5"H x 7.5"W x 13"	18"H x 7.5"W x 13"
Comments	CD network server included. CD directories, and many files are cached on large hard disk for immediate viewing. Tower is accessible, without adding software to existing servers or to clients. Multiple CD towers may be daisy-chained, increasing size of on-line disc library.	Includes caching concentrator, allowing all drives to function under 1 SCSI ID. Six towers may be daisy-chained off 1 SCSI adaptor.
Warranty	1 year	1 year
List Price	$5,845—w/ 4x $6,290—w/ 8x	$3,295

N/A—Not applicable   INA—Information not available

Table Continues →

◼ CD Towers

Manufacturer	**Ten X Technology**	**Ten X Technologies**	**Ultera Systems Inc.**
Model	TenXpert-1System28p	DT 40–109 DT 40–116	C2000–5
OS/NOS Compatibility	NetWare, Windows NT, NFS, Windows 3.1, Windows 95, OS/2,	Any compatible with the standard SCSI interface	DOS, Windows, MAC or Unix
CD-ROM Drives	Seven, 8X 4-CD minichangers	Seven, 4x speed	5
I/O Interface	2 SCSI-2 1 Ethernet twisted pair 1 Ethernet AUI	2 SCSI-2	1 SCSI-2
Controllers per Host System	1 TenXpert-1 server with 1GB hard disk cache	1	1
Redundant Components	Hot swap drives	Hot swap drives	None
Bundled Software	No software needed. Tower is network ready.	None	Works with all authoring software
Enclosure	21.5"H x 7.5"W x 13"	18"H x 7.5"W x 13"	INA
Comments	CD network server included. CD directories, and many files are cached on large hard disk for immediate viewing. Tower is accessible, without adding software to existing servers or to clients. Multiple CD towers may be daisy-chained, increasing size of online disc library.	Includes caching concentrator, allowing all drives to function under 1 SCSI ID. Six towers may be daisy-chained off 1 SCSI adaptor.	Can master up to 5 identical CDs in the time required for one. The CD-R Multi-Master can be used on any DOS, Windows, Mac, or Unix system with a SCSI interface.
Warranty	1 year	1 year	1 year
List Price	$9,325	$2,850/ $6,330	$9,090

N/A—Not applicable   INA—Information not available

End ◼

CD Jukeboxes ■

Manufacturer	CD International	CD International
Model	SQ2100	SQ2800
OS/NOS Compatibility	Windows NT, Unix, Novell	Windows NT, Unix, Novell
CD-ROMDrives	3	5
CD Media Slots	21	29
Magazine Cartridges	None	None
CPU Rrequirements	INA	INA
I/O Interface	1 SCSI-2	1 or 2 SCSI-2
Drive Controller	1 SCSI-2	1 SCSI-2
Controller per Host System	1	1
Redundant Components	Multiple drives, power	Multiple drives, power
Bundled Software	Smart CD, CD Vision, LAN Manager, Data Manager (all optional)	Smart CD, CD Vision, LAN Manager, Data Manager (all optional)
Enclosure	13.5"H x 9.45"W x 17"D	18"H x 9.45"W x 17"D
Comments	Fast access to many CDs	CD-R, 2 hard disks, fast access to many CDs
Warranty	1 year	1 year
List Price	$3,700	$5,900

Manufacturer	CD International	CD International	DISC Inc.
Model	SQ4000	SQ2801	D300–1, D600–2, D630–1, D1260–2
OS/NOS Compatibility	Windows NT, Unix, Novell	Windows NT, Unix, Novell	Unix, Windows, Windows NT, NetWare, and others
CD-ROMDrives	10	4	2–32
CD Media Slots	40	28	1–1478
Magazine Cartridges	INA	INA	Mailbox slot and magazine loading
CPU Rrequirements	INA	INA	82GB to 961GB
I/O Interface	1 BNC, RJ-7, 1 SCSI, 1 monitor	1 BNC or RJ-7, 1 SCSI, 1 monitor	SCSI–2
Drive Controller	SCSI	SCSI	INA
Controller per Host System	1–2	1	INA
Redundant Components	Multiple drives	Multiple drives, power	Dual robotics, dual electronics, dual power supply
Bundled Software	Optional	Optional	None
Enclosure	29"H x 9"W x 18"D	18"H x 9.45"W x 17"D	3 x 9 SL: 74.5"H x37.5"W x26" 6 x 9 DS: 74.5"H x 37.5"W x 36" 6 x 9 SL: 74.5"H x 55"W x 26" 6 x 9 DS: 74.5"H x 55"W x36"
Comments	Network-ready built-in CPU, disks and all software	Network-ready built-in CPU, disks and all software	DISC's CD jukeboxes, an automated CD drive array, incorporate both CD-ROM and CD-Recorder drives; they are available with up to 32 drives and up to 1478 caddy mounted cartridges.
Warranty	1 year	1 year	1 year parts
List Price	$12,900	$9,900	INA

N/A—Not applicable   INA—Information not available

Table Continues →

■ CD Jukeboxes

Manufacturer	Luminex Software	Luminex Software	Luminex Software
Model	LSX-CDJ-50	LSX-CDJ-100	LSX-CDJ-150
OS/NOS Compatibility	Netware, Windows NT/LAN Manager, Unix, AppleTalk	Netware, Windows NT/LAN Manager, Unix, AppleTalk	Netware, Windows NT/LAN Manager, Unix, AppleTalk
CD-ROMDrives	1	4	1
CD Media Slots	50	100	150
Magazine Cartridges	1	5	3
CPU Rrequirements	INA	INA	INA
I/O Interface	1 SCSI	1 SCSI	1 SCSI
Drive Controller	SCSI	SCSI	SCSI
Controller per Host System	1	1	1
Redundant Components	None	None	N/A
Bundled Software	Fire Series	Fire Series	Fire Series
Enclosure	9.5"W x 12.6"H x 15.3"D	9"W x 25"H x 17.3"D	8.6"W x 20"H x 23"D
Comments	With the Luminex LSX SCII expander, each jukebox requires 1 SCSI ID on the server.	With the Luminex LSX SCII expander, each jukebox requires 1 SCSI ID on the server.	With the Luminex LSX SCII expander, each jukebox requires 1 SCSI ID on the server.
Warranty	1 year+	1 year+	1 year
List Price	$3,995	$10,995	$19,995

Manufacturer	MDI	Microboards	Microboards
Model	CD-Express Library	DataWrite 500	DataWrite 100
OS/NOS Compatibility	Netware	Windows NT, Novell, Unix (HP, Sun, PC based)	Windows NT, Novell, Unix (HP, Sun, PC based)
CD-ROMDrives	4	1–4	1–4
CD Media Slots	150 slots	500	100
Magazine Cartridges	4	5	2
CPU Rrequirements	16MB RAM, 2MB disk	16MB RAM, dedicated 2.2GB hard disk	16MB RAM, dedicated 2.2GB hard disk
I/O Interface	2 SCSI-2	5 SCSI	5 SCSI
Drive Controller	ASPI compliant	ASPI compatible	ASPI compatible
Controller per Host System	Up to 5	4	4
Redundant Components	None	None	None
Bundled Software	SCSI Express (optional)	Smart CD for ACCESS, Integrated Recording from Smart Storage	Smart CD for ACCESS, Integrated Recording from Smart Storage
Enclosure	20"H x 8.6"W x 23"D	453 x 1159 x 507 mm	26.3 x 477 x 585 mm
Comments		Features a storage capacity of 330GB, and is fully supported by the Smart Storage jukebox management software for Windows NT, Novell, and UNIX. Can be recordable.	Averages 5 to 7 seconds to unload/load a disc. It is also fully by Smart Storage software. Can be recordable.
Warranty	1 year	1 year with on-site maintenance contracts available from Micro-Boards Technology, Inc.	1 year on-site maintenance contracts available
List Price	$19,995	$26,995	$15,995

N/A—Not applicable   INA—Information not available

CD Jukeboxes ■

Manufacturer	NSM Jukebox	NSM Jukebox
Model	CDR 100XA	Mercury 20/40
OS/NOS Compatibility	Windows, Windows NT, NetWare, OS/2, UNIX, and MS DOS	Windows, Windows NT, NetWare, OS/2, UNIX, and MS DOS
CD-ROMDrives	1	2/4
CD Media Slots	100	150
Magazine Cartridges	2	3
CPU Rrequirements	16MB RAM, 500MB hard disk drive	16MB RAM, 500MB hard disk drive
I/O Interface	SCSI-2	SCSI-2
Drive Controller	RS-232	RS-232
Controller per Host System	16 max.	16 max.
Redundant Components	None	None
Bundled Software	Smart Storage, IXOS, Miles Apart, Celerity Systems, and others	Smart Storage, IXOS, Miles Apart, Celerity Systems, and others
Enclosure	18.5"W x 14.3"H x 8.5"D	8.6"W x 20"H x23"D
Comments	Two magazines of 50 CD's each slide out for easy exchange. This model can be combined with multiple jukeboxes for added storage capacity.	
Warranty	1 year	1 year
List Price	$7,000	$16,000/$17,000

Manufacturer	NSM Jukebox	SMS Data Products Group
Model	Mercury 40 NET	DCM101
OS/NOS Compatibility	NetWare	NetWare, Windows NT
CD-ROMDrives	4	4
CD Media Slots	150	150
Magazine Cartridges	3	3
CPU Rrequirements	Novell 3.1X or higher	INA
I/O Interface	10BASE-T or BNC	2 dual SCSI-2II
Drive Controller	None	SCSI-2
Controller per Host System	4 max.	1–4
Redundant Components	None	None
Bundled Software	DiscView Pro	Optional
Enclosure	8.6"W x 20"H x 23"D	519 (H) x 218 (W) x 587 mm
Comments	Enables users to access CD-ROM data from any workstation on the network. It uses a plug-and-play connection to the Novell network via a BNC cable and BNC connector. It features embedded network controller and a separate SCSI interface, and supports Novell 3.11 and 4.x networks.	
Warranty	1 year	1 year
List Price	$21,000	$14,012

N/A—Not applicable   INA—Information not available

Table Continues →

■ CD Jukeboxes

Manufacturer	SMS Data Products Group	SMS Data Products Group
Model	DCD01	S700, CMAX and (7) DCN101S700, CMDP and (7) DCN101 S700 and (7) DCN101
OS/NOS Compatibility	Netware, Windows NT	Netware, Windows NT
CD-ROMDrives	2	7
CD Media Slots	200	28
Magazine Cartridges	None	None
CPU Rrequirements	INA	None
I/O Interface	2 SCSI-2	Network direct, dual SCSI-II
Drive Controller	INA	INA
Controller per Host System	1	1
Redundant Components	INA	Power supplies (optional 2nd), fans, hot-swappable drive, and (except for S700 and (7) DCN101) connectivity modules
Bundled Software	Optional	Optional
Enclosure	434 (H) x 236 (W) x 457 mm	10.25"W x 20"H x 22"D
Comments	The jukebox rack mounts horizontally into a Series 3000 and 5000 frame available to provide access to 200 discs.	The S700 is a scalable, modular and upgradable system with plug-and-play network-direct Ethernet and Token Ring connectivity modules for all environments, hot-swappable CD-ROM, CD-R and multi-disk changer drives. UL listed, CE compliant, FCC-B.
Warranty	1 year	1 year
List Price	$4,999	$8,474 $8,474 $7,450

Manufacturer	Ten X Technology	Ten X Technology
Model	TenXpert-8 System/150R	TenXpert-8 System/150P
OS/NOS Compatibility	Netware, Windows NT, NFS, Windows 3.1, Windows 95, OS/2, Unix	Netware, Windows NT, NFS, Windows 3.1, Windows 95, OS/2, Unix
CD-ROMDrives	3 CD readers (4K) 1 CD recorder (4K)	4
CD Media Slots	150	150
Magazine Cartridges	3	3
CPU Rrequirements	No CPU requirements, jukebox is network ready	No CPU requirements, jukebox is network ready
I/O Interface	2o SCSI-2, 1 Ethernet twisted pair, 1 Ethernet AUI	2 SCSI-2, 1 Ethernet twisted pair, 1 Ethernet AUI
Drive Controller	TenXpert-8 server with 4GB hard disk cache	TenXpert-8 server with 4GB hard disk cache
Controller per Host System	1	1
Redundant Components	None	None
Bundled Software	None	None
Enclosure	23"H x 8.6"W x 23"D	23"H x 8.6"W x 23"D
Comments	CD network server included. Network clients may read and write CDs over the network. CD directories are cached in large hard disk for immediate viewing, without disk swapping. Jukebox is network accessible, without adding software to existing servers or to clients.	CD network server included. Network clients may read and write CDs over the network. CD directories are cached in large hard disk for immediate viewing, without disk swapping. Jukebox is network accessible, without adding software to existing servers or to clients.
Warranty	1 year	1 year
List Price	$30,720	$26,720

N/A—Not applicable   INA—Information not available

E n d ■

Disk Subsystems

Manufacturer	Amdahl	Andataco	Andataco
Model	LV6 4500	ESP-DK-IS(w/disk)	ESP-RS-IS
OS/NOS Compatible	Solaris, HP-UX, AIX, SVR4, NT	Unix, Windows NT	Unix, Windows NT
Number of Disk Drives per Enclosure	1–30	1–3	1–8
Drive Form Factor	3.5"	3.5" or 5.25"	3.5" to 5.25"
Drive Capacity	4.3GB	Up to 9GB	Up to 9GB
Total Capacity	129GB	Up to 27GB	Up to 27GB
Cache	288MB multipurpose memory	INA	INA
Bundled Host Adapter	PCI, SCSI-III	INA	INA
Transfer Rates Average Access Time	2 X 40MB/sec front end 5 x 40MB/sec back end	40MB/sec 8/9.5 ms	40MB/sec 8/9.5 ms
Redundant Components	Power source, power supplies, controllers, cache	Hot swap drives	Power supplies, fans, hot-swap drives
Bundled Management Software	A+LV5 configuration and monitoring software	Optional	Web Storage Manager allows local and remote monitoring through a Netscape GUI.
Modularity	4GB disk drive canister 20–120GB LSM 387GB Data center	Yes, standard canisters (RSEs)	Yes, modular canisters (RSEs) and power supplies
Enclosure	72" H x 19"W x 30"D 74"H x 19"W x 30"D	5.5"H x 8.38" W x 16.5"D	5.25"H x 19"W x 25.63"D
Comments	Ultra SCSI support, front and back end; no single points of failure; full redundancy and hot-plugability; centralized remote storage management	Environmental monitoring with visual and audible alarms indicating fan, temperature and power supply problems. Cableless connection using SCA drives. I/O activity indicator and hot swap above each drive. Modular building blocks house disk, tape, CD-ROM, and optical drives.	RAID—Ready Design with components. Completely cableless utilizing SCA technology. Environmental monitoring with visual and audible alarms indicating fan, temperature, and power supply problems.
Warranty	1 year	1 year	1 year
List Price	Variable from $49,950 with 20GB to $118,185 with 100GB	$595 (w/drives); $11,515 (w/three 9.1 GB drives)	$1,813 (w/out drives) $30,900 (w/eight 9.1GB drives)

Manufacturer	Andataco	ATTO
Model	ESP-TS-IS(w/disk)	SiliconDisk II
OS/NOS Compatible	Unix, Windows NT	OS independent
Number of Disk Drives per Enclosure	1–24	1
Drive Form Factor	3.5" and 5.25"	5.25
Drive Capacity	Up to 9GB disk drives	Up to 4GB
Total Capacity	Up to 216 GB	Up to 20Gb
Cache	N/A	INA
Bundled Host Adapter	N/A	Ultra SCSI
Transfer Rates Average Access Time	40MB/sec 8–9.5 ms	Up to 80MB/sec
Redundant Components	Power supplies, fans, hot-swap drives	Power, disk
Bundled Management Software	Web Storage Manager allows local and remote management of unit through a Netscape-based GUI.	None

N/A—Not applicable   INA—Information not available

Table Continues →

■ Disk Subsystems

Manufacturer	Andataco	ATTO
Modularity	Yes, modular canisters (RSEs)	
Enclosure	22.25"H x 8.25"W x 26.38"D	3.75"H x 10"W x 11"D
Comments	RAID—Ready design with redundant components. Completely cableless utilizing SCA technology. Visual and audible alarms indicating fan, temperature and power supply problems. True hot-plug drives.	Dual-ported solid-state subsystem. 22,000 I/O per sec
Warranty	1 year	INA
List Price	$2,595 (w/o drives) $89,900 (full with 24–9GB drives)	From $4,500

Manufacturer	Box Hill	Eclipse Technologies
Model	Mod Box 5000	Mariner 2
OS/NOS Compatible	Unix, Windows NT	OS/NOS independent
Number of Disk Drives per Enclosure	1	6 per enclosure; 42 for up to 7 enclosures combined to make an array
Drive Form Factor	3.5" and 5.25"	3.5
Drive Capacity	1–9GB	Up to 8GB
Total Capacity	1–9GB	Up to 300GB
Cache	INA	None
Bundled Host Adapter	SCCI-2, EISA, ISA, or PCI	None bundled. Works with any fast and wide differential SCSI host adapter
Transfer Rates Average Access Time	45–66MB/sec 11ms	16.7MB/sec Sustained (RAID III) 20MB per sec burst
Redundant Components	Power, fan, hot-swap drives	Drives, fans, power supplies (dual) and single or dual hot swappable array controllers
Bundled Management Software	Optional	GUI configuration and management software optionally SNMP network management via LAN/WAN
Modularity	Yes	Yes. Modular drive trays, power supplies, controllers and fans
Enclosure	FH: 4.2"H x 10"W x 14"D HH: 2.1"H x 10"W x 14"D	7"H x 16"W x 16.7"D
Comments	Fault tolerant with Box Hill RAID solution; table top or rackmount	Uses Optix—patented technology for performance instead of cache. Hot swappable array controllers standard, optional, SNMP network management via LAN/WAN
Warranty	3–5 year	2 year
List Price	$500-$50,000	Starting at $9,995 without drives

Manufacturer	Integrix, Inc.	Megadrive Systems
Model	RD10 storage subsystem	Enterprise E-8
OS/NOS Compatible	Solaris 3.5 Sun OS/Windows NT	Macintosh PC, RS-6000, SGI, and most workstations
Number of Disk Drives per Enclosure	1–6	Max 8 slots: 3.5 (1 slot) and 5.25 (2 slots)
Drive Form Factor	3.5	3.5 and 5.25
Drive Capacity	Up to 4GB	Up to 9GB
Total Capacity	Up to 24GB	Up to 36GB
Cache	8–128MB	INA
Bundled Host Adapter	Optional 5 bus-fast/wide SCSI	SCSI

N/A—Not applicable   INA—Information not available

Disk Subsystems ■

Manufacturer	Integrix, Inc.	Megadrive Systems
Transfer Rates Average Access Time	17MB/sec INA	20 to 80MB/sec. 7ms
Redundant Components	Hot swap drives, can be RAID enabled, hot-spare drive	Power, fan, hot-swap drives
Bundled Management Software	RaidStar management GUI	Optional
Modularity	Yes	Yes
Enclosure	3.1"H x 16.4"W x 16.1"D	17.3"H x 7"W x 14"D
Comments		
Warranty	1 year	2 year
List Price	$12,500	INA

Manufacturer	Megadrive Systems	Megadrive Systems
Model	MR 5 and MK 5	MR/10
OS/NOS Compatible	Macintosh PC, RS-6000, SGI, and most workstations	Macintosh PC, RS-6000, SGI, and most workstations
Number of Disk Drives per Enclosure	1–6	1–11
Drive Form Factor	3.5	3.5
Drive Capacity	1–4.2GB	1–4.2GB
Total Capacity	5–21+GB	5– 42+GB
Cache	Up to 128MB	Up to 128MB
Bundled Host Adapter		
Transfer Rates Average Access Time	10MB/sec 7.8–9.3ms	17MB/sec. 7ms
Redundant Components	Power, fan, hot-swap drives	Power, fan, hot-swap drives
Bundled Management Software	OpenWindows 3.5 (standard)	Yes
Modularity	Yes, standard canister	Yes
Enclosure	17.3"H x 7"W x 14"D	15.5"H x 20.5"W x 19"D
Comments		
Warranty	3 year	2 year
List Price	INA	INA

Manufacturer	Micronet Technology	Micronet Technology
Model	DataDock Express	DataDock and DataDock 525
OS/NOS Compatible	Windows NT, Windows 95, Windows 3.1, and Mac	Windows NT, Windows 95, Windows 3.1, and Mac
Number of Disk Drives per Enclosure	1	2
Drive Form Factor	3.50	3.25 and 5.25
Drive Capacity	Up to 9GB	230MB to 16GB depending on device (hard disk, tape, optical, and other removable devices)
Total Capacity	9GB	Up to 24GB (for 6 bays)
Cache	N/A	INA

N/A—Not applicable   INA—Information not available

Table Continues →

■ Disk Subsystems

Manufacturer	Micronet Technology	Micronet Technology
Bundled Host Adapter	Purchase from Micronet $99 SRP	$99 SRP/purchase separately from Micronet
Transfer Rates Average Access Time	Fastest—8.0ms Slowest—28ms	Fastest—8.0ms Slowest—28ms
Redundant Components	Hot-swappable drive modules	Hot-swappable drive modules
Bundled Management Software	Comes with host adapter	Provided with host adapter
Modularity	Yes	Yes
Enclosure	3" x 5" x 6"	3.50—5" x 8 3/8" x 11" 5.25—6" x 10" x 11 3/8"
Comments	Excepts all 3.50 DataDock modules.	Designed to handle a variety of 3.50" and 5.25" devices (removable hard drive, DAT, Magneto Optical, SyQuest, Jazc modules, and disk arrays) for the Macintosh.
Warranty	3 years	3 years (Dock) 1–3 years (Modules)
List Price	$189 SRP	Starts at $735 SRP

Manufacturer	Nstor Corp., Inc.	Nstor Corp., Inc.	Nstor Corp., Inc.
Model	Nstor CR2	Nstor CR6	Nstor CR6
OS/NOS Compatible	Novell NetWare 3.x, 4.x, Windows NT, OS/2, SCO Unix	Novell NetWare 3.x, 4.x, Windows NT, OS/2, SCO Unix	Novell Netware, Windows NT, OS/2, SCO Unix
Number of Disk Drives per Enclosure	1–2	4–6	3–8
Drive Form Factor	3.5	3.5	3.5
Drive Capacity	2–4GB	2GB	2–4GB
Total Capacity	Up to 8GB	Up to 12GB	Up to 32GB
Cache	4MB standard, upgrade to 8GB	8MB	8–32MB
Bundled Host Adapter	Order separately	PCI-SCSI	Order separately
Transfer Rates Average Access Time	10–20MB/sec 9ms	10–20MB/sec 9ms	20MB/sec 9ms
Redundant Components	Fans, hot swap, power supplies, hot-swap drives	Fans, hot swap, power supplies, hot-swap drives	Fans, hot swap, power supplies, hot-swap drives
Bundled Management Software	INA	StorView software for GUI remote interface alert, manager, for Windows NT server	StorView software for GUI remote interface alert, manager, for Windows NT server
Modularity	Yes, stackable cabinet	Yes, hot-swap disk drives	Yes, hot-swap disk drives
Enclosure	5.35"H x 10.75"W x 11.2"D	7.5"H x 12.5"W x 12.5"D	7"H x 16.75"W x 23.25"L (rack) 7"H x 18.7"W x 23"L (tower)
Comments			
Warranty	5 year	5 year	5 year
List Price	Starts at $1,995	Starts at $9,825	Starts at $7,960

Manufacturer	Procom Technology	Procom Technology
Model	LANForce RDT9-B960P	LANForce R2000
OS/NOS Compatible	NetWare, Windows, Unix, OS/2	NetWare, Windows NT, OS/2, Unix, Mac
Number of Disk Drives per Enclosure	2–7	3–56
Drive Form Factor	3.5	3.5 + 5.25

N/A—Not applicable   INA—Information not available

Disk Subsystems ■

Drive Capacity	Up to 4GB	Up to 9GB
Total Capacity	Up to 28GB	Up to 500GB/rack
Cache	Up to 32MB	Up to 512MB
Bundled Host Adapter	PCI-SCSI-2	SCSI-2 not bundled
Transfer Rates Average Access Time	Up to 28MB/sec	18MB/s 6–8.3ms
Redundant Components	Drives, power supplies, fans	Drives, power supplies, fans
Bundled Management Software	Yes, Global array manager	N/A
Modularity	Yes, drive canister	Yes, drives, host channels
Enclosure	19" x 22" x 10"	22.25" x 7.3" x 22.44"
Comments	RAID configurable hardware-based, fault tolerant	RAID configurable hardware-based, fault tolerant
Warranty	1 year	1 year
List Price	$2,995–$15,000	$2,995–$250,000

Manufacturer	**Quantum Corp.**	**Seek Systems**
Model	Atlas II	Seek Array $450
OS/NOS Compatible	Novell Netware, Windows 95, Windows NT	Most Unix, Windows NT, DOS, OS/2, Mac, SCSI users
Number of Disk Drives per Enclosure	1	2–32
Drive Form Factor	3.5	5.25"
Drive Capacity	2.27, 4.55, or 9.1GB	1–9GB
Total Capacity	Formatted 2.2, 4.5 and 9.1	Up to 288GB
Cache	5121K	Up to 128GB
Bundled Host Adapter	SCSI	SCSI-2
Transfer Rates Average Access Time	8bit/16bit 30/40MB/s	Up to 20MB/sec
Redundant Components	None	Power, fan, drive, canister, drivers, controller (optional), and battery backup (optional)
Bundled Management Software	None	Is on firmware and accessible through an RS-port
Modularity	Standard canister form factor. Standard 3.5	Uses industry standard canisters
Enclosure	N/A	40"H x 22"W x 22"D
Comments		Pedestal or rackmount. Fault tolerant. Scaleable. Smaller sizes available. Multiple disk channels
Warranty	Up to 5 year	1 year enclosure 5 year disk drives
List Price	2.2GB: $694 4.5GB: $1,099 9.1GB: $1,699	$.75 to $2.00 per MB

Manufacturer	**Seek Systems**	**Seek Systems**
Model	Seek Array 460	Seek Xcelerator
OS/NOS Compatible	Most Unix, Windows NT, DOS, OS/2, Mac, SCSI users	Most Unix, Windows NT, DOS, OS/2, Mac

N/A—Not applicable   INA—Information not available

Table Continues →

■ Disk Subsystems

Number of Disk Drives per Enclosure	2–32	1–64
Drive Form Factor	5.25"	5.25"
Drive Capacity	Up to 9GB	1–4GB
Total Capacity	Up to 288GB	Up to 256GB
Cache	Up to 128GB	Up to 1GB
Bundled Host Adapter	SCSI-2	SCSI-2
Transfer Rates Average Access Time	Up to 20MB/sec	Up to 20MB/sec Over 1000 I/Os per sec
Redundant Components	Power, fan, drive, canister, drivers, controller (optional), and powerFail/Battery backup (optional)	Power, fan, drive, canister, drivers, controller (optional), and powerFail/Battery backup (optional)
Bundled Management Software	Is on firmware and accessible through an RS-port	Is on firmware and accessible through an RS-port
Modularity	Uses industry standard canisters	Uses industry standard canisters
Enclosure	40"H x 22"W x 22"D	15"H x 15"W x 16"D
Comments	Pedestal or rackmount. Fault tolerant. Scalable. Smaller sizes available. Multiple disk channels	Up to 1GB of solid state disk can be used to eliminate bottlenecks when accessing your disk storage sub system
Warranty	1 year enclosure 5 year disk drives	1 year enclosure 5 year disk drives
List Price	$.75 to $2.00 per MB	$10 to $70 per MB

N/A—Not applicable   INA—Information not available

Disk Subsystems ■

Manufacturer	Stream Logic	Stream Logic
Model	Microdisk LS	Microdisk LT
OS/NOS Compatible	DOS, Windows NT, Mac, OS/2, Unix	DOS, Windows NT, Mac, OS/2, Unix
Number of Disk Drives per Enclosure	1–15	1–15
Drive Form Factor	5.25"	3.5
Drive Capacity	9.1GB	2.1 or 4.3GB
Total Capacity	Up to 136.5GB	Up to 64.5GB
Cache	2MB	2MB
Bundled Host Adapter	None	None
Transfer Rates	10MB/sec	10MB/sec
Average Access Time	12ms	8.9ms
Redundant Components	Hot swap drives	Hot swap drives
Bundled Management Software	Operating system device drivers, format utilities, Macintosh formatting/partitioning software	Operating system device drivers, format utilities, Macintosh formatting/partitioning software
Modularity	Yes	Yes
Enclosure	11"H x 13.8"W x 5.5"D	2.2"H x 8.4"W x 9.6"D
Comments	Stackable, modular, expandable, high capacity storage system	Stackable, modular, expandable, high capacity storage system
Warranty	5 year	5 year
List Price	$3,600+	$1,440

N/A—Not applicable   INA—Information not available   **E n d** ■

■ Optical Drives

Manufacturer	Analog & Digital Peripherals, Inc.	Eastman Kodak	Hewlett-Packard Company
Model	RoadRunner—Rewritable Optical + CD-ROM Reader	System 2000	HP SureStore Optical 2600FX Multifunction Drive
OS/NOS Compatible	OS/2, MS-DOS, Mac, Windows and Windows 95	MVS, Unix, Windows NT, OS/2, Novell, NFS	Windows, Windows 95, UNIX, MS-DOS, Macintosh
Media Type	PD phase change	WORM	MO or WORM
Drive Type	PD rewritable	14" WORM	5.25" Multifunction
Read Only	No	No	Yes
Write Once (WORM)	No	Yes	Yes
Rewriteable	Yes		
Drive Capacity	650MB/sec/1.3GB	14.8GB	2.6GB
I/O Interface	1 SCSI-2 / 1 parallel-EPP, ECP, Bidirectional	SCSI-2	SCSI
Data Transfer Rate-Sustained	SCSI: 1141Kps / Parallel: 600Kps	1MB/sec	INA
Access Times	165ms	170ms	Reads 3.4MB/sec and Writes 1.7MB/sec
Rotational Speed	2,026rpm	1,362–654rpm	INA
Reliability (MTBF)	30,000POH	INA	100,000 hrs.
Bundled Software	Device drivers included for OS/2, DOS, Windows, 95, and Mac	INA	Optional
Power Requirements	Standard 110	530 watts	INA
Comments	Combination system with parallel and SCSI-2 interface for phase change rewriteable optics and CD reader.	Backward compatible, diagnostic keypad	Software drivers and one optical disk are included.
Warranty	1 year	90 day	1 year via HP's Express Exchange Program
Price	$789	INA	$2,995 U.S. List

Manufacturer	Liberty/Fijutsu	Liberty/Fijutsu
Model	30 M0230	115MO1.3/ 115MO2.6
OS/NOS Compatible	Windows 95, Mac, Windows NT, OS2/Warp, Unix	Windows 95, Mac, Windows NT, OS/2, Unix
Media Type	MO	MO
Drive Type	3.5" Magneto-optical	5.25" Magneto-optical
Read Only	No	No
Write Once (WORM)	No	No
Rewriteable	Yes	Yes
Drive Capacity	230MB	1.3GB, 2.6GB
I/O Interface	SCSI-2, parallel port, PCMCIA	SCSI-2, parallel port, PCMCIA
Data Transfer Rate-Sustained	4MB/sec	3MB/sec
Access Times	28ms average	INA
Rotational Speed	3,600rpm	1,900rpm
Reliability (MTBF)	250,000	100,000
Bundled Software	Parallel port software	None
Power Requirements	18 watts	18 watts

N/A—Not applicable   INA—Information not available

Optical Drives ▉

Manufacturer	Liberty/Fijutsu	Liberty/Fijutsu
Comments	4" x 1" x 8" (30) 2" x 4 x 7" (50), Battery option available (50)	2" x 7" x 4", parallel, SCSI, PMCIA
Warranty	1 year	1 year
Price	$699–799	$1,899–$2,699

Manufacturer	Maxoptix	Maxoptix	Maxoptix
Model	T3-1300	T4-1300	T4-2600
OS/NOS Compatible	Netware, DOS, Windows, Windows NT, Unix, and Mac	Netware, DOS, Windows, Windows NT, Unix, and Mac	NetWare, DOS, Windows, Windows NT, Unix, and Mac
Media Type	MO or WORM	MO or WORM	MO or WORM
Drive Type	5.25 Multifunction	5.25 Multifunction	5.25 Multifunction
Read Only			Yes
Write Once (WORM)	Yes	Yes	Yes
Rewriteable	Yes	Yes	No
Drive Capacity	1.3GB	1.3GB	2.6GB
I/O Interface	1 SCSI-2	1 SCSI-2	1 SCSI-2
Data Transfer Rate-Sustained	2.2MB/sec	2.0MB/sec	4.65MB/sec
Access Times	<19ms average 38ms burst	39ms average	<39ms average 75ms burst
Rotational Speed	3,375rpm	3,000rpm	1,900rpm
Reliability (MTBF)	100,000 hrs.	100,000 hrs.	100,000 hrs.
Bundled Software	Optional	Optional	Extensive third-party support
Power Requirements	25 watts	17 watts	17 watts
Comments			ISO standard compliant; backwards compatible with standard 650MB and 1.3GB media. CAD, imaging, digital/audio editing, backup, HSM, prepares graphic applications
Warranty	1 year	1 year	1 year
Price	$1,150	$1,675	$2,025

Manufacturer	MDI	Micronet Technology	Micronet Technology
Model	SE2600	Premiere	Advantage Series
OS/NOS Compatible	Windows NT, Windows 95, OS/2, Netware, DOS	Windows 95, Windows 3.1, Windows NT, Mac Novell 3.x, 4.x	Windows 95, Windows 3.1, Windows NT, Mac
Media Type	MO or WORM	MO	MO
Drive Type	5.25" Multifunction	5.25" MO rewriteable	3.25" and 5.25" rewriteable
Read Only	No	No	No
Write Once (WORM)	Yes	No	No
Rewriteable	Yes	Yes	Yes
Drive Capacity	2.6GB	1.3GB and 2.6GB	230MB-2600MB
I/O Interface	1 SCSI-2	One SCSI-2	One SCSI-2
Data Transfer Rate-Sustained	3.4MB/sec (read) 1.7ms (write)	INA	1 MB/sec
Access Times	35ms	18–39ms	30ms
Rotational Speed	3,000rpm	INA	INA
Reliability (MTBF)	100,000 hrs.	80,000	80,000
Bundled Software	SCSI Express (optional)	Arcada Backup	Arcada Backup

N/A—Not applicable   INA—Information not available

Table Continues →

■ Optical Drives

Manufacturer	MDI	Micronet Technology	Micronet Technology
Power Requirements	36 watts max.	INA	INA
Comments		Features include password protection, verify media, enable/disable drive cache, choice of disk icons and selectable disk interleave.	Offers a variety of cartridges for use with these drives. Average life expectancy greater than 10 years.
Warranty	1 year	2 year	1 year
Price	$1,895 (internal) $1,995 (external)	$1,990–$2,999	$680–$2,590

Manufacturer	MOST, Inc.	Nikon Optical Storage
Model	Jupiter 2	Beluga
OS/NOS Compatible	OS independent	All
Media Type	LIM-DOW, MO, CCW WORM	LIM-DOW, MO, WORM
Drive Type	5 _ MO multifunction	5 _ MO multifunction
Read Only	No	No
Write Once (WORM)	Yes	Yes
Rewriteable	Yes	Yes
Drive Capacity	2.6GB	2.6GB
I/O Interface	SCSI-2	SCSI-2
Data Transfer Rate-Sustained	4MB/sec	4MB/sec average, 10MB/sec burst
Access Times	24ms average 55ms burst	24ms average 55ms burst
Rotational Speed	3,600rpm	3,600rpm
Reliability (MTBF)	100,000	100,000
Bundled Software	N/A	NL
Power Requirements	10 watts	10 watts
Comments	1 pass direct overwrite backward compatible to generations, ISO compliant	Direct overwrite, fully ISO compliant
Warranty	1 year	1 year parts and labor
Price	$2,450	$2,450

Manufacturer	Pinnacle Micro	Pinnacle Micro
Model	Vertex 2.6GB	Apex 4.6GB
OS/NOS Compatible	Most Unix, Windows 95, Windows NT, Windows 3.1x, Mac, OS/2	Most Unix, Windows 95, Windows NT, Windows 3.1x, Mac, OS/2
Media Type	MO	MO or WORM
Drive Type	INA	5.25" Multifunction
Read Only	No	No
Write Once (WORM)	No	Yes
Rewriteable	Yes	Yes
Drive Capacity	2.6GB	4.6GB
I/O Interface	2–50 pin high-density SCSI-2 SCSI-1, fast SCSI-2 compliant	2–50 pin high-density SCSI-2 SCSI-1, fast SCSI-2 compliant
Data Transfer Rate-Sustained	4.3MB/sec	4.3MB/sec
Access Times	19ms	19ms

N/A—Not applicable   INA—Information not available

Optical Drives ■

Manufacturer	**Pinnacle Micro**	**Pinnacle Micro**
Rotational Speed	3,755rpm	2,400rpm
Reliability (MTBF)	150,000 hrs.	150,000 hrs.
Bundled Software	Adaptec EZ-SCSI	Adaptec EZ-SCSI
Power Requirements	INA	INA
Comments	Pinnacle Micro also produces CD Jukebokes using the Vertex 2.6GB optical drives.	Pinnacle Micro also produces CD Jukebokes using the Apex 4.6GB optical drives.
Warranty	1 year	1 year
Price	$1,695	$1,695

Manufacturer	**Plasmon**	**Plasmon**
Model	Cheetah	Cheetah Plus
OS/NOS Compatible	Unix, Windows 95, Windows NT, Windows 3.x, OS/2, Mac	Unix, Windows 95, Windows NT, Windows 3.x, OS/2, Mac
Media Type	MO or WORM,	MO or WORM
Drive Type	5.25" Multi-function	5.25" Multi-function
Read Only Write Once (WORM) Rewriteable	Yes	Yes
Drive Capacity	2.6GB, 2.3GB 1.3GB, 1.2GB 650MB	2.6GB, 2.3GB1.3GB, 1.2GB 650MB
I/O Interface	1 SCSI-2	1 SCSI-2
Data Transfer Rate-Sustained	2MB/sec	4MB/sec
Access Times	2.5ms	2.5ms
Rotational Speed	1,900rpm	3,600rpm
Reliability (MTBF)	>100,000 hrs.	>100,000 hrs.
Bundled Software	Windows 3.x, Windows 95, Windows NT, Mac	Windows 3.x, Windows 95, Windows NT, Mac
Power Requirements	100–240VAC 50/60Hz	100–240VAC 50/60Hz
Comments		
Warranty	1 year	1 year
Price	$1,899 internal $1,999 external	$2,395 internal $2,575 external

N/A—Not applicable   INA—Information not available

Table Continues →

■ Optical Drives

Manufacturer	Sony	Sony
Model	SMO-F541/544	WDD-931
OS/NOS Compatible	Novell 4.1 and Windows NT embedded, Unix (all), OS/2, and Mac	Novell NetWare, Windows 3.1, Windows NT, Unix, OS/2, and Mac
Media Type	5.25" MO and WORM	12" WORM
Drive Type	5.25" Multifunction	12" Write once (alloy recording)
Read Only Write Once (WORM) Rewriteable	No Yes Yes	No Yes No
Drive Capacity	2.6GB	6.55GB
I/O Interface	SCSI-2	SCSI-2
Data Transfer Rate-Sustained	4MB/sec	900K/sec
Access Times	25ms (avg.)	600ms (avg.)
Rotational Speed	3600rpm	760rpm
Reliability (MTBF)	100,000 hrs.	15,000 hrs.
Bundled Software	Software Architect, DOS and Mac Formatter	N/A
Power Requirements	15 watts avg.	1.2A
Comments	S-cache to boost performance with 1MB and 4MB. Rotational eject and low power consumption.	A 100-year projected life
Warranty	1 year, parts and labor	1 year, parts and labor
Price	$2,400 (1MB) $2600 (4MB)	$19,800

CD Recorders ∎

Manufacturer	Hewlett-Packard	Hewlett-Packard
Model	HP SureStore CD-Writer 4020i	HP SureStore CD-Writer 6020i (SCSI)
OS/NOS Compatible	INA	Windows 3.1 and Windows 95
Drive Type	CD Recorder	CD-Recordable-once
Read/Write Capability	1X read/write—Audio: 175KB/sec; Data: 150KB/sec 2X read/write—Audio: 350KB/sec; Data: 300KB/sec 4X read only—Audio: 700KB/sec; Data: 600KB/sec	6X read and 2X write
Drive Capacity	580MB or 680MB	580MB or 680MB
Media Type	580MB or 680MB (63 min. and 74 min.)	580MB or 680MB (63 min. and 74 min.)
I/O Interface	SCSI-2	SCSI-2
Bundled Software	Alchemy Personal, Easy-CD, Easy-CD Audio, Magic Lantern	incat System's Easy-CD Pro for HP; incat System's CD Audio (Voyerta); and IMR Alchemy for HP
Data Transfer Rate	Read: 1X, 2X, 4X (1x=150KB/s Write: 1X, 2X	Read: 1X, 2X 4X, 6X (1x=150kB/s Write: 1X, 2X
Access Times	4X <800ms full stroke <400ms 1/3 stroke	4X <800ms full stroke <400ms 1/3 stroke
Rotational Speed	INA	INA
Power Requirements	Typical 7 watts, Maximum 10 watts	Typical 7 watts, Maximum 10 watts
Comments	Bus-mastering SCSI-2 controller; tray system, no caddy required; up to 4X read; variable write-power laser system; multi-session capable; integrated, automated installation; full software suite; end-user support; extensive compatibility testing; 150,000 hours MTFB. Member of the SureStore Information Storage family.	
Warranty	1 year limited product warranty	1 year product warranty
List Price	INA	INA

Manufacturer	Hewlett-Packard	JVC Engineering
Model	HP SureStore CD-Writer 6020es	JVC Personal Archiver Plus XR-W2010
OS/NOS Compatible	Windows 3.1 and Windows 95	Windows, Windows 95, Windows NT, DOS, MAC
Drive Type	CD Recordable	Internal, External, CD-R Model Minitower, CD-R Model includes HDD
Read/Write Capability	6X read and 2X write	2X Write, 4X Read
Drive Capacity	580MB or 680MB	580MB or 680MB (63 min. and 74 min.)
Media Type	580MB or 680MB (63 min. and 74 min.)	CD-R18, CD-R21, CD-R63, CD-R74
I/O Interface	SCSI	Internal = 1/SCSI External = 2/SCSI Minitower = 2/SCSI
Bundled Software	incat System's Easy-CD Pro for HP; incat System's CD Audio (Voyerta); and IMR Alchemy for HP	Standard = Archiver, EZ-SCSI, SCSI Director, Optional = CD-R Extensions
Data Transfer Rate	Read: 1X, 2X 4X, 6X (1x=150kB/s Write: 1X, 2X	5MB/sec
Access Times	4X <800 ms full stroke <400 ms 1/3 stroke	390ms (Avg.)
Rotational Speed	INA	2120rpm (max.)
Power Requirements	Typical 7 watts, Maximum 10 watts	5V—1.7A 12V—0.3A

N/A—Not applicable   INA—Information not available

Table Continues →

CD Recorders

Manufacturer	**Hewlett-Packard**	**JVC Engineering**
Comments	Designed for SCSI customers who want to share the product among other functional areas or who do not have an open bay in their computer to install the internal drive.	
Warranty	1 year	1 year parts, labor, and technical support
List Price	INA	Internal—$995 External—$1,195 Minitower—$1,695

Manufacturer	**JVC Engineering**	**Liberty/Yamaha**
Model	JVC Personal Rommaker	115CDR4X4
OS/NOS Compatible	Windows, Windows 95, Windows NT, MAC, DOS, Sun, Solaris, HP, SGI, SCO	Windows 95, Windows NT, OS/2, Mac, Unix, SunOS
Drive Type	Internal, External, CD-R Model Minitower, CD-R Model includes HDD Multi-drive CD-R Model	CD Recordable
Read/Write Capability	2X Write, 4X Read	Write once
Drive Capacity	580MB or 680MB (63 min. and 74 min.)	580MB or 680MB
Media Type	CD-R18, CD-R21, CD-R63, CD-R74	580MB or 680MB (63 min. and 74 min.)
I/O Interface	Internal = 1/SCSI External = 2/SCSI Minitower = 2/SCSI Multidrive = 2/SCSI	SCSI-2 parallel PCMCIA
Bundled Software	Rommaker, CD-R Extensions, EZ-SCSI, Alchemy Personal Plus, SCSI Director	Drivers needed Parallel and PCMCIA
Data Transfer Rate	5MB/sec	600 x 600Kbps
Access Times	390ms (Avg.)	<400ms
Rotational Speed	2120rpm (max.)	2–4,000rpm
Power Requirements	5V—1.7A 12V—0.3A	20 watts
Comments		7"(H) x 9"(W) x 2", many I/O options
Warranty	1 year parts, labor, and technical support	1 year
List Price	Internal—$1,895 External—$2,095 Minitower—$2,495	$1,299

Manufacturer	**Liberty/Yamaha**	**MDI**
Model	115CDR2X4	Express Writer
OS/NOS Compatible	Windows 95, Windows NT, OS/2, Mac, Unix	OS/2, DOS, Windows
Drive Type	CD Recordable	CD Recordable
Read/Write Capability	Write once	Write once, read many
Drive Capacity	580MB or 680MB	580MB or 680MB
Media Type	580MB or 680MB (63 min. and 74 min.)	580MB or 680MB (63 min. and 74 min.)
I/O Interface	SCSI-2 parallel PCMCIA	SCSI-2
Bundled Software	Drivers needed Parallel and PCMCIA	Express Writer

N/A—Not applicable   INA—Information not available

CD Recorders ■

Manufacturer	Liberty/Yamaha	MDI
Data Transfer Rate	300 x 600Kbps	300KB/sec sustained
Access Times	<400ms	300ms (avg.)
Rotational Speed	2–4,000rpm	400–1060rpm (recording mode)
Power Requirements	20 watts	8 watts
Comments	7"(H) x 9"(W) x 2", many I/O options	Optional bundled hardware
Warranty	1 year	1 year
List Price	$999	$1,295–$1,695

Manufacturer	Microboards	Microboards
Model	Playwrite 2000	Playwrite 2040
OS/NOS Compatible	Windows, Windows NT, Macintosh, OS/2, Unix	Windows, Windows NT, Macintosh, OS/2, Unix
Drive Type	CD Recordable	CD Recordable
Read/Write Capability	Write once, read many	Write once, read many
Drive Capacity	580MB or 680MB	580MB or 680MB
Media Type	580MB or 680MB (63 min. and 74 min.)	580MB or 680MBB (63 min. and 74 min.)
I/O Interface	SCSI-1	SCSI-1
Bundled Software	Elektroson's Gear, Corel CD Creator, CDR Publisher	Elektroson's Gear, Corel CD Creator, CDR Publisher
Data Transfer Rate	300/KB-sec	300KB/sec
Access Times	250ms	300ms
Rotational Speed	INA	INA
Power Requirements	12 watts	8 watts
Comments		
Warranty	1 year parts/labor 30 day DOA	1 year parts/labor 30 day DOA
List Price	$995	$1,095

Manufacturer	Microboards	Micronet Technology
Model	Playwrite 4000	Master CD Plus
OS/NOS Compatible	Windows, Windows NT, Macintosh, OS/2, Unix	Windows 3.1, Windows 95, Windows NT, Mac
Drive Type	CD Recordable	2X CD Recordable
Read/Write Capability	Write once, read many	Write once
Drive Capacity	580MB or 680MB	580MB or 680MB
Media Type	580MB or 680MB (63 min. and 74 min.)	580MB or 680MB (63 min. and 74 min.)
I/O Interface	SCSI-1	One/SCSI-2
Bundled Software	Elektroson's Gear, Corel CD Creator, CDR Publisher	Standard
Data Transfer Rate	600KB/sec	600KB/sec
Access Times	500ms	390ms (Avg.)
Rotational Speed	INA	INA

N/A—Not applicable   INA—Information not available

Table Continues →

■ CD Recorders

Manufacturer	Microboards	Micronet Technology
Power Requirements	20 watts	8
Comments		Available in 4x and 2x speed, the Master CD series of CD recorders can master a full 650 MB CD in 19 minutes (37 minutes for 2x speed). Data formats supported include ISO 9660, Mac HFS, CD ROM XA, Mac/ISO Hybrid, Generic, Generic XA, Mixed Mode and Audio, Ships with Asarte's Toast CD-ROM Pro.
Warranty	1 year parts/labor 30 day DOA	2 year
List Price	$1,695	$1,195

Manufacturer	Micronet Technology	PLASMON
Model	Master CD Pro	4240
OS/NOS Compatible	Windows 3.1, Windows 95, Windows NT, Mac	Mac, Windows 3.1x, Windows 95, Windows NT
Drive Type	4X CD Recordable	CD Recordable
Read/Write Capability	Write once	Write once
Drive Capacity	580MB or 680MB	748MB(74 min.) 656MB(63 min.)
Media Type	580MB or 680MB (63 min. and 74 min.)	580MB or 680MB (63 min. and 74 min.)
I/O Interface	One/SCSI-2	One SCSI-2
Bundled Software	Standard	Optional
Data Transfer Rate	800KB/sec	4x=615/700KB/sec 2x=307/350KB/sec 1x=154/175KB/sec
Access Times	380ms	350ms
Rotational Speed	INA	CLV
Power Requirements	8	100 to 240VAC 50/60Hz
Comments	Available in 4x and 2x speed, the Master CD series of CD recorders can master a full 650 MB CD in 19 minutes (37 minutes for 2x speed). Data formats supported include ISO 9660, Mac HFS, CD ROM XA, Mac/ISO Hybrid, Generic, Generic XA, Mixed Mode and Audio, Ships with Asarte's Toast CD-ROM Pro.	
Warranty	2 year	1 year parts and labor
List Price	$2,385	INA

Manufacturer	SMS Data Products Group	SMS Data Products Group
Model	DCY101	DCS102
OS/NOS Compatible	NetWare, Windows NT, MS-DOS and Unix	NetWare, Windows NT, MS-DOS and Unix
Drive Type	4X reader 4X recorder	4X reader 2X recorder
Read/Write Capability	Write once	Write once
Drive Capacity	580MB or 680MB	580MB or 680MB
Media Type	580MB or 680MB (63 min. and 74 min.)	580MB or 680MB (63 min. and 74 min.)
I/O Interface	SCSI-2	SCSI-2

N/A—Not applicable   INA—Information not available

CD Recorders ■

Manufacturer	SMS Data Products Group	SMS Data Products Group
Bundled Software	Optional	Gear by Electrosum
Data Transfer Rate	614.4KB/sec	300KB/sec
Access Times	500ms	300ms
Rotational Speed	4X reader 4X recorder	4X reader 2X recorder
Power Requirements	N/A	N/A
Comments	It is considered a Drive Cell component that can be plugged into a S7000 networking tower. The S700 has a dual SCSI chain, which allows for a CD-R drive in the tower of its own SCSI chain. (www.sms.com)	It is considered a Drive Cell component that can be pluggedd into a S7000 networking tower. The S700 has a dual SCSI chain which allows for a CD-R drive in the tower of its own SCSI chain. (www.sms.com)
Warranty	3 year—advance replacement	3 year—advance replacement
List Price	$1,631	$1,308

Manufacturer	Sony	Sony	Teac
Model	CSP-940S	CSP-9411S	CD-R505
OS/NOS Compatible	Windows 3.1, Windows 95, Windows NT, Mac	Windows 3.1, Windows 95, Windows NT, Mac	DOS, Windows 3.x, Windows 95, Windows NT, MAC, Unix
Drive Type	CD-R	CD-R	CD Recordable
Read/Write Capability	Write once	Write once	Write once
Drive Capacity	580MB or 680MB	580MB or 680MB	580MB or 680MB
Media Type	580MB and 680MB (63 min. and 74 min.)	580MB and 680MB (63 min. and 74 min.)	580MB or 680MB (63 min. and 74 min.)
I/O Interface	SCSI-2, SCSI controller not bundled	SCSI-2, SCSI controller not bundled	One SCSI-2/Fast SCSI
Bundled Software	Corel CD Creator (standard)	Corel CD Creator (standard)	None
Data Transfer Rate	Sustained: 600KB (4x) Burst: 2.5MB (async) 4.0MB (sync)	Sustained: 600KB (4x) Burst: 2.5MB (async) 4.0MB (sync)	600Kbps/ 8.47Mbps
Access Times	Full stroke: 400ms (typical, 4x) Random: 250ms (typical, 4x)	Full stroke: 400ms (typical, 4x) Random: 250ms (typical, 4x)	220ms (avg.)
Rotational Speed	Innermost: 2,400rpm (4x) Outermost: 800rpm (4x)	Innermost: 2,400rpm (4x) Outermost: 800rpm (4x)	@400rpm
Power Requirements	Hold track state: +5Vpc<750mA—3.75 watts (max.) +12Vpc <600mA—7.2 watts (max.) Seeking and spin up and write: +5Vpc<1200mA—6.0 watts(max) +12Vpc<1400mA—16.8 watts (max)	12 watts	INA
Comments	Sony's new generation of Spressa CD-R drives makes CD-R discs work like giant floppies. The CDRFS technology brings incremental writing to CD-R discs.	Sony's new generation of Spressa CD-R drives makes CD-R discs work like giant floppies. The CDRFS technology brings incremental writing to CD-R discs.	4x write, 4x read, CD recordable drive with power tray loading capability.
Warranty	1 year parts and labor	1 year parts and labor	1 year parts and labor
List Price	$900	$1050	$999

N/A—Not applicable   INA—Information not available   **End ■**

■ Tape Drives

Manufacturer	**ADIC**	**AIWA CO., LTD** **Sold in USA by AIWA America, Inc.**
Model	8000 Series	TD-S1600
OS/NOS Compatible	Most Unix, OS/2, Windows NT, NetWare	DOS, Windows, Windows 95
Drive Type	4mm DAT	QIC Travan
Total Capacity (Using High-Capacity Media)	8GB	1.6GB compressed
I/O Interface	SCSI-2	Floppy controller
Data Transfer Rate	90MB/min.	9.5MB/min.
Reliability (MTBF)	80,000 INA	100,000 hrs.
Bundled Software	Optional	Arcada backup
Enclosure	3.25"H x 6.75"W x 11"D	Internal (drive measures) 1"H x 4"W x 5.9"D
Comments	Uses both a DDS-1 DAT tape drive and a DDS-2 DAT tape drive. With capacities of up to 8GB per tape and transfer rates up to 90MB/min., the DATa 8000 Series is a reliable backup solution. Compatible with all leading backup software, across popular operating environments.	Includes internal tape drive, 5.25 mount kit, backup software, internal data cable, and installation manual.
Warranty	2 year	2 year
List Price	$1,395–$2,195	$208

Manufacturer	**AIWA CO., LTD** **Sold in USA by AIWA America, Inc.**	**AIWA CO., LTD** **Sold in USA by AIWA America, Inc.**
Model	TD-S3200	TD-P3200
OS/NOS Compatible	DOS, Windows, Windows 95	DOS, Windows, Windows 95
Drive Type	QIC Travan	QIC Travan
Total Capacity (Using High-Capacity Media)	3.2GB compressed	3.2GB compressed
I/O Interface	Floppy controller	PC parallel port
Data Transfer Rate	19MB/min.	19MB/min.
Reliability (MTBF)	150,000 hrs.	100,000 hrs.
Bundled Software	Arcada backup	Arcada backup
Enclosure	Internal (drive measures) 1"H x 4"W x 5.9"D	5.3"H x 1.4"W x 9.3"D
Comments	Includes internal tape drive, 5.25 mount kit, 2MB/sec accelerator card, backup software, internal data cable, and installation manual.	Includes external tape drive, AC adapter with cables, backup software, external data cable, and installation manual.
Warranty	2 year	2 year
List Price	$250	$350

Manufacturer	**AIWA CO., LTD** **Sold in USA by AIWA America, Inc.**	**AIWA CO., LTD** **Sold in USA by AIWA America, Inc.**
Model	GD-B8000	GD-E8000
OS/NOS Compatible	DOS, Windows, Windows 95, NetWare, Windows NT, OS/2, Unix, Mac	DOS, Windows, Windows 95, Netware, Windows NT, OS/2, Unix, Mac
Drive Type	4mm DAT	4mm DAT

N/A—Not applicable   INA—Information not available

Tape Drives ◼

Manufacturer	AIWA CO., LTD Sold in USA by AIWA America, Inc.	AIWA CO., LTD Sold in USA by AIWA America, Inc.
Total Capacity (Using High-Capacity Media)	8GB compressed	8GB compressed
I/O Interface	1 SCSI-2	1 SCSI-2
Data Transfer Rate	48MB/min.	48MB/min.
Reliability (MTBF)	200,000 hrs.	150,000 hrs.
Bundled Software	INA	None
Enclosure	4"H x 1.626"W x 5.961"D	7.008"H x 2.758"W x 10.512"D
Comments	Includes internal tape drive, installation manual, software compatibility guide, free technical support.	Includes external tape drive, SCSI terminator, power cord, stands, software compatibility guide, free technical support.
Warranty	2 year	2 year
List Price	$1,248	$1,582

Manufacturer	AIWA CO., LTD Sold in USA by AIWA America, Inc.	Andataco
Model	GD-S8000	ESP-DK-IS with RSE-Q7000E
OS/NOS Compatible	DOS, Windows, Windows 95, OS/2	HP-UX, Solaris, IBM, SGI, Windows NT
Drive Type	4mm DAT	8 mm
Total Capacity (Using High-Capacity Media)	8GB compressed	40GB compressed or 80 GB compressed
I/O Interface	1 SCSI-2	Two SCSI-2 fast & wide
Data Transfer Rate	48MB/min.	3MB/sec., 6MB/sec. compressed
Reliability (MTBF)	200,000 hrs.	200,000 hrs.
Bundled Software	Novastor, Novaback	N/A
Enclosure	Internal (drive measures) 4"H x 1.626"W x 5.961"D	5.5"H x 8.38"W x 16.5"D
Comments	Includes internal tape drive, 5.25 mount kit, SCSI internal cable, backup software, data cartridge, installation manual, free technical support.	Environmental monitoring with visual and audible alarms indicating fan, temperature and power supply problems. I/O indicator and drive Hot-swap switch above each drive.
Warranty	2 year	1 year enclosure, 2 year drive
List Price	$1,415	$11,600 (includes 2 drives)

Manufacturer	Andataco	Box Hill
Model	ESP-DK-IS with RSE-E8900S	DTH 4
OS/NOS Compatible	HP-UX, Sun-Solaris, IBM, SGI, Windows NT	Unix, Windows NT
Drive Type	DLT	4mm DAT
Total Capacity (Using High-Capacity Media)	70GB compressed	4–8GB
I/O Interface	One SCSI-2, 68-pin	1 SCSI-2
Data Transfer Rate	5MB/sec. native, 10MB/sec. compressed	61.2MB/min.
Reliability (MTBF)	200,000 hrs.	200,000 hrs.
Bundled Software	N/A	Optional

N/A—Not applicable   INA—Information not available

Table Continues →

■ Tape Drives

Manufacturer	Andataco	Box Hill
Enclosure	5.5"H x 8.38"W x 16.5"D	2.1"H x 10"W x 14"D
Comments	Environmental monitoring with visual and audible alarms indicating fan, temperature and power supply problems. I/O indicator and drive Hot-swap switch above each drive.	Configurable in Box Hills' hot-swappable Mod box 5000 chassis
Warranty	1 year enclosure, 2 year drive	1 year
List Price	$16,190 (includes tape drive)	$500–$5,000

Manufacturer	Box Hill	Box Hill
Model	CT 7	CT 20
OS/NOS Compatible	Unix, Windows NT	Unix, Windows NT
Drive Type	8mm	8mm
Total Capacity (Using High-Capacity Media)	7–14GB	20–40GB
I/O Interface	1 SCSI-2	1 SCSI-2
Data Transfer Rate	60MB/min.	360MB/min.
Reliability (MTBF)	160,000 hrs.	200,000 hrs.
Bundled Software	Optional	Optional
Enclosure	2.1"H x 10"W x 14"D	2.1"H x 10"W x 14"D
Comments	Configurable in Box Hills' hot-swappable Mod box 5000 chassis	Configurable in Box Hills' hot-swappable Mod box 5000 chassis
Warranty	1 year	1 year
List Price	$500–$5,000	$500–$5,000

Manufacturer	Box Hill	Box Hill
Model	DLT 3	DLT 4
OS/NOS Compatible	Unix, Windows NT	Unix, Windows NT
Drive Type	DLT	DLT
Total Capacity (Using High-Capacity Media)	15-30GB	20–40GB
I/O Interface	1 SCSI-2	1 SCSI-2
Data Transfer Rate	180MB/min.	180MB/min.
Reliability (MTBF)	80,000 hrs.	80,000 hrs.
Bundled Software	Optional	Optional
Enclosure	4.2"H x 10"W x 14"D	4.2"H x 10"W x 14"D
Comments	Configurable in Box Hills' hot-swappable Mod box 5000 chassis.	Configurable in Box Hills' hot-swappable Mod box 5000 chassis.
Warranty	1 year	1 year
List Price	$500–$5,000	$500–$5,000

N/A—Not applicable   INA—Information not available

Tape Drives ∎

Manufacturer	Cybernetics	Cybernetics
Model	CY-1000	CY-4000
OS/NOS Compatible	Windows NT, OS/2, HP-UX, Solaris	Windows NT, OS/2, HP-UX, Solaris
Drive Type	4mm DAT	DLT
Total Capacity (Using High-Capacity Media)	4GB native; up to 8GB with integral data compression	20GB native; 40GB with integral data compression
I/O Interface	SCSI-2	SCSI-2, single-ended (differential optional)
Data Transfer Rate	778Kps native; 1.5MB/sec. compressed	1.5MB/sec native; 3MB/sec. compressed
Reliability (MTBF)	200,000 hrs.	80,000 hrs.
Bundled Software	Optional	Optional
Enclosure	Single-drive cabinet multi-drive desktop cabinet rackmount	Single-drive cabinet multi-drive desktop cabinet rackmount
Comments	Average search time of <40 seconds. Convenient back-lit display. Data compression, data encryption, accelerated file access (Unix), and digital data recorder options available. Advanced SCSI processor allows two or more drives to work together in a variety of recording modes.	The CY 4000 features the backlit status display and supports the full range of Cybernetics options: data compression, data encryption, accelerated file access (Unix), digital data recorder interface, and the advanced SCSI processor for multi-drive recording in a variety of modes.
Warranty	1 year	2 year
List Price	INA	INA

Manufacturer	Cybernetics	Cybernetics
Model	CY-8000	CY-8900
OS/NOS Compatible	Windows OT, OS/2, HP-UX, Solaris	Windows OT, OS/2, HP-UX, Solaris
Drive Type	8mm	8mm
Total Capacity (Using High-Capacity Media)	25GB and 40GB compressed	20-100 GBcompressed
I/O Interface	SCSI-2, single-ended (differential optional)	SCSI-2, single-ended (differential optional)
Data Transfer Rate	1.5MB/sec., 3MB/sec. compressed	3MB/sec., 9MB/sec. compressed
Reliability (MTBF)	200,000 hrs.	200,000 hrs.
Bundled Software	Wide variety of software packages	Wide variety of software packages
Enclosure	Single-drive cabinet multi-drive desktop cabinet rackmount	Single-drive cabinet multi-drive desktop cabinet rackmount
Comments	Back-lit status display, Advanced Metal Evaporated media, built-in head cleaning mechanism. Advanced SCSI processor allows multi-tape operations in striping, mirroring, cascade, independent, and offline copy/verify modes. Data compression, data encryption, accelerated file access (Unix), and digital data recorder options.	Convenient, back-lit display provides command under execution, transfer rate, compression ratio, tape remaining, and ECC. Advanced SCSI processor, data encryption, accelerated file access, and digital data recorder options available to enhance flexibility and performance.
Warranty	1 year	1 year
List Price	Contact vendor	Contact vendor

N/A—Not applicable   INA—Information not available

Table Continues →

■ Tape Drives

Manufacturer	Cybernetics	Exabyte
Model	CY-9000	Mammoth
OS/NOS Compatible	Windows OT, OS/2, HP-UX, Solaris	Windows NT, OS/2, HP-UX, Solaris
Drive Type	DLT	8mm
Total Capacity (Using High-Capacity Media)	42GB, up to 100GB compressed	20GB 40GB compressed
I/O Interface	SCSI-2, single-ended (differential optional)	1 fast/wide SCSI-2
Data Transfer Rate	3MB/sec., 9MB/sec. compressed	360MB/min. compressed
Reliability (MTBF)	200,000 hrs.	200,000 hrs.
Bundled Software	Wide variety of software packages	None
Enclosure	Single-drive cabinet multi-drive desktop cabinet rack-mount	3"H x 9"W x 11"D
Comments	Back-lit display provides command under execution, transfer rate, compression ratio, tape remaining and ECC. Advanced SCSI processor, data encryption, accelerated file access and digital data recorder options available to enhance flexibility and performance.	Unique capstan-less reel-to-reel tape path. Available with any multilingual LED display.
Warranty	1 year	2 year
List Price	Contact vendor	$6,200

Manufacturer	Exabyte	Exabyte
Model	EXB—8505XL	EXB-8205XL
OS/NOS Compatible	Windows NT, OS/2, HP-UX, Solaris	Windows NT, OS/2, HP-UX, Solaris
Drive Type	8mm	8mm
Total Capacity (Using High-Capacity Media)	7GB 14GB compressed	2.3GB 7GB compressed
I/O Interface	1 SCSI-2	1 SCSI-2
Data Transfer Rate	60MB/min. compressed	32MB/min. compressed
Reliability (MTBF)	160,000 hrs.	160,000 hrs.
Bundled Software	None	Optional
Enclosure	3"H x 9"W x 11"D	3"H x 9"W x 11"D
Comments	Also available as an internal unit.	Also available as an internal unit
Warranty	2 year	2 year
List Price	$2,750	$1,860

Manufacturer	Exabyte	Exabyte
Model	EXB-8700	EXB-8700LT
OS/NOS Compatible	Windows NT, OS/2, HP-UX, Solaris	Windows NT, OS/2, HP-UX, Solaris
Drive Type	8mm	8mm
Total Capacity (Using High-Capacity Media)	7GB 14GB compressed	7GB 14GB compressed
I/O Interface	1 SCSI-2	1 SCSI-2
Data Transfer Rate	60MB/min. compressed	60MB/min. compressed
Reliability (MTBF)	160,000 hrs.	160,000 hrs.

N/A—Not applicable   INA—Information not available

Tape Drives ■

Manufacturer	Exabyte	Exabyte
Bundled Software	Choice of one: Cheyenne ARC Serve, seagate backup director/ backup Exex, Dantz, or Retrospect	None
Enclosure	3"H x 9"W x 11"D	2.5"H x 6.6"W x 9.8"D
Comments	Complete compact 8mm tape drive system includes software	Optional
Warranty	2 year	2 year
List Price	$1,795	INA

Manufacturer	Hewlett-Packard Company	Hewlett-Packard Company
Model	HP SureStore T4I	HP SureStore 2000i/e
OS/NOS Compatible	Windows NT	Novell NetWare, Windows 95, Windows NT, OS/2, HP-UX, SCO UNIX, UNIXware, Macintosh
Drive Type	Travan (TR-4)	DDS
Total Capacity (Using High-Capacity Media)	4GB Native	2GB
I/O Interface	One SCSI-2	One SCSI-2
Data Transfer Rate	514K/sec. or 30MB/min.	Sustained: 183K/sec., Burst: asynch/synch 1.5 MB/sec., 5.0 MB/sec.
Reliability (MTBF)	200,000 hrs.	i: 200,000 hrs. e: 150,000 hrs.
Bundled Software	None	Colorado Backup for Windows and Windows 95
Enclosure	1.7"H x 5.9"W x 8"D	i: 1.6"H x 4"W x 5.9"D e: 3.7"H x 4.6"W x 8.7"D
Comments	Includes drivers for Novell NetWare and Windows NT	
Warranty	2 year	2 year
List Price	$449	i: $904/e: $1,051

Manufacturer	Hewlett-Packard Company	Hewlett-Packard Company
Model	HP SureStore 5000/i/e/eU	HP SureStore 6000/i/e/eU
OS/NOS Compatible	Novell NetWare, Windows NT, Windows 95, Windows 3.x, OS/2, HP-UX, SCO Unix, Unixware, Macintosh	Novell NetWare, Windows NT, Windows 95, Windows 3.x, OS/2, HP-UX, SCO Unix, Unixware, Macintosh
Drive Type	DDS-DC	DDS-DC and DDS-2
Total Capacity (Using High-Capacity Media)	2GB native, 4GB with data compression	4GB native, 8GB with data compression
I/O Interface	One SCSI-2	One SCSI-2
Data Transfer Rate	Sustained: 366 K/sec., Burst: asynch/sync 1.5 MB/sec., 5.0 MB/sec.	Sustained: 1 MB/sec., Burst: asynch/sync 3.0 MB/sec., 7.5 MB/sec.
Reliability (MTBF)	i: 200,000 hrs., e/eU: 150,000 hrs.	i: 200,000 hrs., e/eU: 150,000 hrs.
Bundled Software	Colorado Backup for Windows and Windows 95	Colorado Backup for Windows and Windows 95
Enclosure	i: 1.6"H x 4"W x 5.9"D e/eU: 3.7"H x 4.6"W x 8.7"D	i: 1.6"H x 4"W x 5.9"D e/eU: 3.7"H x 4.6"W x 8.7"D
Comments		
Warranty	2 year	2 year
List Price	i: $1,036 e/eU: $1,183	i; $1,276 e/eU: $1,424

N/A—Not applicable   INA—Information not available

Table Continues →

■ Tape Drives

Manufacturer	Hewlett Packard	Hewlett Packard
Model	HP Colorado T4000es (external) HP Colorado T4000s (internal)	HP Colorado T1000e
OS/NOS Compatible	Windows NT 3.51 (www.hp.com/go/ colorado_support); Windows NT 4.0 (in the OS); Novell NetWare server 3.X, 4.X (Cheyenne); OS/2 (coming Spring '97); Unix (coming Spring '97)	Windows 3.1X, DOS 5.X and higher, small networks Novell, NetWare 2.X, 3>X, LANtastic, Windows for Workgroups
Drive Type	QIC minicartridge/TR4 (8 GB)	TR-1 reads and writes Travan TR-1, QIC-80 Wide, QIC-80XL, QIC-80; Reads QIC-40 tapes
Total Capacity (Using High-Capacity Media)	Using TR4 minicartridge, 4GB native, 8GB compressed (2.1)	Up to 400MB uncompressed/800MB compressed (2.1)
I/O Interface	2/SCSI-2 (external), 1/SCSI-2 (internal)	Parallel interface
Data Transfer Rate	514 K/sec. (31 MB/min.) burst, native	Up to 9.5 MB/min. transfer speed with enhanced parallel port
Reliability (MTBF)	200,000 hrs. (external) 250,000 hrs. (internal)	250,000 hrs. MTBF w/20% tape motion
Bundled Software	Colorado Backup for DOS, Windows, Windows 95	Colorado Backup for Windows, Windows 95, DOS
Enclosure	1.625" x 5.25" (5_ half-height)	9.3"L x 6.3"W x 1.4"H
Comments		Connects to existing parallel port; pass through parallel shares port with printer; supports most popular laptop computers; enhanced parallel ports automatically recognized; internal power supply.
Warranty	2 year limited	2 year limited
List Price	$559 (external) $456 (internal)	$225, $199 street price

Manufacturer	Hewlett Packard	Hewlett-Packard
Model	HP Colorado T3000	HP SureStore DLT30e
OS/NOS Compatible	Windows 3.X, Windows 95, DOS 5.X and higher, small networks Novell, NetWare 2.X, 3.X, LANtastics, Windows for Workgroups, Windows NT 4.0 (applet included in NT OS/2)	Windows NT, OS/2, HU-UX, Solaris, Novell NetWare
Drive Type	Travan TR-3; reads and writes QIC-3020; TR-3, QIC wide-3020	DLT
Total Capacity (Using High-Capacity Media)	With Travan TR-3 minicartridge up to 1.6GB native, 3.2 compressed (2.1)	30GB
I/O Interface	Floppy	SCSI-2
Data Transfer Rate	Up to 19 MB/min. with 2 MB/sec. floppy controller or FC-20 accelerator card	2.5MB/sec.
Reliability (MTBF)	250,000 hour power-on hours with 20% tape motion	80,000 MTBF
Bundled Software	Colorado Backup for Windows 95, Windows, DOS	N/A
Enclosure	3" by 1"	4.88"H x 9"W x 12.75"D
Comments	Optional HP Direct Tape Access (DTA) software enables easy "hard-drive" like storage by allowing the T3000 to be seen as a logical device; includes TR-3 tape in the box.	
Warranty	2 year limited	2 year
List Price	$227, $199 street price	$4,545

N/A—Not applicable   INA—Information not available

Tape Drives

Manufacturer	Hewlett-Packard	Liberty/Seagate
Model	HP SureStore DLT40e	70 DAT 16G
OS/NOS Compatible	Windows NT, OS/2, HU-UX, Solaris, Novell NetWare	Windows 95, Windows NT, OS/2, DOS, Mac, Unix
Drive Type	DLT	DLT
Total Capacity (Using High-Capacity Media)	40GB	16GB
I/O Interface	1 SCSI	SCSI, parallel, PC MCI-A
Data Transfer Rate	3.0MB/sec.	24MB/sec.
Reliability (MTBF)	80,000 MTBF	60,000 hrs.
Bundled Software	N/A	Parallel-port software drivers PCMCIA drivers
Enclosure	124mm (H) x 229mm (W) x 325mm (D)	2"H x 5"W x 7"D
Comments		
Warranty	2 year	1 year
List Price	$6,495	$1,249

Manufacturer	Liberty/Seagate	MDI
Model	70 DAT 4G	SCSI Express DAT Family
OS/NOS Compatible	Windows 95, Windows NT, OS/2, DOS, Mac, Unix	NetWare
Drive Type	DLT	4mm DAT
Total Capacity (Using High-Capacity Media)	4GB	2-8GB
I/O Interface	SCSI, parallel, PC MCI-A	SCSI-2
Data Transfer Rate	22MB/min.	1MB/sec.
Reliability (MTBF)	60,000 hrs.	50,000–200,000 hrs.
Bundled Software	Parallel-port software drivers PCMCIA drivers	LAN Librarian
Enclosure	2"H x 5"W x 7"D	95mmH x 198mmW x 356mmD
Comments		
Warranty	1 year	1 year
List Price	$1,149	$995–$1,845

Manufacturer	MicroNet Technology	MicroNet Technology
Model	Premier ss-D16000	Adavantage ADV2000 Date
OS/NOS Compatible	Windows 95, Windows 3.1, Windows NT, Mac, Novell 3X, 4X	Windows 95, Windows 3.1, Windows NT, Mac, and Novell
Drive Type	4mm DAT	4mm DAT
Total Capacity (Using High-Capacity Media)	16GB	2GB
I/O Interface	1 SCSI-2	1 SCSI-2
Data Transfer Rate	23MB/min.	10MB/min.
Reliability (MTBF)	80,000 hrs.	80,000 hrs.
Bundled Software	Arcada - PC Retrospect for Mac	Arcada; Retrospect for Mac

N/A—Not applicable   INA—Information not available

Table Continues →

■ Tape Drives

Manufacturer	MicroNet Technology	MicroNet Technology
Enclosure	4" x 5" x 9" 5" x 7" x 11 7/8"	2 1/8" x 9" x 11"
Comments	Use HP tape backup drives and are available in capacities up to 16 GB. They conform to standard cable specifications with two 50-pin female connectors, and feature push button SCSI ID select, extended long length tape backup, external termination, 30 second average access and interchangeability of data cartridges. Each system is bundled with Arcada's utility software and includes a drive cable and two blank data cartridges.	Use HP backup drives and are available in capacities of 2GB. The conform to standard cable specifications with two 50-pin female connectors, and feature push button SCSI ID select, extended long length tape backup, external termination, 30 second average access and interchangeability of data cartridges. Each system is bundled with Arcada's utility software and includes a drive cable and two blank data cartridges.
Warranty	2 year	1 year
List Price	Starts at $1,655	$1,030 SRP

Manufacturer	MicroNet Technology	MicroNet Technology
Model	SB30 DLT/NET SB40 DLT/NET	Autoloader JB-DAT 48-6
OS/NOS Compatible	Windows 95, Windows 3.1, Mac, Novell, and NetWare 3X, 4X	Windows 95, Windows 3.1, Windows NT, Mac, Novell 3X, 4X
Drive Type	DLT	4mm
Total Capacity (Using High-Capacity Media)	30–40GB	48GB
I/O Interface	One/SCSI-2	One SCSI-2
Data Transfer Rate	65/80MB/min.	30 MB/min.
Reliability (MTBF)	80,000 hrs.	80,000 hrs.
Bundled Software	Arcada Backup Exec Multi-Server	Arcada—PC Retrospect—Mac
Enclosure	6" x 7" x 12"	4" x 5" x 9" 5" x 7" x 11 7/8"
Comments	Offers high capacity and increased reliability for unattended backup. With sustained data transfer rates of up to 80 MB/min. the system combines advanced linear recording technology, an accurate tape guide system, and an adaptive control mechanism to make the drive the ideal backup companion for mid-range systems, network servers, and high-end workstations.	Safely and automatically backs up and restores up to 48GB of data. Supports DDS 2 compressed and standard DDS data formats. With the six cassette magazine and four 90 meter cassettes provided, users can backup up to 48GB. Combinations of weekly and daily backup tapes can be loaded at the same time. Users can completely backup a network file server without having to change tapes.
Warranty	2 year	2 year
List Price	SRP (starts at) $6,050	$1,655

Manufacturer	NCE Storage Solutions/ Emerald	NCE Storage Solutions/ Emerald
Model	SYS07G/14G	Cheyenne Arc Serve 6
OS/NOS Compatible	Netware, Windows, Windows NT, OS/2	Netware, Windows, Windows NT, OS/2
Drive Type	8mm	4mm DAT
Total Capacity (Using High-Capacity Media)	7 and 14GB	2/4/8GB
I/O Interface	SCSI-1 and SCSI-2	SCSI-2
Data Transfer Rate	Up to 5Mbps, 60GBpm	183–510Kps
Reliability (MTBF)	160,000 hrs.	50,000–200,000 hrs.
Bundled Software	Optional	Cheyenne ARCserve 6 Workgroup or Enterprise

N/A—Not applicable   INA—Information not available

Tape Drives ■

Manufacturer	NCE Storage Solutions/ Emerald	NCE Storage Solutions/ Emerald
Enclosure	2.25"H x 9.75"W 11.5"D	2.5"H x 6.75"W x 9"D
Comments	Server- or workstation-based Backward read Internal or external Cross shipments	Server- or workstation-based Backward read Internal or external Cross shipments
Warranty	1 year	1 year
List Price	$2,995–$3,995	$1,508–$2,985

Manufacturer	NCE Storage Solutions/Emerald	NCE Storage Solutions/Emerald
Model	DAT Drive	Gem Stor
OS/NOS Compatible	Netware, Windows, Windows NT, OS/2	Netware, Windows, Windows NT, OS/2
Drive Type	4mm DAT	4mm DAT
Total Capacity (Using High-Capacity Media)	1/2/4/8GB	2/4/8GB
I/O Interface	SCSI-2	SCSI-2
Data Transfer Rate	183–510K/sec.	183–510K/sec.
Reliability (MTBF)	50,000–200,000 hrs.	50,000–200,000 hrs.
Bundled Software	Cheyenne ARCserve 6 Workgroup or Enterprise	Optional
Enclosure	2.5"H x 6.75"W x 9"D	2.5"H x 6.75"W x 9"D
Comments	Server- or workstation-based Backward read Internal or external Cross shipments	Server- or workstation-based Backward read Internal or external Cross shipments
Warranty	1 year	1 year
List Price	$1,508–$2,985	$1,145–$1,495

Manufacturer	NCE Storage Solutions/Emerald	NCE Storage Solutions/Mountain
Model	DLT Drive	Mountain DAT Drive
OS/NOS Compatible	Netware, Windows, Windows NT, OS/2	Windows, DOS
Drive Type	DLT	4mm DAT
Total Capacity (Using High-Capacity Media)	30 and 40GB	2/4/ 8GB
I/O Interface	SCSI-2	SCSI-2
Data Transfer Rate	183–510K/sec.	183–510K/sec.
Reliability (MTBF)	50,000–200,000 hrs.	50,000–200,000 hrs.
Bundled Software	No	FileSafe for Windows
Enclosure	2.5"H x 6.75"W x 9"D	2.5"H x 6.75"W x 9"D
Comments	Server- or workstation-based Backward read Internal or external Cross shipments	Server- or workstation-based Backward read Internal or external Cross shipments
Warranty	1 year	1 year
List Price	$4,595–$7,995	$1,145–$1,495

N/A—Not applicable   INA—Information not available

Table Continues →

■ Tape Drives

Manufacturer	Overland Data	Quantum Corp.
Model	DLT XT Series	DLT 2000XT
OS/NOS Compatible	DOS, Windows NT, OS/2, RS-6000, Sun, Unix, Netware	Many
Drive Type	DLT	DLT
Total Capacity (Using High-Capacity Media)	30–40GB	15GB–30GB
I/O Interface	1 SCSI-2	SCSI-2
Data Transfer Rate	2.5/3MB/sec.	1.25–2.5MB/sec.
Reliability (MTBF)	225,000 hrs.	80,000 hrs.; head life 10,000 hrs.
Bundled Software	Call	None
Enclosure	7.56"H x 7.5"W x 11.7"D	4.87"H x 9.0"W x 12.75"L
Comments	Other tape format products available	
Warranty	2 year	2 year
List Price	$4,330	$2,665

Manufacturer	Seagate Technology	Seagate Technology
Model	4586 NP DAT Autoloader	TapeStor 8000
OS/NOS Compatible	Windows, Windows NT, DOS, SCO Unix, Apple A/UX, NetWare 4.x, 3.x	NT, NetWare, Windows 3.x, Windows 95, DOS, OS/2, SCO, Unix
Drive Type	4mm	Travan TR4, mini cartridge
Total Capacity (Using High-Capacity Media)	96GB	8GB
I/O Interface	SCSI-2	SCSI-2, SCSI ATA (Enhanced ID5)
Data Transfer Rate	800 K/sec. compressed, 400 K/sec. uncompressed	600/450/300K/sec., uses Fast Sense technology
Reliability (MTBF)	125,000 (2090 data cycle)	200,000 Internal 150,000 External
Bundled Software	Seagate software soft bundle	Seagate Backup
Enclosure	3.2"H x 8"D x 5.7"W	Available in 3.5", 5" and external
Comments	Read while write technology, hardware data compression	Fast Sense technology allows drive to operate at computers fastest data transfer rate. Precision Burst intelligent head positioning system, providing reliable operation at high speed.
Warranty	2 year	2 year
List Price	N/A	N/A

Manufacturer	Seagate Technology	Tecmar Technologies
Model	4324/4326 DAT	Wantek 5200
OS/NOS Compatible	Windows NT, Solaris, Unix, Netware	DOS, Windows NT, OS/2, Sun
Drive Type	4mm DAT	QIC (Full size cartridge)
Total Capacity (Using High-Capacity Media)	4–8GB	2.5GB
I/O Interface	SCSI-2	SCSI-2
Data Transfer Rate	800 K/sec. compressed, 400 K/sec. uncompressed	285K/sec.
Reliability (MTBF)	200,000	80,000 hrs.

N/A—Not applicable   INA—Information not available

Tape Drives ∎

Manufacturer	Seagate Technology	Tecmar Technologies
Bundled Software	Seagate software soft bundle	Optional
Enclosure	Available in 3.5", 5" and external	2.5"H x 8.25"W x 10.75"D
Comments	Read while write technology. Hardware data compression.	
Warranty	2 year	1 year
List Price	N/A	$630–$830

Manufacturer	Tecmar Technologies	Tecmar Technologies
Model	Wantek 5100	Wangdat 3400 DX
OS/NOS Compatible	DOS, Windows NT, OS/2, Sun	Windows NT, OS/2, HP-UX, Solaris
Drive Type	QIC (Full size cartridge)	4mm DAT
Total Capacity (Using High-Capacity Media)	1GB	8GB compressed
I/O Interface	SCSI-2	SCSI-2
Data Transfer Rate	17MB/min.	44MB/min. typical
Reliability (MTBF)	80,000 hrs.	180,000 hrs.
Bundled Software	INA	Optional
Enclosure	2.5"H x 8.25"W x 10.75"D	2.4"H x 6.8"W x 10"D
Comments		Hardware data compression, 1MB buffer DDS-2 format
Warranty	1 year	1 year
List Price	$637	$1,090

Manufacturer	Tecmar Technologies	Tecmar Technologies
Model	Wangdat 3100,3200	Wangtek 5525
OS/NOS Compatible	Windows NT, OS/2, Solaris, HP-UX	Windows NT, OS/2, Solaris, HP-UX
Drive Type	4mm DAT	QIC (full size cartridge)
Total Capacity (Using High-Capacity Media)	4GB compressed	525MB
I/O Interface	SCSI-2	SCSI-2
Data Transfer Rate	22MB/min.	200K/sec.
Reliability (MTBF)	60,000 hrs.	80,000 hrs.
Bundled Software	Optional	Call
Enclosure	2.4"H x 6.5"W x 10"D	2.55"H x 8.25"W x 10.75"D
Comments	Hardware data compression DDS-1 format	Read-after-write data checking
Warranty	1 year	1 year
List Price	$956	$620–$810

N/A—Not applicable   INA—Information not available

End ∎

■ Tape Libraries

Manufacturer	ADIC	ADIC
Model	Scalar Series	VLS DLT Series
OS/NOS Compatible	Most Unix, OS/2, Windows NT, DOS, NetWare	Most Unix, OS/2, Windows NT, DOS, NetWare
Drive/Media Types	DLT	DLT
Drives per Library	4	1
Tapes per Library	48	7
Magazine Capacity	None	7
Library Capacity	3.36TB	490GB
I/O Interface	4 SCSI-2	SCSI-2
Sustained/Peak Data Transfer Rate	300MB/min. (one per drive)	180–600MB/min.
Disk Swap Time	10 secs.	10 secs.
RELIABILITY		
MCBF	1,000,000	1,000,000
MTBF	80,000	80,000
Redundant Components	Drives—hot configurations	None
Bundled Software	None	None
Power Requirements	100–240VAC, 47–63Hz	100–240VAC, 50–60Hz, 1–.5A
Enclosure	40.3"H x 19.5"W x 23.5"D	8"H x 17.4"W x 20.45"D
Comments	The newest model, The Scalar 458, features 58-cartridge positions (including 10 in the media mailbox), barcode reader and four drive bays. The Scalar 448 includes all the features of the Scalar 458 except the 10-position mailbox. Both provide storage capacity of up to 3.36TB of data with sustained throughput speeds of up to 1.2GB/minute (native).	Available in three versions: the model 300, which uses the Quantum DLT2000XT drive, the model 400, with the Quantum DLT4000 drive, and the model 700, with the Quantum 7000 drive. With the XT drive, the VLS DLT300 provides up to 210GB of total storage and an average sustained data transfer rate of 150MB/min.
Warranty	2 year	2 year
Price	$27,750–$93,985	$9,995–$21,995

Manufacturer	ADIC	ADIC
Model	1200 DAT Series	VLS 8mm
OS/NOS Compatible	Most Unix, OS/2, Windows NT, DOS, NetWare	Most Unix, OS/2, Windows NT, DOS, NetWare
Drive/Media Types	4mm	8mm
Drives per Library	1	2
Tapes per Library	12	11
Magazine Capacity	12	11
Library Capacity	96GB	154GB
I/O Interface	One SCSI-2	SCSI-2
Sustained/Peak Data Transfer Rate	22–66MB/min.	60MB/min.
Disk Swap Time	6 secs.	8 secs.
RELIABILITY		
MCBF	INA	100,000
MTBF	80,000	160,000
Redundant Components	None	Dual drives—hot configurations
Bundled Software	None	None

N/A—Not applicable   INA—Information not available   MCBF=mean cycles between failures   MTBF=mean time

Tape Libraries ■

Manufacturer	ADIC	ADIC
Power Requirements	100–240VAC, 50–60Hz, 1–0.5A	100–240VAC, 50–60Hz, 1–.5A
Enclosure	8"H x 17"W x 13.4"D	8"H x 17.4"W x 16.25"D
Comments	Single drive, 4mm DAT libraries that offer all the benefits of ADIC's automation of the data storage process. The 1200C uses DDS-1 format cartridge for a total capacity of 48GB, with transfer speeds of 22 MB/min. ADIC's newest model, the 1200E, incorporates Sony's Quad Speed SDT-7000 DDS-2 drive.	Single or dual drive libraries, all use 11 8mm cartridge magazine for a total of 154GB. The VLS 8mm products offer automated data management, a locking door for data security and automated cleaning and tape rotation. As a dual drive, the VLS 8mm provides data transfer rates up to 120MB/min.
Warranty	2 year	2 year
Price	$4,995–$6,295	$7,595–$11,795

Manufacturer	ADIC	ADIC
Model	800E	VLS 4mm Series
OS/NOS Compatible	Most NetWare, OS/2, Windows NT, DOS	Most Unix, OS/2, Windows NT, DOS, NetWare
Drive/Media Types	4mm	4mm
Drives per Library	1	1–2
Tapes per Library	8	15
Magazine Capacity	8	15
Library Capacity	64GB	120GB
I/O Interface	SCSI-2	SCSI-2
Sustained/Peak Data Transfer Rate	90 MB/min.	90 MB/min.
Disk Swap Time	80 secs.	8 secs.
RELIABILITY		
MCBF	100,000	100,000
MTBF	180,000	80,000
Redundant Components	None	Dual drives—hot configuration
Bundled Software	None	N/A
Power Requirements	100–120/260–240VAC, 50–60Hz	100–240VAC, 50–60Hz 1–5A
Enclosure	3.25"H x 5.75"W x 9.5"D	8"H x 17.4"W x 16.25"D
Comments	Provides up to 64GB storage capacity. Its 8-position magazine stores 8 data tapes and 1 cleaning cartridge with transfer speeds of up to 90 MB/min. User control panel with LCD display shows drive status and allows manual loading and unloading of single cartridges.	Available as either a single or dual-drive DDS-2 DAT tape drive library system, which use a 4mm 15-tape magazine, for a total capacity of 120 GB. As a dual-drive, the VLS 4mm provides data transfer rates up to 180 MB/min.
Warranty	2 year	2 year
Price	$3,395	$7,595–$9,295

Manufacturer	ATL Products	ATL Products
Model	ACL 2/28	ACL 4/52
OS/NOS Compatible	AS/400, S/3X, PC LAN	S/3X, Sun, SGI, IBM, HP, DEC
Drive/Media Types	DLT	DLT
Drives per Library	2	4
Tapes per Library	28	52
Magazine Capacity	28 cartridges	52 cartridges
Library Capacity	560GB	1040GB

N/A—Not applicable   INA—Information not available

Table Continues →

■ Tape Libraries

Manufacturer	ATL Products	ATL Products
I/O Interface	SCSI-2 fast/wide	SCSI-2 fast/wide
Sustained/Peak Data Transfer Rate	1.5MB/sec.	1.5MB/sec.
Disk Swap Time	INA	INA
RELIABILITY		
MCBF	INA	INA
MTBF	170,000 power on hour	170,000 power on hour
Redundant Components	Hot-swap drives	Hot-swap drives
Bundled Software	Call	Call
Power Requirements	160 watts normal, 200 maximum	160 watts normal, 200 maximum
Enclosure	44"H x 23"W x 32"D	44"H x 23"W x 32"D
Comments	Easily scalable to 4 drives and 56 cartridges, 4 cartridge mail slot	2 million cycles demonstrated
Warranty	Onsite 1 year	Onsite 1 year
Price	INA	INA

Manufacturer	AIWA CO., LTD Sold in USA by AIWA America, Inc.	AIWA CO., LTD Sold in USA by AIWA America, Inc.
Model	AL-D210	AL-D220
OS/NOS Compatible	Netware, Windows NT, Unix, OS/2, Mac, Banyan	Netware, Windows NT, Unix, OS/2, Mac, Banyan
Drive/Media Types	4mm DAT	4mm DAT
Drives per Library	1	2
Tapes per Library	17	17
Magazine Capacity	17	17
Library Capacity	136GB	136GB
I/O Interface	2 SCSI-2	1 SCSI-2
Sustained/Peak Data Transfer Rate	60MBpm, sustained to 5MB/sec. burst	60MBpm, sustained to 5MB/sec. burst
Disk Swap Time	15 secs.	15 secs.
RELIABILITY		
MCBF	INA	INA
MTBF	160,000 power on hour	160,000 power on hour
Redundant Components	None	Second drive can be used for redundancy
Bundled Software	None	None
Power Requirements	100/240v	100/240v
Enclosure	8.125"W x 16"H x 12.25"D	8.125"W x 16"H x 12.25"D
Comments	Provides full automation of data backup and management. Reduces operator intervention and frees up valuable disk space by moving files from the server to tape.	Provides full automation of data backup and management. Reduces operator intervention and frees up valuable disk space by moving files from the server to tape.
Warranty	2 year	2 year
Price	$5,995	$7,995

N/A—Not applicable   INA—Information not available

Tape Libraries ■

Manufacturer	Box Hill	Box Hill
Model	Slide Box	DAT Box
OS/NOS Compatible	Unix, Windows NT	Unix, Windows NT
Drive/Media Types	4mm DAT	4mm DAT
Drives per Library	1	1
Tapes per Library	6	12
Magazine Capacity	6	12
Library Capacity	24–48GB	48–96GB
I/O Interface	1 SCSI-2	1 SCSI-2
Sustained/Peak Data Transfer Rate	510K/1MB/sec.	510K/1MB/sec.
Disk Swap Time	INA	INA
RELIABILITY		
MCBF	INA	INA
MTBF	40,000 power on hour	80,000 power on hour
Redundant Components	None	None
Bundled Software	Optional	Optional
Power Requirements	60 watts	60 watts
Enclosure	3.25"H x 5.75"W x 8"D	8"H x 17"W x 13.5"D
Comments	Configures in a hot-swappable, full-height MOD box 5000 chassis.	Rackmountable
Warranty	1 year	1 year
Price	$5,000–$200,000	$5,000–$200,000

Manufacturer	Box Hill	Box Hill
Model	Bread Box	Light Box
OS/NOS Compatible	Unix, Windows NT	Unix, Windows NT
Drive/Media Types	8mm	8mm
Drives per Library	1	1 or 2
Tapes per Library	10	11
Magazine Capacity	10	11
Library Capacity	70–140GB	70–154GB
I/O Interface	1 SCSI-2	1 SCSI-2
Sustained/Peak Data Transfer Rate	500K/1MB/sec.	1MB/2MB/sec.
Disk Swap Time	<25 secs.	INA
RELIABILITY		
MCBF	60,000 hrs.	INA
MTBF	27,000 power on hour	27,000 power on hour
Redundant Components	None	None
Bundled Software	Optional	Optional
Power Requirements	60 watts	60–110 watts
Enclosure	15.5"H x 8.5"W x 17.5"D	Tabletop: 22"H x 9.45"W x 21.4"D Rackmount: 8.75"H x 19"W x 21.13"D
Comments	Box Hill device driver provides full control of all media changer functions.	Rackmountable Bar code reader with scanning software optional
Warranty	1 year	1 year
Price	$5,000–$200,000	$5,000–$200,000

N/A—Not applicable   INA—Information not available   **Table Continues** →

■ Tape Libraries

Manufacturer	Box Hill	Box Hill
Model	Borg Box 2/41 + 4/41	Borg Box 4/81 +.2/81
OS/NOS Compatible	Unix, Windows NT	Unix, Windows NT
Drive/Media Types	8mm	8mm
Drives per Library	2 or 4	2 or 4
Tapes per Library	41	81
Magazine Capacity	41	81
Library Capacity	287–574GB	567–1,134GB
I/O Interface	1 SCSI-2	1 SCSI-2
Sustained/Peak Data Transfer Rate Disk Swap Time	2MB/4MB/sec. <25 secs.	2MB/4MB/sec. None
RELIABILITY		
MCBF	750,000	INA
MTBF	27,000 power on hour	27,000 power on hour
Redundant Components	None	None
Bundled Software	Optional	Optional
Power Requirements	95–145 watts	95–145 watts
Enclosure	25"H x 19"W x 26.75"D	25"H x 19"W x 26.75"D
Comments	Rackmountable Bar code reader with scanning software optional Import/export slot	Rackmountable Bar code reader with scanning software optional Import/export slot
Warranty	1 year	1 year
Price	$5,000–$200,000	$5,000–$200,000

Manufacturer	Box Hill	Box Hill
Model	DLT Five Box	DLT Seven Box
OS/NOS Compatible	Unix, Windows NT	Unix, Windows NT
Drive/Media Types	DLT	DLT
Drives per Library	1	1
Tapes per Library	5	7
Magazine Capacity	5	7
Library Capacity	100–200GB	140–280GB
I/O Interface	1 SCSI–2	1 SCSI–2
Sustained/Peak Data Transfer Rate Disk Swap Time	1.5MB/3MB/sec. 20secs.	1.5MB/3MB/sec. 29secs.
RELIABILITY		
MCBF	INA	INA
MTBF	30,000 power on hour	30,000 power on hour
Redundant Components	INA	INA
Bundled Software	INA	INA
Power Requirements	100 watts	100 watts maximum
Enclosure	11.8"H x 16.3"W x 10.5"D	10.4"H x 8.7"W x 27"D
Comments	Rackmountable Box Hill device driver	Rackmountable Box Hill device driver
Warranty	1 year	1 year
Price	$5,000–$200,000	$5,000–$200,000

N/A—Not applicable   INA—Information not available

Tape Libraries ■

Manufacturer	**Box Hill**	**Box Hill**
Model	Echo Box	DLT Tera Box
OS/NOS Compatible	Unix, Windows NT	Unix, Windows NT
Drive/Media Types	DLT	DLT
Drives per Library	1 or 2	2 or 4
Tapes per Library	10	52
Magazine Capacity	10	52
Library Capacity	150–400GB	1,040–2,080GB
I/O Interface	1 SCSI-2 Fast SCSI-2	1 SCSI-2
Sustained/Peak Data Transfer Rate Disk Swap Time	8MB/10MB/sec. 10 secs.	6MB/12MB/sec. INA
RELIABILITY		
MCBF	500,000 hrs.	INA
MTBF	100,000 power on hour	170,000 power on hour
Redundant Components	None	None
Bundled Software	Tape mirroring software (TMS)	Optional
Power Requirements	120 watts	200 watts max
Enclosure	Rackmount: 7"H x 17"W x 22"D Desktop: 8"H x 19"W x 23"D	44"H x 23"W x 32"D
Comments	2 drive streaming for high-speed backups. Tape mirroring software (TMS) provides real-time mir-roring.	Bar code reader with scanning software. Imports/export slot with 4-cartridge mail box Box Hill device driver
Warranty	1 year	1 year
Price	$5,000–$200,000	$5,000–$200,000

Manufacturer	**Box Hill**	**Box Hill**
Model	DLT Phone Box 9/88	DLT Phone Box 3/264
OS/NOS Compatible	Unix, Windows NT	Unix, Windows NT
Drive/Media Types	DLT	DLT
Drives per Library	9	3
Tapes per Library	88	264
Magazine Capacity	88	264
Library Capacity	1,760–3,520GB	5,280–10,560GB
I/O Interface	1 SCSI-2	1 SCSI-2
Sustained/Peak Data Transfer Rate Disk Swap Time	13.5MB/27MB/sec.	4.5MB/9MB/sec.
RELIABILITY		
MCBF	INA	INA
MTBF	80,000 power on hour	80,000 power on hour
Redundant Components	None	None
Bundled Software	Optional	Optional
Power Requirements	540 watts maximum	480 watts maximum
Enclosure	78.7"H x 28.2"W x 47"D	78.7"H x 28.2"W x 47"D

N/A—Not applicable   INA—Information not available   **Table Continues** →

■ Tape Libraries

Manufacturer	Box Hill	Box Hill
Comments	Pass-thru mechanism and multi-unit controller for addition of expansion unit. Bar code reader with scanning software. Import/export slot with 12-cartridge mailbox.	Pass-thru mechanism and multi-unit controller for addition of expansion unit. Bar code reader with scanning software. Import/export slot with 12-cartridge mailbox.
Warranty	1 year	1 year
Price	$5,000–$200,000	$5,000–$200,000

Manufacturer	Box Hill	Breece Hill Technologies
Model	DLT Phone Box 6/176	Q7
OS/NOS Compatible	Unix, Windows NT	Most Unix, OS/2, Windows NT, DOS
Drive/Media Types	DLT	DLT
Drives per Library	6	2
Tapes per Library	176	28
Magazine Capacity	176	7
Library Capacity	3,520–7,040GB	1.96TB
I/O Interface	1 SCSI-2	SCSI-2
Sustained/Peak Data Transfer Rate	9MB/18MB/sec.	5.4MB/20MB/sec.
Disk Swap Time	INA	10 secs.
RELIABILITY		
MCBF	INA	1,000,000
MTBF	80,000 power on hour	80,000
Redundant Components	None	Drives, power
Bundled Software	Optional	None
Power Requirements	540 watts maximum	220 watts average
Enclosure	78.7"H x 28.2"W x 47"D	28"H x 17.5"W x 28"D
Comments	Pass-thru mechanism and multi-unit controller for addition of expansion unit. Bar code reader with scanning software. Import/export slot with 12-cartridge mailbox.	The Q7 DLT library features a pinpoint laser for cartridge inventory and continuous robotic calibration, comprehensive power out recovery, many customer replaceable units, including all tape drives and electronic assemblies, and 4 removable 7-cartridge magazines for easy off-site storage.
Warranty	1 year	2 year
Price	$5,000–$200,000	$28,000 (DLT2000XT drives)

Manufacturer	Breece Hill Technologies	Breece Hill Technologies
Model	Q47	Q2 15!
OS/NOS Compatible	Most Unix, OS/2, Windows NT, DOS	Most Unix, OS/2, Windows NT, DOS
Drive/Media Types	DLT	DLT
Drives per Library	4	1 or 2
Tapes per Library	60	15
Magazine Capacity	7	10
Library Capacity	4.2TB	1.05TB
I/O Interface	SCSI-2	SCSI-2
Sustained/Peak Data Transfer Rate	5.4MB/20MB/sec.	5 MB/20MB/sec.
Disk Swap Time	12.2 secs.	16 secs.

N/A—Not applicable   INA—Information not available

Tape Libraries ■

Manufacturer	Breece Hill Technologies	Breece Hill Technologies
RELIABILITY		
MCBF	1,000,000	1,000,000
MTBF	80,000	200,000
Redundant Components	Drives, power	Drives
Bundled Software	None	None
Power Requirements	220 watts average	88 watts average
Enclosure	45.75"H x 17.75"W x 28"D	8.75"H x 17.75"W x 24.5"D
Comments	The Q47 DLT library features two media carousels for maximizing capacity, a pinpoint laser for cartridge inventory and continuous robotic calibration, comprehensive power out recovery, many customer replaceable units, and 4 removable 7-cartridge magazines for easy off-site storage.	Available in rackmount, desktop, or deskside configurations, the Q2 15! DLT library features entry-level affordability, a small footprint, patented robotics system, an integrated bar code reader, a removable 10-cartridge magazine, and the ability to stack the units to expand storage capacity.
Warranty	2 year	2 year
Price	$52,000 (4 DLT2000XT drives)	$18,000 *(2 DLT2000XT drives)

Manufacturer	Cybernetics	Cybernetics
Model	CY-TL8-2010	CY- CHS1008
OS/NOS Compatible	Virtually all computer operating systems	Virtually all computer operating systems
Drive/Media Types	8mm	DTF
Drives per Library	2	1
Tapes per Library	10	8
Magazine Capacity	10 cartridges	N/A
Library Capacity	200GB native; 1.0 TB compressed (with one drive)	336GB native; 1.68 TB compressed
I/O Interface	Fast/Wide SCSI	SCSI-2 or RS-232C
Sustained/Peak Data Transfer Rate	3Mbps native; up to 9 Mbps compressed	12Mbps native; 40Mbps compressed
Disk Swap Time	N/A	<6 secs.
RELIABILITY		
MCBF	500,000	INA
MTBF	>200,000	200,000
Redundant Components	None	None
Bundled Software	Wide variety of software packages	Wide variety of software packages
Power Requirements	266 watts (avg.)	1230 watts
Enclosure	Desktop/deskside	Free-standing
Comments	Robotic Control software for Unix systems. Other options include data encryption for security and Advanced SCSI processor which allows two or more drives to work together. Key-locked front door with viewing window. Pressurized, filtered, forced air cooling with redundant fans.	A standard bar code reader provides random access to the data cartridges. Robotic Control software for Unix systems allows users to move, load, and unload tapes without manual tape handling.
Warranty	1 year	1 year
Price	INA	INA

N/A—Not applicable   INA—Information not available   **Table Continues** →

■ Tape Libraries

Manufacturer	Cybernetics	Cybernetics
Model	CY-TL1-2018	CY-CHS9135
OS/NOS Compatible	Virtually all computer operating systems	Virtually all computer operating systems
Drive/Media Types	4mm DAT	DTF
Drives per Library	2	1
Tapes per Library	18	35
Magazine Capacity	N/A	N/A
Library Capacity	72GB native; 144 GB compressed	1.47TB native; 7.35TB compressed
I/O Interface	SCSI-2	SCSI-2 or RS-232C
Sustained/Peak Data Transfer Rate	778Kbps native; 1.5Mbps compressed	12Mbps native; 40Mbps compressed
Disk Swap Time	INA	Tape access time is <6 secs.
RELIABILITY		
MCBF	500,000	INA
MTBF	200,000	200,000
Redundant Components	None	None
Bundled Software	Robotic Control software available; supports most third party software	Robotic Control software available; supports most third party software products.
Power Requirements	200 watts (avg.)	1230 watts
Enclosure	Desktop/deskside	Free-standing
Comments	Robotic Control software for Unix systems. Other options include data encryption for security and Advanced SCSI processor which allows two or more drives to work together. Key-locked front door with viewing window. Pressurized, filtered, forced air cooling with redundant fans.	Provides automated access to up to 7.35TB of data in 7 square feet of floor space. Standard bar code reader provides random access to data cartridges.
Warranty	1 year	1 year
Price	INA	INA

Manufacturer	Cybernetics	Diverse Logistics Inc. (DLI)
Model	CY-CHS9225	Libra-8
OS/NOS Compatible	Virtually all computer operating systems	Windows, Windows 95, Windows NT, OS2, DOS, Novell, all Unix systems, open VMS and ADSM
Drive/Media Types	DTF	4mm DAT
Drives per Library	2	1
Tapes per Library	25	8
Magazine Capacity	N/A	8
Library Capacity	1.05TB native; 5.25TB compressed (one drive)	128GB
I/O Interface	SCSI-2 or RS-232C	1 SCSI-2
Sustained/Peak Data Transfer Rate	12Mbps native; 40Mbps compressed	732Kps and 5MB/sec.
Disk Swap Time	Tape access time is <6 secs.	INA
RELIABILITY		
MCBF	INA	Greater than 65,000 insertions
MTBF	200,000	Greater than 80,000 power on hour
Redundant Components	None	N/A
Bundled Software	Wide variety of software packages	N/A

N/A—Not applicable   INA—Information not available

Tape Libraries ■

Manufacturer	Cybernetics	Diverse Logistics Inc. (DLI)
Power Requirements	1830 watts	100 watts
Enclosure	INA	13"H x 7.9"W x 14"D
Comments	A standard bar code reader provides random access to the data cartridges. Robotic Control software for Unix systems allows users to move, load, and unload tapes without manual tape handling.	High reliability, DAT technology, fast file search, LCD control panel, key lock with security password, only 7 moving parts, and "Clean Stor" environment
Warranty	1 year	1 year
Price	INA	$4,925

Manufacturer	Diverse Logistics Inc. (DLI)	Exabyte Corporation
Model	Libra-16	EXB-210
OS/NOS Compatible	Windows, Windows 95, Windows NT, Novell, all Unix systems, open VMS and ADSM	N/A
Drive/Media Types	4mm DAT	8mm
Drives per Library	1	2
Tapes per Library	16	11
Magazine Capacity	16	10
Library Capacity	256GB	154GB (2:1 compression)
I/O Interface	1 SCSI-2	SCSI-2
Sustained/Peak Data Transfer Rate	732Kps and 5MB/sec.	2MB/10MB/sec. (2:1 compression)
Disk Swap Time	INA	< 10 secs.
RELIABILITY		
MCBF	Greater than 65,000 insertions	750,000
MTBF	Greater than 80,000 power on hour	160,000
Redundant Components	N/A	None
Bundled Software	N/A	Optional
Power Requirements	100 watts	60 watts
Enclosure	13"H x 7.9"W x 14"D	22"H x 9.5"W x 21.4"D
Comments	High reliability, DAT technology, fast file search, LCD control panel, key lock with security password, only 7 moving parts, and "Clean Stor" environment	Collect, protect, and control with 1 or 2 EXB-8505XL drives. Full automation.
Warranty	1 year	2 year
Price	$5,285	Base MSRP $9,250

Manufacturer	Exabyte Corporation	Exabyte Corporation
Model	EXB-220	EXB-10h
OS/NOS Compatible	Unix, Windows NT, Novell, DOS, OS/2	N/A
Drive/Media Types	8mm Mammoth	8mm
Drives per Library	1–2	1
Tapes per Library	20	10
Magazine Capacity	10	10
Library Capacity	400/800*GB *assumes 2:1 compression	140GB (2:1 compression)
I/O Interface	SCSI-2	SCSI-2

N/A—Not applicable   INA—Information not available

Table Continues →

■ Tape Libraries

Manufacturer	Exabyte Corporation	Exabyte Corporation
Sustained/Peak Data Transfer Rate Disk Swap Time	Sustained: 3–6MB/sec., 6–12MB/sec. (assumes 2:1 compression) < 10 secs.	1MB/5MB/sec. (2:1 compression) < 16secs.
RELIABILITY		
MCBF	750,000	>100,000
MTBF	200,000	160,000
Redundant Components	None	None
Bundled Software	Optional	Optional
Power Requirements	Minimum 50 watts Maximum 110 watts	60 watts
Enclosure	Standalone: 22"H x 9.45"W x 21.4"D Rackmount: 8.65"H x 19"W x 21.13"D	15.8"H x 8.5"W x 18.1"D
Comments	Extensive list of standards includes: LCD panel display, front door access to media and drives with keyed lock and security interlock, bar code scanner, interchangeable cartridge magazines, and small footprint in both tower and rackmount configuration.	A compact power tower of storage automation. Reliable robotics, key-lock security. Superior compatibility, worldwide support.
Warranty	2 years	1 year
Price	Base MSRP $19,790	Base MSRP $6,658

Manufacturer	Exabyte Corporation	Exabyte Corporation
Model	EXB-218	EXB-440
OS/NOS Compatible	N/A	Unix, Windows NT, Novell, DOS, OS/2
Drive/Media Types	4mm DAT	8mm Mammoth
Drives per Library	2	2–4
Tapes per Library	19	40
Magazine Capacity	18	10
Library Capacity	152GB (2:1 compression)	800/1,600GB (assumes 2:1 compression)
I/O Interface	SCSI-2	SCSI-2 fast Narrow and differential Single-ended Differential wide
Sustained/Peak Data Transfer Rate Disk Swap Time	1.02MB/15MB/sec. (2:1 compression) < 10secs.	Sustained: 6–12MB/sec., 12–24MB ps (assumes 2:1 compression) < 10 secs.
RELIABILITY		
MCBF	200,000	750,000
MTBF	200,000	200,000
Redundant Components	None	None
Bundled Software	Optional	Optional
Power Requirements	55 watts	Minimum 95 watts, Maximum 145 watts
Enclosure	22"H x 9.5"W x 21.4"D	Standalone: 25.5"H x 19"W x 26.8"D Rackmount: 21"H x 19"W x 26.3"D
Comments	Supports all advanced library functions. 120MBpm throughput. Tower or rackmount.	Extensive list of standards includes: LCD panel display, front door access to media and drives with keyed lock and security interlock, bar code scanner, interchangeable cartridge magazines, and small footprint in both tower and rackmount configuration.
Warranty	2 year	2 year
Price	Base MSRP $7,825	Base MSRP $30,040

N/A—Not applicable   INA—Information not available

Tape Libraries ■

Manufacturer	**Exabyte Corporation**	**Hewlett-Packard Company**
Model	EXB-480	HP Advanced DLT Tape Library 2/28
OS/NOS Compatible	Unix, Windows NT, Novell, DOS, OS/2	HP-UX 10.0
Drive/Media Types	8mm Mammoth	DLT4000/Type IIIXT and Type IV
Drives per Library	2–4	2
Tapes per Library	80	28
Magazine Capacity	10	N/A
Library Capacity	1,600/3,200GB (assumes 2:1 compression)	560GB native/1.1TB compressed
I/O Interface	SCSI-2 fast Narrow and differential Single-ended Differential wide	1 SCSI-2
Sustained/Peak Data Transfer Rate Disk Swap Time	Sustained: 6–12MB/sec., 12–24MB/sec. (assumes 2:1 compression) < 10 secs.	1.5Mbps native/3Mbps compressed INA
RELIABILITY		
MCBF	750,000	1,000,000
MTBF	200,000	Drive: 80,000 hrs. Library: 100,000 hrs.
Redundant Components	None	N/A
Bundled Software	Optional	N/A
Power Requirements	Minimum 95 watts Maximum 145 watts	200 watts typical/260 watts maximum
Enclosure	Standalone: 25.5"H x 19"W x 26.8"D Rackmount: 21"H x 19"W x 26.3"D	36"H x 34"W x 19"D
Comments	Extensive list of standards includes: LCD panel display, front door access to media and drives with keyed lock and security interlock, bar code scanner, interchangeable cartridge magazines, and small footprint in both tower and rackmount configuration.	Fully automated. Patented online drive replacement. Maintenance-free library system.
Warranty	2 year	1 year
Price	Base MSRP $48,080	$49,105 U.S. List

Manufacturer	**Hewlett-Packard Company**	**Hewlett-Packard**
Model	HP Advanced DLT Tape Library 2/48	HP SureStore 12000e
OS/NOS Compatible	HP-UX 10.0	Novell NetWare, Windows NT, 3.x, OS/2, HP-UX, Solaris, AIX
Drive/Media Types	DLT4000/Type IIIXT and Type IV	DDS-2
Drives per Library	2	1
Tapes per Library	48	Six
Magazine Capacity	N/A	8GB with data compression
Library Capacity	960GB native/1.9TB compressed	48GB
I/O Interface	1 SCSI-2	SCSI-2
Sustained/Peak Data Transfer Rate Disk Swap Time	1.5Mbps native/3Mbps compressed INA	Typically 1 MB/sec. with data compression asynch/ synch: 3.0MB/sec., 7.5 MB/sec. 15 secs.
RELIABILITY		
MCBF	1,000,000	INA
MTBF	Drive: 80,000 hrs. Library: 100,000 hrs.	38,000 hrs. on 30% duty cycle

N/A—Not applicable   INA—Information not available

Table Continues →

■ Tape Libraries

Manufacturer	Hewlett-Packard Company	Hewlett-Packard
Redundant Components	N/A	None
Bundled Software	N/A	None
Power Requirements	200 watts typical/260 watts maximum	100–240 V, 0.6A max, 50–60 Hz
Enclosure	36"H x 34"W x 19"D	5.3"H x 6.5"W x 10.6"D
Comments	Fully automated. Industry-leading data availability. Patented online drive replacement. Maintenance-free library system	Configurable six cartridge tape autoloader that provides automated data protection for a broad range of network configurations
Warranty	1 year	2 year express exchange
Price	$61,365 U.S. List	$3,510

Manufacturer	Hewlett-Packard Company	IBM
Model	HP Advanced DLT Tape Library 4/48	Magstar MP
OS/NOS Compatible	HP-UX 10.0	AS/400, AIX—native drivers, most Unix and PC NOS—add-on drives
Drive/Media Types	DLT4000/Type IIIXT and Type IV	Metal Particle
Drives per Library	4	1–2
Tapes per Library	48	20
Magazine Capacity	N/A	10/2
Library Capacity	960GB native/1.9TB compressed	100GB
I/O Interface	One SCSI-2	2 SCSI-2
Sustained/Peak Data Transfer Rate	90MB/min.	INA
Disk Swap Time		8 secs.
	INA	
RELIABILITY		
MCBF	1,000,000	INA
MTBF	Drive: 80,000 hrs. Library: 100,000 hrs.	INA
Redundant Components	N/A	INA
Bundled Software	N/A	Compatible with many top brands
Power Requirements	200W typical/260W maximum	100 to 200VAC
Enclosure	36"H x 34"W x 19"D	8.5"H x 19"W x 30.4"D Rackmountable
Comments	Fully automated. Industry-leading data availability. Patented online drive replacement. Maintenance-free library system.	First in a family of libraries extending up to hundreds of terabytes
Warranty	1 year	3 year
Price	$74,015 U.S. List	Under $15,000

Manufacturer	MDI	Media Logic ADL
Model	SCSI Express DAT Changer	SLA8-base and SLA8-plus
OS/NOS Compatible	Netware	Software/operating systems dependent (Unix, Novell, Windows NT)
Drive/Media Types	4mm DAT	8mm
Drives per Library	1	1 to 6

N/A—Not applicable   INA—Information not available

Tape Libraries ■

Manufacturer	MDI	Media Logic ADL
Tapes per Library	1–6	1–52 tape cartridges in removable magazine
Magazine Capacity	6	14, 28, and 52 cartridge-removable magazines
Library Capacity	48GB	98GB–3.4TB
I/O Interface	SCSI-2	2 SCSI-2 buses for library, 1 additional SCSI bus for MixedMedia Interchange Drawer
Sustained/Peak Data Transfer Rate	7.5MB/sec.	500Kps–18MB/sec.
Disk Swap Time	INA	2 secs. (nominal)
RELIABILITY		
MCBF	100,000	300,000+ for independent drive loading mechanism 500,000+ for DataPak (magazine)
MTBF	40,000	INA
Redundant Components	None	Hot-swap drives and loader mechanism Independent drive loading mechanisms
Bundled Software	LAN Librarian	Optional
Power Requirements	14 watts	350 watts maximum
Enclosure	139mmH x 198mmW x 356mmD	8.75"H x 17"W x 21.75"D
Comments		The SLA product line features unlimited expansion capability, an innovative data handling architecture and integrated MixMedia data interchange. Intelligent features such as drive hot swapping and a program-mable LCD touch screen interface round out the SLA's unique architecture.
Warranty	1 year	1 year
Price	$3,595	$7,470–$27,230

Manufacturer	Media Logic ADL	MicroNet Technology
Model	SLA4-base and SLA4-plus	Autoloader JB-DAT 48-6
OS/NOS Compatible	Software/operating systems dependent (Unix, Novell, Windows NT)	Windows 95, Windows 3.1, Windows NT, Mac, Novell 3X and 4X
Drive/Media Types	4mm DAT	4mm
Drives per Library	1 to 6	1
Tapes per Library	1–65 tape cartridges in removable magazine	6
Magazine Capacity	18, 36, and 65 cartridge-removable magazines	6
Library Capacity	72GB–1.6TB	48
I/O Interface	2 SCSI-2 buses for library, 1 additional SCSI bus for MixedMedia Interchange Drawer	SCSI-2
Sustained/Peak Data Transfer Rate	500Kps– 18MB/sec.	30Mbps
Disk Swap Time	2 secs. (nominal)	INA
RELIABILITY		
MCBF	300,000+ for independent drive loading mechanism 500,000+ for DataPak (magazine)	INA
MTBF	INA	80,000
Redundant Components	Hot-swap drives and loader mechanism Independent drive loading mechanisms	None
Bundled Software	Optional	Arcada-PC Retrospect-Mac
Power Requirements	350 watts maximum	INA
Enclosure	8.75"H x 17"W x 21.75"D	4.5" x 5" x 9.5" 5" x 7.5" x 11.9"

N/A—Not applicable   INA—Information not available

Table Continues →

■ Tape Libraries

Manufacturer	**Media Logic ADL**	**MicroNet Technology**
Comments	The SLA product line features unlimited expansion capability, an innovative data handling architecture and integrated MixMedia data interchange. Intelligent features such as drive hot swapping and a programmable LCD touch screen interface round out the SLA's unique architecture.	The system supports DDS 2 compressed and standard DDS formats. Average file access time is 30 secs.
Warranty	1 year	2 years
Price	$7,365–$25,785	$1,665

Manufacturer	**MTI**	**NCE Storage Solutions/Emerald Systems**
Model	1425	Auto Loader
OS/NOS Compatible	Most Unix, Windows NT, VMS	NetWare, Windows, Windows NT, OS/2
Drive/Media Types	8mm	DLT Autoloader
Drives per Library	1 or 2	1
Tapes per Library	11	N/A
Magazine Capacity	10	5–7 cartridges
Library Capacity	154GB compressed	200- and 280GB
I/O Interface	Up to 3 SCSI-2 or DSSI	SCSI-1, SCSI-2
Sustained/Peak Data Transfer Rate	30–60MB/min.	90MB/sec.
Disk Swap Time	<10 secs.	68 secs.
RELIABILITY		
MCBF	200,000	INA
MTBF	80,000	400,000–500,000
Redundant Components	N/A	None
Bundled Software	N/A	None
Power Requirements	49 watts	82 watts typical/113 max.
Enclosure	22"H x 9.5"W x 21.4"D	External 11.8" x 16.3" x 10.5"
Comments	Optional barcode reader. Rack mount or pedestal. Closed loop serve system for improved reliability.	Random or sequential access. For high-capacity, data backup applications. Cross shipments.
Warranty	1 year	1 year
Price	Contact vendor	$13,496–$16,695

Manufacturer	**Overland Data**	**Overland Data**
Model	Library Xpress LXB	Tape Xpress
OS/NOS Compatible	Windows NT, IBM, AIX, SCO, Solaris, Mac OS, Sun OS, HP-UX	Windows NT, IBM, AIX, SCO, Solaris, Sun OS, HP-UX
Drive/Media Types	1/2"	1/2"
Drives per Library	1–2	1
Tapes per Library	10	60
Magazine Capacity	10 cartridges	60 cartridges
Library Capacity	200GB	144GB + compressed
I/O Interface	1 SCSI-2	1 fast/wide SCSI-2
Sustained/Peak Data Transfer Rate	5–10MB/sec.	3MB/sec. uncompressed
Disk Swap Time	INA	INA

N/A—Not applicable   INA—Information not available

Tape Libraries ■

Manufacturer	Overland Data	Overland Data
RELIABILITY		
MCBF	500,000	150,000
MTBF	10,000–30,000	35,000
Redundant Components	Hot-swap drives	INA
Bundled Software	Optional	Optional
Power Requirements	25 watts	150 watts normal
Enclosure	8"H x 19"W x 23"D (desktop)	52.3"H x 17.8"W x 27.8"D
Comments	Plug-and-play modular design for scaling up capacities/performance	Provides data backup and interchange users with a maximum data storage capacity; medium-size unit at a very low cost.
Warranty	2 year warranty	2 year warranty
Price	$10,995	$28,900

Manufacturer	Qualstar	Qualstar
Model	TLS-2000 Series	TLS-4000 Series
OS/NOS Compatible	Most Unix, NetWare, DOS, OS/2, and Windows NT	Most Unix, NetWare, Windows NT, DOS, OS/2
Drive/Media Types	4mm DAT	8mm, Sony SDX, 8mm Mammoth
Drives per Library	1–4	1–6
Tapes per Library	18–144	10–120
Magazine Capacity	18	10
Library Capacity	72GB–3.5TB	70G –6TB
I/O Interface	2–3 SCSI-2	2–4/SCSI-2
Sustained/Peak Data Transfer Rate Disk Swap Time	9.6 MB/sec. <8 secs.	36 MB/sec. <8 secs.
RELIABILITY		
MCBF	750,000	750,000
MTBF	60,000	60,000
Redundant Components	Fans	Fans
Bundled Software	N/A	Optional
Power Requirements	<280 watts peak	<300 watts
Enclosure	Various	Various/8 models
Comments	4mm tape libraries; 72GB to 1.2TB. Six models. 1–4 drives for concurrent read/write. I/O Port in all models; barcode supported. HP, Sony, Seagate drives. Upgrade to DDS-3. Self-aligning and auto-calibrating; no electrical or mechanical adjustments.	8mm tape libraries; 70 GB to 6 TB. Eight Models. 1-6 drives for concurrent read/write. 36 MB/sec.. I/O Port in all models; barcode supported. Sony SDX or Exabyte drives, including Mammoth, supported. Self-aligning and auto-calibrating; no electrical or mechanical adjustments.
Warranty	2 year	2 year
Price	$8000–$40,000	$8500–$50,000

Manufacturer	Quantum	Seagate Technology
Model	DLT 2500 XT	4586 NP DAT Autoloader
OS/NOS Compatible	OS/NOS compatible	Windows, Windows NT, DOS, SCO Unix, Apple A/UX, NetWare 4.X and 3.X

N/A—Not applicable   INA—Information not available

Table Continues →

■ Tape Libraries

Manufacturer	Quantum	Seagate Technology
Drive/Media Types	DLT	4mm
Drives per Library	INA	1
Tapes per Library	5	12
Magazine Capacity	5	12
Library Capacity	75/150GB	96
I/O Interface	SCSI-2	SCSI-2
Sustained/Peak Data Transfer Rate	1.25/2.5 MB/sec.	800Kbps (compressed)
Disk Swap Time	INA	INA
RELIABILITY		
MCBF	500,000	INA
MTBF	30,000	125,000
Redundant Components	None	Optional
Bundled Software	None	None
Power Requirements	40 watts typical/100 max.	INA
Enclosure	Tabletop version: 11.8"H x 16.3"W x 10.5"L	3.2"H x 5.7"W x 8"
Comments	The Quantum DLT 2500XT tape mini-library is a five-and-seven-cartridge .5 inch library subsystem designed for high-capacity data storage, back-up, and archiving applications in the computer system market.	Read while write technology, hardware data compression
Warranty	2 year	2 year
Price	$4,995	INA

Manufacturer	Ultera System's Inc.
Model	Striper Series TapeArray
OS/NOS Compatible	All
Drive/Media Types	4mm, 8mm, DLT, 3480, etc.
Drives per Library	2–5
Tapes per Library	5 tape auto loaders
Magazine Capacity	5–10
Library Capacity	Up to 560 GB
I/O Interface	1 SCSI-2
Sustained/Peak Data Transfer Rate	2–220 MB/sec. uncompressed
Disk Swap Time	INA
RELIABILITY	
MCBF	INA
MTBF	INA
Redundant Components	None
Bundled Software	None
Power Requirements	INA
Enclosure	Available in varied chassis
Comments	Tape RAID with up to 5 auto changers for large unattended database backup
Warranty	1 year
Price	$6,995

N/A—Not applicable   INA—Information not available

End ■

Optical Jukeboxes ▇

Manufacturer	DISC Inc.	Eastman Kodak
Model	D245–1, D510–2, D525–1, D1050–2	System 2000
OS/NOS Compatible	Unix, Windows, Windows NT, Netware, and others	MVS, Unix, Windows NT, OS/2, Novell, NFS
Drive Type	5.25 MO	14" WORM
Drives per Jukebox	2–16	1–2
Drive Capacity	2.6GB	7,412GB
Media Slots per Jukebox	1–1,054	25–134
Jukebox Capacity	169–1,370GB	370–1,983GB
Media-Loading Options	Mailbox slots	Mail slot
I/O Interface	SCSI-2	SCSI-2, RS-232
Disk Swap Time (MTBS)	8 secs.	5.8 secs.
Redundant Components	Dual robotics, dual electronics, dual power supply	Dual picker
Bundled Management Software	None	Optional
Power Requirements	100–120VAC, 12A or 200–240VAC, 10A 50/60Hz	3,840 watts
Enclosure Size	3x9 SL: 74.5"H x 37.5"W x 26" 6x9 DS: 74.5"H x 37.5"W x 36" 6x9 SL: 74.5"H x 55"W x 26" 6x9 DS: 74.5"H x 55"W x 36"	72"H x 93"W x 35"
Comments	The DocuStore 5.25" optical jukeboxes hold up to 16 drives and 1,054 optical cartridges	Remote diagnostics <3sec, swap time when fully utilizing dual picker
Warranty	1 year parts	90 day
List Price	INA	INA

Manufacturer	Hewlett-Packard Company	Hewlett-Packard Company
Model	HP SureStore Optical 40fx Jukebox	HP SureStore Optical 80fx Jukebox
OS/NOS Compatible	UNIX, OS/2, Windows NT, NetWare and others via 3rd party independent software vendors	UNIX, OS/2, Windows NT, NetWare and others via 3rd party independent software vendors
Drive Type	5.25-inch Multifunction Magneto-Optical	5.25-inch Multifunction Magneto-Optical
Drives per Jukebox	1 or 2	2
Drive Capacity	2.6	2.6
Media Slots per Jukebox	16	32
Jukebox Capacity	41.6	83.2
Media-Loading Options	Mail slot	Mail slot
I/O Interface	One SCSI-2 single-ended or differential	One SCSI-2 single-ended or differential
Disk Swap Time (MTBS)	12 secs.	10 secs.
Redundant Components	None	Online drive replacement
Bundled Management Software	Optional	Optional
Power Requirements	70W typical/100W maximum	210W—240W typical/250W—275W maximum
Enclosure Size	19.5"H x 8.7"W x 29.5"	36.0"H x 33.9"W 19"

N/A—Not applicable   INA—Information not available

Table Continues →

■ Optical Jukeboxes

Manufacturer	**Hewlett-Packard Company**	**Hewlett-Packard Company**
Comments	The 40fx is the entry-level solution for a world of applications that continue to demand more storage and faster access at a reasonable price.	The Model 80fx is expandable to a Model 160fx or Model 200fx with upgrade kits, installable on-site.
Warranty	1 year	1 year
List Price	$6,995–$7,445 U.S. List	$18,000 U.S. List

Manufacturer	**Hewlett-Packard Company**	**Hewlett-Packard Company**
Model	HP SureStore Optical 160fx Jukebox	HP SureStore Optical 200fx Jukebox
OS/NOS Compatible	UNIX, OS/2, Windows NT, NetWare and others via 3rd party independent software vendors	UNIX, OS/2, Windows NT, NetWare and others via 3rd party independent software vendors
Drive Type	5.25-inch Multifunction Magneto-Optical	5.25-inch Multifunction Magneto-Optical
Drives per Jukebox	4	2
Drive Capacity	2.6	2.6
Media Slots per Jukebox	64	76
Jukebox Capacity	166.4	197.6
Media-Loading Options	Mail slot	Mail slot
I/O Interface	One SCSI-2 single-ended or differential	One SCSI-2 single-ended or differential
Disk Swap Time (MTBS)	10 secs.	10 secs.
Redundant Components	Online drive replacement	Online drive replacement
Bundled Management Software	Optional	Optional
Power Requirements	210W—240W Typical/250W—275W maximum	210W—240W Typical/250W—275W maximum
Enclosure Size	36.0"H x 33.9"W x 19.0"	36.0"H x 33.9"W x 19.0"
Comments	The 160fx, along with the 80fx and 200fx, features a two-disk transport system that improves average disk exchange time and online drive replacement which allows a failed drive to be replaced while the jukebox continues operation.	The 200fx, along with the 80fx and 160fx, features a two-disk transport system that improves average disk exchange time and online drive replacement which allows a failed drive to be replace while the jukebox continues operation.
Warranty	1 year	1 year
List Price	$28,215 U.S. List	$22,025 U.S. List

Manufacturer	**Hewlett-Packard Company**	**Hewlett-Packard Company**
Model	HS SureStore Optical 330fx Jukebox	HS SureStore Optical 600fx Jukebox
OS/NOS Compatible	UNIX, OS/2, Windows NT, NetWare and others via 3rd party independent software vendors	UNIX, OS/2, Windows NT, NetWare and others via 3rd party independent software vendors
Drive Type	5.25-inch Multifunction Magneto-Optical	5.25-inch Multifunction Magneto-Optical
Drives per Jukebox	4 or 6	6, 8, 10 or 12
Drive Capacity	2.6	2.6
Media Slots per Jukebox	128	238
Jukebox Capacity	332.8	618.8GB
Media-Loading Options	Mail slot	Mail slot
I/O Interface	One SCSI-2 single-ended or differential	One SCSI-2 single-ended or differential
Disk Swap Time (MTBS)	10 secs.	10 secs.

N/A—Not applicable   INA—Information not available

Optical Jukeboxes ▪

Manufacturer	Hewlett-Packard Company	Hewlett-Packard Company
Redundant Components	Online drive replacement	Online drive replacement
Bundled Management Software	Optional	Optional
Power Requirements	340W typical/560W maximum	340W typical/560W maximum
Enclosure Size	71.1"H x 34.48"W x 29.2"	71.1"H x 34.48"W x 29.2"
Comments	The 330fx can be upgraded to the Model 600fx with an upgrade kit installable on-site. The jukebox provides immediate access to a warehouse of information, ideal for archival and document imaging applications.	The 600fx provides immediate access to a warehouse of information, ideal for archival and document imaging applications. A two-disk transport system improves average disk exchange time and on-line drive replacement allows a failed drive to be replaced while the jukebox continues operation.
Warranty	1 year	1 year
List Price	$37,500–$43,690 U.S. List	$66,000–$84,570 U.S. List

Manufacturer	Maxoptix	Maxoptix
Model	52XT and MX520	MX552 and MX5104
OS/NOS Compatible	Netware, Windows NT, and popular Unix	Netware, Windows NT, and popular Unix
Drive Type	5.25 MO or WORM	5.25 MO or WORM
Drives per Jukebox	1 or 2	2 2 or 4
Drive Capacity	1.3GB 2.6GB	2.6GB
Media Slots per Jukebox	20	52 104
Jukebox Capacity	26GB 52GB	135GB 270GB
Media-Loading Options	Single picker	2-disk transports
I/O Interface	SCSI-2	SCSI-2
Disk Swap Time (MTBS)	3.25 secs 2.5 secs.	3 secs. 4 secs.
Redundant Components	None	None
Bundled Management Software	Optional	Optional
Power Requirements	110 watts	220 watts
Enclosure Size	18"H x 8.25"W x 26" 23"H x 10.5"W x 23.6"	39"H x 14"W x 28.5" 40.5"H x 32"W x 28.5"
Comments	Maximum capacity of 52GB ISO standard compliant, backwards compatible with industry standard 650MB and 1.3GB media.	ISO standard compliant, backwards compatible with industry standard 650MB and 1.3GB media.
Warranty	1 year	1 year
List Price	$5,995	$17,200/ $20,995

N/A—Not applicable   INA—Information not available

Table Continues →

■ Optical Jukeboxes

Manufacturer	Maxoptix	MDI
Model	MX5156 MX5258	SCSI Express
OS/NOS Compatible	Netware, Windows NT, and popular Unix	Netware, DOS, OS/2
Drive Type	5.25 MO or WORM	5.25 MO, multifunctional
Drives per Jukebox	6	1–6
Drive Capacity	2.6GB	2.6GB
Media Slots per Jukebox	156 258	16–238
Jukebox Capacity	450GB 670GB	41–618GB
Media-Loading Options	2 disk transport	Mail slot
I/O Interface	SCSI-2	SCSI-2
Disk Swap Time (MTBS)	4 secs.	8.5 secs.
Redundant Components	None	None
Bundled Management Software	Optional	SCSI Express, EZ Express (HSM software)
Power Requirements	220 watts	100–560 watts max.
Enclosure Size	40.5"H x 32"W x 28.5" 58.25"H x 32"W x 28.5"	19.5"H x 8.7"W x 29.5"
Comments	ISO standard compliant, backwards compatible with industry standard 650MB and 1.3GB media	
Warranty	1 year	1 year
List Price	$44,500/ $60,995	$6,995–$84,570

N/A—Not applicable   INA—Information not available

End ■

Storage Hardware—RAID and Mirrored ■

Manufacturer	AIWA America, Inc.	AIWA
Model	Microarray 2000	Lightening
OS/NOS Compatible	OS dependent	OS independent
Number of Drive Bays	5	6
Number of Drives Installed	3–5	3–6
Drive Capacity	524MB	1/2/4GB
Total Capacity	1–2GB	2–20GB
I/O Interface	SCSI-2, single-ended termination with differential option	Dual SCSI-2
Cache	2MB fault tolerant fast store with error correcting code	8–128 fault tolerant FastStore with error-correcting code
I/O PER SECOND		INA
Sustained	10MB/sec. max	20MB/sec. channel
Burst	INA	40MB/sec. maximum
Hot-Swap Drives	Yes	Yes
Redundant Components	Hot swap drives	Hot-swap hard drives, redundant and power supplies
RAID Controller	Single	Single or dual
RAID Level Supported	3 and 5	3 and 5
Enclosure	3.2"H x 5.75"W x 8"D	8"H x 13.7"W x 18"D
Comments	Fits into an extended 5.25" drive bay	Highspeed RAID class hardware and OS independent
Warranty	5 year	5 year
List Price	$6,400–$8,500	$9,995–$22,800

Manufacturer	AIWA	Amdahl Corporation
Model	RAIDstack	LVS4500
OS/NOS Compatible	System: NetWare 3.12/4.x, Windows NT, most Unix, OS/2 Monitoring software: Windows 3.1, Windows NT, Windows 95, OS/2	Solaris, HP-UX, AIX, SVR4, Windows NT
Number of Drive Bays	3–8 per stack	1–30
Number of Drives Installed	3–6	5 minimum
Drive Capacity	1/2/4/8GB	4.2GB
Total Capacity	2–135GB per stack	20GB to 129GB
I/O Interface	Dual SCSI-2	Two Ultra SCSI channels/LSM: up to 8 data center cabinet
Cache	8–128 ECC cache	64–288MB multi purpose cache
I/O PER SECOND	132MB/sec.	Per Ultra SCSI channel
Sustained		36MB/sec
Burst	INA	40MB/sec
Hot-Swap Drives	Yes	Yes
Redundant Components	Hot-swap hard drives, power supplies, and fans	Hot-swap drives, controllers, power supplies, fans, and power sources
RAID Controller	Single or dual	Dual active/active controllers
RAID Level Supported	0/1/3/5/10/50	0, 1, 0/1, 3, 5 for all supported operating systems

N/A—Not applicable   INA—Information not available

Table Continues →

■ Storage Hardware—RAID and Mirrored

Manufacturer	AIWA	Amdahl Corporation
Enclosure	14.2"H x 6.6"W x 12.2"D	14"H x 25.5"W x 40"D 72"H x 19"W x 30"D
Comments	Expandable using expansion modules containing 2 drives each. Multiple stacks can be daisy-chained to increase captivity.	Ultra SCSI Support front and back end, no single point of failure, full redundancy and hot pluggability, controlled remote storage management
Warranty	5 year	1 year
List Price	$8,300–$22,500	Variable from $49,950 w/20GB to $118,185 w/ 100GB

Manufacturer	Andataco	Andataco
Model	GigaRAID/FT+	ESPR-RS-IS UP RAID Lite
OS/NOS Compatible	Solaris, AIX, HP-UX, IRIX, Windows NT	Unix, IBM-AIX, HP-UX, Sun Solaris, Sun OS, SGI IRIX
Number of Drive Bays	20	8
Number of Drives Installed	Optional	Optional
Drive Capacity	2/4/6/8GB	2/4/9GB
Total Capacity	176GB max.	126GB max.
I/O Interface	Two SCSI-2	2 SCSI-2 68-Pin
Cache	8–64MB	4–64MB
I/O PER SECOND	INA	
Sustained	INA	17MB/sec.
Burst	INA	INA
Hot-Swap Drives	Yes	Yes
Redundant Components	Hot-swap hard drives, power supplies, drive controllers	Hot-swap hard drives, power supplies, fans, drive controllers
RAID Controller	Dual active/active	Single and dual active/passive
RAID Level Supported	0, 1, 0/1, 3, 5	0, 1, 5, 6 (0/1)
Enclosure	14"H x 19"W x 30"D Rack mount, 20 drives	7"H x 19"W x 25.63"D
Comments	ATF and Guardware Software for total failover solution	Hot-swappable power supplies, fans, drives, controllers. Environmental monitoring with visual and audible alarms indicating fan temperature and power supply problems. Completely cableless utilizing SCA technology. RMU Software for remote and local monitoring of RAID unit.
Warranty	3 year	1 year
List Price	$12,000–$15,000	$10,200

Manufacturer	Box Hill	CMD, Clarion, &Ciprico
Model	RAID Box 5300 Turbo	OmniRAID
OS/NOS Compatible	Unix, Windows NT	DOS, NetWare, WinNT, OS/2, SCO Unix, Solaris, AIX, IRIX, HP-UX
Number of Drive Bays	1–7	5–10–20
Number of Drives Installed	2–56	1
Drive Capacity	2/4/9GB	2/4/9GB
Total Capacity	2–504GB	4GB–2TB
I/O Interface	4 SCSI-2	SCSI-2 F/W/D/
Cache	32–256MB read/write back cache	4–512MB

N/A—Not applicable   INA—Information not available

Storage Hardware—RAID and Mirrored ■

Manufacturer	Box Hill	CMD, Clarion, &Ciprico
I/O PER SECOND		
Sustained	60MB/sec.	17.8MB SCSI
Burst	INA	200MB
Hot-Swap Drives	Yes	Yes
Redundant Components	Hard drives, power supplies, fans, drive controllers	Hot/warm-swap drives, power supplies, controllers
RAID Controller	Single or dual with active/standby failover	Single or dual with active or passive failover
RAID Level Supported	5/4/1/0+1	0, 1, 3, 4, 5
Enclosure	FH: 4.2"H x 10"W x 14" HH: 2.1"H x 10"W x 14"	17"H x 6.97"W x 20.4"D
Comments	60MB/sec. aggregate transfer rate, automatic failover configurations, hot-swappable and modular, available with UPS (uninterrupted power supply)	High availability, dual port options, warning and failure alarms, SCSI, Ultra SCSI and filter channel
Warranty	1 year	4 year
List Price	$1,000–$100,000	INA

Manufacturer	Digital Equipment Corp.	Digital Equipment Corp.
Model	Storage Works RAID Array 210	Storage Works RAID Array 230
OS/NOS Compatible	Novell NetWare, Microsoft Windows NT	Novell NetWare, Microsoft Windows NT, Digital Unix
Number of Drive Bays	7–21	7–21
Number of Drives Installed	3 (minimum)	3 (minimum)
Drive Capacity	1.05/3.1/4.3GB	1.05/2.1/4.3GB
Total Capacity	3–90GB	3–90GB
I/O Interface	1 or 3 channel EISA to SCSI-2	1 or 3 channel PCI—SCSI-2
Cache	4–32MB	4MB—32 M 4MB standard
I/O PER SECOND		
Sustained	INA	INA
Burst	INA	Up to 17.8MB per second
Hot-Swap Drives	Yes	Yes
Redundant Components	Hot-swap hard drives, power supplies, and fan modules	Hot-swap hard drives, power supplies, fan module, battery backup for memory cache option
RAID Controller	EISA to SCSI-2 Back plane controller	PCI to SCSI-2, back plane controller
RAID Level Supported	0, 1, 0/1, 5	0, 1, 0/1, 5
Enclosure	22.2"H x 8.2"W x 17"D	22.2"H x 8.2"W x 17"D
Comments	Offers a hardware based, high availability (fault resilient) storage array for EISA based PC servers.	Offers a hardware based, high availability (fault resilient) storage array for PCI based PC servers
Warranty	5 year on drives; 3 years on controller and packaging	5 years on drives; 3 years on controller and packaging
List Price	Starting at $5,318	Starting at $6,335

Manufacturer	Digital Equipment Corp.	Digital Equipment Corp.
Model	Storage Works RAID Array 310	Storage Works RAID Array 410
OS/NOS Compatible	Sun Solaris, Digital Unix, Microsoft Windows NT, Novell NetWare, HP-UX	Sun Solaris, Sun OS, HP-UX, IBM AIX, Digital Unix, Novell NetWare, Microsoft Windows NT
Number of Drive Bays	7–14	24

N/A—Not applicable   INA—Information not available

Table Continues →

■ Storage Hardware—RAID and Mirrored

Manufacturer	Digital Equipment Corp.	Digital Equipment Corp.
Number of Drives Installed	Optional	1
Drive Capacity	1.05./2.1/4.3GB	2.1/4.3GB
Total Capacity	3–60GB	2.1/10.3GB
I/O Interface	2 channel SCSI-2	6 channel SCSI-2
Cache	16MB read/write-back standard	3.2MB read and write-back cache
I/O PER SECOND		
Sustained	INA	INA
Burst	Up to 20MB per second	Up to 20MB per second
Hot-Swap Drives	Yes	Yes
Redundant Components	Hot-swap hard drives, power supplies, fan modules	Hot-swap hard drives, power supplies, fan modules, drive controllers
RAID Controller	Single	Single or dual with active/stand-by failover
RAID Level Supported	0, 1, 0/1, Adaptive 3/5	0, 1, 0/1, Adaptive 3/5
Enclosure	21.4"H x 9.6"W x 20"D	33"H x 18.75"W x 19"D
Comments	Storage Works' entry-level stand-alone RAID subsystem offers exceptional performance and ensures high availability.	The RA410's advanced availability and reliability features match its unbeatable performance.
Warranty	5 years on drives; 3 years on controller and packaging	5 years on hard drives; 3 years on controller and packaging
List Price	Starting at $9,498	Starting at $20,613

Manufacturer	Diverse Logic INC. (DLI)	Diverse Logic INC. (DLI)
Model	Windjammer-S	Ultra-Windjammer-S
OS/NOS Compatible	Windows, Windows 95, Windows NT, OS2, DOS, Novell, Unix, ADSM, and open VMS	Windows, Windows 95, Windows NT, OS2, DOS, Novell, Unix, ADSM, and open VMS
Number of Drive Bays	2–14	2–30
Number of Drives Installed	2–14	2–30
Drive Capacity	2/4/8GB	2/4/8GB
Total Capacity	4–112GB	4–240GB
I/O Interface	3 SCSI-2 fast/ wide	3 40MB/sec. 16-bit Ultra SCSI
Cache	Up to 16MB	N/AN/A
I/O PER SECOND		
Sustained	14MB/sec.	33MB/sec.
Burst	20MB/sec.	40MB/sec.
Hot-Swap Drives	Yes	Yes
Redundant Components	Hard disks	Hard disks
RAID Controller	Single	Single
RAID Level Supported	0 and 1 in all software environments	0 and 1 in all software environments
Enclosure	1.65"H x 5.75"W x 9.58"	1.65"H x 5.75"W x 8"
Comments	Hot-swaps and global hot-swap, no write penalties, LCD display, on-board setup and diagnostics	Hot-swaps and global hot-swap, no write penalties, LCD display, on-board setup and diagnostics, optional differential SCSI interface
Warranty	1 year	1 year
List Price	$1, 995	$2,185

N/A—Not applicable   INA—Information not available

Storage Hardware—RAID and Mirrored ■

Manufacturer	DPT	DPT
Model	SmartRAID IV #PM3334UW	SmartRAID IV #PM3332UW
OS/NOS Compatible	Novell, Windows (3.1x, 95, NT), Vines, SCO Open, Unix, NeXT NEXTSTEP, et al	Novell, Windows (3.1x, 95, NT), Vines, SCO Open, Unix, NeXT NEXTSTEP, et al
Number of Drive Bays	9	9
Number of Drives Installed	Optional	Optional
Drive Capacity	2.1–4.3GB	2.1–4.3GB
Total Capacity	30.1GB: 1 cabinet (RAID 0), max. 73.1GB: 3 cabinets (RAID 5)	30.1GB: 1 cabinet (RAID 0), max. 73.1GB: 3 cabinets (RAID 5)
I/O Interface	Up to SCSI-3 backward compatible	Up to SCSI-3 backward compatible
Cache	Up to 64MB	Up to 64MB
I/O PER SECOND		
Sustained	25MB/sec.	25MB/sec.
Burst	40MB/sec.	40MB/sec.
Hot-Swap Drives	Yes	Yes
Redundant Components	2 modular, hot-swappable power supply/fan units	Hard Disks
RAID Controller	PCI-Ultra/Wide	EISA-Ultra/Wide
RAID Level Supported	0/1/5	0/1/5
Enclosure	21.4"H x 9.6"W x 20.6"	21.4"H x 9.6"W x 20.6"
Comments	Multi-channel, scalable architecture. Scatter/gather, Flash ROM, SCSI device discovery/ inventory, scheduled diagnostics, event notification/ rebuild, drive failure predictions, real-time I/O analysis, tunable cache parameters	Multi-channel, scalable architecture. Scatter/gather, Flash ROM, SCSI device discovery/ inventory, scheduled diagnostics, event notification/ rebuild, drive failure predictions, real-time I/O analysis, tunable cache parameters
Warranty	5 year (tower and drives), 3 years (controller)	5 year (tower and drives), 3 years (controller)
List Price	$6,900 (8GB)	$6,900 (8GB)

Manufacturer	DRA	ECCS
Model	R5X and CLX	Synchronix
OS/NOS Compatible	SCSI-based links for most computers	Windows NT, Unix
Number of Drive Bays	10 internal 38 external	10–30
Number of Drives Installed	3–48	5
Drive Capacity	9GB/21GB	2.1/4.2/9.1GB
Total Capacity	Up to 423	10.5–126GB
I/O Interface	Up to 12 fast/wide SCSI-2, Ultra SCSI	1–2 SCSI-2
Cache	Up to 64MB. Non-volatile write cache 8 or 16MB.	16–224MB configurable, read or write back
I/O PER SECOND		
Sustained	Up to 45MB/sec.	17
Burst	INA	20
Hot-Swap Drives	Yes	Yes
Redundant Components	Hot-swap drives and power supplies (n+1), one controller per drive, multiple hosts, automatic switchover to hot standby.	Hot-swap drives, power, supplies, fan assemblies, global hot save disks
RAID Controller	Single controller with multiple host ports	Single or dual with active/passive failover

N/A—Not applicable   INA—Information not available

Table Continues →

■ Storage Hardware—RAID and Mirrored

Manufacturer	DRA	ECCS
RAID Level Supported	RAID 7	0/1/3/5/10, and non-RAID
Enclosure	14"H x 19"W x 28.5"	INA
Comments	Auto switchover to hot standby disk in event of drive or controller failure. Faster than single disk speed for large or small reads and writes. Performance improves with size. "Back Door Backup™" for high-speed backup of 12MB/sec without host processing.	
Warranty	90 day	3 year
List Price	INA	INA

Manufacturer	Eclipse	Hewlett Packard
Model	Mariner 2	XLR1200 Disk Array w/AutoRaid
OS/NOS Compatible	OS/NOS independent	HP-UX, Windows NT
Number of Drive Bays	6–42	12 one-inch or 6 1.6-inch bays/enclosure
Number of Drives Installed	2–35	Up to 12
Drive Capacity	2/4/8GB	Up to 36GB with 9GB drives
Total Capacity	8–300GB	4/2/9GB drives
I/O Interface	16bit fast/wide differential SCSI-2	SCSI-2 (Fast/wide and Diff.)
Cache	None	16–24MB
I/O PER SECOND		
Sustained	16.7MB/sec	INA
Burst	20 MB/sec	20MB/sec.
Hot-Swap Drives	Yes	Yes
Redundant Components	Drives, Power supplies, array controllers, and fans	R410 5 or mirroring, redundant fans, power supplies, controller w/mirrored cache and redundant battery backup
RAID Controller	Single or dual with auto failover.	Dual, active standby
RAID Level Supported	0/1/3/4/5, and all combinations thereof.	0–5 auto configuring
Enclosure	7"H x 16"W x 16.7"	18"H x 17.8"W x 12.5"D
Comments	GUI configuration and management using serial interface standard, optionally SNMP Netware management via LAN/WAN	AutoRAID offers users ease of implementation through Dynamic Data Migration
Warranty	2 year	Available through OEMS and HP CSO
List Price	$9,995	INA

Manufacturer	MTI Technology	MTI Technology
Model	8300	9200
OS/NOS Compatible	Windows NT	HP-UX, SUNOX, Dec Unix, Solaris, SGI IRIX, IBM AIX, Windows NT
Number of Drive Bays	8	8
Number of Drives Installed	2–8	2–8
Drive Capacity	2.1/4.29GB	2.1/4.29GB
Total Capacity	4.2–34.3 GB	4.2–34.3 GB
I/O Interface	2 SCSI-3	1 SCSI-3

N/A—Not applicable   INA—Information not available

Storage Hardware—RAID and Mirrored ■

Manufacturer	MTI Technology	MTI Technology
Cache	4MB or 8MB Read/Write-back cache (battery backed)	16MB, 32MB, or 64MB Read/Write-back cache (battery backed)
I/O PER SECOND		
Sustained	18MB/sec.	18MB/sec.
Burst	20MB/sec.	20MB/sec.
Hot-Swap Drives	Yes	Yes
Redundant Components	Hot-swap disk drives and power supplies	Hot-swap disk drives and hot-swap power supplies
RAID Controller	Single	Single
RAID Level Supported	0, 1, 0+1, 5	0, 1, 0+1, 5
Enclosure	Rack mount: 5.25"H x 19"W x 22"D	Rack mount: 22.25"H x 7.5"W x 23"D Tower: 22.5"H x 7.5"W x 23"D
Comments	Data consistency check, write-gathering cache	Data consistency check, write-gathering cache
Warranty	1 year	1 year
List Price	$10,000–$22,500	$11,000–$26,000

Manufacturer	MTI Technology	MTI Technology
Model	9300	9500
OS/NOS Compatible	HP-UX, SunOS, Solaris, Dec Unix, SGI IRIX, IBM AIX, Windows NT	HP-UX, SunOS, Solaris, Dec Unix, SGI IRIX, IBM AIX, Windows NT
Number of Drive Bays	8 or 16	8
Number of Drives Installed	2–16	2–8
Drive Capacity	2.1/4.29/9.1GB	9.1GB
Total Capacity	4.2–145.6GB	18.2–72.8GB
I/O Interface	2 SCSI-3	2 SCSI-3
Cache	16MB, 32MB, or 64MB Read/Write-back cache (battery backed)	16MB, 32MB, or 64MB Read/Write-back cache (battery backed)
I/O PER SECOND		
Sustained	18MB/sec.	18MB/sec.
Burst	20MB/sec.	20MB/sec.
Hot-Swap Drives	Yes	Yes
Redundant Components	Hot-swap controllers, drives, power supplies, and fans	Hot-swap drives, power supplies, and fans
RAID Controller	Dual, with active/passive standby failover	Single
RAID Level Supported	0, 1, 0+1, 5	0, 1, 0+1, 5
Enclosure	Rack mount: 8.75"H(or 14") x 19"W x 22"D	Tower: 22"H x 21.5"W x 18"D
Comments	Data consistency check write-gathering cache	Data consistency check write-gathering cache
Warranty	1 year	1 year
List Price	$14,000–$20,000	$22,000–$42,000

Manufacturer	MicroNet Technology	nSTor Corporation, Inc.
Model	DataDock 7000	nStor CR6
OS/NOS Compatible	Platform Independent, All platforms supported	Novell NetWare, Windows NT, OS/2, SCO Unix
Number of Drive Bays	7	6

N/A—Not applicable   INA—Information not available

Table Continues →

■ Storage Hardware—RAID and Mirrored

Manufacturer	MicroNet Technology	nSTor Corporation, Inc.
Number of Drives Installed	1–7	4–6
Drive Capacity	1–9GB	2GB
Total Capacity	63GB per unit (if daisy chained, can be configured up to 6TB)	8–12GB
I/O Interface	SCSI-3 differential	1, Fast/Wide SCSI-2
Cache	Up to 128MB	8MB upgradable to 32MB—write through or write back optional
I/O PER SECOND		
Sustained	14–20MB/sec.	INA
Burst	40MB/sec.	20MB/sec.
Hot-Swap Drives	Yes	Yes
Redundant Components	Hot-swap hard drives, power supplies, drive controllers, and fans	Hot-swap hard drives, load sharing power supplies, and fans
RAID Controller	Single	Single or dual
RAID Level Supported	0, 1, 3, 5, & 0+1	0, 1, 3, 5
Enclosure	18"H x 8.75"W x 21.5"D	12.5"H x 7.5"W x 12.5"L
Comments	Ideal for users who require flexible, reliable, and high-performance RAID 0/1/3/5 solutions with transfer rates up to 40MB/sec. for mission critical server applications for OPI, video, File, and the Internet. Being platform-independent, is compatible with every current platform.	Includes StorView for Windows software for enterprise-wide management, monitoring and control of RAID devices under Novell NetWare, and Alert Manager software for notification under WinNT
Warranty	3 year	5 year
List Price	Starts at $6,499	Starts at $9,825 MSLP

Manufacturer	nSTor Corporation, Inc.	nSTor Corporation, Inc.
Model	nStor CR2	nStor CR8
OS/NOS Compatible	Novell NetWare, Windows NT, OS/2, SCO Unix	Novell NetWare, Windows NT, OS/2, SCO Unix
Number of Drive Bays	2	8
Number of Drives Installed	1 or 2	3–8
Drive Capacity	2/4ZGB	2–4GB
Total Capacity	2–8GB	16–32GB
I/O Interface	2, Fast/Wide SCSI-2	2, Fast/Wide SCSI-2
Cache	8MB upgradable to 32MB—write through or write back optional	4MB, upgradable to 32MB—write through or write back option
I/O PER SECOND		
Sustained	INA	INA
Burst	20MB/sec.	20MB/sec.
Hot-Swap Drives	Yes	Yes
Redundant Components	Hot-swap hard drives and power supplies, dual cooling fans	Hot-swap hard drives, power supplies and fans
RAID Controller	Single or dual (order separately)	Single or dual (order separately)
RAID Level Supported	0, 1, 3, 5	0, 1, 3, 5
Enclosure	5.35"H x 10.75"W x 11"L	Rack: 7"H x 17.7"W x 23.25"L Tower: 18.7"H x 7"W x 23"L
Comments		Can be configured with either a PCI-based or subsystem based RAID controller. Includes StorView RAID management software.

N/A—Not applicable   INA—Information not available

Storage Hardware—RAID and Mirrored ■

Manufacturer	nSTor Corporation, Inc.	nSTor Corporation, Inc.
Warranty	5 year	5 year
List Price	Starts at $1,995 MSLP	Starts at $7960 MSLP

Manufacturer	Seek Systems, Inc.	SMS Data Products Group
Model	Seek Array S450/5460	S700 and (7) DCR101
OS/NOS Compatible	Most Unix, Windows, Windows NT, DOS, OS/2, Mac, and SCSI-compliant OS	Netware, Windows NT, MS-DOS, Mac, Unix
Number of Drive Bays	Up to 32	7
Number of Drives Installed	Minimum of 2	7
Drive Capacity	1/2/4/9/GB	1 gig removable cartridges gig
Total Capacity	Up to 288GB	7 gig at a time
I/O Interface	SCSI I/II/III compatible	2 SCSI-2 chains
Cache	Up to 128MB	256 read/write
I/O PER SECOND		
Sustained	Up to 18MB/sec.	4.73MB/sec
Burst	Up to 20MB/sec.	10 MB/sec
Hot-Swap Drives	Yes	Yes
Redundant Components	Hot-swap hard drive, power, fans, fail over controller	Power supplies (optional second power supply), fans, hot-swappable drives, and connectivity modules
RAID Controller	Up to dual controller with active-active support	Not supplied
RAID Level Supported	0/3/5 hardware, supports Raid, OS (5450) 0/1/0+1/4/5 hardware on most OS	N/A
Enclosure	40"H x 22"W x 22"D	10.25"W x 20"H x 22" The S700 chassis can be configured as a 7-drive tower, or instantly rackmounted; 2 can be configured as a 14-drivetower.
Comments	Supports multiple LANs, fully fault tolerant, very fast read/write cache	Scalable, modular, and upgradable system with hot-swappable drives, redundant cooling fans and power supplies. (www.sms.com)
Warranty	1 year enclosure 5 year disk	3 year—advanced placement
List Price	$.75 to $2.00/MB	$6,554

Manufacturer	SMS Data Products Group	Storage Computer
Model	S700 and (7) DCG101	Storage Server
OS/NOS Compatible	Netware, Windows NT, MS-DOS, Mac, Unix	All Unix, Windows NT, NOS (Netware, Banyan), OS/400, Unisys, Wang, VMS, PrimeOS, Stratus
Number of Drive Bays	7	48
Number of Drives Installed	7	3–48
Drive Capacity	4.2 gig removable cartridges gig	1/2/4/9/23GB
Total Capacity	29.4 gig at a time	3GB–1.1TB
I/O Interface	2 SCSI-2 chains	Up to 48 internal SCSI; 12 external SCSI
Cache	1,024 read/write	256MB
I/O PER SECOND		
Sustained	INA	INA
Burst	INA	INA
Hot-Swap Drives	Yes	Yes

N/A—Not applicable   INA—Information not available

Table Continues →

◼ Storage Hardware—RAID and Mirrored

Manufacturer	SMS Data Products Group	Storage Computer
Redundant Components	Power supplies (optional second power supply), fans, hot-swappable drives, and connectivity modules	Power, supplies, fans, hot-swap drives
RAID Controller	Not supplied	Single
RAID Level Supported	N/A	7
Enclosure	10.25"W x 20"H x 22" The S700 chassis can be configured as a 7-drive tower, or instantly rackmounted; 2 can be configured as a 14-drivetower.	14"H x 16.5"W x 15.3" 9"H x 28.5"W x 14"
Comments	Scalable, modular, and upgradable system with hot-swappable drives, redundant cooling fans and power supplies. (www.sms.com)	Up to 12 heterogenous host connections, multiple hot standbys, fault tolerance, redundant components
Warranty	3 year—advanced placement	90 day
List Price	$15,612	$26,000+

Manufacturer	Storage Computer	Storage Dimension
Model	Storage SuperServer	SuperFlex 3000 DGR/ SuperFlex 3000 DGR Ultra
OS/NOS Compatible	All Unix, Windows NT, NOS (Netware, Banyan), OS/400, Unisys, Wang, VMS, PrimeOS, Stratus	Netware, Windows NT, Solaris, AIX; Intel- and Unix-based servers
Number of Drive Bays	192	7
Number of Drives Installed	12–192	2–7
Drive Capacity	9/23GB	2.1/4.3/9GB
Total Capacity	136GB4.4TB	4.2–63GB
I/O Interface	Up to 192 internal SCSI; 48 external SCSI	Fast/wide SCSI-2/ Wide Ultra SCSI
Cache	76–1,096MB	4–128MB
I/O PER SECOND		
Sustained	40100MB/sec.	17MB/sec.
Burst	INA	20MB/sec.
Hot-Swap Drives	Yes	Yes
Redundant Components	Hot-swap hard drives, power supplies, fans, and power lines	Hot-swap drives, power supplies, and fans
RAID Controller	Configurations available with dual active controllers with automatic failover.	DGR: RAIDCard bus-based controller DGR Ultra: RAIDCard controller
RAID Level Supported	1/3/5/7	0/ 1/0+1/3/5/30/50
Enclosure	24"H x 36"W x 62" 24"H x 36"W x 78" 48"H x 36"W x 78"	6.88"H x 17.38"W x 19.5" Rackmountable
Comments	Multiple hot standby drives, shared storage services, up to 48 host connections, distributed intelligence, repartitioning of storage area to reallocate storage resources as needed, multi-level mirroring, logical volume spanning.	DGR (Dynamic Growth and Reconfiguration) allows for adding capacity and changing RAID levels online. Dual AC inputs. Multiple hot spare capability. Battery-backed cache. Storage management software available.
Warranty	3 year	5 year (disk drives) 3 year (other components)
List Price	$325,000+	$8,700 (DGR with three 2GB drives) $80,000 (DGR Ultra with 21 9GB Ultra drives)

N/A—Not applicable   INA—Information not available

Storage Hardware—RAID and Mirrored ■

Manufacturer	Storage Dimension	StreamLogic
Model	SuperFlex 4000/ SuperFlex 5000 and 5500	RADION LTA
OS/NOS Compatible	Netware, Windows NT, Solaris, AIX; Intel- and Unix based servers	DOS, SCO Unix and SCO ODT, UnixWare, Netware, Windows NT, OS/2, Banyan Vines
Number of Drive Bays	7	Up to 15
Number of Drives Installed	2–7	Up to 15
Drive Capacity	2.1/4.3/9GB	2.16/4.3GB
Total Capacity	4.2–63GB	Up to 64.5GB
I/O Interface	Fast/wide SCSI-2; differential	SCSI-2
Cache	4–32MB	Up to 64MB
I/O PER SECOND		
Sustained	17MB/sec.	4–7MB/sec.
Burst	20MB/sec.	20MB/sec.
Hot-Swap Drives	Yes	Yes
Redundant Components	Hot-swap drives, power supplies, and fans	Hot-swap hard drives
RAID Controller	RAIDFlex SCSI-SCSI controller; dual, hot-swap controllers with active/standby failover (5000, 5500 only)	Single channel, host-based controller
RAID Level Supported	0/1/0+1/3/5	0/1/5/0+1
Enclosure	6.88"H x 17.38"W x 19.5" Rackmountable	Controller: 12.5" x 4.19" 3-high drive stack: 7.6" x 8.4" x 9.6"
Comments	DGR (Dynamic Growth and Reconfiguration) allows for adding capacity and changing RAID levels online. Dual AC inputs. Multiple hot spare capability. Battery-backed cache. Storage management software available.	Tagged command queuing, active termination, global array manager, standby disk support
Warranty	5 year (disk drives) 3 year (other components)	5 year
List Price	$10,000 (SuperFlex 4000 with 3 2GB drives) $70,000 (SuperFlex 5500 with 14 9GB drives)	$7,680+

Manufacturer	StreamLogic	StreamLogic
Model	RADION SpeedStack	RAIDIONplus
OS/NOS Compatible	Macintosh	DOS, NetWare, Windows, Windows NT, OS/2, Unix, Macintosh
Number of Drive Bays	Up to 15	Up to 28
Number of Drives Installed	Up to 15	Up to 28
Drive Capacity	2.16/4.3GB	2.1/4.3/9.1GB
Total Capacity	Up to 64.5GB	Up to 254.8GB
I/O Interface	SCSI-2	SCSI, SCSI-2 or Ultra SCSI
Cache	Up to 128MB	Up to 128MB
I/O PER SECOND		
Sustained	4–7MB/sec.	4–7MB/sec.
Burst	20MB/sec.	40MB/sec.
Hot-Swap Drives	Yes	Yes
Redundant Components	Hard disks	Hot-swap hard drives
RAID Controller	Trillium software	33MHz

N/A—Not applicable   INA—Information not available

Table Continues →

■ Storage Hardware—RAID and Mirrored

Manufacturer	StreamLogic	StreamLogic
RAID Level Supported	0/ 1	0/1/5
Enclosure	5.4" x 8.4" x 9.6"	3-high drive stack: 10.2" x 8.4" x 9.6"
Comments	Pre-configured for Mac, includes drives, host adapter, striping software, and SneakerNet	Supports dynamic expansion, dial-in/dial-out remote management, adaptive caching
Warranty	5 year	5 year
List Price	$4,720+	$7,490+

Manufacturer	Symbios Logic Inc.	Symbios Logic Inc.	Ultera Systems, Inc.
Model	Metastor DS/RM-10	Metastor DS/RM-20E	Striper Tape Array
OS/NOS Compatible	DOS, NetWare, Solaris, HP-UX, Windows NT, Unix 5.4	DOS, NetWare, Solaris, HP-UX, Windows NT, Unix 5.4	INA
Number of Drive Bays	10	20	5
Number of Drives Installed	3–10	3–20	5
Drive Capacity	2/4GB	2/4GB	2–5GB
Total Capacity	6–42GB	6–84GB	2–30GB per tape drive
I/O Interface	1 SCSI-2	2 SCSI-2 F/W	8–120GB
Cache	8, 16, 32, 64MB	32, 64, 128MB non-volatile write back cache	1 SCSI-2 wide
I/O PER SECOND			N/A
Sustained	3.200MB/sec.	INA6550/sec.	17MB/sec.
Burst	14MB/sec. transfer rate	40MB/sec. (transfer rate)	20MB/sec.
Hot-Swap Drives	Yes	Yes	No
Redundant Components	Hot-swap drives and power supplies	Drives, controllers, fans, power supplies, all hot	Tape Drives
RAID Controller	Simple	Single or dual active/active or active/standby	Single
RAID Level Supported	0, 1, 3, 5, and 0/1 combined	0, 1, 3, 5, and 0/1 combined	0/1/3
Enclosure	7.5"H x 19.6"W x 21.5"D	22.5"H x 15.2"W x 32"D	Available in multiple chassis
Comments	Desk-side or rackmount configuration	Desk-side or rackmount configuration	The striper controller stripes data across 2 to 4 drives with an optional parity drive providing data security. Mirroring mode allows the duplication of up to 5 identical tapes at the full speed of the drives. Paired mirroring and off-line copy are also available.
Warranty	5 year	5 year	1 year
List Price	$19,409	$32,665	$6,995

N/A—Not applicable   INA—Information not available

End ■

ZIFF-DAVIS PRESS

11 STORAGE MANAGEMENT SOFTWARE

STORAGE MANAGEMENT SOFTWARE IS a family of related applications that manage files, data, and the storage devices on which they are stored. This software category includes applications, utilities, file systems, and other components that enable storage to achieve better performance, accessibility, and protection from data loss. These are both manual and automated processes.

STORAGE MANAGEMENT SOFTWARE

MOST PEOPLE THINK OF backup and restore as the single storage management application they use. But storage management is much more than this and has a more important role in the network. In fact, it's a common mistake not to recognize that network storage is a key component of the network and the number one cause of unplanned network outages.

Network Storage Architecture

To build a network that is resistant to outages, you have to implement a "network storage architecture" using multiple storage management processes. (Refer to the book *Network Storage Architecture*, Strategic Research Corporation, 1995. The Executive Summary is available on the Internet at http://www.sresearch.com/.) The purpose of storage, as a network component, is to create an environment of high performance, continuous access, and protection from data loss. It takes all three elements—which we call "high data accessibility"—to build a highly available network.

This chapter is organized around the concept of network storage architecture (NSA), since it accurately portrays the role of network storage and storage management and gives you a framework within which to evaluate the many storage management products. This architecture ranks the storage management solutions based on how much they contribute to "high data accessibility." At the top of the pyramid are advanced file system products that transparently replicate data, keeping file systems continuously accessible; at the bottom are "shelf" storage processes such as archive. Figure 11.1 presents a graphical view of the elements that comprise the network storage architecture.

Selecting Storage Management Products

Three important rules go with this network storage architecture approach to selecting storage management products for your network and for specific network applications:

- Measure your network downtime, determining the causes of downtime and the risk of business loss (cost of downtime).

- Implement at least two NSA components.

- Always back up.

You don't need to implement all components of the architecture, but you must implement at least two of them or your NSA is incomplete and backup is still required.

Measure Your Network Downtime

First, you do not have to implement all of the components of the architecture. Each application server or file server has a different set of requirements

STORAGE MANAGEMENT SOFTWARE

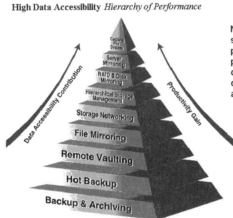

■ **Figure 11.1 The elements of network storage architecture**

High Data Accessibility *Hierarchy of Performance*

Caching File System
Server Mirroring
RAID & Disk Mirroring
Hierarchical Storage Management
Storage Networking
File Mirroring
Remote Vaulting
Hot Backup
Backup & Archiving

Data Accessibility Contribution

Productivity Gain

Network storage is a scalable hierarchy of processes that optimize performance, maintain continuous access to data, and ensure against data loss

based on how critical it is to keep the services of that server available to its users. The number that defines the criticality of a service is called the "cost of downtime." Measure your downtime cost and causes of downtime to determine which processes to implement. (If you don't know how to measure downtime, use the downtime calculator at http://www.sre-search.com.) For example, if you determine that hard-disk related failures are a big contributor to outages, you need a RAID system or at least disk mirroring. (Disk mirroring software is a standard component of the NOS, so it's not covered here.) You also need a robust backup solution to further protect against data loss. You may need other components as well, depending on other data accessibility requirements.

Implement at Least Two NSA Components

The second rule of network storage architecture is that you must implement at least two components of the architecture. Look back at the RAID example. You can spend a lot of money on a RAID system to improve storage integrity and availability, but RAID (or mirroring) alone is inadequate. Remember that disk drives plug into the network "behind" a server. Servers, on average, are unavailable two hours per week because of planned or unplanned outages. So what good does the RAID system do if your company needs access to the data during those two hours?

The solution to this problem is a second element of the network storage architecture called server mirroring. *Server mirroring* creates a "hot

STORAGE MANAGEMENT SOFTWARE

standby" server or a shared storage cluster that allows the standby server to take over when the primary server is unavailable so users still have access to their files and data. Both disk redundancy and server redundancy are required to maintain access to data. Other components of the network can fail as well, potentially requiring other forms of redundancy.

An example is a mail order business that relies on online order processing. If the servers are down or if the site is off line due to a power failure or disaster, the company loses significant business. If a mail order company can't take an order, the customer tends to go to some other competitor rather than come back later. So, what should the company do? They should have local server mirroring as well as a "hot site," which can take over if the local system is unavailable. You can accomplish this with a remote server mirroring process that is kept synchronized in the hot site, or through a remote vaulting process that allows a remote server to be brought online within a few hours, transparently taking over order processing. You have to weigh the cost of protecting the business against the risk of business loss. How many components you deploy is a function of the business requirements of the specific application.

Always Back Up

The third rule is that backup redundancy is still required. No matter which set of processes you put in place, it is foolhardy to stop doing backups. You need this second or third layer of file system redundancy for these key reasons:

- So you can rebuild the file system in case of total loss.

- So you can capture versions of files for historical purposes.

- So you can recover from single file corruption.

Of course, backups don't help if you don't get media off site on a regular basis. An onsite disaster will take the backup media with it, too. To successfully select the appropriate network storage management solutions, you need to use the network storage architecture. Success is defined as maximizing network availability and data accessibility. Otherwise, storage management processes become individual tools you implement to achieve some specific purpose. For example, you might want to set up an optical jukebox to be shared by several applications as near online or archive storage. A media management or library management software package can act as the intermediary between the jukebox and various applications to provide transparent access. In this case, the solution enables you to integrate a piece of hardware into an application, but not to create a robust network architecture. The order of the following product reviews

STORAGE MANAGEMENT SOFTWARE

and feature tables follows the order of the network storage architecture as shown in Figure 11.1.

- Advanced file systems

- Server mirroring and clustering

- Hierarchical storage management (HSM)

- Storage networking

- File mirroring

- Automated remote vaulting

- Network backup and restore

Three additional products—storage resource management, library managers, and CD-ROM networking software—fall at the end of the section because they sit outside the architecture. Other storage management product classes are emerging and will be included in future editions of this guide.

Advanced File Systems

File systems define the way storage is accessed and its physical and logical organization. Each network operating system controls its own, often proprietary, file system. But this native file system is often inadequate for advanced accessibility requirements and several classes of advanced file system products, which mount on top of the native file system have emerged to address these needs. Advanced file systems do everything from improving system performance to managing disk volumes to replicating files to improving data accessibility and protection. Although most of these products are currently UNIX-centric, they are being ported for Windows NT and NetWare. There are three classes of file system products: caching file systems, replicating and journaling file systems, and volume management. Table 11.1 highlights the benefits of these products. The detailed feature tables only cover replicating/journaling and volume management, however, because the sole caching file system product has recently been pulled off the market.

When do you need these different types of file system products? First, caching file systems work best to protect client workstations, replicating data to a local server and eliminating the need for workstation backup except in the case of full system configuration recovery. Caching file systems cache the active data locally at the client, maximizing performance and minimizing network traffic.

STORAGE MANAGEMENT SOFTWARE

■ **Table 11.1   Characteristics of Advanced File Systems**

Function/Benefit	Caching	Replicating/Journaling	Volume Management
Improves Data Protection	X	X	X
Improves Performance	X	X	X
Improves Access to Data	X	X	X
Reduces Network Traffic	X	X	
Synchronizes After Disconnect	X	X	
Fast Server Restore/Rebuild	X	X	
Online Backup System	X	X	
Client HSM	X		
Disk Loading Balancing			X

Replicating and journaling file systems act to improve UNIX file system performance and to journal transactions like a continuous backup. They are used primarily for performance and protection.

Volume management software has a very different role. Its principal function is managing disk performance and load balancing inside large disk arrays. Native file systems only operate on arrays as a single volume. Volume managers get "inside the box," allowing load balancing and performance tuning at a disk drive level.

File system products can work alone or in combination to achieve additional benefits. The following discussion defines the attributes listed in the product comparison tables.

File Access Method and Tracking

Performance	Reliability	Manageability	Scalability	**Flexibility**	Value

If the file system replicates data to multiple locations, it needs to provide the user and any applications with transparent access. It does this by maintaining a database of file locations and system-level processes that generally use the common name space conventions of the native file system. This way access methods don't change. The user just does his or her job and the file system takes over providing access and replication. Some of these file systems also create a global file structure, tying together a broad collection of servers and workstations. In this environment, the access method should not change.

STORAGE MANAGEMENT SOFTWARE

Reconfiguration

Performance   Reliability   **Manageability**   Scalability   Flexibility   Value

When you discover corruption or errors or you need to reconfigure a system, you can use the replicated versions to reconstruct volumes. This means that the replicated version is available to use to recover from an error, provided that the error has not propagated. Look for file systems that have this capability and that can reconfigure the volume dynamically. This activity should have little or no impact on the users.

Backup Capability

Performance   **Reliability**   Manageability   Scalability   Flexibility   Value

You should know two things about backup from an advanced file system: Does it have an impact on normal backup systems and does it offer a new, more efficient way to conduct backup? Make sure any product you select does not have an impact on your backup system. In addition, think hard about the data protection advantages of a journaling file system. In a journal, disk writes are made sequentially and therefore do not overwrite the old data as in native disk file systems. Instead, new data is appended and pointers are shifted to the new records. The old index of pointers is retained and the file system can be scrolled backward by overwriting the pointer index with an older set. This is like an instant restore. Periodically, old pointers are deleted, freeing space on the hard disk.

Security Features

Performance   Reliability   **Manageability**   Scalability   Flexibility   Value

The advanced file system must not open opportunities for security breaches, especially because data is replicated around the network. Many add-on processes like these use the native NOS security methods at a minimum, but others add additional security layers such as kerberos authentication. Either level is generally adequate. If you have broad security concerns, look for add-on security features. Replicated data may be vulnerable.

STORAGE MANAGEMENT SOFTWARE

Scaling Capabilities

Performance   Reliability   **Manageability**   **Scalability**   Flexibility   Value

---

Is this just a local, workgroup solution or can it scale to an enterprise-wide LAN? The issue is not so much product features, but what you need. Being able to combine volumes at a local level may be adequate for most administrative needs.

Server Mirroring and Clustering

Server mirroring is the process of placing redundant file systems on each of two servers and then keeping them synchronized to achieve continuous access to data. Many of the relational database applications refer to server mirroring as "server fault tolerance" or as a "hot-standby" server. An alternative approach to setting up two redundant servers is to externalize the storage and share it between several servers. This way if one server is off line, access to storage is maintained through the alternate. This technique is also called "clustering."

All of these strategies make storage more accessible, but clustering lacks the ability to make server-based processes, such as application serving, continuously available. Table 11.2 lists some of the differences between these various approaches.

The following discussion reviews the attributes listed in the product comparison tables.

Local Server Mirror Configuration

Performance   Reliability   Manageability   **Scalability**   Flexibility   Value

---

The two key issues in system scalability are how many redundant servers are required and whether they can be remote as well as local. Classic Novell SFT-III is a one-to-one, fully fault-tolerant system designed for

---

■ Table 11.2   Server Mirroring Applications

	Server Mirroring	Clustering
Data Continuously Accessible	Yes	Yes
Application Fail Over	Yes	No
Distributed Processing	No	Yes
Storage Networking	Yes	Yes
Shared Storage	No	Yes

STORAGE MANAGEMENT SOFTWARE

mission critical applications requiring continuous operations. (SFT-III can be implemented locally or remotely.) Another less costly approach is to have the standby server supporting many primary servers. This setup is not as resilient, but it is based on the probability that only one server will be down at a time.

Fail Over Methods

Performance	Reliability	Manageability	Scalability	Flexibility	Value

When the primary system is unavailable, the secondary system is supposed to take over providing services to its clients. When this happens automatically and transparently within seconds, the system is called fault tolerant. If manual intervention of some sort is required, the system is called highly available. In a fault-tolerant system, a "heartbeat" monitor allows the standby system to regularly check the pulse of the primary server. If the heartbeat fails, the primary server is considered off line and the standby takes over.

In a highly available system, some failure or error monitor triggers network administration to manually switch over to the standby server. The delay may be in minutes—compared to seconds with a fault-tolerant system. But, depending on the application, the incremental cost may not justify the benefit of fault tolerance.

Operational Modes

Performance	Reliability	Manageability	Scalability	**Flexibility**	Value

Most systems allow administrative control of how tightly the two systems are kept synchronized. When evaluating products, look for flexibility in configuration as well as 100 percent synchronous capabilities, using standard network topologies and protocols. Also consider the scalability of the system. Can it mirror over the distances you need? Consider the advantages of a remote mirror. This becomes an automatic disaster protection system as well. The remote site can take over serving your external clients or act as a hot site in the case of a disaster.

STORAGE MANAGEMENT SOFTWARE

Configuration Management/Error Reporting

Performance	Reliability	**Manageability**	Scalability	Flexibility	Value

You need administrative control. Look for systems that are easy to manage, especially from a centralized console that covers local and remote sites. When errors occur, consider how they are reported and what type of detail is provided. You may be notified of a primary server failure or a mirroring synchronization error. In any case, reporting should be interfaced to your standard network management console. Look for this layer of compatibility.

Hierarchical Storage Management

The role of hierarchical storage management (HSM) is to invisibly manage the millions of files found in a typical network, making other processes more efficient and improving overall productivity. HSM's role is to automate storage management and maximize network performance. It makes significant contributions to high data accessibility.

HSM is highly suited for many environments and applications, especially those with transactional, batch, or aging data. HSM performs three basic functions: It acts as network service, it is integral to client/server applications, and it manages storage for an application server. In the network service role, HSM manages storage on a set of servers and/or workstations. Active files are maintained locally and inactive files are migrated to the back-end store. (The nondisk storage repository—often optical-jukebox- or tape-library-based—is called the *back-end* store or *backing-store*.) The classic applications that use integrated HSM are document imaging and CAD/CAM. When these large file sets are complete or no longer in use, they are immediately moved to the back-end store. Application servers such as database servers, backup or storage servers, and fax-mail servers are good candidates for HSM. All have disk storage pools that fill up with inactive files or records. A directly attached back-end store gives each of these services virtually infinite storage.

The fundamental requirements for implementing HSM are to match the capabilities of the software and the performance of the storage hierarchy to the needs of the application. The measure of performance is transaction rate (I/O rate). Table 11.3 illustrates the needs of a number of different applications. Note that the storage hierarchy under HSM becomes a continuum of performance. Some applications require solid-state drives at the top of their hierarchy to meet the performance requirements.

STORAGE MANAGEMENT SOFTWARE

Others work well with only disk and tape because the performance demands are so low. Table 11.3 also introduces the concept of "Best HSM Level." In Table 11.4, the HSM products are divided into "levels" based on fundamental application needs. An application such as point of sale record keeping has different HSM needs than CAD/CAM. Tables 11.3 and 11.4 are designed to help you purchase a product adequate for your applications. Note that in Table 11.4 these are independent HSM levels. A product does not have to meet these requirements sequentially.

There are over 30 HSM products currently on the market. Make sure to select an experienced and reputable reseller to help with installation and product configuration. The product features tables and the notion of an optimal hierarchy presented in Table 11.3 will help you make the right decisions. The following descriptions of the attributes listed in the features tables should help you understand the differences between these products.

HSM is a strategic product, necessary for managing today's fast growing, mission critical networks. HSM has also been around for over 20 years and all the products are robust. HSM produces many productivity gains and is easy to cost justify. The challenge for the network administrator is simply to begin the evaluation and implementation process. Table 11.4 defines the various levels of hierarchical storage management. Remember that these are functional HSM levels. A product does not have to meet these requirements sequentially.

■ Table 11.3   Optimal HSM Storage Hierarchy

Process	I/O Rate	Best HSM Level	Storage Hierarchy
Video on Demand	>300 I/O per sec.	3,4	SSD or CASD, RAID, tape
Multiuser Database	>100 I/O per sec.	3,4, or 5	SSD or CASD, RAID, slow disk, optical, tape
Fax/E-Mail Server	>50 I/O per sec.	2,3	RAID, optical, tape
Storage Server	>35 I/O per sec.	3,4	RAID, disk, optical, tape
Medical Records	<25 I/O per sec.	3,4	Disk, optical, tape
CAD/CAM	<10 I/O per sec.	3,4	Disk, optical, tape
Student Records	<5 I/O per sec.	1,2	Disk, tape
POS Records	<5 I/O per sec.	1,2	Disk, tape
Manufacturers Product Inspection	<5 I/O per sec.	1,2	Disk, tape

STORAGE MANAGEMENT SOFTWARE

■ Table 11.4 Hierarchical Storage Management Definitions

HSM Level	Functional Parameters	Key Processes
Level 1	Automated file migration with transparent retrieval.	Transparent file migration
Level 2	Real-time, dynamic load balancing of disk space based on multiple predefined thresholds. (Automated transparent space management.) Manages two or more levels of the storage hierarchy (primary and secondary).	Disk threshold balancing Local storage solution
Level 3	Provides for transparent management of three or more levels of the storage hierarchy, not just primary storage. Storage thresholds between different levels in the hierarchy are dynamically balanced and managed. Performs volume management, including media management, job queuing, and device performance optimization. Supports optical and tape devices.	Threshold balancing across multilevel hierarchy Volume management Optical and tape devices
Level 4	Policy management (which includes rules and file classification) and administration at all levels of the hierarchy. Provides for storage management of diverse platforms, extended from file servers to personal workstations and application servers. These services include maintaining the ownership and location of data, thus achieving local transparency.	Policy management Multiplatform distributed solution
Level 5	Object-level management. (Includes structured or nonstructured records and nonfile structures.) Preserves the relationships of objects at all levels in the hierarchy.	Object-centric, not file-centric

> **Media Types and Hierarchies Managed**

Performance   Reliability   Manageability   Scalability   **Flexibility**   Value

A traditional hierarchy includes disk, optical, and tape. But the real issues are how to deploy the product and what you need. Refer to Table 11.3 for suggestions about which media types to use in your hierarchy. If your I/O demands are low, a tape library will be adequate as the back-end store. In the real world, fewer than 2 percent of the files in the back-end repository are ever accessed again, if the rules are set up right. The exception is when you use the back-end store for near-online storage, in a document management application, for instance. Like the number of media types, the hierarchy defines how many layers of storage the HSM process can manage. The requirements are application dependent and should follow the general set of rules outlined in Table 11.3.

STORAGE MANAGEMENT SOFTWARE

Transparent Retrieval and Compatible Backup					
Performance	Reliability	Manageability	Scalability	**Flexibility**	Value

Several retrieval methods are used to affect the appearance of "all files are online at any time." In the PC LAN environments, these are "zero (0)" length files called stub files or phantom files that contain the file name and a pointer to the back-end store. This way, it looks to users as though all their files are online, but the files occupy no online disk space. In UNIX, retrieval methods typically use just the Inode or use symbolic links to a look-up database. All methods work well and there don't seem to be any great differences between them. Here's how they work: When the hidden file is read, it triggers an automatic retrieval from the back-end store. This is why it's crucial to have backup compatibility and compatibility with file system tools such as "Finder," which parse the file system. If every file is retrieved, the system will crash when it runs out of disk space. Look for a solution that is compatible with your backup process or consider purchasing an integrated suite that assures compatibility.

Prestaging					
Performance	Reliability	Manageability	Scalability	Flexibility	Value

One purpose of HSM is to prevent hard-disk volumes from running out of storage space. This process is called file migration. But the common fear is that when an out-of-disk-space event occurs, there will be a huge flurry of network traffic writing data to the repository to free space. Prestaging means that candidate files for migration are selected in advance based on a set of policies such as "these files have not been accessed in more than 90 days." These files are copied to the back-end store during periods of network inactivity. Then when an out-of-disk-space event occurs, no network traffic occurs. The candidate files can be verified if necessary and then the HSM software will delete them, leaving behind an artifact that acts as a pointer to the files' new location in the back-end store.

Level 2 or higher HSM products often use predefined capacity thresholds to prevent out-of-disk-space events from happening. When the disk gets full beyond the upper threshold, prestaged files are deleted until the free capacity is reduced to the lower threshold.

STORAGE MANAGEMENT SOFTWARE

Read-Only Retrieval					
Performance	Reliability	Manageability	Scalability	Flexibility	Value

Typically, when a file is retrieved from the back-end store, it has to reload completely to some local hard disk for a user to access it. In many applications, especially those such as document imaging, the files may be many megabytes in size, causing a significant delay before the file can be used. Then, if the user discovers he or she has the wrong file, that file clogs disk space until migrated again. There is a better way. Read-only retrieval is a preview capability that allows you to read files from the back-end store without committing them to local disk.

Storage Networking

In its simplest form, storage networking is what's called subnetting. A *subnet* is a secondary data path created by adding two network interface cards and cable between two systems that need to share or have greater access to data without loading the primary command and control network. The use of alternate data paths is increasing. New storage networking technologies like clustering, server mirroring, the new serial interface disk drives, and high-speed SCSI extenders and channel connection products are becoming much more the norm in networks where performance and continuous operations are critical.

Some sample implementations will show where these products fit. You build a SCSI cluster between multiple host servers and shared storage by interconnecting the SCSI controller in the disk array and the host adapters on the servers. This is a SCSI network. It takes management software and hardware to implement. SCSI extenders allow you to interconnect shared storage resources, disk tape, or optical over large distances— an example might be a shared tape library or optical jukebox. Channel extenders are similar but are used to interface systems into a mainframe host channel such as FIPS or Escon so the host resources can be shared.

Although storage networking products are largely hardware based, they are covered here because they are integral to building a network storage architecture. Storage networks enable network storage to gain access to dedicated data paths, maximizing data accessibility. You also need

STORAGE MANAGEMENT SOFTWARE

a software component to enable this hardware. These are the key forms of storage networking:

- **Server Mirroring** is used to interconnect two or more servers and keep them synchronized without loading the network backbone. The connection is generally Serial, Ethernet, or FDDI.

- **Clustering** is used to interconnect shared storage between the disk systems and host computers. The connections are usually SCSI or FDDI but will soon be serial using SSA or FC-AL.

- **Serial Devices** such as SSA or FC-AL devices can be interconnected via their serial interfaces, building a storage network.

- **SCSI Extenders** are a hardware interface that allows long-distance SCSI communications. They are often implemented to create device or repository sharing.

- **Channel Extenders** are like SCSI extenders except they interface into mainframe channels at the host end. These are usually FIPS or Escon channels.

The following sections discuss the attributes of storage networking products listed in the product comparison tables.

Network Configurations

Performance	Reliability	Manageability	**Scalability**	**Flexibility**	Value

Most of these products can be implemented within a narrow set of interconnect options. Look for flexibility, distance, compatibility, performance, and fault tolerance when you're making a decision. Serial is the most flexible, allowing various loop configurations and connection into switched fabrics using adapters. SCSI- and Ethernet-based systems are very compatible, but SCSI has limited distance without a SCSI extender. SCSI and serial networks can be very fast, and serial is significantly faster than SCSI, as well as fault tolerant.

Bandwidth

Performance	Reliability	Manageability	Scalability	Flexibility	Value

Bandwidth is the measurement describing performance capability but it is not everything. Performance is also protocol-dependent and limited by other overhead factors. Use this as a gauge but also research specifics on implementation for your particular application and file system requirements.

STORAGE MANAGEMENT SOFTWARE

Reliability Features					
Performance	Reliability	Manageability	Scalability	Flexibility	Value

Some storage networking technologies can be implemented in fault-tolerant configurations. Decide what your requirements are and buy accordingly. It is not the storage network that usually fails, but some adapter or drive at either end. The real reliability question is whether the network has the resilience to route access around a point of failure. Only serial networks can do this.

File Mirroring

File mirroring is a new method of network backup that gives users direct access to their files and file histories. Instead of the traditional tape drive being the primary target for backup files, another disk subsystem acts as the initial repository. This process is a hybrid between server mirroring and backup. While disk and server mirroring are block-level synchronized copies, file mirroring copies at a file level. Its purpose is to make backup transparent and highly available by only capturing files as they change and by keeping versions. A robust file mirroring architecture consists of a hard-disk system that acts as the repository for recent changes and a backup system that captures versions and file histories. When primary server storage is off line, the mirrored volumes are directly accessible, allowing files to be used in place or copied back to the user's workstation. If files are damaged or deleted, historical versions are readily available. No restore is required. Figure 11.2 shows an example.

The available products implement this architecture to varying degrees. Some of the products only create the mirrored copy, and cannot capture historical versions onto a backup. Without versioning, these products are vulnerable. They provide a single online redundant copy that protects from server downtime, but not from file corruption, the number one cause of file restoration.

The following discussion reviews the attributes of file mirroring products.

Configuration					
Performance	Reliability	Manageability	**Scalability**	**Flexibility**	Value

File mirroring systems are designed to support one or more servers. There are two basic configurations available now and a third in development:

- One-to-one, in which there is one mirrored server per primary server protected.

STORAGE MANAGEMENT SOFTWARE

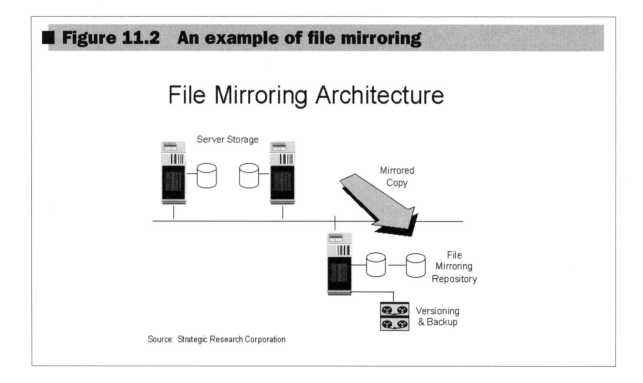

■ **Figure 11.2 An example of file mirroring**

File Mirroring Architecture

Server Storage

Mirrored
Copy

File
Mirroring
Repository

Versioning
& Backup

Source: Strategic Research Corporation

■ Many-to-one, in which many primary servers are protected by one mirroring server.

■ Many-to-many, in which a fault-tolerant configuration spreads the data across many mirroring systems that work in concert. Many-to-many configurations are not yet available.

What is the difference between them? One-to-one systems are tightly coupled and give the best response time, but cost more. Many-to-one are the most economical and are adequate for applications that also use other data protection processes.

Version Retention					
Performance	**Reliability**	Manageability	Scalability	Flexibility	Value

Version retention is a key means of differentiating between products. A backup system such as file mirroring needs to keep versions or the entire system is susceptible to failure in the case of file corruptions. Nonversioning systems have a place, however. They at least keep redundant copies

STORAGE MANAGEMENT SOFTWARE

and perform like server mirroring processes. The disk mirror can recover from outages but that is all. This approach also requires significantly more disk capacity on the mirrored system, especially if it supports many primary servers.

Fail Over Process and File System Access Method

Performance	Reliability	Manageability	Scalability	Flexibility	Value

Unlike server mirroring systems, these systems don't monitor the heartbeat of the primary server and take over file serving and application serving when the primary server is off line. Instead, they are readily accessible, allowing users to continue to access their data on a different server. You can use a network redirector to remap the standby volumes, improving transparency, but this is still not server mirroring.

Automated Remote Vaulting

Automated remote vaulting involves using a backup-like process to transmit data remotely to an alternate site. The objective of remote vaulting is to protect companies or individuals from data loss and to create what is called "business continuance" (in other words, to prevent business operations from being interrupted) when site-level disasters occur.

All businesses must protect themselves from the risk of data loss or the inability to conduct operations due to a disaster. Of the businesses that failed in events like the World Trade Center bombing or the Los Angeles or San Francisco earthquakes, more than 50 percent did so because of their inability to recover their data and get up and running again quickly.

Many companies have discovered that the "remote site" in remote vaulting must be more than 500 miles away to be secure from local disasters. Transmission is usually done via a leased phone line or dial-up service. At the remote site, data may be captured to disk or directly to secondary storage. Usually, a tape library or optical jukebox is used to automate media handling. Through this backup automation, requests for data can be made by the local site and the repository can be used as part of the local data protection system.

Many backup products provide remote vaulting capabilities as well as the automation interfaces. This allows companies to build their own services if they have other sites with which to exchange data. The alternative is to hire a service bureau that specializes in automating remote vaulting. Look for products that transmit only the most critical data. Rarely do you really need to vault application files.

STORAGE MANAGEMENT SOFTWARE

The following discussion reviews the attributes of automated remote vaulting products.

Data Connection					
Performance	Reliability	Manageability	Scalability	Flexibility	**Value**

When you're transmitting data to a remote site, bandwidth is the largest barrier to good performance. Bandwidth is also expensive. Most vaulting products rely on you to purchase the required bandwidth. They just use any available carrier. Internet-based services are the exception. You have to purchase specific products designed to maximize throughput for the Internet.

Remote Backup Method					
Performance	Reliability	**Manageability**	Scalability	**Flexibility**	**Value**

The art to vaulting is reducing the amount of data to be transferred. Compression at the same source yields 2:1 data reduction. Sending incremental backups only and consolidating at the back-end store reduces the load more than 10:1.

Network Backup and Restore

The traditional way of backing up is to make redundant copies of files to tape or optical media to protect against data loss. These media types are used because they are cheaper than hard-disk storage and you can physically move the media off site. Storing data off site assures against disastrous losses. This is a manual method of remote vaulting.

Three major issues confront today's traditional backup and archive methods: How can the process become more reliable, how can it be automated to reduce the labor content and cost, and how can it keep up with the growing capacity? Current network backup processes are not considered very reliable by network administrators. Survey data on PC LANs and UNIX networks continues to indicate that the average number of backup failures is two per week. Seventy to eighty percent of these are caused by open files. You can overcome this problem by using a product like St. Bernard's *Open File Manager,* which gives backup products transparent access to any open file. Regardless of the cause, this is an unacceptably high error rate.

There is a substantial amount of labor involved in media management, administration, scheduling, error handling, and configuration of backups. Studies have determined that the average labor cost of server

STORAGE MANAGEMENT SOFTWARE

backup in distributed networks ranges from $20,000 to $100,000 per year (Strategic Research, *Backup and Archive Profile,* 1996).

You solve the capacity problem by using tape libraries and optical jukeboxes that have large capacities. Libraries and jukeboxes provide automated media handling and queuing across multiple drives, reducing many aspects of backup labor costs.

These three issues (reliability, manual cost, and capacity) are all addressed by backup automation. Reliability is improved because the process runs consistently without human intervention. Labor costs are reduced as a result of automated media management. Capacity growth is covered because of the large backup system capacity.

There are two basic classes of network backup products: network products and enterprise products. Network backup products provide backup services for a single computing environment like PC LAN or UNIX. Enterprise backup products interoperate across computing environments, allowing companies to build centralized backup services for all platforms.

Small companies with few servers commonly place a tape or optical backup system on each server. Backups are often structured as full daily backups for simplicity. In larger sites, backups are more of a shared process with a tape system—often several drives or a small library or jukebox—shared between every three to five servers. Incremental backups of only critical files are more typical. A larger corporation may want to centralize backup on a backup server, requiring an enterprise-class product. A small company may want to keep it simple.

The following discussion reviews the key attributes for backup and restore products:

Centralized Administration

Performance	Reliability	**Manageability**	Scalability	Flexibility	Value

Because most networks use multiple instances of a backup application and multiple drives, it is useful to have a single point of administration. This way you don't have to go to every server and interface with the backup process on each one individually. Through a central administration console, you can establish global policies and schedules, vastly simplifying the management task. If you have more than several systems, consider using a product with this feature.

STORAGE MANAGEMENT SOFTWARE

Open Database Suppport

Performance	Reliability	Manageability	Scalability	**Flexibility**	Value

Relational databases often need to remain on line during backup to maintain user access. Open database backup requires a special interface into each type of database. Many products use SQL Backtrack from DataTool or write their own database agents. This feature is usually sold as an add-on module. Make sure you really need this feature before purchasing the necessary software, and also check that the software supports your databases because each one is unique.

Concurrent and Parallel Recording

Performance	Reliability	Manageability	Scalability	Flexibility	Value

There are two basic ways to maximize backup performance, both of which back up multiple servers to multiple backup devices.

- *Parallel backup* means each server is backing up to a single device, but all are in process at the same time.

- *Concurrent backup,* also called "streaming" or "striping," is a technique of supplying data from multiple sources to a very fast backup device. In network transmission, a single server can rarely feed data fast enough to keep a high-speed backup device fully streaming. The solution is to send data concurrently, from multiple sources. This technique is used to attain backup speeds of greater than 50GB per hour and is essential for backing up very large volumes such as big databases with short backup windows.

Media Management

Performance	Reliability	**Manageability**	Scalability	Flexibility	Value

Media management is a set of software utilities that monitor the number of write passes, media quality, and aging to recommend new media. It is a proactive and automated feature, replacing the system administration time spent in manual media management and error control. Many new generation tape drives report on these media characteristics, but only backup solutions with media management interfaces use the information. If you've experienced tape failures or lost data, this is an essential feature and should be high on your priorities list.

STORAGE MANAGEMENT SOFTWARE

Automatic Archive					
Performance	Reliability	Manageability	**Scalability**	Flexibility	Value

Two automation capabilities are used in the archiving process: the automatic identification of candidate files based on some set of rules, and the use of automated media handling via a tape library or optical jukebox in the archive storage repository. Archive is now an expected feature set for a complete backup solution. It may come bundled or as an add-on.

Network Archiving

Archiving means copying files to some offline storage media and removing them from primary, disk storage. (Archiving is sometimes called "shelf storage.") This frees up disk space and creates long-term storage of valuable data. You archive old files or data that are no longer in use but have some long-term value.

Archiving is usually a manual process but can be automated. Automation has two forms: rules that select candidate files and media handling automation attained from robotics. Automation often allows the archives to remain in a near-online storage repository (library or jukebox) where they can still be accessed.

Most high-end network backup and all enterprise backup products have automated archive capabilities built in as a standard feature. If you are looking for an archive product, look at backup solutions as well since some include archiving features. The products listed in this section are archive solutions only. They may also be part of a product suite.

The following discussion reviews the key attributes of network archiving products.

Library Management					
Performance	Reliability	Manageability	**Scalability**	Flexibility	Value

Library management is the function that maintains the database tracking where the archives are stored. It needs to manage online, offline, and shelf storage media and to have the device drivers to support the major drives and libraries. Check that the software supports your drive technologies. And if you may be moving media to shelf storage, make sure the product can manage media outside the storage devices.

STORAGE MANAGEMENT SOFTWARE

File History Database and Scalability					
Performance	Reliability	Manageability	**Scalability**	Flexibility	Value

It's not important which type of database you use to maintain the backup history unless there are known compatibility issues in your network. However, the size of the database is important if it limits the scalability of your network. Make sure that the products you're considering maintain a secure and scalable history of what is in the archives. Archives can grow rapidly and become unmanageable if you don't have this capability. Also make sure that the database can expunge records that have expired.

File Selection Process					
Performance	Reliability	Manageability	Scalability	**Flexibility**	Value

There are a number of techniques for selecting backup or restore products. Look for systems that allow policy-based selection as well as the normal range of manual approaches.

Storage Resource Management

Storage resource management tools provide administration of various storage resources in the network. These resources are storage components such as disk, tape, or optical. You can manage their availability, capacity loading, performance, connectivity, use, and so on. Storage Resource Managers (SRM) let you administer a network's storage centrally rather than just administering a specific process like backup or archive on each server. SRM is like network management or systems management for storage resources rather than servers or Ethernet.

If you want to improve your network by simplifying manageability, reducing operating costs, and making the environment more resistant to outages, you should use storage resource management. These tools create a central management layer that enables you to manage storage.

The following discussion reviews the key attributes of storage resource management products.

Task Launching					
Performance	Reliability	Manageability	**Scalability**	Flexibility	Value

Task launching is the ability to initiate other applications, such as backup or file migration, based on the occurrence of some threshold event. You set rules/policies in the SRM; when these rules are violated, your predefined

STORAGE MANAGEMENT SOFTWARE

tasks are initiated in response. These tasks range from triggering integrated applications to running predefined command-line scripts. The methodology is less important than the range of applications that the SRM can start and control.

Management Alerts

Performance   Reliability   **Manageability**   Scalability   Flexibility   Value

---

When events or errors occur, the SRM can send alerts to network administration. Alerts are transmitted via SNMP, e-mail, or paging. Look for methods that are consistent and compatible with your other network management consoles.

Removable Media/Library Management Software

To operate devices such as optical jukeboxes or tape libraries, you need a middleware piece of software, generally called a "library manager" and sometimes called a "media manager." This type of software operates between a front-end application like backup or archive and an automated media repository. The library manager intercepts the call for a specific file, looks up the file's location, and issues commands to the jukebox or library manager to mount a specific media and retrieve the requested data. The library manager contains the file history databases, media location database, device drivers for the supported media repositories, and has other management functions. Media management capabilities such as monitoring media aging and error levels are usually built into a library manager.

The following discussion reviews the key attributes of removable media/library management software products.

Online Catalogue and File Tracking

Performance   Reliability   **Manageability**   Scalability   Flexibility   Value

---

Most library managers are middleware and don't have their own administrative interface. Unless you are using a library manager as a stand-alone interface to run a library, this feature is of no use. An online catalog is an online database of file histories or volume set identifications and media locations.

File tracking is the ability of the online catalog to provide complete file versioning and history information along with specific media locations. This feature is crucial for large systems.

STORAGE MANAGEMENT SOFTWARE

Volume Set Compatibility

Performance   Reliability   Manageability   Scalability   **Flexibility**   Value

Files, data, or media-sets that span multiple pieces of media need to be kept together. These are called *volume sets*. Larger libraries or jukeboxes require volume set capability.

Manages Shelf Storage

Performance   Reliability   Manageability   **Scalability**   **Flexibility**   Value

When the repository fills, media is often moved to shelf storage. The librarian must be able to track this media and make requests for specific media if those files are needed again. This feature is especially important if the library supports products like backup or archive where the specific objective of the system is to store media off site. Shelf storage tracking is essential.

Mount Request Queue

Performance   Reliability   Manageability   Scalability   Flexibility   Value

When requests are made for a file, the media manager first determines where the file is stored and then checks whether there is an available drive in which to place the specific media. If multiple requests occur faster than they are filled, a queue forms. Usually, this queue is first in first out (FIFO) unless overridden. A library manager's ability to manage a queue is a good indicator of its scalability.

Media Control Features

Performance   Reliability   Manageability   Scalability   **Flexibility**   Value

Media control defines features such as ownership and specific tape attributes like amount full, amount used, compression information, aging, label protection to prevent improper naming conventions, and other usage information. Any comprehensive and manageable system needs this feature. It is better to buy a set of comprehensive capabilities than to limit yourself on these features.

STORAGE MANAGEMENT SOFTWARE

Media Life Cycle Management

Performance	Reliability	**Manageability**	Scalability	Flexibility	Value

Media life cycle management is the history of the number of times that
the media is recorded and the monitoring of raw error rates to prevent excessive usage and data loss. Life cycle management is a key piece of
media management.

CD-ROM Networking

CD-ROM networking is a class of media drivers and library management
that enables shared CD-ROM access over the network. CD-ROM does
not use a standard disk file system. Consequently, you cannot make CDs
standard network devices without a special device driver. Some of these
interfaces also enable CD recording (CD-R) to CD-R type drives over
the network. These are drives that can record information on special CD
media.

The following discussion reviews the key attributes of CD-ROM networking software products.

CD Recordable Requirements

Performance	**Reliability**	Manageability	Scalability	Flexibility	Value

CD-R drives have a unique recording process that requires a continuous
stream of data. Any interruption ruins the recording, which has to start
over on new media. The recording process requires a dedicated hard disk,
at least 600MB of free space, and a clear channel. Most installations author
on a client, and then transmit the final production across the network to the
dedicated disk volume, which is bus attached to the CD-R drive. If you in-
tend to author on CD-R, you need this type of configuration.

Central Management

Performance	Reliability	**Manageability**	Scalability	Flexibility	Value

What type of central administrative interface is available and what can it
do? If you have many networked CDs or a CD jukebox, you need a single interface. This central administrative interface should enable a single
volume view of the CDs where they appear as directories. It should also
have management tools to administer the CD systems.

Advanced File Systems: Replicating/Journaling

Manufacturer	Digital	Transarc Corporation
Model	Digital Unix	AFS®
Host Server OS	Digital Unix	Solaris, AIX, HP-UX, Digital Unix, IRIX, NT
Client Platforms	Digital UNIX	Solaris, AIX, HP-UX, Windows 3.11, 95, and NT
Server CPU	Alpha workstations and servers	Unix Workstations, Intel
General Description and Benefits	Fast reboot, online maintenance, load balancing, full SMP support	Global file system for joining collections of server and client machines
File Access Method	Digital Unix VFS commands	Standard office applications
File Location Tracking	Fully logged based	File name is independent of the file's location. Automatic tracking databases
Performance Features	INA	Client caching to reduce network load. Callbacks to maintain cache consistency
Reconfiguration	By volumes, no user impact files remain accessible and file names do not change when volumes are moved.	By volumes. No user impact: files remain accessible and file names do not change when volumes are moved.
Backup Compatibility	Compatible with UNIX backup utilities (clump, etc.) and Networker	Backup system for on-line backup (no system downtime)
Security Features	NFS security, access control, support VFS security features	Kerberos authentication with encrypted network transmissions. Access control lists on directories for user and group access.
Availability Features	Always available, online management	Replicates system databases and data
System Management	Central or remote administration	Central administration console
Scaling Capabilities	64-bit architecture, highly scalable	Architecture (cells, volumes) designed to scale, both locally and globally. Excellent performance across wide-area configurations.
Comments	No file size limitations	Supporting infrastructures for high-volume Web servers
Warranty/Service	Standard Digital	Standard contracts
List Price	Starts at $4,200 for utilities (file system bundled with Digital UNIX)	Unavailable

N/A—Not applicable   INA—Information not available

Advanced File Systems: Replicating/Journaling ■

Manufacturer	Transarc Corporation	Veritas
Model	DFS™	Veritas File System (VxFS)
Host Server OS	Solaris, AIX, HP-UX, Digital Unix, IRIX, NT	Channel Product: Solaris 2.4, 2.5, 2.5.1 for SPARC. OEM product on DEC, HP, Novell, Motorola, NCR, NEC, and others
Client Platforms	Solaris, AIX, HP-UX, Windows 3.11, 95, and NT	Same as above
Server CPU	Unix Workstations, Intel	Same as above
General Description and Benefits	Global file system for joining collections of server and client machines	Online backup, online resizing, online defragmentation, extent based allocation, data management API (DMAPI), available on multiple platforms
File Access Method	Standard office applications web browsers	INA
File Location Tracking	File name is independent of the file's location. Automatic tracking databases	INA
Performance Features	Client caching to reduce network load. Callbacks to maintain cache consistency. Log-based physical file system	Extent-based allocation, logging of user data, cache/buffer/allocation management, explicit file alignment
Reconfiguration	By file sets no user impact: files remain accessible and file names do not change when file sets are moved.	Support for greater than 2GB file systems, guaranteed user semantics, Interfaces to VxVM
Backup Compatibility	Backup system for on-line backup (no system downtime)	Compatible with normal backup methods
Security Features	Kerberos authentication with encrypted network transmissions. Access control lists on files and directories for user and group access.	File ownership levels
Availability Features	Replicates system databases and data	Online administration, fast file system recovery, online defragmentation and resizing, online backup, online unmount of failed file systems, panic-free error strategy, sync on close
System Management	Central administration console	GUI and command line
Scaling Capabilities	Architecture (cells, file sets) designed to scale, both locally and globally. Excellent performance across wide-area configurations.	Very scalable, from desktop to Cray
Comments	Supporting infrastructures for high-volume Web sites. Based on DCE standards.	Also sold as VXServerSuite NFS Edition (including VxVM and VxFS) $2,395 (SPARCstation) to $42,395 (Cray)
Warranty/Service	Standard contracts	None
List Price	Unavailable	$1,430 (SPARCstation-5) to $24,930 (Cray)

N/A—Not applicable   INA—Information not available

End ■

Advanced File Systems—Volume Management

	Sun Microsystems/SunSoft	Veritas
Manufacturer	Sun Microsystems/SunSoft	Veritas
Model	Solstice DiskSuite	Veritas Volume Manager (VxVM)
Host Server OS	Solaris 2 (SunOS 4.1.3, 4.1.4) Solaris 2 2.3, 2.4, 2.5)	Channel product: Solaris 2.4, 2.5, 2.5.1 for SPARC. OEM product on DEC, HP, Novell, Motorola, NCR, NEC, and others.
Client Platforms	N/A	Same as above
Server CPU	Sun Solaris SPARC/INTEL	Same as above
General Description and Benefits	Disk array management, data availability, reliability, performance, manageability, reduced administrative costs	Online storage management, mirroring, RAID-5, concatenation, online administration and reconfiguration, hot sparing, performance monitoring, journaling file system
Disk Management and Features	RAID (0,1,5), large file system support, hot spares (online replacement), system monitoring (performance, events to network to management framework)	INA
Reconfiguration	Online partition replacement	Graphical administration interface, dynamic online resizing, spanning of multiple disks, free space pool management for automatic or directed allocation.
Security	Standard Unix securities	Volume wnership
Availability	Replicates system data+dbs. Thru RAID logging UFS for fast system recovery	Online administration, mirroring, RAID-5, hot sparing of disk drives, support for failover (hot-standby) configurations
System Management	Central admin console thru Solaris and thru Solstice domain manager console	GUI and command line
Scaling Capabilities	Multiple instances of admin. interface hundreds to thousands of disks	Very scalable, from desktop to Cray
Comments and Features	Unique "Drag + Drop" metadevice GUI. Mirror design tolerate multiple failures.	Also sold as VXServerSuite NFS Edition (including VxVM and VxFS) $2,395 (SPARCstation) to $42,395 (Cray)
Warranty/Service	90 day or materials/installation. SunServer available if contract purchased	None
List Price	$1,295 and up	$1,430 (SPARCstation-5) to $24,930 (Cray)

N/A—Not applicable   INA—Information not available

Server Mirroring ■

Manufacturer	NonStop Networks, Ltd.	Novell
Model	No*Stop Network-V.4.X	SFT III
Features and Functionality	Data duplicated at point of origin, the client, ensuring no loss of data or any single point of failure.	Mirrored server link card between servers
O/S Compatibility	NetWare 4.1	NetWare 4.11
Server Configuration	486/66 EISA or PC, 16MB RAM	386, 486, 12MB and above
Host Bus	EISA	ISA, EISA, MCA, PCI
Interface	SCSI-2	See above
Protocol	FDDI	IPX
Local Server Mirror Configuration	One-to-one, one-to-many	One-to-one
Remote Server Mirror	Any distance supported at network traffic speed.	2KM, extended via repeaters to 40KM
Failover Method	Fault tolerant	Everything is automatic—client stays connected and apps work with description in event of hardware failure.
Disk Storage	Equal to that requiring mirroring.	2KM, extended via repeaters to 40KM
Protected Servers	Any mix of servers, including SMP and Minis	NetWare 4.11
Software Components	Workstation-based TSR 11K-16K, runs high	License to enable
Operational Modes	Synchronous, semi-synchronous, 100% synchronous remote mirroring, remote mirroring with maximum. I/O lag of 1 per volume.	100% mirrored state
Configuration Management	Servers may be cross-mirrored to maximize throughput, no redundant hardware.	INA
Error Reporting	"Mirror mismatch" reported by file.	Error loss
Comments	Data cannot be lost upon server failure.	INA
Warranty/Service	1 year, free tech support	N/A
List Price	$1,290+ node charges. $365 peer-to-peer.	INA

Manufacturer	Twincom	Vinca Corporation
Model	DualDisk/Network Disk Mirroring	StandbyServer 2.0 for NetWare
Features and Functionality	Mirror up to 16 pairs of disks. After a failure is corrected the "mirror" automatically synchronizes the second disk in the background.	Real-time disk/system mirroring. Auto resynchronization after failures.
O/S Compatibility	All major Unix platforms	NetWare 3x/4x
Server Configuration	INA	Any; must be NetWare capable
Host Bus	INA	EISA, ISA, PCI
Interface	SCSI/IDE	Any
Protocol	TCP/IP	IPX
Local Server Mirror Configuration	INA	One-to-one
Remote Server Mirror	INA	Any distance
Failover Method	Fault tolerant	Fault tolerant—auto failover
High available—manual failover

N/A—Not applicable   INA—Information not available

Table Continues →

■ Server Mirroring

Manufacturer	Twincom	Vinca Corporation
Disk Storage	Identical size	Mirrored partition match between servers
Protected Servers	Major Unix versions	NetWare 3x/4x servers
Software Components	INA	Device driver and NLM-based 5-1,000 user
Operational Modes	Synchronous mirroring	Standard NetWare mirroring across IPX protocol communications cards; WAN link supported
Configuration Management	INA	Duplexed drives across servers, split seek benefit, real-time mirroring at I/O level, read block for WAN environments
Error Reporting	Notifies console continues processing	Use NetWare's console messaging and Vinca error logging on standby machine
Comments	Programs are fully transparent to users and application programs	Additional copy of NetWare not required. No impact to client network. Uses real-time, native disk mirroring.
Warranty/Service	Global tech support	30-day money back guarantee
List Price	$1,495–$5,995	$3,499

Manufacturer	Vinca Corporation	Vinca Corporation
Model	StandbyServer Entry Level for NetWare	StandbyServer Many-to-One for NetWare
Features and Functionality	Real-time disk/system mirroring. Auto resynchronization after failures.	Real-time disk/system mirroring. Auto resynchronization after failures.
O/S Compatibility	NetWare 3x/4x	NetWare 3x/4x
Server Configuration	Any; must be NetWare capable	Any; must be NetWare capable
Host Bus	EISA, ISA, PCI	EISA, ISA, PCI
Interface	Any	Any
Protocol	IPX	IPX
Local Server Mirror Configuration	One-to-one	Many-to-one, one-to-many
Remote Server Mirror	Local	Any distance
Failover Method	Fault tolerant—auto failover High available—manual failover	Fault tolerant—auto failover High available—manual failover
Disk Storage	Mirrored partition match between servers	Total of all protected servers on standby machine
Protected Servers	NetWare 3x/4x servers	NetWare 3x/4x servers
Software Components	Device driver and NLM-based 5-25 user	Device driver and NLM based 5-1,000 user
Operational Modes	Standard NetWare mirroring across IPX protocol communications cards; local only	Standard NetWare mirroring across IPX protocol, communications cards, WAN link supported
Configuration Management	Duplexed drives across servers, split seek benefit, real-time mirroring at I/O level, write throttle for non-dedicated links	Duplexed drives across servers; split seek benefit; real-time mirroring at I/O level; read block for WAN environments
Error Reporting	Use NetWare's console messaging and Vinca error logging on standby machine	Use NetWare's console messaging and Vinca error logging on standby machine
Comments	Additional copy of NetWare not required. No impact to client network. Uses real-time, native disk mirroring.	Additional copy of NetWare not required. No impact to client network. Uses real-time, native disk mirroring.
Warranty/Service	30-day money back guarantee	30-day money back guarantee
List Price	$1,299	$4,999

N/A—Not applicable   INA—Information not available

Server Mirroring ■

Manufacturer	Vinca Corporation	Vinca Corporation
Model	StandbyServer for NT	StandbyServer for OS/2 Warp
Features and Functionality	Real-time disk/system mirroring. User selectable configuration options.	Real-time disk/system mirroring. User selectable configuration options.
O/S Compatibility	NT 3.51 Server+	OS/2 warp, Warp Server
Server Configuration	Intel-based servers running NT 3.51+	Requirements are set by the OS being run
Host Bus	PCI, EISA	ISA, EISA, MCA, PCI
Interface	100Mb Ethernet	100MB Ethernet
Protocol	Proprietary	Proprietary
Local Server Mirror Configuration	One-to-one	One-to-one
Remote Server Mirror	N/A	N/A
Failover Method	Fault tolerant—auto failover High available—manual failover	Fault tolerant—auto failover High available—manual failover
Disk Storage	Mirror partition match between servers	Disk configuration to satisfy disk mirroring requirements of the OS being used.
Protected Servers	Primary server	Any OS/2 Warp, LAN server, or WARP Server
Software Components	Server software, NT services, 1 license per pair of servers	Device drivers and user interface
Operational Modes	Synchronous	Real-time mirroring over 100MB Ethernet
Configuration Management	NT and Vinca administration tools	OS/2 and Vinca administration tools
Error Reporting	NT event logging	Error detecting and reporting through TME 10 NetFinity
Comments	Connects a secondary NT server directly to the primary server. When the main server fails, StandbyServer for NT automatically switches to the secondary machine. Users experience no downtime, and do not need to reattach to the network.	
Warranty/Service	30-day money back gaurantee	30-day money back guarantee
List Price	$3,499	$3,449

■ Server Clustering

Manufacturer	**Digital Equipment Corp.**	**IBM**
Model	Digital Clusters for NT v.1 Da	HA/CMP
O/S Compatibility	Windows NT 3.51, 4.0 Server, WFW 3.11, Windiws 95	AIX
Server Configuration	All Digital Prioris and Alpha Servers, 16MB RAM	Power/PC
Host Bus	PCI	MCA, PCI
Interface	SCSI-2	SCSI-2, serial
Protocol	FDDI, 10BASE-T, 100BASE-T	Ethernet, Token Ring, FDDI, ATM, FCS
Local Server Mirror Configuration	Mirror supported via subsystem RAID	One-to-one, one-to-many
Remote Server Mirror	Not supported	In plan
Failover Method	Automatic and manual failover on per-disk basis	Auto failover multiple ways 2-way—8-way
Disk Storage	Multiple SCSI Buses/max limit of NT storage	To 4TB
Protected Servers	Pairs of cluster members	Any AIX server
Software Components	2 cluster server license/unlimited client	Server software
Operational Modes	Asynchonous, both servers and the subsystem RAID provide mirroring and striping	Synchronous, asynchronous
Features and Functionality	Commodity Hardware, off the shelf SCSI storage, independent disk failover, automatic fail back to pricing, cluster management GUI, script failure, SQL, Oracle and NTFS failover	INA
Configuration Management	GUI administrator, non-disruptive	BSPOC-cluster single point of control, single service image
Error Reporting	NT Event Log, user specified notification user scripting	SNMP
Comments	Cluster alias for transport recomment, client browsing, software only solution, dual heartbeat/SCSI and LAN, can detect disk failures SCSI adapter failures RAID controlling failure, can set independent failover groups and policies, manual load balancing on both center servers	
Warranty/Service	INA	INA
List Price	$995/per server license	$4,000–$20,000

N/A—Not applicable   INA—Information not available

Server Clustering ■

Manufacturer	**Tandem Computers**	**Hewlett Packard**
Model	Cluster Availability Solution (CAS)	MC/Service Guard
O/S Compatibility	Windows NT Server version 4.0	HP-UX 10.0 or later
Server Configuration	Pentium Pro, PCI, dual network	HP 9000 servers
Host Bus	PCI	HP 9000 servers
Interface	SCSI, Ethernet, ServerNet (Q197)	Fast Wide SCSI, Single Ended SCSI,HP-FL
Protocol	TCP/IP	Ethernet, FDDI, Token Ring LANs
Local Server Mirror Configuration	Dual host SCSI, h/w RAID 1, 10, 5, 50	One-to-one, one-to-many
Remote Server Mirror	INA	Campus LAN
Failover Method	Automatic fault detection and failover on server, O/S or application failures	Fault-tolerant, auto failover
Disk Storage	Equal to largest single server	Each node in active-standby may vary
Protected Servers	Any mix of PC servers running	Any max. of up to 8-HP9000 servers
Software Components	Server Software	Each node licenses one copy—HP also offers special implementation tool kits
Operational Modes	Active-standby (one server active), active-active (both servers active), nonidentical or identical node	Active-active or active-standby
Features and Functionality	Active-active Microsoft SQL Server environment with automated failover. Cluster IP addresses with client location transparency over routed or hard-wired networks. User selectable application failover policies. Easy and powerful customization of recovery and health management procedures.	High Availability for mission critical apps: Fast detection of failure, fast restoration of applications, availability during hardware/software maintenance, provides protection beyond single nod failures, workload balancing
Configuration Management	Windows NT GUI. Definition of resource dependence hierarchy for individual application or application pair. Logical disk volume definition and management. Ownership protection of logical volumes.	"Clusterview" works with HP Openview and other management products.
Error Reporting	Windows NT event log	Through HP Open View, problem prediction, detection and resolution
Comments	Redundant network to eliminate false failovers	HP-UX 10.0 or later
Warranty/Service	Standard media defects; optional incidence blocks and professional services	N/A
List Price	$1,995 per server	INA

N/A—Not applicable   INA—Information not available

End ■

■ Hierarchical Storage Management

Manufacturer	**Alphatronix**	**Cheyenne Software**
Model	Inspire Migrator	Cheyenne HSM for Netware
HSM Levels	1,2,4	1, 2
Host Server OS	Solaris 2.4 or higher	Netware 3.1X, 4.1
Client Platforms Supported	Solaris, any Unix NFS	Any client supported by Netware
Manages Storage on Servers and/or Clients	Client and server	Servers only
Media Types Managed	Hard Disk, optical, and tape	Hard disk, read/write, optical, worm, and tape
Hierarchies Managed	Unlimited	Unlimited number of hierarchies, each hierarchy can have up to 3 levels of storage.
Type of Security	Sun Microsystem's Native O/S security	Netware Native Security
Reporting	Yes	Yes
Transparent Retrieval	Yes, works with NFS	Yes
Compatible Backup Application	Inspire backup, any Unix backup	ARCserve 5.01g or greater
Prestaging	Yes	No
Allows Read-Only Access on Retrieve	Yes	No
Comments	Part of integrated suite of storage management products	Uses Novell's Real-time Data Migrator (RTDM)
Warranty/Service	INA	INA
List Price	INA	Base-1 server—$6,995 Add 1–4 servers—$495–$1495

Manufacturer	**CommVault Systems**	**Computer Associates Int'l Inc.**
Model	HSM	CA-Unicenter/OSM (Open Storage Manager)
HSM Levels	1, 2, 3, 4, 5	1, 2
Host Server OS	INA	AIX, Solaris, HP-UX
Client Platforms Supported	INA	Any system with NFS
Manages Storage on Servers and/or Clients	Clients and servers	Clients and servers
Media Types Managed	Hard disk and optical	Hard disk, optical, tape
Hierarchies Managed	3	16
Type of Security	Native Unix security	Integrates with Native Security and CA-Unicenter Security
Reporting	Yes	Yes
Transparent Retrieval	Yes	Yes (U node intercept)
Compatible Backup Application	"ABARS" software	CA-Unicenter
Prestaging	INA	Yes

N/A—Not applicable   INA—Information not available

Hierarchical Storage Management ■

Manufacturer	CommVault Systems	Computer Associates Int'l Inc.
Allows Read-Only Access on Retrieve	No	No—Full access privileges are restored as they were when file was archived
Comments	Provides data on optical indrive file system format. Only un-migrates file if file is modified, no reverse-migration storm.	Media overwrite protection through integration w/CA-Unicenter tape mgmt., multi-level policy-based solution manages infrequently accessed files.
Warranty/Service	INA	INA
List Price	INA	INA

Manufacturer	EMASS	Knozall Systems, Inc.
Model	DataMgr	FileWizard 3
HSM Levels	1, 2, 3, 5	1, 2, 4
Host Server OS	Novell, Windows NT	Netware
Client Platforms Supported	INA	Windows 95
Manages Storage on Servers and/or Clients	Server and Client (Unix)	Server only
Media Types Managed	Hard disk and optical	Anything that can be mounted as a volume
Hierarchies Managed	O/S security	Unlimited
Type of Security	Yes	Netware Native
Reporting	INA	No
Transparent Retrieval	Legato, Smarch, all third party packs	Yes
Compatible Backup Application	Yes	None
Prestaging	Yes	No
Allows Read-Only Access on Retrieve	Yes	No
Comments	Optical or tape drivers at additional costs	Analyzes and provides reports and graphs on duplicate, unused, etc., files.
Warranty/Service	90 day	90-day money back guarantee
List Price	$2000–$5000	$695 first server $495 each additional server

Manufacturer	Legato	LSC, Inc.
Model	STORSUITE	SAM-FS
HSM Levels	3	1, 2 ,3, 4
Host Server OS	Solaris, AIX, HP-UX	Solaris
Client Platforms Supported	Solaris, AIX, HP-UX	Any system with NFS plus others
Manages Storage on Servers and/or Clients	Clients and servers	Server and clients
Media Types Managed	Hard disk and optical	Hard disk, tape, and optical

N/A—Not applicable   INA—Information not available

Table Continues →

■ Hierarchical Storage Management

	Legato	LSC, Inc.
Manufacturer	Legato	LSC, Inc.
Hierarchies Managed	2	Solaris native security
Type Of Security	Native OS Security	Yes
Reporting	Yes	4
Transparent Retrieval	Yes	AXXiON NetBackup, CAM SM-arch, others
Compatible Backup Application	Network	Yes
Prestaging	Yes	Yes
Allows Read-Only Access on Retrieve	No	Yes
Comments		Transportable media. Associative Staging™ checksum direct access.
Warranty/Service	90 day	90 day warranty, software support available
List Price	$25,000	$6,000 and up

	Novell, Inc.	OpenVision Technologies, Inc.
Manufacturer	Novell, Inc.	OpenVision Technologies, Inc.
Model	HCSS	Axxion-HSM
HSM Levels	INA	1, 2, 4
Host Server OS	NetWare 4.x	Sun, HP
Client Platforms Supported	N/A	Sun, HP
Manages Storage on Servers and/or Clients	Servers only	Both
Media Types Managed	Hard disk and magnetic optical	Most devices
Hierarchies Managed	Novell directory services security	8
Type of Security	No	None
Reporting	2	Yes
Transparent Retrieval	Any SMS application	Yes
Compatible Backup Application	No	Axxion-Netbackup
Prestaging	Yes	Yes
Allows Read-Only Access on Retrieve	No	Yes
Comments	Access to space usage and console parameters, utilization thresholds set for migration.	
Warranty/Service	Included with NetWare 4.x	INA
List Price	Included with NetWare 4.x	$20,000 server $150+ client

N/A—Not applicable   INA—Information not available

Hierarchical Storage Management ■

Manufacturer	**PLATINUM Technology, Inc.**	**Software Partners/32, Inc.**
Model	PLATINUM NetArchive	Hierarchy
HSM Levels	1, 2, 3, 4	1, 2, 3
Host Server OS	Sun, HP	VMS, OpenVMS
Client Platforms Supported	HP/UX 9.x and 10.0x, Sun OS 4.1x, Solaris 2.3, 2.4 and 2.5, or any system with NFS	OpenVMS, VAX/Alpha
Manages Storage on Servers and/or Clients	Both	Clients and servers
Media Types Managed	Hard disk, 5.25 magneto optical, and tape (4mm, 8mm. and DLT).	Tape and optical
Hierarchies Managed	Unlimited	3
Type of Security	OS's native as well as built-in enhanced file security.	Native VMS security
Reporting	Yes	Yes
Transparent Retrieval	Yes, stub file is placed at the original file location	From optical or mag disk
Compatible Backup Application	Integrated with NetArchive Backup Agent for enhanced functionality or bypass mode option can be used with any other third party backup product	"Tapesys" software
Prestaging	No	No
Allows Read-Only Access on Retrieve	Yes	Yes
Comments	Heterogeneous operating system support for both client and server. Distributed storage environment provides automatic load balancing and fault tolerant operations.	RAM disk processing, seamless access, automatic archiving, automatic retrieval
Warranty/Service	90-day warranty. Onsite consulting and training also available.	90 day
List Price	Server site license is $2,000 per OS, no client limits.	$1,350 and up

---

N/A—Not applicable   INA—Information not available

E n d ■

■ Storage Network: Extenders

Manufacturer	CNT	Luminex
Model	Channellink	LSX
Key Function	Mixed channel cnterconnects LAN/WAN support	Serves purpose of SCSI expander, allowing 7 SCSI devices to be supported as one host SCSI-ID.
Architecture	SCSI, ESCON, Bus and Tag	SCSI-II, transparent to network/host
OS Compatible	Unix, Windows NT	OS independent
Standard Conformance	SCSI-1 and 2	SCSI-2
Network Configurations and Distance	Point-to-point Multi-point (up to 1000s of miles)	Standard SCSI
Bandwidth	20MB/sec. (SCSI) 17MB/sec. (ESCON) 4.5MB/sec. (Bus and Tag)	10MB/sec.
Protocols	All	All
Implementation	Vendor setup and service	Auto configuration
Software Requirements	None	SCSI-II compliant drives that support Logical Unit Numbers (LUNs)
Management Tools	SNMP, Netview	None required
Scalability (nodes)	256	Supports 7 drives for each host SCSI-ID
Reliability Features	Hot Swap Power Node remove/replace	Drive dependent
Comments		
Warranty/Service	INA	1 year
List Price	INA	$795

N/A—Not applicable   INA—Information not available

End ■

File Mirroring ■

Manufacturer	CloneStar Software	Horizons Technology, Inc.
Model	REFLECT	Version 4.5
OS Compatibility	DOS/Windows/NetWare	NetWare 3.x and 4.x
File Mirroring Configuration	One-to-one logical disk mirror	One-to-one, many-to-one, cross mirroring. One-to-many.
Host/Client Requirements	Client <9K RAM	Console module requires Windows 3.1, Windows 95, Windows NT, or Windows for Workstations. Server module requires NetWare 3.x or 4.x and 500K RAM.
Version Retention	Yes	5-10 minutes some manual intervention
Failover Process	Auto or manual	Auto or manual
File System Access Method	Uses underlying OS or redirector	Direct access to backup server
Comments	No physical dependencies; primary/mirror can be different types NOS independent	
Warranty/Service	30 day	INA
List Price	$99 (single user) $1,995 (250 user)	INA

Manufacturer	Network Specialists, Inc.	Network Integrity, Inc.
Model	Double-Take	LANtegrity for NetWare
OS Compatibility	NetWare 3x, 4x; Windows NT 3x,4x	LANtegrity server requires NetWare 4.1, 3.x and/or 4.x for protected servers
File Mirroring Configuration	One-to-one, many-to-one, one-to-many	One-to-one, one-to-many
Host/Client Requirements	Server: 32MB RAM, disk space equal to all protected server volumes	Intel-compatible, 486/66 EISA or better, hard drive minimum of 2GB
Version Retention	Version 2.01, every file and cache change	INA
Failover Process	Automatic or manual failover	15secs automatically
File System Access Method	Restore full, partial or use backup server as failover	Full online restore capabilities
Comments	Open file, file delta, protocol independent TCP, Ethernet, ISDN, etc.	Protects against all kinds of errors even software error and data corruption. Includes continuous backup and online archive for file restore.
Warranty/Service	Multi-platform support in backup mode—NT and NetWare on one backup server	90 day
List Price	$1,875 for one source and one backup server	$4,950 for 100 users

N/A—Not applicable   INA—Information not available

Table Continues →

■ File Mirroring

Manufacturer	Octopus Technologies, Inc.	Vinca	Vinca
Model	Octopus Server 2.0 W/SuperASO	StandbyServer 2.0	Many-to-one Standby Server
OS Compatibility	Windows NT, Windows 95	NetWare 3.x, 4.x	NetWare 3.x, 4.x
File Mirroring Configuration	Over LAN or WAN there are no limitations	One-to-one	Many-to-one, one-to-many
Host/Client Requirements	Any NT certified hardware	StandbyServer must be NetWare capable. Disks must be able to be mirrored to primary server.	StandbyServer must be NetWare capable. Disks must be able to be mirrored to primary server.
Version Retention	Can be configured	All disk images updated in real-time to standby server.	All disk images updated in real-time to standby server.
Failover Process	Instant/server groups can also be protected	Failover time is 1-3 minutes automatic.	Failover time is 1-3 minutes automatic.
File System Access Method	INA	Full system restoration	Full system restoration
Comments (unique features)	Completely user transparent, automatic switch over, 24 x 7 server availability, no special hardware required, back office certified	Uses dedicated high speed link—no impact to network	Uses dedicated high speed link—no impact to network
Warranty/Service	30 days; additional plans available	30-day money back guarantee	30-day money back guarantee
List Price	$1,248	$3,499	$4,799

N/A—Not applicable   INA—Information not available

End ■

Automated Remote Vaulting ■

Manufacturer	**IBM**	**McAfee**
Model	ADSM-Disaster Recovery Manager	Webstor
Host OS/Nos	MUS, AIX	Windows95/Windows NT
Client Platforms Supported	All	Windows 95,Windows NT
Data Connection	Digital Service Unit via ISDN phone line to off-site location	Any line that supports FTP over PPP
Remote Backup Method	Incremental backups	Full, incremental
Backup Open Databases	Yes	No
File History Logs	Server data backup dada base and log	Yes
User Initiated Retrieval	Administrator and user	Yes
Security of Backed-Up Data Transmitted	Password: 2-way verify	Automatic encryption (blowfish algorithim)
Virus Scanning	No	No
Comments	DRM features, up-to-date vaulting	Selects only user created data for offsite protection
Warranty	Life of product	90 day
List Price of Service	N/A	$65

Manufacturer	**Octopus Technologies, Inc.**	**Rimage Telvaulting**	**Software Partners/32, Inc.**
Model	Octopus 2.0	System 1000 (for Novell) System 1000NT (for NT)	SafetyPosit
Host OS/Nos	Windows NT/Windows 95	NetWare, NT, MS-DOS	Sun OS, Sun Solaris, HP-UX, IBM AIX, DEC Unix
Client Platforms Supported	Windows NT , Windows 95	NetWare, NT, MS-DOS, UNIX	Sun OS, Sun Solaris, HP-UX, IBM AIX, DEC Unix, Windows NT
Data Connection	Any NT supported	Digital Service Unit via ISDN to off-site location. Also analog modem & 28.8 analog line.	Internet
Remote Backup Method	Real time, full or incremental	Daily incremental. Optional full backup.	Automatic full or incremental backups
Backup Open Databases	Yes—can backup all open files	NO	Yes, with third party software
File History Logs	INA	Master log on client disk	Searchable local history database
User Initiated Retrieval	Either can be configured	Automatic backups; User initiated retrievals	Yes
Security of Backed-Up Data Transmitted	INA	Automatic encryption	RSA encryption and node authentication
Virus Scanning	None	Automatic scanning and notification	No
Comments	One to one, one to many, many to many, many to one (all over LAN or WAN)	Last copy of all files updated daily on optical jukeboxes. Data Archived to CDR and returned to direct	Comes complete with software for backup and restore and archiving
Warranty	30 day—1 year standard or premium	3 Year—System purchases, continued—suscriber service	INA
List Price of Service	$1,248	Minimum monthly service $150	$9.95 per month and up

N/A—Not applicable   INA—Information not available   **End ■**

■ Network Backup

Manufacturer	Arback Networks Inc.	Boole & Babbage Storage Division	Cheyenne Software
Model	ARBACK	Stage 3	ARCserve 6 for NetWare
Product Class (Network or Enterprise)	Network	Enterprise	Network
Host Server OS	Novell 3.x, 4.x	MVS	NetWare 4.1x/3.1x
Client Supported (Servers or Workstations)	Novell, Windows 3.1/95, DOS	Netware 4.x/3.x, Windows NT, OS/2, Sun OS, Solaris 4.x, HP-UX all supported natively.	Macintosh, Windows NT, SCO Unix, SCO UnixWare, SUN (Sparc and x86), IBM/AIX, HP-/UX, SGI IRIX
Installation	Automated configuration	Partially automated	Automated-single install for multiple servers
Centralized Administration	Yes	Yesæ Via Cheyenne, Legato, Seagate, HP backup products	Yes
Management Reporting	History file, log files, console message	MVS console messages, activity logfiles, SMF records. Activity logs and database reporting, e-mail and SNMP available on Cheyenne, Legato, or Seagate partners.	INA
Open Relational Database Support	No	Cheyenne add-on (Oracle, Sybase, Lotus Notes, SAP R/3, Gupta, MS SQL Server); Seagate add-on (MS SQL Server); Legato/SQL Backtrack add-ons (Oracle, Sybase, Informix); St. Bernard Open File, Manager add-on	Oracle 7, Sybase SQL Server v4.x, v10, Centura (formerly Gupta) SQL Base 5.2.1, BTI Btrieve 6.x
Remote Vaulting	Yes	Yes	No
Data Compression	Yes	Yes	Hardware only
Concurrent Recording	INA	Yes	No
Parallel Recording	INA	Yes	Yes
File Migration/HSM	No	Add-on at MVS (DFSMS. DFHSM, DMS/OS, SAMS, DISK, FDR/ABR)	Additional integrated product
Media Management	Integrated	INA	Integrated through advanced features such as tape pooling, automatic tape naming, and bar code reader support
Automatic Archive	Yes	Yes	Yes, through archive job and file grooming
Drive Types Supported	Tape, optical	MVS DASD, tape, optical	Disk, tape, optical
Library/Loader/ Jukebox	Optical and tape, add-on, module	Mainframe DASD or mainframe tape	Optional module
Security	Password protection, data encryption, limited user/server access, controlled device access	Password protection, limited user access, virus protection, controlled device access available through Cheyenne, Seagate, or Legato on client side, through RACF, ACF/2, Top Secret on MVS host side.	SNMP alerts, log files, pager, and fax through Faxserve add-on, integration with NMS, OpenView, NetView, Insight Manager Caps OK? "Faxserve," "OpenView," "NetView," Insight Manager"
Comments	Automatic centralized server/station backup, decentralized restore	Emulates changer device to network backup products and does not replace them. Session file transfers via Enterprise Transport for Linking and Communicating. Duplexed control (index) file on MVS or offsite. Provides for local and mainframe backups in parallel streams. Uses existing storage management. Utilites on mainframe.	Disaster recovery option, RAID fault tolerance option, backup agent for open files, on-line backup of cc:Mail post offices

N/A—Not applicable   INA—Information not available

Network Backup ■

Manufacturer	Arback Networks Inc.	Boole & Babbage Storage Division	Cheyenne Software
Warranty/Service	1 year	1 year service agreement	30- day money back guarantee, / free technical support
List Price	$4,995+	Host/server from $7,500 Network/client from $2,900	Workgroup edition $795 Enterprise edition $1,895

Manufacturer	Commvault	Commvault
Model	ABARS	Netvault
Product Class (Network or Enterprise)	Network	Network
Host Server OS	Solaris, Sun OS	Solaris, Sun OS
Client Supported (Servers or Workstations)	DOS, Mac, AIX, HP-UX, VMS, Vines, Sun OS, Solaris, Netware	AIX, HP-UX, VMS, Sun OS, Solaris, Netware, Windows NT, DEC-Unix, IRIX, DGUX, SVR4, SCO
Installation	Semi-custom	Automatic
Centralized Administration	Yes	Yes
Management Reporting	E-mail, log files, pager, console, SNMP, ad hoc reporting	SNMP
Open Relational Database Support	Yes, Oracle, Sybase, Informix	Yes, Oracle, Sybase, Informix
Remote Vaulting	No	Yes
Data Compression	Yes (power press)	Yes, Data Tools interface
Concurrent Recording	Yes	Yes
Parallel Recording	Yes	Yes
File Migration/HSM	Add-on, integrated data migration	No
Media Management	Integrated	Integrated
Automatic Archive	Add-on, integrates	Yes
Drive Types Supported	Tape, optical	Tape, optical
Library/Loader/ Jukebox	Tape and optical	Tape and optical
Security	Password protection, server/client, authentication, write protection	Native NOS
Comments	Integrated suite with backup, archive, HSM, and media management	Integrated suite with backup, archive, HSM, and media management
Warranty/Service	Professional services available	Professional services available
List Price	$5,000–$30,000	$4,000+

Manufacturer	Computer Associates International	Dantz Development Corp.
Model	CA-Unicenter	Retrospect and Remote Pack for Windows NT
Product Class (Network or Enterprise)	Enterprise	Network
Host Server OS	Windows NT, Unix, OS/2, Netware, Tandem, AS/400	Mac OS, Windows NT, Windows 95
Client Supported (Servers or Workstations)	Windows NT, OS/2, Unix	Automated configuration

N/A—Not applicable   INA—Information not available

Table Continues →

■ Network Backup

Manufacturer	Computer Associates International	Dantz Development Corp.
Installation	Automated configuration	Yes
Centralized Administration	Yes	E-mail, pager, log files, console messages
Management Reporting	E-mail, pager, SNMP, all possible through CA-Unicenter Event Management.	No
Open Relational Database Support	Yes, CA-DB on Unix and OS/2, SQL/server on Windows NT	No
Remote Vaulting	Only on Unix	Yes
Data Compression	Yes	Yes
Concurrent Recording	No	No
Parallel Recording	Yes	Yes
File Migration/HSM	Yes, add-on, CA-Unicenter OSM option	Integrated
Media Management	Yes, integrated	Integrated
Automatic Archive	Yes	INA
Drive Types Supported	Tape, optical	Disk, tape, optical
Library/Loader/Jukebox	Yes. Basic provided with base product. Advanced provided through OSM option.	Client/server password protection, network-data transfer encryption, limited user access, controlled device access
Security	Secured commands, optical encryption	Back-up server, Easy Script
Comments	Full and incremental file backups across entire network.	60-day money back guarantee; free tech support
Warranty/Service	Unlimited	INA
List Price	Unavailable	Retrospect: $249 Remote (5/10/50 pack): $169/$249/$1,095

Manufacturer	Digital Equipment Corp.	DOROTECH
Model	NetWorker Save & Restore	DOROSTORE 2.1
Product Class (Network or Enterprise)	Network	Network
Host Server OS	Digital Unix or Alpha M	SOLARIS 2.x, HP/UX 9 & 10
Client Supported (Servers or Workstations)	Digital Unix, HP, Sun, IBM, Solaris, Macintosh, Windows NT or 95, NetWare	PC/Windows, Windows NT, NT, Novell 3.12, & 4, SCO, Sun OS, Solaris, HP/UX, AIX, IRIX, ULTRIX, OSF/1, AUSPEX, UNISYS, NCR, SEQUENT, PYRAMID, CONVEX
Installation	Preconfigured defaults	Semi-Automated
Centralized Administration	Yes	Yes, and multiserver capabilties
Management Reporting	INA	GUI, Log files, e-mail, console message, 1/3 party pagers
Open Relational Database Support	Oracle	Yes, Oracle 7.X
Remote Vaulting	Yes	Yes
Data Compression	Yes	Yes at CLIENT
Concurrent Recording	INA	Yes
Parallel Recording	INA	Yes

N/A—Not applicable   INA—Information not available

Network Backup ■

Manufacturer	Digital Equipment Corp.	DOROTECH
File Migration/HSM	No	Yes
Media Management	Yes, integrated	Integrated (IEEE Model)
Automatic Archive	Add-on	Yes as standard
Drive Types Supported	Disk, tape, optical	Tape
Library/Loader/ Jukebox	Add-on	Tapes (8mm, DLT,SVHS, 34XX), STK
Security	End to end data verification, encryption	Passwords, limited user access, quotas, user and applications access control, logical filter previous to physical deletion
Comments	Networker technology on 64 bits	Multiserver/multiclient, client throughput control and disk buffering for backup and archive, on demand backup and restore, on demand cross platform restore, IEEE and Moses compliant, backup speed on mono-processor
Warranty/Service	Software product services are available	3 months, hot line, remote support
List Price	$1,000 for NT server $2,500 for Unix server	From $14,000 for 1 backup server, 10 clients, 100GB to site licenses

Manufacturer	EMC Corporation	Emprise Technologies
Model	EDM (EMC Data Manager)	Stage 3 3.0
Product Class (Network or Enterprise)	Network	Enterprise
Host Server OS	Solaris	MVS
Client Supported (Servers or Workstations)	SAP, Windows NT, NetWare, SVR4, OSF, Ultrix, DGUX, HP-UX, AIX, Solaris, SunOS, Pyramid	Netware 4.x/3.x, Windows NT, OS/2, Solaris, HP-UX
Installation	Manual	Configuration generation utility
Centralized Administration	yes	Mainframe and LAN backup product
Management Reporting	GUI Interface manages reporting messages	E-mail, SNMP, pager, console message
Open Relational Database Support	Yes, Oracle, Sybase, Informix	Oracle, Informix, Sybase, SAP r/3, NW SQL, SQL Server, NW Btrieve
Remote Vaulting	Yes	Yes
Data Compression	Yes	Yes
Concurrent Recording	Yes	Yes
Parallel Recording	Yes	Yes
File Migration/HSM	Available	Yes, via LAN-based HSM
Media Management	Integrated	Integrated
Automatic Archive	Yes	Yes
Drive Types Supported	Tape	MVS DASD
Library/Loader/ Jukebox	Tape	Jukebox software required
Security	Password protection, limited user access controlled device access.	MVS dataset security, password and userid, data encryption and virus protection also provided

N/A—Not applicable   INA—Information not available

Table Continues →

■ Network Backup

Manufacturer	EMC Corporation	Emprise Technologies
Comments	RAID's Disk Array manages data placement, Remote Maintenance, 24 hour phone support.	Disaster recovery management, high performance options, interface to Cheyenne, Legato, and Seagate backup applications
Warranty/Service	1 year	1 year
List Price	$115,000–$525,000	$1,000–$25,000

Manufacturer	IBM	Innovation Data Processing
Model	ADSM	FDR/Upstream
Product Class (Network or Enterprise)	Enterprise	Enterprise
Host Server OS	AIX,Sun SOLARIS 2.5, NT & NetWare	MVS mainframe
Client Supported (Servers or Workstations)	DOS, NetWare, WINDOWS,Windows NT, NOVELL 3.12, & 4, SCO, SUNOS OS/2,Mac, SOLARIS, HP/UX, AIX, IRIX, ULTRIX, CONVEX, MVS,IRIX	Netware, OS/2, Vines, AIX, Windows NT
Installation	Program Assisted	Automated configuration
Centralized Administration	Yes	Yes
Management Reporting	Proprietary	Generalized report program can be customized to report to all upstream functions, log files, console messages
Open Relational Database Support	Yes	Oracle, Lotus Notes, DB/Z
Remote Vaulting	Yes	Yes
Data Compression	Yes/add-on	Yes
Concurrent Recording	Yes	Yes
Parallel Recording	Yes	Yes
File Migration/HSM	Yes/add-on	Yes
Media Management	Integrated	Upstream mainframe DASD mmanagement or use existing tape and disk management
Automatic Archive	Integrated	Yes
Drive Types Supported	Disk, tape, optical	MVS DASD, tape
Library/Loader/ Jukebox	Yes	Tape Silos/ATLs
Security	Password Protection, 2-way verification	Mainframe security honors PC LAN security, userid and password protection. Personalization limits user access.
Comments	Proprietary database, backup to disk. Disaster recovery manager	Automatic duplicate file support, forward merge backup, migration, vaulting, ultra workstation backup, local backup storage
Warranty/Service	Disaster Recovery Manager	Full warranty
List Price	INA	INA

Manufacturer	Interlink Computer Science, Inc.	Legato	MTI
Model	Harbor 4 Backup	Networker	Backup Unet
Product Class (Network or Enterprise)	Enterprise	Enterprise	Network

N/A—Not applicable   INA—Information not available

Network Backup ■

Manufacturer	Interlink Computer Science, Inc.	Legato	MTI
Host Server OS	WNS/XA, MUS/ESA, OS/390	Windows NT, Netware, Solaris, HP-UX, AIX	Sun OS, Solaris, HP-UX, AIX, IRIX, DEC Unix, SCO
Client Supported (Servers or Workstations)	DOS 4.0, Windows 3.1,3.11, Windows 95, NT Server for Intel 3.5, NT Workstation for Intel 3.5, OS/2 2/0, OS/2 WARP, AT&T system V for Intel 4.0, HP-UX 9.0 & 10.0, IBM AIX 3.2 & 4.1, Solaris 2.4, SunOS 4.1, DEC Unix AXP, DG-UX	Windows NT, NetWare 4.xX/ 3.xX, Sun OS, HP-UX, AIX	Sun OS, Solaris, HP-UX, AIX, IRIX, DEC Unix, SCO, Windows NT
Installation	Transparent between Host and LAN	Automated configuration	GUI-based
Centralized Administration	Yes	Yes	Yes
Management Reporting	Yes	E-mail, pager, SNMP, log files, console messages	E-mail, log files, console message
Open Relational Database Support	Oracle, SYBASE	Oracle 7, Informix	No
Remote Vaulting	Distributed Storage Servers	No	Yes
Data Compression	Yes	Yes	Yes
Concurrent Recording	INA	Yes	Yes
Parallel Recording	INA	Yes	Yes
File Migration/HSM	Yes, DFSMS/MVS,DFHSM,DMS/ OS,ABR,ASM2	Option	No
Media Management	Transparent	Smart media	Yes and integration with Oasis Media software
Automatic Archive	Available	Option	No
Drive Types Supported	Disk, tape, optical	Disk, tape, optical	Tape, optical
Library/Loader/ Jukebox	Distributed storage server optional	Tape and optical, add-on module	Yes and integration with Oasis RLM
Security	RACF, TOP SECRET, ACF2	Password protection, data encryption	Password protection, data encryption, Internet access controls, controlled device access
Comments	HARBOR Distributed storage servers, harbor transport gateway, fault tolerance	Opentape interchangeable media	Distributed client/server architecture lets manual operation survive any system failure.
Warranty/Service	INA	90 day	Annual packages available
List Price	$25,000	$750–$8,000	$2,000

Manufacturer	NCE Storage Solutions/Emerald Systems	NCE Storage Solutions/Emerald Systems
Model	Xpress Librarian	EmSAVE
Product Class (Network or Enterprise)	Network	Network
Host Server OS	DOS 3.3-6.0.x, Netware 4.1x/3.1x, Windows	Windows/DOS 3.x +, Netware 3.x +
Client Supported (Servers or Workstations)	NetWare 4.x/3.x, Windows 3.x, Windows for Workgroups	Netware 4.x/3.x, Windows 3.x, WG
Installation	Automated configuration	Automated configuration
Centralized Administration	Workstation-based	Workstation-based

N/A—Not applicable   INA—Information not available   **Table Continues** →

■ Network Backup

Manufacturer	NCE Storage Solutions/Emerald Systems	NCE Storage Solutions/Emerald Systems
Management Reporting	Log files, workstation messages	Log files, workstation messages
Open Relational Database Support	No	No
Remote Vaulting	No	No
Data Compression	Yes	No
Concurrent Recording	No	No
Parallel Recording	Yes	No
File Migration/HSM	No	No
Media Management	Integration	No
Automatic Archive	No	No
Drive Types Supported	Tape, optical	Tape, optical
Library/Loader/Jukebox	Yes	No
Security	Workstation-based package	Workstation-based package
Comments	Backs up NDS for Netware 4.1	Optional auto-loader support
Warranty/Service	Free telephone support	Free telephone support
List Price	$565	$375

Manufacturer	Network Systems	OpenVision Technologies, Inc.
Model	CAM/EBF	Axxion—NetBackup
Product Class (Network or Enterprise)	Enterprise	Network
Host Server OS	MVS and Solaris	Unix-most versions, Windows NT
Client Supported (Servers or Workstations)	30+ clients	Windows, Windows NT, most Unix platforms, Mac, Netware
Installation	Centrally administered	Automated installation across all servers and clients
Centralized Administration	Yes	Yes
Management Reporting	Log files, console messages	Yes, with Axxion-event manager, optional module
Open Relational Database Support	Oracle, Sybase	Oracle, Informix, Sybase
Remote Vaulting	Yes	Yes
Data Compression	Yes	Yes
Concurrent Recording	Yes	Yes
Parallel Recording	Yes	Yes
File Migration/HSM	No	With Axxion HSM
Media Management	MVSDFHSM, Solaris, integrated	Yes
Automatic Archive	User-initiated	Yes
Drive Types Supported	Disk, tape, optical	Disk, tape, optical
Library/Loader/Jukebox	Tape library, tapes, disk	Yes

N/A—Not applicable   INA—Information not available

Network Backup ■

Manufacturer	Network Systems	OpenVision Technologies, Inc.
Security	Password protection, limited user access, controlled device access	Data encryption optional, module available Spring 1997
Comments		
Warranty/Service	90 day (warranty) 24 hrs. x 7 days per week (service)	INA
List Price	Server: $8,500–$22,500 Client: $50–$4,000	Server: $8,500 Client: $50

Manufacturer	Platinum Technology Inc.	SCH Technologies/Storage Tek	Seagate
Model	Platinum NetArchive	REEL backup 4.0	Backup Exec
Product Class (Network or Enterprise)	Network	Network	Network
Host Server OS	HP-UX 9.x and 10.0x, Sun OS 4.1x, Solaris 2.3/ 2.4/2.5, IBM, AIX 4.1	Most Unix platforms	Netware 4.x/3.x
Client Supported (Servers or Workstations)	HP-UX 9.x and 10.0x, Sun OS 4.1x, Solaris 2.3/ 2.4/2.5, IBM, AIX 3.2/4.1	Most Unix platforms	Netware 4.x/3.x, Windows 3.1/ 95, DOS OS/2, other optionals
Installation	Automated configuration	SCH System Engineers	Automated configuration
Centralized Administration	Yes	Yes	Yes
Management Reporting	E-mail, pager, log files, console messages	E-mail, reports, log files, console	Log files, console messages
Open Relational Database Support	Proprietary, moving to Oracle in late 1996	Internal B-Tree	No
Remote Vaulting	Yes	Yes	No
Data Compression	Yes	Yes-hardware	For tape drive
Concurrent Recording	INA	Yes	INA
Parallel Recording	INA	Yes	INA
File Migration/HSM	Tightly integrated with NetArchive HSM agent as add-on option	Future add-on	No
Media Management	Integrated. Manages online and offline locations, bar code, media compaction, overwrite protection	Integrated	Integrated
Automatic Archive	Tightly integrated with NetArchive HSM agent as add-on option	Integrated	Yes
Drive Types Supported	Disk, tape, optical	Disk, tape, optical	Tape, optical
Library/Loader/ Jukebox	Disk drives, many 4mm, 8mm, and DLT tape drives and tape libraries, 5.25 magneto optical jukeboxes	Tape drive, stacker, robotic support	No
Security	Operating system native security as well as built-in enhanced file security which assigns a new world-unique name to each file and passes a security key to the client for each restoration to ensure proper authorization when accessed. Data encryption option.	Password protection, limited permissions, media verification	Password protection, data encryption, limited user access, controlled device access, virus protection (optional)

N/A—Not applicable   INA—Information not available

Table Continues →

■ Network Backup

Manufacturer	Platinum Technology Inc.	SCH Technologies/Storage Tek	Seagate
Comments	Automatic file duplication for disaster recovery capabilities and file relocation services. Shares storage resources with backup and migrated data. Data stored in tar-compatible format. Heterogeneous OS support for both client and server agents.	High performance direct and network attached devices	32-bit backup for Windows NT
Warranty/Service	90-day warranty. 8AM-5PM Mon.—Fri.or 7days/ week, 24hrs./day optional.	Annual support, upgrade program	Free telephone support
List Price	Client: $2,000	$1,500–$32,000	$695–$1,295

Manufacturer	Seagate Software	Software Partners/32, Inc.
Model	Storage Manager	Storage Center
Product Class (Network or Enterprise)	INA	Network
Host Server OS	Netware 4.x/3.x, Windows NT	Sun OS, Sun Solaris, HP-UX, IBM AIX, DEC Unix
Client Supported (Servers or Workstations)	NW, Windows NT, DOS, Windows, Windows 95, Mac, OS/2, Unix	Sun OS, Sun Solaris, HP-UX, IBM AIX, DEC Unix, Windows NT
Installation	Server- and client-based, client-based	Shell Script
Centralized Administration	Yes	No
Management Reporting	SNMP, e-mail, MHS, MAPI, log files, alert palette	E-mail, pager, log files, and console message
Open Relational Database Support	No	Partial
Remote Vaulting	No	Yes
Data Compression	No	Yes
Concurrent Recording	INA	Yes
Parallel Recording	Yes	Yes
File Migration/HSM	Yes	Yes
Media Management	Integrated	Yes
Automatic Archive	Yes	Yes
Drive Types Supported	Tape, optical	Tape, optical
Library/Loader/ Jukebox	Tape and optical (add-on-module)	Tape, optical
Security	Password protection, limited user access	RSA encryption and node authentication, access control list
Comments	Integrated backup, archiving, and HSM solution	Redundant tape drives and backup servers, redundant copies of master database
Warranty/Service	90-day money back guarantee	90 day
List Price	INA	$1,875 and up

N/A—Not applicable   INA—Information not available

Network Backup ■

Manufacturer	Software MogulsSoftware	Spectra Logic
Model	SM-arch	Alexandria
Product Class (Network or Enterprise)	INA	Network
Host Server OS	Most Unix	Unix
Client Supported (Servers or Workstations)	Most Unix, DOS, Windows NT, Macintosh and more.	Unix, Windows NT
Installation	Tapes	Scripts
Centralized Administration	Yes	Yes
Management Reporting	E-mail, event logging, detailed messaging, status screens	INA
Open Relational Database Support	No	Proprietary with SQL Access
Remote Vaulting	No	Yes
Data Compression	Yes	Yes
Concurrent Recording	Yes	No
Parallel Recording	Yes	Yes
File Migration/HSM	No	No
Media Management	Integrated	Yes
Automatic Archive	Optional	INA
Drive Types Supported	Tape, optical	Tape, optical
Library/Loader/ Jukebox	4mm,8mm,DLT,Robotics,Tape/Optional Libraries	Yes
Security	Password protection; data encryption; administration defined user privileges, virus protection.	13 levels of application security
Comments	Also available for Windows NT, remote device support	For large networks and RDBMS
Warranty/Service	90 day telephone, e-mail, fax	90 days/includes optional maintenance
List Price	$1,000–$4,000 server	$1,500–$18,000

N/A—Not applicable   INA—Information not available

Table Continues →

■ Network Backup

Manufacturer	Vinca	Workstation Solutions
Model	SnapShot Server	Quick Restore V2.1
Product Class (Network or Enterprise)	Network	Network
Host Server OS	Netware 4.x/3.x	Unix
Client Supported (Servers or Workstations)	Netware 4.x/3.x	Unix, Windows NT
Installation	Floppy diskinstall on standby machine	Optional automated configuration
Centralized Administration	Yes	Yes
Management Reporting	N/A	Log files, console messages, e-mail
Open Relational Database Support	Yes, Btrieve Oracle Sybase. All databases that run in a Netware environment	Yes
Remote Vaulting	Yes	Yes
Data Compression	No	Yes
Concurrent Recording	INA	No
Parallel Recording	INA	Yes
File Migration/HSM	Supported	No
Media Management	Supported	Integrated
Automatic Archive	Supported	Yes
Drive Types Supported	Tape, optical	Tape, optical
Library/Loader/Jukebox	Supported	Tapes standalones, libraries, bar code readers, ADI on modules
Security	Console is password locked	Password protection, limited user access, controlled device access
Comments	Backup facilitatoræpresents data image to standard backup engines	Online indexing database, automatic clean-up tools, industry (DOSIX-component) standard
Warranty/Service	30-day money back guarantee	90 day
List Price	$999	$1,500+

N/A—Not applicable   INA—Information not available

Network Archive ■

Manufacturer	Arback Networks, Inc.	Bull Worldwide Information Systems
Model	Arback	Epoch Backup 3.4
Integrated or Standalone Application	Standalone	Integrated with ISM/ Open Master
Host Server OS	Novell 3.x, 4.x	AIX 3.2.5, AIX 4.1
Client OS	Windows 3.1, Windows 95, DOS	Most UNIX, Windows NT, NetWare, OS/2, DOS/ Windows connected to NetWare
Archive Hardware	Optical drive tour, optical jukeboxes	Disk, DLT, HP optical jukeboxes 3480
Archive Media Supported	2.6GB and optical drive	5.25 magneto optical, 8mm tape with w/3480
Library Management	N/A	Online and offline data HSM
File History Database Type	N/A	Ingres SQL database
Database Scalability	N/A	No limit
File Selection Process	Manual	Manual and policy- based
Administration Interface	GUI	GUI (XII)
Retrieval Access	Administrator and client	Administrator
Retrieval Interface	GUI	GUI on UNIX
Performance	Supports high-speed networks; automatic backup scheduling for all servers and stations	Supports Ethernet and FDDI simultaneous and multi- plexed on many tapes. Configurable to optimize backups
Comments	Automatic station backup, decentralized restore	HSM, Archicol integrated off-line media management. Automated client install and configure.
Warranty/Service	1 year	Bull WIS support plans
List Price	$4,985 (base unit)	$9,000 for 5 UNIX clients

Manufacturer	CommVault Systems	NovaStor
Model	3D Archive	NovaNet
Integrated or Standalone Application	Integrated with the CommVault Suite	Integrated with Novell libraries
Host Server OSs	Sun OS, Solaris	NetWare 3.x and higher
Client OSs	DOS, Mac, AIX, HP-UX, Sun OS, Solaris, Vines, VMS	DOS, Windows, OS/2
Archive Hardware	MO or WORM drives & jukeboxes	Tape drives and libraries
Archive Media Supported	5.25 MO or Warm, and 12" Warm	SCSI tape
Library Management	Online and shelf storage	Manages online
File History Database Type	Unix	INA
Database Scalability	Unlimited	INA
File Selection Process	Policy and manual	Manual, automatic
Administration Interface	GUI and command line	GUI, character- based

N/A—Not applicable   INA—Information not available

Table Continues →

■ Network Archive

Manufacturer	CommVault Systems	NovaStor
Retrieval Access	Direct by any authorized user	Anyone
Retrieval Interface	Command line	GUI, character- based
Performance	Direct access via the 3D file system	Supports high-speed networks; direct access and file sharing by various workstations
Comments	Uses a 3D file system over NFS which allows a time dimension providing online access to file versions and histories.	Password protection, random stacker support, NDS support, SMS compliant, QFA
Warranty/Service	Professional services offered	INA
List Price	$5,000–$30,000	Single server—$299 (single server) 50 user—$399 (50 user) 1,000 user—$699 (1,000 user)

Manufacturer	NovaStor	NovaStor
Model	NovaDisk	NovaWorks CD-ROM
Integrated or Standalone Application	Part of a product suite	Part of a product suite
Host Server OSs	INA	INA
Client OSs	Windows 95/NT	DOS, Windows 3.x, Windows 95, OS/2, Mac
Archive Hardware	Removable media Jaz, Zip, MO, Bernouli, etc.	Tape drives, tape libraries
Archive Media Supported	3.5", 5.25", hard drive, MO, Floptical, etc.	MO, SCSI, QIC
Library Management	INA	INA
File History Database Type	INA	INA
Database Scalability	INA	INA
File Selection Process	Manual, automatic	Manual, automatic
Administration Interface	GUI, command line	GUI, command line
Retrieval Access	Anyone	Anyone
Retrieval Interface	GUI, character line	GUI, character line
Performance	Supports high-speed networks and; Supports high-capacity devices, as well as any removable media available.	Supports high-speed networks and high- capacity devices
Comments	NovaRoot disaster recovery	NovaRoot disaster recovery
Warranty/Service	INA	INA
List Price	$99	$119

N/A—Not applicable   INA—Information not available

Storage Resource Management ■

Manufacturer	High Ground Systems, Inc.	PDC
Model	SRM:™ Applications	DiskInfo
General Description and Benefits	Provides a comprehensive Storage Resource Management (SRM) infrastructure and application set that increases data availability over its lifecycle and a framework for Data Mover ISVs to take advantage of the same tools.	Analyzes disk utilization and ownership. A reporting and analyzing tool.
Tools	INA	File access, profiles user and ownership attributes
Client/Server Platforms Supported	Windows NT Server	Sun OS, Solaris, SGI, Auspex, HP-UX, AIX
Administration Console OS	Windows NT Server	Motif-based, Unix
Hardware Requirements	Intel- and Alpha-based systems	Any Unix client
Client Agent Requirements	SRM:™ consumer node software	Agent on each managed client or server
Task Launching	Logic-driven failover, load balancing, media management, replication, alerts	None
Management Alerts	SNMP alerts	None
Device Support	Disk, tape, optical, removable disk	Disk only
Reporting	SRM: Media Lifecycle™, SRM: Source Monitor™, SRM: Media Conversion™, SRM: Server Backup™, SRM: Disaster Recovery™, SRM: Planner™, SRM: Vault™, SRM: Weather Station™	Charts and graphs
Comments	HighGround's SRM:™ Applications bring comprehensive SRM tools to developers and users of data mover applications on Windows NT networks	1 license per network
Warranty/Service	INA	INA
List Price	INA	INA

N/A—Not applicable   INA—Information not available

Table Continues →

■ Storage Resource Management

Manufacturer	**Sterling Software**	**W. Quinn Assoc.**
Model	SAMS: Expert	Storage Advisor
General Description and Benefits	Provides central multiplatform management of file usage, capacity leading, load-balancing, and utilization in an expert, interactive, policy-driven system	Manages usage, utilization, sets policies, monitors events, capacity load balancing and planning
Tools	Capacity planning, space utilization, file system monitoring and analysis, policy management tools, file aging profiling, task launching based on rules and policies	Storage object and configuration management, comprehensive reporting policy management, event monitor, trend analysis, hotline tracking
Client/Server Platforms Supported	Unix (AIX 4.14, HP-UX 9.04, Sun OS 4.13, Solaris 2.4), Windows NT 3.51 or higher, Netware 3.11 or higher	Open VMS, Digital Unix, Windows NT, HP-UX, Solaris, AIX, Windows 95, SCO, Linux
Administration Console OS	Windows 95, OS/2	AXP or VAX
Hardware Requirements	Intel PC, DOS 3.3 and higher, OS/2 Warp Connect with Windows OS/2	AXP, VAX, x86, Sparc, HP, IBM
Client Agent Requirements	Agent on each managed client or server	Agent on each managed client or server
Task Launching	Can launch any storage application from a command line script	None
Management Alerts	SNMP alerts	SNMP alerts
Device Support	All disk for monitoring, no tape or optical	Disk-based
Reporting	Interactive queries, custom and noted report templates	Interactive standard, custom reports and trend analysis
Comments (unique features)	A consistent, interactive view of Unix, Windows NT, and Netware environments from a storage perspective	Sold in 3 modules: Reports, Lights out, Advanced (with other W. Quinn products Q*file and Disk Master
Warranty/Service	3 year	INA
List Price	Starts at $15,000	INA

Removable Media/Library Manager ∎

Manufacturer	Alphatronix	Artecon
Model	Inspire SME	Arkstak
Host Server OS	Solaris	Sun OS, AIX
Clients Platforms Supported	Solaris	Same as host
Library Tapes Managed	Exabyte, ATL, HP, Breece Hill, Storage Tek	Exabyte, HP, Conner,
Media Types Managed	4mm, 8mm, DLT, optical	8mm, 4mm
Manages Online Media	Yes	Yes
Manages Shelf Storage	Yes	No
Online Catalogue	Yes	No
File Tracking	Yes	No
Volume Set Compatibility	Yes	No
Mount Request Queue	Yes	No
Media Control Features	Yes	Yes
Media Life Cycle Management	Yes	No
Security	None	No
Reporting	Yes	No
Database Structure	Proprietary	No
Limit on Number of Media	Unlimited	Based on stacker size
Remote Vaulting Capability	Yes	No
Software Integrates With	Works with most Unix based	N/A
Comments		Simple GUI for tape stacking libraries
Warranty/Service	INA	90 day
List Price	INA	$1,295

Manufacturer	Artecon	Aviv
Model	ArkEOD	ALM
Host Server OS	Sun OS, AIX	DEC VMS
Clients Platforms Supported	Same as host	None
Library Tapes Managed	Optical	Exabyte, STIC, Quantum, ATL
Media Types Managed	Optical	8mm, 3480, 3490, DLT
Manages Online Media	Yes	Yes
Manages Shelf Storage	No	Yes

N/A—Not applicable   INA—Information not available

Table Continues →

■ Removable Media/Library Manager

Manufacturer	Artecon	Aviv
Online Catalogue	No	No
File Tracking	No	No
Volume Set Compatibility	No	No
Mount Request Queue	Yes	No
Media Control Features	Yes	Yes
Media Life Cycle Management	No	No
Security	No	No
Reporting	No	No
Database Structure	No	Proprietary
Limit on Number of Media	No	Unlimited
Remote Vaulting Capability	No	No
Software Integrates With	INA	PSA, BacPlus
Comments		Robust CLI interface
Warranty/Service	90 day	30 day
List Price	$995	$3,000

Manufacturer	Dallastone Jax	MTI
Model	Dallastools	Oasis Media
Host Server OS	HP-UX, AIX, IRIX, Solaris, ATFG, Windows NT, Windows 95	NT, Unix
Clients Platforms Supported	HP-UX, AIX, IRIX, Solaris, ATFG, Windows NT, Windows 95, Netware, Vines, Mac, UMS, other Unix	NT, Unix
Library Tapes Managed	Exabyte, ADIC, ATL, Storage Tek, IBM, HP, Breece Hill	Open interface plus via RLM
Media Types Managed	4mm, 8mm, DLT, 3480, 3490, optical	Any
Manages On-line Media	Yes	Yes
Manages Shelf Storage	Yes	Yes
Online Catalogue	Yes	Yes
File Tracking	Yes	No
Volume Set Compatibility	No	Yes
Mount Request Queue	No	Yes
Media Control Features	Yes	Yes
Media Life Cycle Management	Yes	Yes
Security	Yes	Yes
Reporting	Yes	Yes
Database Structure	Public	SQL

N/A—Not applicable   INA—Information not available

Removable Media/Library Manager ■

Manufacturer	Dallastone Jax	MTI
Limit on Number of Media	Unlimited	Unlimited
Remote Vaulting Capability	Yes	Yes
Software Integrates With	Dallastools	Open
Comments	Move media software may be used with Dallastools or TAR, CPIO, and other backup software	
Warranty/Service	18% of list price	INA
List Price	$1,000–$50,000	INA

Manufacturer	MTI	Veritas Software
Model	Oasis RLM	NRML
Host Server OS	WNT, AIX, Solaris, HP-UX, OpenVMS, DEC Unix	AIX, HP/UX, Solaris, NT, (2Q/97)
Clients Platforms Supported	WNT, AIX, Solaris, HP-UX, OpenVMS, DEC Unix	AIX, HP/UX, Solaris, NT, (2Q/97)
Library Tapes Managed	Exabyte, ATL, Quantum, Breece Hill, Digital	Exabyte, ADIC, HP-Optical, Odetics, 4mm Autochanger, any SCSI Library
Media Types Managed	8mm, DLT, 34xx, 35xx	Yes
Manages Online Media	Yes	Yes
Manages Shelf Storage	Yes	Yes
Online Catalogue	Yes, integrates with media manager, software	No
File Tracking	No	Yes
Volume Set Compatibility	No	Yes
Mount Request Queue	No	Yes
Media Control Features	No	Yes
Media Life Cycle Management	No	Yes
Security	N/A	Yes
Reporting	Log, console, e-mail	Yes
Database Structure	Open SQL	Object-oriented—Proprietary
Limit on Number of Media	Unlimited	Unlimited
Remote Vaulting Capability	No	Yes
Software Integrates With	Legato, Oasis NetBackup, AutoSoftware (HSM), Backup Unet	Native system utilities (TAR/JUMP/CPIO), others in the future
Comments	Distributed control of all libraries from any workstation, asynchronous detection, automated policies for maintenance, operational access and scenerio	Network transparent access to all drives and media. (Remote Drive Access across Hetero hosts). Library sharing among simultaneous applications. Bar code Reader support. Centralized—Graphical view of all network resources, complete API, CLI, GUI. Complete command level interface enables to write scripts
Warranty/Service	1 year	Unlimited, requires support contract
List Price	$2,000+	$100–$30,000

N/A—Not applicable   INA—Information not available

End ■

■ CD Networking

Manufacturer	**Luminex**	**Luminex**
Model	Fire Series for Unix	Fire Series for Multinet
General Description	Network oriented performance features, providing seamless client access to CD-ROMs in towers and jukeboxes	Combines Fire Series for Unix with multi-protocol connectivity to solve CD-ROM networking requirements in complex local-area and wide-area heterogeneous networks
OS Compatible	Sun OS 4.13, Sun Solaris 2.3/2.4/2.5 (Sparc and Intel); IBM AIX 3.2x/4.1, HP-UX 9.x/10.x, SGI, IRIX	Sun OS 4.13, Sun Solaris 2.3/2.4/2.5 (Sparc and Intel); IBM AIX 3.2x/4.1, HP-UX 9.x/10.x, SGI, IRIX
Server Configuration	INA	INA
CD-ROM Controller Interface	SCSI-2; 1 SCSI ID for each 7 drives, or each jukebox	SCSI-2; 1 SCSI ID for each 7 drives, or each jukebox
CD-ROM Drives	CD-ROM towers from 7-96 drives. Jukeboxes with 50, 100, 150, 300, 500 discs	CD-ROM towers from 7-96 drives. Jukeboxes with 50, 100, 150, 300, 500 discs
CD-Recordable and Hard Disk Drive Requirements	No CD-R	No CD-R
Communication Protocols	TCP/IP	TCP/IP, IPX/SPX, LAN Manager, NetBEUI, AppleTalk
Installation	INA	INA
Central Management	Yes	Yes
Operation Features	All CD-ROMs mounted simultaneously, Configurable CD-ROM volume grouping, permanent migration caching options, Unix network, security and access privileges	Configurable CD-ROM volume grouping, migration caching options, network administration
Security	Utilizes security features native to the server	Utilizes security features native to the server
Comments		
Warranty/Service	3 year, Phone, e-mail, Website	3 year Phone, e-mail, Website
List Price	$1,000 and up	$1,000 and up

Manufacturer	**Luminex**	**Meridian Data**
Model	Fire Series for NetWare	CD Net Software
General Description	An intuitive, full-featured solution for networking CD-ROMs in a drive tower or jukebox can be presented as directories within a single NetWare volume	Shared CD-ROM access and management; shared CD-ROM
OS Compatible	NetWare 3.11 and higher	NetWare 3.12/4.1 or higher, Windows NT/3.51 or higher
Server Configuration	INA	Intel 486/33, 32MB minimum. 2MB hard disk
CD-ROM Controller Interface	SCSI-2; 1 SCSI ID for each 7 drives, or each jukebox	SCSI-2 with 100% Adaptec ASPI-compliant device driver
CD-ROM Drives	CD-ROM towers from 7-96 drives. Jukeboxes with 50, 100, 150, 300, 500 discs	Up to 56 per server
CD-Recordable and Hard Disk Drive Requirements	None	Requires a dedicated SCSI-2 hard disk drive with a minimum capacity of 700MB to be connected to the same host. NetWare 3.12/4.1 or higher
Communication Protocols	TCP/IP, IPX/SPX	IPX/SPX, TCP/IP, Net BEUI
Installation	INA	Turnkey and active servers available. Detects the attached CD-ROM drives and automatically creates a CD-ROM server.

N/A—Not applicable   INA—Information not available

CD Networking ■

Manufacturer	Luminex	Meridian Data
Central Management	Yes	Views and manipulates the network-wide CD-ROM job queue and maintains logfile history for recorded CD jobs
Operation Features	Drag-and-drop management, integrates fully with NetWare, CD-ROM volume sets, client launch utility, CD-ROM jukebox support, jukebox reserve time	Create user accounts. Users can log on using NetWare log in command. Map multiple CD-ROMs to drive letter. Manage all resources across multiple servers from one administrative workstation. Vines 6.0 higher
Security	Utilizes security features native to the server	NetWare, Windows NT and Vines compatible
Comments		Multiple CD volume grouping; common network/NT client
Warranty/Service	Unlimited Phone, e-mail, Website	1 year
List Price	$1,000 and up	NetWare: starts at $795 BT: starts at $995 Vines: $6 995

Manufacturer	MDI (Micro Design)	MDI (Micro Design)
Model	SCSO Express 3.0 NetWare	CD-Express Connect
General Description	Shared CD-ROM access across network	LAN Attach CD-ROM Server
OS Compatible	NetWare 3.x, 4.x	NetWare, NT, Unix, Web
Server Configuration	Intel 386DX, 16MB min., 5MB hard disk	NA
CD-ROM Controller Interface	SCSI-II, ASPT-Compliant device driver	NA
CD-ROM Drives	One or more CD-ROMs, up to 56 drives in single host adapter	Up to 7 drives
CD-Recordable and Hard Disk Drive Requirements	NA	NA
Communication Protocols	IPX/SPX	IPX,TCP/IP, and SMB over IP
Installation	Detects the attached CD-ROM drives, and automatically creates a CD-ROM file	Detects the attached CD-ROM drives, and automatically configures itself as a CD-ROM server.
Central Management	Central Management and Remote from Workstation	Central Management and Remote
Operation Features	NDS support, Subscription handling, create CD-ROM groups (up to 200 CDs per volume), on disk directory for faster access to CD Jukebox	Multiple Client Access, Map all CD-ROMs into single group, Express Admin Software for administration, draws no resources from existing file servers
Security	NetWare's Security features	Optional software which permits or denies access to CD volumes. Password-Based
Comments	Includes magneto optical support	Also available for Windows NT. Web browser to access CDs
Warranty/Service	1 year	1 year
List Price	$595–$3,995	$995–$4,395

Manufacturer	Novell, Inc.	Ornetix	Smart Storage
Model	CD ROM.nlm	CD-Vision/CD-Commander	SmartCD versions:
General Description	Shared CD ROM Access and shared CD ROM recording capabilities	CD Networking Software	Network CD access, Network CD recording, Network CD recording and access
OS Compatible	NetWare v3.12 and higher	NetWare 2.x/3.x/4.x, Windows NT/3.51 and higher	NetWare, Windows NT, Unix

N/A—Not applicable   INA—Information not available

Table Continues →

■ CD Networking

Manufacturer	Novell, Inc.	Ornetix	Smart Storage
Server Configuration	Hardware to support NetWare plus disk/mounted CD	N/A	Intel 486/33 16MB RAM standard Unix processor
CD-ROM Controller Interface	SCSI or ATAPI/IDE	N/A	All SCSI CD-ROM drives, CD min-ichangers and most CD jukeboxes, most CD recorders and CD-record-able jukeboxes
CD-ROM Drives/ Libraries	Unlimited	Share up to 448 drives, changers, towers, and jukeboxes	NA
CD-Recordable and Hard Disk Drive Requirements	NA	N/A	NA
Communication Protocols	IPX/SPX	Supports standard protocol	All supported by network operating system
Installation	Detects the attached CD-ROM drives, CD mount command	Detects the attached CD-ROM drives and creates a CD-ROM server	Detects and attaches CD devices
Central Management	Console commands mountable	Use CD-Commander to install and manage all your CD titles and CD-Vision servers	Creates centralized icons at the desktop for access. Maintains job queue for CD recording
Operation Features	Users can log on using NetWare login command, Map CD-ROM volumes to drive letters, Access and use the CD-ROM drives using DOS and Windows	Log in and map clients on the fly. Virtual Volume support. Automatic CD title mounting. Off-load all CD traffic from the server and clients. Installs in less than 5 minutes. Icon toolbar.	Users get all standard network operating system security. Simultaneous recording and access capabilities for CD-recordable juke-boxes. High volume recording capabilities utilizing CD recorders and autoloading mechanisms. API toolkit available for imbedding system
Security	NetWare compatible. Login security and user access to specific CD's controlled with Network's syscon utility in NetWare 3.1 and controlled with Novell Directory Service security in NetWare 4.1 and higher.	Title and server access security. CD-ROM drive eject security	Available by specific network oper-ating system
Comments	Support disk caching options	No need to install memory hungry NLM or TSR	Access to CD devices as single drive letter from DOS, Windows, Windows 95, Windows NT, Mac, Unix.
Warranty/Service	Included in NetWare 3.12 and higher	45 day. Complete technical assis-tance available.	1 year
List Price	Included in NetWare 3.1 and higher	$795–$3,395	Starts at $495

Manufacturer	SMS Data Products Group, Inc.	SMS Data Products Group, Inc.
Model	AFCMS1	AFCSM2
General Description	Provides network access to CD ROM devices	Provides network access to CD ROM devices
OS Compatible	NetWare 3.11/3.12/ 4.0/4.01	NetWare 3.11/3.12/ 4.0/4.01
Server Configuration	IBM PC-compatible 80386 or higher processor, 16MB RAM, 90MB hard drive	IBM PC-compatible 80386 or higher processor, 16MB RAM, 90MB hard drive
CD-ROM Controller Interface	Most standard SCSI controllers	Most standard SCSI controllers
CD-ROM Drives/ Libraries	500 CDs or 196 drives	500 CDs or 196 drives
CD-Recordable and Hard Disk Drive Requirements	N/A	N/A

N/A—Not applicable   INA—Information not available

CD Networking ■

Manufacturer	SMS Data Products Group, Inc.	SMS Data Products Group, Inc.
Communication Protocols	Default IPX, SPX	Default IPX, SPX
Installation	Load software and follow instructions	Load software and follow instructions
Central Management	Automatically prepares and mounts; allows networked CD-ROM to appear as subdirectories; drag-and-drop management features.	Automatically prepares and mounts; allows networked CD-ROM to appear as subdirectories; drag-and-drop management features.
Operation Features	Automatically prepares and mounts CDs; client support for DOS, Windows, Mac and OS/2; integrates caching, security and usage of CDs.	Automatically prepares and mounts CDs; client support for DOS, Windows, Mac and OS/2; integrates caching, security and usage of CDs.
Security	Fully integrated NetWare security	Fully integrated NetWare security
Comments		Create a limited independent Novell server for CD-ROMs
Warranty/Service	1 year	1 year
List Price	$549	$1,396 (50 user license)

Manufacturer	SMS Data Products Group, Inc.	SMS Data Products Group, Inc.
Model	AFCNOSNT	AFCSW3
General Description	Provides network access to CD ROM devices	Provides network access to CD ROM devices
OS Compatible	Windows NT 3.51	Banyan Vines 4.11 or greater
Server Configuration	IBM PC-compatible 100 MHz Pentium, 32MB RAM, 1GB hard drive	386/33 or better, 4MB RAM, 20MB hard drive
CD-ROM Controller Interface	Most standard SCSI controllers	Most standard SCSI controllers
CD-ROM Drives/ Libraries	No limitation (limited by hardware)	270 simultaneous connections to 24 drives
CD-Recordable and Hard Disk Drive Requirements	N/A	N/A
Communication Protocols	Server-dependent	Server-dependent
Installation	Load software and follow instructions	Load software and follow instructions
Central Management	Virtual File System allows CDs to be put in a single point subdirectory and viewed in a virtual directory tree.	Windows-based menu and remote monitor console features
Operation Features	INA	No memory overhead with the ability to share drives simultaneously
Security	Fully integrated NT security	For volume, directory, and file levels
Comments	Provides flexible CD-ROM networking management software for towers and jukeboxes. Views directories on CD-ROM without mounting the CDs and aggregates the same CDs under single or multiple drive letters.	Gives Vines users the ability to have shared access to mounted drives located anywhere on the network.
Warranty/Service	1 year	1 year
List Price	$1,495	$2,055

N/A—Not applicable   INA—Information not available

Table Continues →

■ CD Networking

Manufacturer	Ten X Technology	Ten X Technology	Ten X Technology
Model	TenXpert-1 Server	TenXpert-4 Server	TenXpert-8 Server
General Description	CD access in a multiple OS and NOS environment	Shared CD reading and writing in a multiple OS and NOS environment	Shared CD reading and writing in a multiple OS and NOS environment
Os Compatible	NetWare 3.x/4.x, Windows NT, Windows 95, NFS, OS/2, Windows 3.1, Unix	NetWare 3.x/4.x, Windows 95, Windows NT, NFS, OS/2, Windows 3.1, Unix	NetWare 3.x/4.x, Windows NT, Windows 95, OS/2, NFS, Windows 3.1, Unix
Server Configuration	1GB hard disk cache, 10MBps Ethernet controllers	2GB hard disk cache, 10MBps Ethernet controller	4GB hard disk cache,
CD-ROM Controller Interface	SCSI-2	SCSI-2	SCSI-2
CD-ROM Drives/ Libraries	Maximum 42 drives	Maximum 168 drives	Maximum 250 drives
CD-Recordable and Hard Disk Drive Requirements	No hard disk requirements (recording not offered with this model)	No additional hard disk required	Records to standalone or internal to a jukebox, CD-R drives
Protocols	IPX/NCP, IP/NFS	IPX/NCP, IP/NFS	IPX/NCF, IP/NFS
Installation	Plug 10BASE-T cable into hub from RJ-45 or AUI port	Plug 10BASE-T cable into hub from RJ-45 or AUI port	Plug 10BASE-T cable into hub from RJ-45 or AUI port
Central Management	Done through GUI.Complete control of user access, CD grouping, cache usage, etc. Also monitors network usage and performances.	Done through GUI. Complete control of user access, CD grouping, cache usage, etc. Also monitors network usage and performance.	Done through GUI. Complete control of user access, CD grouping, cache usage, etc. Also monitors network usage and performance
Operation Features	CDs automatically added or removed from online catalog when discs are inserted or removed. Latest CD-server features may be downloaded free from the Ten X Web site.	Supports reading and writing CDs over the network. CDs automatically added or removed from online catalog when discs are inserted or removed. Latest CD-server features may be downloaded free from the Ten X Web site.	Supports CD readers, recorder and NSM jukeboxes. No software to install on existing servers or clients. CDs automatically added or removed from online catalog when discs are inserted or removed. Latest features may be downloaded free from the Ten X Web site.
Security	NetWare compatible. Login security and user access to specific CDs controlled, if desired.	NetWare compatible. Login security and user access to specific CDs controlled, if desired.	NetWare compatible. Login security and user access to specific CDs controlled, if desired
Comments	1GB hard disk cache. No software to install	Hard disk cache. No software to install. Read and write CDs over the network.	Hard disk cache. No software to install. Read and write CDs from the network.
Warranty/Service	30-day money back guarantee. 1 year parts and labor.	30-day money back guarantee. 1 year parts and labor.	30-day money back guarantee. 1 year parts and labor.
List Price	$2,995	$5,495	$11,725

N/A—Not applicable   INA—Information not available

12 OTHER NETWORK HARDWARE

THIS CHAPTER DISCUSSES some of the additional items you need to put together a network. The first is power protection. These products protect your network equipment from damage or downtime due to power irregularities. Because printing is an important network function, network printers are also discussed here. In addition, you'll also learn about modems, important network peripherals that are instrumental in remote communications. Finally, you'll find out about network test equipment (cable testers and protocol analyzers). Such devices can help you troubleshoot network problems and save you time in the process.

OTHER NETWORK HARDWARE

Power Protection

We often take power for granted, not surprisingly, since it is available to us 99 percent of the time, 24 hours per day, seven days a week. But to keep sensitive equipment up and running you need to pay special attention to power sources. Power interruptions or severe fluctuations can cause disruption or even damage your equipment. Even quick dips in voltage can cause a system to go down. All your computer equipment should have some level of power protection.

Levels of Power Protection

Performance	Reliability	Manageability	**Scalability**	Flexibility	**Value**

There are various levels of power protection. The first level is a surge protected power strip, an inexpensive item you're probably familiar with. This device protects equipment from voltage spikes that could damage it, and is a common level of power protection for individual workstations. A step up is power conditioning, which filters power from electrical interference in addition to providing surge protection. Power regulators provide surge protection and power filtering, and also provide a precise voltage output even though power going into the device may vary approximately ±15 volts. This assures a more stable power source for equipment that may be sensitive to the minor power fluctuations that are not uncommon in most business environments.

Uninterruptable power supplies (UPS) offer the highest level of power protection. Many of these devices perform all of the functions of other power protection devices, but also have a battery that continues to supply power for a limited period of time if total power is lost. UPS devices have become standard equipment for protecting critical hardware such as server systems. All servers should be on some kind of UPS system to protect them from damage and prevent them from going down should the power go out. If you want to continue network operations during an outage, you need to supply backup power to all the components in the chain (hubs, routers, workstations, and so on).

UPS Types

Performance	**Reliability**	**Manageability**	Scalability	Flexibility	Value

UPS devices are either online or standby. In an online device, power goes to the battery and the battery supplies power while being charged. This method regulates voltage and conditions power as well as providing

OTHER NETWORK HARDWARE

power in the event of power failure. In standby devices, the battery is engaged only when a disruption to the power source occurs. These units may or may not provide power conditioning and regulation, but most do.

Power and Battery Consumption					
Performance	Reliability	Manageability	**Scalability**	Flexibility	Value

UPS devices have a range of power capabilities, from $175 single-server bread box units to those costing tens of thousands of dollars that have the power to protect just about everything on the network. The key factors are the battery size and how much power consumption can be accommodated. The more power drain on a battery, the less time the UPS can keep power available. Your local power conditions are a factor in deciding your needs here. If you experience short and frequent outages during business hours, you need to protect all your equipment for short periods. If you have less frequent but longer outages, the servers alone may need protection and automatic shutdown if power is not restored after a certain amount of time.

Power Management Features					
Performance	Reliability	**Manageability**	Scalability	Flexibility	**Value**

Power monitoring and management features differentiate UPSs. Most units have some LEDs to indicate basic power conditions such as whether power is on battery, whether there is an overload condition, or whether the battery needs replacing. In addition, the unit may emit a tone whenever source power is lost and battery operations are engaged. Network UPS systems come with a serial connection or network connection (or both) to report unit status and enable software to take action according to power-related events. For example, if there's a power outage, a message might appear on the administrator's console to notify him or her of the condition. If power is not restored within 15 minutes, the software begins downing the server properly before battery power runs out. Of course, when power is restored, the unit switches back to the regular power source. Incorporating power management software also enables you to analyze your power usage and environment. This makes it easier to plan and efficiently invest in the necessary equipment.

OTHER NETWORK HARDWARE

Network Printers

Because sharing printers is a valuable network capability, vendors have responded with printers designed specifically for that purpose. Unlike personal printers, network printers have built-in network connections. Network printers are also constructed for heavy use. Choosing a network printer involves determining both the print features and connectivity features you need. This chapter covers monochrome laser printers, which make up the bulk of the network printing market.

Print Speed and Resolution

Performance   Reliability   Manageability   Scalability   **Flexibility**   **Value**

Two key printer features are print resolution and print speed. Print resolution, or print quality, is measured in dots per square inch (dpi). The typical network laser printer offers 400 to 600 dpi. This is very crisp detail for any text and suitable for basic graphics needs. Higher resolutions are offered for graphic-intensive applications to provide better gray shades and transitions. If you primarily print text, 600 dpi offers more than adequate print clarity.

Print speed is measured by how many pages per minute (ppm) are printed. A printer's speed varies depending on the file size, the complexity of the print job, the printer memory (RAM), and the resolution at which you are printing. A text document prints faster than one loaded with graphics because there is less information to process. The print speed rating shown in product literature is almost always the printer's *maximum* speed based on text page printing, unless stated otherwise. A printer has internal memory to process print requests and is often upgradable. These days 4Mb is about minimum and about 12MB lets you handle typical text and graphics with good speed. Most printers have multiple resolution settings and higher resolutions take a bit longer to print. Twelve pages per minute (for text printing) is about the minimum for network printers today; most are in the 12 to 16 ppm print range, which is suitable for the typical printing needs of a 20 person workgroup. High-end printers are capable of 20 to 30 ppm and are well-suited for larger workgroups, high print volumes, or heavy graphics use.

Paper Handling

Performance   Reliability   Manageability   Scalability   **Flexibility**   Value

---

If you use different types of paper, paper handling is an important feature. Multiple bins (most often two) switchable at the user station are convenient for choosing between letterhead and just plain paper, for example. Paper size can also be an issue when you use the same printer for letter, legal, or large

OTHER NETWORK HARDWARE

format printing. Sheet capacities are similar among machines of the same
class (high-volume printers can of course handle larger amounts of paper).

Connectivity Features

Performance　　Reliability　　**Manageability**　　Scalability　　**Flexibility**　　Value

---

A printer is classified as a network printer if it has a built-in option for
network connection (network adapter card). The choice in cards may be
important—check whether there's an option for either Ethernet or Token-
Ring. The next level of connectivity is the printer's communication protocol support. These include IPX/SPX (Novell), TCP/IP, Appletalk, and others. Because print jobs may come from different sources, you might want
to be able to autoswitch between protocols. In addition, a choice in cards
should include a choice in connectors. Multiple cable connectors on the
same card give you greater flexibility if the printer ends up in a different
department on another cabling system. A multiport printer may accept
print jobs from its serial, parallel, or network card by sensing the signal
and switching to the appropriate port. Other issues of print connectivity
may be managed from print manager software that comes with the unit.

Printer Emulation

Performance　　Reliability　　Manageability　　Scalability　　**Flexibility**　　Value

---

Print information can come in different forms and the printer must be
able to translate this information into print form. This capability is called
printer emulation. Postscript is an increasingly popular emulation because
of its ability to handle both text and graphics well. But there are other
popular protocols, such as the Hewlett-Packard LaserJet protocol, that a
printer should be able to handle. Some applications only support certain
printer emulations. Most network printers support multiple printer emulations and can autoswitch between them.

Print Management

Performance　　Reliability　　**Manageability**　　Scalability　　**Flexibility**　　Value

---

All printers have some sort of visual display and controls to make setting
changes right at the printer. But because network printers are hooked
into the network, it makes sense to manage them remotely when possible.
The more printer settings and connectivity aspects that you can manage
remotely through software, the better. This saves time and effort for both

OTHER NETWORK HARDWARE

the user and the network administrator. Some printer vendors supply software for extensive print management but most rely on the NOS and workstation operating systems for remote management functions.

The two things to manage are printer functions and network connections. Printer functions include resolution settings, paper bins, and so on. Some monitor toner and paper levels remotely, alerting users before they print and telling administrators so the toner and/or paper can be replenished. Managing connections includes monitoring connection status and print activity, and reporting on these factors. Reporting may include SNMP messages to network management applications. Software can also provide variable levels of security that can lock printer settings from user changes or even access.

Duty Cycle

Performance	**Reliability**	Manageability	Scalability	Flexibility	Value

High-volume printing requires well-constructed equipment, but not all network printers need to be able to print thousands of pages per day. Before buying, you need to estimate how many pages per month are printed by the workgroup sharing the printer. Printers have a "duty cycle" rating measured in maximum recommended print pages per month. Exceeding the maximum places undue stress on the machine, possibly shortening its life or causing premature failure. The duty cycle rating helps you choose a printer that can meet the volumes you need.

Modems

Modems have become an integral part of networking. They can be the key link to connecting other LANs, tying in a remote user, providing access to the Internet, or enabling PC-based faxing. Modems translate digital signals into analog signals for transmission over telephone lines and translate them back into digital signals on the other end. Modem technology has developed rapidly. Reliability and speed continue to improve and we seem to have a new widespread standard every six to eight months. Modems are commonly installed at user workstations, but they are increasingly being installed in file servers and dedicated communications servers for distributed access, easier management, and improved security, since these important communication tools are becoming more critical to business and network operations.

Baud Rate

Performance	Reliability	Manageability	Scalability	Flexibility	Value

The baud rate is the actual speed at which electrical signals can be passed and received. The common speeds are 14.4 Kbps and 28.8 Kbps; 28.8 Kbps

OTHER NETWORK HARDWARE

is preferred for new purchases. Actual transmission speeds are often double that through the use of compression built into the unit. High-speed modems are used for specialized connections, usually between LANs passing large amounts of data. The communications between modems are at the highest supported rate of both modems, so a faster modem automatically switches to a slower speed to communicate with a slower modem.

Compatibility

Performance   Reliability   Manageability   Scalability   **Flexibility**   Value

Telecommunications can be tricky and modems can seem like mysterious gremlins whose faulty connections have no apparent explanation. Compatibility between like modems is never a problem, but most modems end up connecting to other modems of different brands and even different speed capabilities. In most cases, this isn't a problem, but some modems tend to be make connections more reliably than others. This can be due to emulation capabilities, recognized AT command set, handling of line interference, and other factors. Most vendors don't list compatible modems because the term "AT-compatible" is widely used to mean compatibility with all modems that use the AT command set developed by Hayes. Buyers often choose a modem with brand name and a reputation for reliability, which includes compatibility and a high rate of successful connections.

Feature Distinctions

Performance   Reliability   **Manageability**   Scalability   **Flexibility**   Value

Aside from speed, modems seem more alike than different. They are based on the same communications standards and perform much like other modems in the same class. An internal modem requires a software interface to tell the user connections and configuration information. External modems, on the other hand, usually have a series of LEDs that provide some of this information right on the unit itself. These LEDs can be handy when you're troubleshooting and cannot access information through software. Modems should also be able to redial failed connections. This feature can save you time and effort when you're establishing new connections.

When you place a modem on a network, there may be high demands on its use. In this situation, the modem's reliability becomes important, as does its ability to perform a wide range of tasks. Most modems now support fax transmissions for PC-based faxing. From the network manager's point of view, it can be critical to be able to manage modems remotely, especially if they are on servers in different parts of the building, or even at other sites. If you plan to use the modem on leased lines, look for a

OTHER NETWORK HARDWARE

modem that specifically supports this capability, and be prepared to spend more. Such modems run close to $1,000 in many cases.

Warranty					
Performance	Reliability	Manageability	Scalability	Flexibility	**Value**

Most of us are using 14.4 Kbps or 28.8 Kbps modems at our stations or a server. These types of modems usually cost under $300, and are not worth repairing if something goes wrong. Therefore the warranty becomes an important feature. If you have a three-year warranty, you know that the modem will be replaced for free if anything goes wrong with it within the warranty period. If it fails after the three-year warranty period, you don't care because it has served its function long enough and by that time you're probably ready to upgrade to a faster unit. Warranties range from 90 days to a lifetime. Three years buys good protection. A lifetime warranty sounds nice, but you will undoubtedly upgrade long before that.

Test Equipment

Installing and maintaining network equipment require testing and troubleshooting. When you install, you need to test as you go from the physical layer (cabling, connectors, and so on) to the application layers. When existing networks experience problems, testing usually goes the other way, starting at the application layer and moving down to the physical layer. You can perform application layer analysis with software such as the NOS network management applications, or other software tools. But to test cable connections and analyze the data packets that are sent, you need specialized equipment.

Cable testers and protocol analyzers are the two key types of network test equipment. Cable testers are usually hand-held devices that let you carry out a series of tests to ensure that the cable connection is functioning properly for data transmissions. You can use them to troubleshoot faulty wires, improper connector installations, electrical interference, and so forth. A protocol analyzer can be software, hardware, or a combination of both that examines network traffic at the protocol layer, analyzing data packets for integrity and traffic flow. These analyzers help isolate problem devices, such as a system sending packets too slowly or identifying the last protocol transfer before a network failure, possibly offering important clues to the problem. Both cable testing and protocol analysis monopolize the use of the connections being tested.

OTHER NETWORK HARDWARE

Cable Tests

Performance   Reliability   Manageability   Scalability   **Flexibility**   Value

Most cable test equipment conforms to the Technical Services Bulletin (TSB) standard for cable testing. This standard calls for testing in four areas: wire mapping (the continuity of physical connections), link length (the length of the cable connection), attenuation (the signal power lost as the signal travels across distances), and cross talk (electrical interference from other wires or external factors). Although most products use the same methods for testing in these areas, the reporting features and level of detail provided can vary. Of course, different units may test different types of cables and accommodate different cable connectors.

You may also want to be able to measure the difference in time it takes for a wire pair to reach its destination. These minute differences, known as "skew," can be a problem if the skew is high enough to affect the success of the transmission. This is particularly true for high-speed technologies that split signals across wire pairs and reassemble them at their destination. Skew is measured in nanoseconds and tolerances vary depending on protocol.

Protocol Analyzer Types

Performance   Reliability   Manageability   **Scalability**   **Flexibility**   Value

You can perform protocol analysis with software and a network interface card (NIC). This method is the least expensive because it allows you to use an existing computer to do the processing and reporting. However, most NICs are designed to read only packets addressed to them, so you need to get a NIC that can read all traffic—referred to as operating in "promiscuous mode." Software compatibility and system performance are important issues to consider.

The other solution is to go with a self-contained device that includes all the necessary integrated components. These devices vary from boxes that plug into a CPU for monitor display and storage to complete portable computer systems dedicated to protocol analysis. Such devices usually offer better performance than software solutions because everything is integrated and performing a single function, and components like the NIC are specifically designed for protocol analysis (with onboard memory and so on).

Protocol Analyzer Features

Performance   Reliability   **Manageability**   Scalability   Flexibility   **Value**

Protocol analyzers have a common set of analysis features but may run on different platforms and may be more or less extensible to WAN

OTHER NETWORK HARDWARE

environments. All protocol analyzers provide packet-level analysis, particularly of the packet headers, which contain source and destination information. Products may have different filtering capabilities—the ability to filter out unwanted packets to analyze and display in reports.

Some protocol analyzers can help you diagnose problems rather than just present reports on packet information. Problem diagnosis goes beyond presenting filtered packets, in addition making determinations about what is wrong or what needs fixing. You may get a reference to a symptom and diagnoses table or an indication about which particular piece of equipment is causing the problems. Such features help point network administrators in the right direction, rather than leaving them on their own to sort through the mounds of information these devices collect. In addition, being able to automate test procedures and preferred form of output saves time and effort, particularly if you perform protocol analysis infrequently and you have to relearn how to use the device.

Test Reporting

Performance	Reliability	**Manageability**	Scalability	Flexibility	Value

For cable testers, readouts are fairly standard, with limited graphics on an LCD screen that is part of the unit. Protocol analyzers are different, however. These devices not only troubleshoot but provide a host of statistical information about network traffic. Flexible graphic displays can be quite valuable in illustrating subtleties. You might be able to filter data in various ways and choose from several graphic styles. At minimum, you want a generous amount of predefined reports if customization is not an option.

Compatibility

Performance	**Reliability**	Manageability	Scalability	Flexibility	Value

For cable testing, compatibility is straightforward. You need to determine the cable types and category levels it will test and what connector types it will accommodate and test. Cable testers usually test either fiber or copper cabling exclusively.

Be sure that the protocol analyzer is compatible with the protocols you need. This includes the sublayers of NOS protocols. For instance, IPX/SXP compatibility should also mean that the device can analyze related Novell protocols such as NCP and NDS to be a more complete solution. A narrow range of compatible protocols may not be an issue for you if your network is homogenous.

■ Uninterruptible Power Supply

Manufacturer	**Alpha Technologies**	**APC**
Model	CFR Series UPS	MX and MX5000
Type	Online	Line interactive
INPUT		
VAC/Watts	120VAC/1087 watts	208/240 VAC, 60Hz
Range	-25%, +10%	-25% to +15%
OUTPUT		
VAC/Watts	120VAC/1000watts	120/208/240VAC
Regular Balanced	+/-5%	+/-5%
Regular Unbalanced	± 1%	INA
Efficiency	92%	>93%
Overload Capacity	150% for 10 min. 200% for 5 secs.	Capacity: 3000/2250 (MX3000), 5000/3750 (2) (MX5000)
Typical Runtime (Full/Half Load)	13 min./30 min.	7/18 min. (3000) 8/20 min. (5000)
Recharge Time	5 hrs.	1.2 hrs. (3000), 2.7 hrs. (5000)
User Replaceable	Yes	Yes
Hot-Swappable	No	Yes
LEDs	Low battery, line present/failure	Battery
Audible Alerts	Battery power source, overload condition	Yes
Bundled Software and Features (Standard or Optional)	N/A	SNMP via APC SNMP Adapter. Power Chute® plus for automatic shutdown and reboot, administrator notification, scheduling of self tests (optional for $69-$200).
Outlets	4 5-1SR	1/L14-30R, 2L6-30R, 6/5-15R
Safety	UL/CSA	UL per 1778, CSAper C22.2, TUV per IEC 950
Dimensions	8.5"W x 21"H x 22"	17.8"H x 13.8"W x 17.8" 9.1"W x 6.9"H x 17.8": (battery pack)
Weight	174 lbs.	40-45 lbs. (Electronics module), 104-130 lbs. (Isolation), 64 lbs. each (batteries)
Comments	Expandable backup time to 8 hrs., complete isolation	Consists of 3 modules: an isolation module, an electronics module, and external battery pack(s). Designed for use with multiple servers. Additional batteries can be added for extended runtime. Intelligent bypass and Intelligent Serial Interface.
Warranty/Service	2 year	2 years with lifetime equipment protection. Tech support also available.
List Price	$1,985	$3,499 (MX3000) $5,199 (MX5000)

Manufacturer	**Best Power**	**Best Power**
Model	Fortress Series	UNITY/I Single Phase
Type	Line interactive	Line interactive
INPUT		
VAC/Watts	120 or 230VAC	200/208/220/230/240 VAC
Range	92-136VAC or 196-254VAC	INA
OUTPUT		
VAC/Watts	120 or 230VAC	200/208/220/230/240 VAC
Regular Balanced	± 3%	± 3%
Regular Unbalanced	INA	INA
Efficiency	95%	95%-96%

N/A—Not applicable   INA—Information not available

Uninterruptible Power Supply ■

Manufacturer	Best Power	Best Power
Overload Capacity	Circuit breaker protected	150% surge
Typical Runtime (Full/Half Load)	5/15 min.-12/33 min.	8 min.-19 min. @ .75
Recharge Time	3-5 hrs.	2.5-5 hrs.
User Replaceable	Yes (some models)	No
Hot-Swappable	No	Nes
LEDs	Alarm, battery, line	Line, battery, bypass, alarm
Audible Alerts	14 alarms, distinguished by 4-character display	19 alarm conditions distinguished on a digital display
Bundled Software and Features (Standard or Optional)	Standard: power management, and safe shutdown Optional: SNMP adapter	Standard: power management, and safe shutdown Optional: SNMP adapter
Outlets	4 to 6 output	Hardwired
Safety	UL, CUL, CSA	UL, CUL, CSA, and TUV
Dimensions	6.5"H x 5.25"W x 15.5" to 17"H x 8"W x 23"	29"H x 10.5"W x 25.75"
Weight	28-155 lbs.	200-480 lbs.
Comments		External battery cabinets available for extended running
Warranty/Service	2 year	2 year
List Price	$549–$3,599	$3,799–$7,099

Manufacturer	Clary Corp	Clary Corp	Computer Power
Model	LI Series	Elite Series	Survivor TSO
Type	Line interactive	Double conversion online	Online
INPUT			
VAC/Watts	120VAC (US), 220VAC (EUR)	120-240VAC	120VAC
Range	+17%, -23%	+10%, -25%	+15-20%
OUTPUT			
VAC/Watts	120VAC-220VAC	3-5KVA	120VAC
Regular Balanced	+/- 5%	INA	+/- 2%
Regular Unbalanced	+/- 5%	+/-3%	INA
Efficiency	98%	83/87%	90% full load
Overload Capacity	125% for 10 min. 150% for 30 secs.	110% for 10 min. 120% for 25 secs.	Normal: 150% for 1 hr Emergency: 130% for 5 min.
Typical Runtime (Full/Half Load)	8 min./20 min.	18 min./50 min.	Full: 6-15 min. Half: 15-40 min.
Recharge Time	4-5 hrs.	4-5 hrs.	10 min.-1 hr
User Replaceable	No	Yes	No
Hot-Swappable	No	No	No
LEDs	Load, low battery, replace, online	32 character alphanumeric LCD	Overload, replace battery, isolated output
Audible Alerts	Summary, on battery, overload, replace battery		None
Bundled Software and Features (Standard or Optional)	Standard: Power Monitor Plus Optional: All OS shutdown	Standard: Power Monitor Plus Optional: All OS shutdown	SNMP capable, software available for all popular networks and operating systems
Outlets	3-6	5-9	6
Safety	UL and CSA, C66	UL and CSA	UL 1778 listed
Dimensions	6.0"H x 5.1"W x 15.9" to 15"H x 7.3"W x 19.7"	28.4"H x 10.3"W x 23.6" 36.4"H x 15.4"W x 26.8"	Varies

N/A—Not applicable   INA—Information not available

Table Continues →

■ Uninterruptible Power Supply

Manufacturer	Clary Corp	Clary Corp	Computer Power
Weight	21-104lbs	235-652lbs.	Varies
Comments	Other models available	Other models available	
Warranty/Service	1 year	1 year	10 year pro-rated
List Price	$477–$1,997	$5,575–$7,421	$3,145+

Manufacturer	Controlled Power	Controlled Power
Model	Series LT	Series MD
Type	Online	Online
INPUT		
VAC/Watts	250VA-2.1KVA	3.1KVA7.5KVA
Range	-40%, +10%	-40%, +10%
OUTPUT		
VAC/Watts	250VA-2.1KVA	3.1KVA7.5KVA
Regular Balanced		
Regular Unbalanced	+/- 3%	+/- 3%
Efficiency	90%	90% @ full load
Overload Capacity	125% for 10 min.	125% for 10 min.
Typical Runtime (Full/Half Load)	20 min./50 min.	12 min./32 min.
Recharge Time	3 hrs.	3 hrs.
User Replaceable	Yes	Yes
Hot-Swappable	No	No
LEDs	Load, charge, capacity, input voltage, output voltage	Load, charge, input voltage, output voltage
Audible Alerts	Variety of conditions- user selectable	User selectable
Bundled Software and Features (Standard or Optional)	Real-time monitoring	Real-time monitoring
Outlets	6	6
Safety	UL and CSA approved	UL and CSA
Dimensions	8"W x 17.5"H x 17.5"D	8"W x 17.5"H x 17.5"D
Weight	64 lbs	64 lbs
Comments	Expandable, provides isolation and power conditioning	Expandable, provides isolation and power conditioning. Additional run-time available.
Warranty/Service	1 year	1 year
List Price	$1,165+	$3,695+

Manufacturer	DELTEC	DELTEC
Model	PowerWorks RS	PowerRite Max
Type	Online	Line interactive
INPUT		
VAC/Watts	120 or 240 VAC	120 or 230 VAC
Range	-27%- +22%	-35%- +20%
OUTPUT	Power levels (VA rating)	Power levels (VA rating)
VAC/Watts	2.1, 3.1, 5.0, 6.0KVA	450, 700, 1000, 1500 VA
Regular Balanced	+2%, -2%	+6%, -10%
Regular Unbalanced	N/A	N/A

N/A—Not applicable   INA—Information not available

Uninterruptible Power Supply ■

Manufacturer	DELTEC	DELTEC
Efficiency	92%	96%
Overload Capacity	INA	INA
Typical Runtime (Full/Half Load)	8-12 min./22-37 min.	5-8 min./14-26 min.
Recharge Time	Less than 3 hrs.	Less than 4 hrs.
User Replaceable	No	Yes
Hot-Swappable	No	Yes
LEDs	Input level, operation status, battery level, load level, battery service	Power on, input level, operation status, battery level, load level, battery service, site wiring fault
Audible Alerts	Battery power source, overload condition	Battery power source, battery service, overload condition
Bundled Software and Features (Standard or Optional)	Power Mgt. Software, SNMP adapter (optional), sequential shutdown, unattended shutdown of all network devices, e-mail, paging capabilities	Windows 95 PNP driver, Power Mgt. Software: sequential, unattended shutdown of all network devices, e-mail and paging capabilities
Outlets	4-14 outputs, 1 input	4 or 6 outputs, 1 input
Safety	UL, CSA	UL, CSA, EN 50091-1
Dimensions	16"W x 6.8"H x 24"D 16"W x 6.8"H x 24"D 6.8"W x 17.5"H x 24"D (rack)	4.6"W x 6.4"H x 14.8"D 7"W x 8.8"H x 17.1"D
Weight	125-180 lbs.	22-55 lbs.
Comments	Advanced Battery Mgt. Extends battery life, extended battery packs	Network/modem surge protection, ABM technology, SNMP option, load scheduling, redundant power supply
Warranty/Service	10 year prorated(3 full)	10 year prorated(2 full)
List Price	Starts at $2,525	Starts at $299

Manufacturer	DELTEC	DELTEC
Model	PowerRite Pro	PowerRite Plus
Type	Line interactive	Off-line/standby
INPUT		
VAC/Watts	120 or 230 VAC	120 or 230 VAC
Range	-25%- +25%	-14%- +21%
OUTPUT	Power levels (VA rating)	Power levels (VA rating)
VAC/Watts	450, 600, 1000, 1500, 2000, 2200, 3000 VA	220, 300, 420, 500 VA, 650 VA
Regular Balanced	+6%, -10%	N/A
Regular Unbalanced	N/A	N/A
Efficiency	96%	99%
Overload Capacity	INA	INA
Typical Runtime (Full/Half Load)	6-14 min./18-43 min.	5-10 min./20-30 min.
Recharge Time	3 to 6 hrs.	Less than 6 hrs.
User Replaceable	No	No
Hot-Swappable	No	No
LEDs	Power on, input level, battery level, load level, comm port, battery service, site wiring fault	Power on, battery service, site wiring fault
Audible Alerts	Battery power source, overload	Battery power source, Low battery, service battery
Bundled Software and Features (Standard or Optional)	Optional Power Mgt. Software: sequential, unattended shutdown of all network devices, saves work in progress, e-mail, paging capabilities	Optional Power Mgt. Software: orderly shutdown, unattended shutdown, incident logs, diagnostics
Outlets	4 or 6 outputs, 1 input	2 or 4 outputs, 1 input

N/A—Not applicable   INA—Information not available

Table Continues →

■ Uninterruptible Power Supply

Manufacturer	DELTEC	DELTEC
Safety	UL, CSA, VDE	UL, CSA, VDE
Dimensions	4.5"W x 6.5"H x 15.7"D 7"W x 9"H x 16.7"D	3.4"W x 6.0"H x 13.5"D 4.7"W x 6.0"H x 14.2"D
Weight	25-53 lbs.	14-20 lbs.
Comments	Advanced battery management (ABM) extends battery life, rackmount units available	Advanced Battery Management (ABM) extends battery life, start on battery capability
Warranty/Service	10 year prorated(2 full)	5 year prorated (2 full)
List Price	Starts at $399	Starts at $119

Manufacturer	Exide Electronics Group, Inc.	Exide Electronics Group, Inc.
Model	NetUPS model 450VA (700VA and 1000VA also available)	NetUPS model 1500VA (700VA and 1000VA also available)
Type	Line interactive	Line interactive
INPUT		
VAC/Watts	110, 120, 127 VAC Normal	110, 120, 127 VAC Normal
Range	78-144 VAC w/out using batteries	78-144 VAC w/out using batteries
OUTPUT		
VAC/Watts	450-280	1500-960
Regular Balanced	-10%, +6%	-10%, +6%
Regular Unbalanced	INA	INA
Efficiency	96%	96%
Overload Capacity	200% of full load for 15 cycles, 110% for 2 min.	200% of full load for 15 cycles, 110% for 2 min.
Typical Runtime (Full/Half Load)	6-18 min.	6-18 min.
Recharge Time	Less than 4 hrs.	Less than 4 hrs.
User Replaceable	Yes	Yes
Hot-Swappable	Yes—front panel hot swappable for all models	Yes—front panel hot swappable for all models
LEDs	Input voltage status, battery charge condition, load capacity, communications activity, potential battery failure, site wiring faults, system normal. Bar graphs for input level, battery charge.	Input voltage status, battery charge condition, load capacity, communications activity, potential battery failure, site wiring faults, system normal. Bar graphs for input level, battery charge.
Audible Alerts	Alarm horn for other than normal conditions	Alarm horn for other than normal conditions
Bundled Software and Features (Standard or Optional)	Lansafe III Power Mgt. Software. Controls, monitors and configures UPS. Provides unattended system shutdown.	Lansafe III Power Mgt. Software. Controls, monitors and configures UPS. Provides unattended system shutdown.
Outlets	(4) 5-15R	(6) 5-15R
Safety	UL 1778, CSA C22.2 No. 107.1, UL 1449 rated MOV	UL 1778, CSA C22.2 No. 107.1, UL 1449 rated MOV
Dimensions	6.4"H x 4.6"W x 14.8"D	8.8"H x 7"W x 17.1"D
Weight	24 lbs.	50 lbs.
Comments	Perfect for computer networking environments. Protects critical equipment from surges, brownouts and power outages. User configurable front panel w/ RJ11/45 modem/data line surge protection. Available in both 50- and 60Hz. Competitively priced.	Perfect for computer networking environments. Protects critical equipment from surges, brownouts and power outages. User configurable front panel w/ RJ11/45 modem/data line surge protection. Available in both 50- and 60Hz. Competitively priced.
Warranty/Service	2 years, parts and labor	2 years, parts and labor
List Price	$329	$775

N/A—Not applicable   INA—Information not available

Uninterruptible Power Supply ■

Manufacturer	Exide Electronics Group, Inc.	Exide Electronics Group, Inc.
Model	Powerware Prestige 650 (800 also available)	Powerware Prestige 1000 (800 also available)
Type	Online	Online
INPUT		
VAC/Watts	120 VAC Normal	120 VAC Normal
Range	85-144 VAC (full load); 75-144 VAC (half load) w/out using batteries	85-144 VAC (full load); 75-144 VAC (half load) w/out using batteries
OUTPUT		
VAC/Watts	650-445	1000/700
Regular Balanced	+/-3%	+/-3%
Regular Unbalanced	INA	INA
Efficiency	85%	85.7%
Overload Capacity	105% indefinite/106% to 110%—4 min./greater than 110%—4 secs.	105% indefinite/106% to 110%—4 min./greater than 110%—4 secs.
Typical Runtime (Full/Half Load)	15-45 min.	8-24 min.
Recharge Time	4 hrs. to 80% capacity	4 hrs. to 80% capacity
User Replaceable	Yes	Yes
Hot-Swappable	Yes—hot swappable extended battery packs	Yes—hot swappable extended battery packs
LEDs	Normal, bypass, battery, overload	Normal, bypass, battery, overload
Audible Alerts	Alarm horn for other than normal conditions	Alarm horn for other than normal conditions
Bundled Software and Features (Standard or Optional)	OnliNet software is user configurable and provides unattended shutdown of the operating system. Allows scheduled shutdown and restarts of system on any size network. Can be used on mixed networks such as Novell and UNIX.	OnliNet software is user configurable and provides unattended shutdown of the operating system. Allows scheduled shutdown and restarts of system on any size network. Can be used on mixed networks such as Novell and UNIX.
Outlets	(4) 5-15R	(4) 5-15R
Safety	UL 1778, CSA C22.2 No. 107.1: EN50091-1	UL 1778, CSA C22.2 No. 107.1: EN50091-1
Dimensions	9.9"H x 5.6"W x 15.8"D	9.9"H x 5.6"W x 15.8"D
Weight	28.5 lbs.	28.5 lbs.
Comments	Perfect for power protection for servers, workstations, office equipment and light industrial applications. Ready to use straight out of the box. The continuous online power provides clean, reliable power to protect critical equipment. Connectivity via Ethernet and Token Ring SNMP adapter.	Perfect for power protection for servers, workstations, office equipment and light industrial applications. Ready to use straight out of the box. The continuous online power provides clean, reliable power to protect critical equipment. Connectivity via Ethernet and Token Ring SNMP adapter.
Warranty/Service	2 year, parts and labor	2 year, parts and labor
List Price	$699	$889

Manufacturer	Hewlett-Packard	Hewlett-Packard
Model	600VA	900VA
Type	Line interactive	Line interactive
INPUT		
VAC/Watts	120 VAC/420 watts	120 VAC/630 watts
Range	-22%,+10%	-22%,+10%
OUTPUT		
VAC/Watts	120 VAC/400 watts	120 VAC/600 watts
Regular Balanced	+/-5%	+/-5%
Regular Unbalanced	+/-5%	+/-5%
Efficiency	95% typical @ full load	95% typical @ full load
Overload Capacity	105% alarm 110% shutdown	105% alarm 110% shutdown

N/A—Not applicable   INA—Information not available

Table Continues →

■ Uninterruptible Power Supply

Manufacturer	Hewlett-Packard	Hewlett-Packard
Typical Runtime (Full/Half Load)	6 min./17 min.	11 min./28 min.
Recharge Time	4 to 5 hrs. typical	4 to 5 hrs. typical
User Replaceable	No	No
Hot-Swappable	No	No
LEDs	Line or battery, battery replace, overload, fault, low battery	Line or battery, battery replace, overload, fault, low battery
Audible Alerts	On battery, overload, low battery	On battery, overload, low battery
Bundled Software and Features (Standard or Optional)	Power Mgt. SW (standard): SNMP agents, OpenView application, auto-shutdown, UPS status and monitoring, historical graphs, diagnostics	Power Mgt. SW (standard): SNMP agents, OpenView application, auto-shutdown, UPS status and monitoring, historical graphs, diagnostics
Outlets	4 outputs, 1 input	4 outputs, 1 input
Safety	UL and CSA approved	UL and CSA approved
Dimensions	4.8"W x 7.7"H x 13.5"D	6.5"W x 9.5"H x 17.5"D
Weight	28 lbs.	48 lbs.
Comments	Warranty upgrades, cables and software included	Warranty upgrades, cables and software included
Warranty/Service	2 year express exchange	2 year express exchange
List Price	$319	$489

Manufacturer	Hewlett-Packard	Hewlett-Packard
Model	1000VA	1250VA
Type	Online	Line interactive
INPUT		
VAC/Watts	120VAC/82Watts	120VAC/900 watts
Range	-22%,+10%	-22%,+10%
OUTPUT		
VAC/Watts	120VAC/700 watts	120VAC/850 watts
Regular Balanced	+/-3%	+/-5%
Regular Unbalanced	+/-3%	+/-5%
Efficiency	85% typical at full load	95% typical at full load
Overload Capacity	105% to 150% for 10 secs.	105% alarm 110% shutdown
Typical Runtime (Full/Half Load)	10 min./22 min.	6 min./20 min.
Recharge Time	2 to 4 hrs. typical	4 to 5 hrs. typical
User Replaceable	No	No
Hot-Swappable	No	No
LEDs	Line or battery, battery capacity, battery replace, overload, fault, low battery, load usage	Line or battery, battery replace, overload, fault, low battery
Audible Alerts	On battery, overload, low battery	On battery, overload, low battery
Bundled Software and Features (Standard or Optional)	Power Mgt. SW (standard): SNMP agents, OpenView application, auto shutdown, UPS status and monitoring, historical graphs, diagnostics	Power Mgt. SW (standard): SNMP agents, OpenView application, auto shutdown, UPS status and monitoring, historical graphs, diagnostics
Outlets	4 outputs, 1 input	4 outputs, 1 input
Safety	UL and CSA approved	UL and CSA approved
Dimensions	8"W x 9"H x 20.8"D	6.5"W x 9.5"H x 17.5"D
Weight	48 lbs.	48 lbs.

N/A—Not applicable   INA—Information not available

Uninterruptible Power Supply ■

Manufacturer	Hewlett-Packard	Hewlett-Packard
Comments	Warranty upgrades, cables and software included and expandable batteries	Warranty upgrades, cables and software included
Warranty/Service	2 year express exchange	2 year express exchange
List Price	$519	$649

Manufacturer	Hewlett-Packard	IntelliPower Inc.
Model	2100VA	BrightUPS
Type	Online	Online, double conversion
INPUT		
VAC/Watts	120VAC/1700 watts	115VAC, 800 watts
Range	-22%,+10%	-25%, +22%
OUTPUT		
VAC/Watts	120VAC/1500 watts	115VAC/733 watts
Regular Balanced	+/-3%	+3%
Regular Unbalanced	+/-3%	+3%
Efficiency	85% typical at full load	92%
Overload Capacity	105% to 150% for 10 secs.	115% continuous 1000% .15 sec., 500% .3 secs.
Typical Runtime (Full/Half Load)	9 min./20 min.	8 min./20 min.
Recharge Time	2 to 4 hrs. typical	2–3 hrs. typical
User Replaceable	No	Yes
Hot-Swappable	No	Yes
LEDs	Line or battery, battery capacity, battery replace, overload, fault, low battery, load usage	Battery capacity, input volt, output load, service battery, ground fault, on battery
Audible Alerts	On battery, overload, low battery	Loss of utility, low battery, service battery, ground fault
Bundled Software and Features (Standard or Optional)	Power Mgt. SW (standard): SNMP agents, OpenView application, auto-shutdown, UPS status and monitoring, historical graphs, diagnostics	Open protocol, optional auto-shutdown, power history, diagnostics & UPS control, SNMP
Outlets	4 outputs, 1 input	5
Safety	UL & CSA approved	UL, ANSI C62.41
Dimensions	8"W x 13.8"H x 20.8"D	5"H x 17"W x 16"D
Weight	87 lbs.	45 lbs.
Comments	Warranty upgrades, cables and software included and expandable batteries	Online—double conversion, single or dual input models, rack mountable, ext. battery packs
Warranty/Service	2 year express exchange	1 year standard 2–5 year optional
List Price	$1,179	$849

Manufacturer	Liebert Corp.	Liebert Corp.
Model	UPStation S3 16KVA	UPStation S 8.0KVA
Type	Online	Online
INPUT		
VAC/Watts	208–240VAC	170–264VAC
Range	-18%, +27%	INA
OUTPUT		
VAC/Watts	$\pm$ 1%	240/110VAC

N/A—Not applicable   INA—Information not available

Table Continues →

■ Uninterruptible Power Supply

Manufacturer	Liebert Corp.	Liebert Corp.
Regular Balanced	INA	INA
Regular Unbalanced	INA	INA
Efficiency	INA	INA
Overload Capacity	Based on configuration	150%, 10 secs. 125%, 10 min.
Typical Runtime (Full/Half Load)	Based on configuration	10 min./40 min.
Recharge Time	Based on configuration	8 hrs. maximum
User Replaceable	No	No
Hot-Swappable	No	No
LEDs	UPS metering, control and status	Metering, control and status, including event logging
Audible Alerts	For all out-of-spec conditions	For out-of-spec conditions
Bundled Software and Features (Standard or Optional)	SiteNet 1 Shutdown interface, SiteNet 2 Monitoring software, SiteNet SNMP software, SiteNet Integrator Multi-function Monitoring software.	Optional SiteNet SNMP Internal Agent allows for remote control and monitoring of connected equipment.
Outlets	4 output, 1 input	4 output, 1 input
Safety	UL 1778, CSA 22.2, IEEE 587 CAT A and B	UL 1778, CSA 22.2, IEEE 587 CAT A and B
Dimensions	62" x 29" x 26"	18" x 27" x 29"
Weight	700 lbs.	560 lbs.
Comments	Provides power protection for large network clusters, industrial, and telecommunications equipment	Communications capabilities designed to make the S 8.0KVA a fully interactive network node
Warranty/Service	2 year	2 year
List Price	$15,600+	$7,164+

Manufacturer	Liebert Corp.	Liebert Corp.	Liebert Corporation
Model	PowerSure 250 VA	UPStation D 900 VA	UPStation GX 1500 VA
Type	Offline	Line interactive	Online
INPUT			
VAC/Watts	120VAC/150 watts	120VAC/630 watts	120VAC/1,050watts
Range	90–135VAC	+10%, –28%	+10%, -20%
OUTPUT			
VAC/Watts	120VAC ± 5%	120VAC	120VAC
Regular Balanced	INA	INA	INA
Regular Unbalanced	INA	INA	INA
Efficiency	97% at normal mode	96% at full load	82%
Overload Capacity	115%	200% for 5 secs., 120% for 1 min., 150% for 1 cycle, 125% for 5 secs.	150% for 10 cycles 120% for 1 sec.
Typical Runtime (Full/Half Load)	10 min./30 min.	6 min./12 min.	10 min./18 min.
Recharge Time	8 hrs.	8 hrs. maximum	4 hrs.
User Replaceable	Yes	No	No
Hot-Swappable	Yes	No	No
LEDs	On/off button, AC light	On/off, on-battery, fault, boost, replace battery, load, battery capacity	Battery capacity, load, battery operation, UPS fault condition
Audible Alerts	Low battery, site wiring fault, over-power, overload short circuit	For all out-of-spec conditions	For all out-of-spec conditions

N/A—Not applicable   INA—Information not available

Uninterruptible Power Supply ■

Manufacturer	Liebert Corp.	Liebert Corp.	Liebert Corporation
Bundled Software and Features (Standard or Optional)	SiteNet 1 Shutdown interface safely shuts down applications, logs power events, and features on-screen graphs to monitor power history.	Optional SiteNet internal SNMP warns users of on-battery conditions, safely shuts down applications, provides on-screen graphs, and logs power events.	Three levels of communications capability: SiteNet 1 Shutdown interface, SiteNet 2 Monitoring software, SiteNet SNMP software, SiteNet Integrator Multi-function Monitoring software
Outlets	2 output, 1 input	6 output, 1 input	4 output, 1 input
Safety	UL and CSA approved	UL1778, UL1449, CSA IEEE 587 CAT.A	UL 1449, IEEE
Dimensions	12"W x 21"H x 19"	10.5" x 6.9" x 17.8"	7" x 17" x 21"
Weight	12.8 lbs.	55 lbs.	83 lbs.
Comments	High-frequency UPS designed for protection of critical loads	Designed for PCs, network servers, and peripherals	Designed as a versatile UPS for network and telecommunications applications.
Warranty/Service	2 year	2 year	2 year
List Price	$173+	$779	$1,314

Manufacturer	Tripp Lite	Tripp Lite
Model	Smart Pro UNISON	Smart Pro DataCenter UPS
Type	Online	Line interactive
INPUT		
VAC/Watts	120VAC	208/240VAC in
Range	-15%, +10%	-25%, +15%
OUTPUT		
VAC/Watts	120VAC, 450-2000 VA	120+208/240 VAC out, 3000 VA +5000 VA
Regular Balanced	ANSI C84.1	ANSI C84.1
Regular Unbalanced	INA	INA
Efficiency	95% or better	95% or better
Overload Capacity	N/A	N/A
Typical Runtime (Full/Half Load)	5 min./10 min.	15 min./30 min., expandable
Recharge Time	4-6 hrs.	4-6 hrs.
User Replaceable	No	Yes
Hot-Swappable	No	Yes
LEDs	Online, on battery, battery replace, overload, voltage correct	Online, on battery, maintenance bypass, battery replace, overload, voltage correct
Audible Alerts	On battery, battery self test	Battery swap, on battery, battery self test
Bundled Software and Features (Standard or Optional)	Multiple operating system software and cabling is included on CD-ROM with complete power management (alarm logs, shutdown, reboot, SNMP, UPS statistics, etc.).	Multiple operating system software and cabling is included on CD ROM with complete power management (alarm logs, shutdown, reboot, SNMP, UPS statistics, etc.).
Outlets	Varies depending on model	14 AC(12-120V; 2-208/240V)
Safety	UL	UL, CSA, CE
Dimensions	Varies depending on model	8"W x 23"H x 22"D
Weight	Varies depending on model	84-126 lbs. without batteries
Comments	Fully regulated voltages, frequency and waveform output	Expandable battery, multiple LAN ports standard
Warranty/Service	2 year/$100,000 connected equipment coverage	2 year/$75,000 connected equipment coverage
List Price	$599–$1,999	$2,799–$4,199

N/A—Not applicable   INA—Information not available

Table Continues →

■ Uninterruptible Power Supply

Manufacturer	Tripp Lite	Tripp Lite
Model	Smart Pro Series	BC Pro Series
Type	Line interactive	Line interactive
INPUT		
VAC/Watts	120VAC	120VAC
Range	-25%, +15%	N/A
OUTPUT		
VAC/Watts	120VAC/280 VA to 3000 VA	120VAC(450-1400 VA)
Regular Balanced	ANSI C84.1	N/A
Regular Unbalanced	INA	INA
Efficiency	95% or better	95% or better
Overload Capacity	N/A	N/A
Typical Runtime (Full/Half Load)	10 min./20 min.	20 min./10 min.
Recharge Time	2-4 hrs.	4-6 hrs.
User Replaceable	No	No
Hot-Swappable	No	No
LEDs	Online, on battery, battery replace, overload, voltage correct	Online, on battery, battery replace, overload
Audible Alerts	On battery, battery self test	On battery, battery replace
Bundled Software and Features (Standard or Optional)	Multiple operating system software and cabling is included on CD-ROM with complete power management (alarm logs, shutdown, reboot, SNMP, UPS statistics, etc.)	Optional CD-ROM software for multiple operating systems
Outlets	Varies depending on model	Varies depending on model
Safety	UL, CSA, CE	UL, CSA
Dimensions	Varies depending on model	Varies depending on model
Weight	Varies depending on model	Varies depending on model
Comments	Some models have expandable batteries, multiple LAN ports, track mount, hot swap	Small footprint, low price, full surge, and noise protection
Warranty/Service	2 years/$50,000 connected equipment coverage	2 years/$25,000 connected equipment coverage
List Price	$299–$2,299	$199–$569

Manufacturer	ViewSonic	ViewSonic
Model	Opti-UPS 1000E	Opti-UPS 1400E
Type	Line interactive	Line interactive
INPUT		
VAC/Watts	88—149VAC	88—149VAC
Range	120VAC +/-12%	120VAC +/-12%
OUTPUT		
VAC/Watts	120VAC/1000VA	120VAC/1400VA
Regular Balanced	N/A	N/A
Regular Unbalanced	N/A	N/A
Efficiency	95%	95%
Overload Capacity	150 % for 10 min. 110% continuous	150 % for 10 min. 110% continuous
Typical Runtime (Full/Half Load)	4 min./ 12 min.	4 min./ 12 min.
Recharge Time	5 hrs. maximum	5 hrs. maximum
User Replaceable	Yes	Yes

N/A—Not applicable   INA—Information not available

Uninterruptible Power Supply ■

Manufacturer	ViewSonic	ViewSonic
Hot-Swappable	Yes	Yes
LEDs	6 LED array: boost, buck, power status, battery, load, replace battery	6 LED array: boost, buck, power status, battery, load, replace battery
Audible Alerts	On battery, low battery, overload, replace battery	On battery, low battery, overload, replace battery
Bundled Software and Features (Standard or Optional)	Included: Power Management Suite CD-ROM and cable for NetWare, Windows NT/95/3.x, DOS. Optional: SNMP	Included: Power Management Suite CD-ROM and cable for NetWare, Windows NT/95/3.x, DOS. Optional: SNMP
Outlets	4	4
Safety	UL and CUL, Microsoft and Novell	UL and CUL, Microsoft and Novell
Dimensions	5.5" x 16.8" x 7.7"	5.5" x 16.8" x 7.7"
Weight	35.3 lbs.	43 lbs.
Comments	Plug-and-play, RJ-11 Internet protection, site wiring indicator, smart communications, and software	Plug-and-play, RJ-11 Internet protection, site wiring indicator, smart communications, and software
Warranty/Service	3 year limited/ $25,000 connected	3 year limited/ $25,000 connected
List Price	$459	$579

Manufacturer	ViewSonic	ViewSonic
Model	Opti-UPS 100E	Opti-UPS 420E
Type	Line interactive	Line interactive
(Input)		
VAC/Watts	88149VAC	88149VAC
Range	120VAC +/-12%	120VAC +/-12%
(Output)		
VAC/Watts	120VAC/650VA	120VAC/420VA
Regular Balanced	N/A	N/A
Regular Unbalanced	N/A	N/A
Efficiency	95%	95%
Overload Capacity	150% for 10 min. 110% continuous	150% for 10 min. 110% continuous
Typical Runtime (Full/Half Load)	5 min./12 min.	5 min./12 min.
Recharge Time	5 hrs. maximum	8 hrs. maximum
User Replaceable	Yes	Yes
Hot-Swappable	Yes	Yes
LEDs	6 LED array: boost, buck, power status, battery, load, replace battery	1 LED array: power status, battery status, load,
Audible Alerts	On battery, low battery, overload, replace battery	On battery, low battery, overload, replace battery
Bundled Software andFeatures (Standard or Optional)	Included: Power Management Suite CD-ROM and cable for Netware, Windows NT/95/3.x, DOS. Optional:SNMP	Included: Power Management Suite CD-ROM and cable for Netware, Windows NT/95/3.x, DOS. Optional: SNMP
Outlets	4	2
Safety	UL and CUL, Microsoft and Novell	UL and CUL, Microsoft and Novell
Dimensions	5.5" x 16.8" x 7.7"	4.1" x 10.4" x 5.6"
Weight	35.3 lbs	16.3 lbs
Comments	Plug-and-play, RJ-11 Internet protection, site wiring indicator, smart communications, and software.	Plug-and-play, RJ-11 Internet protection, site wiring indicator, smart communications, and software.
Warranty/Service	3 year limited/ $25,000 connected	3 year limited/ $25,000 connected
List Price	$299	$199

N/A—Not applicable   INA—Information not available

Table Continues →

■ Uninterruptible Power Supply

Manufacturer	**ViewSonic**
Model	Opti-UPS 280E
Type	Line interactive
INPUT	
VAC/Watts	88149VAC
Range	120VAC +/-12%
OUTPUT	
VAC/Watts	120VAC/280VA
Regular Balanced	N/A
Regular Unbalanced	N/A
Efficiency	95%
Overload Capacity	150% for 10 min. 110% continuous
Typical Runtime (Full/Half Load)	18 min./6 min.
Recharge Time	8 hrs. maximum
User Replaceable	Yes
Hot-Swappable	Yes
LEDs	1 LED array: power status, battery status, load,
Audible Alerts	On-battery, low battery, overload, replace battery
Bundled Software and Features (Standard or Optional)	Included: Power Management Suite CD-ROM and cable for Netware, Windows NT/95/3.x, DOS. Optional: SNMP
Outlets	2
Safety	UL and CUL, Microsoft and Novell
Dimensions	4.1" x 10.9" x 5.6"
Weight	14.7 lbs
Comments	Plug-and-play, site wiring indicator, smart communications, and software
Warranty/Service	3 year limited/ $25,000 connected
List Price	$119

N/A—Not applicable   INA—Information not available

Power/Line Conditioners

Manufacturer	Controlled Power Company	Controlled Power Company
Model	Series 700	Series 800
Input VAC	120/208/240/480/600VAC	120/208/240/480VAC
Output VAC	120/208/240/480/600VAC	120/208/240/480VAC
Maximum Output	500KW	25KW
Efficiency	95-97% typical	Greater than 90% typical full load
Overload Capacity	500% non-continuous	150% non-continuous
LEDs	INA	INA
Outlets	Up to 16 outlets	Up to 16 outlets
Safety	UL and LSA Approved	UL and LSA Approved
Dimensions	21.5"W x 30"D x 29"H	8.5"W x 9.5"H x 12.75"D
Weight	34.4 lbs	29l bs
Comments	Input and output breakers, power distribution, bypass switch	Wide input range, input and output breakers, power distribution. Plug and play and hardwired
Warranty/Service	1 year	1 year
List Price	From $3,500	From $370

Manufacturer	Tripp Lite	Tripp Lite	Tripp Lite
Model	LS Series	LC Series	LCR 2400
Input VAC	87-140 VAC	87-140 VAC	87-140VAC
Output VAC	120 VAC	120 VAC	120VAC
Maximum Output	600 to 1200 watts	1200 to 2400 watts	2400 watts
Efficiency	95% or better	95% or better	95% or better
Overload Capacity	N/A	N/A	N/A
LEDs	Input voltage, protected, line fault	Input voltage, protected, line fault	Input voltage, protected, line fault
Outlets	Varies depending on model	4 or 6, depends on model	14 outlets
Safety	UL	UL	UL
Dimensions	Varies depending on model	Varies depending on model	5.5"H x 19"W x 5"D
Weight	Varies depending on model	Varies depending on model	24 lbs.
Comments	Portable, full surge and noise suppression	Portable, full surge and noise suppression	Rack mount, 12-foot line cord, ISO bar surge suppression
Warranty/Service	2 year/$25,000 connected equipment coverage	2 year/$25,000 connected equipment coverage	2 year/$25,000 connected equipment coverage
List Price	$129–$159	$229–$399	$399

N/A—Not applicable   INA—Information not available

End ■

■ Printers

Manufacturer	CIE America	Hewlett-Packard	Hewlett-Packard
Model	CI-30 Thunderbolt	LaserJet 4MV	LaserJet SN
General Description	High-speed laser printer providing high-volume on-demand printing with full paper handling capabilities including duplex, sorter and up to ledger size paper support.	Workgroup desktop printer for mid volume printing environments. Features Resolution Enhancement technology (RET), Jet Admin and Jet Direct.	Designed for black printing in mid-size workgroup. Features HP PCL 6 for better graphics output.
MEMORY (RAM)			
Standard	32MB Model 1 and 2; 64MB Model 3 and 4. No additional memory needed.	12MB	4MB
Maximum	INA	44MB	66MB
Printing Technology	Laser	Laser	Laser
Maximum Resolution DPI	600 x 600	600 x 600	600 x 600
Rated Page Per Minute (ppm) Engine Speed	30	16	12
Duty Cycles	200,000 pages per month	50,000	35,000
Color or Monochrome	Monochrome	Monochrome	Monochrome
Printer Languages Supported	PCL5e and Adobe PostScript	Adobe Postscript Level 2, PCL 5 with HP-GL12	PCL 6
Network Protocols Supported	TCP/IP, IPX/SPX, EtherTalk, LocalTalk	TCP/IP, IPX, EtherTalk	TCP/IP, IPX/SPX
Interface Jack	RJ-45 and BNC	Twisted pair and BNC	Twisted pair and BNC
Network Interfaces	Ethernet 10MB	Ethernet and LocalTalk	Ethernet 10MB
Printer Interfaces	Bi-directional Parallel, LocalTalk and Network Connections	Bi-Tronics parallel	Bi-directional parallel
Auto-switching between Incoming Ports	Yes	Yes	Yes
Auto Emulation	Yes	Yes	Yes
Comments	Statement through Ledger paper sizes are standard. Optional 2000 sheet input, duplex, 750 sheet single job stacker, 1500 sheet dual job stacker; 20-bin sorter.	Offers an internal hard disk option, 11 x 19 wide format pages, supports 12 network operating systems.	Optional duplex unit, optional envelope feeder, 350 standard input capacity/800 max.
Warranty	120 day on-site	1 year	1 year
List Price	$15,995	$3,549	$1,929

Manufacturer	Hewlett-Packard	Hewlett-Packard
Model	LaserJet 5Si MX	LaserJet 5M
General Description	Designed for black printing in high-volume, large workgroups	Designed for black printing in mid-size workgroups. Features HP PCL 6 for better graphics output.
MEMORY (RAM)		
Standard	12MB	6MB
Maximum	76MB	52MB
Printing Technology	Laser	Laser
Maximum Resolution DPI	600 x 600	600 x 600
Rated Page Per Minute (ppm) Engine Speed	24	12

N/A—Not applicable   INA—Information not available

Printers ■

Manufacturer	Hewlett-Packard	Hewlett-Packard
Duty Cycles	100,000	35,000
Color or Monochrome	Monochrome	Monochrome
Printer Languages Supported	PCL, Adobe Postscript Level 2	PCL 6, Adobe Postscript Level 2
Network Protocols Supported	TCP/IP, IPX/SPX, EtherTalk	TCP/IP, IPX/SPX, EtherTalk
Interface Jack	Twisted pair and BNC	Twisted pair and BNC
Network Interfaces	Ethernet 10MB/LocalTalk	Ethernet 10MB/LocalTalk
Printer Interfaces	Bi-directional parallel	Bi-directional parallel
Auto-switching between Incoming Ports	Yes	Yes
Auto Emulation	Yes	Yes
Comments		Optional duplex unit, optional envelope feeder, 350 standard input capacity/800 max.
Warranty	1 year	1 year
List Price	$4,899	$2,229

Manufacturer	Hewlett-Packard	Hewlett-Packard
Model	Color LaserJet 5M	DeskJet 1600CM
General Description	Designed for corporate workgroups. Features Image RET 1200, Colorsmart software, HP FontSmart, Jet Direct and Jet Admin software	Designed to handle everyday black and color printing demands of small to mid-size workgroups. Features HP's Resolution Enhancement technology (RET) and ColorSmart software.
MEMORY (RAM)		
Standard	36MB	6MB
Maximum	76MB	70MB
Printing Technology	Laser	Inkjet
Maximum Resolution DPI	300 x 300, but Image RET 1200 generates output in the 1200dps Class.	b/w = 600 x 600 c/r = 300 x 300
Rated Page Per Minute (ppm) Engine Speed	b/w -= 10 c/r = 2-3	b/w = 9 c/r = 4
Duty Cycles	30,000	12,000
Color or Monochrome	Color	Color
Printer Languages Supported	Postscript Level 2, PCL 5 with HP-GL12	Adobe Postscript Level 2, Enhanced PCL 5 with HP-GL12
Network Protocols Supported	TCP/IP, IPX/SPX, EtherTalk	TCP/IP, IPX/SPX, EtherTalk
Interface Jack	Twisted pair and BNC	Twisted pair and BNC
Network Interfaces	Ethernet/LocalTalk (optional: Token Ring)	Ethernet/LocalTalk via Jet Direct card
Printer Interfaces	Bi-Tronics parallel	Bi-Tronics parallel
Auto-switching between Incoming Ports	Yes	Yes
Auto Emulation	Yes	Yes
Comments	Image RET 1200 uses sophisticated color control and precise blending techniques to produce 1200ppm equivalent image quality.	Comes standard with 180-sheet input tray and 100-sheet output tray. Optional 500-sheet paper feeder. Print cartridges: Cyan, Magenta, Yellow, and Black
Warranty	1 year	1 year
List Price	$9,195	$2,749

N/A—Not applicable   INA—Information not available

Table Continues →

■ Printers

Manufacturer	IBM	IBM
Model	Network 4312 M	Network 4312 M
General Description	MICR-enhanced for printing any MICR-encoded documents on blank cut-sheet paper stock.	MICR-enhanced for printing any MICR-encoded documents on blank cut-sheet paper stock. Designed for medium to large work groups.
MEMORY (RAM)		
Standard	2MB	2MB
Maximum	66MB	66MB
Printing Technology	Laser	Laser
Maximum Resolution DPI	300 x 300	300 x 300
Rated Page Per Minute (ppm) Engine Speed	12ppm	17ppm
Duty Cycles	35,000	65,000
Color or Monochrome	Monochrome	Monochrome
Printer Languages Supported	PCL5e, PostScript, AFD/1PDS	PCL5e, PostScript, AFD/1PDS
Network Protocols Supported	TCP/IP, IPX/SPX	TCP/IP, IPX/SPX
Interface Jack	INA	INA
Network Interfaces	Ethernet Twinix, Coax, Token Ring	Ethernet Twinix, Coax, Token Ring
Printer Interfaces	Serial, parallel	Serial, parallel
Auto-switching between Incoming Ports	Yes	Yes
Auto Emulation	Yes	Yes
Comments	Duplex optional, additional paper trays optional	Duplex optional, 2 media input trays optional
Warranty	1 year	1 year
List Price	$2,399	$3,286

Manufacturer	Kyocera Electronics	Kyocera Electronics
Model	FS-1600+	FS-1600+
General Description	It is a member of the new FS-Series+ printer line that includes support for SNMP and plug-and-play systems management tools for simple printer installation and maintenance.	It is a member of the new FS-Series+ printer line. The 1550+ accommodates several paper options including barcodes and labels.
MEMORY (RAM)		
Standard	2MB	1MB
Maximum	66MB	5MB
Printing Technology	LED	LED
Maximum Resolution DPI	600 x 600	600 x 600
Rated Page Per Minute (ppm) Engine Speed	10ppm	10ppm
Duty Cycles	25,000 pages	25,000 pages
Color or Monochrome	Monochrome	Monochrome
Printer Languages Supported	PCL5e, Diablo 630, IBM Proprinter X24E, Epson LQ-850, Line Printer, PostScript2-KPDL2	PCL5e, Diablo 630, IBM Proprinter X24E, Epson LQ-850, Line Printer, PostScript2-KPDL2
Network Protocols Supported	SNMP	SNMP

N/A—Not applicable   INA—Information not available

Printers ■

Manufacturer	Kyocera Electronics	Kyocera Electronics
Interface Jack	IEEE 1284 compatible	IEEE 1284 compatible
Network Interfaces	Ethernet, Token Ring, or Local Talk	Ethernet, Token Ring, or Local Talk
Printer Interfaces	INA	INA
Auto-switching between Incoming Ports	Yes	Yes
Auto Emulation	Yes	Yes
Comments		
Warranty	1 year or 300,000 pages	1 year or 300,000 pages
List Price	$1,995	$1,545

Manufacturer	Lexmark International	Lexmark International
Model	Optra E / Optra Ep	4039 10plus
General Description	Personal laser printers for business and home with a space saving format. Launches page while data transfer is in progress.	An entry priced desktop laser printer
MEMORY (RAM)	N/A	N/A
Standard	Optra E: 1MB Optra Ep: 2MB	2MB
Maximum	Optra E: 5MB Optra EP: 6MB	10MB
Printing Technology	Laser	Laser
Maximum Resolution DPI	600 x 600	600 x 600
Rated Page Per Minute (ppm) Engine Speed	6ppm	10ppm
Duty Cycles	Up to 10,000 pages per month	Up to 25,000 pages per month
Color or Monochrome	Monochrome	Monochrome
Printer Languages Supported	Enhanced PCL 5 emulation. (Ep includes PostScript Level 2 emulation)	PostScript Level 2 and enhanced PCL emulations
Network Protocols Supported	IPX/SPX, AppleTalk, TCP/IP, DLC/LLC	IPX/SPX, AppleTalk, TCP/IP, DLC/LLC
Interface Jack	N/A	N/A
Network Interfaces	Token Ring, 10BASE2 and T	Token Ring, 10BASE2 and T
Printer Interfaces	Optional: IEEE 1284, serial RS-232C/RS-422, and MarkNet for infrared connectivity	IEEE 1284, serial RS-232C/RS-422, and optional MarkNet for infrared connectivity
Auto-switching between Incoming Ports	Yes	Yes
Auto Emulation	Yes	Yes
Comments	150-sheet input tray, 100-sheet output bin, optional 250-sheet second tray, MarkVision printer management utility standard	Optional paper trays and second drawers. MarkVision printer management utility standard
Warranty	1-year Lexexpress	1-year Lexexpress
List Price	$699/$949	$1,249

Manufacturer	Lexmark International	Lexmark International
Model	Optra R / Optra Rn+	Optra R+
General Description	1200dpi laser printers for desktops and small workgroups	Dual-tray desktop laser printer with support for 5 automatic input sources
MEMORY (RAM)	N/A	N/A

N/A—Not applicable   INA—Information not available

Table Continues →

■ Printers

Manufacturer	Lexmark International	Lexmark International
Standard	4MB	4MB
Maximum	64MB	64MB
Printing Technology	Laser	Laser
Maximum Resolution DPI	1200 x 1200	1200 x 1200
Rated Page Per Minute (ppm) Engine Speed	16 8ppm (1200 x 1200)	16 8ppm (1200 x 1200)
Duty Cycles	Up to 35,000 pages per month	Up to 35,000 pages per month
Color or Monochrome	Monochrome	Monochrome
Printer Languages Supported	Enhanced PCL emulation and PostScript Level 2 emulations	Enhanced PCL emulation and PostScript Level 2 emulations
Network Protocols Supported	IPX/SPX, AppleTalk, TCP/IP, DLC/LLC	IPX/SPX, AppleTalk, TCP/IP, DLC/LLC
Interface Jack	N/A	N/A
Network Interfaces	Token Ring, 10BASE2 and T	Optional Internal Network Adapter, Token Ring, 10BASE2 and T
Printer Interfaces	Optional: IEEE 1284, serial RS-232C/RS-422, and MarkNet for infrared connectivity	Optional:IEEE 1284, serial RS-232C/RS-422, and MarkNet for infrared connectivity
Auto-switching between Incoming Ports	Yes	Yes
Auto Emulation	Yes	Yes
Comments	150-sheet input tray, 100-sheet output bin, optional 250-sheet second tray, MarkVision printer management utility standard	150-sheet input tray, 100-sheet output bin, optional 250-sheet second tray, MarkVision printer management utility standard
Warranty	1-year Lexexpress	1-year Lexexpress
List Price	$1,549/$1,849 (Rn+)	$1,849

Manufacturer	Lexmark International	Lexmark International
Model	Optra Lx+ / Optra Lxn+	Optra N 240 / 245
General Description	Laser printer designed for high volume and large workgroups	Large capacity laser printers designed for high volume and departmental printing
MEMORY (RAM)	N/A	N/A
Standard	4MB	4MB/16MB
Maximum	64MB	64MB
Printing Technology	Laser	Laser
Maximum Resolution DPI	1200 x 1200	600 x 600
Rated Page Per Minute (ppm) Engine Speed	16 8ppm (1200 x 1200)	24ppm (letter), 13ppm (tabloid)
Duty Cycles	Up to 75,000 pages per month	100,000 pages per month
Color or Monochrome	Monochrome	Monochrome
Printer Languages Supported	Enhanced PCL 5 emulation. (Ep includes PostScript Level 2)	PostScript Level 2 and enhanced PCL emulations
Network Protocols Supported	IPX/SPX, AppleTalk, TCP/IP, DLC/LLC	IPX/SPX, AppleTalk, TCP/IP, DLC/LLC
Interface Jack	N/A	N/A
Network Interfaces	Token Ring, 10BASE2 and T	Token Ring, 10BASE2 and T Internal Network Adapter (245)

N/A—Not applicable   INA—Information not available

Printers ■

Manufacturer	**Lexmark International**	**Lexmark International**
Printer Interfaces	Optional: IEEE 1284, Serial RS-232C/RS-422, and MarkNet for infrared connectivity	IEEE 1284, Serial RS-232C/RS-422, and MarkNet for infrared connectivity
Auto-switching between Incoming Ports	Yes	Yes
Auto Emulation	Yes	Yes
Comments	150-sheet input tray, 100-sheet output bin, optional 250-sheet second tray, MarkVision printer management utility standard	Processor: 50MHz Intel i960. MarkVision printer management utility standard. Optional 2000-sheet input drawer.
Warranty	1-year Lexexpress	1-year LexOnSite
List Price	$1,549/$1,849	$3,399/$4,199

Manufacturer	**Lexmark International**	**Lexmark International**
Model	Optra C / CPRO	Color Jetprinter 4079 plus
General Description	Photographic-quality printing with color	Color and saturated-black printer that supports 11" x 17" paper and full-bleed tabloid
MEMORY (RAM)	N/A	N/A
Standard	8MB /32MB	4MB
Maximum	64MB	36MB
Printing Technology	Laser	Inkjet
Maximum Resolution DPI	600 x 600	360 x 360 with ColorGrade
Rated Page Per Minute (ppm) Engine Speed	12ppm monochrome 3ppm color	Up to 1ppm (color) Up to 1.7ppm (black draft)
Duty Cycles	15,000 per month	
Color or Monochrome	Color and monochrome	Color
Printer Languages Supported	PostScript Level 2 and enhanced PCL, color and GL (plotter) emulations	PostScript Level 2, color and GL (plotter) emulations
Network Protocols Supported	IPX/SPX, AppleTalk, TCP/IP, DLC/LLC	IPX/SPX, AppleTalk, TCP/IP, DLC/LLC
Interface Jack	N/A	N/A
Network Interfaces	Token Ring, 10BASE2 and T Internal Network Adapter (245)	Token Ring, 10BASE2 and T Internal Network Adapter (245)
Printer Interfaces	IEEE 1284, Serial RS-232C/RS-422, and MarkNet for infrared connectivity	IEEE 1284, Serial RS-232C/RS-422, and MarkNet for infrared connectivity
Auto-switching between Incoming Ports	Yes	Yes
Auto Emulation	Yes	Yes
Comments	MarkVision printer management utility standard. Optional 250-sheet second drawer assembly. ERR	MarkVision printer management utility standard
Warranty	1-year LexOnSite	1-year LexOnSite
List Price	$6,849/$7,999	$3,199

Manufacturer	**Okidata**	**Okidata**
Model	OL1200	OL1200/PS
General Description	INA	INA
MEMORY (RAM)		
Standard	2MB, 4MB	6MB
Maximum	32MB	INA

N/A—Not applicable   INA—Information not available

Table Continues →

■ Printers

Manufacturer	Okidata	Okidata
Printing Technology	INA	INA
Maximum Resolution DPI	600 dpi	600 dpi
Rated Page Per Minute (ppm) Engine Speed	12ppm	12ppm
Duty Cycles	24,000 pages per month	24,000 pages per month
Color or Monochrome	monochrome	monochrome
Printer Languages Supported	PCL	PostScript 2
Network Protocols Supported	INA	INA
Interface Jack	INA	INA
Network Interfaces	Ethernet, Token Ring	LocalTalk, EtherTalk
Printer Interfaces	INA	INA
Auto-switching between Incoming Ports	INA	INA
Auto Emulation	INA	INA
Comments	Supports 8.5x11 and 8.5x14	Supports 8.5x11 and 8.5x14
Warranty	INA	INA
List Price	$1,499	$1,839

Manufacturer	Olympus Image Systems, Inc.	Olympus Image Systems, Inc.
Model	PagePlex 24	PagePlex 32
General Description	Designed for high-speed, high-volume printing, providing long duty cycles for general applications, bar code, label, MCR forms, and document image processing	Designed for high-speed, high-volume printing, providing long duty cycles for general applications, bar code, label, MCR forms, and document image processing
MEMORY (RAM)		
Standard	8MB	8MB
Maximum	28MB	28MB
Printing Technology	Electron Imaging	Electron Imaging
Maximum Resolution DPI	300 x 300	300 x 300
Rated Page Per Minute (ppm) Engine Speed	24ppm	32ppm
Duty Cycles	125,000 pages a month	200,000 pages a month
Color or Monochrome	Monochrome	Monochrome
Printer Languages Supported	PCL 5	PCL 5
Network Protocols Supported	TCP/IP, IPX/SPX, AppleTalk	TCP/IP, IPX/SPX, AppleTalk
Interface Jack	RJ-45, BNC	RJ-45, BNC
Network Interfaces	10BASE-T, 10BASE2	10BASE-T, 10BASE2
Printer Interfaces	Parallel, RS-232C/422	Parallel, RS-232C/422
Auto-switching between Incoming Ports	Yes	Yes
Auto Emulation	Yes	Yes
Comments	1,000- and 2,000-sheet input feeders, 2,000-sheet stacker, 5- and 10-bin mailbox sorters, internal hard disk drives, NetDirect Ethernet Interface	1000- and 2000-sheet input feeders, 2000-sheet stacker, 5- and 10-bin mailbox sorters, internal hard disk drives, NetDirect Ethernet Interface

N/A—Not applicable   INA—Information not available

Printers

Manufacturer	Olympus Image Systems, Inc.	Olympus Image Systems, Inc.
Warranty	1 year parts and labor	90 day
List Price	$6,295	$10,995

Manufacturer	QMS	QMS
Model	QMS 2425 Print System	Magicolor CX Laser Printer
General Description	Combines a high-performance 100MHz processor w/ QMS crown technology and extensive document handling capabilities, making it an ideal advanced network printing solution	The Magicolor CX Laser Printer offers fast, high-quality color printing. The printer also offers advanced networking features, broad media support, and many color control capabilities.
MEMORY (RAM)		
Standard	2 models available 8MB, 24MB	4 models available 8MB, 20MB, 32 MB, 40MB
Maximum	128MB	64MB
Printing Technology	Laser	Laser
Maximum Resolution DPI	600dpi standard 1200dpi optional	8MB=600dpi monochrome, 300dpi color 20MB=600dpi monochrome & color 32MB=600dpi monochrome & color 40MB=1200dpi monochrome & color
Rated Page Per Minute (ppm) Engine Speed	24ppm	12ppm monochrome 3-6ppm color
Duty Cycles	100,000 pages per month	5,000 color pages month 20,000 monochrome
Color or Monochrome	Monochrome	Color
Printer Languages Supported	GL/2, HP PCL, 5C, PostScript 2, HP-GL 7475A/7550/ Draft Master, line printer	HP-GL, GL/2, HP PCL, 5C, PostScript, PostScript 2
Network Protocols Supported	NetWare IPX/SPX, EtherTalk, TCP/IP, OS/2 LAN manager/LAN server/Net OEUI, Windows 3.1x, Windows NT, Windows 95, NetBIOS/NetBEUI	NetWare IPX/SPX, EtherTalk, TCP/IP, OS/2 LAN manager/LAN server/Net OEUI, Windows 3.1x, Windows NT, Windows 95, NetBIOS/NetBEUI, (optional w/8MB & 20MB models. EtherTalk available w/ Ethernet only)
Interface Jack	10BASE-T & Thin w/Ethernet, STP/UTP w/ Token Ring	10BASE-T & Thin w/Ethernet, STP/UTP w/ Token Ring
Network Interfaces	Ethernet standard (Token Ring, DECnet-TCP/IP & LocalTalk optional)	Ethernet, Token Ring (Choice of either Ethernet or Token Ring w/32MB & 40MB models. These are optional on 8MB & 20MB models) DECnet-TCP/IP & Local optional
Printer Interfaces	Parallel—standard, serial—optional	RS232C serial, Centronics parallel
Auto-switching between Incoming Ports	Yes—standard	Yes—standard
Auto Emulation	Yes—standard	Yes—standard
Comments	Supports paper sizes: 8.5x11, 8.5x14, ledger, C5 envelopes, A3, A4, A5, B4, B5 statement, universal, DL, monarch, C5, and Com 10 envelopes (advanced paper handling features available)	250 sheet out-put tray with face down out-put. Supports several paper sizes. Envelope tray available.
Warranty	1 year on-site	1 year on-site
List Price	$5,499 (8MB) $6,999 (24MB)	$5,799 (8MB) $6,499 (20MB) $7,999 (32MB) $8,499 (40MB)

Manufacturer	Textronix	Textronix
Model	Phaser 550	Phaser 350
General Description	Fast, high-volume, high capacity desktop color laser printer. Prints color pages at 5ppm & monochrome at 14ppm. True 1200 x 1200dpi, built-in Textronix PhaserLink software.	Color laser-class printer that is half the price of competitive laser-class color printers, and can print a full color page at half the cost of other laser-Class color printers

N/A—Not applicable   INA—Information not available

Table Continues →

■ Printers

Manufacturer	Textronix	Textronix
MEMORY (RAM)		
Standard	8MB	8MB
Maximum	76MB	24MB
Printing Technology	Color laser	Solid ink
Maximum Resolution DPI	1200 x 1200dpi	600 x 300dpi
Rated Page Per Minute (ppm) Engine Speed	5ppm color, 14ppm monochrome	6ppm (both color & monochrome)
Duty Cycles	N/A	N/A
Color or Monochrome	Color	Color
Printer Languages Supported	True Adobe PS level 2, HP-GL emulation, PCLS monochrome emulation	True Adobe PS level 2, HP-GL emulation, PCLS monochrome emulation
Network Protocols Supported	Novell NetWare, EtherTalk, TCP/IP, Token Ring	Novell NetWare, EtherTalk, TCP/IP, Token Ring
Interface Jack	Bi-directional parallel standard, LocalTalk, serial, Ethernet, Token-Ring are optional	Bi-directional parallel standard, LocalTalk, serial, Ethernet, Token-Ring are optional
Network Interfaces	Ethernet, Token Ring, LocalTalk	Ethernet, Token Ring, LocalTalk
Printer Interfaces	Bi-directional parallel standard, LocalTalk, serial, Ethernet, Token-Ring are optional	Bi-directional parallel standard, LocalTalk, serial, Ethernet, Token-Ring are optional
Auto-switching between Incoming Ports	Yes	Yes
Auto Emulation	Yes	Yes
Comments	Textronix PhaserLink, Web-based printer management built-in. Tekcolor dynamic correction allows you to print the colors you want.	Tekcolor dynamic correction allows you to print the colors you want & is a Web-based printer mgt. tool. PhaserLink software is standard with the Phaser 350.
Warranty	1 year	1 year
List Price	$6,995 U.S. List	$6,995 U.S. List

Manufacturer	Xerox	Xerox
Model	Docuprint 4517 & 4517mp	XPrint 4915 Plus
General Description	The DocuPrint 4517 offers extensive and advanced set of options and accessories for a black-and-white network laser printer, allowing flexible configuration for workgroup specific needs. DocuPrint 4517mp comes with an additional 4MB of memory (six total), an Ethernet network interface card and Adobe PostScript Level 2.	Xprint 4915 Plus is an entry-level color laser printer that allows paper capacities of up to 1,750 sheets. Xerox Intelligent Color technology automatically applies the best printing method for different page elements, ensuring excellent image quality.
MEMORY (RAM)		
Standard	2MB	16MB
Maximum	64MB	48MB
Printing Technology	Laser	Laser
Maximum Resolution DPI	1200 x 600 dpi	1200 x 300 dpi
Rated Page Per Minute (ppm) Engine Speed	17	3ppm color, 12ppm black
Duty Cycles	50,000 pages per month	15,000 pages per month
Color or Monochrome	Monochrome	Color
Printer Languages Supported	HP PCL, PostScript 2, PCL-5E	PCL-5E, PostScript 2
Network Protocols Supported	INA	INA

N/A—Not applicable   INA—Information not available

Printers ∎

Manufacturer	Xerox	Xerox
Interface Jack	Parallel	Parallel, Serial, LocalTalk
Network Interfaces	Ethernet, Token Ring, LocalTalk	Ethernet, Token Ring
Printer Interfaces	INA	INA
Auto-switching between Incoming Ports	Yes	Yes
Auto Emulation	Yes	Yes
Comments	Operating with a 1,350 paper unit capacity. Optional features include: network interface cards; a confidential mailbox/collator for a network printer; and a low cost, user-installed duplex unit.	The unit's standard 16MB RAM can be expanded to 48MB, and an optional media server can be installed for direct printing.
Warranty	1 year	1 year
List Price	$1,835	$4,995

Manufacturer	Xerox	Xerox
Model	XPrint 4920 Plus	XPrint 4925 Plus
General Description	The Xprint 4920 Plus provides high-quality "all-in-one" printing with true 600x600dpi resolution. The unit produces black-only pages at per-page cost comparable to monochrome printers.	The Xprint 4925 Plus is an advanced color document printer that produces complete document sets. Designed for networked workgroups where high productivity and quality are critical.
MEMORY (RAM)		
Standard	16MB	24MB
Maximum	48MB	48MB
Printing Technology	Laser	Laser
Maximum Resolution DPI	600 dpi	600 dpi
Rated Page Per Minute (ppm) Engine Speed	3ppm color, 12ppm black & white	3ppm color, 12ppm black & white
Duty Cycles	15,000 pages per month	15,000 pages per month
Color or Monochrome	Color	Color
Printer Languages Supported	PCL-5E, PostScript 2	PCL-5E, PostScript 2
Network Protocols Supported	INA	INA
Interface Jack	INA	INA
Network Interfaces	Ethernet, Token Ring	Ethernet, Token Ring
Printer Interfaces	INA	INA
Auto-switching between Incoming Ports	Yes	Yes
Auto Emulation	Yes	Yes
Comments	Supports paper capacities of up to 1,750 sheets, Xerox Intelligent Color technology automatically applies the best printing method for different page elements, ensuring excellent image quality, the unit's standard 24MB RAM expands to 48MB; a standard 340MB collation disk enables full document-set printing, optional media server is available.	Supports paper capacities of up to 1,750 sheets, Xerox Intelligent Color technology automatically applies the best printing method for different page elements, ensuring excellent image quality, the unit's standard 24MB RAM expands to 48MB; a standard 340MB collation disk enables full document-set printing, optional media server is available.
Warranty	1 year	1 year
List Price	$7,295	$8,995

N/A—Not applicable   INA—Information not available

End ∎

■ Modems

Manufacturer	**ARIEL Corp.**	**ARIEL Corp.**
Model	TI-Modem	CTI-Modem
Compatibility	V.34-28.8, V.32bis, V.32, V.22bis, V.23, V.21, Bell 212A, Bell 103J	V.34-28.8, V.32bis, V.32, V.22bis, V.23, V.21, Bell 212A, Bell 103J
Configuration	ISA, EISA, VME bus, PCI Bus	ISA, EISA, VME bus, PCI Bus
Compressions	CC ITT V.42bis, MNP5, MNP10 & MNP10 EC	CC ITT V.42bis, MNP Class5
Error Correction	CC ITT V.42 CAMP, V.42 cellular, MNP2, MNP4	CC ITT V.42, V.42 cellular, MNP Class 2-4
Data Format	N/A	N/A
Transmission Lines Supported	N/A	N/A
Facsimile Compatibility	Group 3	Group 3
Operating Speeds	.3-28.8Kbps	.3-19.2Kbps
Flash EpROM	No	No
Remote Callback	Yes	Yes
Automatic Redial	Yes	Yes
Comments	12 or 24 modems on one CARD-ISA Bus slot, MUIP/SCSA Computer Telephone Interface	16 modems on one CARD-ISA Bus slot, MVIP/SCSA Computer Telephone Interface
Warranty	INA	INA
List Price	$13,500	$10,000

Manufacturer	**Boca Research**	**Boca Research**
Model	V.34 Boca Modem	V.34 Boca Modem
Compatibility	ITU: 33.6, V.34, V.32bis, V.32, V.22bis, V.22, V.21, V.23, Bell 212A, 102	ITU: 33.6, V.34, V.32bis, V.32, V.22bis, V.22, V.21, V.23, Bell 212A, 102
Configuration	ISA	Standalone External
Compressions	N/A	N/A
Error Correction	N/A	N/A
Data Format	Asynchronous	Asynchronous
Transmission Lines Supported	Dial-up	Dial-up
Facsimile Compatibility	Group 3	Group 3
Operating Speeds	0.3-33.6Kbps	0.333.6Kbps
Flash EpROM	No	No
Remote Callback	No	No
Automatic Redial	Yes	Yes
Comments	Communications software and free trial Internet online services included	Communications software and free trial Internet online services included
Warranty	5 year	5 year
List Price	$207	$234

Manufacturer	**Boca Research**	**Boca Research**
Model	PRO16 Corp.	PRO16 Rack
Compatibility	ITU: 33.6, V.34, V.32bis, V.32, V.22bis, V.22, V.21, V.23, Bell 212A, 103	ITU: 33.6, V.34, V.32bis, V.32, V.22bis, V.22, V.21, V.23, Bell 212A, 103
Configuration	Standalone External	Rackmount
Compressions	N/A	N/A

N/A—Not applicable   INA—Information not available

Modems ■

Manufacturer	Boca Research	Boca Research
Error Correction	N/A	N/A
Data Format	Asynchronous, synchronous, serial, binary	Asynchronous, synchronous, serial, binary
Transmission Lines Supported	Dial-up or leased line	Dial-up or leased line
Facsimile Compatibility	Group 3	Group 3
Operating Speeds	0.3-33.6	0.333.6
Flash EpROM	Yes	Yes
Remote Callback	Yes	Yes
Automatic Redial	Yes	Yes
Comments	Full security	Full security Hot-swappable Redundancy SNMP managed
Warranty	5 year	5 year
List Price	$549	$4,449 8 bundle $8,949 16 bundle

Manufacturer	Bravo	Bravo
Model	1042E	2042E / 2042EX
Compatibility	IBM parallel, Centronics parallel, IEEE P1284, bi-directional parallel	RS-232 and V.24 serial
Configuration	Standalone, external and rackmount	Standalone, external and rackmount
Compressions	N/A	N/A
Error Correction	Parallel	RS-232 and V.24 serial
Data Format	Parallel	Serial (all formats and protocols)
Transmission Lines Supported	5 volts	Up to ± 25 volts
Facsimile Compatibility	N/A	N/A
Operating Speeds	Up to 500Kbps	Up to 120Kbps
Flash EpROM	No	No
Remote Callback	No	No
Automatic Redial	No	No
Comments	Distances to 3,000 feet	Built-in surge protection, LED monitor display, RJ-45, DB 25, and Screw terminal connections
Warranty	1 year	1 year
List Price	$109	2042E: $149 2042EX: $179

Manufacturer	D-Link Systems	D-Link Systems
Model	DM-288	DME-288T
Compatibility	V.34, V.32, V.32bis, V.21, V.22, V.22bis, Bell 212, 103,	V.34, V.32, V.32bis, V.21, V.22, V.22bis, Bell 212, 103,
Configuration	PCMZA	PCMCIA
Compressions	V.92bis, MNP 2-5	V.92bis, MNP 2-5
Error Correction	V.42	V.42
Data Format	Asynchronous: 8, 9, 10 Synchronous: not supported	Asynchronous: 8, 9, 10 Synchronous: not supported
Transmission Lines Supported	Dial/Voiceline: 10dBm	Dial/Voiceline: 10dBm

N/A—Not applicable   INA—Information not available

Table Continues →

■ Modems

Manufacturer	D-Link Systems	D-Link Systems
Facsimile Compatibility	V.17, V.29, EIA/TIA578 Class 1	V.17, V.29, EIA/TIA578 Class 1
Operating Speeds	0.3-57.6Kbps	0.3-57.6Kbps
Flash EpROM	Yes	Yes
Remote Callback	No	No
Automatic Redial	Yes	Yes
Comments	Fax-modem	Ethernet fax-modem
Warranty	5 year	INA
List Price	$279	INA

Manufacturer	E-Tech Research	E-Tech Research
Model	PC 288MX	E 288MX
Compatibility	ITU-T V.34, V.32 terbo, V.32 bis, V.32, V.23, V.22bis, V.22, V.21	ITU-T V.34, V.32 terbo, V.32 bis, V.32, V.23, V.22bis, V.22, V.21
Configuration	Internal	External
Compressions	V.42bis, MNP5	V.42bis, MNP5
Error Correction	V.42	V.42
Data Format	Asynchronous	Asynchronous Synchronous
Transmission Lines Supported	Dial-up: 10dBm	Dial-up: 10dBm
Facsimile Compatibility	Class I and II	Class I and II
Operating Speeds	0.3-28.8Kbps	0.3-28.8Kbps xxx
Flash EpROM	No	No
Remote Callback	No	Yes
Automatic Redial	No	No
Comments	Diagnostic testing, memory for 10 phone numbers	Diagnostic testing, remote configuration, password protection, memory for 10 phone numbers, call progress display
Warranty	2 year	2 year
List Price	$169	$249

Manufacturer	E-Tech Research	E-Tech Research
Model	PC 1414UX	PC 1414VMX
Compatibility	ITU-T V.32bis, V.32, V.23, V.22bis, V.22, V.21	ITU-T V.3bis, V.32, V.23, V.22bis, V.22, V.21
Configuration	Internal	Internal, voice
Compressions	V.42bis, MNP5	V.42bis
Error Correction	V.42bis	V.42
Data Format	Asynchronous	Asynchronous
Transmission Lines Supported	Dial-up: 10dBm	Dial-up: 10dBm
Facsimile Compatibility	Class II fax	Class II fax
Operating Speeds	0.3-14.4Kbps	0.3-14.4Kbps
Flash EpROM	No	No
Remote Callback	No	No
Automatic Redial	No	No

N/A—Not applicable   INA—Information not available

Modems ■

Manufacturer	E-Tech Research	E-Tech Research
Comments	Diagnostic testing, memory for 3 phone numbers, call progress display	Diagnostic testing, memory for 10 phone numbers, call progress display
Warranty	2 year	2 year
List Price	$69	$89

Manufacturer	Farallon	MagicRAM, Inc.
Model	LAN/Modem PC Card	PC card 28.8 Fax/Modem
Compatibility	V.34, V.32, terbo, V.32 bis, V.32, V.23, V.22 bis, V.22, V.21, Bell 212A, Bell 103	CCITT V.34, V.32bis, V.32, V.23, V.22 bis, V.22, Bell 212A, Bell 103
Configuration	INA	PCMCIA
Compressions	V.42 bis; MNP5	V.42bis, MNP 5
Error Correction	V.42; MNP levels 2-4	V.42
Data Format	INA	Full duplex binary asynchronous, asynchronous 7,8,9,10 including start, stop bits
Transmission Lines Supported	INA	10dBm
Facsimile Compatibility	Group 3, Class 1 & 2 faxing	CCITT Group 3, EIA Class 1 & 2
Operating Speeds	10Mbps	0.3 to 28.8Kbps
Flash EpROM	Flash ROM upgradable	No
Remote Callback	Through software	Yes
Automatic Redial	Through software	Yes
Comments	Comes with a free twin pack of Timbuktu 2.0	
Warranty	5 year	5 year
List Price	$499	$179

Manufacturer	Motorola	Motorola
Model	Premier 33.6	BitSURFR
Compatibility	ITU V.34, V.32bis, V.32, V.22bis, V.21, Bell 21217, 1L3, V.33, V.29, V.27	V.120, V.11C. AIMUX, Clear Channel
Configuration	External/ISA	External
Compressions	MNP 2-5, ITU, V.42/V.42bis	N/A
Error Correction	MNP 2-5; ITU V.42/V.42bis	V.120
Data Format	Synchronous (external only)	Asynchronous 10 bits Synchronous
Transmission Lines Supported	Dial-up 10dBm permissive Leased line: 6-15dBM	N/A
Facsimile Compatibility	ITU Group III compatible when used with Class 1 fax software	N/A
Operating Speeds	33.6Kbps	2.4-115.2Kbps
Flash EpROM	Yes	No
Remote Callback	Yes	No
Automatic Redial	Yes	No
Comments		Built-in NT1, compatible with Macs, Windows, standard RJ-3.7
Warranty	5 year	5 year
List Price	$495	$375

N/A—Not applicable   INA—Information not available

Table Continues →

ZIFF-DAVIS PRESS

■ Modems

Manufacturer	Motorola	Motorola
Model	BitSURFR PC	BitSURFR D.O
Compatibility	V.120, V.110, AIMUX, Clear Channel, Synchronous Bonding	V.120, V.11, MLDP, AIMUX, Clear Channel, PPP, Bonding
Configuration	ISA	ISA/External
Compressions	N/A	N/A
Error Correction	V.120	V.120
Data Format	Asynchronous 10 bits Synchronous	Asynchronous 10 bits Synchronous
Transmission Lines Supported	N/A	N/A
Facsimile Compatibility	N/A	N/A
Operating Speeds	2.4-115.2Kbps	2.4-115.2Kbps
Flash EpROM	No	Yes
Remote Callback	No	No
Automatic Redial	No	No
Comments	Built-in NT1, U interface, standard RJ-3.7	Available for Mac, Windows, built-in NT1, supports custom calling features
Warranty	5 year	5 year
List Price	$375	$495

Manufacturer	Motorola	Motorola
Model	ModemSURFR	OnlineSURFR Int.
Compatibility	ITU V.34, V.32bis, V.32, V.22bis, V.22, V.23, V.21; Bell 212, 103	ITU V.34, V.32bis, V.32, V.22bis, V.22, V.21; Bell 212, 103
Configuration	ISA/External	ISA
Compressions	ITU, V.42bis, MNP 5	ITU, V.42bis, MNP 5
Error Correction	V.42, MNP 2-5	V.42, MNP 5
Data Format	Asynchronous: 115, 200bps	Asynchronous: 115, 200bps
Transmission Lines Supported	10dBm permissive	10dBm permissive
Facsimile Compatibility	ITU Group III compatible, compatible with all Class 1 and 2 fax software packages	ITU Group III compatible, compatible with all Class 1 fax software
Operating Speeds	.3-28.8Kbps	.3-28.8Kbps
Flash EpROM	No	No
Remote Callback	No	No
Automatic Redial	No	No
Comments	PC or Mac, comes with online software, children's educational CD-ROM and video games	Caller ID, phone and directory, comes with Internet Web browser software, e-mail and Newsreader, FTP
Warranty	5 year	5 year
List Price	$200 (ISA) / $240 (EXT)	$215

Manufacturer	Motorola	Motorola
Model	OnlineSURFR External	VoiceSURFR 28.8 Internal
Compatibility	ITU V.34, V.32bis, V.32, V.22bis, V.22, V.21; Bell 212, 103	ITU, V.34, V.32bis, V.32, V.22bis, V.22, V.21; Bell 212, 103
Configuration	Desktop	ISA
Compressions	ITU, V.42bis, MNP 5	ITY, V.42bis, MNP 5

N/A—Not applicable   INA—Information not available

Modems ∎

Manufacturer	Motorola	Motorola
Error Correction	V.42 MNP 2-5	V.42 MNP 5
Data Format	Asynchronous: 115, 200bps	Asynchronous: 115, 200bps
Transmission Lines Supported	10dBm permissive	10dBm permissive
Facsimile Compatibility	ITU Group III compatible, compatible with all Class 1 fax software	ITU Group III compatible, compatible with all Class 1 fax software
Operating Speeds	.3-28.8Kbps	.3-28.8Kbps
Flash EpROM	No	No
Remote Callback	No	No
Automatic Redial	No	No
Comments	Comes with: Internet Web browser software, e-mail and Newsreader, FTP and Gopher, a complete Internet guide	Voice mail/answering machine, full duplex speaker phone, caller ID, Internet survival kit, phone and directory
Warranty	5 year	5 year
List Price	$250	$225

Manufacturer	Multi-Tech Systems, Inc.	Multi-Tech Systems, Inc.
Model	MT1432BA	MT1432BLR MTR1432BR
Compatibility	V.32bis and slower with AT&T 212A	V.32bis and slower with AT&T 212A
Configuration	Standalone/External	Rackmount
Compressions	MNP 5, V.42bis	MNP 5, V.42bis
Error Correction	V.42	V.42
Data Format	Asynchronous Synchronous	Asynchronous Synchronous
Transmission Lines Supported	Dial-up, 2-wire leased	Dial-up, 2-wire leased, 4-wire leased Dial-up, 2-wire leased
Facsimile Compatibility	V.17 and Group 3	V.17 and Group 3
Operating Speeds	0.3-14.4Kbps	0.3-14.4Kbps
Flash EpROM	Not flashable	Not flashable
Remote Callback	Yes	Yes
Automatic Redial	Yes	Yes
Comments	Remote configuration, UUCP Spoofing, AS/400 settings, and 10-number storage for automatic dialing	Remote configuration, UUCP Spoofing, AS/400 settings, and 10-number storage for automatic dialing
Warranty	5 year	2 year
List Price	$749	$740 $690

Manufacturer	Multi-Tech Systems, Inc.	Multi-Tech Systems, Inc.
Model	MT1432LT	MT1432MR
Compatibility	V.32bis and slower with AT&T 212A	V.32bis and slower with AT&T 212A
Configuration	Type II PCMCIA	Managed/Rackmount
Compressions	MNP 5, V.42bis	MNP 5, V.42bis
Error Correction	V.42	V.42
Data Format	Asynchronous	Asynchronous: 8, 9, 10, or 11 bits; Synchronous: serial, binary
Transmission Lines Supported	Dial-up	Dial-up, 2-wire leased, 4-wire leased

N/A—Not applicable   INA—Information not available

Table Continues →

■ Modems

Manufacturer	Multi-Tech Systems, Inc.	Multi-Tech Systems, Inc.
Facsimile Compatibility	V.17 and Group 3	V.17 and Group 3
Operating Speeds	0.3-14.4Kbps	0.3-14.4Kbps
Flash EpROM	Flashable	Flashable
Remote Callback	No	Yes
Automatic Redial	Yes	Yes
Comments	Remote configuration, DTMF tone detection, and 10-number storage for automatic dialing	Remote configuration, UUCP Spoofing, AS/400 settings, caller ID, and 10-number storage for automatic dialing
Warranty	2 year	2 year
List Price	$299	$2,999

Manufacturer	Multi-Tech Systems, Inc.	Multi-Tech Systems, Inc.
Model	MT1432MU MT1932BL	MT1932ZDX MT1932ZPX2
Compatibility	MU: V.32bis and slower with AT&T 212A BL: V.32 terbo and slower with AT&T 212A	V.32 terbo and slower with AT&T 212A
Configuration	Standalone/External	Standalone/External 16-bit ISA bus
Compressions	MNP 5, V.42bis	DX: N/A PX2: MNP 5, V.42bis
Error Correction	V.42	V.42
Data Format	MU: Asynchronous: 8, 9, 10, or 11 bits BL: Asynchronous: 8, 9, 10, or 11 bits; Synchronous: serial, binary	Asynchronous: 8, 9, 10, or 11 bits
Transmission Lines Supported	MU: Dial-up BL: Dial-up, 2-wire leased, 4-wire leased	Dial-up
Facsimile Compatibility	V.17 and Group 3	V.17 and Group 3
Operating Speeds	0.3-14.4Kbps 0.3-19.2Kbps	0.3-19.2Kbps
Flash EpROM	Flashable Not flashable	Not flashable
Remote Callback	No Yes	No
Automatic Redial	Yes	Yes
Comments	MU: Remote configuration, UUCP Spoofing, and 10-number storage for automatic dialing BL: Remote configuration, UUCP Spoofing, AS/400 settings, DTMF tone detection, and 10-number storage for automatic dialing	Remote configuration, DTMF tone detection, and 2-number storage for automatic dialing
Warranty	5 year	10 year
List Price	$699 $799	$198

Manufacturer	Multi-Tech Systems, Inc.	Multi-Tech Systems, Inc.
Model	MT2834BA MT2834BC	MT2834BL MT2834BLR
Compatibility	V.34bis and slower with AT&T 212A	V.34bis and slower with AT&T 212A
Configuration	Standalone/External 16-bit ISA bus	Standalone/External Rackmount
Compressions	MNP 5, V.42bis	MNP 5, V.42bis
Error Correction	V.42	V.42

N/A—Not applicable   INA—Information not available

Modems ■

Manufacturer	Multi-Tech Systems, Inc.	Multi-Tech Systems, Inc.
Data Format	BA: Asynchronous: 8, 9, 10, or 11 bits; Synchronous: serial, binary BC: Asynchronous: 8, 9, 10, or 11 bits	Asynchronous: 8, 9, 10, or 11 bits; Synchronous: serial, binary
Transmission Lines Supported	Dial-up, 2 wire-leased Dial-up	Dial-up, 2-wire leased, 4-wire leased
Facsimile Compatibility	V.17 and Group 3	V.17 and Group 3
Operating Speeds	0.3-33.6Kbps	0.3-33.6Kbps
Flash EpROM	Flashable	Flashable
Remote Callback	Yes	Yes
Automatic Redial	Yes	Yes
Comments	BA: Remote configuration, UUCP Spoofing, AS/400 settings, DTMF tone detection, and 10-number storage for automatic dialing BC: Remote configuration, UUCP Spoofing, DTMF tone detection, and 10-number storage for automatic dialing	Remote configuration, UUCP Spoofing, AS/400 settings, caller ID, DTMF tone detection, and 10-number storage for automatic dialing
Warranty	5 year	5 year 2 year
List Price	$799 $449	$849 $790

Manufacturer	Multi-Tech Systems, Inc.	Multi-Tech Systems, Inc.
Model	MT2834BR MT2834LT	MT2834MR MT2834MR-PSTN
Compatibility	V.34bis and slower with AT&T 212A	V.34bis and slower with AT&T 212A
Configuration	Rackmount Type II PCMCIA	Managed/rackmount
Compressions	MNP 5, V.42bis	MNP 5, V.42bis
Error Correction	V.42	V.42
Data Format	BR: Asynchronous: 8, 9, 10, or 11 bits; Synchronous; serial, binary LT: Asynchronous: 8, 9, 10, or 11 bits	Asynchronous: 8, 9, 10, or 11 bits; Synchronous; serial, binary
Transmission Lines Supported	Dial-up, 2-wire leased Dial-up	MR: Dial-up, 2-wire leased, 4-wire leased MR-PSTN: Dial-up
Facsimile Compatibility	V.17 and Group 3	V.17 and Group 3
Operating Speeds	0.3-33.6Kbps	0.333.6Kbps
Flash EpROM	Flashable	Flashable
Remote Callback	Yes No	Yes
Automatic Redial	Yes	Yes
Comments	BR: Remote configuration, UUCP Spoofing, AS/400 settings, caller ID, DTMF tone detection, and 10-number storage for automatic dialing LT: Remote configuration, DTMF tone detection, and 10-number storage for automatic dialing.	Remote configuration, UUCP Spoofing, AS/400 settings, caller ID, DTMF tone detection, and 10-number storage for automatic dialing.
Warranty	2 year 5 year	2 year
List Price	$740 $399	$3,199 $2,999

Manufacturer	PairGain Technologies, Inc.	Trendware Int'l
Model	Megabit Modem 768	TFM-288P
Compatibility	INA	V.34

N/A—Not applicable   INA—Information not available

Table Continues →

Modems

Manufacturer	PairGain Technologies, Inc.	Trendware Int'l
Configuration	Standalone/External, Campus-Star plug-in module	PCMIA
Compressions	N/A	V.42, MNP 2-4bis
Error Correction	CRC-32	V.42
Data Format	Ethernet	Asynchronous 8, 9, 10, 11 bits
Transmission Lines Supported	+ 13.5dBm dedicated	10dBm permissive
Facsimile Compatibility	No	CCITT Group 3
Operating Speeds	768Kbps (bi-directional)	300-33.6Kbps info OK this cell and next?
Flash EpROM	Yes	Yes
Remote Callback	N/A	No
Automatic Redial	N/A	No
Comments	Bridging Routing	
Warranty	5 year	5 year
List Price	Starting at $995	$299

Manufacturer	Trendware Int'l	US Robotics
Model	TEM-288T	Courier I-Modem with ISDN/V.34
Compatibility	V.34, Ethernet 10BASE- T	ISDN: ITU-TV.120, V.110, PPP, MLPPP Analog: V.34, V.32bis, V.FL, V.3L terbo, V.32 to 300bps
Configuration	PCMIA	External ISA
Compressions	V.42, MNP 2-4	ISDN: STAL, Ascend, Microsoft Analog: V.42bis, MNP5
Error Correction	V.42	ISDN: V.120 ANALOG: V.42, MNP2-4
Data Format	Asynchronous 8, 9, 10, 11 bits	7E1, 7O1, 7M1, 751, 7N2, 8N1, synchronous
Transmission Lines Supported	10dBm permissive	9dBm maximum; sensitivity -43dBm ± 2dBm
Facsimile Compatibility	CCITT Group 3	Group 3, Class 1 + 2.0
Operating Speeds	300-33.6Kbps	ISDN: 56, 64-128Kbps Analog: 300-33.6Kbps
Flash EpROM	Yes	Yes
Remote Callback	No	Yes
Automatic Redial	No	Yes
Comments	Ethernet 10BASE-T adapter combination	Universal connect, turbo PPP, remote configuration, integrated NT1, integrated V.34 modem, compression, dial security, dynamic voice override.
Warranty	5 year	5 year
List Price	$399	$495+

Manufacturer	US Robotics	US Robotics
Model	Courier V.Everything IV.34	Sportster ISDN 128K
Compatibility	V.34, V.FC, V.32 terbo, V.32bis, HST, V.32, V.22, V.23, V.21, Bell 212A down to 300bps	Synchronous PPP, Multilink PPP
Configuration	External, ISA, PCMCIA	ISA
Compressions	V.42bis, MNP 5	Ascend, Microsoft, Stac

N/A—Not applicable   INA—Information not available

Modems ■

Manufacturer	US Robotics	US Robotics
Error Correction	V.42, MNP 2-4 US Robotics HST	INA
Data Format	7E1, 7O1, 7M1, 751, 7N2, 8N1, synchronous	Sync PPP
Transmission Lines Supported	-9dBm max sensitivity: -43dBm + 2dBm	INA
Facsimile Compatibility	6 Groups, Class 1 and 2.0	INA
Operating Speeds	300-33.6Kbps	56/64/112/128Kbps
Flash EpROM	Yes	Through host drivers
Remote Callback	Yes	Yes
Automatic Redial	Yes	Yes
Comments	Quick connect, caller ID, ASL (adaptive speed leveling), distinctive ring, remote configuration, plug-and-play, dial security	Integrated NT1, Windows 95, TAPI simultaneous voice and data, dynamic voice override, integrated analog device port
Warranty	5 year	5 year
List Price	$345	INA

Manufacturer	Xircom, Inc.	Xircom, Inc.
Model	CreditCard Ethernet + Modem 33.6	CreditCard Modem 33.6
Compatibility	V.34 from 2.4 to 33.6Kbps V.32 terbo 19.2 & 16.8Kbps V.32bis at 14.4, 12, 9.6, 7.2Kbps uncoded at 4.8Kbps V.32 at 9.6Kbps uncoded at 4.8Kbps V.22bis at 2.4Kbps V.22 at 1.2Kbps V.23 at 1.2, .75Kbps Bell 212A at 1.2Kbps	V.34 from 2.4 to 33.6Kbps V.32 terbo 19.2 & 16.8Kbps V.32bis at 14.4, 12, 9.6, 7.2Kbps uncoded at 4.8Kbps V.32 at 9.6Kbps uncoded at 4.8Kbps V.22bis at 2.4Kbps V.22 at 1.2Kbps V.23 at 1.2, .75Kbps Bell 212A at 1.2Kbps
Configuration	PCMCIA Interface	PCMCIA Interface
Compressions	V.42bis (4:1) or MNP level 5 (2:1)	V.42bis (4:1) or MNP level 5 (2:1)
Error Correction	V.42/MNP levels 2-4	V.42/MNP levels 2-4
Data Format	Asynchronous: 8	Asynchronous: 8
Transmission Lines Supported	Dial up 10dBm permissive	Dial up 10dBm permissive
Facsimile Compatibility	Group 3, EIA/IA Class 1 & Class 2	Group 3, EIA/IA Class 1 & Class 2
Operating Speeds	12Kbps to 33.6Kbps	12Kbps to 33.6Kbps
Flash EpROM	Yes	Yes
Remote Callback	Not built into hardware but is supported if communications software supports it	Not built into hardware but is supported if communications software supports it
Automatic Redial	Not built into hardware-but can be supported	Not built into hardware-but can be supported
Comments	Combined Ethernet LAN adapter and 33.6Kbps modem in a single PC card, Digital Line Protection with Digital Line Alert, Cellular upgradeable, certified for international use, MiniDock connector, LEDs, includes Delrina WinFax Lit and WinComm Lite	Digital Line Protection with Digital Line Alert, Cellular upgradeable, certified for international use, MiniDock connector, LEDs, includes Delrina WinFax Lit and WinComm Lite,
Warranty	Lifetime	Lifetime
List Price	CreditCard Ethernet+Modem 33.6: (10BASE-T) $359 (10BASE-T/10BASE-2) $399 (10BASE-T MiniDock) $359 (10BASE-T/10BASE-2) International $449	CreditCard Modem 33.6 $259 CreditCard Modem 33.6 International $309 CreditCard Modem 33.6+Cellular $309

N/A—Not applicable   INA—Information not available

Table Continues →

■ Modems

Manufacturer	Xircom, Inc.	Xircom, Inc.
Model	CreditCard Ethernet + Modem 28.8	CreditCard Modem 28.8
Compatibility	V.34 from 2.4 to 33.6Kbps V.32 terbo 19.2 & 16.8Kbps V.32bis at 14.4, 12, 9.6, 7.2Kbps uncoded at 4.8Kbps V.32 at 9.6Kbps uncoded at 4.8Kbps V.22bis at 2.4Kbps V.22 at 1.2Kbps V.23 at 1.2, .75Kbps Bell 212A at 1.2Kbps	V.34 from 2.4 to 33.6Kbps V.32 terbo 19.2 & 16.8Kbps V.32bis at 14.4, 12, 9.6, 7.2Kbps uncoded at 4.8Kbps V.32 at 9.6Kbps uncoded at 4.8Kbps V.22bis at 2.4Kbps V.22 at 1.2Kbps V.23 at 1.2, .75Kbps Bell 212A at 1.2Kbps
Configuration	PCMCIA Interface	PCMCIA Interface
Compressions	V.42bis (4:1) or MNP level 5 (2:1)	V.42bis (4:1) or MNP level 5 (2:1)
Error Correction	V.42/MNP levels 2-4	V.42/MNP levels 2-4
Data Format	Asynchronous: 8	Asynchronous: 8
Transmission Lines Supported	Dial up 10dBm permissive	Dial up 10dBm permissive
Facsimile Compatibility	Group 3, EIA/IA Class 1 & Class 2	Group 3, EIA/IA Class 1 & Class 2
Operating Speeds	12Kbps to 28.8Kbps	12Kbps to 28.8Kbps
Flash EpROM	Yes	Yes
Remote Callback	Not built into hardware-but is supported if communications software supports it	Not built into hardware-but is supported if communications software supports it
Automatic Redial	Supported if communications software supports it	Supported if communications software supports it
Comments	Digital Line Protection with Digital Line Alert, Cellular upgradeable, certified for international use, modem LED software utility, includes Delrina WinFax Lit and WinComm Lite, Full duplex Ethernet, Advanced Look-Ahead Pipelining, SNMP agent	Digital Line Protection with Digital Line Alert, Cellular upgradeable, certified for international use, modem LED software utility, includes Delrina WinFax Lit and WinComm Lite
Warranty	Lifetime	Lifetime
List Price	CreditCard Ethernet+Modem 28.8: (10BASE-T) $359 (10BASE-T/10Base-2) $399	$259

Manufacturer	ZYPCOM, Inc.	ZYPCOM, Inc.
Model	Z34-RX	Z32-SE
Compatibility	ITU-T: V	ITU-T: V.32bis, V.32, V.22bis, V.22, V.21, V.23; AT&T: V.32 Terbo, 212A
Configuration	Dual modem Rackmount	Standalone/External
Compressions	V.42bis, MNP 5	V.42bis, MNP 5
Error Correction	V.42, MNP 2-4	V.42, MNP 2-4
Data Format	Asynchronous: 8, 9, 10, 11 bits Synchronous: serial, binary	

Transmission Lines Supported	Dial-up: -10dBm permissive,
	  2-and 4-wire leased line,
	  -6 to -15dBm selectable
		Dial-up: 10dBm permissive
		2-wire leased line,
		-6 to -15dBm selectable

Facsimile Compatibility	CCITT Group 3 fax machines and fax-modems	CCITT Group 3 fax machines and fax-modems
Operating Speeds	33.6Kbps/0.3Kbps	0.3-19.2Kbps
Flash EpROM	Yes	No
Remote Callback	Yes	Yes
Automatic Redial	Yes	Yes
Comments	Z960NM network management, side channel for remote control	Side channel for remote control

N/A—Not applicable   INA—Information not available

Modems ■

Manufacturer	ZYPCOM, Inc.	ZYPCOM, Inc.
Warranty	2 year/24 hour exchange	2 year
List Price	$1,498 (dual modem)	$419

Manufacturer	ZYPCOM, Inc.	ZYPCOM, Inc.
Model	Z32t-SX	Z32t-RX
Compatibility	ITU-T: V.32bis, V.32, V.22bis, V.22, V.21, V.23; AT&T: V.32 Terbo, 212A	ITU-T: V.32bis, V.32, V.22bis, V.22, V.21, V.23; AT&T: V.32 Terbo, 212A
Configuration	Standalone/External	Dual modem Rackmount
Compressions	V.42bis, MNP 5	V.42bis, MNP 5
Error Correction	V.42, MNP 2-4	V.42, MNP 2-4
Data Format	Asynchronous: 8, 9, 10, 11 bits Synchronous: serial, binary	Asynchronous: 8, 9, 10, 11 bits Synchronous: serial, binary
Transmission Lines Supported	Dial-up: 10dBm permissive 2-wire leased line -6 to -15dBm selectable	Dial-up: 10dBm permissive 2-wire leased line -6 to -15dBm selectable
Facsimile Compatibility	CCITT Group 3 fax machines and fax-modems	CCITT Group 3 fax machines and fax-modems
Operating Speeds (high/low Ks)	0.3-19.2Kbps	0.3-19.2Kbps
Flash EpROM	No	No
Remote Callback	Yes	Yes
Automatic Redial	Yes	Yes
Comments	Side channel for remote control	Z960NM network management, side channel for remote control
Warranty	2 years/24 hour exchange	2 year/24 hour exchange
List Price	$629	$1,258 (dual modem)

Manufacturer	ZYPCOM, Inc.	ZYPCOM, Inc.
Model	Z32b-SE	Z32b-SX
Compatibility	ITU-T: V.32bis, V.32, V.22bis, V.22, V.21, V.23; AT&T: 212A/103	ITU-T: V.32bis, V.32, V.22bis, V.22, V.21, V.23; AT&T: 212A/103
Configuration	Standalone/External	Standalone/External
Compressions	V.42, MNP 5	V.42, MNP 5
Error Correction	V.42, MNP -24	V.42, MNP -24
Data Format	Asynchronous: 8, 9, 10, 11 bits Synchronous: serial, binary	Asynchronous: 8, 9, 10, 11 bits Synchronous: serial, binary
Transmission Lines Supported	Dial-up: 10dBm permissive 2-wire leased line -6 to -15dBm selectable	Dial-up: 10dBm permissive 2-wire leased line -6 to -15dBm selectable
Facsimile Compatibility	CCITT Group 3 fax machine and fax-modems	CCITT Group 3 fax machine and fax-modems
Operating Speeds	14.4Kbps/0.3Kbps	14.4Kbps/0.3Kbps
Flash EpROM	No	No
Remote Callback	Yes	Yes
Automatic Redial	Yes	Yes
Comments	Side channel for remote control	Side channel for remote control
Warranty	2 year	2 year/24 hour exchange
List Price	$389	$549

N/A—Not applicable   INA—Information not available

Table Continues →

■ Modems

Manufacturer	ZYPCOM, Inc.	ZYPCOM, Inc.	ZYPCOM, Inc.
Model	Z34-SE	Z34-SX	Z32b-RX
Compatibility	ITU: V.34, V.32bis, V.32, V.22bis, V.22, V.21, V.23, V.29, V.17 ATT: V.32 terbo, 212/103	ITU: V.34, V.32bis, V.32, V.22bis, V.22, V.21, V.23, V.29, V.17 ATT: V.32 terbo, 212/103	ITU-T: V.32bis, V.32, V.22bis, V.22, V.21, V.23; AT&T: 212A/103
Configuration	Standalone External	Standalone External	Standalone/External
Compressions	V.42bis, MNP 5	V.42bis, MNP 5	V.42, MNP 5
Error Correction	V.42, MNP 2-4	V.42, MNP 2-4	V.42, MNP -24
Data Format	Asynchronous: 8, 9, 10, 11 bits, Synchronous, serial, bindery	Asynchronous: 8, 9, 10, 11 bits, Synchronous, serial, bindery	Asynchronous: 8, 9, 10, 11 bits Synchronous: serial, binary
Transmission Lines Supported	Dial-up: -10dBm permissive 2-wire leased line: -6 to 15dBm selectable	Dial-up: -10dBm permissive 2-and 4-wire Leased line: -6 to 15dBm selectable	Dial-up: 10dBm permissive 2-wire leased line -6 to -15dBm selectable
Facsimile Compatibility	CCITT Group 3 fax machines and fax-modems	CCITT Group 3 fax machines and fax-modems	CCITT Group 3 fax machine and fax-modems
Operating Speeds (high/low Ks)	33.6Kbps/0.3Kbps	33.6Kbps/0.3Kbps	14.4Kbps/0.3Kbps
Flash EpROM	Yes	Yes	No
Remote Callback	Yes	Yes	Yes
Automatic Redial	Yes	Yes	Yes
Comments	Side channel for remote control	Side channel for remote control	Z960 NM network management, side channel for remote control
Warranty	2 year	2 year/24 hour exchange	2 year/24 hour exchange
List Price	$499	$749	$1,098

Test Equipment ■

Manufacturer	Adtech, Inc.	AG Group, Inc.
Model	AX/4000 ATM Test System	EtherPeek™
General Description	Modular, multi-port ATM test system with test cell generation, full rate analysis & network impairment emulation.	Ethernet packet-level network traffic and protocol analyzer to troubleshoot and debug multi-protocol networks.
Form Factor	Mainframe or portable	Software
Network Platforms	INA	Macintosh, Windows
Network Topology	INA	Ethernet, Fast Ethernet
NOS	INA	NOS independent
Communication Protocol	ATM, AAL, Q.2931, UNI 3.0/3.1	AppleTalk, TCP/IP, NetBEUI
Interfaces	14 interfaces up to 622 MBPS OC-12c	Ethernet (thinnet, thick, twisted-pair)
Readout/Display	Status LEDs plus Windows control interface	Standard
Testing Features	Up to 16 ports ATM traffic generation ATM network impairment emulation Full rate analysis	ProtoSpecs filtering, real-time decodes of WAN and encapsulated LAN protocols, stress and monitor tests, performance tuning, troubleshooting test
Reporting Features	Real time statistics and histograms of up to 16 filtered substreams per port	Real-time traffic graph and statistics export to text file
Comments	For multi-port ATM performance testing. Has SVC signaling support, Windows interface included, but can be controlled from any ANSI C platform.	Pinpoints network, bottlenecks, finds hardware and software faults, identifies routing and addressing problems, name-to-address mapping, event trigger and filtering mechanism
Warranty	1 year	90 day
Price	Starting $14,700	SRP $995

Manufacturer	Datacom Technologies	Digitech Industries, Inc.
Model	NETcat 2200	LAN 900
General Description	PC-controlled analyzer & cable tester	The LAN 900 provides Fast Ethernet, FDDI/ CDDI, Ethernet and Token Ring protocol analysis for PCM-CIA, PCI and ISA Pcs
Form Factor	Hand held	PC-based boards and systems
Network Platforms	PC under Windows 3.1/95	DOS, Unix, Windows
Network Topology	Ethernet	Ethernet, Fast Ethernet, FDDI/CDDI, Token Ring
NOS	NOS Independent	NOS independent
Communication Protocol	IPX, IP, Vines, AppleTalk, DEC NET	DECnet, NFS, IBM, Novell, IP/IPX, Vines, TCP/ IP, XNS, AppleTalk, ISO
Interfaces	RS232-c, RJ45, BNC	10BASE-T, 100BASE-T, AUI, 10BASE1, ANSI X.3TIR, SMT 7.3, dual attach
Readout/Display	Backlighted graphical LCD	PC dependent
Testing Features	Cable tester, NIC/Hub tester, network monitor, automatic diagnosis of NetWare login problems, autofile server/user discovery	The LAN 900 line offers detailed decodes of all common LAN protocols, Real-time monitor of stats and traffic, network analysis by station address and protocol type
Reporting Features	Hand-held saved reports include 500 cable tests, NetWare login tests and traffic tests, PC-saved reports include protocol mix, utilization baseline, packet errors, frame types, top senders/receivers, IPX routing	Same as above plus Expert system. The LAN 900 line includes stats and traffic capture, as well as playback and multi-layered filter.
Comments	Complete cable test per IEEE Ethernet or TIA 568 cable std., complete NIC/Hub test including transmit/receive, AC or NiMH battery pack, TCP/IP option includes IP PING and IP name/address resolution	For local and remote expert protocol and network analysis of Ethernet, Fast Ethernet, FDDI/CDDI and Token Ring, Digitech offers a broad array of protocol analyzers and network management tools.
Warranty	1 year	1 year and labor
Price	$2,995 U.S. list	Starts at $4,900

N/A—Not applicable   INA—Information not available

Table Continues →

■ Test Equipment

Manufacturer	Digitech Industries, Inc.	DIGILOG
Model	WAN 900	NETforager
General Description	The WAN 900 line of protocol analyzers offers real-time capture, emulation, analysis, and troubleshooting.	Long-term network performance analysis system
Form Factor	PC-based boards and systems	Distributed
Network Platforms	DOS, Unix, Windows	Unix
Network Topology	WANs	Ethernet, Token Ring
NOS	NOS independent	NOS independent
Communication Protocol	Asynchronous, BSC, x.25/x.75, SNA, QLLC, frame relay, ISDN, SLIP, PPP, asynchronous PPP, routing, LAN encapsulated	SNMP, UDD, IP
Interfaces	RS-232, RS-449, DS3/DS1, ISON PRI, V.35, V.36/V.10/V.11, RS-530, X.21, T1, FT2, E1, FE1, and 4w DDS, ATM, OC3, MSSI/DXI	RS-232, built-in modem
Readout/Display	PC dependent	None
Testing Features	The WAN 900 protocol analyzers offer integrated interfaces, real time decoders, stats analysis, filters, stats, traps and triggers for all major WAN and encapsulated LAN protocols.	Ping sweeps, long-term histories of SNMP MIB variables
Reporting Features	Features an intuitive user interface, autoconfigure, canned tests, pre-written emulation scenarios and softkey menus requiring fewer keystrokes.	MIB II- and RMON-based reports of network performance
Comments	For local and remote expert protocol and network analysis of WANs. Digitech offers a broad array of protocol analyzers and network management tools.	NETforager manager configures and gathers performance data from remote NETforager nodes. The node polls network elements for interesting MIB data and performs a first level of data reduction.
Warranty	1 year parts and labor	1 year
Price	Starts at $4,900	Manager: $4,995 Node: $5,995

Manufacturer	Fluke Corporation	Fluke Corporation
Model	670 Series LANMeter	680 Series Enterprise LANMeter
General Description	Combines commonly used troubleshooting functions of protocol analyzers with the functions of a cable tester.	A portable network troubleshooting tool using SNMP to access information stored in managed devices.
Form Factor	Hand-held	Hand-held
Network Platforms	N/A	N/A
Network Topology	Ethernet and/or Token Ring including switched environments	Direct connection to Ethernet and/or Token Ring
NOS	NOS independent	NOS independent
Communication Protocol	N/A	N/A
Interfaces	Ethernet, Token Ring and RJ-45, RS 232 communications/printer	Ethernet, Token Ring and RJ-45, RS-232 communications/printer
Readout/Display	240 x 128 pixel bit-mapped LCD, 19 color-coded LED indicators for utilization and status	240 x 128 pixel bit-mapped LCD, 19 color-coded LED indicators for utilization and status
Testing Features	Real-time monitoring of network health including utilization, error, collision, and broadcast rates. Identification of error types and sources. NIC/HUB hardware and cable testing.	Includes all testing features of the 670 Series LANMeters. TCP/IP Internet test features using SNMP to access standard MIB I/II, transmission MIB and RMON information from any managed device on the network.
Reporting Features	Datalog feature collects statistical network data. Optional HealthScan software package allows PC data upload and provides 5 reports	Datalog feature collects statistical network data. Optional HealthScan software package allows PC data upload and provides 5 reports

N/A—Not applicable   INA—Information not available

Test Equipment ■

Manufacturer	Fluke Corporation	Fluke Corporation
Comments	Battery and AC powered; Novell Netware tests include server lists, file and packet statistics, routing analysis; TCP/IP tests include ICMP monitor, ping and trace route; Banyan Vines test suite.	Automatic TCP/IP configuration using DHCP or BOOTP; automatic discovery of routers, IP servers, SNMP agents and local hosts; NetBIOS tests suite supports Windows NT, Windows 95, IBM LAN Server, and OS/2 environments.
Warranty	1 year	1 year
Price	Starts at $6,495	Starts at $8,495

Manufacturer	Fluke Corporation	Frontline Test Equipment
Model	68X Series Enterprise LANMeter Switch Wizard	Ethertest®
General Description	A portable tool for troubleshooting switched network environments. Available as an option or upgrade to the Fluke Enterprise LANMeter	Ethernet LAN analyzer. Provides network traffic statistics and decodes. Comes with your choice of PCMCIA or ISA card.
Form Factor	Hand-held	INA
Network Platforms	N/A	DOS
Network Topology	Ethernet and/or Token Ring including switched environments	Ethernet
NOS	NOS independent	N/A
Communication Protocol	N/A	N/A
Interfaces	Ethernet, Token Ring and RJ-45, RS-232 communications/printer	INA
Readout/Display (LED, LCD, other)	240 x 128 pixel bit-mapped LCD, 19 color-coded LED indicators for utilization and status	INA
Testing Features	SwitchWizard uses SNMP to access standard MIB I/II, transmission MIB and RMON information from switches, displaying statistics on up to 8 ports simultaneously	7-layer decodes for most protocols; locates duplicate IPs; filter on MAC or IP addresses protocols and errors; tracks error-generating nodes.
Reporting Features	Datalog feature collects statistical network data. Optional HealthScan software package allows PC data upload and provides 5 reports including utilization, collision and error analysis, protocol distribution and top traffic contributors.	Sets alarms; saves captured data; generates traffic; Protocol Definition Language—create your own decode; detailed summary of network usage and errors.
Comments	Battery and AC powered; capable of displaying information from any switch, anywhere on the network	
Warranty	1 year	Lifetime on hardware
Price	$995	$2,995

Manufacturer	Fluke Corporation	General Software
Model	One Touch Network Assistant	EtherProbe v. 2.10
General Description	The One Touch Network Assistant makes it easy to prove network connectivity on both 10Mbps and 100Mbps Ethernet Networks.	Software-based, Ethernet protocol analyzer. Provides for real-time traffic capture and protocol decoding. Source code available.
Form Factor	Hand-held	PC platform
Network Platforms	Embedded	Runs from DOS
Network Topology	Ethernet (One Touch-10), Ethernet, Fast Ethernet (One Touch—10/100)	Ethernet, Fast Ethernet
NOS	NOS Independent	Netware, LAN Manager, General Software's embedded LAN
Communication Protocol	TCP/IP, IPX/SPX, NetBIOS, DECnet, Appletalk	TCP/IP, IPX/SPX, NCP, Xerox IDP/XNS, IEEE 802.2/ 802.3, NetBEUI
Interfaces	RS-232-C	Ethernet, NIC
Readout/Display	LCD Backlit display touch screen, 4 LEDs	PC or laptop monitor

N/A—Not applicable   INA—Information not available   **Table Continues →**

■ Test Equipment

Manufacturer	**Fluke Corporation**	**General Software**
Testing Features	Verify critical network resources (routers, servers), Verify network components (NICs/Hub), Network Health (Utilization, Errors, Collisions, Broadcast), Cable test, Wire map	Capture triggers on alarm activation; 45 programmable alarms (utilization alarms, file sharing request alarms, protocol usage alarms); programmable traffic generations
Reporting Features	Cable map results, component IP or MAC addresses, individual tests for hubs and adapter cards are available	Netware-style interface; on-the-fly address and protocol filtering; DLC name management; summary level, detail and hexidecimal protocol display; real-time statistics displayed during capture.
Comments	Verifies network connectivity with a single touch	Source code permits additional protocol decoding or graphical display; Crynwr Packet Driver support for popular NICs; Includes free NIC.
Warranty	1 year (extended warranty is available)	N/A
Price	$3,695	$995 (source code $500)

Manufacturer	**Novell, Inc.**
Model	LANalyzer for Windows 2.2
General Description	Network analysis solution for efficient network management, users can detect, repair & prevent network problems through a graphical, dashboard interface.
Form Factor	Windows software that runs on any standard PC or laptop that supports Windows 3.1 or Window 95
Network Platforms	Platform independent
Network Topology	Ethernet, Fast Ethernet, Token Ring
NOS	Runs on any NOS, has extra capabilities when used with NetWare
Communication Protocol	Native NetWare suite: IPX/SPX, NCP, NDS, RIP, SAP and others. AppleTalk suite: ATP, AFP, RTMP, ZIP, and others. TCP/IP suite: IP, TCP, RIP, OSPF, NFS, SNMP, and others. NFS, SNA
Interfaces	RS232
Readout/Display (LED, LCD, other)	Color monitor
Testing Features	Real time decodes of LAN protocols, Network Trending, alarm logging and explanations, alarm thresholds, active name gathering, packet filtering
Reporting Features	Trending data exportable to standard spread-sheet programs to generate reports.
Comments	Supports Novell Directory Services to automatically retrieve user names from NetWare 3 & 4 servers.
Warranty	90 day
Price	$1,495 U.S.

Manufacturer	**RADCOM EQUIPMENT, INC.**	**RADCOM EQUIPMENT, INC.**
Model	RC-88W	RC-88WL
General Description	Entry-level WAN analyzer operating at 256Kbps	WAN/LAN analyzer operating at 256Kbps on WANs and 10 or 4/16Mbps on LANs
Form Factor	Portable, weighing less than 2 kg. (4 lbs.)	Portable, weighing less than 2 kg. (4 lbs.)
Network Platforms	Windows based (Windows 3.1, WFW 3.11, Windows 95)	Windows based (Windows 3.1, WFW 3.11, Windows 95)
Network Topology	Ethernet, Token Ring	Ethernet, Token Ring
NOS	NOS Independent	NOS Independent
Communication Protocol	WAN: LAPB, LAPD, HDLC, SDLC, Frame Relay, X.25, SNA, SMDS/DXI, ISDN. Customized and other protocols are also available.	WAN: LAPB, LAPD, HDLC, SDLC, Frame Relay, X.25, SNA, SMDS/DXI, ISDN. LAN and LAN over WAN: Ethernet, Token Ring, IGRP, PPP suite, TCP/IP suite, FDDI, ISO/OSI. Customized and other protocols are also available.

N/A—Not applicable   INA—Information not available

Test Equipment ■

Manufacturer	**RADCOM EQUIPMENT, INC.**	**RADCOM EQUIPMENT, INC.**
Interfaces	V.35, V.24/RS-232, RS-449, RS-530, X.21/V.11, ISDN/BRI(S/T), ISDN/BRI(U), E1/FE1 & ISDN/PRI, T1/FT1, & ISDN/PRI, 10BASE-2, 10BASE-T, 10BASE-5, Token Ring STP, Token Ring UTP	V.35, V.24/RS-232, RS-449, RS-530, X.21/V.11, ISDN/BRI(S/T), ISDN/BRI(U), E1/FE1 & ISDN/PRI, T1/FT1, & ISDN/PRI, 10BASE-2, 10BASE-T, 10BASE-5, Token Ring STP, Token Ring UTP
Readout/Display	Windows GUI	Windows GUI
Testing Features	Frame Relay User/Network Analysis, User/Network Simulation. Simultaneous Two-Channel Operation. Encapsulation and SMDS Analysis. SNA Analysis ISDN Simulation. FUNI Analysis.	Frame Relay User/Network Analysis, User/Network Simulation. Simultaneous Two-Channel Operation. Encapsulation and SMDS Analysis. SNA Analysis. ISDN Simulation. FUNI Analysis.
Reporting Features	Online/Offline Analysis Process Display: Bar/Pie Chart Calculation: Average, Total, Per Cycle Frame Relay: Distribution, Congestion Analysis: Frame Distribution (Tabular), Protocol Distribution	Online/Offline Analysis Process Display: Bar/Pie Chart Units: Frames, Bytes Y-Axis: Value, Percent WAN Frame Level: Distribution of Frame status, length, and direction Erroneous Frames, Frame Distribution (Tabular)
Comments	RISC processor (I960). 8MB RAM on board. Performance: WAN-up to 2Mbps monitor and simulation with a 10 μsec time stamp resolution.	RISC processor (I960). 8MB RAM on board. Performance: WAN-up to 2Mbps monitor and simulation with a 10 μsec time stamp resolution.
Warranty	1 year hardware, free software upgrades for 2 years	1 year hardware, free software upgrades for 2 years
Price	Starting at $3,700	Starting at $7,500

Manufacturer	**RADCOM EQUIPMENT, INC.**	**RADCOM EQUIPMENT, INC.**
Model	RC-100W	RC-100WL
General Description	High-performance WAN analyzer operating at 2Mbps	WAN/LAN analyzer operating at 2 MBPS on WANs and 10 or 4/16Mbps on LANs
Form Factor	Portable and lightweight, weighing less than 2 kg. (4 lbs.)	Portable and lightweight, weighing less than 2 kg. (4 lbs.)
Network Platforms	Windows based (Windows 3.1, WFW3.11, and Windows 95)	Windows based (Windows 3.1, WFW3.11, and Windows 95)
Network Topology	Ethernet, Token Ring	Ethernet, Token Ring
NOS	NOS Independent	NOS Independent
Communication Protocol	WAN: LAPB, LAPD, HDLC, SDLC, Frame Relay, X.25, SNA, SMDS/DXI, ISDN Frame-based ATM: FUNI, ATM/DXI, Signaling Customized protocols available on request.	WAN: LAPB, LAPD, HDLC, SDLC, Frame Relay, X.25, SNA, SMDS/DXI, ISDN, IGRP, PPP suite, TCP/IP suite, FDDI, ISO/OSI, DECnet, XNS, Novell, Banyan Vines, 3Com, AppleTalk, Sun Lan Manager, DLSW, NetBIO
Interfaces	V.35, V.24/RS-232, RS-449, RS-530, X.21/V.11, ISDN/BRI(S/T), ISDN/BRI(U), E1/FE1 & ISDN/PRI, T1/FT1, & ISDN/PRI, Ethernet 10BASE-2(BNC), Ethernet 10BASE-T, Ethernet 10BASE-5(AUI), Token Ring STP, Token Ring UTP	V.35, V.24/RS-232, RS-449, RS-530, X.21/V.11, ISDN/BRI(S/T), ISDN/BRI(U), E1/FE1 & ISDN/PRI, T1/FT1, & ISDN/PRI, Ethernet 10BASE-2(BNC), Ethernet 10BASE-T, Ethernet 10BASE-5(AUI), Token Ring STP, Token Ring UTP
Readout/Display	Windows GUI	Windows GUI
Testing Features	Frame Relay User/Network Analysis, User/Network Simulation. Simultaneous Two-Channel Operation. Encapsulation and SMDS Analysis. SNA Analysis. ISDN Simulation. FUNI Analysis Frame Relay User/ Network Analysis.	Frame Relay User/Network Analysis, User/Network Simulation. Simultaneous Two-Channel Operation. Encapsulation and SMDS Analysis. SNA Analysis. ISDN Simulation. FUNI Analysis Frame Relay User/ Network Analysis.
Reporting Features	Online/Offline Analysis Process. Display: Bar/Pie Chart. Calculation: Average, Total, Per Cycle. Frame Relay: Distribution, Congestion Analysis: Frame Distribution (Tabular). Protocol Distribution.	Online/Offline Analysis Process. Display: Bar/Pie Chart. Calculation: Average, Total, Per Cycle. Frame Relay: Distribution, Congestion Analysis: Frame Distribution (Tabular). Protocol Distribution.
Comments	RISC processor (I960). 8MB RAM on board. Performance: WAN-up to 2Mbps monitor and simulation with a 10 μsec time stamp resolution.	Real-time and offline statistics. Online and offline data processing. MS-Windows user interface with mouse or keyboard control, complete context-sensitive help.
Warranty	1 year hardware, free software upgrades for 2	1 year hardware, free software upgrades for 2
Price	Starting at $7,000	Starting at $12,000

N/A—Not applicable   INA—Information not available

Table Continues →

■ Test Equipment

Manufacturer	**RADCOM EQUIPMENT, INC.**	**RADCOM EQUIPMENT, INC.**
Model	RC-200-C	PRISM200
General Description	ATM analyzer capable of operating at speeds from 1.5 to 155Mbps	High-end ATM analyzer
Form Factor	Portable and lightweight, weighing less than 2 kg. (4 lbs.)	Portable and lightweight, weighing less than 2 kg. (4 lbs.)
Network Platforms	Windows based (Windows 3.1, WFW3.11, and Windows 95)	Windows based (Windows 3.1, WFW3.11, and Windows 95)
Network Topology	Ethernet, Token Ring	Ethernet, Token Ring
NOS	NOS Independent	NOS Independent
Communication Protocol	ATM: Cell types: AAL0, AAL1, AAL2, AAL3/4, AAL5, OAM, RM, SMDS, SIP-L2 WAN over ATM: Frame Relay, X.25, SNA, SMDS, ISDN Audio-Visual over ATM: MPEG-1, MPEG-2, circuit emulation Customized protocols available on request	ATM: Cell types: AAL0, AAL1, AAL2, AAL3/4, AAL5, OAM, RM, SMDS, SIP-L2 WAN over ATM: Frame Relay, X.25, SNA, SMDS, ISDN Audio-Visual over ATM: MPEG-1, MPEG-2, circuit emulation Customized protocols available on request
Interfaces	I55 MBPS SONET OC-3/SDH STM-1 multi-mode fiber, single-mode fiber,UTP-5, electrical versions. 100 MBPS TAXI (4B/5B encoding). 45Mbps DS-3 (HEC and PLCP mapping.	Line Interface Units: ATM: Sonet OC-3C, SDH STM-1, DS-3 and DS-1, E3 and E1, TAXI and 25 MBPS UTP. WAN: Multitype V.35, V.24 (RS-232), X.21, RS-530, RS-449, E1, T1.
Readout/Display	Windows GUI	Windows GUI
Testing Features	ATM Signaling Simulation. ATM Signaling Protocol Analysis. LAN Emulation Protocol Analysis, LAN/WAN over ATM Protocol Encapsulation Analysis, Quality of service testing. Audio-Visual Services over ATM Analysis. User Programming Library.	ATM Signaling Simulation. ATM Signaling Protocol Analysis. LAN Emulation Protocol Analysis, LAN/WAN over ATM Protocol Encapsulation Analysis, Quality of service testing. Audio-Visual Services over ATM Analysis. User Programming Library.
Reporting Features	ATM: Frame Distribution by Status, Length, Direction (tabular). Traffic Distribution by VPI/VCI, VPI, VCI, AAL. Error Distribution by VPI/VCI. Ethernet: Network Traffic Activity (pairs).	ATM: Frame Distribution by Status, Length, Direction (tabular). Traffic Distribution by VPI/VCI, VPI, VCI, AAL. Error Distribution by VPI/VCI. Ethernet: Network Traffic Activity (pairs).
Comments	RISC processor (i960), ATM SAR. Real-time unit connects with any PC via the printer port. Includes one line interface unit containing two receive and two transmit ports.	RISC processor (i960), ATM SAR. Real-time unit connects with any PC via the printer port. Includes one line interface unit containing two receive and two transmit ports.
Warranty	1 year hardware, free software upgrades for 2 years	1 year hardware, free software upgrades for 2 years
Price	Starting at $15,000	Starting at $35,000

Manufacturer	**Scope Communications, Inc.**	**Tekelec**
Model	Frame Scope 802	Chameleon Open
General Description	Hand-held network analyzer for Token Ring or Ethernet LANs	A portable protocol analyzer providing simultaneous, full-bandwidth testing of LAN, WAN, and broadband networks.
Form Factor	Hand-held	Portable desktop
Network Platforms	Ethernet, Token Ring	Unix
Network Topology	Ethernet, Token Ring	ATM, Ethernet, Fast Ethernet, high-speed WAN (HSSI), Token Ring, ISDN, FDDI, SMDS, frame relay.
NOS		Sun interactive
Communication Protocol	TCP/IP, IPX, AppleTalk, Novell, DECnet, Banyan	TCP/IP, OSI, DECnet, Novell Netware, AppleTalk, XNS, STP, NFS, XTP, and Banyan Vines
Interfaces	UTP, AUI, Type 1, RJ-45, Coax	RS-232, V.35, V.36, X.21, T-1/E-1, OC-1, OC-3, DS-3 (T3/E3).
Readout/Display	LCD display with back lighting	X-Windows
Testing Features	Tests Netware server reachability and configuration; ping test data path across any Internet; troubleshooting test; measures response time	Simultaneous, full-rate simulation and analysis (up to 6 various protocols); real-time decode of LAN and encapsulated WAN networks; load generation to verify network operations; store and replay traffic for future analysis

N/A—Not applicable   INA—Information not available

Test Equipment ■

Manufacturer	Scope Communications, Inc.	Tekelec
Reporting Features	All error and traffic statistics for all stations; simultaneous traffic generation and network monitoring; protocol tracking by station or whole network	INA
Comments	AC power and battery powered; easy to use Autotest; IP and network troubleshooting tools; pocket-sized; complete kit tests Token Ring and Ethernet in one system.	Designed to allow customers to test numerous, complex protocols and technologies as their networks grow, without investing in additional testing equipment.
Warranty	1 year	1 year
Price	$2,750 (EN or TR) $3,995 (EN and TR combo)	$22,000

Manufacturer	TTC	TTC
Model	LANHAWK 3750A	FIREBERD 500
General Description	FDDI Expert analyzer	Portable Internetwork analyzer for WAN and LAN protocols
Form Factor	PC Card	Portable, modular
Network Platforms	Windows NT	MS, Windows
Network Topology	FDDI	Ethernet, Token Ring, FDDI, TI/G/Data interfaces
NOS	INA	Independent
Communication Protocol	RPC	INA
Interfaces	Handled by NT	Ethernet, Token Ring, FDDI, TI/G/Data interfaces
Readout/Display	Windows 95 or Windows NT	Color VGA display
Testing Features	Real-time all the time; xpert analysis/ statistics; intelligent ring map; Event management and display, SNMP access, Client/server architecture.	Simultaneous LAN and WAN analysis; Real-time decodes on WAN, LAN, and encapsulates protocols; traffic generation and emulation for ISDN; BERT on all WAN interfaces.
Reporting Features	Customizable reports for all Applets (ring statistics, station statistics, Event Leg)	Multiple real-time statistics (WAN); multiple LAN statistics, Logging of all statistics, remote access via SNMP or Reachout
Comments	Seamless integration with client/server architecture, full 100MBPS bandwidth, manages multiple rings and servers from a single client, captures/decodes all FDDI data and notifies user of any problems	Full PC functionality, multi-testing of WAN with LAN analysis
Warranty	3 year	3 year
Price	$8,950	$25,000–$60,000

Manufacturer	TTC	TTC
Model	FIREBERD 300	NETLENS 3000
General Description	Portable Internetwork analyzer for WAN and LAN protocols	Portable ISDN and signaling analyzer
Form Factor	Portable, modular	Portable, modular
Network Platforms	INA	DOS
Network Topology	Ethernet, Token Ring, TI/G/Data interfaces	ISDN PRI, BRI, SS7/TI/G/V.35
NOS	Independent	INA
Communication Protocol	INA	INA
Interfaces	Ethernet, Token Ring, FDDI, TI/G/Data interfaces	RS-232/RS-449 TI/EI
Readout/Display	Color VGA display	LCD display with status LEDs
Testing Features	Simultaneous LAN and WAN analysis; real-time decodes on WAN, LAN, and encapsulates protocols; traffic generation and emulation for ISDN; BERT on all WAN interfaces	Real-time protocol decodes; dial port analysis; extensive, simple display filtering

N/A—Not applicable   INA—Information not available

Table Continues →

■ Test Equipment

Manufacturer	**TTC**	**TTC**
Reporting Features	Multiple real-time statistics (WAN), Multiple LAN statistics, Logging of all statistics, Remote access via SNMP or Reachout	Multiple decodes
Comments	Full PC functionality Multi-testing of WAN with LAN analysis	Portable, modular In-depth analysis of ISDN, SS7 and wireless signaling protocols
Warranty	3 year	3 year
Price	$14,000–$25,000	$15,000

Manufacturer	**TTC**	**TTC**
Model	FIREBERD 4000	FIREBERD 6000
General Description	Communications Analyzer	Communications Analyzer
Form Factor	Benchtop/Portable	Benchtop/Portable
Network Platforms	N/A	N/A
Network Topology	N/A	N/A
NOS	N/A	N/A
Communication Protocol	INA	INA
Interfaces	RS232 Async/IEEE 488	RS232 Async/IEEE 488
Readout/Display	8 lines of 32 characters each	8 lines of 32 characters each
Testing Features	T1/FT1, 2M/N, 64k, RS232, V.35, TS 449, X.21, HSSI, DS3, EIA530, DDS-LL, DDS DSOA/B, MIL 188, 6.703 64k BERT. Signal and datacom analysis.	T1/FT1, 2M/N, 64k, RS232, V.35, TS 449, X.21, HSSI, DS3, EIA530, DDS-LL, DDS DSOA/B, MIL 188, 6.703 64k BERT. Frame relay, ISDN BRI, ATM. Jitter, signal and datacom analysis.
Reporting Features	RS-232 print outs	RS-232 print outs
Comments	Modular test set. Wide selection of interface modules. Easy-to-use, multi-access transmission testing.	Modular test set. Features for circuit switched, packet mode, and switched services testing. Focuses on wide area data services testing and advanced transmission testing.
Warranty	3 year	3 year
Price	$5,995 and up	$8,495 and up

N/A—Not applicable   INA—Information not available

End ■

Cable Testing ■

Manufacturer	CeLAN Technology, Inc.	CeLAN Technology, Inc.
Model	FlexCHECK-BNC	FlexCHECK-UT
General Description	Provides diagnostic information on free cable and installed cable runs	Provides diagnostic information on patch cable and installed cable runs
Form Factor	Hand-held	Hand-held
Cables Tested	Thin coax and thick coax	Category 3,4,5
Network Topology	Ethernet	Ethernet, Token Ring
Connector Types	BNC	RJ45
Readout/Display	LED	LED
Testing Features	Tests available: Shorts, opens, and continuity	Tests available: Shorts, opens, and continuity
Reporting Features	Concise LED display	Concise LED display
Comments	Battery powered—two units can be used together to test installed hidden cable runs	Battery powered—two units can be used together to test installed hidden cable runs
Warranty	30 day	30 day
Price	$49	$39

Manufacturer	Datacom Technologies	Datacom Technologies
Model	LANcat Vx	NETcat 800
General Description	Category 5 Cable Tester and TalkSet	LAN Cable Tester
Form Factor	Hand-held	Hand-held
Cables Tested	TIA 568A cat 3, 4, 5 cable	TIA 568A cat 3, 4 cable
Network Topology	Ethernet, Token Ring	Ethernet, Token Ring
Connector Types	RS232C, RJ45, BNC	RJ45, BNC
Readout/Display	Backlighted graphical LCD	4 line x 16 character LCD
Testing Features	Automatic 2-way NEXT measurements, tests multi-mode/single-mode fiber with FIBERcat option, UL verified performance, Ethernet traffic monitor.	Identifies all wiring errors, pre-programmed Autotest test suite checks all critical electrical parameters, tests wiremap, length, NEXT, attenuation, ACR, noise, identifies location of cable damage, simple pass/ fail results.
Reporting Features	1000 Autotest Reports, 30 hour time log of Ethernet traffic, output to PC/printer	None
Comments	Half-duplex, 2-way voice communications over test link, graphic display at both ends of test set, 20 second Autotest, plug-in modules for adaption to 110 blocks, BIX blocks, ALL-LAN, fiber	Battery powered, Ethernet Traffic monitor measures utilization, collisions, simple to use
Warranty	1 year	1 year
Price	$4,395 U.S. List	$895 U.S. List

Manufacturer	DiCon Fiberoptics	Fiber Instruments Sales
Model	GP 700 FO Switch/Tester	OV-1 Optical Verifier
General Description	High precision low loss optical switch used for cable & component testing, remote fault locating & optical signal routing	Multi-function fiber optic field tester includes power meter, LED/laser source, ORL, visual fault locator and talk capability
Form Factor	Rackmount, "19" Benchtop, "10"	Hand-held
Cables Tested	Fiberoptic single-mode & fiberoptic multi-mode	Multi-mode & single-mode fiber optic cable
Network Topology	FDDI, Sonet, SDH, ATM	LAN, WAN, FDDI, STAR, SONET
Connector Types	FC, FC/APC, SC, SC/APC, ST, ST/APC	ST, FC, SC fiber optic connectors
Readout/Display	Manual front panel vacuum fluorescent display. Continuously showing current position of all switches.	LED

N/A—Not applicable   INA—Information not available

Table Continues →

■ Cable Testing

Manufacturer	DiCon Fiberoptics	Fiber Instruments Sales
Testing Features	For automated testing of cable, components, & active devices in remote fiber testing systems, a 1xN switch is used to isolate fiber cable faults in networks during installation and routing maintenance monitoring.	Visual fault detection loss, optical return loss, talk, up to 80km
Reporting Features	Insertion loss, back reflection, fault location	
Comments	Configurations available are 1xN, 2xN, MxN, MxN directional matrix, MxN distributional matrix, & custom switching systems. Controls are manual, GPIB & RS232.	AC/DC and battery powered
Warranty	1 year	2 year
Price	$2,995 U.S. List	$895–$2,995

Manufacturer	FLUKE	FLUKE
Model	FLUKE 610 LAN CableMapper	FLUKE 620 LAN CableMeter
General Description	The 610 CableMapper provides a fast, easy way to verify UTP cabling per EIA/TIA 568 standards & detect split pairs—something no other wiremapper can do.	The 620 LAN CableMeter verifies connections of LAN cables without requiring a remote connector or another installation expert at the other end of the cable.
Form Factor	Hand-held	Hand-held
Cables Tested	Category 3, Category 4, Category 5	LocalTalk, Type1, Type 3,Category 3, Category 4, Category 5, thin coax, and thick coax.
Network Topology	Ethernet, Token Ring	Ethernet, Token Ring
Connector Types	RJ-45	RJ-45, BNC
Readout/Display	Single 16-segment character display shows the cable identifier number and the type of fault found. LEDs indicate pass or fail for each pair.	Backlit, two-line LCD display reports pass/fail conditions and additional diagnostics.
Testing Features	Tests available: shorts, opens, wire map, reversed polarity, split pairs, near-end cross-talk and crossed pairs. Tests performed to 10MHz.	Tests available: shorts, opens, wire map, reversed polarity, split pairs, distance to fault, length and crossed pairs.
Reporting Features	INA	INA
Comments	Battery-powered unit, easy one button testing, allows user to identify one termination point from the other.	Battery-powered unit with a 50-hour life.
Warranty	1 year (extended warranty available)	1 year (extended warranty available)
Price	$395	$795

Manufacturer	FLUKE	FLUKE
Model	FLUKE 650 LAN CableMeter	FLUKE 652 LAN CableMeter
General Description	The 650 LAN CableMeter provides specific diagnostic information, together with detailed cable performance analysis and certification of standard or custom cable types.	With a 20MHz range and bright, backlit display, the 652 LAN CableMeter provides a complete suite of tests and compares results to EIA/TIA and IEEE-802.
Form Factor	Hand-held	Hand-held
Cables Tested	Category 3, Category 4, Category 5, thin coax, and thick coax.	LocalTalk, Type 1, Type 3, Category 3, Category 4, Category 5, thin coax, and thick coax.
Network Topology	Ethernet, Token Ring	Ethernet, Token Ring
Connector Types	RJ-45, BNC	RJ-45, BNC
Readout/Display	64-character four-line LCD display	Four line, 64-character LCD with backlight
Testing Features	Tests available: shorts, opens, reversed polarity, split pairs, near-end cross-talk, attenuation, signal-to-noise ratio, impedance, length, and Ethernet traffic. Tests performed to 10MHz.	Tests available: shorts, opens, wire map, reversed polarity, split pairs, near-end cross-talk, attenuation, signal-to-noise ratio, impedance, length, Ethernet traffic and crossed-pair. Tests performed to 20MHz.

N/A—Not applicable   INA—Information not available

Cable Testing ∎

Manufacturer	FLUKE	FLUKE
Reporting Features	Printed reports document Cable Certification and Traffic Activity via the serial printer port. Stores results from as many as 50 tests for later print-out.	Stores up to 400 test results for printing via the 652's serial port. Results are compared to IEEE-802 & EIA/TIA 568 Commercial Building Telecommunications Wiring Standards and may be printed out for future reference.
Comments	Replaceable 9V battery or AC line operation. Measures installed cable for compliance with the EIA/TIA 568 Commercial Building Telecommunications Wiring Standard.	AC or battery-powered unit. Shuts down automatically when left idle for 15 minutes to prolong battery life. O'SCOPE mode allows the user to view TDR pulses and reflections with an oscilloscope.
Warranty	1 year (extended warranty available)	1 year (extended warranty available)
Price	$1,795	$2,395

Manufacturer	FLUKE	Harris Corporation, Network Support System	Harris Corporation, Network Support System
Model	FLUKE DSP-100 LAN CableMeter	25600-001	25600-002
General Description	The DSP-100 LAN CableMeter is the first digital cable tester for certifying Cat 5 cabling, and is the only tester to meet TIA Level II accuracy requirements for both the Basic Link and Channel configurations.	The LanMaster data clamp instantly detects and displays network activity without a direct electrical connection to the network.	The LanMaster data clamp instantly detects and displays network activity without a direct electrical connection to the network.
Form Factor	Hand-held, rugged yellow overmold	Hand held	Hand held
Cables Tested	LocalTalk, Type 1, Type 3, Category 3, Category 4, Category 5, thin coax, and thick coax, single-mode fiber, multi-mode fiber, plastic fiber, and delay skew.	UTP, STP and coax	UTP, STP and coax
Network Topology	Ethernet, Token Ring	Ethernet, 10 Base-T, 4Mbs Token Ring, 16Mbs Token Ring, Ethertalk	Ethernet, 10 Base-T, 4Mbs Token Ring, 16Mbs Token Ring, Ethertalk
Connector Types	RJ-45, BNC, other adapters available	Non-intrusive clamp	Non-intrusive clamp
Readout/Display	Graphic LCD, 240 x 200 bit mapped display with backlight.	110x32 graphic LCD display, 10 LED indicators & audible status monitor	110x32 graphic LCD display, 10 LED indicators & audible status monitor
Testing Features	Tests available: shorts, opens, wire map, reversed polarity, split pairs, near-end cross-talk, attenuation, signal-to-noise ratio, impedance, location of NEXT fault, and Ethernet traffic.	Traffic monitoring and logging, verify connectivity, measures network segment loading	Traffic monitoring and logging, verify connectivity, measures network segment loading
Reporting Features	Stores test results up to 500 links for later printing or downloading to a computer. Each link's test result may be uniquely labeled for future reference. Connects to an Epson™ or HP™ LaserJet printer for fast hardcopy results.	Instantaneous average and peak measurements, network statistics, collision indicator, average traffic log over time	Instantaneous average and peak measurements, network statistics, collision indicator, average traffic log over time, data down load via RS232
Comments	Battery-powered unit. New additions include a free upgrade adding the capability to test to 155MHz, and a new Fiber Optic Testing Option.	AC and battery powered (wall plug-in transformer included)	AC and battery powered (wall plug-in transformer included)
Warranty	1 year (extended warranty available)	18 months from the date of manufacture	18 months from the date of manufacture
Price	Starts at $3,795	$750	$900

N/A—Not applicable   INA—Information not available

Table Continues →

■ Cable Testing

Manufacturer	MilesTek Inc.	Nortech Fibronic Inc.	Nortech Fibronic Inc.
Model	40-30041 Uni-Network Tester	5500 Series	Lynx
General Description	Checks continuity of individual wires of a patch cord or an installed cable	Fully automated single-mode fiber optic Multi-Meter, a single-connector feature eliminates the need to make repeated connections to the same link while performing bi-directional, end-to-end loss tests. It also integrates talk-set option.	Mini OTDR, Fault locator
Form Factor	Hand-held	Hand-held	Hand held
Cables Tested	Category 3-5, coax, modular	Single-mode & multi-mode fibers	Single-mode & multi-mode fibers
Network Topology	Ethernet	LAN/WAN Networks, SONET, FDDI, etc.	LAN/WAN Networks, SONET, FDDI, etc...
Connector Types	RJ45, RJ11 and coax with optional adapter	ST, FC, SC, ST/APC, FC/APC, SC/APC, other	VFO, FC/PC, EC, others...
Readout/Display	LED	Large 240x64 pixel LCD, with graphic capability	Large LCD dot matrix 320x240pts (96x72mm)
Testing Features	Tests for opens, shorted, crossed, reversed, transposed, and split-wiring faults	Power, loss, fault location, light source, voice communication	OTDR, fault location, distance to breaks, full trace capability
Reporting Features	None	Stores as many as 500 test results	None
Comments	9V battery	AC or battery-powered unit. Batteries can be recharged while the unit is in operation.	NiCad battery-powered with 6 hours autonomy, interface RS232C, rugged, compact and easy to use.
Warranty	1 year	1 year warranty on defective material and workmanship	1 year warranty on defective material and workmanship
Price	$75 and $3 for optional coax adapters	From $2,095 U.S.	From $295 U.S.

Manufacturer	Nortech Fibronic Inc.	Nortech Fibronic Inc.	Nortech Fibronic Inc.
Model	MOP Series	MOS Series	MOT Series
General Description	Miniature Optical Power Meter. It adapts to any brand of DMM, transforming it into a versatile fiber optic Power-Meter.	Miniature Optical Source. When used with MOP, you can measure attenuation through any single or multi-mode fiber optic link inexpensively.	Miniature Optical Talk Set, with digital-quality voice transmission, multi-mode LED transmission. LED 850nm, LED 1300nm, LASER 1310nm, LASER 1550nm. Can be operated as a light source.
Form Factor	Hand-held	Hand-held	Hand-held with head set
Cables Tested	Single-mode & multi-mode fibers	Single-mode & multi-mode fibers	Single-mode & multi-mode fibers
Network Topology	LAN/WAN Networks, SONET, FDDI, etc.	LAN/WAN Networks, SONET, FDDI, etc...	LAN/WAN Networks, SONET, FDDI, etc...
Connector Types	SMA, ST, FC, SC, Biconic	SMA, ST, FC, SC	ST, FC, SC
Readout/Display	Calibrated analog output (voltage)	LED	LED
Testing Features	Power	Loss (light source), fault location	Voice communication, loss (light Source)
Reporting Features	Depends on user supplied meter	None	None
Comments	Battery life of more than 200 hours, rugged, compact and easy to use	Rugged, compact, and easy to use	Rugged, compact, and easy to use
Warranty	1 year warranty on defective material and workmanship	1 year warranty on defective material and workmanship	1 year warranty on defective material and workmanship
Price	From $189 U.S.	From $209 U.S.	From $295 U.S.

N/A—Not applicable   INA—Information not available

Cable Testing ■

Manufacturer	Noyes Fiber Systems	Noyes Fiber Systems
Model	MLP 4-2	MLP 5-2
General Description	Fiberoptic loss test kit for multi-mode and single-mode fibers	Fiberoptic loss test kit for multi-mode and single-mode fibers
Form Factor	Hand-held	Hand-held
Cables Tested	Fiber optic, multi-mode, single-mode	Fiber optic, multi-mode, single-mode
Network Topology	N/A	N/A
Connector Types	ST, SC, and FC	ST, SC, and FC
Readout/Display	LCD	LCD
Testing Features	Verify transmitter output power, measure optical loss on links	Verify transmitter output power, measure optical loss on links
Reporting Features	Displays power in dBm and loss in dB	Displays power in dBm, mW and loss in dB
Comments	9V battery operated	9V battery operated, data storage with PC software
Warranty	1 year	1 year
Price	$1,545	$1,940

Manufacturer	Noyes Fiber Systems	Noyes Fiber Systems	Scope Communications, Inc.
Model	OFL 100 MM	OFL 100 DM	WireScope 155
General Description	Optical time domain reflectometer for multi-mode fiber	Optical time domain reflectometer for multi-mode fiber	Qualifies cable for networks up to 155 MHz. It includes an Autotest time of 14 seconds, qualifies cable for 20 network specifications, and offers fiber test capabilities.
Form Factor	Portable	Portable	Hand-held
Cables Tested	Multi-mode fiberoptic	Multi-mode fiberoptic	LocalTalk, Type 3, Category 3-5, thin coax, thick coax, and multi-mode fiber
Network Topology	N/A	N/A	N/A
Connector Types	ST, SC, and FC	ST, SC, and FC	BNC Intelligent Test Port with adapters: RJ45 Modular Plug, RJ45 Modular Jack, 110, Northern Telecom BIX, Krone HiBand, IBM Type 1, and Twinax.
Readout/Display	LCD	LCD	Backlit graphics LCD display with contrast controls
Testing Features	Tests fibers for length and locates breaks. 850 nanometer operation.	Tests fibers for length and locates breaks. 850 and 1300 nanometer operation.	Shorts, opens, wire map, reversed polarity, split pairs, near-end crosstalk, attenuation, signal-to-noise ratio, impedance, ambient noise, propagation delay, delay skew, TIA-TSB-67, ISO 11801, 20 network-specific pass/fail profiles, loop resistance, and lobe insertion
Reporting Features	LCD displays length and break location. Backscatter trace available through software.	LCD displays length and break location. Backscatter trace available through software.	Local results storage: Up to 500 Autotests (summary reports, flash memory equipment for easy software updating). Remote results storage (via ScopeData): Full plots can be stored for all tests. Total limited only by disk space.
Comments	PC software provides full fiber certification. Battery and AC operation.	PC software provides full fiber certification. Battery and AC operation.	AC or battery powered, removable/rechargeable NiCd battery, built in fast charger extends number of charges by eliminating memory effect.

N/A—Not applicable   INA—Information not available

Table Continues →

■ Cable Testing

Manufacturer	Noyes Fiber Systems	Noyes Fiber Systems	Scope Communications, Inc.
Warranty	1 year	1 year	Limited one year warranty (extended warranty available)
Price	$4,995	$7,495	$4,995 for complete analyzer kit

Manufacturer	UNICOM Electric, Inc.	UNICOM Electric, Inc.
Model	TRT-018 TP Cabling System Tester Kit	UNITRACK
General Description	Designed to detect either STP or UTP cable assembly errors. LEDs indicate shorts, breaks, and miswires in STP/UTP cables.	Will map any 8 wire combination end to end. It can locate up to 12 different locations at one testing.
Form Factor	Hand-held or hung	Hand-held
Cables Tested	Shield twisted-pair and unshield twisted-pair	Both twisted-pair and flat cable
Network Topology	Token Ring	Twisted-pair
Connector Types	Data connectors & RJ45 jack	RJ45
Readout/Display	LED	32-character LCD-2 line
Testing Features	Test open shorts, breaks, grounding open and miswires in STP/UTP cables and indicate data connector shorting ban failure in STP cables.	Instant display of results on 2 lines of 16 characters. Shows wiring information for different mapping combinations. Wire mapping, remote locating and patch cord testing all-in-one.
Reporting Features	INA	INA
Comments	Battery powered	Light weight hand held tester weighing 8oz. Battery powered, lasting up to 6 hrs. of continuos testing.
Warranty	1 year	1 year
Price	$85	$188

Manufacturer	Wavetek Corporation	Wavetek Corporation
Model	LANTEK Pro Series	Flash Mini-OTDR
General Description	LAN tester meets TIA and ISO standards (user can select either standard for customization) so cable types & tests suites can be adapted to user's specific needs.	Maximizes field performance by conducting functions of full-sized OTDR's but weighs only 4 lbs. Available in both single-mode and multi-mode.
Form Factor	Durable hand-held unit	Durable hand-held unit
Cables Tested	LocalTalk, Type 1&3, Categories 3,4,5, thin coax, thick coax, single-mode, multi-mode, and plastic fiber	Single-mode, multi-mode, and plastic fiber
Network Topology	AppleTalk, LocalTalk, Ethernet, 10BASE-T, Fast Ethernet, Token-Ring, ATM	FDDI, Fiber Channel, Soret ATM
Connector Types	RJ-45 (plug & jack), BNC-coax, Twin-Ax, IBM Type 1A, Token-Ring	FC/PC, ST, VFO, SC, PFO, DIN, biconic
Readout/Display	Graphical LCD	Graphical LCD
Testing Features	Line mapping, length, DC loop, capacitance, attenuation, ACR, Dual NEXT™ return loss, delay, level-II accuracy (all Autotest functions)	Event detection, location, power loss, ghost detection, level-II accuracy
Reporting Features	Tester stores up to 500 Autotests that can be printed or downloaded to your PC for later use. Results can also be sorted.	Field-collected data can be printed or stored using internal memory or built-in PCMCI card slot and memory cards. Data can also be downloaded directly to a PC or printer.
Comments	With the Fiberkit option, fiberoptic cable power loss capability is added to the LANTEK Pro. Fiber cabling connection can be verified with the same LANTEK Pro as for copper cable.	Simple user interface. Software package provides additional testing options.
Warranty	1 year	1 year
Price	$4,620	$9,300 to $14,900

N/A—Not applicable   INA—Information not available

A   CONTACT LIST

THIS APPENDIX IS A contact list of all the companies
whose products are mentioned in this buyer's guide. The
companies are listed in alphabetical order by name, and we
also provide the address, telephone number followed by fax
number, and Web address (if available).

DIRECTORY OF MANUFACTURERS, VENDORS, AND SUPPLIERS

Accton Technology
1962 Zanker Road
San Jose, CA 95112
800-926-9288, 408-452-8988

AccuLan
558 Oakmead Parkway
Sunnyvale, CA 94086
408-245-3300, 408-245-3390
www.acculan.com

Adaptec
691 S. Milpitas Blvd.
Milpitas, CA 95035
408-945-8600, 408-957-7150
www.adaptec.com

Addtron Technology Company
46712 Fremont Blvd.
Fremont, CA 94538
510-770-0120, 510-770-0171
www.addtron.com

ADIC
10201 Willows Road
Redmond, WA, 98052
206-881-8004 , 206-881-2296
www.adic.com

The ADM Group
477 Madison Avenue, 17th Floor
New York, NY 10022
212-371-4900, 212-750-7419
www.admgroup.com

Advanced Media Services, Inc.
10 Upton Drive
Wilmington, MA 01887
800-466-0813, 508-658-1877
www.industry.net/adv.media

AG Group
2540 Camino Diablo, Suite 200
Walnut Creek, CA 94596
510-937-7900, 510-937-2479
www.aggroup.com

AIWA
800 Corporate Drive
Mahwah, NJ 07430
201-512-3629, 201-512-3704
www.aiwa.com

Alexander LAN
100 Perimeter Road
Nashua, NH 03063
603-880-8800, 603-880-8881
www.alexander.com

Alfa Netcom
477 Valley Way
Milpitas, CA 95035
408-934-3880, 408-934-3883
www.alfaInc.com

Allied Telesyn International
950 Kifer Road
Sunnyvale, CA 94086
408-730-0950, 408-736-0100
www.alliedtelesyn.com/index.htm

Alphatronix
4022 Stirrup Creek Drive
Research Triangle, NC, 27709
919-544-0001, 919-544-4079
www.alphatronix.com

ALR, Inc.
9401 Jeronimo Road
Irvine, CA 92718
714-581-6770, 714-581-9240
www.alr.com

Amdahl Corporation
1250 E. Arques Avenue
Sunnyvale, CA 94088
408-746-6000, 408-773-8833
www.amdahl.com

AMP
P.O. Box 3608
Harrisburg, PA 17105
800-835-7240, 910-727-5858
www.amp.com/networking

Analog & Digital Peripherals, Inc. (ADPI)
P.O. Box 499
Troy, OH 45373
513-339-2241, 513-339-0070
www.adpi.com

Andataco
10140 Mesa Rim Road
San Diego, CA 92121
619-453-9191, 619-453-9294
www.andataco.com

Annexus Data Systems
10559 Lansford Lane
San Diego, CA 92126
800-505-0019, 619-530-0096

Antares Microsystems
160B Albright Way
Los Gatos, CA 95030
408-370-7287, 408-370-7649
www.antares.com

Apple Computer, Inc.
1 Infinite Loop
Cupertino, CA 95014
408-996-1010, 408-974-0275
www.apple.com

APT Communications
9607 Doctor Perry Road, Suite 107
Ijamsville, MD 21754
800-842-0626, 301-874-5255
www.aptcom.com

Arback Networks, Inc.
297 Labrosse Road
Pointe-Claire, PQ, CA
514-630-3728, 514-694-6973

Archtek America Corporation
18549 Gale Avenue
City of Industry, CA 91748
818-912-9800, 818-912-9700
www.archtek.com

Artecon, Inc.
6305 El Camino Real
Carlsbad, CA 92009
619-931-5500, 619-931-5527
www.artecon.com

Artisoft, Inc.
2202 N. Forbes Blvd.
Tucson, AZ 85745
602-670-7100, 602-670-7101
www.artisoft.com

Asante Technologies
821 Fox Lane
San Jose, CA 95131
408-435-8388, 408-432-1117
www.asante.com

Asarte Fiber Networks
2555 55th Street, Suite 100
Boulder, CO 80301
303-443-8778, 303-449-2975
www.starswitch.com

Astea International
55 Middlesex Turnpike
Bedford, MA 01730
617-275-5440, 617-275-1910
www.astea.com

ATL Products
1515 S. Manchester
Anaheim, CA 92802-2907
714-780-7827, 714-780-7799
www.atl.com

Attachmate Corporation
3617 131st Avenue S.E.
Bellevue, WA 98006
206-644-4010, 206-747-9924
www.attachmate.com

ATTO Technology, Inc.
40 Hazelwood Drive #106
Amherst, NY 14228
716-691-1999, 716-691-9353
www.atta.com

Aurora Technologies
176 2nd Avenue
Waltham, MA 02154
617-290-4800, 617-290-4844
www.auratek.com

Auspex Systems, Inc.
5200 Great America Parkway
Santa Clara, CA 95054
408-986-2000, 408-986-2020
www.auspex.com

Automated Systems Methodologies, Inc. (ASM)
703 Grand Central
Clearwater, FL, 34616
813-449-8200, 813-531-7510
www.asmgator.com

Aviv Corporation
4 Fourth Avenue
Burlington, MA 01803
617-270-6900, 617-270-5727
www.aviv.com

DIRECTORY OF MANUFACTURERS, VENDORS, AND SUPPLIERS

Axent Technologies
2400 Research Blvd., Suite 200
Rockville, MD 20850
301-258-5043, 301-330-5756
www.axent.com

Axis Communications, Inc.
4 Constitution Way, Suite G
Woburn, MA 01801-1030
617-938-1188, 617-938-6161
www.axisanc.com

Banyan Systems, Inc.
120 Flanders Road
Westborough, MA 01581-1035
508-898-1000, 508-898-1755
www.banyan.com

Baranof Software, Inc.
85 School Street #101
Watertown, MA 02172
617-926-6626, 617-926-6636
www.baranof.com

BASS Micro Industries
6 Bendix
Irvine, CA 92618
800-677-0707, 714-457-8825

Belden Wire & Cable Company
P.O. Box 1980
Richmond, IN 47375
317-983-5200, 317-983-5294

Bindview Development
3355 W. Alabama, 12th Floor
Houston, TX 77098
713-789-0882, 713-881-9200

Blue Ocean Software
15310 Amberly Drive, Suite 250
Tampa, FL 33647
813-977-4553, 813-979-4447
www.blueocean.com

BMC Software
2101 City West Blvd.
Houston, TX 77042
713-918-8800, 713-918-8000
www.bmc.com

Boole & Babbage Storage Division
3131 Zanker Road
San Jose, CA 95134
408-526-3000, 408-526-3053
www.boole.com

Box Hill Systems Corporation
161 Avenue of the Americas
New York, NY 10013
212-989-4455, 212-989-6817
www.boxhill.com

BrainTree Technology, Inc.
200 Cordwaner Drive
Norwell, MA 02061
617-982-0200, 617-982-8076
www.bti.com

Breece Hill Technologies
6287 Araphoe Avenue
Boulder, CO 80303
303-449-2673, 303-449-1027
www2.csn.net/breece_hill/

BreezeCom
2195 Faraday Avenue, Suite A
Carlsbad, CA 92008
619-431-9880, 619-431-2595
www.breezecom.com

The Bristol Group
100 Larkspur Landing Circle #200
Larkspur, CA 94939
415-925-9250, 415-925-9278
www.bg.com

Brooktrout Technology, Inc.
410 First Avenue
Needham, MA 02194
617-449-4100, 617-449-9009
www.brooktrout.com

Bull Worldwide Information Systems
13430 North Black Canyon Highway
Phoenix, AZ 85209
602-862-8000, 602-862-6973
www.bull.com

Calculus, Inc.
3250 Sharon Park Drive, Suite M
Menlo Park, CA 94025
415-854-3130, 415-854-1248

CALLWARE Technologies, Inc.
2323 Foothill Drive
Salt Lake City, UT 84109
801-486-9922, 801-486-8294

Canary Communications
1851 Zanker Road
San Jose, CA 95112
408-453-9201, 408-453-0940
www.canarycom.com

Castelle
3255-3 Scott Blvd.
Santa Clara, CA 95054
408-496-0474, 408-492-1964
www.castelle.com

Cayman Systems
100 Maple Street
Stoneham, MA 02180
617-279-1101, 617-438-5560
www.cayman.com

CCNS, Inc.
48531 Warm Springs Blvd. #413
Fremont, CA 94539
510-438-9635, 510-440-0419

CD International
128A York Street
Kennebunk, ME 04043
207-985-6370, 207-985-6467
www.cybertours.com/cdi

CeLan Technology
2323 Calle Del Mundo
Santa Clara, CA 95054
408-988-8288, 408-988-8289

Champlain Cable
12 Herculus Drive
Colchester, VT 05446
802-654-4200, 802-654-4224

Chase Research, Inc.
545 Marriot Drive #100
Nashville, TN 37214
615-872-0770, 615-872-0771
www.chaser.com

ChatCom, Inc.
9600 Topanga Canyon Blvd.
Chatsworth, CA 91311
818-709-1778, 818-882-9134
www.chatcom.com

CheckPoint Software
400 Seaport Court, Suite105
Redwood City, CA 94063
415-562-0400, 415-562-0410
www.checkpoint.com

Cheyenne Software
3 Expressway Plaza
Roslyn Heights, NY 11577
516-484-5110, 516-484-1853
www.cheyenne.com

Cinco Networks
1340 Center Drive, Suite 103
Atlanta, GA 30338
770-671-9272, 770-390-9947
www.cinco.com

Cisco Systems
170 West Tasman Drive
San Jose, CA 95134
800-553-6387, 408-526-4100
www.cisco.com

Citrix Systems, Inc.
210 University Drive #700
Coral Springs, FL 33071
305-755-0559, 305-341-6880
www.citrix.com

CloneStar Software
24102 Palo Dura
Hockley, TX 77447
713-256-1632, 713-373-5619

CNet Technology
2199 Zanker Road
San Jose, CA 95131
408-954-8000, 408-954-8866
www.cnet.com.tw

Cogent Data Technologies
15375 S.E. 30th Place #310
Bellevue, WA 98007
206-603-0333, 206-603-9223
www.cogentdata.com

DIRECTORY OF MANUFACTURERS, VENDORS, AND SUPPLIERS

Communication Devices, Inc.
1 Forestmann Court
Clifton, NJ 07011
201-772-6997, 201-772-0747
www.commdevices.com

CommVault Systems
1 Industrial Way W., Bldg. D
Eatontown, NJ 07724
908-935-8000, 908-935-8040

Compaq Computer Corporation
P.O. 692000
Houston, TX 77269-2000
713-374-4619, 713-378-1442
www.compaq.com

CompuServe Network
5000 Arlington Center Blvd.
Columbus, OH 43220
614-457-8600, 614-457-0438
www.compuserve.com

Computer Associates International
1 Computer Associates Place
Islandia, NY 11788
516-342-5224, 516-342-5734
www.cai.com

Computer Network Technology Corporation
605 Highway 169 North, Suite 800
Minneapolis, MN 55441
612-797-6000, 612-797-6800
www.cnt.com

Computone Corporation
1100 Northmeadow Parkway #150
Roswell, GA 30076
800-241-3946, 770-664-1510
www.computone.com

Concord Communications
33 Boston Post Road West #400
Marlboro, MA 01752
508-460-4646, 508-481-9772
www.concord.com

Concurrent Computer Corporation
2101 W. Cypress Creek Road
Ft. Lauderdale, FL 33309-1892
954-974-1700 , 954-977-5580

Control Data Corporation
4201 N. Lexington Avenue
Arden Hills, MN 55126
612-482-6736, 612-482-2000
www.cdc.com

Corollary, Inc.
2802 Kelvin Avenue
Irvine, CA 92714
714-250-4040, 714-250-4043
www.corollary

Cray Communications
9020 Junction Drive
Annapolis Junction, MD 20701
800-367-2729, 301-317-7535
www.craycom.com

CrossCom
450 Donald Lynch Blvd.
Marlborough, MA 01752
800-388-1200, 508-229-5535
www.crosscomm.com

CrossWind Technologies
1505 Ocean Street #1
Santa Cruz, CA 95060
408-469-1780, 408-469-1750
www.crosswind.com

CSS Laboratories
1641 McGaw Avenue
Irvine, CA 92714
714-852-8161, 714-852-0410
www.csslabs.com

Cubix Corporation
2800 Lockheed Way
Carson City, NV 89706
702-888-1000, 702-888-1001
www.cubix.com

CyberAccess, Inc.
9700 Rockside Road #110
Valley View, OH 44125
216-524-5005, 216-524-5001
www.cyberacc.com

Cyberguard Corporation
2101 W. Cypress Creek Road
Fort Lauderdale, FL 33309
954-977-5615, 954-973-5160

Cybermation
80 Tiverton Court, Suite 400
Markham, Ontario, L3R 0G4
Canada
905-479-4611, 905-479-5474
www.cybermation.com

Cybernetics
111 Cybernetics Way
Yorktown, VA 23693
804-833-9100, 804-833-9300

CyberSAFE
1605 NW Sammamish Road #310
Issaquah, WA 98027-5378
206-391-6000, 206-391-0508
www.cybersafe.com

Cylink
910 Hermosa Court
Sunnyvale, CA 94086
408-735-5800, 408-735-6643
www.cylink.com

C-Spec
20 Marco Lane
Dayton, OH 45458
513-439-2882, 513-439-2358
www.c-spec.com

Dallastone, Inc.
2 Cote Lane
Bedford, NH 03110
603-647-8168, 603-624-2466

Danaware Data A/S Markham Computer
One South Ocean Blvd. #301
Boca Raton, FL 33432
407-394-3994, 407-394-3844
www.mcc-usa.com

Dantz Development Corporation
4 Orinda Way, Building C
Orinda, CA 94563
510-253-3000, 510-253-9099
www.dantz.com

Data Research & Applications, Inc.
9041 Executive Park Drive #200
Knoxville, TN 37923
423-690-1345, 423-693-5468

DataTools
3340 Hillview Ave.
Palo Alto, CA, 94304
415-842-9100 , 415-842-9101

Dayna Communications
849 West Levoy Drive
Salt Lake City, UT 84123-2544
801-269-7200, 801-269-7363
www.dayna.com

Dell Computer Corporation
2214 West Braker Lane, Suite D
Austin, TX 78758
800-854-6245, 512-728-3653
www.dell.com

Devcom Mid-America, Inc.
2603 W. 22nd Street #23
Oakbrook, IL 60521
708-574-3600, 708-572-0508
www.devcom.com

Develcon Electronics Unlimited
856 51st Street
Saskatoon, Saskatchewan 57K 5C7
Canada
306-933-3300, 306-931-1370
www.develcon.com

DiCon Fiberoptics
1331 Eighth Street
Berkeley, CA 94710
510-528-0427, 510-528-1519

Digi International
1101 Renbren Road East
Minnetonka, MN 55343
612-943-9020, 612-943-5398
www.digi.com

Digital Equipment Corporation
550 King Street
Littleton, MA 01460-1289
800-486-711, 508-486-7417
www.digital.com

Digital Pathways, Inc.
201 Ravendale Drive
Mountain View, CA, 94043
415-964-0707, 415-961-7487
www.digpath.com

DIRECTORY OF MANUFACTURERS, VENDORS, AND SUPPLIERS

Digital Products, Inc.
411 Waverly Oaks Road
Waltham, MA 02154-8414
617-647-1234, 617-647-4474
www.digprod.com

Disc, Inc.
372 Turquoise Street
Milpitas, CA 95035
408-934-7000, 408-934-7007
www.discjuke.com

Distinct Corporation
12901 Saratoga Avenue #4
Saratoga, CA 95070
408-366-8933, 408-366-0153
www.distinct.com

Diverse Logistics, Inc. (DLI)
2862 McGaw Avenue
Irvine, CA 92714
800-345-6432, 714-476-0714
www.dilog.com

Dorotech
344 Avenue Georges Clemenceau
92000 Nanterre, France
011-331-46148807, 011-331-40999794

DPT
140 Candace Drive
Maitland, FL 32751
407-830-5522, 407-260-5366
www.dpt.com

Dynatech Communications, Inc.
12650 Darby Brook Court
Woodbridge, VA 22192
703-494-1400, 703-494-1920
www.dynatech.com

D-Link Systems
5 Musick
Irvine, CA 92718
714-455-1688, 714-455-2521
www.dlink.com

Eastman Kodak Company
343 State Street
Rochester, NY 14650
716-724-4000, 716-588-0561
www.kodak.com

Eccs, Inc.
One Sheila Drive, Building 6A
Tinton Falls, NJ 07724
908-747-6995, 908-747-6542
www.eccs.com

Eclipse Technologies, Inc.
547 Oakmead Parkway
Sunnyvale, CA 94086
408-523-5700, 408-523-5749

EFA Corporation
3040 Oakmead Village Drive
Santa Clara, CA 95051
408-987-5400, 408-987-5415
www.efacorp.com

Efficient Networks
4201 Spring Valley Road #1200
Dallas, TX 75244
214-991-3884, 214-991-3887
www.efficient.com

Elegant Communications, Inc.
4 King Street West #1101
Toronto, Ontario M5H 1B6,
Canada
416-362-9772, 416-362-8324
www.elegant.com

EMC Corporation
171 South Street
Hopkinton, MA 01757
508-435-1000, 508-497-6904
www.emc.com

Emprise Technologies
3117 Washington Pike
Bridgeville, PA 15017
412-257-9060, 412-257-9012
www.emprise.com

Emerging Technologies, Inc.
900 Walt Whitman Road
Melville, NY 11747
516-271-4525, 516-271-4814
www.etinc.com

Emulex Corporation
3535 Harbor Blvd.
Costa Mesa, CA 92626
714-662-5600, 714-513-8266
www.emulex.com

Engage Communication
9053 Soquel Drive
Aptos, CA 95003
408-688-1021, 408-688-1421
www.engage.com

Equinox Systems, Inc.
1 Equinox Way
Sunrise, FL 33351
954-746-9000, 954-746-9101
www.equinox.com

Equisys USA
1951 Airport Road, Suite 202
Atlanta, GA 30341
770-457-0703, 770-457-9500
www.tspco.com

Esker, Inc.
350 Sansome Street #210
San Francisco, CA 94104
415-675-7777, 415-675-7775
www.esker.com

Evergreen Systems
120 Landing Court
Novato, CA 94945
415-897-8888, 415-897-6158
www.eversys.com

Exabyte Corporation
1685 38th Street
Boulder, CO 80301
800-392-2983, 303-417-5500
www.exabyte.com

Excel Computers
3330 Earhart Drive #212
Carrollton, TX 75006
214-980-7098, 214-980-0375
www.flash.net/~excel

Extended Systems
7 East Beall
Bozeman, MT 59715
800-235-7576, 406-587-9170
www.extendsys.com

E-Mail, Inc.
2245 East Colorado Blvd., Suite 180
Pasedena, CA 91107
818-403-1999, 818-351-4719
www.emailinchp.com

Falcon Systems, Inc.
1417 North Market Blvd.
Sacramento, CA 95834
800-326-1002, 916-928-9355
www.falcons.com

FaxBack, Inc.
1100 N.W. Compton Drive, Suite 200
Beaverton, OR 97006
800-329-2225, 503-690-6399
www.faxback.com

Faximum Software, Inc.
1497 Marine Drive Suite 300
Vancouver, British Columbia, V7T 1B8,
Canada
604-925-3600, 604-926-8182
www.faximum.com

Fibronics
16 Esquire Road
North Billerica, MA 01862-2590
800-553-1552, 508-667-7262
www.fibusa.com

FORE Systems
2115 O'Neil Drive
San Jose, CA 95131
408-955-9000, 408-955-9500
www.fore.com

Fotec
151 Mystic Avenue
Medford, MA 02155
800-537-8254, 617-396-6155
www.std.com/fotec

FSA Corporation
1011 First Street S.W., Suite 508
Calgary, Alberta, T2R 1J2
Canada
403-264-4822, 403-264-0873
www.fsa.ca

FTP Software, Inc.
2 High Street
N. Andover, MA 01845
508-685-4000, 508-794-4488
www.ftp.com

Fujitsu America, Inc.
3055 Orchard Drive
San Jose, CA 95134
408-432-1300, 408-432-1318

DIRECTORY OF MANUFACTURERS, VENDORS, AND SUPPLIERS

FutureSoft
12012 Wickchester Lane #600
Houston, TX 77079
713-496-9400, 713-496-1090
www.fst.com

Galacticomm, Inc.
4101 S.W. 47th Avenue, Suite 101
Fort Lauderdale, FL 33314
954-583-5990, 954-583-7846
www.gcomm.com

GammaLink
1314 Cheaspeake Terrace
Sunnyvale, CA 94089
408-744-1400, 408-744-1900
www.gammalink.com

Gandalf Technologies, Inc.
130 Colonnade Road South
Nepean, Ontario, K2E 7M4
Canada
800-426-3253, 609-461-4074
www.gandalf.ca

General Datacom
1579 Straits Turnpike
Middlebury, CT 06762
203-574-1118, 203-758-8507
www.gdc.com

Help Desk Technology
1976 Lapad Court
Mississauga, Ontario, L5L 5R1
Canada
905-608-0523, 905-608-2199
www.helpstar.com

Heroix Corporation
120 Wells Avenue
Newton, MA 02159
617-527-1550, 617-527-6132

Hewlett-Packard
P.O. Box 58059
Santa Clara, CA 95051
800-752-0900

Highground Systems, Inc.
1300 Massachusetts Ave. #205
Boxborough, MA 01719
508-263-5588, 508-263-5565

Hooleon Corporation
411 South 6th Street, Building B
Cottonwood, AZ 86326
520-634-4503, 520-634-4620
www.hooleon.com

Horizons Technology, Inc.
3990 Ruffin Road
San Diego, CA 92123-1826
619-292-8331, 619-292-9439
www.horizons.com

HT Communications
4480 Shopping Lane
Simi Valley, CA 93063
805-579-1700, 805-522-5295

Hypercom Network Systems
2851 W. Kathleen Road
Phoenix, AZ 85023
602-866-5399, 602-866-5380
www.hypercom.com

IBM
Old Orchard Road
Armonk, NY 10504
800-426-3333, 520-574-4600
www.ibm.com

Icon Resources, Inc.
1050 N. State Street #210
Chicago, IL 60610
312-573-0142, 312-573-0143

ImageNet Ltd
10 HaKishon Street, 51203
Bnei Brak, ISRAEL
972-357-83178, 972-357-83180

Infinite Technologies
11433 Cronridge Drive
Owings Mills, MD 21117
410-363-1097, 410-363-3779
www.ihub.com

Informative Graphics
706 E. Bell Road #207
Phoenix, AZ 85022
602-971-6061, 602-971-1714
www.infograph.com

InMagic, Inc.
800 W. Cummings Park
Woburn, MA 01801
617-938-4442, 617-938-6393
www.inmagic.com

Innovation Data Processing, Inc.
275 Patterson Avenue
Little Falls, NJ 07424
201-890-7300, 201-890-7147
www.innovationdp.fdr.com

Integrix, Inc.
2001 Corporate Center Drive
Newbury Park, CA 91320
805-375-1055, 805-376-1001
www.integrix.com

Intel Corporation
5200 N.E. Elam Young Parkway
Hillsboro, OR 97124
503-696-8080, 503-264-0123
www.intel.com

Intellicom, Inc.
20415 Nordoff Street
Chatsworth, CA 91311
818-407-3900, 818-882-2404
www.csintel.com

Intergraph Computer Systems
One Madison Industrial Park
Huntsville, AL 35807
205-730-2000, 205-730-6011
www.intergraph.com

Interlink Computer Sciences, Inc.
47370 Fremont Blvd.
Fremont, CA 94538
510-657-9800, 510-659-6381
www.interlink.com

Intrak, Inc.
9999 Business Park Avenue, Suite B
San Diego, CA 92131
619-695-1900, 619-271-4989
www.intrak.com/intrak

Intrusion Detection, Inc.
49 Glen Head Road
Glen Head, NY 11545
516-674-4800, 516-674-2458
ww.intrusion.com

Ipsilon Networks, Inc.
2191 East Bayshore Road #100
Palo Alto, CA 94303
415-846-4600, 415-855-1414
www.ipsilon.com

Ipswitch, Inc.
81 Hartwell Avenue
Lexington, MA 02173
617-676-5700, 617-676-5710
www.ipswitch.com

ISOTRO Networks
875 Carling Avenue #200
Ottawa, Ontario, K1S 5P1
Canada
613-722-1921, 613-722-1997
www.isotro.com

JVC
5665 Corporate Avenue
Cypress, CA 90630
800-995-4582, 714-261-9692

Kelaur Netcom Corporation
326 Meadowrue Lane
Batavia, IL 60510
708-879-6131, 708-879-9178

Kingston Technology Corporation
17600 Newhope Street
Fountain Valley, CA 92708
714-435-2600, 714-435-1879
www.kingston.com

Knozall Systems
375 E. Elliot Road #10
Chandler, AZ 85225-1130
602-545-0006, 602-545-0008
www.tesi.com

KTI Networks
7400 Harwin Drive #120
Houston, TX 77036
713-266-3891, 713-266-3893
www.ktinet.com

LANart Corporation
145 Rosemary Street
Needham, MA 02194
617-444-1994, 617-444-3692
www.lanart.com

DIRECTORY OF MANUFACTURERS, VENDORS, AND SUPPLIERS

LANCast
12 Murphy Drive
Nashua, NH 03062
603-880-1833, 603-881-9888

LANcity Corporation
200 Bulfinch Drive
Andover, MA 01810
508-682-1600, 508-682-3200

Landings Technology Corporation
163 Water Street, Unit A2, Merrill Block,
Exeter, NH 03833
603-772-4500, 603-772-0141

LanOptics, Inc.
2445 Midway Road, Building 2
Carrollton, TX 75006
214-738-6900, 214-738-6999
www.lanoptics.com

LANSource Technologies
221 Dufferin Street #310A
Toronto, Ontario, M6K 3J2
Canada
416-535-3555 , 416-535-6225
www.lansource.com

LANtronix
15353 Barranca Parkway
Irvine, CA 92618
714-453-3990, 714-450-7229
www.lantronix.com

Lanworks Technology, Inc.
gd2425 Skymark Ave. Unit 4
Mississauga, Ontario, L4W 4Y6
Canada
905-238-5528 , 905-238-9407
www.lanworks.com

LAN-ACES, Inc.
12777 Jones Road #481
Houston, TX 77070
713-890-9787, 713-890-9731
www.lan-aces.com

Larscom
4600 Patrick Henry Drive
Santa Clara, CA 95054
408-988-6600, 408-986-8690
www.larscom.com

Laser Communications
1848 Charter Lane, Suite F
Lancaster, PA 17601
717-394-8634, 717-396-9831
lasercomm.com/lasercomm

LeeMah DataCom Security Corporation
6200 Paseo Padre Parkway
Fremont, CA 94555
510-608-0600, 510-608-0688
www.leemah.com

Legato Systems, Inc.
3145 Porter Drive
Palo Alto, CA 94304
415-812-6000, 415-812-6032
www.legato.com

Liberty Inc./Fujitsu
120 Saratoga Avenue #82
Santa Clara, CA 95051
408-983-1127, 408-243-2885
www.libertyinc.com

Liebert Corporation
1050 Dearborn Drive
Columbus, OH 43229
800-877-9222, 614-841-6973
www.liebert.com

Linksys
17401 Armstrong Avenue
Irvine, CA 92714
714-261-1288, 714-261-8868
www.linksys.com

Livingston Enterprises
6920 Koll Center Parkway, Suite 220
Pleasanton, CA 94566
800-458-9966, 510-426-8951
www.livingston.com

LSC, Inc.
4211 Lexington Avenue N.
St. Paul, MN 55126
612-482-4535, 612-482-4595
www.lsci.com

Lucent Technology
475 South Street, Room S-05A
Morristown, NJ 07962
908-559-4200, 908-559-1996
www.lucent.com

Luminex Software, Inc.
6840 Indiana Avenue #130
Riverside, CA 92506
909-781-4100, 909-781-4105
www.luminex.com

Madge Networks
2310 N. First Street
San Jose, CA 95131-1011
408-955-0700, 408-955-0970
www.madge.com

Magic Ram, Inc.
1850 Beverly Blvd.
Los Angeles, CA 90057
213-413-9999, 213-413-0828
www.magicram.com

Magic Solutions
10 Forest Avenue
Paramus, NJ 07652
201-587-1515, 201-587-8005
www.magicsolutions.com

Markham Computer Corporation
One South Ocean Blvd. #301
Boca Raton, FL 33432
407-394-3994, 407-394-3844
www.mcc-usa.com

Maximum Strategy, Inc.
801 Buckeye Court
Milpitas, CA 95035-7408
408-383-1600, 408-383-1616
www.maxstrat.com

Maxoptix
3342 Gateway Blvd.
Fremont, CA 94538
510-353-9700, 510-353-1845
www.maxoptix.com

Maxtech Corporation/GVC Corporation
400 Commons Way
Rockaway, NJ 07866
201-586-3008, 201-586-3308
www.maxcorp.com

McAfee Associates, Inc.
2710 Walsh Avenue
Santa Clara, CA 95051
408-988-3832, 408-970-9727
www.mcafee.com

Media Logic ADL, Inc.
1965 North 57th Court
Boulder, CO 80301
303-939-9780, 303-939-9745
www.adlinc.com

Megadrive
489 S. Robertson Blvd.
Beverly Hills, CA 90211
310-247-0006, 310-247-8118
www.megadrive.com

Meridian Data, Inc.
5615 Scotts Valley Drive
Scotts Valley, CA 95066
800-748-0920, 408-438-6816
www.meridian-data.com

Micro Design International
6985 University Blvd.
Winter Park, FL 32792
407-677-8333, 407-677-8365
www.mdi.com

Microboards Inc. of America
1480 Park Road, Suite B
Chanhassen, MN 55317
612-470-1848, 612-470-1805

Microcom
500 River Ridge Drive
Norwood, MA 02062
617-551-1000, 617-551-1968
www.microcom.com

Microdyne Corporation
3601 Eisenhower Avenue
Alexandria, VA 22304
703-329-3700, 703-329-3722
www.mcdy.com

Micronet Technology, Inc.
80 Technology
Irvine, CA 92718
714-453-6000, 714-453-6001
www.micronet.com

Microplex Systems Ltd.
8525 Commerce Court
Burnaby, British Columbia, V5A 4N3
Canada
604-444-4232, 604-444-4239
www.microplex.com

DIRECTORY OF MANUFACTURERS, VENDORS, AND SUPPLIERS

Microsoft Corporation
One Microsoft Way
Redmond, WA 98052
800-426-9400, 206-936-7329
www.microsoft.com

Microsystems
2500 Highland Avenue, Suite 350
Lombard, IL 60148
708-261-0111, 708-261-9520
www.sysdraw.com

Microwave Bypass Systems
72 Sharp Street, Unit C8
Hingham, MA 02043
617-337-2005, 617-337-0544

Milkyway Network Corporation
2650 Queensview Drive, Suite 255
Ottawa, Ontario, K2B 8H6
Canada
613-596-5549, 613-596-5615
www.milkyway.com

Mitron Computer, Inc.
574 Weddell Drive, Suite 8
Sunnyvale, CA 94089
800-713-6888, 408-752-8989
www.mitron.com

Modular Industrial Solutions (MIS)
1729 Little Orchard Street
San Jose, CA 95125-1039
408-971-0910, 408-971-0763
www.icp-oem.com

Most, Inc.
11205 Knott Avenue, Suite B
Cypress, CA 90630
714-898-9400, 714-373-9960

Motorola, Information Systems Group
20 Cabot Blvd.
Manfield, MA 02048-1193
508-261-4000, 508-337-8744
www.mot.com

MTI
100 Carpenter Drive, Suite 200
Sterling, VA 20164
703-709-1122, 703-904-7861
www.mti.com

Multi-Tech
2205 Woodale Drive
Mounds View, MN 55112
800-328-9717, 612-785-9874
www.multitech.com

Nashoba Networks
9 Goldsmith Street
Littleton, MA 01460
508-486-3200, 508-486-0990
www.nashoba.com

NBase Switch Communications
8943 Fullbright Avenue
Chatsworth, CA 91311
818-773-0900, 818-773-0906
www.nbase.com

NCE Storage Solutions
9717 Pacific Heights Blvd.
San Diego, CA 92121
619-658-9720, 619-452-3271
www.ncegroup.com

NCR Corporation
1529 Brown Street
Dayton, OH 45479
513-445-5000, 513-445-1893
www.ncr.com

NEC Technologies, Inc.
1414 Massachusetts Avenue
Boxborough, MA 01719
800-632-4636, 508-264-8673
www.nec.com

Net Manage, Inc.
10725 N. De Anza Blvd.
Cupertino, CA 95014
408-973-7171, 408-257-6405
www.netmanage.com

Net Partners
9665 Chesapeake Drive #350
San Diego, CA, 92123
619-505-3020, 619-495-1950
www.netpart.com

NetFrame Systems, Inc.
1545 Barber Lane
Milpitas, CA 95035
408-474-1000, 408-474-4190
www.netframe.com

NetLock
1801 Hughes Drive
P.O. Box 34028
Fullerton, CA 92633
714-446-2354, 714-446-2311
www.netlock.com

NetPlus Software, Inc.
47 Wake Robin Road
Sudbury, MA 01776
508-443-6043, 508-443-0638

Netscape Communications Corporation
501 E. Middlefield Road
Mountain View, CA 94043
415-528-2555, 415-528-4140
www.home.netscape.com

NetSuite
321 Commonwealth Road #300
Wayland, MA 01778
508-647-3100, 508-647-3112
www.netsuite.com

Network Analysis Center
45 Executive Drive, Suite GL3
Plainview, NY 11803
800-765-4622, 516-576-3269
www.nacmind.com

Network Appliance
319 N. Bernardo Avenue
Mountain View, CA 94043
415-428-5271, 415-428-5151
www.netapp.com

Network Express, Inc.
305 E. Eisenhower Parkway, Suite 200Ann
Arbor, MI 48108
313-761-5005, 313-995-1114
www.nei.com

Network General Corporation
4500 Bohannon Drive
Menlo Park, CA 94025
415-473-2000, 415-321-0855
www.ngc.com

Network Integrity, Inc.
201 Boston Post Road West
Marlborough, MA 01752
508-460-6670, 508-460-6771
www.netint.com

Network Peripherals, Inc.
1371 McCarthy Blvd.
Milpitas, CA 95035
408-321-7300, 408-321-9218
www.npix.com

Network Products Corporation
1440 West Colorado Blvd.
Pasadena, CA 91107
818-441-6504, 818-440-0879
www.networkproducts.com

Network Specialists, Inc.
80 River Street #5B
Hoboken, NJ 07030
201-656-2121, 201-656-2727
www.nsisw.com

Network Systems Corporation
7600 Boone Avenue North
Minneapolis, MN 55428
612-424-4888, 612-424-2853
www.network.com

Network-1 Software & Tech.
909 Third Avenue
New York, NY 10022
800-638-9751, 800-638-1329
www.network-1.com

Nikon Optical Storage Division
1399 Shoreway Road
Belmont, CA 94002
415-508-4659, 415-508-4600
www.mo-nikon.com

Niwot Networks, Inc.
1880 S. Flatiron Court, Suite M
Boulder, CO 80301
303-444-7765, 303-444-7767
www.niwot.com

Nonstop Networks Ltd.
20 Waterside
New York, NY 10010
212-481-8488, 212-779-2956

NORDX/CDT
150 Boulevard Montreal/Toronto
Lachine,Quebec, H8S 1B6-
Canada
514-639-2345, 514-639-2573
www.nordx.com

DIRECTORY OF MANUFACTURERS, VENDORS, AND SUPPLIERS

Northern Telecom
2221 Lakeside Blvd.
Richardson, TX 75082
800-466-7835, 800-598-6726
www.nortel.com

NovaStor Corporation
80-B West Cochran Street
Simi Valley, CA 93065
805-579-6700, 805-579-6710
www.novastor.com

Novell, Inc.
122 East, 1700 South
Provo, UT 84606
800-453-1267, 801-228-9517
www.novell.com

Noyes Fiber Systems
Eastgate Park, Route 106
Belmont, NH 03220
603-528-7780, 603-528-2025

NSM Jukebox
1158 Tower Lane
Bensonville, IL 60106
630-860-5100, 630-860-5144

NStore Corporation
450 Technology Park
Lake Mary, FL 32746-6203
407-829-3600, 407-829-3638
www.conner.com

N.E.T.
800 Saginaw Drive
Redwood City, CA 94063
415-366-4400, 415-366-5675
www.net.com

Octopus Technologies, Inc.
301 Oxford Valley Road #102-A
Yardley, PA 19067
215-321-8750, 215-321-8755
www.octopustech.com

On Technology
One Cambridge Center, 6th Floor
Cambridge, MA 02142
617-374-1400, 617-374-1433
www.on.com

Ontrack Data Recovery, Inc.
6321 Bury Drive, Suites 13-21
Eden Praire, MN 55346
800-872-2599, 612-937-5750
www.ontrack.com

OpenVision Technologies
7133 Koll Center Parkway, Suite 200
Pleasanton, CA 94566
510-426-6400, 510-426-6486
www.ov.com

Optical Cable Corporation
5290 Concourse
Roanoke, VA 24019
800-622-7711, 540-265-0724
www.occfiber.com

Optimal Networks
1057 East Meadows Circle
Palo Alto, CA 94303
415-845-6333, 415-845-6363
www.optimal.com

Oracle Corporation
500 Oracle Parkway
Redwood Shores, CA 94065
415-506-7000, 415-506-7200
www.oracle.com

Overland Data, Inc.
8975 Balboa Avenue
San Diego, CA 92123-1599
800-729-8725, 619-571-0982
www.ovrland.com/~odisales

Pacific Data Products
9855 Scranton Road
San Diego, CA 92121
800-737-7117, 619-552-0889
www.pacdata.com

PairGain Technologies
14402 Franklin Avenue
Tustin, CA 92680-7013
800-370-9670, 714-832-9924
www.pairgain.com

Paralon Technologies, Inc.
Key Tower, 700 5th Avenue
Seattle, WA 98104
800-727-2566, 206-641-1347
www.paralon.com

Patton Electronics
7622 Rickenbacker Drive
Gaithersburg, MD 20879
301-975-1000, 301-869-9293
www.patton.com

PC Guardian Security
1133 Francisco Blvd. East
San Rafael, CA 94901
800-288-8126, 415-459-1162
www.pcguardian.com

PDC
1002 W. 9th Avenue
King of Prussia, PA 19406
610-265-3300, 610-265-2165

Penril Datability Networks
1300 Quince Orchard Blvd.
Gaithersburg, MD 20878
800-473-6745, 301-921-8376
www.penril.com

Performance Technology, Inc.
315 Science Parkway
Rochester, NY 14620
716-256-0200, 716-256-0791
www.pt.com

Personal Cipher Card Corporation
3211 Bonnybrook Drive North
Lakeland, FL 33811
941-644-5026, 941-644-1933

Pinacl Communications, Inc.
Cross Westchester Executive Park
Elmsford, NY 10523
914-345-8155, 914-345-2807

Pinnacle Micro, Inc.
19 Technology Drive
Irvine, CA 92718
800-553-7070, 714-583-7070
www.pinnaclemicro.com

Pivotal Networking
7246 Sharon Drive
San Jose, CA 95129
408-777-0336, 408-777-0337
www.pivnet.com

Plaintree Systems
9 Hillside Avenue
Waltham, MA 02154
800-370-2724, 617-290-0963
www.plaintree.com

Plasmon Data
2045 Junction Avenue
San Jose, CA 95131
800-445-9400, 408-474-0111
www.plasmon.com

Plasmon Data, Inc.
9625 W. 76th Street, Suite 100
Eden Prairie, MN 55344
800-451-6845, 612-946-4141
www.plasmon.com

Platinum Technology, Inc.
1815 South Meyers Road
Oakbrook Terrace, IL 60181
800-442-6861, 708-691-0718
www.platinum.com

Plexcom, Inc.
2255 Agate Court
Simi Valley, CA 93065
805-522-3333, 805-583-4764

Polywell Computers, Inc.
1461-1 San Mateo Avenue
South San Francisco, CA 94080
800-999-1278, 415-583-1974
www.polywell.com

Preferred Systems, Inc.
250 Captain Thomas Blvd.
West Haven, CT 06516
800-222-7638, 203-937-3032
www.prefsys.com

Premenos Corporation
1000 Burnett Avenue, 2nd Floor
Concord, CA 94520
800-426-3836, 510-602-2024
www.premenos.com

Procom Technology
2181 Dupont Drive
Irvine, CA 92612
800-800-8600, 714-852-1221
www.procom.com

DIRECTORY OF MANUFACTURERS, VENDORS, AND SUPPLIERS

Professional Help Desk
800 Summer Street, Suite 500
Stamford, CT 06901
800-474-3725, 203-356-7900
www.prohelpdesk.com

Protec Microsystems, Inc.
297 Labrosse
Pointe-Claire, Quebec, H9R 1A3
Canada
800-363-8156, 514-694-6973
www.protec.com

Proteon, Inc.
9 Technology Drive
Westborough, MA 01581
800-830-1300, 508-366-7930
www.proteon.com

Proxim, Inc.
295 North Bernardo Avenue
Mountain View, CA 94043
800-229-1630, 415-960-1984
www.proxim.com

QMaster Software Solutions
840 7th Avenue S.W. #1620
Calgary, Alberta, T2P 3G8
Canada
403-264-8322, 403-265-5307
www.qmaster.com

Qualstar Corporation
6709 Independence Avenue
Canoga Park, CA 91303
800-468-0860, 818-592-0116
www.qualstar.com

Quantum Corporation
333 South Street
Shrewsbury, MA 01545
508-770-3111, 508-770-3738

Quarterdeck Corporation
13160 Mindanao Way, 3rd Floor
Marina Del Ray, CA 90292
310-309-3700, 310-309-4218
www.quarterdeck.com

Quintus Corporation
47212 Mission Falls Court
Fremont, CA 94539
510-624-2800, 510-770-1377
www.quintus.com

RAD Data Communications
900 Corporate Drive
Mahwah, NJ 07430
800-444-7234, 201-529-5777

RadVision
900 Corporate Drive
Mahah, NJ 07430
201-529-4300, 201-529-3516
www.radvision.com

Ragula Systems, Inc.
404 East 4500 South Street Suite A22
Salt Lake City, UT 84107
800-724-8521, 801-281-0317
www.ragula.com

Raptor Systems, Inc.
69 Hickory Drive
Waltham, MA 02154
617-487-7700, 617-487-6755
www.raptor.com

RDC Communications Ltd.
11 Beit Hadfus Street
Jerusalem, Israel, 95483

RDC Networks
551 Foster City
Foster City, CA 94404
415-577-8075, 415-577-8077
www.rdccom.com

Regal Electronics
4251 Burton Drive
Santa Clara, CA 95054
408-988-2288, 408-988-2797
www.regal.com

Renex Corporation
2750 Killarney Drive
Woodbridge, VA 22192
800-497-3637, 703-878-4625
www.renex.com

Rimage Corporation
7725 Washington Avenue South
Minneapolis, MN 55439
612-944-8144, 612-944-7808
www.rimage.com

RNS—Rockwell Network Systems
7402 Hollister Avenue
Santa Barbara, CA 93117-2590
800-262-8023, 805-968-6478
www.rns.com

Rose Electronics
10707 Stancliff
Houston, TX 77099
800-933-9343, 713-933-0044

Russell Information Sciences
35 Journey Road
Aliso Vigao, CA 92656
714-362-4000, 714-362-4040
www.russellinfo.com

Salix Systems
9345 Byron Street
Schiller Park, IL 60176
800-725-4948, 847-678-7676
www.salix.com

SAS Institute, Inc.
SAS Campus Drive
Cary, NC 27513
919-677-8000, 919-677-8123
www.sas.com

SCH Technology
895 Central Avenue
Cincinnati, OH 45202
800-729-8649, 513-579-1064
www.sch.com

Seagate
36 Skyline Drive
Lake Mary, FL 32746
407-333-7500, 407-262-8116
www.arcada.com

Seagate Software
37 Skyline Drive, Suite 1101
Lake Mary, FL 32746
800-327-2232, 407-333-7730
www.arcada.com

Sealevel Systems, Inc.
P.O. Box 830
155 Technology Place
Liberty, SC 29657
864-843-4343, 864-843-3067
www.sealevel.com

SecureNet Tech, Inc.
19101 36th Avenue W., Suite 211
Lynnwood, WA 98036
800-673-3539, 206-776-2891
www.securenet.com

Seek Systems, Inc.
11014 120th Avenue N.E.
Kirkland, WA 98033
800-790-7335, 206-822-3898
www.seek.com

Sequent Computer Systems
15450 South West Koll Parkway
Beaverton, OR 97006-5903
800-854-0428, 503-578-9890
www.sequent.com

Serengeti Systems Inc.
2306 Lake Austin Blvd.
Austin, TX 78703
800-634-3122, 512-480-8729
www.serengeti.com

SFA DataCom
7450 New Technology Way
Fredrick, MD 21703
800-270-2669, 301-694-6279
www.sfa.com

Shiva Corporation
28 Crosby Drive
Bedford, MA 01730
612-270-8300, 617-270-8599
www.shiva.com

Siemens Nixdorf Printing Systems
5600 Broken Sound Blvd.
Boca Raton, FL 33487
800-523-5444, 407-997-3352

SilCom Technology, Inc.
5620 Timberlea Blvd.
Mississauga, Ontario, L4W 4M6
Canada
800-388-3807, 905-238-4976
www.silcomtech.com

Silicon Graphics
2011 Shoreline Blvd.
Mountain View, CA 94043
415-933-1980, 415-933-4731
www.sgi.com

DIRECTORY OF MANUFACTURERS, VENDORS, AND SUPPLIERS

Simpact, Inc.
9210 Sky Park Court
San Diego, CA 92123
800-746-7228, 619-565-4112
www.simpact.com

Smart Storage
100 Burtt Road
Andover, MA 01810
508-623-3300, 508-623-3310
www.smartstorage.com

SMS Data Products Group, Inc.
1501 Farm Credit Drive
McLean, VA 22102-5004
800-331-1767, 703-356-5167
www.sms.com

SoftArc, Inc.
100 Allstate Parkway
Markham, Ontario, L3R 6H3
Canada
800-364-1923, 905-415-7151
www.softarc.com

SoftLinx, Inc.
234 Littleton Road
Westford, MA 01886
800-899-7724, 508-392-9009
www.softlinx.com

Software Artistry, Inc.
9449 Priority Way, West Drive
Indianapolis, IN 46240
800-795-1993, 317-574-5867
www.softart.com

Software Management Associates
15600 JFK Blvd., Suite 17
Houston, TX, 77032
713-442-4882, 713-442-6826
www.sma.com

Software Moguls, Inc.
12301 White Water Dr. #160
Minnetonka, MN 55343
612-933-8790, 612-932-6736
www.millcom.com/smoguls/

Software Partners, Inc.
447 Old Boston Road
Topsfield, MA 01983
508-887-6409, 508-887-3680
www.sp32.com

Sonic Systems
575 N. Pastoria
Sunnyvale, CA 94086
800-535-0725, 408-736-7228
www.sonicsys.com

Sony Corporation of America
3300 Zanker Road
San Jose, CA 95134
888-476-6972, 408-954-8339
www.sony.com

Sony Electronics, Inc.
3300 Zanker Road
San Jose, CA 95134
800-476-6972, 800-766-9022
www.sony.com

Sound Ideas of America, Inc.
Fountain Court, Suite 23
Bartonsville, PA 18321
717-688-9511, 717-688-9611

Southwest Microwave
2922 South Roseville Street
Tempe, AZ 85282
602-968-5995, 602-894-1731
www.primenet.com

Spartacom
1951 Airport Road
Atlanta, GA 30341
770-455-0701, 770-457-9500
www.tspco.com

Spectra Logic Corporation
1700 N. 55th Street
Boulder, CO 80301
303-449-7759, 303-939-8844
www.spectralogic.com

Spectrix Corporation
106 Wilmot Road, Suite 250
Deerfield, IL 60015-5150
800-710-1805, 847-317-1517

Spyglass, Inc.
1240 East Viehl Road
Maperville, IL 60563
800-647-8901, 630-505-4944
www.spyglass.com

Stallion Technologies, Inc.
2880 Research Park Drive, Suite160
Soquel, CA 95073
800-347-7979, 408-477-0444
www.stallion.com

Standard Microsystems Corporation
80 Arkay Drive
Hauppauge, NY 11788
516-435-6900, 516-273-5550
www.smc.com

Sterling Software
11050 White Rock Road #100
Rancho Cordova, CA 95670-6095
916-635-5535, 916-635-5604
www.sterling.com

Storage Computer Corporation
11 Riverside Street
Nashua, NH 03062-1373
603-880-3005, 603-889-7232
www.storage.com

Storage Dimensions
1656 McCarthy Blvd.
Milpitas, CA 95035
408-954-0710, 408-944-1200
www.storagedimensions.com

Stream Logic
21329 Nordhoff
Chatsworth, CA 91311
818-701-8400, 818-701-8410
www.streamlogic.com

St. Bernard Software
15175 Innovation Drive
San Diego, CA 92128
619-676-2277, 619-676-2299
www.stbernard.com

Sun Microsystems
2550 Garcia Avenue
Mountain View, CA 94043-1100
415-960-1300, 415-336-7751
www.sun.com

SunSoft, Inc.
7150 Campus Drive #150
Colorado Springs, CO 80920
719-528-4600, 719-548-1009

SVEC Computer Corporation
2691 Richter Avenue, Suite 130
Irvine, CA 92606
800-756-7382, 714-756-1340
www.svec.com

Symantec Corporation
2500 Broadway, Suite 200
Santa Monica, CA 90404-3063
310-453-4600, 310-453-0636
www.symantec.com

Symetrical Technologies
600 Herndon Parkway
Herndon, VA 22170
800-532-2224, 703-478-6690

Symplex Communications
5 Research Drive
Ann Arbor, MI 48103
800-327-9926, 313-995-1564
www.symplex.com

SysKonnect, Inc.
1922 Zanker Road
San Jose, CA 95112
800-752-3334, 408-437-3866
www.syskonnect.com

Systemetrics, Inc.
120 Appleton Street
Cambridge, MA 02138
617-868-8308, 617-868-5906
www.system.com

TAC Systems
1035 Putman Drive
Huntsville, AL 35816
800-659-4440, 205-721-0242
www.tac.com

Tally Systems
P.O. Box 70
Hanover, NH 03755
800-262-3877, 603-643-9366
www.tallysys.com

Tandem Computer Corporation
19191 Vallco Parkway #4-26
Cupertino, CA 95014-0724
408-285-6000
www.tandem.com

DIRECTORY OF MANUFACTURERS, VENDORS, AND SUPPLIERS

Tatung Science & Technology, Inc.
1840 McCarthy Blvd.
Milpitas, CA 95035
800-695-5902, 408-383-0886
www.tsti.com

Teac America, Inc.
7733 Telegraph Road
Montebello, CA 90640
213-726-0303, 213-727-7652

Technical Communication Corporation
100 Domino Drive
Concord, MA 01742-2892
508-287-5100, 508-371-1280
www.tccsecure.com

Tecmar Technologies, Inc
1900 Pike Road, Building E
Longmont, CO 80501
800-422-2587, 303-776-1698
www.tecmar.com

Telco Systems
63 Nahatan Street
Norwood, MA 02062
617-551-0300, 617-551-0539
www.telco.com

Telebit Corporation
1 Executive Drive
Chelmsford, MA 01824
800-835-3248, 508-656-9415
www.telebit.com

TenX Technology, Inc.
13091 Pond Springs Road, Suite B-200
Austin, TX 78729
800-922-9050, 512-918-9495
www.tenx.com

Teubner & Associates
623 S. Main Street
Stillwater, OK 74074
405-624-2254, 405-624-3010
www.teubner.com

Texas Microsystems, Inc.
5959 Corporate Drive
Houston, TX 77036
800-627-8700, 713-541-8226
www.texasmicro.com

3Com Corporation
5400 Bayfront Plaza
Santa Clara, CA 95052
408-764-5000, 408-764-5001
www.3com.com

Thunderbyte Corporation
49 Main Street, Suite 300
Massena, NY 13662
315-764-1616, 315-764-1620
www.thunderbyte.com

Thunderstone EPI, Inc.
11115 Edgewater Drive
Cleveland, OH 44107
216-631-8544, 216-281-0828

Touchstone Software Corporation
2124 Main Street, Suite 250
Huntington, CA 92648
800-531-0450, 714-960-1886
www.checkit.com

Transitional Technologies, Inc.
5401 E. La Palma Avenue
Anaheim, CA 92807
714-693-1133, 714-693-0225
www.ttech.com

Traveling Software
18702 N. Creek Parkway, Suite 102
Bothell, WA 98011
800-343-8080, 206-485-6786
www.travsoft.com

TRENDware International, Inc.
2421 West 205th Street, Suite D-102
Torrance, CA 90501
310-328-7795, 310-328-7798
www.trendware.com

Tricord Systems, Inc.
2800 Northwest Blvd.
Plymouth, MN 55441-2625
612-557-9005, 612-557-8403
www.tricord.com

Triticom
P.O. Box 46427
Eden Prairie, MN 55344
612-937-0772, 612-937-1998
www.triticom.com

TTI-wireless (Transformation Technique)
17830 Engle Wood Road #17
Cleveland, OH 44130
800-860-2519, 216-243-9045
www.rflink.com

Twincom USA
1120 S. Point Parkway, Building B
Shreveport, LA 71105
800-234-8088, 318-868-0788

UB Networks
3990 Freedom Circle
Santa Clara, CA 95054
800-777-4526, 408-970-7337
www.ub.com

Ultera Systems, Inc.
26052 Merit Circle, Suite 106
Laguna Hills, CA 92653
714-367-8800, 714-367-0758

UNICOM Electric, Inc.
11980 Telegraph Road, Suite103
Santa Fe Springs, CA 90670
800-346-6668, 310-946-9167
www.conectors.com

Uniplex Software
715 Sutter Street
Folsom, CA 95630
415-577-8789, 415-577-9373
www.unitext.com

Unisys Corporation
2700 North 1st Street
San Jose, CA 95134
408-434-4702, 408-434-2131
www.unisys.com

US Robotics
8100 N. McCormick Blvd.
Skokie, IL 60076
800-245-5020, 847-933-5400
www.usr.com

USA Communications
493-9 Johnson Avenue
Bohemia, NY 11716
800-724-5434, 516-244-5725

Verilink
145 Baytech DriveSan Jose, CA 95134
800-837-4546, 408-262-6260
www.verilink.com

Veritas Software Corporation
1600 Plymouth Street
Mountain View, CA 94043
415-335-8000, 415-335-8050

Vinca Corporation
1815 S. State Street #4000
Orem, UT 84058
801-223-3100, 801-223-3107
www.vinca.com

Vivid Image
2311 West 205th Street, Suite 103
Torrance, CA 90501
310-618-0274, 310-618-1982
www.vivid.com

V-Systems, Inc.
32232 Paseo Adelanto, Suite 100
San Juan Capistrano, CA 92675
800-556-4874, 714-489-2486
www.vsi.com

W. Quinn Associates
1835 Alexander Bell Drive, Suite 330
Reston, VA 20191
703-758-0707, 703-758-0727
www.wquinn.com

Wandel & Golterman
P.O. Box 13585
Research Triangle Park, NC 27709
800-729-9441, 919-941-5751
www.wg.com

Wang Software
4760 Walnut Street
Boulder, CO 80301
303-444-4018, 303-546-4219

WaveAccess
1 Apple Hill, Suite 203
Atick, MA 01760
508-653-3646, 508-653-3306
www.waveaccess.com

DIRECTORY OF MANUFACTURERS, VENDORS, AND SUPPLIERS

Webster Computer Corporation
16040 Redwood Lodge Road
Los Gatos, CA 95030
408-353-5252, 408-357-2550
www.webstercc.com

Whitaker-Xyplex
295 Foster Street
Littleton, MA 01460
800-338-5316, 508-952-4702
www.xyplex.com

White Pine Software, Inc.
40 Simon Street
Nashua, NH 03060
603-886-9050, 603-886-9051
www.wpine.com

Wi-LAN, Inc.
300-801 Manning Road N.E.
Calgary, Alberta, T2E 8J5
Canada
800-258-6876, 403-273-5100
www.wi-lan.com

Workstation Solutions, Inc.
One Overlook Drive
Amherst, NH 03031
603-880-0080, 603-880-0696
www.worksta.com

WRQ, Inc.
1500 Dexter Avenue N.
Seattle, WA 98109
206-217-7500, 206-217-0293
www.wrq.com

XCd, Inc.
3002 Dow Avenue, Suite 110
Tustin, CA 92780
800-923-9538, 714-573-7084

Xerox Corporation
800 Long Ridge Road
Stanford, CT 06904
203-968-3000, 203-968-4312
www.xerox.com

Xircom
2300 Corporate Center Drive
Thousand Oaks, CA 91320
800-438-4526, 805-376-9311
www.xircom.com

XLNT Designs, Inc.
15050 Avenue of Science, Suite 200
San Diego, CA 92128
800-818-9568, 619-487-9768
www.xlnt.com.

Xylogics
53 Third Avenue
Burlington, MA 01803-9927
800-225-3317, 617-221-0170
www.xylogics.com

Zenith Data Systems
300 Concord Road
Billerica, MA 01821
508-294-2011, 508-294-3054
www.zds.com

Zephyr Development Corporation
Summit Tower
Houston, TX 77046-1104
800-966-3270, 713-623-0091
www.zephyrcorp.com

APPENDIX

B EVALUATION TOOLS

THIS APPENDIX CONTAINS THREE forms you can use to
help make buying decisions easier. You can copy these forms
and use them repeatedly. In addition, the CD-ROM packaged
with this book includes a spreadsheet for calculating the cost
of network downtime. Other software-based tools, including
an online downtime calculator, are available on the Network
Buyer's Guide on the Internet (http://www.sresearch.com/).

EVALUATION TOOLS

This appendix includes the following forms:

- **Product Evaluation Worksheet**. This form lets you organize your thoughts on products to make a more quantifiable comparison of product attributes.

- **Software Licensing Worksheet**. This form provides a way to organize comparative price information on software licensing. You write in your requirements and fill in vendor licensing information from vendor-supplied price sheets.

- **Equipment Cost Worksheet**. This form helps you assess the total cost of equipment purchases, including factors such as installation and maintenance.

Product Evaluation Worksheet

To make a good buying decision you need to understand the differences between products and make value judgments based on those differences. This is true for comparing both features and products. For instance, you determine the product's strengths and weaknesses by its capabilities relative to similar products. But you also need to determine which features are of greatest value to you and weigh them accordingly. The Product Evaluation Worksheet lets you organize the features you want to compare and rank them accordingly.

How to Use

Follow these steps to use the Product Evaluation Worksheet:

1. Select a similar group of products to compare.

2. Decide what features to use to measure criteria, such as performance, reliability, and so forth.

3. Determine what is average among the group for each comparative measure. Use this average as a reference in your ranking.

4. Rank criteria based on the product's features by comparing them to the average for the group. In the notes area explain the rank.

5. Add the individual rankings to calculate the total score. Use the individual ranking and total score for comparison.

Example

The following example is a comparison of tape libraries. The first criteria ranked is performance. Suppose you decide to use the tape drive's transfer rate to measure performance and you determine that the typical transfer rate is 3MBs for products in this class. You then rank each product from 1 to 10 in relation to the average for the group. You repeat the process for the different features and criteria. The form provides space for adding your own criteria and features to measure them by.

EVALUATION TOOLS

Product Evaluation Worksheet Sample

Manufacturer	Sample	Sample	Sample
Model	**Model A**	**Model B**	**Model C**
Performance Rank	8	9	7
Performance	4MB/sec transfer rate	5.4MB/sec transfer rate	3MB/sec transfer rate
Reliability Rank	8	6	9
Reliability	160,000 hrs mean time be-tween failures	80,000 hrs MTBF	170,000 hrs MTBF
Scalability Rank	9	8	7
Scalability	Up to 80 cartridges	Up to 60 cartridges	Up to 52 cartridges
Compatibility Rank	7	7	9
Compatibility	All major operat-ing systems	All major operating systems	All major operating systems; archiving HSM software
Flexibility Rank	7	7	9
Flexibility	Preconfigured	Preconfigured	User-configured
Tech Support Rank	8	7	8
Tech Support	2–year warranty	1–year warranty; cus-tomer replace units	2–year warranty
Price Rank	8	6	9
Price	$48,080	$50,130	$47,090
Capacity Rank	7	7	7
Capacity	Up to 1.12TB	Up to 4.2TB	Up to 1.0TB
Total Score:	62	61	65

EVALUATION TOOLS

Software Licensing Worksheet

It can be cumbersome to calculate the necessary software licenses for some network environments. Even more difficult is comparing product licenses as they would specifically apply to your network. For example, one product may have lower per workstation license costs, but may require workstation purchases in blocks of 100, possibly making it more expensive if you just need another 60 licenses. The Software Licensing Worksheet will help you compare software costs using your current network configuration as the guideline.

How to Use

Follow these steps to use the Software Licensing Worksheet:

1. Use one form for each network operating system that will host the software, and list the number of servers and clients you need licensing for.

2. Use the vendor price sheets to determine the necessary licensing for your network and complete the form.

3. Use the completed form to assess the license component fees and the totals in making a price evaluation.

Example

The example shows 5 servers and 175 clients as the current NetWare installation. Sample A offers a client/server package and sample B is priced simply by the number of servers and clients required. Both offer client packs but Sample A sells client packs in units of 100 whereas sample B allows an exact match to needed client licenses. Both offer maintenance agreements that include technical support and related services, but sample A also includes a year of upgrades free of charge.

EVALUATION TOOLS

Software Licensing Worksheet Sample

CURRENT SYSTEM:

NOS: NetWare
# of Servers: 5
# of Clients: 175

Manufacturer Model	Sample A Sample A	Sample B Sample B
Client/Server Package $	1 server, 100 users $4,950	N/A N/A
Additional Servers $	4 servers $2,000	5 servers $5,000
Additional Clients $	100 pack $1,600	150 pack plus 25 $1,750
Maintenance Agreement $	Extended (based on purchase price) $1,500	Extended (based on number of servers) $1,000
Upgrades $	1 year included 0	1 year $500
Other $	N/A N/A	N/A N/A
Total Cost	$10,050	$8,250

EVALUATION TOOLS

Equipment Cost Estimation Worksheet

The cost of network equipment can appear straightforward. But purchases have hidden costs such as installation and maintenance time. You also need to consider how long the equipment will be in use, its depreciation, and its value at the end of its useful period. Understanding these factors when you buy will help you make a sound purchase decision. The Equipment Cost Estimation Worksheet will help you take these factors into consideration.

How To Use

Follow these steps to use the Equipment Cost Estimation Worksheet:

1. Enter purchase price information and associated costs such as annual service agreements and upgrade packages.

2. Estimate the number of hours it will take to install and maintain the equipment. Use an hourly rate to assess this time and to include it in the total equipment cost.

3. Estimate the life of the product to calculate its depreciation value and/or salvage value at the end of its life.

Example

The example shows how the purchase price is followed by various additional costs related to the purchase. The annual service contract is included in the first year so no price is listed. Installation is estimated at 7 hours and comes to $210 based on a $30 per hour rate (the rate should be a fully burdened labor rate, which includes benefits, overhead, and so on). Annual maintenance refers to equipment repairs and servicing. Annual administrative costs refer to time spent managing device operations. The product is estimated to have a five year usable life, no depreciation benefits were calculated but it is estimated that the item will be worth $5,000 at the anticipated time of replacement or retirement.

EVALUATION TOOLS

Equipment Cost Estimation Worksheet Sample

Manufacturer/Model	Sample Company/Sample Model		Cost
Purchase Price	**60 slot, 90GB, 2 drives**		**$19,450**
Annual Upgrades	No policy		$0
Annual Service Contract	1 year onsite included		$0
Installation Cost	7 hrs @ $30/hr =		$210
Annual Maintenance Costs	25 hrs @ $50/hr =		$1,250
Annual Administrative Costs	25 hrs @ $50/hr =		$1,250
Other:			$0
Total Cost			$25,515
Depreciation/ Product Life	Deductible? Y/N 5 Yrs	Annual Deduction Value	
Salvage Value			$5,000

EVALUATION TOOLS

Product Evaluation Worksheet

Manufacturer			
Model			
Performance Rank			
Performance			
Reliability Rank			
Reliability			
Scalability Rank			
Scalability			
Compatibility Rank			
Compatibility			
Flexibility Rank			
Flexibility			
Tech Support Rank			
Tech Support			
Price Rank			
Price			
Capacity Rank			
Capacity			
Total Score:			

EVALUATION TOOLS

Software Licensing Worksheet
CURRENT SYSTEM:

NOS:
\# of Servers:
\# of Clients:

Manufacturer/ Model:			
Client/Server Package			
$			
Additional Server Licenses			
$			
Additional Client Licenses			
$			
Maintenance Contract			
$			
Upgrades			
$			
Other			
$			
Total Cost			

EVALUATION TOOLS

Equipment Cost Worksheet

Manufacturer/Model		Cost
Purchase Price		
Annual Upgrades		
Annual Service Contract		
Installation Cost	___ Hrs @ $___ /hr. =	
Annual Maintenance Costs	___ Hrs @ $___ /hr. =	
Annual Administrative Costs	___ Hrs @ $___ /hr. =	
Other Fees		
Total Cost		
Depreciation	Deductible? (Y)/N ___ years ___	Annual Deduction Value	
Salvage Value		$

C CD-ROM CONTENTS

THIS BOOK IS PACKAGED with a CD-ROM that includes a complete version of this printed text, several software tools, and expanded company profiles take from the Network Buyer's Guide on the Internet. The files are organized into three main directories for your convenience. Programs may have different system requirements, which are listed under the appropriate headings.

CD-ROM CONTENTS

The Electronic Version of This Book

This guide includes a wealth of information on network-related products. The enclosed CD lets you review this information in a convenient electronic form. The electronic version of the book comes with text search capabilities to help you quickly find just what you are looking for. To get started, go to the readme.txt file on the CD.

System Requirements:

- Windows 3.*x* with a minimum of 8MB of RAM

- Windows 95/NT with a minimum of 16MB of RAM

Software-Based Buying Tools

It can be a chore to determine what you need to buy and to integrate the networking equipment you purchase. There's a growing market for software tools to help you plan a network, create a network map, analyze your network to assess what you might need, and so on. This CD comes with two software tools that provide cutting edge buying assistance. These are functional programs, not demonstration programs, but some of their capabilities may not be available unless you decide to purchase the product.

C/S Solutions Advisor by Interpose Incorporated

It is increasingly important for IS administrators to be able to cost justify purchases, but it is often difficult to come up with quantifiable results. You have to weigh many factors, including user productivity and maintenance. C/S Solutions Advisor is a tool to help you cost justify the purchase of networking equipment. This program lets you input information about your network to calculate many of the costs that are difficult to measure. In addition, it lets you consider a range of possible scenarios. For instance, you can try adding certain equipment to see its potential cost savings. The data used for calculations is derived from empirical study by industry research organizations. The product is designed to analyze networks of any size. For a more detailed description of the program and installation instructions, consult the readme.wri file under the SOFTWARE\CSSA\ directory on the CD.

System Requirements:

- A computer with an 80386 or higher processor

- MS-DOS operating system version 5 or later

- A minimum of 8MB of RAM

- A minimum of 4MB of free hard-disk space

- Microsoft Windows 95 or Windows 3.1*x* running in enhanced mode

CD-ROM CONTENTS

- VGA or higher resolution video

- A mouse or other compatible pointing device

- Attachment to a Novell NetWare 3 or 4 server
  (if Analyze Environment Discovery is used)

CANE by Imagenet Corporation

Network planning software is beginning to be recognized and widely used as the products become more sophisticated and well integrated with all the necessary components. CANE is especially well-suited for helping you buy network equipment. It includes robust planning features such as network mapping, performance simulation, integrity checking, and others. In addition, it lets you choose actual products from a large database. The database includes price information so you can get a good idea of the cost of your installation based on the products you choose. Of course, you can add products that are not already in the database (the version on this CD has a limited database). You can use CANE to plan for a network of any size, but its price and power make it especially well-suited for networks of 200 or more client stations. For a more detailed description of the program and installation instructions, see the readme.txt file under the SOFTWARE\CANE directory on the CD.

System Requirements:

- A Pentium computer with at least 32MB of RAM

- A hard disk with at least 65MB of free disk space

- Super VGA with 800x600 resolution (256 colors)

- MS Windows NT Workstation version 3.51 or higher

Detailed Company Profiles   The Network Buyer's Guide (NBG) on the Internet (http://www.sresearch.com) provided some of the groundwork for this book. Among other things, the NBG supplies company profiles of networking and storage vendors. These are included on the CD-ROM so you can gain access to them easily without having to connect to the Internet. (You can also get to the Web site from this portion of the CD if you have an Internet connection.) To access the profile information, double-click on home.htm in the HTML directory on the CD. You should also be able to open the file from within your Web browser application. The home page explains how to use this section of the CD. You need a Web browser to view this section of the CD, and you need Internet access to link to the NBG on the Internet.

GLOSSARY

alpha channel   The upper 8 bits of a 32-bit data path in some graphics adapters. The alpha channel is used by some software for controlling the color information contained in the lower 24 bits.

10Base2   IEEE's specifications for running Ethernet over thin coaxial cable.

10Base5   IEEE's specifications for running Ethernet over thick coaxial cable.

10BaseT   IEEE's specifications for running Ethernet over unshielded twisted-pair wiring.

3+Open   A family of 3Com networking products built around the LAN Manager file/print server. 3+Open includes connectivity, messaging, and network management services.

3174   A new version of the 3274 terminal cluster controller.

3270   The generic name for the family of interoperable IBM system components—terminals, printers, and terminal cluster controllers—that can be used to communicate with a mainframe by means of the SNA or bisync protocols. All of these components have four-digit names, some of which begin with the digits 327.

3274/3276   The most commonly used cluster controller. This device links as many as 32 3270-type terminals and printers to a mainframe front-end processor.

3278   The most commonly used terminal in the 3270 family. It features a monochrome display and offers a limited graphics set.

3279   A color terminal that is part of the 3270 family.

3287   The current series of printers in the 3270 equipment family.

3705   A common front-end processor, typically used to link several 3274s to a mainframe.

3725   A common front-end processor, intended for linking groups of cluster controllers to a mainframe.

GLOSSARY

3745   A new communications controller that combines the functions of a cluster controller and a front-end processor. The 3745 can interface simultaneously with as many as 8 Token-Ring networks, 512 terminals or printers, and 16 1.544-megabit-per-second communications lines.

802.X   The Institute of Electrical and Electronics Engineers (IEEE) committee that developed a set of standards describing the cabling, electrical topology, physical topology, and Access Scheme. In other words, the 802.X standards define the physical and data-link layers of LAN architectures. IEEE 802.3 is the work of an 802 subcommittee that describes the cabling and signaling for a system nearly identical to classic Ethernet. IEEE 802.5 comes from another subcommittee and similarly describes IBM's Token-Ring architecture.

A/D converter   A device that converts analog signals to digital.

access method   A protocol that determines which device in a local area network has access to the transmission media at any instant. CSMA/CD is an example of an access method. IBM uses the same term for specific kinds of communications software that include protocols for exchanging data, constructing files, and other functions.

access protocol   The traffic rules that LAN workstations abide by to avoid data collisions when sending signals over shared network media; also referred to as the media-access control (MAC) protocol. Common examples are carrier sense multiple access (CSMA) and token passing.

accessibility   See *data accessibility*.

ACK   A positive acknowledgment control character. This character is exchanged between system components when data has been received without error. The control character is also used as an affirmative response for setting up a communications exchange. ACK is also used as the name of a message containing an acknowledgment.

acoustic coupler   The portion of a modem that physically holds a telephone handset in two rubber cups. The cups house a small microphone and speaker that "talk" and "listen" to the telephone handset.

active version   The most recent copy of a file stored in a storage pool. Such a file is exempt from deletion until a storage management process detects that the user has either replaced the file with a newer version or has explicitly deleted the file from the workstation.

GLOSSARY

ADCCP (Advanced Data Communications Control Procedures) A bit-oriented ANSI-standard communications protocol. It is a link-layer protocol.

address A unique memory location. Network interface cards and CPUs often use shared addresses in RAM to move data from each card to the PC's processor. The term "address" can also refer to the unique identifier for a particular node in a network.

Address Resolution Protocol (ARP) A protocol within the Transmission Control Protocol/Internet Protocol (TCP/IP) suite that "maps" IP addresses to Ethernet addresses. TCP/IP requires ARP for use with Ethernet.

administrative console A management utility that allows administrators to control and monitor the managed application or hardware through an independent administrative interface.

Advanced Communications Function (ACF) An IBM program package to allow the sharing of computer resources through communications links. ACF supports SNA.

Advanced Communications Service A large data communications network developed by AT&T.

AFP (AppleTalk File Protocol) Apple's network protocol, used to provide access between file servers and clients in an AppleShare network. AFP is also used by Novell's products for the Macintosh.

alphanumeric Characters made up of letters and numbers; usually contrasted with graphics characters made up of dots in terminal emulation.

analog Commonly refers to transmission methods developed to transmit voice signals. These methods were designed only for the bandwidth of the human voice (up to about 3 kHz); this limits their capability to pass high-speed digital signals.

ANSI (American National Standards Institute) An organization that develops and publishes standards for codes, alphabets, and signaling schemes.

API (application program interface) A set of standard software interrupts, calls, and data formats that application programs use to initiate

GLOSSARY

contact with network services, mainframe communications programs, or other program-to-program communications. For example, applications use APIs to call services that transport data across a network.

APPC (Advanced Program-to-Program Communications) An IBM protocol analogous to the OSI model's session layer; it sets up the necessary conditions that enable application programs to send data to each other through the network.

APPC/PC An IBM product that implements APPC on a PC.

AppleTalk An Apple networking system that can transfer data at a rate of 230 kilobytes per second over shielded twisted-pair wire. Superseded by the term LocalTalk.

application layer The highest (seventh) level of the OSI model. It describes the way that application programs interact with the network operating system.

applications processor A special-purpose computer that enables a telephone system to furnish special services such as voice mail, messaging services, and electronic mail.

archive To erase files from primary storage (disk) after a copy has been stored on tape or other secondary media. The intent is long term storage where the media contents remain unchanged. Archiving is also referred to as "retirement" or "shelving." Archive also refers to long term storage for legal protection of the "state of the data" at specific points in time.

ARCnet (Attached Resources Computing) A networking architecture (marketed by Datapoint Corporation and other vendors) using a polling bus architecture, usually on coaxial cable.

ARPANET (Advanced Research Projects Agency Network) A network originally sponsored by the Defense Advanced Research Projects Agency (DARPA) to link universities and government research centers. The TCP/IP protocols were pioneered on ARPANET.

ARQ A control code that calls for the retransmission of a block of data.

array driver A software program that makes use of the host or server processor to perform disk array functions.

GLOSSARY

array processor   A special-purpose computer contained in a disk array system that uses its own dedicated processor to manage array functions, including striping and error correction.

array   A group of storage devices controlled in such a way as to provide higher data transfer rates, higher data availability, or both. The array is treated as a single volume by the operating system. The array may be subdivided into several volumes to configure the storage system.

ASCII (American Standard Code for Information Interchange)   The data alphabet used in the IBM PC to determine the composition of the 7-bit string of 0s and 1s that represents each character (alphabetic, numeric, or special).

ASR (automatic send/receive)   A term left over from teleprinters that punched messages on paper tape. Now, "ASR" is sometimes used to indicate any terminal that has a storage capability.

asynchronous   A method of transmission in which the time intervals between characters do not have to be equal. Start and stop bits are added to coordinate the transfer of characters.

attenuation   The decrease in power of a signal transmitted over a wire, measured in decibels. As attenuation increases, the signal decreases.

automated remote vaulting   Intended to allow a business to continue to operate in the face of a disaster or network outage. Automatically adds a layer of data protection by backing up network information and keeping it in another facility, preferably many miles away.

automatic archive   The automation capabilities that can be brought to the archive process are two: automatic identification of candidate files based on some set of rules, and the use of automated media handling via a tape library or optical jukebox in the archive storage repository.

Automatic File Redundancy Checking (AFRC)   The process of scanning the network for identical files on the basis of file name, file size, file content, and any other criteria that distinguish differences between files. You can reduce the backup load an estimated 20 to 35 percent by not backing up redundant files. The file history database can be updated to identify all occurrences, ownerships, and locations of duplicates.

GLOSSARY

Automatic Number Identification (ANI)   A feature that passes a caller's ten-digit telephone number over the network to the customer's premises so that the caller can be identified.

availability rate   The availability rate is the percentage of time a server can respond to client requests. You obtain the rate by multiplying the average number of outages during a given period by the average downtime per outage during the same period, dividing this by the number of hours in the period, and subtracting the result from 100 percent.

availability   The probability that a system is available at a given instant. In the context of a server, this function expresses the expected percentage of time a system is available to respond to client requests. See network availability, high system availability, and continuous operation.

background program or process (background mode)   A program that performs its functions while the user is working with a different program. Communications programs often operate in background mode. They can receive messages while the user works with other programs. The messages are stored for later display.

backup file consolidation   The ability for the backup software to re-create a full backup every time an incremental backup is performed.

backup server   A computer and storage system that provides backup and restore services for the network as a network resource.

backup version   A file, directory, or file space that a user has backed up and that resides in a backup storage pool in data storage. Although there may be more than one backup version of a file in the storage pool, only one is considered the active version. See active version and inactive version.

backup/archive client   A client to a backup/archive process. Usually, there is an agent code resident on the client that allows the controlling application to provide backup/archive services.

backup   A function that creates a redundant copy of files to a secondary storage pool (usually offline media) in case the original files are damaged, are accidentally deleted, or are no longer accessible.

Balun (BALanced Unbalanced)   An impedance-matching device that connects a balanced line (such as a twisted-pair line) and an unbalanced line (such as a coaxial cable).

GLOSSARY

bandwidth   The range of frequencies a circuit will pass. Analog circuits typically have a bandwidth limited to that of the human voice (about 300 Hz to 3 kHz). The square waves of a digital signal require a higher bandwidth. The higher the transmission rate, the greater the bandwidth requirement. Fiber-optic and coaxial cables have excellent bandwidths. Also, in common usage, bandwidth refers to the upper limit of the rate that information can be transferred over a network.

base address   The first address in a series of addresses in memory, often used to describe the beginning of a network interface card's I/O space.

baseband   A network that transmits signals as a direct-current pulse rather than as variations in a radio-frequency signal. A nonmultiplexed signal, resulting in a single channel monopolizing the bandwidth of the transmission media.

Basic-Rate Interface (BRI)   The ISDN standard governing how a customer's desktop terminals and telephones can connect to the ISDN switch. It specifies two B-channels that allow 64-kilobits-per-second simultaneous voice and data service, and one D-channel that carries call information and customer data at 16 Kbps.

baud   A measure of transmission speed; the reciprocal of the time duration of the shortest signal element in a transmission. In RS-232C ASCII, the signaling element is 1 bit.

BBS (bulletin board system)   An electronic message system.

BCD (binary-coded decimal)   A coding scheme using a 6-bit (six-level) code.

B-Channel   A "bearer" channel that carries voice or data at 64 kilobits-per-second in either direction and is circuit-switched.

benchmark test   A program used to measure system speed or throughput.

bindery   A database maintained by Novell's NetWare operating system that holds information on users, servers, and other elements of the network.

GLOSSARY

bisynchronous communications (BSC) This protocol is one of the two commonly used methods of encoding data for transmission between devices in IBM mainframe computer systems. Data characters are gathered in a package called a frame, which is marked by 2 synchronization bits (bisync). The more modern protocol is SDLC.

bit The smallest unit of information. In digital signaling, this commonly refers to a 0 or a 1.

block A number of characters transmitted as a group.

BNC connector A small coaxial connector with a half-twist locking shell.

boot A read-only memory (ROM) chip allowing a workstation to communicate with the file server and to read a DOS boot program from the server. Stations can thus operate on the network without having a disk drive.

bps Bits per second.

bridge An interconnection device, sometimes working within a PC and sometimes within a special-purpose computer, that can connect LANs using similar or dissimilar data links such as Ethernet, Token-Ring, and X.25. Bridges link LANs at the data-link layer of the OSI model. Modern bridges read and filter data packets and frames, and they pass traffic only if the address is on the same segment of the network cable as the originating station.

broadband Refers to a network that carries information riding on carrier waves rather than directly as pulses, providing greater capacity at the cost of higher complexity. These carrier waves split the bandwidth of the transmission channel into separate channels capable of carrying unique data transmissions simultaneously.

broadcast To send a message to all stations or an entire class of stations connected to the network.

brouter A device that combines the functions of a bridge and a router. Brouters can route one or more protocols, such as TCP/IP and XNS, and bridge all other traffic. Contrast with bridge, router, and gateway.

GLOSSARY

buffer   A temporary storage space. Data may be stored in a buffer as it is received, before or after transmission. A buffer may be used to compensate for the differences between the speed of transmission and the speed of processing.

buffered repeater   A device that amplifies and regenerates signals so they can travel farther along a cable. This type of repeater also controls the flow of messages to prevent collisions.

bus topology   A "broadcast" arrangement in which all network stations receive the same message through the cable at the same time.

byte   A group of 8 bits.

C   A programming language used predominantly by professional programmers to write applications software.

cache   An amount of RAM set aside to hold data that is expected to be accessed again. The second access, which finds the data in RAM, is very fast.

cache memory   A portion of memory dedicated to collecting and holding related data until a processing or a storage module is ready to process it. The intent is to improve the overall system performance. Cache for a disk drive is usually implemented as fast semiconductor memory. See *read cache* and *write cache*.

caching file system   An advanced, distributed file system that also has HSM (hierarchical storage management) capabilities. Its objective is improved workstation performance, network data accessibility, and workstation storage management.

call packet   A block of data carrying addressing and other information that is needed to establish an X.25 switched virtual circuit (SVC).

carrier signal   A tone or radio signal modulated by data, usually for long-distance transmission.

cartridge   A tape cartridge is a media housing in which the supply of tape is spooled onto two hubs; a supply hub and a tape-up hub. The cartridge itself forms a significant portion of the tape path.

GLOSSARY

CCITT X.25 Recommendation   An international standard defining packet-switched communication protocols for a public or private network. The recommendation is prepared by the Comite Consultatif International Telegraphique et Telephonique (CCITT). Along with other CCITT recommendations, the X.25 Recommendation defines the physical-, data-link-, and network-layer protocols necessary to interface with X.25 networks. The CCITT X.25 Recommendation is supported by most X.25 equipment vendors, but a new CCITT X.25 Recommendation is published every four years.

CCS 7   A network signaling standard for ISDN that incorporates information from databases to offer advanced network services.

CD networking   Software that allows a network to access a CD-ROM drive, tower, or jukebox.

central administration   A feature of network or enterprise software that allows a distributed process to be controlled from an administration console. Control can reside both locally and remotely either at any point or at multiple points in the enterprise.

central office (CO)   The telephone-switching location nearest to the customer's premises. It serves the businesses and residences connected to its loop lines.

channel   A path between sender and receiver that carries one stream of information. (A two-way path is a circuit.)

channel extenders   A type of storage network similar to SCSI extenders except they interface into mainframe channels at the host end. These are usually FIPS or Escon channels.

character   One letter, number, or special code.

CICS (Customer Information Control System)   This IBM software runs on a mainframe and makes a variety of services available for application programs. It furnishes easy ways for programs to enter mainframe files and find data within them.

circuit switching   A method of communicating in which a dedicated communications path is established between two devices, the bandwidth is guaranteed, and the delay is essentially limited to propagation time. The telephone system uses circuit switching.

GLOSSARY

clear packet   A block of data containing a command that performs the equivalent of hanging up the telephone.

client platforms   The computer platforms from which the file or media catalog can be accessed and specific requests can be made.

client/server computing   A computing system in which processing can be distributed among "clients" on the network that request information and one or more network "servers" that store data, let clients share data and programs, help in printing operations, and so on. The system can accommodate stand-alone applications (word processing), applications requiring data from the server (spreadsheets), applications that use server capabilities to exchange information among users (electronic mail), and applications providing true client/server teamwork (databases, especially those based on Structured Query Language, or SQL). Before client/server computing, a server would download an entire database to a client machine for processing. SQL database applications divide the work between machines, letting the database stay on the server.

client   A recipient of services in a client/server application. Clients can be workstations or other servers.

cluster controller   A computer that sits between a group of terminals and the mainframe, gathering messages and multiplexing over a single link to the mainframe.

clustering   A technique for configuring servers using software and hardware that allows sharing of processing, mass storage, and other resources under a single management domain. Clustering offers high data accessibility by allowing access to shared storage even when various components fail.

CMIP (Common Management Information Protocol)   An OSI-based structure for formatting messages and for transmitting information between data-collection programs and reporting devices. CMIP was developed by the International Standards Organization and designated as ISO 9596.

CMOT (CMIP Over TCP/IP)   An Internet standard defining the use of CMIP for managing TCP/IP networks.

GLOSSARY

coax or coaxial cable   A type of network media. Coaxial cable contains a copper inner conductor surrounded by plastic insulation and then a woven copper or foil shield.

codec (coder/decoder)   A device that transforms analog voice signals into a digital bit stream (coder) and digital signals into analog voice (decoder) using pulse-code modulation.

collision   An attempt by two units to send a message at one time on a single channel. In some networks, the detection of a collision causes all senders to stop transmissions, while in others the collision is noticed when the receiving station fails to acknowledge the data.

collocation   A process that attempts to keep all data belonging to a single client node on a minimal number of sequential access media volumes within a storage pool. The purpose of collocation is to minimize the number of volumes that must be accessed when a large amount of data must be restored.

command line interface   A type of user interface in which commands are specified on the command line instead of through a graphical user interface (GUI).

common carrier   A transmission company (such as a telephone company) that serves the general public.

communications controller   A programmable computer dedicated to data communications and serving as the "front end" in the IBM SNA network.

communications protocol   See *transport protocol*.

compression   See *data compression*.

concentrator   See *wiring hub*.

concurrency   The ability of backup software to allow a storage device to receive data from more than one source at a time, interleaving the data streams.

contention   The condition that occurs when two or more stations attempt to use the same channel at the same time.

GLOSSARY

continuous operation   The elimination or masking of all planned and unplanned system outages by the use of high system availability or fault tolerance.

control character   A character used for special signaling; often not printed or displayed, but causing special functions such as the movement of paper in a printer, the blanking of a display screen, or "handshaking" between communicating devices to control the flow of data.

controller   A physical module that interprets signals sent between the host processor and a peripheral device.

COW interface (character-oriented Windows interface)   An SAA-compatible user interface for OS/2 applications.

cps   Characters per second.

CPU (central processing unit)   The functional "brain" of a computer; the element that does the actual adding and subtracting of 0s and 1s that is essential to computing.

CRC (cyclic redundancy check)   A numeric value derived from the bits in a message. The transmitting station uses one of several formulas to produce a number that is attached to the message. The receiving station applies the same formula and should derive the same number. If the numbers are not the same, an error condition is declared.

crosstalk   The spillover of a signal from one channel to another. In data communications it is very disruptive. Usually, careful adjustment of the circuits eliminates crosstalk.

CRT (cathode ray tube)   A video screen.

CSMA (carrier sense multiple access)   A media-sharing scheme in which stations listen in to what's happening on the network media; if the cable is not in use, a station is permitted to transmit its message. CSMA is often combined with a means of performing collision detection—hence CSMA/CD.

current loop   An electrical interface that is sensitive to current changes rather than voltage swings; used with older teleprinter equipment.

GLOSSARY

cursor The symbol indicating the place on the video screen where the next character will appear.

customer premises equipment (CPE) A general term for the telephones, computers, private branch exchanges, and other hardware located on the end user's side of the network boundary, established by the Computer Inquiry II action of the Federal Communications Commission.

D/A converter A device that changes digital pulses into analog signals.

data access protocol A specialized protocol used by Digital Equipment Corporation.

data accessibility A term defining the system requirements for network storage as continuous access to files and data, high performance, and protection from data loss.

data compression The process of condensing the data through utilization of algorithms to save storage space. The original data is decompressed when read back into memory.

data packet In X.25, a block of data that transports full-duplex information via an X.25 switched virtual circuit (SVC) or permanent virtual circuit (PVC). X.25 data packets may contain up to 1,024 bytes of user data, but the most common size is 128 bytes (the X.25 default).

data reconstruction The process of re-creating data that was contained on a drive that has failed from information contained on the remaining drives in a RAID system.

data set This term can mean a file, or a "set" of data. It is also the name the telephone company often uses for a modem.

data transfer rate (drive) The maximum data rate from the drive to the controller. The rate is a function of several parameters, including the interface transfer rate, the bus bandwidth, and the buffer output rate from the drive.

database backup Specifically refers to the backup of large relational databases. These databases are unique because of their record-based file system. Traditional file-centric backup may not work well because large databases may never close or because there is too much data to transfer.

GLOSSARY

Three methods of backup are typically used: an image backup of the raw disk partition, backup of database log files, or backup using the database's native application.

database structure   The underlying database engine on which the file and media database runs.

datagram   A packet of computer-generated information that includes a complete destination address provided by the user, not the network, along with whatever data the packet carries.

data-link control   A communications layer in SNA that manages the physical data circuits.

data-link layer   The second layer of the OSI model. Protocols functioning in this layer manage the flow of data leaving a network device and work with the receiving station to ensure that the data arrives safely.

DB-25   The designation of a standard plug-and-jack set used in RS-232C wiring: 25-pin connectors, with 13 pins in one row and 12 in the other row.

DCE (data communications equipment)   Refers to any X.25 network component that implements the CCITT X.25 standard.

D-channel   The "data" channel of an ISDN interface, used to carry control signals and customer call data in a packet-switched mode. In the basic-rate interface (BRI), the D-channel operates at 16 kilobits per second; in the primary-rate interface (PRI), the D-channel is used at 64 Kbps.

DDCMP (Digital Data Communications Message Protocol)   A byte-oriented, link-layer protocol from Digital Equipment Corporation, used to transmit messages over a communications line.

DDD (direct distance dialing)   Use of the common long-distance telephone system.

DECnet   A communications protocol and line of networking products from Digital Equipment Corporation, compatible with Ethernet and a wide range of systems.

delay commonly   A pause in activity. Delay can also be a kind of distortion on a communications circuit. Specifically, it is the property of an electrical circuit that slows down and distorts high-frequency signals. Devices called equalizers slow down the lower frequencies and "equalize" the signal.

GLOSSARY

demodulation   The process of retrieving data from a modulated carrier wave; the reverse of modulation.

dial-up line   A communications circuit established by dialing a destination over a commercial telephone system.

differential backup   A process that backs up data that has been modified or added since the last full backup. This approach means that only two tapes are required for a full restore.

digital   In common use, on/off signaling; signals consist of 0s and 1s instead of a great multitude of analog-modulated frequencies.

direct access storage device (DASD)   A storage device in which access time is effectively independent of the location of the data. DASD refers to magnetic disk in the mainframe environment.

disaster recovery   A set of rules and procedures that allow a computer site to be put back in operation after a disaster has occurred. Moving backups off site is the minimum basic precaution for disaster recovery. The remote copy is used to recover data when the local storage is inaccessible after a disaster.

disk duplexing   See *disk mirroring*.

disk mirroring   A data redundancy technique in which data is recorded identically on multiple separate disk drives at the same time. When the primary disk is off line, the alternate takes over, providing continuous access to data. Defined as a RAID 1 configuration.

disk-based backup   The process of sending backup data to hard-disk storage rather than directly to tape. The backup storage pool on disk is a cache, managed for fast restore capability. Background copies are made to tape or to a remote vault. This is also referred to as "hot backup."

DISOSS (Distributed Office Supported System)   An integrated package of electronic-mail and document-preparation programs from IBM, designed for IBM mainframe computer systems.

distortion   Any change to the transmitted signal. Distortion can be caused by crosstalk, delay, attenuation, or other factors.

GLOSSARY

Distributed Systems Architecture (DSA)   A Honeywell architecture that conforms to the Open Systems Interconnection model proposed by the ISO. It supports X.25 for packet switching and X.21 for packet-switched and circuit-switched network protocols.

downtime   A amount of time during which users cannot use part or all of the network for any reason.

DQDB (Distributed Queue Dual Bus)   A proposed IEEE 802.6 standard for metropolitan-area networks (MANs).

driver   A software program that interfaces between portions of the LAN software and hardware.

DTE (data terminal equipment)   Any end-user device that can access an X.25 network using the CCITT X.25 standard, LAP/LAB, and X.25 PAP.

duplex   In communications circuits, duplex means the ability to transmit and receive at the same time; also referred to as full duplex. Half-duplex circuits can receive only or transmit only. In terminals, duplex means a choice between displaying locally generated characters and echoed characters.

duplexing   A configuration in which several elements of a system or subsystem are duplicated in addition to the disk drive—for example, a controller, a host adapter, a power supply. See *mirroring*.

duty cycle   The period of time of continuous operation. For a server, the duty cycle may be 24 hours per day, 7 days per week, 365 days per year.

EBCDIC (Extended Binary Coded Decimal Interchange Code)   The data alphabet used in all IBM computers except the PC; it determines the composition of the 8-bit string of 0s and 1s representing each character (alphabetic, numeric, or special).

echo suppressor   A device used to eliminate the echo effect of long-distance voice transmission circuits. This suppressor must be disabled for full-duplex data transmission; the modem answer tones turn the suppressor off automatically.

GLOSSARY

echoplex   A method of transmission in which characters are echoed from the distant end and the echoes are presented on the terminal; this provides a constant check of the communications circuit to the user.

ECMA (European Computer Manufacturers' Association)   A trade association that provides input to international standards-forming organizations.

EDI (electronic data interchange)   The communication of orders, invoices, and similar transactions electronically between organizations.

EIA (Electronic Industries Association)   An organization of U.S. manufacturers of electronic parts and equipment. The organization develops industry standards for the interface between data-processing and communications equipment.

EISA (Extended Industry Standard Architecture)   A PC bus system that serves as an alternative to IBM's Micro Channel Architecture (MCA). The EISA architecture, backed by an industry consortium headed by Compaq, is compatible with the IBM AT bus; MCA is not.

elevator seeking   A method of optimizing the movement of the heads on the hard disk in a file server.

EMA (Enterprise Management Architecture)   Digital Equipment Corporation's company-specific architecture, conforming to ISO's CMIP.

emulation   Simulation of a system, function, or program.

encryption   The coding of data into an unreadable form; decoding is restricted by password, user access, or other means. Some software allows decoding to be transparent to the authorized user, while data is unreadable to the unauthorized user.

enterprise data management software   A class of software that builds on network data management software, adding the capabilities of interoperating and providing backup and restore services across multiple, heterogeneous computing environments such as PCs, UNIX, midrange systems, or mainframes.

enterprise storage management   A family or suite of related processes and applications that manage storage devices plus files and data as enterprise resources across heterogeneous environments. Storage

GLOSSARY

management applications range from asset management to hierarchical storage management.

equalization   Balancing of a circuit so that it passes all frequencies with equal efficiency.

Ethernet   A network cable and access protocol scheme originally developed by Xerox, and now marketed mainly by Digital Equipment Corporation and 3Com.

EtherTalk   The Apple Ethernet adapter for the Macintosh II computer. It is also the software driver used by the Macintosh to communicate with Ethernet adapters.

expiration   The process by which files are identified for deletion because their expiration date or retention period has passed.

facsimile (fax)   The transmission of page images by a system that is concerned with patterns of light and dark rather than with specific characters. Older systems use analog signals; newer devices use digital signals and may interact with computers and other digital devices.

fail over   The process of shifting operations from an online system to an alternate or redundant system after a failure. The fail over process may be automatic (as in fault-tolerant systems) or manual (as in high availability systems).

fault   A physical or logical break in a communications link.

fault management   One of the five basic categories of network management defined by the International Standards Organization (ISO). Fault management is used for the detection, isolation, and correction of faults on the network.

Fault tolerance   The ability for a system to remain operational, sometimes in a degraded mode, even though one or more elements of the system have failed. Fault tolerance is obtained through the use of redundant components or modules. Fault-tolerant systems have automatic fail over to the redundant components. See fail over.

FCC   Federal Communications Commission.

GLOSSARY

FDDI (Fiber Distributed Data Interface)   A specification for fiber-optic networks operating at 100 megabits per second. FDDI uses wiring hubs, and the hubs are prime candidates to serve as network monitoring and control devices.

FEP (front-end processor)   A computer that sits between groups of cluster controllers and the mainframe, concentrating signals before they are transmitted to the mainframe.

fiber optics   A data-transmission method that uses light pulses sent over glass cables.

field   A particular position within a message frame. Positions are labeled as the control field, flag field, and so on. Bits in each message have a meaning for stations on the network.

file and software distribution   The ability to configure and broadcast software across the network. There are many levels to this application set. The simplest is the ability to recognize revision levels of software installed on the network and to broadcast upgrades so that revision levels can be maintained automatically.

file lock   See *locking.*

file migration   File migration is an automated process in which candidate files are removed from primary storage, leaving an artifact such as a phantom (or stub) file or symbolic link in place of each file. Candidate files are automatically identified for removal based on their inactivity or file type. When the phantom file is read, it triggers a transparent retrieval from the secondary storage pool.

file mirroring   A method of network backup that gives users direct access to their files and file histories on a secondary storage pool. Copies of users' files are stored on a network attached disk volume. When the file or storage server is off line, users' files are still accessible. No restore is required. No intervening application is in the way. Files can be copied directly to the local workstation or used in place.

file recall   The return of migrated files from the lower level of the storage hierarchy to a higher level in response to user access request or in accordance with preset rules.

GLOSSARY

file server   A type of server that holds files in private and shared directories for LAN users. See *server.*

file system   The organized body of rules and processes governing storage at the operating system level. File systems define the manner in which storage is accessed and its physical and logical organization. The term "file system" also describes a common logical volume, as in a partition or a repository.

file tracking   The ability of the online catalog to provide complete file versioning and history information along with specific media locations.

file transfer   The practice of moving files from one storage medium to another.

file/disk grooming   Maintenance and management of files and disk space on servers and workstations.

flow control   A convention used to regulate communications between two nodes. Hardware and software techniques are available.

foreign exchange   A telephone line that represents a local number in a calling area quite removed from the telephone's actual termination. If your office is in the suburbs but many of your customers are in the city, you might have a foreign exchange line with a city telephone office.

four-wire circuit   A transmission arrangement in which two half-duplex circuits (two wires each) are combined to make one full-duplex circuit.

frame   A data packet on a Token-Ring network. Also denotes a data packet on other networks such as X.25 or SNA.

frequency converter   In broadband cable systems, the device that translates between the transmitting and receiving frequencies.

frequency-agile modem   A modem used on some broadband systems that can shift frequencies to communicate with stations in different dedicated bands.

frequency-division multiplexing   A technique for combining many signals on one circuit by separating them in frequency.

GLOSSARY

frequency-shift keying   A transmission method using two different frequencies that are shifted to represent the digital 0s and 1s; used in some common modems.

FTAM (File Transfer Access and Management)   An OSI protocol that provides access to files stored on dissimilar systems.

FTP (File Transfer Protocol)   A protocol that describes how one computer can host other computers to allow transferring files in either direction. Users can see directories of either computer on the host and perform limited file-management functions. Software for the FTP client function is usually a part of TCP/IP packages for the PC; some vendors also provide FTP host software for the PC. See *TFTP*.

full backup   A backup of all files on a storage device. If files or directories have been excluded from backups, they will not be contained in a full backup. See backup, differential backup, incremental backup, and partial backup.

full duplex   The ability for communications to flow both ways over a communications link at the same time.

functional-management layer   A communications layer in SNA that formats presentations.

gateway   A device that translates between dissimilar network architectures—such as a IPX/Ethernet network and an IBM/AS400 network—allowing shared information. The gateway is not just the point of entry but the device that translates and manages the union. It can serve as a shared point of entry from a local area network into a larger information resource such as a large packet-switched information network or a mainframe computer.

GOSIP (Government OSI Profile)   The U.S. government's version of the OSI protocols. GOSIP compliance is typically a requirement in government networking purchases.

graphical user interface (GUI)   A type of user interface that combines graphics and the use of pointing devices, menu bars, overlapping windows, and icons.

ground   An electrically neutral contact point.

GLOSSARY

half duplex   Alternating transmissions; each station can either transmit or receive, not both simultaneously. In terminals, "half duplex" describes the condition when a terminal displays its own transmissions instead of a remote-end echo. The term also refers to the configuration option in some modems allowing local character echo.

handshaking   Exchange of control codes or specific characters to control data flow.

HDLC (High-Level Data Link Control)   A comprehensive standard developed by the International Standards Organization (ISO). It is a bit-oriented link-layer protocol.

hierarchical storage management (HSM)   The process of automatically storing data on the lowest cost devices that can support the performance required by the applications. To users, data storage never fills and file access, regardless of location in the storage hierarchy, is completely transparent. The software automatically manages multiple levels of the storage hierarchy. See *file migration*.

high migration threshold   A percentage of the storage pool capacity that identifies when the software can start migrating files to the next available storage pool in the hierarchy. Contrast with low migration threshold. See migration.

high systems availability   A configuration that has loosely coupled redundancy and requires the manual transfer of control to switch from one configuration to another. See *fault tolerance*.

high-speed modem   A modem operating at speeds from 2,400 to 9,600 bits per second.

HLLAPI (High-Level-Language Application Program Interface)   A scripting language (that is, a set of verbs) that allows programmers to build transparent interfaces between 3270 terminals and applications on IBM mainframes.

host backup server   The backup server that is the central repository in an enterprise data management architecture. Local backup servers ship data to the host backup server. The host backup server can be located anywhere in the enterprise and on any platform that will support the requirements.

GLOSSARY

hot backup   In the database world, this term means a live, "hot" backup while the database is open and in use. As a general backup practice, "hot backup" is used to describe a disk-to-disk backup (instead of disk-to-tape). Restoration from disk is so fast that it is called "hot." See *disk-based backup.*

hot spare (or online spare)   A component that is present in the system but is not normally used until another component fails. (May apply to a drive, a power supply, and so on.) At this time the hot spare is automatically substituted for the failed component.

hot swap   The ability to exchange a defective equipment component without shutting down the equipment. (May apply to a drive, a fan, a power supply, and so on.)

HotFix   A Novell program that dynamically marks defective blocks on the hard disk so they will not be used.

HSM   See *hierarchical storage management.*

Hz (hertz)   Cycles per second.

I/O bound   A condition where the operation of the I/O port is the limiting factor in program execution.

I/O   Input/output.

I/O Operations Per Second (IOPS)   A generic measure of I/O performance. To be meaningful, the type and operation mixture of I/O must be specified as well, such as read IOPS.

ICMP (Internet Control Message Protocol)   The TCP/IP process that provides the set of functions used for network-layer management and control.

IEEE 802   A large family of standards for the physical and electrical connections in local area networks, developed by the IEEE (Institute of Electrical and Electronics Engineers).

IEEE 802.1D   An IEEE media-access-control-level standard for inter-LAN bridges linking IEEE 802.3, 802.4, and 802.5 networks.

GLOSSARY

IEEE 802.2   An IEEE standard for data-link-layer software and firmware for use with IEEE 802.3, 802.4, and 802.5 networks.

IEEE 802.3 10Base2   This IEEE specification matches the thin Ethernet cabling. It designates a 10-megabit-per-second signaling rate, a baseband signaling technique, and a maximum cable-segment distance of 185 (nearly 200) meters.

IEEE 802.3 10BaseT   An IEEE standard describing 10-megabit-per-second twisted-pair Ethernet wiring using baseband signaling. This system requires a wiring hub.

IEEE 802.3 10Broad36   This IEEE specification describes a long-distance type of Ethernet cabling with a 10-megabit-per-second signaling rate, a broadband signaling technique, and a maximum cable-segment distance of 3,600 meters.

IEEE 802.3 1Base5   An IEEE specification matching the older AT&T StarLAN product. It designates a 1-megabit-per-second signaling rate, a baseband signaling technique, and a maximum cable-segment distance of 500 meters.

IEEE 802.4   This IEEE specification describes a LAN using 10-megabit-per-second signaling, token-passing media-access control, and a physical bus topology. It is typically used as part of networks following the Manufacturing Automation Protocol (MAP) developed by General Motors. This is sometimes confused with ARCnet, but it is not the same.

IEEE 802.5   This IEEE specification describes a LAN using 4- or 16-megabit-per-second signaling, token-passing media-access control, and a physical ring topology. An IBM variation is used by IBM's Token-Ring systems.

IEEE 802.6   This IEEE standard for metropolitan-area networks (MANs) describes what is called a Distributed Queue Dual Bus (DQDB). The DQDB topology includes two parallel runs of cable—typically fiber-optic cable—linking each node (typically a router for a LAN segment) using signaling rates in the range of 100 megabits per second.

impedance   An electrical property of a cable, combining capacitance, inductance, and resistance, and measured in ohms.

GLOSSARY

inactive files   Files or data that are no longer in use. Criteria for determining inactive files are based on the length of time since their last access. Files may be "stable" (read-access only) or "dormant" (no access). In most file systems, inactive files occupy 80 percent of the storage space.

incremental backup   An operation that backs up all data that has been modified or added since a given date. The date is usually the date of the last full or incremental backup.

IND$FILE   A mainframe editing utility, commonly used to make PC-to-mainframe file transfers; a logical unit in an SNA network that addresses and interacts with the host.

interface   An interconnection point, usually between pieces of equipment.

Internet   A collection of networks and gateways including ARPAnet, MILnet, and NSFnet (National Science Foundation net). Internet uses TCP/IP protocols. Originally used for academic research, the Internet has become a worldwide communications tool for anyone with a computer, a modem, and an access account through a service provider. The World Wide Web (WWW) is now widely used to establish a business presence online, providing everything from marketing to customer service.

interrupt   A signal that suspends a program temporarily, transferring control to the operating system when input or output is required. Interrupts may have priority levels, and higher priority interrupts take precedence in processing.

IP (Internet Protocol)   A standard describing software that keeps track of the Internet address for different nodes, routes outgoing messages, and recognizes incoming messages.

IPX (Internet Packet Exchange)   NetWare's native LAN communications protocol, used to move data between server and/or workstation programs running on different network nodes. IPX packets are encapsulated and carried by the packets used in Ethernet and the similar frames used in Token-Ring networks.

IPX/SPX   Internetwork Packet Exchange/Sequenced Packet Exchange. IPX/SPX is Novell NetWare's proprietary communication protocol.

GLOSSARY

IRQ (interrupt request)   A computer instruction that causes an interruption of a program running on the CPU for an I/O task.

ISDN (Integrated Services Digital Network)   As officially defined by the CCITT, "a limited set of standard interfaces to a digital communications network." The result is a network that offers end users voice, data, and certain image services on end-to-end digital circuits.

ISO (International Standards Organization)   A Paris-based organization that developed the Open Systems Interconnection (OSI) model.

jam signal   A signal generated by a card to ensure that other cards know that a packet collision has taken place.

JBOD (just a bunch of disks)   This refers to a disk drive array configuration in which there is no redundancy.

jumper   A plastic and metal shorting bar that slides over two or more electrical contacts to set certain conditions for operation.

K   Used in this book to represent a kilobyte (1,024 bytes).

kernel   The heart of an operating system, containing the basic scheduling and interrupt handling, but not the higher level services, such as the file system.

LAN Manager   The multiuser network operating system co-developed by Microsoft and 3Com. LAN Manager offers a wide range of network-management and control capabilities.

LAN Manager/X (LM/X)   LAN Manager for the UNIX environment.

LAN Server   IBM's proprietary OS/2-based network operating system. LAN Server is compatible with LAN Manager, which was codeveloped by Microsoft and 3Com.

LAP-B link access procedure (balanced)   The most common data-link control protocol used to interface X.25 DTEs with X.25 DCEs. X.25 also specifies a LAP, or link access procedure (not balanced). Both LAP and LAP-B are full-duplex, point-to-point bit-synchronous protocols. The unit of data transmission is called a frame; frames may contain one or more X.25 packets.

GLOSSARY

leased line   A communications circuit reserved for the permanent use of a customer; also called private line.

library manager   A library manager sits as a piece of middleware between a backup, archive, or some other application and an automated media repository such as an optical jukebox or tape library. The library manager intercepts the call for a specific file, looks up the file's location, and issues commands to the jukebox or library manager to mount a specific media and retrieve the data requested. The library manager contains the file history databases, media location database, device drivers for the supported media repositories, and has other management functions. Media management capabilities are usually built in to a library manager. A library manager is a superset of functions to a media manager.

life cycle management (tape)   A process of tracking and monitoring the number of times that the media is recorded or certain zones are overwritten (this translates into the number of passes over the heads). Management also requires the monitoring of raw error rates to prevent excessive usage and data loss.

light-wave communications   Usually, communications using fiber-optic cables and light generated by lasers or light-emitting diodes (LEDs). The phrase can also refer to systems using modulated light beams passing through the air between buildings or other adjacent locations.

link layer   The second layer in the OSI architecture. This layer takes data from the higher layers, creates packets, and sends them accurately out through the physical layer.

local area network (LAN)   A network in which a set of devices are connected to one another for local (restricted geographical area) communication and can be connected to other networks.

Local Area Transport (LAT)   A DECnet protocol used for terminal-to-host communications.

local backup server   A CPU and storage pool that acts as a centralized backup device and repository for a set of workstations and servers in a network. Multiple local backup servers are tied together and act synchronously to provide backup for the network under central control. Data may be ported off site to a host backup server. Administration is

GLOSSARY

performed for all local backup servers either locally or from the host backup server.

local loop   The connection between a customer's premises and the telephone company's central office.

local   Refers to programs, files, peripherals, and computational power accessed directly in the user's own machine rather than through the network.

LocalTalk   The 230.4-kilobit-per-second media-access method developed by Apple Computer for use with its Macintosh computer.

locking   A method of protecting shared data. When an application program opens a file, file locking either prevents simultaneous access by a second program or limits such access to "read only." DOS Versions 3.0 and higher allow an application to lock a range of bytes in a file for various purposes. Because DBMS programs interpret this range of bytes as a record, this is called "record locking."

lost revenue   The opportunity cost, whether real or hidden, of server downtime or of the productivity loss attributable to users managing their own storage.

low migration threshold   A percentage of the storage pool capacity that specifies when the migration or retrieval of files to the next storage pool in the hierarchy can stop. Contrast with high migration threshold. See *file migration*.

low-speed modem   A modem operating at speeds up to 600 bits per second.

LU 6.2 (Logical Unit 6.2)   In IBM's SNA scheme, a software product that implements the session-layer conversation specified in the Advanced Program-to-Program Communications (APPC) protocol.

MAC (media-access control)   See *access protocol*.

mainframe   A large centralized computer.

Mainframe-Link   A file transfer product that provides a bridge between existing network data management backup applications running on the network and the mainframe-based data center. This software relies on the

GLOSSARY

local backup software for all functionality at the client side and provides a robust management environment on the mainframe. A Mainframe-Link appears as a device driver under the backup destination options within the local backup scheduler. Network backup may be made to a local tape drive or to the mainframe.

MAN (metropolitan area network)   A public high-speed network (100 megabits per second or more) capable of voice and data transmission over a range of 25 to 50 miles (40 to 80 kilometers).

MAP (Manufacturing Automation Protocol)   A token-passing bus LAN originally designed by General Motors and now adopted as a subset of the IEEE 802.3 standards.

mark   A signaling condition equal to a binary 1.

MAU   See *medium attachment unit* and *Multistation Access Unit.*

MCA (Micro Channel Architecture)   The basis for IBM Micro Channel bus, used in high-end models of IBM's PS/2 series of personal computers.

media control   A set of features and commands that monitor specific tape attributes such as amount full, amount used, compression information, aging, label protection to prevent improper naming conventions, and other usage information.

media management   A set of software commands that monitors the number of write passes or uses other techniques to monitor media quality and aging to recommend new media. It is a proactive and automated feature, allowing preventative media failures and requiring less system administrator time in manual media management and error control.

media   Plural of medium; the cabling or wiring used to carry network signals. Typical examples are coaxial, fiber-optic, and twisted-pair wire.

media types managed   Optical or tape media are common. There are many types of tape media that are supported by libraries; 3490, DLT, 8 MM, 4 MM, and VHS (VLDS).

media-sharing LAN   A network in which all nodes share the cable using a media-access control (MAC) scheme. Contrast with circuit switching or packet switching.

GLOSSARY

Medium Attachment Unit (MAU)   A transceiver that attaches to the AUI port on an Ethernet adapter and provides electrical and mechanical attachments to fiber-optic, twisted-pair, or other media.

medium-speed modem   A modem operating between 600 and 2,400 bits per second.

message switching   A routing technique using a message store-and-forward system. No dedicated path is established. Rather, each message contains a destination address and is passed from source to destination through intermediate nodes. At each node, the entire message is received, stored briefly, and then passed on to the next node.

MHS (Message Handling Service)   A program developed by Action Technologies and marketed by that firm and Novell to exchange files with other programs and send files out through gateways to other computers and networks. It is used particularly to link dissimilar electronic-mail systems.

MIB (management information base)   A directory listing the logical names of all information resources residing in a network and pertinent to the network's management.

midsplit   A type of broadband cable system in which the available frequencies are split into two groups, one for transmission and one for reception. This requires a frequency converter.

migration   See *file migration*

mirroring   See *disk mirroring, file mirroring,* or *server mirroring.*

mission critical   A term used to identify applications that are critical to business operations. If these applications are not available the company suffers significant lost revenue or productivity losses. Examples are accounting programs, order entry, and customer or sales databases.

modem (modulator/demodulator)   A device that translates between electrical signals and some other means of signaling. Typically, a modem translates between direct-current signals from a computer or terminal and analog signals sent over telephone lines. Other types of modems handle radio frequencies and light waves.

GLOSSARY

modem eliminator   A wiring device designed to replace two modems; it connects equipment over a distance of up to several hundred feet. In asynchronous systems, this is a simple cable.

modified   A backup parameter that indicates that the file is considered for backup only if it has changed since the last backup. A file is considered changed if the date, size, owner, or permissions have changed.

modulation   A process of varying signals to represent intelligent information. The frequency, amplitude, or phase of a signal may be modulated to represent an analog or digital signal.

mount request queue   When requests are made for a file, the media manager looks first at where the file is stored and then checks whether there is an available drive in which to place the specific media. If multiple requests occur faster than they are filled, a queue forms.

MTBDL (mean time between data loss)   The average time between data loss due to failure. In the RAID applications, this depends on the probability of a second drive failure before the first drive failure can be repaired. See also *MTDA*.

MTBF (mean time between failures)   The average amount of time before any component in the system will fail. Component failure may or may not cause the system to fail. This parameter reflects the frequency of repair the system will require.

MTDA (mean time to data availability)   The average time required for nonredundant components to fail, causing data to be inaccessible without losing it.

MTRF (mean time to reduced functionality)   The average time required for a component to fail in any way that causes reduced system functionality, but allows continued access to data.

MTTR (mean time to repair)   A statistical figure indicating the average time spent on the machine by a service technician to fix a problem.

multiple name spaces   The association of several names or other pieces of information with the same file. This allows renaming files and designating them for dissimilar computer systems such as the PC and the Mac.

GLOSSARY

multiple parallel backup   The ability to manage multiple jobs (backup/restore) at the same time by keeping multiple tape drives operating in parallel.

Multiple Virtual Storage (MVS)   One of the family of IBM operating systems for the System/370 or System/390 processor, such as MVS/ESA.

multipoint line (or multidrop line)   A single communications link for two or more devices shared by one computer and more than one terminal. Use of this line requires a polling mechanism.

Multistation Access Unit (MAU)   IBM's name for a Token-Ring wiring concentrator.

N Connector   The large diameter connector used with thick Ethernet cable.

NAK (negative acknowledgment)   A control code indicating that a character or block of data was not properly received. See *ACK*.

named pipes   A technique used for communications between applications operating on the same computer or across the network. It includes a relatively easy-to-use API, providing application programmers with a simple way to create interprogram communications using routines similar to disk-file opening, reading, and writing.

NCP   Stands for NetWare Core Protocol, the data format of the requests NetWare uses to access files. Also stands for Network Control Program, special IBM software that runs in a front-end processor and works with VTAM on the host computer to link the application programs and terminal controllers.

NDIS (Network Driver Interface Specification)   A device driver specification co-developed by Microsoft and 3Com. Besides providing hardware and protocol independence for network drivers, NDIS supports both DOS and OS/2, and offers protocol multiplexing so that multiple protocol stacks can coexist in the same host.

near online storage   The position in the storage hierarchy between primary (online) storage and offline storage. Nearline storage is accessible in seconds to minutes through the use of automated robotics-based media handling. No human intervention is required.

GLOSSARY

NetBIOS (Network Basic Input/Output System) A layer of software originally developed by IBM and Sytek to link a network operating system with specific hardware. It can also open communications between workstations on a network at the transport layer. Today, many vendors either provide a version of NetBIOS to interface with their hardware or emulate its transport-layer communications services in their network products.

NetVIEW IBM's company-specific network-management and control architecture. This architecture relies heavily on mainframe data-collection programs and also incorporates PC-level products running under OS/2.

NetWare A popular series of network operating systems and related products made by Novell.

network A continuing connection between two or more computers that facilitates sharing files and resources.

network archives To erase files from primary storage (disk), after a copy has been stored on tape or other secondary media. The intent is long-term storage where the media contents remain unchanged. Also referred to as "retirement" or "shelving." "Archive" also refers to long-term storage for legal protection of the "state of the data" at specific points in time.

network availability A measure of network uptime. High network availability is a term designed to convey the message that 100 percent network uptime is very desirable. Most networks only achieve 96 percent uptime due to planned and unplanned outages.

network backup Making copies of files on the network, usually to an offline storage medium such as tape or optical. The purpose is to be able to recover files that are damaged, accidentally deleted, or no longer accessible.

network backup software Software application capable of providing backup and restore of network files for servers and clients. It is flexible and has many features such as tape catalogs, tape libraries, and the support for many storage devices.

network data management software Backup software that includes high performance backup and restore features and that manages data and

GLOSSARY

files in the network. Features such as disk-based database/librarian, automated archiving, and file migration set it apart from network backup.

Network File System (NFS)   One of many distributed-file-system protocols that allow a computer on a network to use the files and peripherals of another networked computer as if they were local. This protocol was developed by Sun Microsystems and adopted by other vendors.

network layer   The third level of the OSI model, containing the logic and rules that determine the path to be taken by data flowing through a network. Not important in small LANs.

network management tools   Software used to monitor network processes, including network I/O rate, communications, and connectivity.

network storage architecture   An integrated hierarchy of storage-related processes with the objective of achieving high data accessibility. See data accessibility.

network storage resource   A storage pool that every client in the network can access. Its access is completely transparent to the user, whether the storage is online or nearline.

Network-Addressable Unit (NAU)   In SNA, a device that can be the source and destination of messages.

NFS (Network File System)   See *Network File System*.

NLMs (NetWare Loadable Modules)   Applications and drivers that run in a server under Novell's NetWare 386 and can be loaded or unloaded on the fly. In other networks, such applications could require dedicated PCs.

NMP (Network Management Protocol)   A set of protocols developed by AT&T to exchange information with and control the devices that govern various components of a network, including modems and T1 multiplexers.

NNTP (Network News Transport Protocol)   An extension of the TCP/IP protocol that provides a network news transport service.

node   A connection or switching point on the network.

GLOSSARY

ODI (Open Data-link Interface)   A standard interface for transport protocols, allowing them to share a single network card without any conflicts.

OfficeVision   IBM's set of applications designed to bring a uniform user interface to the company's various lines of computing products. OfficeVision works in conjunction with IBM's Systems Application Architecture.

offline media   Media placed external to an automated repository such as an optical jukebox or tape library. Media may be on-the-shelf or in a vault.

online catalog   An online database of file histories or volume set identifications and media locations.

online   Connected to a network or a host computer system.

online media   Media mounted internal to an automated repository such as an optical jukebox or tape library.

ONMS (Open Network Management System)   Digital Communications Associates' architecture for products conforming to ISO's CMIP.

open file backup   The backup of open files (files that may be accessed or modified during backup). The file must remain static for backup, but be available for reading and writing.

Open Systems Interconnection (OSI)   A model for networks developed by the International Standards Organization, dividing the network functions into seven connected layers. Each layer builds on the services provided by those under it.

OpenView   Hewlett-Packard's suite of a network-management application, a server platform, and support services. OpenView is based on HP-UX, which complies with AT&T's UNIX system.

opportunity cost   The cost associated with opportunities that are foregone by not putting the firm's resources to their highest valued use. It relates to downtime in that companies are not only paying users' wages for nonproductivity during server downtime, but also forego earnings that those users would otherwise be generating. In terms of storage management,

GLOSSARY

opportunity cost refers to the time spent by users managing their own storage when they should be doing their assigned tasks.

OPT (Open Protocol Technology)   Novell's strategy for complete protocol independence. NetWare supports multivendor hardware with this approach.

OS/2 (Operating System/2)   An operating system developed by IBM and Microsoft for use with Intel's microprocessors. Unlike its predecessor, DOS, OS/2 is a multitasking operating system.

OS/2 Extended Edition   IBM's proprietary version of OS/2; it includes built-in communications and database-management facilities.

OSF (Open Software Foundation)   A consortium of industry leaders working to standardize the UNIX operating system.

OSI   See *Open Systems Interconnection.*

outage   See *planned outage* and *unplanned outage.*

OverVIEW Proteon   Architecture for products conforming to SNMP.

packet   A block of data sent over the network transmitting the identities of the sending and receiving stations, error-control information, and a message.

packet filter   A feature of a bridge that compares each packet received with specifications set by the network administrator. If the packet matches the specifications, the bridge can either forward or reject it. Packet filters let the administrator limit protocol-specific traffic to one network segment, isolate electronic-mail domains, and perform many other traffic-control functions.

packet switching   A transmission technique that maximizes the use of digital transmission facilities by transmitting packets of digital data from many customers simultaneously on a single communications channel.

PAD (packet assembler/disassembler)   An X.25 PAD. A hardware-and-software device, sometimes inside a PC, that provides users access to an X.25 network. CCITT Recommendations X.3, X.28, and X.29 define the PAD parameters, terminal-to-PAD interface, and PAD-to-X.25 host interface.

GLOSSARY

PAP (packet-level procedure)   A protocol for the transfer of packets between an X.25 DTE and an X.25 DCE. X.25 PAP is a full-duplex protocol that supports data sequencing, flow control, accountability, and error detection and recovery.

parallel transmission   Simultaneous transmission of bits down parallel wires; for example, byte parallel transmission requires eight wires. See serial port.

parallel/concurrent   Parallelism is the capability to manage multiple jobs (backup/restore) at once by keeping multiple tape drives operating simultaneously. Concurrence allows a storage device to receive data from more than one system at a time, interleaving the data streams.

parity check   A self-checking code employing binary digits in which the total number of ones (or zeros) in each coded expression is always either even or odd. A check may be made for even or odd parity as a means of detecting errors in the system.

parity   The state of a binary-coded character under a system in which a character having an even number of digits is assigned the code 0 and one having an odd number is assigned the code 1. A parity bit is used to check the accuracy of data. For example, in RAID, the combined binary values of the striped bytes or sectors creates a parity character. Parity is used to recover data in the event that one drive in array fails.

partial file backup   A backup in which only the changes to a file (usually blocks or records) are copied to backup media rather than the entire file. This assumes that an older version of the entire file has already been copied to backup media.

passive head end   A device that connects the two broadband cables of a dual-cable system. It does not provide frequency translation.

PBX (private branch exchange)   A telephone system serving a specific location. Many PBX systems can carry computer data without the use of modems.

PDS (Premise Distribution System)   AT&T's proprietary building-wide telecommunications cabling system.

GLOSSARY

peer-to-peer resource sharing   An architecture that lets any station contribute resources to the network while still running local application programs.

physical layer   The lowest layer of the OSI model. It consists of network wiring and cable and the interface hardware that sends and receives signals over the network.

PING (Packet Internet Groper)   An exercise program associated with TCP/IP and used to test the Internet communications channel between stations.

pipe   A communications process within the operating system that acts as an interface between a computer's devices (keyboard, disk drives, memory, and so on) and an applications program. A pipe simplifies the development of application programs by "buffering" a program from the intricacies of the hardware or the software that controls the hardware; the application developer writes code to a single pipe, not to several individual devices. A pipe is also used for program-to-program communications.

planned outage   A planned event in which a server is unavailable to its users for reasons such as software upgrades, hardware upgrades, and preventative maintenance.

polling   A method of controlling the transmission sequence of communicating devices on a shared circuit by sending an inquiry to each device asking whether it wishes to transmit.

presentation layer   The sixth layer of the OSI model, which formats data for screen presentation and translates incompatible file formats.

Presentation Manager   The portion of the operating system OS/2 that provides users with a graphical rather than a character-based interface. The screens are similar to those of Microsoft Windows.

Primary-Rate Interface (PRI)   In ISDN, the specification for the interface at each end of the high-volume trunks linking PBX and central-office facilities or connecting network switches to each other. The primary rate consists of 23 B or "bearer" channels (operating at 64 kilobits per second) and a D or "data" channel (also functioning at 64 Kbps). The combined signal-carrying capacity is 1.544 megabits per second—equivalent to that of a type T1 channel.

GLOSSARY

print server   A computer on the network that makes one or more attached printers available to other users. The server usually requires a hard disk to spool the print jobs while they wait in a queue for the printer.

print spooler   The software that holds print jobs sent to a shared printer over a network when the printer is busy. Each file is saved in temporary storage and then printed when the shared printer is available.

PROFS (Professional Office System)   Interactive productivity software developed by IBM that runs under the VM/CMS mainframe system. PROFS is frequently used for electronic mail.

propagation delay   The delay between the time a signal enters a channel and the time it is received. This is normally insignificant in local area networks, but it becomes a major factor in satellite communications.

protocol   A specification that describes the rules and procedures that products should follow to perform activities on a network, such as transmitting data. If they use the same protocols, products from different vendors can communicate on the same network.

PSDN packet   Switched data network.

PU (physical unit)   In an SNA network, usually a terminal or printer connected to the controller.

public data network   A commercially owned or national-monopoly packet-switched network, publicly available as a service to data-processing users.

pulse-code modulation (PCM)   A common method for digitizing voice signals. The bandwidth required for a single digitized voice channel is 64 kilobits per second.

PVC   See *VC (virtual circuit)*.

query language   A programming language designed to make it easier to specify what information a user wants to retrieve from a database.

queue   A list formed by items in a system waiting for service. An example is a print queue of documents to be printed in a network print server.

GLOSSARY

RAID level   A number designating the general configuration of an array. RAID configurations are generally defined from levels 0 through 5. The use of RAID 0 for a configuration that offers no redundancy is a misnomer.

RAID   This term originally stood for Redundant Array of Inexpensive Disk Drives. Today, it stands for Redundant Array of Independent Disk Drives. A technique for using drives as a group to improve performance, data availability, or both.

RAM (random access memory)   Also known as read-write memory; the memory used to execute application programs.

read cache   A cache segment dedicated to saving information read from the disk drives, on the assumption that this data will be soon requested again by the system. The system will initiate further disk accesses only if the desired information is not located in the cache. See *cache memory.*

read/write ratio   The ratio of read operations to write operations in a typical host system workload. This is important to the performance criteria of some configurations that are inefficient in write intensive environments, as are some RAIDs.

read-only access to migrated data   The normal retrieval process automatically writes the file back to primary storage. If the user is scanning a large number of files, this procedure can rapidly overload the primary file system. Read-only access is an alternative that reads the files from the migration storage pool directly into memory and does not write to disk unless the user chooses to do so. This way, the unused files can be discarded without affecting disk storage.

recentralization   The process of physically consolidating or bringing servers together under centralized administration. See central administration.

record locking   A feature that excludes other users from accessing (or sometimes just writing to) a record in a file while the first user is accessing that record.

redirector   A software module loaded into every network workstation; it captures application programs' requests for file- and equipment-sharing services and routes them through the network for action.

GLOSSARY

redundancy   The use of modules that are not necessary for normal system operation. They get substituted for (or can perform the same function as) another component, allowing the system to remain operational if the component fails.

reliability   The likelihood of a hardware component or software program failing within a given period of time.

remote vaulting   The software has the ability to transmit over phone lines or via direct connection with other sites, and manage that data, essentially treating remote site data as a client system or visa versa.

removable media/library manager   A library manager sits as the piece of middleware between a backup, archive, or some other application and an automated media repository such as an optical jukebox or tape library. The library manager intercepts the call for a specific file, looks up the files location and issues commands to the jukebox or library manager to mount a specific media and retrieve the data requested. The library manager contains the file history of databases, media location database, device drivers for the supported media repositories and other management functions. Media management capabilities are usually built in to a library manager. A library manager is a superset of functions to a media manager.

repeater   A device that amplifies and regenerates signals so they can travel on additional cable segments.

reporting   The ability to develop reports on access, media status, and other management requests.

restart packet   A block of data that notifies X.25 DTEs that an irrecoverable error exists within the X.25 network. Restart packets clear all existing SVCs and resynchronize all existing PVCs between an X.25 DTE and X.25 DCE.

restore   A function that allows users to copy files from the backup storage pool to an online storage device.

retrieve   A function that allows users to copy files from the archived storage media to an online storage device.

reverse channel   An answer-back channel provided during half-duplex operation. It allows the receiving modem to send low-speed

GLOSSARY

acknowledgments to the transmitting modem without breaking the half-duplex mode. This is also used to arrange the turnaround between modems so that one ceases transmitting and the other can begin.

RF (radio frequency) A generic term referring to the technology used in cable television and broadband networks. It uses electromagnetic waveforms, usually in the megahertz (MHz) range, for transmission.

RFS (Remote File Service) One of the many distributed-file-system network protocols that allow one computer to use the files and peripherals of another as if they were local. Developed by AT&T and adopted by other vendors as a part of Unix V.

ring A network connection method that routes messages through each station on the network in turn. Most ring networks use a token-passing protocol, which allows any station to put a message on the network when it receives a special bit pattern.

RJ-11/RJ-45 Designations for commonly used modular telephone connectors. RJ-11 is the 8-pin connector used in most voice connections. RJ-45 is the 8-pin connector used for data transmission over twisted-pair telephone wire.

RJE (Remote Job Entry) A method of submitting work to an IBM mainframe in a batch format. Although it has been superseded by the 3270 system, it is still widely used in some installations.

RO (receive-only) Refers to a one-way device such as a printer, plotter, or graphics display.

ROM (read-only memory) Memory containing preloaded programs that cannot be rewritten or changed by the CPU.

router An interconnection device that is similar to a bridge but serves packets or frames containing certain protocols. Routers link LANs at the network layer of the OSI model. Modern routers handle multiple protocol stacks simultaneously and move packets or frames onto the right links for their destinations. For example, an X.25 router will wrap an Ethernet packet back into an Ethernet system.

RPC (Remote Procedure Call) A set of software tools developed by a consortium of manufacturers and designed to assist developers in creating distributed applications. These tools automatically generate the code

GLOSSARY

for both sides of the program (client and server) and let the programmer concentrate on other portions of the application.

RS-232C   An electrical standard for the interconnection of equipment established by the Electrical Industries Association; the same as the CCITT code V.24. RS-232C is used for serial ports.

RS-449   An EIA standard that applies to binary, serial synchronous, or asynchronous communications systems.

RU (request unit or response unit)   A message that makes a request or responds to one during a session.

SAA (Systems Application Architecture)   A set of specifications written by IBM describing how users, application programs, and communications programs interface. SAA represents an attempt to standardize the look and feel of applications and the methods they use to communicate.

scalable   A scalable system is capable of growing through additions of modular increments, without necessitating major modification to the original system.

SCSI (Small Computer System Interface)   An intelligent bus level device interface. It defines a standard I/O bus and a set of high-level I/O commands.

SCSI extenders   Hardware interfaces that allow long distance SCSI communications after implemented to create device or repository sharing.

SDLC (synchronous data link control)   The data-link layer of SNA, SDLC is a more efficient method than the older bisync protocol when it comes to packaging data for transmission between computers. Packets of data are sent over the line without the overhead created by synchronization and other padding bits.

security features   Security features include operator access privileges, authorization levels, and password control to limit access to unauthorized files and data.

selective backup   A function that allows the backup program to include files in or exclude files from backup during a full or incremental backup operation.

GLOSSARY

serial port   An I/O port that transmits data 1 bit at a time—contrasted with a parallel transmission, which transmits multiple bits (usually 8) simultaneously. RS-232C is a common serial signaling protocol.

serial device   SSA or FC-AL devices can be interconnected via their serial interface, building a storage network.

Server   A computer with a large power supply and cabinet capacity. A server can also refer to any computer on a network that makes file, print, or communications services available to other network stations.

server mirroring   The process of placing and maintaining redundant file systems on each of two servers. The alternate server may be local or remote. When the primary server is off line, the alternate takes over, providing continuous access to data and network services.

session layer   The fifth layer of the OSI model, which sets up the conditions whereby individual nodes on the network can communicate or send data to each other. The functions of this layer are used for many purposes, including determining which side may transmit during half-duplex communications.

session   The name for the connection between a mainframe terminal (or a PC emulating a mainframe terminal) and the mainframe itself when they are communicating. The number of sessions that can be run simultaneously through a LAN gateway is limited by the gateway software and the hardware configuration.

SFT (system fault tolerance)   The capability to recover from or avoid a system crash. Novell uses a Transaction Tracking System (TTS), disk mirroring, and disk duplexing as its system recovery methods.

shelf storage   Media placed external to an automated repository. Requests to mount this media require manual intervention.

SMB (Server Message Block)   A distributed-file-system network protocol that allows one computer to use the files and peripherals of another as if they were local. Developed by Microsoft and adopted by IBM and many other vendors.

SMTP (Simple Mail Transfer Protocol)   A protocol that describes an electronic mail system with both host and user sections. Many companies sell host software (usually for UNIX) that will exchange SMTP mail with

GLOSSARY

proprietary mail systems, such as IBM's PROFS. The user software is often included as a utility in TCP/IP packages for the PC.

SNA (Systems Network Architecture) IBM's scheme for connecting its computerized products so that they can communicate and share data.

SNADS (SNA Distribution Services) An IBM protocol that allows the distribution of electronic mail and attached documents through an SNA network.

SNMP (Simple Network Management Protocol) A structure for formatting messages and for transmitting information between reporting devices and data-collection programs; developed jointly by the Department of Defense, industry, and the academic community as part of the TCP/IP protocol suite.

space The signal condition that equals a binary 0.

SPX (Sequenced Packet Exchange) An enhanced set of commands implemented on top of IPX to create a true transport-layer interface. SPX provides more functions than IPX, including guaranteed packet delivery.

SQL (Structured Query Language) A formal data sublanguage for specifying common database operations such as retrieving, adding, changing, or deleting records. SQL is pronounced "sequel."

STA (Spanning Tree Algorithm) A technique based on an IEEE 802.1 standard that detects and eliminates logical loops in a bridged network. When multiple paths exist, STA lets a bridge use only the most efficient one. If that path fails, STA automatically reconfigures the network so that another path becomes active, sustaining network operations.

standby server A redundant server that is not necessarily operational in normal conditions, but takes over through manual intervention when an outage occurs on the primary server.

star topology A network connection method that hooks up all links to a central node.

StarLAN A networking system developed by AT&T that uses CSMA protocols on twisted-pair telephone wire; a subset of 802.3.

GLOSSARY

start bit   A data bit used in asynchronous transmission to signal the beginning of a character and indicate that the channel is in use. It is a space signal lasting only for the duration of 1 bit.

stop bit   A data bit used in asynchronous transmission to signal the end of a character and indicate that the channel is idle. It is a mark signal lasting at least for the duration of 1 bit.

storage hierarchy   A logical ordering of the storage devices. Generally, the ordering is based on the speed, access time, cost, and capacity of the devices. Typically, each storage pool is associated with a different type of storage device; online disk, optical jukebox or tape library, or offline tape.

storage management   Not a single application, but a family of related products that manage files, data, and the storage devices on which they are stored. Storage management includes applications, utilities, file systems, and other components that enable storage to achieve better performance, accessibility, and protection from data loss. These are both manual and automated processes.

storage networking   The establishment of a secondary network that ties the storage devices together with a high-speed link. Storage traffic can now pass in the background without affecting network traffic.

storage pool   A named collection of storage volumes, whether online, nearline, or offline.

storage server   An application server placed on the network as a shared resource for multiple workgroups, providing a centralized storage repository. Storage servers have two roles in the network. First, they offer shared storage services as a large repository and/or centralized storage management services. Second, they run storage management applications for the network. Their configuration typically consists of a CPU with multiple I/O channels, many gigabytes of disk storage, and tape libraries and/or optical jukeboxes.

store and forward   See *message switching*.

streams   An architecture introduced with UNIX System V, Release 3.2, that provides for flexible and layered communication paths between processes (programs) and device drivers. Many companies market applications and devices that can integrate through streams protocols.

GLOSSARY

striping The process of recording data across multiple disks rather than on one drive. Data is divided into segments, each of which is written to successive drives.

strobe An electrical pulse used to call for the transfer of information.

subnetting Configuring servers by using alternate data paths to reduce network traffic and promote data accessibility in case of a single path failure. Subnets are typically constructed as a dedicated Ethernet subnetwork between two systems. All that is required are two NICs and cable.

superserver A high-capacity server with fault-tolerant disk storage subsystems.

SVC See *VC (virtual circuit)*.

sync character A character (two or more in bisync) sent from a transmitting station for synchronizing the clocks in transmitting and receiving stations.

synchronous Refers to a transmission system in which characters are synchronized by the transmission of initial sync characters and a common clock signal. No stop or start bits are used.

systems management utilities Software that is used to monitor specific system factors such as disk performance, operations/ workload, configuration, and capacity. Often used as a synonym for network management.

T interface A standard basic-rate interface using four copper wires.

T1 A 1.544-megabit-per-second communications circuit provided by long-distance communications carriers for voice or data transmission. T1 lines are typically divided into 24 64-kilobit channels.

tap A connector that couples to a cable without blocking the passage of signals down the cable.

TCAM (Telecommunications Access Method) An IBM system for controlling communications.

GLOSSARY

T-connector   A coaxial connector, shaped like a T, that connects two thin Ethernet cables while supplying an additional connector for a network interface card.

TCP (Transmission Control Protocol)   A specification for software that bundles and unbundles sent and received data into packets, manages the transmission of packets on a network, and checks for errors. Popular TCPs include TCP/IP (commonly used in UNIX networks) and IPX/SPX (Commonly used in PC LANs).

TCP/IP (Transmission Control Protocol/Internet Protocol)   A set of communications protocols that has evolved since the late 1970s, when it was first developed by the Department of Defense (DOD). Because programs supporting these protocols are available on so many different computer systems, they have become an excellent way to connect different types of computers over networks.

Telex   An international messaging service, marketed in the United States by Western Union.

TELNET   A terminal-emulation protocol. Software supporting TELNET usually comes as a utility in a TCP/IP package, and all TELNET programs provide DEC VT-100 terminal emulation. Many companies either provide or allow other add-in emulators.

Terminal Adapter (TA)   An ISDN phone or a PC card that emulates one. Devices on the end of a basic-rate interface line are known as terminals.

terminator   A resistor used at each end of an Ethernet cable to ensure that signals do not reflect back and cause errors. It is usually attached to an electrical ground at one end.

TFTP (Trivial File Transfer Protocol)   A simplified version of FTP that transfers files but does not provide password protection or user-directory capability. It is associated with the TCP/IP family of protocols.

thick Ethernet   A cabling system using relatively stiff, large-diameter cable to connect transceivers. The transceivers connect to the nodes through flexible multiwire cable.

thin Ethernet   A cabling system using a thin and flexible coaxial cable to connect each node to the next node in line.

GLOSSARY

TIC (Token-Ring Interface Coupler)   An IBM device that allows a controller or processor to attach directly to a Token-Ring network. This is an optional part of several IBM terminal cluster controllers and front-end processors.

Time Domain Reflectometry (TDR)   A method of sending a radio pulse down a wire or cable to detect a shorted or open condition. High-priced devices can pinpoint a fault within inches; lower-priced devices often provide widely varying results when they try to pinpoint the distance to a fault.

Time-Division Multiplexing (TDM)   A method of placing a number of signals on one communications circuit by allocating the available time among competing stations. Allocations may be on a microsecond basis.

token passing   An access protocol in which a special message (token) circulates among the network nodes, giving them permission to transmit.

Token-Ring   The wire and the access protocol scheme whereby stations relay packets in a logical ring configuration. This architecture, pioneered by IBM, is described in the IEEE 802.5 standards.

TOP (Technical and Office Protocol)   An implementation of OSI standards in office and engineering environments. TOP, developed by Boeing and other firms, employs Ethernet specifications.

topology   The map or plan of the network. The physical topology describes how the wires or cables are laid out, and the logical or electrical topology describes how the messages flow.

TP-4 (Transport Protocol 4)   An OSI layer-4 protocol developed by the National Bureau of Standards.

transceiver   A communicating device capable of transmitting and receiving.

Transmission Control   The layer in SNA that controls sessions and manages communications.

transparent retrieval   Transparent retrieval is the ability of the users to access all their files and data as if they were on line. Some methods leave a stub or phantom file, which has the same name as the migrated file. When the application begins to read the file, the stub triggers a

GLOSSARY

retrieval. Control is returned to the users along with a message, so that they can do something else while the retrieval occurs.

transport layer   The fourth layer of the OSI model. Software in this layer checks the integrity of and formats the data carried by the physical layer (1), managed by the data layer (2), and perhaps routed by the network layer (3).

transport protocols   The communications protocols that operate across the network transport layer.

tree   A network arrangement in which the stations are attached to a common branch or data bus.

TTS (Transaction Tracking System)   A log of all file activity in NetWare.

twisted-pair Ethernet   See *IEEE 802.3 10BaseT.*

twisted-pair wiring   Cable comprised of two wires twisted together at six turns per inch to provide electrical self-shielding. Some telephone wire—but by no means all—is twisted-pair.

Type 3 cable   An unshielded twisted-pair wire that meets IBM specifications for use in 4-megabit-per-second Token-Ring networks.

U Interface   A standard basic-rate interface using two copper wires.

UDP (User Datagram Protocol)   A TCP/IP protocol describing how messages reach application programs within a destination computer. This protocol is normally bundled with IP-layer software.

UNIX   A multitasking, multiuser operating system for minicomputers that was developed by AT&T and has enjoyed popularity among engineering and technical professionals. UNIX is finding new uses as the basis of file-server operating systems for networks of PCs.

UNMA (Unified Network Management Architecture)   AT&T's company-specific architecture conforming to the ISO's CMIP.

unplanned outage   An unplanned event in which a server is unavailable to its users for reasons such as disk drive failures, software glitches, and power outages.

GLOSSARY

uptime   The period of time when a system is available to respond to client requests. The converse of downtime. See *network availability, high system availability, downtime,* and *continuous operation.*

UUCP (UNIX-to-UNIX Copy Program)   A standard UNIX utility used for information exchange between two UNIX nodes.

VAN (value-added network)   A privately owned packet-switched network whose services are sold to the public. See *PSDN.*

VC (virtual circuit)   An X.25 VC is a PAP logical connection between an X.25 DTE and an X.25 DCE. X.25 supports both switched VCs (SVCs) and permanent VCs (PVCs). SVCs are analogous to dial-up lines; that is, they allow a particular X.25 DTE to establish a connection with different X.25 DTEs on a per-call basis. By contrast, PVCs are analogous to leased lines because they always connect two X.25 DTEs.

versions   A maximum number of copies of files and directories retained for redundancy. Backup creates many versions until a file is no longer active.

VINES (Virtual Networking Software)   A UNIX-based network operating system from Banyan Systems.

virtual circuit   A temporary connection path, set up between two points by software and packet switching, that appears to the user to be available as a dedicated circuit. This "phantom" circuit can be maintained indefinitely or can be ended at will.

virus protection   A program feature or application that screens data for computer viruses, disinfects them in the process, and then notifies the system administrator of the problem, actions taken, and/or suggested actions.

virus   Computer viruses are malicious or just irritating programs that attach themselves to other files or programs and can cause everything from random video screen problems to data loss and system failure. They are created by computer hackers and distributed unknowingly by attachment to files, floppy disks, or networked data.

voice channel   A transmission path usually limited to passing the bandwidth of the human voice.

GLOSSARY

volume set   Related files, data, or media-sets. They may span multiple pieces of media and need to be kept together.

VTAM (Virtual Telecommunications Access Method)   An IBM standard for software that runs on the host mainframe computer and works with the Network Control Program to establish communications between the host and the cluster controllers. Among other things, VTAM sets the pacing and LU characteristics.

wide area network (WAN)   A network linking computers, terminals, and other equipment over a large geographic area.

wideband modem   A modem that operates at over 9,600 bits per second.

wideband   Refers to a channel or transmission medium capable of passing more frequencies than a standard 3-kHz voice channel.

wiring hub   A cabinet, usually mounted in a wiring closet, that holds connection modules for various kinds of cabling. The hub contains electronic circuits that retime and repeat the signals on the cable. The hub may also contain a microprocessor board that monitors and reports on network activity.

workstation   A desktop computer that performs local processing and accesses LAN or WAN services.

write cache   A cache segment used to accumulate data before writing to the drive on the theory that a single large write operation is more efficient than several smaller transfers.

X Window   A network-based windowing system that provides a programmatic interface for graphic window displays. X Window permits graphics produced on one networked workstation to be displayed on another.

X.25   A CCITT standard that describes how data is handled in and how computers can access a packet-switched network.

X.400   The CCITT designation for an international electronic-mail distribution system.

X.500   The CCITT designation for a directory standard to coordinate the dispersed file directories of different systems.

GLOSSARY

X/Open   A consortium of computer-industry vendors, chartered to specify an open system platform based on the UNIX operating system.

XNS (Xerox Network Services)   A multilayer protocol system developed by Xerox and adopted, at least in part, by Novell and other vendors. XNS is one of the many distributed-file-system protocols that allow network stations to use other computers' files and peripherals as if they were local.

INDEX

INDEX

INDEX

INDEX

INDEX

INDEX

INDEX

INDEX

INDEX

INDEX

INDEX

INDEX